Scholastic
904 Sylvan Ave.
Englewood Cliffs
N. J. 07632

American Education Publications AEP
Education Center
Columbus, Ohio 43216

Read 7, 8, 9

Characterization - List of 9 basic methods p. 193

Dictionary in thirds
   A - E
   F - P
   Q - Z

J. N. Hook has long been associated with the University of Illinois, where he received his doctorate and served for a number of years as Professor of English and Counselor in the Teaching of English. Dr. Hook has also played a significant role in the improvement and advancement of English teaching throughout the nation, having served as Executive Secretary of the National Council of Teachers of English, Coordinator of Project English for the U.S. Office of Education, and director of a number of federal projects aimed at improving the preparation of teachers of secondary school English and stating its performance objectives. He is co-author of *Modern English Grammar for Teachers* and of *Handbook of Representative Performance Objectives in English: Grades 9–12*, both published by The Ronald Press Company, as well as a number of high school textbooks.

The Teaching of High School English

J. N. HOOK

UNIVERSITY OF ILLINOIS

FOURTH EDITION

THE RONALD PRESS COMPANY · NEW YORK

Library of Congress Catalog Card Number: 70–179563
PRINTED IN THE UNITED STATES OF AMERICA

To the thousands who helped

Preface

The Teaching of High School English has been written to inform both the neophyte and the experienced teacher about the present state of our knowledge in this field. It is a textbook for students preparing to teach the English language and its literature in junior and senior high schools, as well as a reference book for in-service teachers.

This book stresses application rather than theory, presenting a large number of specific suggestions and tested classroom procedures. Some of these have been drawn from my own years of teaching in high school, college, and university, but many more have been derived from the teaching experience of others and from research, especially that of the past decade. Varied though the suggestions and recommendations are, I believe that they add up to a coherent theory.

The teaching of English in the junior and senior high schools continues to change rapidly. Among the many recent developments are the increased stress on improvisation and dramatization, the tendency toward teaching rich English language content rather than only grammar and usage, greater freedom in the range of literary materials, greater emphasis on process (e.g., the process of writing), and the formulation of objectives stated in terms of what the student does rather than in terms of abstract content.

It has been my privilege during the past two decades to play some part in the still-developing secondary English curriculum, first as Executive Secretary of the National Council of Teachers of English, and later as coordinator and director of federally sponsored projects dealing with curriculum and methods. Meanwhile hundreds of other researchers were making their substantive contributions to the improvement of the secondary school program. Even more significantly, thousands of junior and senior high school teachers were trying new things in their classrooms—unconventional literary selections and new approaches to literature, language, and composition. The result has been high school English programs which, though still far from perfect, are much more interesting to students and in many ways more resultful than the programs of past decades. Many problems still remain; many questions are yet unanswered. Nevertheless the profession may point pridefully to its accomplishments.

My indebtedness to others is very great. I can utter only a blanket "Thank you" to the editors of professional magazines, to speakers at professional meetings, to the sometimes inspired and inspiring high school teachers whose classes I have visited, to my own undergraduate and graduate students who are planning to become teachers, and to the hundreds of other teachers who, knowingly or unknowingly, have assisted me. One special "Thank you" goes to Mrs. Barbara Taylor, who as a graduate student at the University of Illinois was largely responsible for the material in the chapter on film. Another special "Thank you" goes to my secretary, Mrs. Charlotte Lake, for her patient and efficient work with the manuscript. And a final word of thanks goes to two people I have often neglected: my wife, Rachel, and my son, Jay, who as a high school student is now being taught by users of earlier editions of this book.

J. N. HOOK

Urbana, Illinois
February, 1972

Contents

The Teaching of
High School English

1

The Changing World
of the English Teacher

THE CHANGING SOCIETY

Toward the Third Hundred Million

In 1949, when the first edition of this book appeared, the population of the United States was about 148,000,000, or about 50 persons per square mile. By 1960 the figure had grown to 178,000,000 or about 60 per square mile. In the late sixties we passed 200,000,000, or about 70 per square mile. Demographers expect a quarter-billion by 1980, or 86 per square mile. And in 1990 or a little later the United States may have 300,000,000 inhabitants, more than double the 1949 figure, or about 100 persons per square mile.

If the 100 persons were evenly distributed, each would have 6.4 acres to call his own—more than ample room to stretch out his arms without hitting a neighbor. But of course they won't be evenly distributed, since few people live in deserts or on mountain tops or in corn fields. Because of human gregariousness and for economic reasons, most of the 300,000,000 will live in or near cities, as indeed is true among the 200-plus million we already have. As early as 1966, Washington, D.C., had 13,246 persons per square mile—a severely limited number of square feet per person—and Harlem and other areas in all major cities were much more crowded than that.

3

Megalopolitan areas will expand and become more densely populated—contiguous urban sprawls stretching from Boston to New York and Philadelphia and Baltimore and Washington and beyond, or from Chicago to Detroit, Toledo, and Cleveland, or in the California coastal area from San Francisco to the Mexican border. Perhaps, as is proposed in *The New City* by the National Committee on Urban Growth Policy, there will also be 110 new communities, housing 20,000,000 people, by the year 2000—ten of them with a million or so people each, and the others averaging a mere 100,000.

English teachers are usually not much interested in statistics, and may ask "So what?" with regard to all these numbers. The answer is that increased urbanization means different problems for the schools, the need for reappraising objectives in English and other subjects, the throwing out of some familiar materials and the addition of some that are new, a fresh look at motivation and methodology. When people are crowded together, their desires and their needs and their reactions are not the same as when they have elbow room. Even their values may differ. (Cats when crowded together are much more pugnacious than are dispersed cats; the actual flow of adrenalin is much greater.)

The process of urbanization, like other sociological processes, is one of change. In decades and centuries now past, a teacher could with some assurance give instruction that he knew would be useful to his students when they became thirty or forty or sixty years old, because he knew that the world they would later live in would not differ greatly from the world they inhabited as children. But today's instruction must be geared to change, must prepare students to adjust to change and to become change agents themselves. John W. Gardner has said it this way:

> If we indoctrinate the young person in an elaborate set of fixed beliefs, we are ensuring his early obsolescence. The alternative is to develop skills, attitudes and habits of mind and the kinds of knowledge and understanding that will be the instruments of continuous change and growth on the part of the young person. Then we will have fashioned *a system that provides for its own continuous renewal*.[1]

An Age of Uncertainty

Once upon a time God was in His heaven, and all was more or less right with the world. There was no doctrine of relativity, in

---

[1] John W. Gardner, *Self-Renewal: The Individual and the Innovative Society*, as quoted in Neil Postman and Charles Weingartner, *Linguistics: A Revolution in Teaching* (New York, 1966), p. 43.

science or anything else. Einstein had not yet lived, nor had Darwin. People believed in absolutes. They were sure they could define "right" and "wrong," even though not everyone pursued the former and eschewed the latter. They thought they could define absolutes of excellence in literature, art, and music, as well as in human conduct. Certainties stood mountainlike; a person awoke each morning, and they were always there.

Today all is different. Churches are reconsidering their purposes, and some of them are effecting changes much more profound than those of the Reformation. Mathematicians teach that the base-ten system is only one of many possible; in a base-three or a base-four system, two plus two does not equal four, so even that supposedly undeniable truth has been denied, and in the computer-used binary system the number two does not even exist. Experimentation in music, art, and literature has revealed varieties or possibilities of excellence undreamed of by the classicists and their successors. Moral codes are changing; they appear to be developing toward the principle that anything an individual does is all right if it does not harm others. Few people today live a life of quiet acquiescence: if they sense that something is wrong, they protest, demonstrate, rebel.

The "eternal verities," physical and other, are going. We can still count on gravity and on the daily progress of the sun from horizon to horizon, but not on much else. The certainty of a plenitude of fresh air is vanishing; many of our streams and lakes are so polluted that one cannot swim in them; even the ocean's oyster and scallop beds have been largely ruined by waste-disposal. Time-honored aphorisms are being eroded: our thrift-minded ancestors said "A penny saved is a penny earned" and "Early to bed and early to rise / Makes a man healthy, wealthy, and wise," but today universal thrift would be considered bad for the economy, and night-people are often as healthy, wealthy, and perhaps as wise as day-people.

In earlier periods few persons wondered whether mankind would survive. Almost everyone was sure that man would last at least until a heaven-imposed Judgment Day. Today questions about man's survival are real and constant, as the shadow of annihilation becomes apparent to more and more human beings.

The age of uncertainty poses new problems for teachers. Should we live, laugh, and be merry with our students because tomorrow we may all die together? Should we proceed with business as usual, hoping that the old will somehow return and replace the new, teaching as we were taught and what we were taught? Should we assume the attitude that questions about pollution, morals, racial bias, and the like do not really concern us English teachers, because we are employed to teach spelling, punctuation, and the structure of the short story? Or should we assume that we have a part in the struggle for survival, in the search for new verities, in the process of change, in what may amount to a redefinition of man in relation to himself and his universe?

If we answer "No" to all those questions except the last, the challenge is greatest, our job most difficult. But answering "Yes" to any of the first three questions may lead only to a dead end—a very dead end.

Explosions

The explosion of knowledge is a now-familiar phenomenon. It has been estimated that the sum total of human knowledge doubles in ten years. Scientific frontiers press outward in all directions. Technology provides new foods, new toys, new household gadgets; it whizzes us ever faster across or above the earth's surface and carries men ever deeper into space. Medicine finds new cures for old diseases. Psychologists probe further into the complexities of the human nervous system.

All to what purpose? Why is man? What is man? Why and what are a man and a woman, a boy and a girl? Where are we going? Where should we try to go? For centuries people have asked such questions, but now more often than ever. So much of modern life seems a purposeless scurry, activity for activity's sake. The term "rat race," though not a twentieth century coinage, was seldom used in our language before. Young people in particular are increasingly asking hard questions. Many answer them to their own satisfaction, but others become discouraged, lacking enough information and inspiration to find answers that they can accept, in effect dropping out of humanity before they have been fully in.

Never before has mankind needed so much to prevent dropouts. Never before has mankind needed so many dreamers, so many seers (see-ers). We are an age strong in analysis, weak in synthesis. We can penetrate an atom, but we cannot find a human soul, which is presumably much larger.

 That's what the humanities, in contrast to the sciences, are about (or should be about). Soul-seeking. Goal-seeking. Imagining. Dreaming. Synthesizing. Trend-describing. Understanding. Deepening. Philosophizing. Defining. Enjoying. Loving. Living.

But they haven't been—at least not enough. Scholars in the humanities have taught their students to analyze and to quantify, not to humanize and seldom to dream. For proof, look at the title of almost any doctoral dissertation. Or look at almost any of the questions asked of students by their literature textbooks, or listen to the questions in almost any English class. Of course there must be some "hard" knowledge, but there must also be fancy and imagination and the soft webstuff of dreams.

The explosions of scientific knowledge and technology will no doubt continue and increase, as knowledge flows from knowledge. But we humanists need to contribute to other and milder and less observable but much greater explosions—explosions within man—if a nearer approach to brotherhood, to humanness, is to come into being, if man is to survive without living underground in abandoned subways—going back to the cave.

THE SCHOOL

Each autumn *Saturday Review* gleans figures from the U. S. Office of Education and the National Education Association and publishes them under such a heading as "The Magnitude of the American Educational Establishment." In 1970, "more than sixty-one million Americans engaged full-time as students, teachers, or administrators in the nation's educational enterprise." [2]

In 1970–71, according to these figures, the nation supported 30,810 secondary schools, enrolling 15,000,000 students, who were taught by 1,013,000 teachers exclusive of administrators and supervisors. The nation's educational budget was about seventy billion dollars.

Some contrasts with earlier years are enlightening. According to U. S. Office of Education statistics, in 1900 only 94,883 students were graduated from high school (and only 27,410 from all the nation's colleges and universities—fewer than the total now enrolled in a single large university). Even in 1949–50, only six and a half million students were enrolled in grades 9–12. An enrollment projection for 1985 anticipates almost seventeen million high school students and almost twelve million college students.[3]

[2] "The Magnitude of the American Educational Establishment (1970–71)," *Saturday Review*, Sept. 19, 1970, p. 67.

[3] U. S. Bureau of the Census, *Pocket Data Book: USA 1967* (Washington, D.C.: U. S. Government Printing Office, 1967), p. 148.

In addition to such statistics, there is other evidence concerning changes in schools. School construction is a major business. School buildings are now nearly all well built, well lighted and heated and cooled—pleasant places in which to work. Only a relatively few schools now provide the dingy, bleak, uncomfortable surroundings that once were typical. Libraries and laboratories are generally well stocked, as are many classrooms. Television sets and various kinds of projectors abound. Physically, then, most schools are far superior to those of the past.

In general, too, administrators and teachers have had more years of schooling than ever before. The uncertificated teacher is a rarity, and most secondary teachers have had at least a little college work beyond the baccalaureate; the number with a master's degree increases steadily.

Secondary school teachers now are much more specialized than they were in the past. When I began teaching in high school in the 1930's, one of my fellow-graduates had to teach seven different subjects, and I myself taught English and speech, was the librarian, advised the school newspaper and annual, coached all the plays, was a class sponsor, sold tickets at football games, and served as official scorer at basketball games. Today, typically, a teacher teaches "his" subject and perhaps has one or two co-curricular responsibilities. As a result of this trend, a person preparing to teach may get much deeper and broader preparation in his own special field, instead of spreading his study thinly over a variety of fields. In addition, schools are increasingly using differentiated staffing, with teachers' aides and with other persons employed for special tasks.

Teachers' salaries, once abysmally low, have in most places risen faster than the cost of living. Even though most teachers still do not make as much money as plumbers, electricians, and bricklayers, and far less than medical doctors, the gains have been considerable.

Curricular offerings are much richer in the majority of schools than they ever were before. In the typical small high school of the thirties, students had the opportunity to study English (the same English for everybody), history and civics and perhaps economics, one or at most two foreign languages (usually Latin), physiology and botany and zoology and chemistry and physics (often only one semester of each), mathematics, home economics, physical education, and possibly music and art (though these were often only co-curricular). A school today, in contrast, may offer two dozen or more courses in English and speech, a rich variety of social sciences, four or five foreign languages, in-depth work in science and mathematics, varied programs in home economics and physical education, music, art, psychology, philosophy, business and secretarial work, shop or agriculture, health science, radio and television, and driver education, and special work for those with mental or physical handicaps.

Educational research, some trivial and some important, has made available to teachers a vast amount of data that can be useful. Although much of this research reaches the conclusion "no statistically significant difference," we do have an array of hard facts on which to base many of our educational decisions.[4]

In summary, then, most of our schools are in many ways much better than those known to our parents, grandparents, or great-grandparents. We have come a long way from the shabby buildings of the past, with their lack of books and equipment, their underprepared and underpaid staff, their slender curricular offerings, and their general lack of research bases. The American people today support their schools much better than before.

But despite today's advantages, not everything is perfect. Gross inequalities still exist: some buildings are still poor, some schools lack books and equipment, some teachers are poorly prepared, some curricular offerings are almost archaic. Even in the "better" schools, some instruction is bad, and too little advantage is taken of research findings. Many children still drop out at the minimum legal age, usually because the schools have failed to motivate them, to reach them where they are. Many others stay in school, go through the necessary motions in order to graduate, perhaps even go to college, but never become deeply interested in learning and do not develop in proportion to their ability.

THE STUDENTS

The American dream of education for all young people has become a reality. Over ninety-nine per cent of children between the ages of six and sixteen are listed on school rolls; the major exceptions are those whose physical or mental health makes school attendance impossible, and even those children are generally given special treat-

[4] The U. S. Office of Education *Research in Education* summarizes hundreds of research studies each month.

ment of some sort. Over half of today's high school graduates go on to some form of higher education, and the proportion continues to grow.

At one time, just a little over a century ago, there were no high schools. When such schools did come into existence, they were for a long time regarded as for the few, not for the majority. A number of states did not have minimum school-leaving ages until the present century; these ages now vary from sixteen to eighteen, and there is talk of making some of them higher.

Educating all American youth obviously means educating a wide variety of American youth. They come in various colors, shapes, and sizes. They are the children of millionaires, the children of parents on government welfare, and especially the children of parents who are not very rich or very poor. Some come from homes that attach a high value to education, others from homes where schooling is considered unnecessary or even downright undesirable. Some parents are themselves well educated, but the average parent has spent only about ten years in school.

Most of the children share certain environmental characteristics. Since they have never lived through a depression, few of them know what hunger is, they have never of necessity worn rags, they have never seen their fathers trudging the streets looking for work. And since they, like their younger teachers, are of a post-world-war generation, relatively few of them have felt the sickening fear that a father or a brother will be killed in combat, the feeling of helplessness that exists when much of a world is burning and one can do nothing to extinguish the flames. They are in a sense a soft generation, for they have not known the hardships of the pioneers, most of them have never grasped a hoe handle or a broom, many have been given so many luxuries that they cannot distinguish luxury from necessity.

They are a mobile generation. From the natal crib in the hospital to the four-on-the-floor that some of them drive to school, they have been on wheels. Although a few, especially in urban or rural ghettos, have seldom been over a few miles from home, some have been in a dozen or a score of states, and many have traveled abroad. Hence they have seen much more of the world than their parents had, a generation ago. Many have lived in six or eight communities as their fathers' work changed. Some have attended a dozen

schools. Because they have seen so much, many have become blasé
if not sophisticated.

They do know more than earlier teen-agers. They grew up star-
ing at television, and despite its flaws, TV is a powerful educator.
Some of them learned to read via commercials for shampoo and beer.
By television they have been taken to distant lands and into space,
into family brawls and gang warfare and dope addiction and music
good or bad and hospitals and offices and. . . . They have seen on
the picture tube the faces of presidents, murderers, soldiers, prosti-
tutes, comedians, singers, poets, artists, laborers. . . . They have
learned the superficialities of countless crafts and innumerable ways
of life. They have learned little or nothing in depth, but the breadth
of their vicarious experience is considerable.

Most have grown up in highly permissive homes. The legendary
stern father and the demanding mother have nearly disappeared.
Children stay up late, and a few years afterward they stay out late.
They are given an allowance to spend as they please, instead of having to work to earn money that must then be accounted for. They
start dating early, little girls wear brassieres before they need them,
and many a mother provides her daughter with the Pill or closes
her eyes when the daughter filches a supply from the bottle. Movies
are frank and explicit: honeymooners or other lovers are followed
into the bedroom. Magazines are no less lurid. The eyes of many
a teen-ager are old; they have seen so much. Many teen-age bodies
have undergone erotic experiences that their grandparents did not
know existed, and many youngsters have experimented with drugs
as their forebears tried smoking cornsilk or that first cigarette behind
the barn.

But despite all this, many young people retain a sturdy idealism.
Much of the unrest of youth can be accounted for by the fact that
the world is not the perfect place that the young believe it should
and can be. Though many of their complaints deal with trivia or
are based on inadequate information, and though many of their proposed solutions seem completely impracticable, they have a right
to protest, and the future shape of society is dependent upon how
successful they will be in effecting reforms. They see injustice, and
they are right to protest against it. They see dangers of a war that
can annihilate them, and they are right in crying "I want to live!"
If youth believed that injustice, war, tyranny, hunger, and constant

fear are inevitable, then such things would indeed be inevitable. The hope of tomorrow lies in the idealism of today, guided into rational and potentially productive channels.

As in every generation, the abilities of individuals differ. Some learn quickly, some slowly. Some will never master more than a fraction of what we can offer them, but others will far outstrip their teachers. Some will become drivers of taxis, and they will serve society well if they are considerate and resourceful drivers. Some will be carpenters, and we need quality housing. Some will be secretaries, and we need more and better secretaries. Some will become research scientists, doctors, lawyers, teachers, professors, and political leaders; we never have enough highly able people in these occupations. Most will become parents, and the world needs wiser parents. As we teachers think of the future contributions of our students to society, we may well remember Browning:

> All service ranks the same with God:
> . . . there is no last nor first.

THE ENGLISH TEACHERS

As students do, teachers vary in color, shape, and size, and in intellectual quality, emotional control, and past experiences. Obviously they vary more in age than students do—from about twenty to about seventy.

In a single English department, one may find:

Mrs. Maternal, who loves the kids and who has their confidence and their confidences.
Miss Rigid (Frigid?), the martinet.
Mr. Hailfellow, everybody's friend.
Mr. Esthete, "That is all ye know on Earth, and all ye need to know."
Miss Specialist, who relates everything to the eighteenth century.
Mrs. Gush, "Isn't this beautiful!"
Mr. Anatomist, "Now let's analyze the poem line by line."
Mr. Techno, worshiper of the machine.
Mr. Linguist, superb at drawing sentence tree-diagrams.
Miss Creative, guide of many young Creatives.
Mr. Bircher, ultraconservative, "We must preserve the purity of the English language."

and if the department is lucky, several Balances, who have many of the best and few of the worst qualities of all the others.

A departmental meeting at which each teacher utters his beliefs freely can be quite an experience. There is value, though, in diversity within a department, because each teacher may be able to contribute something worth while both to departmental meetings and to work with students. (There may be one or two exceptions in the list above!)

Most English teachers are better prepared today than they used to be, although the nearly fifty per cent who have only a college minor in English are likely to be relatively limited in their knowledge of the subject unless they have studied extensively on their own. Standards for certification have been rising gradually, especially with regard to requirements in subject-matter fields.

Two major studies of English teacher preparation have been completed in recent years. One of these, the English Teacher Preparation Study, was sponsored by the Modern Language Association, the National Council of Teachers of English, and the National Association of State Directors of Teacher Education and Certification. The second involved cooperative research by twenty Illinois colleges and universities. Although the studies differ in detail, they are in basic agreement. The following points are derived from the conclusions of the Illinois study and are detailed in Chapter 2.

1. In regard to language, English teachers should be familiar with at least the history of the English language and modern English grammar, and preferably also with general linguistics, lexicography, principles of usage, semantics, psycholinguistics, and especially dialectology.
2. English teachers should take at least one and preferably two courses in advanced composition.
3. Study of the teaching of reading is imperative.
4. Although preparation in literature is generally rather strong, these areas often need strengthening: applied criticism, literary backgrounds (history, mythology, folklore, the Bible), world or comparative literature, and literature written especially for young people.
5. Basic speech and oral interpretation are essential.
6. Teachers who plan to work with special groups, such as slow learners, the academically talented, or students for whom English is a second language, need special preparation for their tasks.
7. Methods of teaching English, not just general methods, should be included in the preparatory program. Effective supervision is obviously desirable.

8. It is important for teachers to understand and be able to apply principles of evaluation.

It is clear that not all teachers presently employed possess the breadth and depth of preparation that these two major studies describe as needed. Nevertheless, the studies are being used widely as guides, and as their recommendations are put into effect, English teachers will become increasingly strong.[5]

Because of the need for so much breadth and depth, a high proportion of secondary school English teachers take graduate work in summer sessions, in evening or Saturday classes, or during sabbaticals. A few states and a number of individual school systems now require five years of preparation. The days are long past when a teacher could teach if he had only a year or two more study than his most advanced students.

Besides knowledge of subject matter and ways to teach it, teachers need to know a great deal about young people—their basic characteristics, their development, their rapidly changing mores. Although collegiate study of educational psychology or adolescent development can be revealing, it must be supplemented by frequent observation. For that reason, more and more teacher-education programs require visits to schools and also incorporate current films or videotapes showing students in class. Micro-teaching (videotaping of the prospective teacher working with a small group) is also frequent; it enables the young teacher to re-observe the students and to examine and analyze his own performance in this pre-student-teaching activity.

THE SUBJECT

Years ago (and even today in some schools) the content of English was rather simply defined as selected masterpieces of English and American literature, grammar and usage, and composition. Most students in the secondary schools read approximately the same literature, studied the same principles of grammar and usage, and wrote compositions on similar topics.

But times have changed and are changing here too. The content of the literature curriculum is no longer only or mainly the selections

[5] *What Every English Teacher Should Know* (Champaign, 1970) is a popularized NCTE publication based in part upon the Illinois study; it places emphasis upon the necessity of knowing students well.

in an anthology; some schools do not even use an anthology. Much
of the material is in paperbacks, which sometimes can be purchased
in the school's own bookstore. Magazines and newspapers are often
employed as sources for some of the reading material. There is no
list of "classics" that every student is expected to read, and even
though *Julius Caesar, Macbeth, Great Expectations,* "The Rime of
the Ancient Mariner," and a few other works may appear repeatedly,
there is much less commonality in curriculum guides than was once
the case.

Much of the literature studied is less innocuous than that formerly read—less "pretty," maybe less "clean," certainly more realistic.
Although censorship problems exist in many schools, frank and revealing and essentially honest books like Salinger's *Catcher in the
Rye* or Ellison's *Invisible Man* are included in many curriculums.
"WASP" literature (white Anglo-Saxon Protestant) has been joined
by works written by members of every ethnic group and of every
cultural and religious heritage. And a book need not be fifty or a
hundred years old to be included: many works of the present decade
or even the present year are being taught. Instead of being limited
to a highly restricted list, today's students may encounter almost
anything in the whole range of literature, old or new.

Books written especially for young people, if the books are of
good quality, are often included; the so-called "junior novel" has a
place of high regard in many classes. Nor does the literature for
today's schools come only from England and America: Europe, Asia,
Australia, and Africa are often represented. Provincialism is thus
slowly reduced.

In the study of the English language there has been a similar
broadening. Once this study was poverty-stricken. It meant only
the analysis of sentences (parsing, diagraming, underlining, the
naming of parts) and drill on "correct" usage. Today, with the ad-
vent first of structural and then of transformational grammar, the
analytical system has been greatly changed, and the purpose of
grammatical study is frequently defined as cultural rather than
merely utilitarian. There is less assurance about "correctness"; principles of usage are discussed in terms of the real world of today
rather than in terms of the prescriptivism inherited from the eighteenth century.

The study of dialectology—especially American geographical dialects—has entered many a curriculum; this study combats the as-

sumption that someone who speaks differently is in some way an inferior being. Semantics, which has moved up and down in school popularity, seems again to be on the upswing; one of its values is that it analyzes the use of language to sway people. And history of the English language—a study once confined largely to Ph.D programs—is enriching many high school students' awareness of how and why language changes and his knowledge of why some of the seeming oddities of English exist.

The emphasis in composition is shifting toward self-discovery and toward attempts at placing in order some parts of a student's world. We are moving away from rigid and often identical-for-all assignments such as "For Friday write four hundred words of analysis of this poem." Today's students have greater freedom in what they write about. Increasingly, instruction emphasizes the process of writing, and teachers realize that the process is not the same for every writer; principles of organization, which were once a major focus, tend to appear as byproducts.

The whole subject of English is being redefined. The participants in the Dartmouth Conference, despairing of defining English in terms of subject matter, concluded that "English" is what happens in English classes. In the twentieth-century swing of the pendulum, English was once defined as subject-matter content; then, with the Progressive Education movement and the child-centered school, the focus was on what happened to the child; with Sputnik, we swung back to "solid knowledge"; Dartmouth moved us back to what happens inside the child. All these forths-and-backs might be amusing if they did not have such serious implications. Do we teach the child, or do we teach the subject? There can be only one answer: we do both. We teach the child something; we teach something to the child. Lack of significant subject matter could result in a glib generation with nothing to say. Lack of attention to the development of children could result in a perpetuation of a system in which the majority of young people are turned off by literature and by most other subjects that schools have stressed. The child and the subject have to be combined in every assignment, in every discussion, in every hour of school.

THE TOOLS

English teachers today have more tools and materials to work with than ever before. A big problem, in fact, lies in choosing, from the wealth available, those items that will contribute most to the education of the young. Some school systems have employees whose task it is to screen and to make recommendations; it is easily a full-time job merely to examine and evaluate the books, A-V aids, and other items that the ingenuity of American publishers and manufacturers create for school use.

The foremost source of help to English teachers is the National Council of Teachers of English. Founded in 1911 with only a few dozen charter members, this organization has since grown to over an eighth of a million members and subscribers. Major advancements in English teaching since 1911 are linked inseparably with the history of the NCTE.

The first issue of the *English Journal* appeared in January, 1912. Since that time the Council's list of periodicals has been swelled by *Elementary English*, for elementary teachers, *College English* and *College Composition and Communication* for college teachers, *Abstracts of English Studies* for anyone interested in concise summaries of scholarly work, *Research in the Teaching of English*, which reports research relevant to the classroom, and *English Education*, first published in 1969 as an aid to the preparation of teachers. The *English Journal* is the most widely read professional publication for high school English teachers, many of whom regard it as indispensable if they are to keep up with present trends.

In addition to professional journals, the Council makes available surveys and research by sixty or so committees and commissions, and distributes various books, pamphlets, literary maps, recordings, filmstrips, and other teaching aids. Perhaps even more important, the Council has gradually assumed considerable professional leadership, working both by itself and in cooperation with other national organizations and the federal government for higher standards in teacher education and for improvement of the curriculum.

Commercial publishers bring out scores of new English textbooks each year. Some of these are hardly distinguishable from their predecessors, but others are based upon recent research or upon someone's innovative thinking. Most of the books are bright and cheerful, and are illustrated well but not superfluously; some are accompanied by teachers' manuals, filmstrips, maps, disk or tape recordings, tests, and the like.

Audio-visual aids for today's schools are abundant. In contrast, when I began teaching, my class had only chalk and blackboards, plus shared access to a creaking wind-up phonograph with a few

NCTE-produced records of Lindsay, Sandburg, and others reading their own poems. Today the well-equipped classroom has radio, television, record player, tape recorder, filmstrip projector, film projector, overhead projector, opaque projector, maps, dictionaries, a classroom library, and perhaps much more. Some schools have individual learning carrels equipped with screens for viewing videotapes, and perhaps furnished also with recording equipment, microfiche readers, and the like.

The completely mechanized school is not yet with us, though some technologists dream of it and plan for it. In its "ideal" form, it would have individual learning booths in which students would be seated before an array of pushbuttons and gauges slightly less awesome than those in the cockpit of an airliner. A computer in the subterranean regions would determine what each student should study next, and as the student worked on each item he would press the response buttons he judged appropriate. The ever-alert computer would keep him informed of his progress, provide simpler or more advanced learning experiences as need became apparent, and keep a permanent record of his accomplishment. Occasionally the student would be permitted to crawl out of his cubicle for exercise or for a form of group therapy that old-fashioned persons referred to as class discussion.

In direct contrast to the trend toward mechanization, however, is a tendency toward greater student involvement and interaction. Here the tools are not machines but students' minds and emotions. The emphasis is upon pantomine, improvisation, dramatization, oral reading, discussion, creative writing.

We may be on the verge of a big battle between those who favor increased mechanization and those who have been impressed by the deliberations of the 1966 Dartmouth Conference, as described in John Dixon's *Growth Through English*.[6]

More and more textbook companies have been taken over by IBM, Xerox, Raytheon, and other corporate giants which foresee a huge school market for their products as they develop more machines ("hardware") and more materials ("software") to feed into those machines. The technologists argue that conventional schools have been inefficient and often unsuccessful in their teaching endeavors, and that with computerized controls and individually prescribed

[6] Reading, England: National Association for the Teaching of English, 1967, 120 pp. (Available from NCTE.)

learning tasks each child can be brought along as rapidly as is possible for him. Opponents argue that interaction among children—learning to get along together on this crowded planet—is more important than learning superficial skills and tucking away various pieces of factual information. The machine, they say, may father other machines, encased in human bodies; they believe that it cannot develop warm, responsive, kindly, cooperative human beings.

No one can say for sure how the battle will turn out. One possibility is that to the machines will be entrusted much of the instruction in the mechanical, easily measurable parts of our subject, such as spelling, punctuation, capitalization, or metrics. We have unquestionably been wasteful and inefficient in teaching such things. But the machines may be rightly ignored in much of our work, such as dramatization, the discussion of literature, the creation of a piece of writing—the particularly human and humanistic aspects of our instruction.

2

The English Teacher
and His Work

WHAT MAKES A GOOD ENGLISH TEACHER?

Baseball men assert that pitching is seventy-five per cent of the game. A team with poor pitching almost never wins a championship. Similarly it may be argued that teaching is about seventy-five per cent responsible for the success of a school. No matter how fine the building, the equipment, or the administration, unless the quality of the instruction is high, the school will be relatively unsuccessful. So in this section we shall glance at the qualities desirable in a good teacher.

Human Qualities

The success of a teacher depends in large part upon his personal qualities. Although knowledge and skills are also of great importance, every successful teacher today is successful because of what he *is*, not simply because of what he *knows*.

The capable English teacher is first of all a human being. He teaches one of the humanities; he is a humanist; and he never forgets the relationship of the words *humanities, humanist,* and *human.* A person's language is one of his most essential human characteristics, and literature represents the highest reach of language. It deals with people. Always the English teacher is dealing with people, then: in his teaching of literature, in his instruction in language, in his guidance to students as they put together sentences, paragraphs, and longer pieces to communicate with people. The science teacher may measure and weigh and count, but the English teacher often teaches those things to which no existent yardsticks can apply.

The English teacher realizes that he is a member of society and that, like almost everyone else, he has something to contribute to the betterment of society. He does not consider himself superior to his students except in his knowledge of a specialized subject matter. He knows that he merely happens, through an accident of chronology, to be older and more experienced and better trained in some one phase of knowledge. With William Lyon Phelps, he knows also that every student in his classroom is better informed concerning some subjects than he is. For these reasons the teacher does not pose as the final authority on life and life's problems; he does not assume an air of superiority.

"We are all engaged in a great search," he says in effect. "We are searching for the purpose of life and for the purposes of each of our lives. This is the great human quest. Where are we going? Why are we going? Who are we searchers? How can we survive? What are the reasons for survival? What can we do to make tomorrow brighter than today?"

Vera P. John, of Yeshiva University, emphasizes the constant need for reassessment of educational goals in a rapidly changing society. She refers especially to two goals, both of which require humanness and humaneness in teachers: "One goal is the preparation of children to become 'permanent learners.' . . . A second objective is to prepare children to enjoy an adulthood of vastly increased leisure. Here, the need to develop human beings with many-sided interests, talents, and curiosities is obvious." [1]

Respect for One's Work

Although he is always ready to grant that the work of others can be as significant as his own, the successful English teacher nevertheless has a deep sense of the worthwhileness of his own work. He does not teach commas simply because the course of study says that he should, or teach Shakespeare because Shakespeare is always taught in English, or teach oral English because he does not have

[1] *English Language Teaching*, Jan., 1970.

to prepare lessons for the days when students make speeches. He teaches these things and everything else because of what they can do for his students. He teaches his students to organize their thoughts, to express themselves clearly in an age when clarity of thought and statement may save humanity from extinction, and to understand the thoughts and statements of other persons in the classroom, in a distant state, on the other side of the world, or in another century. Teaching those things is important. A word is only a group of sound waves or inky curlicues, a punctuation mark is only an ink spot, and a printed sentence is only a conglomeration of curlicues and spots—until teacher and student make of them something meaningful, a representation of man's ability to think thoughts bigger than himself. From ink in students' pens and from ink that was once wet on a printing press, the teacher helps to create constructive thoughts, orderliness, understanding. His is a job that challenges by its bigness.

Tolerance

The teacher tries to make his students tolerant of those unlike themselves. To do so, he must himself be tolerant. Not just in the narrow sense of enduring, but in the broader sense of trying to see the point of view of others.

It isn't easy. Brought up in one kind of environment, wearing one color of skin, having at least enough mental ability to get through college, and having been exposed there or elsewhere to some of "the finer things of life," he may face students from different environments, with different pigmentation, sometimes of limited mentality, and often with little awareness of what the teacher thinks of as culture. The contrasts are too much for some teachers. There are too many things for them to understand.

But the effort must be made. It is a creative effort, akin to that of an author who must understand and portray persons very unlike himself. John Steinbeck was a brilliant man; one measure of his brilliance is that in *Of Mice and Men* he wrote sympathetically and convincingly about the dim-witted Lennie Small. Just as the Steinbecks must understand the Lennies, so teachers must try to understand and to help those very unlike themselves—the slow, the lonely geniuses, the obstreperous, the shy, the foreign-born, the ghettodwellers, and (perhaps hardest of all) the indifferent.

Adaptability

John Holt has written,

What children need, even just to make a living, are qualities that can never be trained into a machine—inventiveness, flexibility, resourcefulness, curiosity, and, above all, judgment.[2]

Students' success in developing such qualities clearly depends in part upon having teachers who possess the qualities. And many teachers do. They do not simply move through a routine of pouring knowledge from their own brimming pitchers into the students' little cups.

In short, the successful English teacher is adaptable. Perhaps he grew up in New York City and is teaching in Littleville. Maybe he was born on a Nebraska farm and is teaching in Los Angeles. Possibly the school has had three different principals in the past three years. Maybe at nine o'clock the teacher has a class of super-par college-preparatory students, and at ten o'clock a class of slow, uninterested ninth graders who read a simple poem by John Masefield and get only a vague idea that it is about ships. Regardless of the contrasts he faces, the teacher must be flexible enough to do the right thing at the right time. He can lead his college prep seniors through a stimulating discussion of why Hamlet was Hamlet, and spend the next hour in helping the freshmen comprehend Masefield the Incomprehensible. The day before the big game, he can relate some of the items in the lesson to the only topic that at the moment interests nine-tenths of the class, and yet help the students to learn as much as usual. When the class mood is a rollicking one, the teacher can be frolicsome, too, and when war or other shadows emerge from the nebulous world that students often successfully ignore, he can be as serious as an owl in hearing their opinions.

B. J. Mandel says that teachers must be adaptable and must help their students to adapt readily to whatever they may face in their futures: "More and more it seems to me that one cannot predict what will be of educational value. All one can do is create an environment conducive to self-directed exploration and discovery."[3]

[2] "Why We Need New Schooling," *Look*, 34:1 (Jan. 13, 1970), p. 52.
[3] *Literature and the English Department* (NCTE, 1970).

Alertness

Related to adaptability—prerequisite to it—is alertness. The successful English teacher is physically and mentally alert. Alertness makes him eager, imaginative. He is not a dead fish. He teaches because he likes to teach, and he wants to make his teaching as effective as possible because it's more fun that way. So he experiments—tries first this, then that. Scientific accuracy? Possibly. Control groups? Could be. But whether or not his experimentation is scientific, he works imaginatively to improve his teaching. He never teaches a course twice in exactly the same way. Beneath his calmness he is restless, pioneering; goaded by his drive to serve better than ever before, westering he explores.

The teacher's imaginativeness reveals itself often in creative writing—not necessarily for publication, but for writing's effect upon him. He likes to write; he must write. And he knows that he can best help to interpret literature if he himself has suffered a few of the pangs of literary parturition. More important, he knows that through writing he can better understand the difficulties of the thirty-three juniors who have a composition due on Friday. So the teacher fills a desk drawer with his poems, his essays, his stories, his first draft of The Great American Novel, and then he starts on another drawer.

Sense of Humor

The teacher, being truly human, has a sense of humor. Learning is apparently something like digestion. A person digests more readily if mealtime is enjoyable, but if a person is tense at his meals, his food gives him indigestion. A classroom is similar to a dining room; the teacher is the host.

So the successful teacher says in effect, "In my classroom, smiles will not be unholy or laughter blasphemous. I'll try to be as good fun in class as I think I am at a party. It's a happy coincidence that _human_ and _humor_ are so much alike. What lifts human beings above the other animals? A musician may say that it's his musical ability, a scientist that it's his possession of a useful thumb, a linguist that it's his flexible use of language, a minister that it's his religion, and a historian that it's knowing the events of the past. But fifty million American kids and I know that man became man the first time he ever laughed at anything more subtle than another's misfortune. It's human to have a sense of humor. A class shouldn't become riotous, but a few laughs per day do any class good. And the teacher, too. As somebody once said, 'He who laughs—lasts.' "

Professional Attitude

The capable teacher is professional in his outlook. That means that he wants to improve the profession, help others who are in it, bring other capable persons into it. It implies that, although he tries to improve the working conditions of his profession, he will not whine about them or boast about how much more money he could make in industry. Being professional means that he subscribes to professional magazines, attends worthwhile professional meetings (without spending much time shopping), and backs worthy professional activities. It includes his own carefully formulated code of professional ethics. And it means that he regards his work—the enrichment of the minds and spirits of youth—as the finest way he has of defending his right to existence—of justifying the ways of a man *Milton* to God.

Academic and Professional Qualifications

Even though personal qualifications are important, no one can deny the need for a well-stocked mind and for familiarity with educational principles and procedures. Professor Ralph Boas, writing in the *English Leaflet* long ago, commented, "There is something fatal about the human mind which particularly affects teachers, so *Note* that all too often one finds enthusiasm and vitality without any sound basis in scholarship, or else pedantic scholarship without any real imagination or human sympathy."

Like Professor Boas, you no doubt have observed many instances of the dichotomy of which he spoke. But you have probably not been so unfortunate that you have failed to meet teachers who combined praiseworthy personal qualities with exact and extensive *Blue ribbon* knowledge and with ability to share that knowledge. They are the *teachers* blue-ribbon teachers in your collection.

The April, 1968, issue of the *English Journal* is devoted to English teacher preparation and includes, along with a history, a nine-page set of "Guidelines for the Preparation of Teachers of English," prepared under the joint sponsorship of the Modern Language Association, the National Council of Teachers of English, and the National Association of State Directors of Teacher Education and Certification. The Guidelines, as well as the history, are worth studying.

A somewhat more concise set of guidelines was prepared cooperatively, with financial support from the U. S. Office of Education, by representatives of twenty Illinois colleges and universities who made a five-year study (1964–69) of needed improvements in English teacher preparation. That list is reproduced here (see pp. 28–32), from the final report of the project, since it may be useful as a checklist that you may want to use to ascertain areas for your own future study.

The beginning teacher who has read the foregoing pages may feel that impossible ideals have been set up. Rest assured, they are not impossible, although obviously not even the best teachers possess all the qualifications in equal degree. I have sat in the classrooms of many teachers who have possessed in considerable measure the personal, academic, and professional qualifications that have just been summarized. Being in those classrooms was an agreeable experience. The students were alert and friendly. There was no feeling of tension. Learning was cooperative; it was enjoyable. Students were learning constantly, and learning not just facts but also much of what John Holt recommended in an earlier quotation—inventiveness, flexibility, resourcefulness, curiosity, and judgment.[4]

ORGANIZING FOR THE TASK

In Chapter 1, pages 12–16, you read a brief overview of a modern English teacher's responsibilities in the teaching of literature, language, and composition. We shall now take a further look at aims and relate them to curricular patterns that are often followed in order to carry on the work with reasonable efficiency.

The Aims That Are Shared

Some responsibilities are common to all teachers in secondary schools. Such responsibilities are usually listed as the general aims

---

[4] For a detailed look at desiderata for English teacher preparation, see a small book by J. N. Hook, Paul H. Jacobs, and Raymond D. Crisp, *What Every English Teacher Should Know* (NCTE, 1970). The introduction emphasizes the characteristics of children and of teachers, and the five subsequent chapters deal with desirable knowledge of language, written composition, literature, oral communication, and teaching methodology.

of the school, and statements of such aims are almost as numerous as schools themselves.

Discussion of the basic aims of education goes on and on. More and more teachers are coming to believe that building the capability of making independent judgments in varied circumstances is most important of all. Charles Weingartner, for example, says that students may find it difficult to survive in tomorrow's world if they are led to expect certainty or stability. They need to learn to make decisions, not to be told what to do. "It would seem reasonable that education . . . should focus on helping students to develop mastery of such concepts as relativity, probability, contingency, and process." [5]

Most widely known of the statements is the set of seven "Cardinal Principles" promulgated over a half-century ago by what was then the U. S. Bureau of Education. According to these principles, the secondary teacher needs to guide his students toward the following goals: (1) health, (2) command of fundamental processes, (3) worthy home membership, (4) vocation, (5) citizenship, (6) worthy use of leisure, and (7) ethical character. All secondary teachers share in working toward these goals. The English teacher has partial responsibility for each goal. The study of literature may contribute to mental health. Reading and writing are two of the fundamental processes. What a student reads, as well as his interactions with his teachers and fellow students, may affect his family relationships. His reading will probably affect his vocational choice, and his success in English may determine in large measure his success in his vocation. Discussions of ethics and of morals, and the understanding of human beings that he gains from literature, may influence a student as a citizen. In an age of increasing leisure, what a student learns from his reading may affect the way he spends the hours away from his job. The standards of rightness revealed in literature, the fact that in English class a student can discover dramatically that both ideas and actions have consequences, may help to develop his ethical character. Teachers of other subjects contribute in their own ways to the realization of the seven "Cardinal Principles," but the English teacher's contribution is certainly no less than theirs.

[5] *Florida English Journal,* Dec., 1969.

1. KNOWLEDGE OF LANGUAGE

Minimal	Good	Superior
An understanding of how language functions	A detailed understanding of how language functions, including knowledge of the principles of semantics	
A reasonably detailed knowledge of one system of English grammar and a working familiarity with another system	A detailed knowledge of at least two systems of English grammar	
A knowledge of the present standards of educated usage; a knowledge of the various levels of usage and how those levels are determined	A thorough knowledge of levels of usage; some knowledge of social and geographical dialects; a realization of the cultural implications of both usage and dialect	Sufficient knowledge to illustrate richly and specifically the areas listed under "good"
	A knowledge of the history of the English language, with appropriate awareness of its phonological, morphological, and syntactic changes	

2. KNOWLEDGE AND SKILL IN WRITTEN COMPOSITION (IMAGINATIVE AND EXPOSITORY)

Minimal	Good	Superior
Ability to recognize such characteristics of good writing as substantial and relevant content; organization; clarity; appropriateness of tone; and accuracy in mechanics and usage	A well-developed ability to recognize such characteristics of good writing as substantial and relevant content; organization; clarity; appropriateness of tone; and accuracy in mechanics and usage	In addition to "good" competencies, a detailed knowledge of theories and history of rhetoric and of the development of English prose

A basic understanding of the processes of composing writings of various types	Perception of the complexities in the processes of composing writings of various types	Perception of the subtleties, as well as the complexities, in the processes of composing writings of various types
Ability to analyze and to communicate to students the specific strengths and weaknesses in their writing	Ability to analyze in detail the strengths and weaknesses in the writing of students and to communicate the analysis effectively	Ability to give highly perceptive analysis of the strengths and weaknesses in the writing of students, to communicate this exactly, and to motivate students toward greater and greater strengths
Ability to produce writing with at least a modicum of the characteristics noted above	Proficiency in producing writing with at least considerable strength in the characteristics noted above	Proficiency in producing writing of genuine power; ability and willingness to write for publication

3. KNOWLEDGE AND SKILL IN LITERATURE

Minimal	Good	Superior
An awareness that all literature is a reflection of the human condition.		
Acquaintance with the most important works of major English and American authors	Familiarity with the important works of major English and American authors; knowledge of the characteristics of various genres and of major works in English and American literature in the genres	In addition to the "good" competencies: Intensive and extensive knowledge of one or more major authors and of at least one genre and one period; knowledge of major works of selected foreign writers, both ancient and modern, and of comparative literature
Awareness of the patterns of development of English and American literature from their beginnings to the present	As part of the awareness of patterns of development, a knowledge of such backgrounds of English and American literature as history, the Bible, mythology, and folklore	

Ability to read closely an unfamiliar literary text of average difficulty with comprehension of its content and salient literary characteristics

Ability to read closely an unfamiliar literary text of above-average difficulty with good comprehension of its content and literary characteristics

Familiarity with, and ability to make pertinent applications of, major critical theories and schools of criticism

✳ Familiarity with a considerable body of literature suitable for adolescents of varying abilities and backgrounds

---

4. KNOWLEDGE AND SKILL IN ORAL COMMUNICATION

Minimal	Good	Superior
An understanding of the place of oral communication in the teaching of English	An understanding of the principles of group discussion, group dynamics, oral reporting, panel discussions, classroom dramatizations, and choral reading; an understanding of the relationships between speaking and other facets of English	
An awareness of the role of listening in communication	A knowledge of current information relative to listening techniques	In addition to the "good" competencies: touches of expertise and showmanship that a professional speaker, oral interpreter, or actor possesses
An ability to speak with clarity and in conformity with present standards of educated usage	An ability to speak clearly and effectively, and in conformity with present standards of educated usage; an ability to recognize the virtues of divergence in language	
An ability to read aloud well enough for ready comprehension	An ability to read aloud well enough to convey most aspects of the interpretive art—meaning, mood, dominant emotions, varying emotions, overtones, and variety	

5. KNOWLEDGE AND SKILL IN THE TEACHING OF ENGLISH

Minimal	Good	Superior

A knowledge and appreciation of students as individuals
Creative approaches to meeting the social responsibility of teaching English to all youth

Minimal	Good	Superior
Some understanding of basic principles of educational psychology	Knowledge of educational psychology, especially of the learning process and adolescent psychology	Competence in the knowledge and application of educational psychology; detailed knowledge of the stages of language growth in children and youth
Introductory knowledge of American secondary education	Knowledge of the philosophy, organization, and educational programs of American secondary education now and in historical perspective	
A basic understanding of the content, instructional materials, and organization of secondary English programs	A good understanding of the content, instructional materials, and organization of secondary English programs, and of the role of English in the total school program	A thorough understanding of the content, instructional materials, and organization of secondary English programs, and of the role of English in the total school program; knowledge of principles of curriculum development in English
A basic knowledge of ways to teach English, with an awareness of the importance of developing assignments that guide students in their study of language, written and oral communication, and literature	A wide knowledge of effective ways to teach English, to select and adapt methods and materials for the varying interests and maturity levels of students, and to develop a sequence of assignments to guide and stimulate students in their study of language, written and oral communication, and literature	A thorough knowledge of the most effective ways to teach English, to select and adapt methods and materials for the varying interests and maturity levels of students, and to develop sequential assignments that guide, stimulate, and challenge students in their study of language, written and oral communication, and literature

Minimal	Good	Superior
A basic understanding of the uses of mass media and multimedia approaches in the teaching of English	Knowledge of ways to select and use mass media and multimedia approaches to enhance the teaching of English	Sophistication concerning the selection and use of mass media and multi-media approaches to enrich the teaching of English
Some knowledge of corrective and developmental reading techniques	Moderate knowledge of corrective and developmental reading techniques	A relatively thorough knowledge of corrective and developmental reading techniques
Understanding of basic principles of evaluation and test construction in English	Broad understanding of basic principles of evaluation and test construction in English	Thorough understanding of basic principles of evaluation and test construction in English

A somewhat more specific list of general objectives is this one, prepared as a guide for the Champaign, Illinois, public schools:

1. To master the basic skills of reading, writing, mathematics, and speech.
2. To develop the ability to think clearly, critically, and creatively.
3. To acquire a desire for knowledge that will lead to continued growth and to the best development of one's potentialities for the common good.
4. To develop a respect for high moral values and to incorporate them into a personal code of living.
5. To understand the rights and duties of members of a democratic society in order to become responsible citizens.
6. To gain a knowledge of our history and an appreciation of our culture.
7. To acquire an understanding of the people and culture of other countries.
8. To develop respect for other persons and to be able to live and work cooperatively with them.
9. To develop habits of safe and healthful living, including the wholesome use of leisure time.
10. To develop skills, understanding, and attitudes that will help one to make a constructive contribution to society.
11. To learn about the natural resources of the world and to develop a feeling of social responsibility toward their use and conservation.
12. To understand the significance of the family for the individual and society, and to strive to become a worthy family member.

The central purpose of the educational program defined by these objectives is that boys and girls be helped to develop their intellectual skills to a degree which is consistent with their present and potential capacities—that they be taught to think logically, critically, and creatively. Our students must be able to solve problems of the present and problems of the future.

Our teachers and administrators accept the responsibility for translating these objectives and high purposes into day to day educational practice. They deal with knowledge, meanings, generalizations, and useful concepts. Knowledge is organized and presented as subject matter. This subject matter receives regular and constant scrutiny to insure that what is taught is what is most worth knowing. A process of continuing evaluation, selection, expansion, and elimination is always underway.

The staff is concerned not only with what is taught but how it is taught. Today's student must learn better, more rapidly, and with more efficiency than ever before. More and more, our students are being led to inquire into problems and discover answers, shades of meanings, and relationships for themselves.

This concern with better selection of subject matter and with improved methodology of teaching begins with individual teachers in the classroom.

The English teacher's share in attaining each of these twelve objectives is obvious. But it must be remembered that his is not the sole responsibility. These objectives he shares, but beyond these he has his own task, which is unique and which no other teacher can perform, though other teachers can supplement it: the task of helping students to understand the nature of language, to use it as a tool for the sending and receiving of messages, and to employ it in comprehending the best that has been written so far by the best minds of men.

Obviously aims like those recommended by John Holt—inventiveness, flexibility, resourcefulness, curiosity, and judgment—must be shared aims, too. The English teacher can contribute to the realization of each, but so can and should every other teacher in the school.

The slogan "Every teacher a teacher of English" is high in motive but unattainable in general practice. The simple fact is that few teachers of other subjects know enough about language and literature to teach them. They have necessarily specialized in other subjects and have had insufficient time, even if they had the will, to master English in addition to their specialty. In two ways, however, the teachers of other subjects may and should reinforce the work of the English teacher, just as he is constantly reinforcing or supplementing their work. One of the ways is for these other teachers to let students know that they regard good English as important. They can insist on good organization, correct spelling, accurate punctuation and capitalization, and usages in accord with those most generally approved today. Second, the teachers of other subjects have the responsibility of teaching the vocabulary, spelling, and special reading skills required by their subjects. They are responsible, for instance, for definition, pronunciation, and spelling of such words as *theorem, enzyme, appellate,* and *pizzicato.* The mathematics teacher is responsible for instruction in reading an algebra problem—a very different thing from reading a short story. The social studies teacher is responsible for instruction in reading graphs—a very different thing from reading poetry. To such an extent every teacher may be a teacher of English.

The Aims That Are Unique

Several decades ago a researcher listed all the aims for English teaching that he could find in print. The result: 1,581 aims, ranging from a vaguely phrased "Teach appreciation" down to "Teach proper attitudes toward proper care of the teeth." If his count were brought up to date, the number might reach 2,000 or even 3,000. But in most schools there are only 180 school days per year. To attain 2,000 or 3,000 aims is impossible. Needed is a reachable goal or a group of closely interrelated reachable goals.

Yet school and community pressures are hostile to such simplicity. The home and the church have abrogated some of the responsibilities once assumed to be theirs. Increasingly, instruction in etiquette, in courtesy, in relations between the sexes, and in moral values has been relinquished to the schools. Each time when a new task for the schools is suggested, somebody observes that the task involves reading, writing, speaking, and listening; he then suggests that, because of this involvement, the English class is the logical place to insert this new material. If teen-age telephone habits are bad, for example, a unit on using the telephone is recommended for the English classes, because telephoning means using the language. If an article in a national scientific magazine proposes (as at least one did) that much or most of the reading in secondary English be about science, hosts of scientists and laymen applaud, urging that the reform be instituted at once. School administrators are assailed again and again with pleas of "Do this!" "Include this!" "Give this high priority!" Servants of the community, the administrators oblige as well as they can. They turn to their English teachers, saying, "There's a chance here for students to read and write and speak about something that the community wants to have read and written and spoken about. Will you try to incorporate it in your program, please." And the English teachers look through the course of study to see what can best be sacrificed so that they can include instruction in

> The health that is dental and the health that is mental
> (Good-bye, good-bye to the transcendental);
> The importance of space and the Martian race
> (And Browning goes, frowning, from his place);

The pageant we need for the Bicentennial
(And so we lose a Hardy perennial).

Increasingly, though, English teachers have been resisting the intrusion of what is not germane to their work. They are learning to say no—politely, but still *no*. Their hands will be strengthened when they reach closer agreement about what is truly germane.

Somewhat competitive theories exist among English teachers about what really belongs in an English program, and these theories obviously are tied in closely with aims.

One theory is that anything at all may be included in English if it furthers the development of the individual student. Teachers in experimental British schools (which will be discussed later) tend toward this theory, and often move along without much plan. Theirs is a *carpe diem* philosophy. This says, in brief, that any topic involving the use of language is apropos and may be introduced at any time that seems suitable. Bicentennial celebrations and this week's cricket match or yesterday's great train robbery, being of current interest, are therefore appropriate and easily motivated subjects for reading, writing, speaking, and listening. The children, say the defenders of this theory, will learn because they want to learn, and if some of the usual content of English is missing (such as Romantic poetry or the semicolon), it doesn't really matter, because the children are learning about things more meaningful and important to them.

A second theory holds that the English teacher's task is to improve *communication*. Communication is divided into two parts.

COMMUNICATION

Sending	Receiving

Each of these is in turn subdivided:

COMMUNICATION

Sending		Receiving	
Speaking	Writing	Listening	Reading

This four-part division does not necessarily mean, though, that each section will be equally emphasized in the classroom. Reading is broadly enough defined to include the reading and study of literature, to which the proponents of the communication theory would devote perhaps as much as a half of the time. Writing and speaking both involve study of the language (as do listening and reading to some extent), but, since writing skills seem to take longer to develop than do speaking skills, there is a tendency to devote more attention to the language of writing. In general, though, substantive study of language (its history, dialects, etc.) is frequently somewhat neglected by followers of this theory.

Ernest R. Wall attempts to broaden the traditional understanding of communication, as do many other modern teachers who would step outside the boundaries of the diagram above. "English teachers," says Wall, "must investigate the contents, the techniques, and the structures of the new communications, the emotional, as well as verbal and intellectual, communication; they must determine the traditional skills worth retaining and adapt them to the new technology; and, above all, they must accept the fact that written expression, though still important and essential, is just *one* of *many* methods of communication available today." [6]

The *tripod* theory says that instruction should encompass language, composition, and literature as equal partners in the English curriculum. Language includes study of such things as history, grammar, usage, semantics, lexicography, and dialectology. Composition refers especially but not exclusively to written work. Literature means literary materials, not today's newspaper or an article in *Popular Mechanics*. During the 1960's, especially in institutes for teachers, this tripod theory was emphasized, and until the Dartmouth Conference raised doubts in some people's minds, it was the focal point for much curricular revision.

In mathematics, *unified field theory* refers to a concept of Albert Einstein concerning electromagnetism and gravitation. We may borrow the term for English to designate the belief that English is and should be a unified field, addressed to enhancing student's experiences with and through language, and using those experiences to gain insights into themselves and the society in which they live. The definition of the unifying force, however, has been debated.

[6] *Maryland English Journal, Fall,* 1968.

Some professional leaders argue that language or rhetoric is the unifying force, and that the English curriculum should be language-centered, while others assert that literature should be the center. Those favoring the emphasis on language or rhetoric advocate intensive and extensive study of the English language, much writing on language topics, and much literary study concerned with the author's use of language and rhetoric. Those who favor a literary center contend that writing should be mainly on literary topics, and that students may best improve their use and appreciation of language by wide and deep reading. Despite such differences of opinion, though, the belief that English is a seamless garment rather than a mixture of three or four or many things has attracted considerable attention in recent years.

The Point of View of This Book

It is not intended here to arbitrate among these four theories, and indeed they are not mutually exclusive. A teacher may find himself in a school where the departmental philosophy is essentially any one of the four, or some combination of them; or there may be no clear philosophy.

Any one of the four may be adequate. The first, stressing as it does the interaction between the student and the content, has been gaining in popularity; it is the foundation-stone of much modern instruction in England, and has been strongly advocated in the United States by James Moffett.[7] The other three differ from one another more in emphasis than in essentials. The communication theory stresses the interrelatedness of the sending and receiving of oral and written "messages," including literature; the tripod theory pays relatively little attention to speaking and listening, much to literature and written composition and language as subjects for intensive study; the unified field theory says that speaking, listening, writing, and reading may all be studied through their common denominator, language or rhetoric, or through their common greatest exemplification, literature.

The point of view of the writer of this book is somewhat eclectic. It may be summarized as follows:

[7] *Teaching the Universe of Discourse* and *A Student-Centered Language Arts Curriculum, Grades K–13: A Handbook for Teachers* (Boston: Houghton Mifflin Co., 1968).

Philosophy
Hooks
summing up

1. English is a man-made tool, not important in itself. (Similarly, a hammer or an airplane is a man-made tool, important only when it is used.) The importance of a language lies in its use for determining and furthering the ends of an individual and of society.
2. <u>Objectives</u> for English-learning are necessary. Lack of objectives is aimlessness. If one does not know where he is going, he cannot ever tell whether he has arrived. Whatever objectives there are must stress the interaction of student and content, of student and student, of student and the society in which he lives.
3. <u>Planning</u> is better than planlessness. But plans should never be so tight that they admit no flexibility; the unexpected often pays rich dividends; the concept of serendipity should be clear in every teacher's mind.
4. The functioning of the English language should be given daily attention, sometimes as a thing in itself, often as a key to the clarity and effectiveness of composition and literature.
5. Students should be steadily exposed to the best literature they are capable of understanding reasonably well.
6. Students should have regular practice in using the language through a <u>planned</u> but flexible <u>sequence</u> of <u>oral</u> and <u>written compositions.</u>

The implementation of any theory requires some sort of organizational pattern, or curricular plan. Descriptions of three patterns are given in the sections that follow.

The Block Concept of Curriculum

Most popular concept

In effect, knowledge is conceived of as assignable to blocks, which are piled one upon another as a child moves through school (see the diagram below). In schools without homogeneous grouping, all seventh grade children, for example, study the same block, which therefore must be thought of in terms of capabilities of an average child (though within the class some adaptation is possible). In homogeneously grouped classes, as the diagram on page 39 shows, the blocks for the average level correspond to those for the heterogeneous groups, but low-level ninth graders may be taking less advanced work than average-level seventh graders, and high-level seventh graders may be taking more advanced work than average-level ninth graders. This concept of the curriculum, particularly when applied in homogeneous groups, has proved useful and workable and is still the concept most frequently used as a basis for curriculum planning.

Heterogeneous Classes

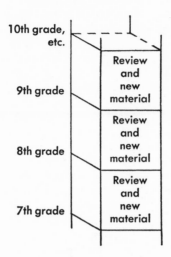

The Spiral Cone Concept

In *The Process of Education* (1960) Jerome Bruner wrote in favor of beginning fundamental instruction in each significant topic at the earliest possible age, returning to it and developing it in later grades. He asserted that even very young children can be taught the basic principles of almost anything. He referred to the process of starting instruction early and then returning to the same topic in higher grades as a "spiral curriculum."

Bruner, in his book, did not develop in any detail the theory of the spiral curriculum. He might or might not have subscribed to the idea that the best image is that not of an ordinary spiral but of a spiral cone.

The concept of the spiral cone may be clarified by the diagram on page 41 and by the following paragraphs:

In the primary grades the level of difficulty of material presented is low, and the coverage is narrow. As the children grow older, they are introduced to more difficult material, they do more with it, and they cover more of it. Hence curriculum coverage rises and broadens simultaneously.

Different children of the same chronological age will be at different places on the cone. If the differences are not great, they may be accommodated by simple adjustments in the quality of material presented. (In the illustration,

Homogeneous Classes

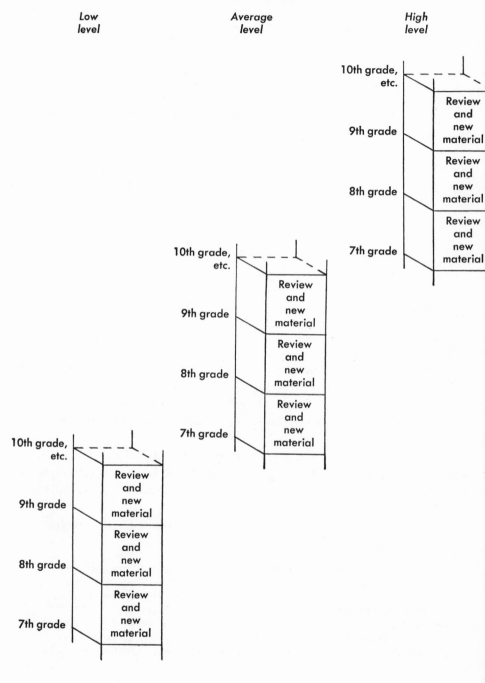

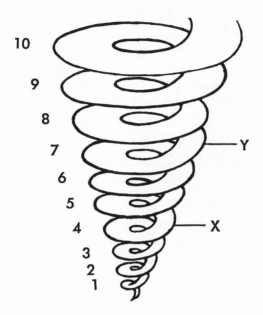

for instance, less able children who are on the sixth ring of the spiral may be visualized as being on the inside of the cone, covering a limited amount of material of sixth-ring difficulty; their more able classmates will be on the outer edge, covering more material.) But when differences between children of the same age are considerable, when two children are at widely separated points on the spiral, they cannot be expected to master identical work. Of two ten-year-old children, for instance, one may be at point X on the spiral, the other at point Y. Through varied assignments, grouping, or a rather drastic revision of our usual concepts of grade level, it is possible to provide for each child what he needs at the particular point he has reached on the spiral.

. . . If all children were of equal ability and could progress at the same rate, it would be a relatively simple matter to decide upon a subject-matter sequence that would be logical. But since children (happily) are not identical, they are not all ready for the same learnings at the same time. The spiral cone concept provides for sequential progress in subject matter without ignoring variations in children.[8]

If the spiral cone concept were ever fully realized, it would have far-reaching effects upon education. It would involve an upward extension of the ungraded primary system, in which children in their first three years are taught what they need to be taught, without regard to whether the materials or skills are traditionally first, second, or third grade. A child who reads early, for example, is moved

[8] J. N. Hook, "The Emerging English Curriculum," *The American Behavioral Scientist*, Nov., 1962, p. 36.

quickly into third grade materials or even above; a child who is slow in learning to read stays with the simplest work until he has mastered it. For several years such schools as those in Melbourne, Florida, have experimented with ungraded classes in either the elementary or the secondary schools, with notably excellent results. If the plan is carried to its logical culmination, some children of fifteen or sixteen may reach the top rung of the secondary spiral in all subjects, pass college entrance examinations, and go to college at an age considerably below average. Other students, for whom high school represents terminal education, may have reached only a relatively low rung because of lack in ability or in motivation; after twelve years of elementary and secondary education, they would receive their high school diplomas but would not proceed to college, because their test results would be too low. On the other hand, a student who after twelve years had almost reached a college-level rung could, if he wished, attend secondary school for an additional year without being sneered at for falling behind the rest of his class; in an ungraded system such designations as "sophomore" or "senior" are scarcely needed.

Among the specific implications of the spiral cone for English departments, perhaps the most important is also the most obvious: the need to plan the sequence of content. A second implication is flexibility of scheduling, so that whatever a given group of students (often of different age levels) needs, could be offered to it.

The Individual-Growth Concept of Curriculum

Every teacher no doubt realizes that children grow at individual rates, both physically and mentally. Usually growth is not steady; rather, it occurs in spurts. Parents who keep monthly records of a child's height often discover that in some months or even quarters change is barely perceptible, but that at other times the child grows an inch or more in a very short time. There is evidence that mental growth occurs similarly. And within a class at any given time, some children are growing very rapidly while others hardly seem to "improve" at all; in the next month or two, however, the fast may slow down for a while and the slow may speed up.

In intellectual growth, though, despite what has just been said, some children's average rate is much faster than that of others—even though the rate appears not to be steady for anyone. Therefore child A may over a year's time advance much more than child B does, and over a period of several years a mental age differential of two or three years may increase to five or six.

Because of such realities in growth-patterns, in recent years more and more attention has been given to what is in effect the development of curriculums for individuals. Although classes are still held and students share a number of activities, the same behavioral objectives are not selected for and by each student. There are common general objectives—the direction of movement is essentially the same—but the specific behaviors expected from child A and child B are not the same, and the tasks performed by each may differ greatly.

Highly elaborate plans for differentiation of instruction are being formulated, and no doubt will attract considerable attention throughout the seventies and eighties. One of these, being developed, with millions of dollars of commercial funds, by a large staff in California, and being tried out in a number of schools throughout the nation, uses sophisticated batteries of tests to find the present status of each student in a number of aspects of English and later includes many additional measurements to ascertain the new levels of achievement. The tasks assigned to, or chosen by, each student are selected in light of the present stage of his development, as well as in the light of his individual career goals. The student often works alone on these tasks, sometimes he works in small groups, and at times a whole class or group of classes may assemble for discussion, a film showing, or some other appropriate activity. The individual tasks may vary greatly, including among others such things as programmed instruction, preparing a paper or an oral report or even making a film, reading a poem or a story, working on matters of grammar or usage or punctuation, and many more.

In such a school the teacher's role is different from that in the more traditional plans. In fact, he does comparatively little "teaching" as that term is usually defined. Instead, he is primarily a learning coordinator, who interprets test results, helps each student select appropriate tasks, decides which groups may best work together for a while, makes sure that suitable materials are available for the diverse activities of his students, and spends much time in conferring individually or in small groups with students. A tradition-bound teacher, accustomed to being in the front of the room at all times, "the cynosure of all eyes," may at least for some time be uncomfortable in a school that defines his role in this new way. But some such plan for individualization may well become standard before very long, and the teacher who possesses the adaptability mentioned early in this chapter should be able to adjust to it without too much pain.

This system has the advantage of providing suitable tasks for individuals, and a pace of work geared to each, in accordance with his present achievement and his present learning rate. It thus differs markedly from the somewhat lockstep procedures of the conventional class. It may have disadvantages, too. For example, it diminishes the amount of student interaction within a class (and students do learn much from one another). It also necessitates a greater wealth of readily available materials. And it presupposes a teacher who can manage so many circus rings at one time.

This chapter has described some of the changes in the English teacher's role that have been occurring in recent years. Change, as everyone knows, is inevitable, but its rate has been accelerating in the past decade or so. In 1968, reviewing developments in the previous ten years, Michael Shugrue wrote:

> The educational system . . . is in the process of tremendous change. The English teacher caught up in that change at the school or college level must respond by developing new skills and acquiring new knowledge. Most of all, he will have to prove himself flexible as the traditional, comfortable, familiar classroom in the neighborhood school is challenged and changed.[9]

THE IDEA BOX

Purpose stated!

The Idea Box, which you will find at the end of this chapter and each succeeding one, has three purposes: (1) To suggest teaching devices of proved worth, besides those discussed in the chapter itself; (2) to mention other aids, materials, articles, or books that offer additional help; and (3), for classes of prospective teachers, to provide items (sometimes controversial) for discussion. A very large proportion of the articles summarized are in the *English Journal*, both because that magazine is readily available and because it emphasizes the practical as well as the theoretical.

As Louis Zahner once said, ". . . no classroom practice is sound unless it stems from sound theory and can be traced back to it." The practices in the Idea Box appear to be based on sound theory, though

[9] *English in a Decade of Change*, p. 176.

it cannot be claimed that all are of equal merit, and certainly some are controversial or even contradictory of others. The Idea Boxes contain many more tactics and techniques than any one teacher can or should try. However, from the riches each teacher may select the ideas that best fit his temperament and the needs of the classes he instructs. What will work well for one teacher in one situation may work less well in other circumstances, but every idea presented here has been *Note* ✗ used successfully in somebody's classroom.

The items in the Idea Boxes following Chapters 2 and 3 are less specific than those in the rest of the book because of the broad topics of these two chapters.

What Do Today's Students Really Want To Know?

Usually not what we want to teach them. So Charles F. Greiner asked them, "If you could have the answers to any three questions, what would those questions be?" They asked some deep ones! Greiner helped them find answers, or partial answers, or hypotheses. "Hook-Up, Plug In, Connect," *English Journal*, LVIII (Jan., 1969), 23.

Facilitation of Learning

According to psychologist Carl R. Rogers, teachers should not teach; they should "facilitate learning." Education can improve tremendously and unrest can decrease, he says, if we stop closing our ears to "honest feedback" from students. One thing that they constantly call for is greater control over their own education. Teachers can help them to attain reasonable goals they establish for themselves.

Preparing Students for Leisure Time

As leisure time increases, for many it is only a blank to be endured. Robert G. Lambert says we can help young people to get ready for leisure by discussing the problem directly, by encouraging intelligent listening (to dramas, for instance), by teaching "the way words work" so that students will be less likely prey for demagogues, by teaching wise choices in the mass media, by making reading more enjoyable, and by encouraging writing for fun. "The Forty-Year Coffee Break," *English Journal*, LV (Sept., 1966), 768.

The Teacher as Intermediary

The following diagram depicts one interpretation of the role of the teacher, conceived of here as an intermediary, a facilitator of learning:

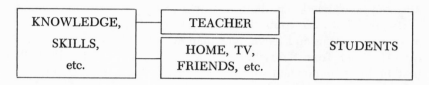

In Defense of the Humanities

"To report to and be knowledgeable about painting and architecture, music and poetry, fiction and philosophy, the course of history and the beauty of nature—and to form from all these responses and knowledges a system and a pattern that is one aspect of a coherent personality—that is the goal." Walter Hipple, *Indiana English Journal* (Winter, 1969).

Why Some Students Hate English

Robert Hogan, NCTE executive secretary, tells of a second-grader who as his "composition" wrote, "Sometimes I wish I was dead." The teacher's only reaction was to cross out *was* and replace it with *were*.

How To Nonteach

Ramble. Lecture. Read aloud from the assigned text. Play records without pre-auding. Make discussions a pooling of ignorance. Robert Coard describes the five techniques of nonteaching in *Kappa Delta Pi Record* (April, 1965).

To Stifle Creativity

Too many teachers and parents stifle creativity by imposing these ten commandments, claims Stanley Krippner, *Gifted Child Quarterly* (Autumn, 1967):

1. Everything thou doest must be useful.
2. Everything thou doest must be successful.
3. Everything thou doest must be perfect.
4. Everyone thou knowest must like thee.
5. Thou shalt not prefer solitude to togetherness.
6. Remember concentrated attention and keep it holy.
7. Thou shalt not diverge from culturally imposed sex norms.
8. Thou shalt not express excessive emotional feeling.
9. Thou shalt not be ambiguous.
10. Thou shalt not rock the cultural boat.

"Understanding Means Predicting"

If you understand something, you can predict pretty accurately what will come next, or what will be the consequence of an act, R. K. MacDonald of Montana believes. If you know how to spell *donkeys*, you can predict *journeys*. If you've read well several O. Henry stories, you can make some predictions about the characters, plot, and style in the next one. (Teachers of the new math often build on this fact, by giving students sets of numbers in which they are to predict the next: 1 3 6 10 ? .) *English Journal*, LV (Nov., 1966), 1066.

What Is Aptitude?

According to John Carroll, formerly of Harvard, *aptitude* refers to the amount of time required for a person to master a concept, skill, etc. The curricular implications of this fact—if it is a fact—are considerable.

Emphasizing the Process in Learning

In *Process as Content*, J. C. Parker and L. J. Rubin divide learning into these components: (1) intake operations (listening, looking, reading, note-taking, charting, identifying, etc.); (2) manipulative operations (comparing, verifying, interpreting, modifying, classifying, etc.); (3) applicative operations (deciding, solving, constructing, performing, etc.). Perhaps in English we over-emphasize the first and pay too little attention to the others.

What Is Cheating?

Lynn L. Weldon argues that unless the quality and quantity of memorization are what is being measured, a student who uses notes should not be considered to be cheating. A revolutionary concept, but worth considering; after all, what should we be testing—memorized details or an understanding of patterns? *Clearing House* (April, 1966).

"Helping Slow Learners Achieve Success"

"One year's crop of dropouts costs the American taxpayers $500,000,-000 in welfare costs during their lifetime." And Judge James Lincoln of Detroit says, "The only thing concerning these kids about which I am absolutely sure is that those who get in trouble have never had any success experiences." The article by Ethel Tincher suggests a few ways to attain success; e.g., journals, frequent change of pace, no lectures, much use of AV aids. *English Journal,* LIV (April, 1965), 289.

Do You Teach Mexican-Americans?

Luis F. Fernandez, in "Teaching English to the Culturally Disadvantaged Mexican-American Student," sympathetically describes such students and suggests ways to teach them most effectively. *English Journal,* LVII (Jan., 1968), 87.

The Maligned Football Player

Football players, in Iowa at least, are better-than-average students in English, history, science, and mathematics. In twenty-four high schools with very good football records, Russell M. Eidsmoe reports in *School Activities* (Nov., 1963), football players made a 2.443 grade-point average (on a four-point basis) while the non-players made only a 2.166.

"Kari's Handicap—The Impediment of Creativity"

Kari tried "to synthetize all the elements of her world into relevance," so that an algebraic solution was "symbolic poetry that rhymes in the symmetry of logic." She was the only student who defended the heroine in the *The Scarlet Letter* "for having the courage to be apart from the society." But school tried relentlessly to warp her into a common mold. Robert E. Samples told her story in *Saturday Review* (July 15, 1967), and it is reprinted in a fine collection of articles on creativity, *Readings on Creativity and Imagination in Literature and Language* (NCTE, 1968).

Help From Other Departments

The Virginia State Board of Education recommends that (1) teachers in all subject areas encourage pupils to apply principles of effective writing in all writing assignments; (2) in preparing examinations, teachers in all subjects consider the appropriateness of one or more essay-type questions; (3) spelling and composition be given due consideration in grading pupils in all subject fields.

Now part of Ky Curriculum for Soc. Studies

Role of the Department Chairman

Orientation of new teachers is one of the important jobs of a department chairman, says Paul S. Nelson of Franconia, N. H., "Orientation of New English Teachers," *English Journal,* LVII (March, 1969), 409.

Lasting Issues

In "Passing Strange," Dennis W. Crow of Sandy, Ore., says that though progress in teaching is undeniable, many old problems still exist. To prove his point, he quotes dozens of parallel passages from the first issue of the *English Journal* (Jan., 1912), and from 1967 and 1968 issues.

3

Planning—For the Year, the Month, and the Day

To sequence effectively for coherence and continuity

In Chapter 2 we have looked at curricular theories for English, at basic ways of organizing heterogeneous materials and heterogeneous concepts for heterogeneous students. Choosing from among the various alternatives is normally the function of the whole English department, because it involves broad philosophical considerations. Or it may be the task of a special curriculum committee, which may or may not be granted a certain amount of released time or summer employment to do its work. Seldom, except in a very small school, is it the responsibility of just one teacher of English.

But within whatever basic framework the department has agreed upon, each teacher generally has considerable freedom and responsibility. He plans the segments of work, often in the form of units, and tries to mesh the segments so that they have reasonable continuity and coherence. Within the units he works out—in greater or less detail—lesson plans for the week or the day. And, within the range of the principles adopted by his department or his school, he decides upon and puts into practice his own system of evaluation.

These matters are the concern of this chapter. In later chapters we shall become increasingly specific.

PLANNING OF UNITS

Answers to the question "What is a unit?" may vary widely. One teacher said, "I'm teaching a unit on Frost's 'Death of the Hired Man' today." To her a unit meant simply having students read and discuss a single poem and perhaps bring in some related material. In contrast, in a Minnesota rural elementary school all eight grades worked for a whole year on a "unit" called "Improving Our School," with all the elementary subjects incorporated in the work. More typically, though, the term *unit* refers to an organized study, lasting from one week to eight weeks and centered upon a given theme or topic, to which everything in the unit is in some way related.

Some units are devoted almost entirely to composition, others to literature, to language study, or to oral work. Some may center on drama, on dramatic re-creation, on the short story, on the paragraph, on the history of the English language in America or on any of hundreds of other things. It is most often characteristic of a good unit, though, that it combines work in reading, writing, listening, and speaking. Even though it may center upon, say, eighteenth-century satire it provides students with an opportunity to talk and write and hear, and to look at the language as language and not just as literature.

The number of possible subjects for units, as has just been implied, is limitless. Very often a concept is central, such as "Caution vs. cowardice," "What makes a plot?," "How authors delineate characters," or "The essence of tragedy." A linguistic item may be the focus: "English in Chaucer's time," "Emotive and reportorial language," "The versatile verb," "Do you speak a dialect?," etc. Skills may sometimes be stressed, as in "Reading for greater comprehension" or "Learning to write good letters." A large number of unit topics are suggested in The Idea Box, pages 70–72.

Even teachers who do not use the term *unit*, unless they adhere completely to the *carpe diem* practices discussed on page 35, generally employ some kind of planning. If they did not, the work in the English classroom would probably consist of many unrelated snippets. But the amount of planning may vary widely.

It was once the practice of some teachers (often at the bidding of administrators) to plan the organization of a unit to the last detail. Their lesson plans within the unit indicated that five minutes would be devoted to this, ten minutes to that, and so on. The teacher gathered every scrap of material in advance. Little or nothing was left to student initiative. The class moved in rigid conformity to schedule, regardless of whether or not the desired outcomes had been reached.

Then, under the leadership of a few "progressive" educators, some teachers went to the other extreme, that of near planlessness. In effect, they appeared before their classes, asked "What shall we do today [or during the next four weeks]?" took a vote, and did whatever the majority of students said they wanted to do, regardless of its apparent suitability to usual aims of an English course. If the students wanted to read and discuss comic books, they did that; if they wanted to spend their time in planning for a school function, they did that.

Of course there was learning in both the carefully planned and the virtually unplanned units. Students learn in spite of themselves and their teachers. But the present tendency is toward planning that is flexible enough to permit some alteration in accord with legitimate student requests or unexpected developments.

Joint planning by teachers and students exists in various modifications in some schools. Student participation in such planning is most likely to consist of assistance in selection of specific learning activities, or perhaps in choosing between two or more equally appropriate topics for units. When students have had some voice (a genuine voice) in such decisions, their motivation is likely to be better. Some teachers therefore give students much opportunity to choose individual and group behavioral objectives, to choose and gather materials, and to be creative in designing activities. A number of teachers like to employ student committees, each of which is responsible for part of the work of the unit.

In a well-planned unit, not all students are doing exactly the same things. Some of the reading and exercises are performed in common, but individual and group work, tailored to special needs, is also included.

More than books should be used in most units. Movies and filmstrips often fit in. The making of a film by students may be useful for teaching principles of plotting, characterizing, and writing of dialogue. Sometimes, through coincidence, radio or television programs are appropriate. Magazines, newspapers, and radio or TV scripts may often be used. Occasionally a field trip is desirable. Outside speakers, or teachers in other departments, may be invited to talk to the class. The students' own activities may be varied. The good unit does possess much variety, life, interest. It is as a rule infinitely preferable to the old day-to-day assignment routine: "Tomorrow study pages fifty-eight to sixty-seven."

Details of unit planning vary, but the following description is reasonably typical.

1. *Scope:* a general statement of what will be covered and what apparently related material will be excluded.

2. *Objectives:* a list of desired outcomes. Objectives are often subdivided into general and specific. The general should not be huge and amorphous, such as "Learn to be a better citizen." Instead they should be general only in that they exclude concrete detail; e.g., "Learn to be tolerant of those whose home backgrounds differ from ours." The objectives are normally stated in terms of the outcomes for students; i.e., not *teach* but *learn*. With today's emphasis on behavioral objectives, the statements are likely to be in terms of the specific behaviors expected of students during the work and at its end.[1]

3. *Activities:* the specific reading, writing, problems, laboratory experiments, field trips, and other experiences that will be included. These activities form the basis of separate, more detailed lesson plans which develop each activity or group of activities fully enough for a day's classwork. Often the first activity is an "initiating" or "introductory" or "motivational" one intended to arouse students' interest and support and provide essential background. The last activity is called "culminating" in current jargon and is intended to summarize or in some other way bring to a head all the other activities. It may be combined with 5, Evaluation. Activities may be varied to provide for individual differences; if so, the unit should show how this is to be accomplished.

4. *Resources:* the books and other text or library materials, *realia*, audiovisual aids, laboratory equipment, field trips, and anything else needed for successful completion of the unit. Often the resources are divided into those for student use and those for the teacher.

5. *Evaluation:* the ways in which the success of the students and the success of the teacher may be judged.[2]

Many schools today are making use of "modules," which may be considered either extended units or short courses. In a modular plan, students register for a given number of weeks in a module that will concentrate on a particular area of English. Upon completion of the module, they register for another, perhaps with a

[1] Two useful and readable (and short!) books on behavioral objectives: Norman E. Gronlund, *Stating Behavioral Objectives in the Classroom* (New York: The Macmillan Co., 1970). Robert F. Mager, *Developing Attitude Toward Learning* (Palo Alto, Calif.: Fearson Publishers, 1968). Another especially valuable book, though the statements are not usually in behavioral terms, is Arnold Lazarus and Rozanne Knudson, *Selected Objectives for the English Language Arts, Grades 7–12* (Boston: Houghton Mifflin Co., 1967).

[2] J. N. Hook, *Hook's Guide to Good Writing: Grammar, Style, Usage* (New York: The Ronald Press Company, 1962) p. 482.

different teacher. R. Baird Shuman describes a plan in which during each twelve weeks each student takes for four weeks a "substantive" course (history of the language, history of the novel, literary criticism, etc.), for another four weeks a "skill" course (reading, speech, technical writing, etc.), and for the remaining four weeks, an "appreciation" course (genre, major author, literature of protest, etc.). With counsel, students select their own modules; teachers teach in their specialties.[3] In the same issue, J. N. Hook describes modules of a semester or a half-semester in length, with students' choices assisted by diagnostic tests to show what would be most profitable for each. Each module, though it would emphasize one component, would include some literature, some composition, and some study of language.

One of the most exciting curricular developments is a variation of the modular plan: the APEX program at Trenton, Michigan. Students, regardless of age or year in school, may choose any course offered. There are, however, five "phases," from basic to advanced; any student may take whatever he believes he is ready for. Courses run a semester each. Individualized Reading, Composition I, and Reading Techniques rank high in popularity.[4]

Still another variation, described by Dorothy Wright,[5] is a plan being used at Athens, Ohio, High School. Students may drop a regularly scheduled subject for nine or eighteen weeks and substitute for it a "Quest" project, which may involve research or creation, with the student responsible for carrying out his project with minimal guidance. Such a program, although it appears most suitable for the college-bound, may also help other students to develop initiative and to learn how to learn independently.

Such independent study is becoming more and more common. Scarsdale, New York, as reported by Franklin G. Myers,[6] permits students to embark on ten-week investigations on such topics as Ferlinghetti, How Television Works, or Is There a Point in Existing? David W. Berg called independent study a "Transfusion for Anemic English Programs."[7]

[3] University of Toledo *Educational Comment* for 1968.
[4] A book describing the program in detail may be purchased from the school. A brief account by Donald F. Weise appeared in the *English Journal*, Jan., 1970.
[5] *English Journal*, Jan., 1970.
[6] *English Journal*, Feb., 1970.
[7] *Ibid.*

DIAGNOSIS, LESSON PLANS, AND EVALUATION

Diagnosis

Faced with his four or five classes—perhaps 100 or 175 students —the beginning teacher may feel a temporary bafflement. How can he get to know these young people? How can he discover what they are and what they need to learn?

The principal's or counselor's files will probably yield some in- *Basic* formation concerning the age, background, physical handicaps, *Information* academic records, test scores, etc., of most of the students. It is usually inadvisable, though, to spend much time in studying these records until one gets to know the students fairly well in class. The mere reading of a hundred or so sets of data will leave in one's mind no clear impression about individuals unless one is already somewhat familiar with each student. Therefore, except for a brief preliminary examination of the records, the files may be ignored for a few weeks. Then, if the teacher wishes specific information about individuals, he may ask permission to consult the files again. What he finds there should be taken with some salt, however, and should not be regarded as final.

For example, the file may show that freshman Herbert had difficulties in passing some of his subjects in the seventh and eighth grades, that his IQ is 97, and that disciplinary action was once taken when Herbert stole a ball-point pen. To the teacher, Herbert has seemed a pleasant, well-behaved boy who is capable of doing at least average work. In this instance, the teacher's judgment *may* be more reliable than the statistical data, for the simple reason that Herbert is an adolescent and that adolescents change rapidly. Perhaps Herbert, in a moment of adolescent irresponsibility, did steal a ball-point pen; he should not, however, be regarded as a confirmed thief whose every movement must be watched. Perhaps his IQ is slightly below normal, but psychologists today are aware that the IQ test scores are not entirely reliable and that the IQ may change somewhat over a period of years. The process of growing up may have caused Herbert's troubles in eighth grade English; perhaps now he is mature enough that those troubles are lessened. In other *Teacher* words, data of the sort usually in the principal's office need to be *observation* supplemented by personal observation; these data may be of considerable value at times, but they should never cause a teacher to decide that one student is hopeless, that another is a genius, or that a third is doomed to mediocrity.

The advice just given is of great importance. Studies made in the late 60's suggest strongly that students tend to live up to teachers' expectations. Students whose teachers have been informed that they are capable of making great strides often do make great strides. Other students, whose teachers are told that they are "hopeless," often do act as though they have no hope, and they accomplish little. The teachers' pre-established attitudes ("prejudiced" attitudes in the etymological sense of pre-judging) are frequently revealed unintentionally or unconsciously to the students, and they tend to react in the ways that the teachers have shown they are expected to react.

Within his classroom the teacher has a number of ways of learning about individuals. He should learn students' names quickly, for obvious reasons. The easiest way to do so is to make a temporary seating chart at the first class meeting. Fifteen or twenty minutes' homework studying each chart, plus a quick review before class, should enable him to call each student by name on the second day. The students will be pleased that they have so quickly lost their anonymity; they will be happy that they are not addressed as "the boy in the green shirt" or "the last girl in the row" or "yes, you"; and they will immediately gain respect for the teacher. If the teacher wishes to change or discard the seating arrangement after he has learned to attach the right name to the right face, he may, of course, do so.

After learning students' names, the teacher may begin making mental notes of individuals' characteristics. The notes are for the sake not of classifying but of understanding. Thus the teacher may note that George seems sullen in class and rather hostile toward the other students; the teacher will then be on the alert to discover the reasons for George's attitude and eventually to plan a little campaign to make George more cooperative. Or Helen may appear to be unusually intelligent and well informed; the teacher may search for ways of making use of Helen's intelligence for the benefit of both Helen and the rest of the class.

How a student talks, how he reads aloud, how he listens, how willing he is to contribute to class discussion, what information he brings in from his own background, how he reacts to a literary selection—all these are straws in the wind, bits of evidence that will help the teacher to understand him. Particularly valuable, though, is noting what and how he writes. In a page or two of a student's writing, one can find much more than the fact that the student does not know how to punctuate or to spell "there." One may discover his ambition, hopes, fears; much of his background; glimmerings of his developing philosophy of life.

student autobiography

Besides learning about students from administrators' data and from observation in class, the teacher may—and should—if there is time—talk with the students individually. The subject of conversation is relatively unimportant; it may be schoolwork, but it may almost as well be football or clothes or a movie or anything else. From such conversation the teacher may draw valid conclusions about what a student is and what he needs.

There are also numerous standardized tests available for diagnostic purposes. Such tests are of value as indications of what points need to be stressed in whatever units are planned.

Lesson Plans

A lesson plan is a fairly detailed outline of the work proposed by the teacher for a single class period. Some department heads, supervisors, or principals require that lesson plans be turned in for a week or two weeks in advance, so that in case of the teacher's illness a substitute will know what is to be covered. In other schools no such requirement exists.

Ordinarily it is desirable for beginning teachers to make more detailed lessons plans than experienced teachers need. For the experienced teacher a statement that covers the purpose, the materials, and the main points to be included is enough. Many old-timers, in fact, carry their lesson plans in their heads. But the beginner will feel more comfortable and probably do a better job if he has outlined each lesson rather carefully, even though he should expect to be flexible in following the plan.

No specific kind of outline will cover all lesson plans. Most often, though, the following three points will be covered:

Objective or Objectives.   These should be limited enough to be attained in the period. Usually they will represent a small segment of the objectives of the total unit and will be phrased in behavioral terms.

Activities. These generally include (1) an introduction that relates the day's topic to previous work, or presents the beginnings of new material and (2) a chronological ordering of the things to be done during the hour, together with key questions to be asked if discussion is involved. If the class works in groups, the tasks for each group are specified.

Materials Needed. This is simply a list of any books, pictures, recordings, or other materials the teacher should be sure to have in class.

Many beginning teachers dread the prospect of running out of material before the class period ends. Actually, as experienced teachers know, this seldom happens. The reverse is more likely: the bell will ring before the work planned for the hour is completed. Nevertheless, the beginner will have more peace of mind if he has available a supply of ten- or fifteen-minute fillers that can be slipped into any vacant time-slot that may unexpectedly appear. These fillers may be quite varied, and need not be closely correlated with any given lesson, since students like variety. Among the numerous possibilities are these: a very short story or an easy poem that can be read aloud and briefly discussed; a useful exercise in spelling or punctuation or some other mechanical matter; an improvised dramatic sketch by students, perhaps related to recently studied literature; playing part of a literary recording or one on dialects; writing in a journal, or other brief writing; and of course that old standby, using the last few minutes for work on the next assignment, with the teacher available to provide help as needed.

Evaluation

William H. Evans and Jerry Walker discuss at length some of the recent variations from usual evaluative procedures.[8] Among other devices, they discuss the use of lay readers for compositions, conferences with students, student correction of themes, emphasis upon mastery of a process rather than of a product, the use of cumulative grids, class discussions, and individual projects.

The use of behavioral objectives, which are increasingly discussed and employed in today's schools, involves built-in evaluative techniques. In such objectives the emphasis is upon what the student

[8] *New Trends in the Teaching of English in Secondary Schools* (Chicago: Rand McNally & Co., 1966).

does as a result of instruction—not just what facts he is able to regurgigate. Thus, in the first outgrowth of a federally supported study conducted at three Midwest universities,[9] each objective requires the student to do something observable: analyze, draw, read aloud, justify, describe, write, act out, find in a dictionary, explain relationships etc. Such evaluation is constant, a regular ingredient of all activities, and is far removed from the conventional pencil and paper test.

Every teacher needs to give considerable thought to evaluation, even before entering the classroom. How will he be able to determine whether his classes are making satisfactory progress? Upon what bases shall he grade the work of individuals?

The first of these questions is somewhat easier to answer than the second. The teacher may ascertain class progress in a number of ways. For one thing, he may, at the end of a semester or year, roughly estimate the progress of the class toward the attainment of the objectives that have been set up. That is, he will re-examine the objectives and draw conclusions concerning how fully they have been reached. The important point to remember is that any measurement should be in terms of the predetermined behavioral objectives: To what extent do students evince the behaviors that were selected? (It is surprising that many teachers teach one thing but test something else.) A comparison of paragraphs or longer pieces of writing prepared by the students at the beginning and the end of each term is often enlightening. Likewise, a consideration of improvement in students' ability to make well-organized and reasonably well-delivered oral presentations is possible, particularly if a few recordings are made at the beginning and again at the end of the term. Increased maturity of response to literature can be observed at least subjectively, as can the willingness to read without prodding. Certain less tangible but no less important aspects of improvement can hardly be measured but should be thought about: such things as class spirit, cooperativeness, willingness to assume responsibility, initiative, judgment, tolerance, and understanding and employment of democratic principles.

The basis for evaluating the work of individuals is often determined by the administration. In some schools no student who attends class with fair regularity is permitted to fail. In others a

[9] *Representative Performance Objectives in English: A Preliminary Catalog* (1970).

grading curve must be followed by all teachers: perhaps 15 per cent A's, 20 per cent B's, 30 per cent C's, 20 per cent D's, and 15 per cent F's. In such a system the top 15 per cent must be given A's, even though some do not deserve this mark of distinction, or even though more than 15 per cent have displayed consistent excellence; likewise, 15 per cent must fail, even though they may have been fairly successful in reaching the objectives of the course. In a large number of schools, written comments are superseding grades; at the end of the course the student either is or is not given credit. Much could be said in favor of this plan, although some teachers complain that it destroys the initiative of potentially superior students to whom grades are an incentive. In still other systems the administrators have other rules of thumb concerning grading, rules which of course the teacher must follow whether or not he agrees with the principles involved.

But suppose that you—not "the teacher" but *you*—suppose that you may decide for yourself how you will separate the sheep from the goats. How will you determine who passes, who fails, who is "average," who deserves the coveted top marks?

You will doubtless find that making individual evaluations, "passing out grades," is the most painful part of teaching. Here is Edwin, slow, inaccurate, retarded in reading, but cooperative, likable and hardworking; he ranks near the bottom of the class in almost everything he tries. Must Edwin be given an F? Here is Joan, who almost never exerts herself but does work of consistently high quality. Should Joan be given an A, or should the top grades go usually to students like William, who is less able but more conscientious and who through strenuous effort does first-quality work? If Clara ranked very low at the beginning of the term, but now does work as good as that of the majority of the class, should she be given a B because of her marked improvement, a C because she is now doing C work, or a D because the average of all her grades is D? Several students are exactly on the borderline between two grades; either grade could be justified. Should you give them the higher or the lower grade?

Unfortunately there are no pat answers to questions like these. The plan of writing comments instead of grades on report cards eliminates many such problems; at the end of the term, only the decision to pass or to fail must be made, and since relatively few students are generally near failure, only a small number of decisions must be reached. But if your school does not employ the pass-fail system of grading, you have to decide about Edwin, Joan, William, Clara, and the others.

Most helpful will be a definite interpretation of what each grade means. You may not agree with the definitions that follow, but they may serve as a guide to your further thinking.[10]

A

The grade of A is distinctly a mark of superiority. It represents much more than mere competence in meeting assignments. There is a "plus factor" involved: The A student not only does what is expected of him but goes beyond it. He dares to be himself; he dares to use his initiative; he does not require prodding. Even his occasional failures are magnificent failures; like the late Babe Ruth, he strikes out with a mighty swing. He works well with the group and often assumes leadership in group undertakings.

The grade of B indicates a high level of accomplishment, with the "plus factor" diminished. It represents less originality, less artistry, less depth of analysis than the A; yet all three qualities are sometimes present. A student may receive a B because he is in ability an A student who has not lived up to his potentialities, or because he is in ability a C student who has worked hard enough to pull himself up by his own bootstraps, or because he is an able student who does most things well but does not possess a sufficient amount of ability, initiative, or aggressiveness to merit an A. The B student usually cooperates well with the group and sometimes assumes leadership.

"C"

The grade of C represents mediocrity of accomplishment (in the old sense of *"mediocris,"* meaning "in a middle state"). The student who is given a C has done what he was asked to do, but probably little more, possibly a little less. The quality of his accomplishment is neither high nor low. Sometimes a C is given a student poorer than average in ability who has worked hard enough to deserve it; sometimes it is given to a capable student who does not try to live up to his ability. Usually, though, the C goes to the student who is not very high or very low in native ability, energy, and productiveness. The C student cooperates fairly well with the group but rarely volunteers to lead.

The grade of D covers a multitude of sins such as carelessness, indifference, sluggishness, or laziness. Or it may come as the re-

[10] If your school uses a numerical rather than an alphabetical system, substitute 92–100 for A, 84–91 for B, 76–83 for C, 68–75 for D, below 68 for F.

sult of virtually insurmountable handicaps such as low native ability, slowness in learning, or physical defects, over which neither teacher nor student has much control. Or the D may result from lack of reading skill, lack of ability to speak and write well, or inability to concentrate—all of which may be subject to correction. The D student is often pathetically eager to learn and hence may cooperate well; sometimes, though, he may be surly and resentful until the teacher gets his confidence. Only in the few areas where he believes himself skillful is he willing to accept leadership.

The grade of F indicates indifference and failure to try. It is not given to the student who plugs away, doing his pitiful best. In high school English (not necessarily in mathematics and kindred subjects) everyone who tries conscientiously to reach the objectives of the course deserves to pass. But the one who regularly loafs, who apparently does not care, who procrastinates, who fails to cooperate, who does not do the work that others do, deserves an F.

Now for a few additional comments. It is wise to talk about standards of grading with your classes. Perhaps you and they can draw up a list of criteria, maybe a modification of the one you have just read; the students will then understand that a grade is not the result of the teacher's whim. Ask your classes what they believe you should do in borderline cases. Their answer may be that such decisions must be based upon little things that otherwise might not be considered: such things as the score on a spelling test, a voluntary report in literature, extra care in revision of written work, etc. Or the class may decide that the student's cooperativeness and willingness to accept responsibility should determine whether he ought to receive the higher or the lower grade.

Beginning teachers tend to give too many high grades, especially at the start of the year. They are often surprised that so many students are bright and cooperative, and as a result they give mostly A's and B's. Then, as the year moves on and their understanding of the students increases, the grades begin falling, to the detriment of class morale. It is much better to grade conservatively at the start, giving few A's and B's and many C's and D's (always accompanied by constructive suggestions for improvement). Then, when the students who are really doing superior work have clearly emerged from the pack, they may be given suitable rewards. And, of course, when a student who normally does C or D work makes a spurt, he too should be rewarded.

A large number of F's, however, is usually a greater criticism of the teacher than of the class. If many students fail to try, the teacher is not supplying adequate motivation. In such cases, strenuous introspection is in order and a change of tactics is usually indicated.

As a rule, the quality of work that a student does in the last few weeks of a term should have greater bearing upon the final grade than should the work of the first few weeks. Thus, in the case of Clara, who was mentioned on page 60, the final grade should probably be a C, since she has been doing C work during the last few weeks.[11]

If a school has adopted the spiral cone concept explained on pages 39–41, there are special implications for grading. The only A's would be given to students who have considerably surpassed the norms of accomplishment for their age. B's and C's, however, could go to any students who are working conscientiously, even though their level of accomplishment is below average for their age. The grade of D would represent general sloppiness and indifference. An F would be given rarely, and only to a student who hardly tried at all and who was frequently absent without excuse. Such a grading system would provide strong motivation for the less able student, since he would know he could make B's by hard work. Restricting A's to students of high accomplishment would motivate able students. Since with wide adoption of the spiral cone concept, colleges would rely mainly on entrance examinations for admitting students, the fact that many students of average or even below-average ability might have B grades would not matter; they could enter the college of their choice only if they passed required tests.

It is too bad, really, that grades must be given, because it seems unfair that any student should be rewarded or marked down be- _I agree_ cause of his innate characteristics or his home environment. He has no control over these, but they have a large share in determining whether his grades are high or low. But many administrators say that grades must be given, colleges ask about class rank, businessmen inquire about grades, some parents prefer grades because they appear less equivocal than written comments, and many students have themselves come to feel cheated unless their achieve-

[11] Further discussion of the grading of written work is included in Chapter 8.

ment is capsulized in a symbol. Those of us who dislike and distrust grades (preferring written statements or fairly detailed check-lists) may agitate for change, but there is great opposition to over-come. In the meantime, we can try to make grading as fair as the system permits.

THE IDEA BOX

"Criteria for Evaluating High School English Programs"

Paul H. Jacobs has prepared this widely used checklist, using headings on organization and procedures, the whole curriculum, literature, language, written and oral composition, reading, speech, evaluation, facilities, materials, and teacher qualifications. *English Journal*, LVII (Dec., 1968), 1275.

A Principle for a Curriculum

"The best preparation for a period of rapid change consists of a firm grounding in those things *least* likely to change or that will change most slowly. Many of the subjects that seem at the moment to be most 'practical' are the very ones that will soon be outmoded by the swift march of events." Paul Woodring, *General Electric Forum*, IV, No. 3 (Oct.–Nov., 1961).

Evaluating a Curriculum Guide

An NCTE Committee (Dorothy Davidson, chairman) offers a checklist for evaluating a school's curriculum guide. "Trends in Curriculum Guides," *English Journal*, LVII (Sept., 1968), 890.

"Begin With the Three -CY's"

Curriculum revision in English today should begin with a concern for adequate attention to each of the three -cy's: literacy, oracy (oral language), and mediacy (study of modern media). So Bryant Fillion argues, *English Journal*, LIX (Nov., 1969), 123.

"The Inductive Teaching of English"

Erwin R. Steinberg and others present a rationale for inductive teaching, along with several examples. *English Journal*, LV (Jan., 1966), 139.

British "Projects"

British schools often have students working on individual projects that involve reading, writing, and speaking. The first two or three periods may be spent in gathering material and planning its presentation (which may be by means of writing, dramatization, tape-recording or what have you), and other periods may be used in anticipating possible difficulties, reporting on progress, and presenting the finished product. Geoffrey Summerfield presents detailed suggestions in *Topics in English*, B. T. Batsford Ltd., London, 1965.

Three Roles for Teachers and Students

"Role I. The Teacher Tells: The Student Memorizes and Stores."
"Role II. The Teacher Molds: The Student Conforms."
"Role III: The Teacher Stimulates: The Student Teaches Himself."

G. Robert Carlsen condemns the first two, and applauds the third, saying that much of the progress made in science and mathematics teaching is attributable to it. *"How* Do We Teach?" *English Journal*, LIV (May, 1965), 364.

What High School Teachers Can Learn From Elementary

1. The importance of knowing the backgrounds of individual children.
2. Use of bulletin boards, pictures, and other concrete material.
3. Avoidance of the question-answer ("catechism") recitation.

Sheila Schwartz, "Help Needed by High School Student Teachers," *English Journal*, LIV (Sept., 1964), 547.

Worth Asking Yourself When You Make An Assignment

1. Will the work arouse wholesome curiosity?
2. Will it build rather than kill interest?
3. Will it help students to think?
4. Will it improve expression?
5. Will it teach cooperation and promote an interest in others?

To Prevent Dropouts

1. Use a term like "career curriculum" for the "general" curriculum.
2. Plan as carefully for the potential dropout as for the college prospect.
3. "Give as much genuine recognition for non-academic accomplishment as for academic."

4. Overhaul required reading lists; don't sniff at *Popular Mechanics* or *Consumer Reports*.
5. Use more contemporary works: Updike, Roth, etc.
6. Teach more cross-disciplinary studies: American Studies, English-Contemporary Affairs.

So suggests Robert J. Graham, "The English Teacher: A Major Cause of School Drop-outs," *English Journal*, LIV (Oct., 1965), 629. Question: How fair is the title Professor Graham chose?

Teaching the Potential Dropouts

In a class of ninth grade boys who had become completely antagonistic to school, Mary Bramer of Elgin, Illinois, found that it took weeks to win their cooperation and even then it was sporadic and that they seldom pushed themselves hard. But things like these succeeded: (1) teaching "the subtle concept of mood with the movie *Phoebe,* a dilemma of an unwed mother"; (2) "asking each to make a [cut-and-paste] symbol of himself in the form of a coat of arms"; (3) preparation of collages of pictures from *Life* and *Look,* with a group poem based on each collage; (4) in connection with *To Kill a Mockingbird,* "we talked the book" and "The day of the trial I passed around a can containing one paper saying 'jury foreman,' eleven saying 'jury member,' and the rest blank; I taught my best lesson in discrimination when I refused to let the one Negro class member draw, saying, 'I'm sorry, but this is 1935; no Negroes serve on juries in Alabama in 1935.'" (From a personal letter.)

Suggestions for Slow Learners

Among Nancy Steinbeck's suggestions for teaching slow learners are these: (1) Use at least two or three different activities per period. (2) Give a question or two to look for in reading. (3) Learn vocabulary from context. (4) Use committee work frequently. (5) Use panel discussions for book reports. (6) Encourage value judgments. (7) Write many short paragraphs, very few long compositions. "Avoid Babysitting with Basics," *English Journal*, LIV (May, 1965), 438.

The Slightly Educable

It has been estimated that as many as 20 per cent of students (excluding mental defectives) can never master material of above fifth or sixth grade difficulty. To require such students to undertake reading or other assignments permanently beyond their capacity is folly.

Yet they may be taught reading and language skills that will help them to develop into useful citizens.

Guidelines for English for the Disadvantaged

Writing in the *Journal of Negro Education* (Summer, 1964), Eunice Newton suggests these and other guidelines: (1) Concern for reading should be dominant. (2) "Experiencing" should be the basic activity. (3) The thinking processes (relating, generalizing, classifying, modifying) should be stressed. (4) Many AV materials should be used.

In the *New Jersey English Leaflet* (Jan., 1964), Seymour Spiegel lists the following: (1) Compare the student's achievements with his own past ones, not someone else's. (2) Do not give letter grades for skill work. (3) Encourage reading of *anything*. (4) Relate material to students' own lives. (5) Use students' own writing in teaching usage. (6) Have a classroom library with varied types of material. (7) Use a reading text with short selections. (8) Make use of pantomime, music, drawing, and other means of expression.

A Useful Magazine for Slow Learners

Scope, a weekly magazine published by Scholastic Magazines, Inc., offers help in reading, composition, and language study for junior high students with fourth to sixth grade reading levels. It has high interest level and often imaginative ideas.

"Combatting Apathy: Literature and the General Class"

"Naturally I don't want any student to read indiscriminately or without understanding or sensitivity, but the first step to making people thoughtful readers is to make them readers." George Ehrenhaft supplies a list of books read by his "general" seniors. *English Journal*, LIX (Sept., 1969), 845.

Stimulating the Academically Talented

Phyllis Peacock lists these ways of stimulating superior students: "(1) not *more* but *more challenging* activities; (2) new ideas, new ways of treating traditional materials; (3) emphasis on 'power-to-do,' not accumulation of facts; (4) challenge to do *extensive* reading; (5) challenge to do *intensive* reading; (6) a great variety of written work to gain power in analyzing, organizing, and thinking creatively; (7) extensive vocabulary growth." *North Carolina English Teacher* (Oct., 1959).

The Gifted Become Experts

C. P. Rossier finds it useful in teaching gifted students to enable each to attain a degree of mastery in a certain literary or linguistic area. "It contributes to pride in his own accomplishment and to status in the eyes of his fellow students." (It should help in teaching individual study, too.) Each student, along with his classwork, takes on an individual project for the semester or year, makes progress reports, and prepares a final paper. *Clearing House,* XXXIII (March, 1959), 415.

An Ungraded Program for Superior Students

High-ability tenth, eleventh, and twelfth year students are admitted to a special ungraded program at Schenley High School, Pittsburgh, described as follows: "Since the basic structure of the course is a three-year sequence of thematic units, a student may enter the class at the beginning of any sequence. The student's progress toward intellectual maturity in English is marked, not by changing grade level designations or by speed, but by his reading of the more difficult selections for group and independent reading, his understanding of the subtler points of both content and style in the literature read, and his demonstration of increasing mastery of speaking and writing skills." (From an unpublished report.) Three units are based on language, three on literary types, one on literature and the fine arts, and thirteen on universal themes in literature; writing and speaking are incorporated in all units.

In Deep

The Detroit English Experimental Plan (DEEP) allows a day for oral work, a day for writing, a day for work in a programmed text, two days for independent reading. Each teacher has one day free for conferences. According to some reports, students read more, write more, make higher scores on tests.

"Project Freedom"

For six weeks students in Mrs. Jacquelyn Carr's San Mateo, Calif., classes could read anything they wanted, write anything they wanted, and determine their own grades. Says Mrs. Carr, "Most of the students did more work on their own than when directed by a teacher." *English Journal,* LIII (March, 1964), 202.

Small Groups

Here are some tasks in which small groups may profitably engage: (1) pick a composition from their group to read to the class, (2) work on a problem common to the group, (3) edit one another's compositions, (4) practice oral usage with mimeographed or taped material, (5) plan a playlet or other work, (6) explore ideas for composition, (7) work with a filmstrip, (8) listen and react to a recording. See Joanne Dale, "Working with Groups in the English Classroom," *English Journal*, LIV (Jan., 1965), 39.

Problems for Small Groups

In Cleveland Heights, Ohio, small groups choose different problems to work on in connection with a literary work and then share their findings. L. B. Freyman and B. L. Van Sickle, "Individualizing Instruction," *NEA Journal* (Nov., 1966).

"The Unit Method"

In a philosophical presentation, George H. Henry suggests that in the unit method, six "intellectual operations must be in evidence." Among them: "There must be some personal experience of discovery of a relation. . . . The pupil must be so taught as to see the open-ended nature of what he thinks he knows—concepts, like 'tragedy,' being planned over a period of years." *English Journal*, LVI (March, 1967), 401.

Planning a Unit

In the *Missouri English Bulletin* (May, 1964) Paul Krueger describes eight steps in unit planning: (1) Selecting the experience. (2) Determining the basic content. (3) Determining common reading selections. (4) Determining selections for individual reading. (5) Determining meaningful writing activities. (6) Determining oral activities. (7) Compiling a list of spelling and vocabulary words. (8) Determining language skills which can be taught in relation to the unit.

Units for Use in Teaching the College-Bound

12,000 Students and Their English Teacher (published in 1968 by the College Entrance Examination Board) includes good sample units and suggestions for teaching *The Old Man and the Sea*, *The Bridge of San Luis Rey*, *Stalky & Co.*, *A Separate Peace*, "The Tell-Tale Heart," "The Rocking-Horse Winner," "Gooseberries," "A Rose for Emily," "The

Dead," *J. B.*, *The Glass Menagerie*, as well as a number of poems. Units on the language and on composition are also included.

Suggested Topics For Units

Topics for units are endless. The headings and specific topics listed here are only representative. The choice of topics depends upon students' grade level and interests, the relationship to other work of the course, the material covered in earlier years, the amount of time available, the significance of the topic for these students, and the availability of material.

Most of the suggested topics can be developed with a central literary core (perhaps to include some works suggested by students). Writing and other individual work, as well as discussion and class projects, can be built into nearly all of them. Some topics require considerable library and community resources and much use of those resources by students; others may be based upon readings in an anthology or in readily available paperbacks.

The Concerns of People

What everybody hopes for (or The world we want)
What everybody worries about
Finding a satisfactory occupation
A wholesome family life (or A house vs. a home)
What a friend can be
The role of humor in modern life
Fair play
Anti-war literature
Days of hunger, nights of dread
Attaining and keeping self-respect
What is an educated person? (or The further education I need)

The problems of a crowded city
Toward racial harmony
Varied searches for God
How do I know it's love? (or Does sexual attraction equal love?)
Ideals of marriage
There's always a generation gap
How I'll bring up my children
What makes people human?
Making the most of each twenty-four hours
What is the happiness we pursue?
What is success (greatness, beauty, goodness, etc.)?

Our Country and Its Literature

With the explorers
Life in colonial days
The Revolutionary (or other) era
The seafarers
They sought gold
"O pioneers!"
Great moments in freedom

Iron horses and others
"America the Beautiful"
What to do about "America the Ugly"
This state of ours
They had to be brave
Smokestacks

The early American short story

Changing themes in American poetry

The world of Hawthorne (or another literary figure)

"Varied carols I hear"

The dreams of modern writers

Young heroes and heroines

Life in the American city (or countryside)

Literature looks at politics and government

The duties of a citizen

American ideals

Other Parts of the World

When the West was young

"A wet sheet and a flowing sea"

"This is the forest primeval"

Holidays in foreign lands

When the world was very young

Travel in an armchair

Our neighbors in foreign lands

The inscrutable (?) Orient

Latin-American (or other) literature

How to be a citizen of the world

England sings

England's theatrical heyday

Early English literature

War stories from England

English satirists

Nature poetry in England

What are the British writing about, today?

The Qualities of Literature

"The play's the thing"

Why poetry?

Literature of fantasy

"My dear Watson"

Science fiction

Historical fiction

What makes a good short story?

The structure of novels

What is a ballad?

Poems of feeling

Rhythms for moderns

What makes a literary work endure?

Relationships of literature to other arts

Modern songs as literature

Skills

Talking together

For reading aloud

The art of conversation

Telephone etiquette

Giving directions

Manners of today (social graces)

How to study

Telling stories

Panels for information

Making announcements

Letters in our lives

First aid for thinking

Interviews

How systematic is English spelling?

Making sentences behave

The English Language

Using words to influence people (semantics)

How advertisers sway us

The story of British English

The story of American English
How the English sentence works
How words get into the language
What can happen to a word
American dialects
Attempts at spelling reform
Modern conventions in usage
American Idioms

How language use determines style
Words of power
Language as related to thinking
How people (places) got their names
Writing for personal pleasure
Euphemisms

English—Not in a Vacuum

Adventure ho!
Great moments in science
Man with a test tube
Where is technology taking us?
What the past gave us
When the world was very young
Inventors and inventions

Literature and music (painting, etc.)
English in your life's work
Literary prophets (stories about the future) *Sci Fi*
Explorers of space
Mankind—how and why?

The Media and Mass Entertainment

You are tuned to channel—(a critique of television)
What happened to radio?
Daily, including Sunday
Movies as an art form
The modern magazine
The story of printing

Living with—or in spite of—the media
Personal hobbies vs. spectator sports
Mass entertainment as a common denominator
How the media could be improved

 Varieties of Units

Joseph Mersand, in *High Points* (April, 1965) classifies units thus: (1) skill-emphasizing, (2) concentrating on a single work, (3) concentrating on a genre, (4) based on works of one author or a group of authors, (5) based on a theme, (6) based on a single topic, (7) based on students' problems (e.g., Getting Ready for My Life's Work), (8) aimed toward a culminating project (e.g., producing a play).

Using Community Resources

Learning need not be confined within four walls. Robert F. Kinder suggests using town libraries, museums, newspaper plants, art galleries, theaters, "a spot in town that was once a way station for stagecoach riders," an abandoned farmhouse or a ghost village, railway station and bus depots, governmental offices, and human resources such as writers, publishers, or leaders of minority groups. *Challenges to Meet: Guidelines for Building English Language Arts Curriculums, 9–12,* published by the Connecticut State Dept. of Education, 1969. (This book is excellent for reference by teachers building or revising a curriculum.)

"Try An Attitude Survey"

A great deal may be learned about one's students, says Paul T. McCalib of St. Cloud State College, by surveying their personal attitudes concerning some of the social problems treated by literature. He illustrates with a survey on attitudes toward sharing by marriage partners, related to *Giants in the Earth*. *English Journal*, LV (Dec., 1966), 1175.

Lesson Plans

Joseph Mersand, in *High Points* (June, 1965) says that good lesson plans consider objectives (immediate and long-range), the nature of the class, the content, available materials, teaching procedures, and learning activities.

What's a Good Question?

Among characteristics of good questions listed by Allen Ornstein, *Chicago Schools Journal* (Feb., 1965), are these: (1) Stimulation of thought, not just recall. (2) Questions in sequence. (3) Variation in length and difficulty. (4) Questions asked by students, not just the teacher. (5) Questions asked non-volunteers and disruptive students. (6) Use of a few pivotal questions. (7) Writing the aim of the lesson as a question, a problem to be solved.

Three Types of Questions

Questions may be classified in many ways. One is this: *Level I*—Concrete (factual—who, what, when, where). *Level II*—Abstract (probing relationships, finding main ideas, making inferences, evaluating ideas). *Level III*—Creative (open-ended, like "What would happen if . . . ?" or "What other uses could be made of this?"). *Illinois English-Reading Newsletter* (Sept., 1969).

Dangers in Humanities Programs

In humanities programs John R. Searles finds "curricular clutter," "slanting and imbalance," and too little teaching of skills. "Are Humanities Programs the Answer?" *English Journal*, LIV (March, 1965), 175. In the same issue, other articles applaud humanities programs.

Seminars for Seniors

In a humanities course in Castleton-on-Hudson, N.Y., two seniors present a paper at each meeting; these papers serve as the focus for discussion. Literature, music, and art are included. Richard E. Bamberger, "Involving Students in a Humanities Class," *English Journal,* LVII (Jan., 1968), 34.

"Humanities: From Aeschylus to Antonini"

In a delightful article, Adele H. Stern of Montclair, N.J., attacks some humanities programs, but concludes, "Where will they learn that everything a human being does, his song, his marble, his words, reveal what he is, and that this revelation has been repeated and repeated from the beginning to the now? Where will he learn all this if not in the Humanities class?" *English Journal,* LVIII (May, 1969), 676. In the following article, however (p. 681), Edward J. Gordon attacks humanities courses as thin and scattergunned, if not scatterbrained.

Recreating a Decade

Seniors in Mount Hermon, Mass., relived "the Roaring 20's" by seeing films, listening to Edward R. Murrow's "I Can Hear It Now," reading books by Frederick L. Allen, John Dos Passos, Eugene O'Neill, F. Scott Fitzgerald, E. E. Cummings, and others, and leading class discussions of the period. K. Kelly Wise, "The Senior Seminar at Mount Hermon." *English Journal,* LIV (Dec., 1965), 830.

Pros and Cons of Team Teaching

Favorable: Fewer preparations per teacher; more thorough preparations; cross-fertilization of teachers; playing from each teacher's strongest suits; provision for individual differences in small groups; greater variety in presentations; economical use of films, etc.; more student responsibility for his own learning; useful practice in listening to lectures, note taking, etc.; fairer evaluation of students; ease in administering tests.

Unfavorable: Intensive preparation required for large-group presentations; difficulty of recognizing student lack of understanding in large groups; need for reaching many kinds of students with a single presentation; tendency to make teaching too subject-centered; revisions and reorientation required each time team personnel changes; occasional incompatibility of team members; loss of close teacher-student relationship; disciplinary problems in large groups; danger that lectures will constitute basis for all testing; in some schools, lack of suitable rooms and equipment.

Five Types of Team Teaching

1. Part- or full-time helpers (lay readers, secretaries, audio-visual helpers, etc.).
2. Trading (informal exchanges of class hours to capitalize on teachers' individual strengths).
3. Cross-departmental (use of specialists in other departments such as history and music, for certain purposes).
4. Coordinated teaching (with team members as equal partners in planning and in assuming responsibilities according to their specialties).
5. Hierarchy (one teacher, the "team leader," responsible for major presentations and supervision of the whole team).

Team Teaching Has Many Forms

Florence M. Diesman describes the varieties she observed in 21 schools. *English Journal,* LIII (Nov., 1964), 617.

Requisites for Team Teaching

"Members of the team should like and respect each other as a person and as a teacher; recognize each other's and his own strengths and weaknesses; compliment and complement each other; be flexible and ready to change plans or to help each other in reading papers, making out grade cards, filling out reports and forms, or in scheduling parent conferences; and, above all, must have a sense of humor that enables him or her to laugh at mistakes and carry on from there." Julia Matcha and Don Kenyon, "Trying Out for a Team?" *English Journal,* LVII (March, 1968), 416.

Language-Teaching Games and Contests

For teaching children up to age twelve or thirteen, W. R. Lee (an Englishman) has prepared this book of suggested oral games, pronunciation games, reading and writing games, and spelling games. In defense of games, the author says, ". . . what great difference is there between 'work' and 'play' when concentration is sharply focused and the learner's energies stretched to the full?" Oxford University Press, 1965.

Separatism or Integration

Should the literature of Blacks and other minority groups be taught separately from the rest or integrated into the mainstream? This question is related to the larger one, unanswered yet by Blacks themselves, of separatism or integration into the society.

Each year the NCTE publishes a new booklet on *Classroom Practices in Teaching English*—a useful compilation of tested and often innovative procedures. The 1969–1970 edition concerned "Minorities: Communicating the Dream's Responsibility." Although no such publication can answer a gigantic sociological question like "separatism or integration," this issue does show what some teachers are doing to guarantee adequate attention to groups that happen to be outnumbered in the United States. (We sometimes forget that that's what a minority is—an outnumbered group—and that in many of our roles every human being is in a minority.)

Student Self-Evaluation

At the University of Chicago Laboratory School, reports to parents are supplemented each quarter by students' own evaluation of their learning.

"Evaluation of Published English Tests"

This booklet by Susan Wood, under the direction of Robert C. Pooley, describes and evaluates a large number of widely used tests. Available from the Wisconsin State Department of Public Instruction, Madison.

What Do You Do the Last Five Minutes?

Beginning teachers often agonize over the possibility that they may exhaust the day's lesson and still have time left. It is a good idea to have a reservoir of ideas for such a situation, even though it will not exist often. Ted Hipple offers a score of ideas in "Twenty Five-Minute Teaching Topics," *English Journal,* LV (Nov., 1966), 1094. There's a sequel in the Dec., 1967, issue, with twenty more topics.

4

The Improvement
of Reading

BASIC PRINCIPLES

First Principle: Reading Is Complex

If reading consisted merely of pronouncing printed words, reading problems would almost cease to exist. Even with a relatively unphonetic language like English, daily short periods of instruction would in a few months or years enable a person to "read."

But pronouncing words is not reading. Reading involves apprehending as much as possible of the meaning and emotion and purpose of the writer. It involves thinking about the meaning, emotion, and purpose, relating them to what one already knows. It often involves enjoyment. With today's knowledge of electronics it is at least theoretically possible to construct a machine that can scan a printed page and reproduce vocally every word on the page. But that machine could not really read, for the mental reaction that is the most important part of reading would be missing.

Some children in our schools are like this hypothetical machine. They know most or all the words on the page, but they cannot tell except in very general terms what they have read.

Goethe, when he was already elderly and famous, said, "The dear ＊Goethe
people do not know how long it takes to learn to read. I have been

at it all my life, and I cannot yet say that I have reached the goal."
And Goethe is believed to have been one of the most intelligent men
of all time! Yes, reading is complex.

Take the apparently simple items of speed and comprehension,
for example. Hundreds, even thousands, of articles have been written about speed and comprehension in reading, and some exorbitant
claims have been made. Some persons, it is said, have learned to
read up to 10,000 words a minute. (That would mean, according
to some calculations by Professor V. E. Leichty of Michigan State,
that a book about the size of the one you have in your hands could
be read in seventeen minutes.) The theoretical maximum—with a
machine to turn pages—is 40,000 words a minute. But somewhere
comprehension fails to keep pace with speed. For most persons,
reading easy material, that somewhere is in the 250 to 500 WPM
(words per minute) range. Speed is not the sole criterion of excellence in reading; neither is comprehension. Rather, quickness of
comprehension marks the able reader. In contrast, the poor reader
grasps the meaning slowly if at all.

In the 1960's, according to the *Thirteenth Yearbook* of the National Reading Conference, a study of Michigan high schools revealed that about one third of the students did not read well enough
to do the work expected in high school classes, and about two thirds
of such students had not received any reading instruction designed
to overcome their handicaps.

The problem of teaching reading is complicated because no two
persons will or can react in exactly the same way to the same set of
black stimuli on the white page. Tom and Jerry, next-door neighbors of the same age, may look alike, but note a small part of the
tremendous array of possible differences that may make Tom a poor
reader, Jerry a good one:

Tom	*Jerry*
Has somewhat defective vision	Has traveled little
Has an IQ of 105 [1]	Lives in an almost bookless house

[1] Although IQ scores are mentioned frequently in this chapter, it must be stressed
that such scores are by no means totally significant as measurements of mental ability
or potential. Instruments for measuring intelligence have never become sufficiently
refined to measure all aspects of intelligence, and many of them are so constructed
that they favor people who read well or who have had certain types of cultural experiences. An IQ score must, then, be regarded only as a partial index to that complicated thing we call "intelligence."

Is mainly interested in autos and sports
Wants to become an automobile mechanic
Likes practical jokes
Thinks school a waste of time
Moves his lips when he reads
Reads everything at same speed
Read two books last year
Has excellent vision
Has an IQ of 115

Has traveled extensively
Lives in a house with a good library
Has wide interests
Wants to become a lawyer
Likes puns and limericks
Likes school moderately well
Does not move his lips in reading
Varies speed of reading
Read twenty-five books last year

Second Principle: Everyone Can Read Better

Perhaps Tom will never become as good a reader as Jerry, because Tom's characteristics and environment are unlikely to change enough to enable him to catch up. But, helped by good teachers, Tom can learn to stop moving his lips, to vary his reading speed, to become interested in books about autos and sports and some other subjects, and to carry some books and magazines into his bookless home.

Jerry, however, although he is already an able reader, can become still more able. In fact, the chances are that the gap between him and Tom will steadily increase, even though Tom's improvement is considerable. Jerry can increase his vocabulary, his speed of comprehension, his retention of details, his ability to find main ideas, his ability to skim, his ability to draw conclusions, his understanding of people in literature, his ability to find material, his expressiveness in reading aloud, and undoubtedly some of his other partially developed skills.

Everyone—even you, presumably an excellent reader—can read better. So many skills are involved in reading that no one can have reached his potential in all of them.

Because of the increased realization of this fact, most high schools now stress what is called *developmental reading*. Instead of assuming as formerly that students have mastered reading in the elementary schools, high school teachers attempt to develop for each student the skills in which he is least proficient.

Such reading does not necessitate a separate course, although some schools do have such courses, perhaps taught by specialists in reading. Developmental reading can be stressed in science, social studies, mathematics, and especially in English classes.

Third Principle: To Read Well, One Must Want to Read Well

Unless Tom can be led to realize that reading can bring him something that he wants or needs, he will probably never learn to read well. And if Jerry complacently believes that he knows all about reading, his improvement is not likely to be great. Motivation, then, becomes a key.

For motivation, teachers need to consider why students read at all. According to a study reported by Robert Emans and Gloria Patyk,[2] recreation is the chief reason for reading. In second place is information, which boys seek more often than girls do. Esthetic reasons rank low. Poor readers like to be able to identify with a character—with, for example, the baseball player who steals home with the winning run, or with the girl who succeeds against odds in entering a nursing career.

The principles for motivating better reading may be summarized in the form of six axioms:

Axiom 1. Each student should understand what reading can do for him. People read either for pleasure or for information or both. A student may be led to increase his reading skill if he can be shown that reading, both now and later, can contribute to his pleasure and to the knowledge that he himself requires or will require.

Example A. Louis. Age fourteen. IQ 85. Eighth grade. Fifth grade reading level. Failed third grade. Would probably leave school at sixteen and become an unskilled laborer. Working slowly and with easy materials pertaining to sports and model airplanes, in which Louis was especially interested, the teacher was able to help the boy convince himself that newspapers, magazines, and even a few books could give him pleasure. Special help in technique made reading less burdensome for him. Through a unit on democracy at work, Louis (and the rest of the class) became aware that good citizens need to keep informed about political, social, and economic issues. During the year, Louis' reading ability increased to seventh grade level, and his attitude toward reading was improved.

Example B. Mabel. Age fifteen. IQ 101. Tenth grade. Tenth grade reading level. Not a college prospect. Mabel had no strong reading interests, although she voluntarily read local news, motion picture magazines, and love stories. The teacher led Mabel to see that news did not have to be local to be interesting, showed that some love stories are more realistic and worthwhile than those Mabel had been reading, and interested the girl in fiction and non-fiction pertaining to home life and home problems. Mabel's reading ability

[2] *Journal of Reading*, Feb., 1967.

improved only one year in two semesters, but she was choosing *Good House-keeping* and *Seventeen* instead of *Romantic Mirror*.

Example C. Charles. Age sixteen. IQ 135. Eleventh grade. College reading level. A prospective lawyer. The teacher's task with Charles was to show him the value of certain reading skills in which he was least strong: skimming for central ideas or for specific points, determining word meanings from context, and varying his speed according to the material. The teacher also helped him to see that wide reading of adult books would assist him in preparing for his legal career.

Axiom 2. Each student should know how well he reads. This implies that students' reading should be tested at regular intervals. Although most educators consider it generally wise to withhold from students their IQ scores, they do not say the same thing about scores on reading tests. It seems inadvisable to post scores of students, but each should be told privately what the tests show about his own reading. If his score is low, he should be given encouragement and advice designed to help him improve. If it is high, he should be shown that further improvement is possible and desirable. Every student should be in competition, not with other students but with himself.

Axiom 3. Each student should know that his reading can be improved.[3] The experienced teacher will be able to tell the child about similar former students whose reading ability was bettered. The inexperienced teacher can find brief case histories in some of the items listed in The Idea Box, pages 109 ff. If a student's reading ability is very low, the teacher can encourage him by referring to whole classes of poor readers whose reading improved much more rapidly than would have been expected. If the student is already rather proficient, the test results will certainly show that some of the skills may be further developed.

The teacher may find it useful to chart the results of the subparts of students' reading test scores, and in a "so-what" column indicate suggested courses of action to cope with specific difficulties. The results need not be kept secret from the students, each of whom may look at what is in effect a diagnostic chart with recommended remedies.[4]

[3] Sometimes improvement is contingent upon the elimination or reduction of physical handicaps. The teacher needs to watch particularly for defects in vision or hearing and recommend appropriate medical care.

[4] For details, see Thomas D. Horn, ed., *Reading for the Disadvantaged: Problems of Linguistically Different Learners* (New York: Harcourt Brace Jovanovich, 1970), p. 214.

Axiom 4. Each student should be kept aware of his progress.
Simple, teacher-made tests should be administered frequently, and
standardized tests given at regular intervals—two or three times each
year. Although there is usually insufficient time for a conference
after each test, the teacher should encourage the students by giving
evidence of individual progress, and may occasionally be able to
pay a sincere compliment to the whole class on its improvement.

Axiom 5. Reading materials should be appropriate. Intrinsic
worth, interest, and degree of difficulty should all be considered.
Quality must not be sacrificed. There is such a plenitude of well-
written, exciting material that it is totally unnecessary to use school
time for reading anything of poor quality. This does not mean that
practice materials must be "Literature," but they should be worthwhile.

Many studies have been made of the reading interests of young
persons. John J. De Boer summarized many of the findings:

> Boys like vigorous action-exploration, pursuit, conflict, triumph, surprise.
> They like the David-and-Goliath type of story, the real life or fictional hero in
> either the Edison or Daniel Boone category. Often they enjoy stories of sports
> and science. Many come to love Stevenson, Dickens, Dumas, Mark Twain.
> Girls, on the other hand, read stories of home and school life, romantic love,
> careers for women, mystery stories, and sentimental fiction. Girls are more
> likely to read boys' books than boys are to read girls' books.
> Curiously, the factors of intelligence and socioeconomic status do not
> markedly affect young people's interests.[5]

Jo M. Stanchfield studied the reading preferences of eighth grade
boys, listing in rank order fifty types of subjects. The top ten were
explorations and expeditions, outdoor life, tales of fantasy, everyday-
life adventures of boys, historical fiction (with some characters of
their own age), sea adventure, sports and games, war, humor, and
science fiction. At the bottom were teen-age romance, fairy tales,
music, family and home life, plays, art, and poetry.[6]

An Iowa study that covered grades seven through twelve was
based on the responses of 510 students to the question "If you could
have an author write a story-to-order for you, what would you have
him put in it?" The following table summarizes the most frequent
replies:

[5] "What Does Research Reveal About Reading and the High School Student?"
English Journal, XLVII (May, 1958), 277–78.
[6] "The Reading Interests of Eighth-Grade Boys," *Journal of Developmental Reading,* V (Summer, 1962), 256–65.

Junior high boys:

Mystery	16%
Sports	15%
Science fiction	15%
Adventure	15%
Animal stories	13%
Sea stories	10%

Senior high boys:

Adventure	46%
Mystery	25%
Sea stories	25%
Comedy	24%
Historical	23%
Science fiction	21%

Junior high girls:

Romance	65%
Mystery	20%
Career	12%
Comedy	11%

Senior high girls:

Romance	66%
Career	36%
Mystery	32%
Adventure	30%
Comedy	28% [7]

adventure

Mystery

In a somewhat similar study, reported by J. Harlan Shores in *The Reading Teacher* (April, 1964), high school students were asked, in effect, "If you were to be given a book, what would you like it to be about?" Mystery and adventure again topped the list, and there was considerable interest in biography and historical fiction, while reading on "personal and social adjustment questions" also ranked high. There was comparatively little interest in war stories, humor, classics, poetry, and westerns.

Thomas G. Devine recommends the following: (1) Make sure that reading materials are appropriate. (2) Take advantage of teachers' manuals. (3) Use the supplementary materials. (4) Use a variety of materials. (5) Create materials (exercises, activities, games, etc.).[8] For classes of the ingenious teacher who has enough time (if there is such a person), the creation of materials may be especially useful, since students appreciate any special effort that teachers make to help them, and also because such materials can be specifically geared to the needs of a given class.

On the average, eighth graders read more than does anyone else *Note* of any age. Ninth-grade reading drops remarkably. Paul Diederich hypothesizes that one reason may be that ninth-grade teachers too often make an abrupt switch from juveniles to "classics." We teachers, he says, may "introduce students to adult reading through authors like Scott, Eliot, and Dickens when we should have used

[7] Mary L. Smith and Isabel V. Eno, "What Do They Really Want to Read?" *English Journal*, L (May, 1961), 343–45.

[8] "What Does Research in Reading Reveal about Materials for Teaching Reading?" *English Journal*, Sept., 1969.

authors like Agatha Christie, Carter Dickson, Rex Stout, P. G. Wodehouse, Clarence Day, and James Thurber." [9]

Most high school students prefer a simple style, brevity, and straight-forwardness; they dislike difficulty, wordiness, slow movement, monotony, sentimentality, and lack of worthwhileness.

An experienced teacher can estimate fairly well the difficulty of a selection. He knows that students find a selection difficult if the vocabulary is beyond them, if the word order is unusual, if sentences are long and complex, if statements are highly compressed, if the language is strongly metaphorical, and if abstractions are numerous. Should you be dubious about your own ability to judge difficulty, you might apply some such scale as the Lorge formula, which involves counting the number of words in a sample passage, and the number of sentences, prepositional phrases, and "hard words" in that passage.

One caution is imperative, though: A teacher is responsible for helping his students grow. If *all* reading materials are based only on their current interests, growth is slowed unnecessarily. Always the good teacher is introducing his students to materials that, in both difficulty and significance of content, are just a little above the students' present levels.

Axiom 6. The classroom atmosphere should be pleasant. Learning is most efficient when the environment is friendly and free from tension. Even in a rather gloomy, unattractive building, the attitude of the teacher can make a class cheerful and cooperative.

Fourth Principle: Many Teachers Share in the Responsibility for Improving Reading

If there is any one feature of the total reading program about which the experts are in agreement, it is that all the high school teachers have a share in the responsibility, even though the major part of the burden falls upon the teacher of English. In summarizing the experts' idea of an ideal all-school developmental program (which no school yet claims to have achieved) Margaret J. Early lists these ten points. Note that teachers of subjects other than English have responsibility in numbers 1, 3, 4, 5, and 7, and possibly in one or two more:

[9] *English Journal,* Sept., 1969.

1. Continuous instruction in reading skills from kindergarten to grade twelve for *all* pupils.
2. Integration of reading skills with other communication skills: writing, speaking, and listening.
3. Specific instruction by subject-matter teachers in *how to read and study* in their special fields, using the basic reading materials of their courses.
4. Cooperative planning by all teachers so that skills will not be overlooked or overstressed.
5. Adjusted reading materials in all subjects for slow, average, and superior students.
6. Guidance in free reading.
7. Emphasis on the uses of reading as a source of information, as an aid to personal and social development, and as a means of recreation.
8. Corrective or remedial instruction for seriously retarded readers.
9. Measurement of growth in skills by means of standardized and informal tests; study of students' application of techniques in all reading tasks.
10. Evaluation of the uses of reading through study of the amount and quality of voluntary reading; study of effect on achievement in all school subjects; effect on percentage of drop-outs.[10]

Examples may make this point more specific. Social studies teachers should give suggestions on how to read and study social studies material, and should teach students how to interpret maps, graphs, and charts. Music teachers, in addition to teaching the reading of music, should be sure that students can read and understand such terms as *pianissimo* and *glissando;* teachers of health and physical education should teach necessary technical vocabulary. Science and mathematics teachers, in addition to giving specific vocabulary instruction, need to teach the peculiar skills involved in reading problems and formulas. All teachers who require reports should help students learn to locate and use appropriate materials.

Fifth Principle: There Is No Single Right Way to Teach Reading

Perhaps this principle is a corollary of the first, that reading is complex. Research has shown repeatedly that students may improve their reading abilities when taught by various methods or

[10] "About Successful Reading Programs," *English Journal,* XLVI (Oct., 1957), 395.

combinations of methods. Unfortunately some researchers or experimenters, loving their own brainchildren best, have tended to make exaggerated claims for the methods they have used successfully. Thus machine users, for instance, being able to demonstrate that students improve speed and perhaps comprehension through mechanical aids, have urged that reading accelerators be lined along the walls like slot machines in Las Vegas. Some persons who favor phonetics would apparently ignore everything else. Some who think that small vocabularies are poor readers' biggest handicaps would spend day after day on vocabulary-building devices. Some have found that extensive reading, unaccompanied by any formal instruction, may result in considerable gains, and hence have argued that all that is needed is to turn children loose in a library. And so on, ad infinitum.

The significant point is that there is a degree of truth in most of the claims. However, each of the dozens of recommended methods is likely to lead to a special—and rather limited—sort of improvement. The best program, then, it would seem, would be a balanced one that borrows some parts from each of the proved methods.

That is the kind of program outlined in the rest of this chapter. It is based on the five principles of which you have just read. It presupposes an interested school administration, and cooperation from other teachers as recommended in the fourth principle. It describes special help for special cases, then attempts to suggest some of the many ways in which reading instruction can be brought into the English classroom, and finally considers how the student can be helped to help himself through extensive out-of-school reading.

READING IN SPECIAL CLASSES

Various Types of Special Classes

In a free society, with local control of schools, it is to be expected that organizational patterns will differ widely, because of peculiar local conditions and also because of the varying beliefs and understandings of administrators and leading teachers. The weakness of such diversity is that inevitably some patterns will be inferior to others; the strength is that opportunities to experiment are constantly present almost everywhere, and out of countless experiments may evolve a system that many communities can accept and find effective.

In a study of 107 special reading-improvement programs in Illinois high schools, Loren V. Grissom found three patterns in operation. In Group One were schools that provided special, ability-grouped English classes in which much emphasis was placed on reading. Schools in Group Two offered one- to two-semester reading classes in addition to the regular English classes, and tried to place in them those students whose reading levels were below the levels that intelligence tests and other measures showed to be possible for them. The schools (usually large) in Group Three made varied provisions, typically including remedial English-reading classes for low-ability classes, special reading classes for students reading below their ability levels, and voluntary, non-credit clinic periods for students deficient in certain skills and for college-preparatory students who wanted to become better readers.[11] Today, with more and more schools making use of six- or nine-week modules of instruction, several such modules might well incorporate instruction in specialized facets of reading.

Classes for Needlessly Retarded Readers. These are usually the readers whose reading levels are one or more years below their apparent ability, as measured by intelligence tests and other means. For instance, if a ninth grader with an IQ of 100 is reading at sixth or seventh grade level and if he seems to have no serious visual or other handicaps, he would be a candidate for such a class. Such readers are very numerous.

Ordinarily, the special classes for such students are treated as temporary substitutes for regular English work. For instance, twenty ninth graders are put into the special class for a semester or at most a year, and they receive English credit for the reading course. Perhaps ideally they should take both English and reading, but most school programs are too crowded to permit such doubling up. At the end of a semester or a year, if the teaching has been successful, most of the students will have made sufficiently substantial gains that they will have approached their potential as of that time. For instance, ninth grader Carol, IQ 90, may have started the term with sixth grade reading ability and finished it with eighth. That, for Carol, would represent her present potential. If her IQ were 100 or 110, though, it would be hoped that she would reach the ninth grade reading level or above as a result of the corrective instruction.

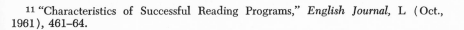

[11] "Characteristics of Successful Reading Programs," *English Journal,* L (Oct., 1961), 461–64.

In this type of special class, the teacher attempts to find, through diagnostic tests, the major reading weaknesses of the individuals and of the whole class. Geared to the entire class is instruction in those reading skills in which most of the students are deficient. This instruction is supplemented by some individual assignments and activities, intended to help students overcome weaknesses not shared by the majority.

Organization of such classes varies considerably. Here are a few examples of patterns followed in some schools:

X 1. Non-credit reading laboratory—selected students sent there two or three hours a week, during study periods; individualized instruction, geared to specific needs of each student.

2. Workshop—taken for credit either in addition to or in place of English; enrolment limited to fifteen or twenty per period; both group and individual instruction.

X 3. Reading period—one period a week taken from regular English class, for intensive work on reading improvement.

4. Concentrated work on reading—typically a three- or four-week period, sometimes in summer, when other work is laid aside for group and individual work on reading problems.

X 5. Daily reading session in English—fifteen or twenty minutes a day devoted to instruction and practice in reading.

6. Elective reading course—student initiative, both for electing the course and planning work for self-improvement; this may be a six- or nine-week module.

Classes for Mentally Retarded or Otherwise Handicapped Readers. Among the eighth grade students in one school are Clayton and Dolores, with reported IQ's of 76 and 78; Joachim, who has just arrived in the United States and knows no English; Blanche, with a serious speech defect; Glenn, with a serious visual defect; Bill, with a drunken father and an irresponsible mother, no interest in school, and a record with the juvenile courts; and Louise, who has never been more than two miles from home, and who is responsible for most of the care of several younger brothers and sisters. All feel lost in regular classes, yet their needs are obviously not the same. No single formula will help all of them, but the school cannot afford the individual tutelage that might make each of them a better reader, a better student, a more productive adult citizen.

Some schools would put Clayton and Dolores and other mentally handicapped children into special classes called "General English" or something else; in those classes the work would be sufficiently simple that the slow learners could succeed with it reasonably well. Clayton and Dolores can hardly be expected ever to read up to their grade level; their potential, as eighth graders, is probably about fourth grade level. Their other language skills are likely to be comparable.

But suppose that Clayton and Dolores stay in "General English" all through school. And suppose further that they or their parents think they should go on to college. (After all, they have a high school diploma, haven't they?) This kind of situation exists fairly frequently. In fairness to colleges, to other students, and to Clayton and Dolores, the school administration should state clearly, with reasons, that Clayton and Dolores are not suited for college work. A good guidance program in the school should steer them toward technical training rather than toward college.

Some schools would keep Clayton and Dolores in regular classes, and in small high schools there may be no other solution. In that case the teacher must realize that much of the work will pass over their heads, but that many special assignments within their reach are possible. Dolores and Clayton may profit especially from well-conceived group work. They may also have special abilities that can be developed and that can bring them enthusiastic acceptance by their fellows. (I once taught a constantly clowning Clayton who became so proficient in giving humorous readings that he won a county championship.)

If the school has enough students like Joachim, the new arrival, they may be put together into a class for foreign students. Much work is now being done to improve the teaching of English as a second language. New York City, in particular, has worked out detailed plans for teaching the large number of Puerto Ricans and others to whom English is almost an unknown language. Los Angeles and other places in the West and Southwest are also working steadily on methods of teaching their Spanish-speaking students in particular. The techniques are specialized ones and cannot be described here.

Blanche and Glenn, with their severe defects in speech and vision, probably need first some specialized doctors' care that few schools can provide. The school can, however, help in making arrangements with appropriate local, county, or state authorities. Then Blanche and Glenn may be placed in a class small enough for considerable individual help. (Writing in the *Saturday Review* for

August 22, 1970, Senator Abraham Ribicoff said, ". . . when one large metropolitan hospital recently gave medical examinations in a ghetto junior high school, 20 per cent of the students were found to have hearing and sight problems. Because nobody had ever examined them before, many had spent half their public school lives in schools for the retarded.")

Bill has an emotional problem caused by family troubles. A psychologist who works with the school may be helpful. So may a teacher, if the teacher can find one small opening in Bill's armor, one interest that can be capitalized upon, one subject that Bill is willing to read a little about. If Bill's intelligence is about normal, he may well be placed for a while in a reading class for the needlessly retarded. Otherwise he may be provided for in a "General English" class or even in a regular one.

Louise, the girl with limited experience, obviously needs reading materials that will give her some hints about the rest of the world. She will probably find herself in the same class with Bill. Both of them may profit from and find interesting some stories about other young people with problems similar to theirs.

Perhaps the severely handicapped children like the seven we have just observed pose the biggest problem that teachers encounter. Many, perhaps most, of such children, though, can be sufficiently helped that they can contribute wholesomely to society. The teaching and other assistance that they need are expensive, but it is better to spend a few hundred dollars annually on Bill now than to spend a few thousand dollars a year to keep him in prison later. It is more economical to spend generously for the others now than it is to maintain them the rest of their lives as public wards.

Classes for the Gifted. In Gouverneur, New York, the rather small high school has offered "efficiency classes" for sophomores, juniors, and seniors who are in the top fifth in intelligence. These classes were intended to help the most able students reach their potential. From such students the majority of tomorrow's leaders will come, yet in most schools they have insufficient opportunity to grow as much as they are able. Gouverneur's efficiency classes stressed efficient reading and study skills. Each student selected five fields of specialization, and, under guidance, read extensively in these fields and concurrently was given instructions in developing the reading skills in which he was least advanced.

Other schools are conducting different experiments in an attempt to find ways of taking down the bars that surround the most able students in many places. These experiments are among the very significant ones in twentieth-century America.

Devices Used in Special Classes

Only a book devoted solely to reading can explain in detail the various methods and devices employed. Here we can look at just a few of them, in summary form, under three headings.

Learning Methods of Word Attack. Phonics teaches a child to "sound out" many words. Research has shown that the phonics approach works best with words that are already in the child's speaking vocabulary.[12] In addition to learning the usual sounds of letters, the student needs to learn the sounds of such consonant combinations as *bl, st, str, ng,* and *gr,* and such diphthongs as *aw* and *ou.*

Obviously, though, we do not want the child to have to sound out the same word again and again. Perhaps he uses his knowledge of phonics and learns the word *belong,* let us say. He should, later, through the use of flashcards and similar elementary techniques, be helped to recognize *belong* at a glance. Still later he may be helped to read at a glance a group of words, like *belong to me,* in which the word appears.

A number of reading workbooks contain picture aids and other devices for increasing each student's ability to recognize words.

Increasing Speed. The slow, word-by-word reader often fails to grasp the meaning because the phrases and clauses never take shape in his mind. He may understand "John-and-Paul-came-to-the-bridge," but, if the sentence contains a few more phrases and clauses, he loses the entire thought. Speed in itself is not a very important goal, but as a tool of comprehension it is.

Students should be told how one reads. As you know, the eye does not glide smoothly along from left to right but moves in a series of little jumps. The more jumps, or pauses, the less speed. Students may be given simple, teacher-made or class-made exercises such as flashcard exercises or groups of phrases arranged vertically on the page; the purpose is to learn to take in the whole phrase at a glance. Working in pairs, students may observe each other's eye

12 Paul A. Witty and Robert A. Sizemore, "Phonics in the Reading Programs," *Elementary English,* XXXII (Oct., 1955), 355–70.

movements, as the reader tries consciously to read each line with the fewest possible fixations.

Reading in which the student forces himself to read at his top speed is often productive. For this purpose the material selected should be very easy, preferably two grades or more below the student's reading level. It should be on a subject interesting to the student. With such material the student can be encouraged to compete against himself, keeping time charts and figuring out his own reading speed.

The usefulness of tachistoscopes, pacers, and other machines has been hotly debated. Undeniably, boys especially are fascinated by them, so motivation is made easier. Undeniably also, their use can result in greatly increased reading speed. However, doubters say that the increased speed is not uniformly transferred to reading done without the machine, that just as great gains may be made by reading easy material at top speed, that the acquired high speed is not necessarily retained, and that after a couple of years the gains in comprehension, which accompanied the machine-made increase of speed, may disappear. Robert M. Guinevan says that some students are highly motivated by machines, but that the emphasis upon speed may induce the habit of reading everything as rapidly as possible.[13] The upshot of the discussion appears to be that machines are useful, especially for motivation, but not indispensable. Robert Karlin, in his *Teaching Reading in High School*,[14] reported that of twelve studies that compared results of "machine reading" with those from "natural reading," eleven showed no greater gains in reading rate for the students who used the machines.

Improving Comprehension. Frederick B. Davis listed the following types of comprehension: defining words as used in the context, understanding the pattern of organization, identifying the main thought, finding answers to questions discussed in the passage, drawing inferences, recognizing literary devices, identifying the tone or mood, and determining the writer's purpose or viewpoint.[15]

Direct questioning, on whichever of these types a class is ready for, is often the best and simplest approach; for example, "What is

[13] *Education Summary*, Aug. 12, 1967.
[14] Indianapolis: Bobbs-Merrill, 1964.
[15] "Comprehension in Reading," *Baltimore Bulletin of Education*, XXVIII (Jan.–Feb., 1951), 16–24.

the main thing the author says about seashells?" "What is the meaning of *sound* as the author uses it?" "Can you figure out the meaning of *bivalve* from the way the author describes it?" "What does he say causes the roaring that we hear when we hold a large shell to our ear?" "How many kinds of shells does he name?" "What are the two main classes of these shells?" "What shows you that the author loves the sea?"

Many variations are possible, including the writing of a title for the passage, writing a "headline" about it, thinking of other words the author could have used to express the same idea, thinking of another possible pattern of organization, adding to what the author says, choosing the best summary sentence, reducing each of the author's sentences to a word or a phrase, and discussing how the passage would have been different if the author's purpose or viewpoint had been different.

Sister Jean Patice, C. S. J., suggests that unorthodox reading materials may help in building comprehension: catalogs, directories, and magazines like *Sports Illustrated*.[16] For example, students may use the Yellow Pages to get information about where they could get help for a broken waterpipe or repairs for an air conditioner. And a catalog can lead to reading about things they'd like to own.

READING IN REGULAR ENGLISH CLASSES

On the high school level much of the teaching of reading takes place in regular English classes, most often in connection with the study of literature. Chapters 5, 6, and 7 of this book treat in some detail the teaching of literature; if the recommendations in those chapters are followed, improvement in reading ability will almost inevitably result. There are, though, some specific techniques that a teacher may consciously employ with the improvement of reading as his major goal. It is the purpose of this section to discuss those techniques. However, much more experimentation is necessary before we shall know the very best ways of incorporating reading instruction in the regular English program while still teaching adequately everything else that must be included. Perhaps as much as 95 per cent of the research so far reported has dealt with special

16 *Minnesota English Newsletter*, Nov., 1967.

classes or individual problems rather than with reading in the regular English class.

The well-balanced English program includes some reading done in common by the whole class or by sizable groups within the class, and also reading done by individuals or by small groups. In this section we shall concern ourselves especially with reading in common.

Before the Students Read

A reading program is likely to be most effective if the teacher knows how well each student already reads, if students' interest is aroused, and if students' probable difficulties with assigned selections are anticipated.

Testing. Some schools as a matter of general practice give all entering students a reading test. Some give such tests annually, to measure each student's growth. Some give them at the beginning and end of each year.

If your school tests reading regularly, you should study the test results for your students. Do not look only at the total scores, but also at the scores on various parts of the test. These parts vary according to the test given but are likely to have such classifications as speed, word comprehension, sentence comprehension, paragraph comprehension, finding answers to questions, selecting main ideas, drawing inferences, and observing organization. If you find that most of your students are especially weak in certain of the items tested, you may slant your instruction somewhat toward those items.

If your school does not have an established and consistent testing program in reading, perhaps you can arrange one for your classes. It is probably best to plan to give different forms of the same test at the beginning and the end of the same year. The comparison may please you or humble you, and may affect your teaching in subsequent years.

Do not be reluctant to talk with your classes about the kinds of things that reading tests measure—and why. Analysis of the parts may help your students to understand more clearly the components of reading skill.

Skills To Be Emphasized. In Pennsylvania, instruction in reading skills is legally required in grades seven and eight. A number of junior high schools have chosen to emphasize these skills:

1. Word Recognition Techniques
   a. Meaning aids
   b. Visual and structural aids
   c. Auditory and phonetic aids
2. Comprehension Abilities: reading to
   a. Retain information
   b. Organize
   c. Evaluate
   d. Interpret
   e. Appreciate
3. Basic Study Skills
   a. Locating information
   b. Use of general references
   c. Use of visual materials
   d. Organizing
4. Basic Meaning Development
   a. Paragraph meaning and organization
   b. Word meaning [17]

In later grades, these skills may be developed further, and more advanced skills such as skimming and "reading between the lines" may be added.

Building an Interest in a Selection. You yourself read with the liveliest mind and the greatest understanding that which interests you. Your students are no different. They will start an assignment —and complete it—with most success if they have a glimpse in advance of what it may mean to them.

Often a simple factual question is enough, or a question that relates the selection to the students' lives, or one that poses a problem. Here are a few examples, related to familiar pieces of American literature:

(Irving's "Rip Van Winkle") If you had gone to sleep twenty years ago and woke up today, what changes would you soon be aware of?

(Henry's "Speech in the Virginia Convention") All of you have heard "Give me liberty or give me death!" What caused Patrick Henry to give the famous speech ending with that sentence?

(Hawthorne's "The Minister's Black Veil") How would you react if your minister or one of your teachers started wearing a black mask to church or school?

(Poe's "The Purloined Letter") If you wanted to hide a letter in your room so that very thorough searchers could not find it, where would you put it?

(Peattie's "What Life Means—An Answer in Nature") Ruling out such things as bombs, what is man's greatest weapon?

Sometimes a little background information—a kind of quick stage setting—can provide the impetus for careful and intelligent reading. For example, for the Donald C. Peattie selection, you might tell the class that Mr. Peattie spent three years studying intensively the ani-

[17] U. Berkley Ellis, "Developmental Reading in Junior High School," *Journal of Developmental Reading,* VI (Autumn, 1962), 41–49.

mals and plants in a single square mile of land near Chicago. From his observations of insects and small animals he not only learned much about them but also about human beings. "Can any of you think of anything that we might learn about ourselves by watching ants or bees or chipmunks?"

Sharing of students' experiences may also whet a desire to read a selection. One teacher knew, for instance, that one of the boys in her class had done a little amateur panning for gold during the past summer. Before her class read Jack London's "All Gold Canyon," she asked this student to relate his experiences to the class and explain just how panning is done.

Louise Rosenblatt stressed the importance of student participation in reading experience:

> We do not learn *about* Lear, we share, we participate in Lear's stormy induction into wisdom. In *Huckleberry Finn,* we do not learn *about* conditions in the pre-Civil War South; we live in them, we see them through the eyes and personality of Huck. . . . Whether it be a light-hearted lyric of Herrick's or a swiftly-paced intellectual comedy of Shaw's or a brooding narrative of Hardy's, a reading is of necessity a participation, a personal experience.[18]

Anticipating Difficulties. It is not possible to anticipate all the difficulties that individual students may conceivably encounter in their reading. However, a teacher can reduce some of the problems. The amount of such anticipatory assistance should be greater for young students and slow-learning groups than for older students and quick learners.

Suppose that reading tests or the teacher's observations have revealed that a class has difficulty in understanding organization and grasping main ideas. A brief outline, mimeographed or placed on the board, may be of considerable help. For a variation, especially useful with exposition, the numbers of main and supporting points may be supplied, with the students to fill them in: I . . . . A . . . . B . . . . II . . . . , etc. Or a list of key questions, each pointing toward the main idea of a section, may be prepared.

Questions about the meaning of important paragraphs or sentences may also be presented to the class in advance to help them improve comprehension still more. It is especially desirable to ask questions about paragraphs and sentences that *must* be understood if the student is to comprehend the selection.

[18] *English Journal,* Nov., 1966.

There are differences of opinion about trying to anticipate difficulties with vocabulary. Some teachers like to pick out a few of the
important "hard" words and define them in advance. Others argue *General*
that new words are best learned in context. You may want to ex- *Vocabulary*
periment to see which method you prefer. Any general work that *works*
the class does in vocabulary building (see Chapter 12) is valuable
for reading as well as for writing, speaking, and listening.

If you use an anthology for the central reading material of the
course, do not overlook one source of help that can save you hours *Teachers*
and hours of preparation. That is the teachers' handbook, which is *Handbook*
available as a companion to several of the best anthologies. One
such handbook contains 504 pages, crammed with aids and suggestions. For every selection or group of selections, the authors of the
handbook have prepared background information, an explanation
of possible procedure, and a suggested assignment that guides the
student's reading, as well as ideas for class discussion and follow-up.
You will not find useful in your classes every suggestion in a handbook, but judicious choice can save time and enrich teaching.

Unusual Techniques. Sometimes unorthodox teaching devices
increase motivation and contribute to reading improvement. For
example, in Sousa Junior High School, Port Washington, New York,
seventh graders with a reading range from 3.5 to 5.0 had an opportunity to produce a videotape. They found that to do so they had
to locate a topic, "do research" (i.e., a great deal of reading on the
topic), prepare graphics, write a script, practice reading the script,
record a run-through, evaluate this practice tape, and make a final
tape. The quality of their work "far surpassed" initial quality, and
test scores showed gains.[19]

For another example, the Wilbur L. Cross High School in New
Haven, Connecticut, gave forty students in grades nine to twelve
a six-week unit on films, using as texts *The Filmviewer's Handbook*
and *Exploring the Film*, as well as having many appropriate paperbacks available. The visuals were TV commercials and four movies:
*The Last Angry Man, Requiem for a Heavyweight, On the Water-
front*, and *Raisin in the Sun*. Students responded enthusiastically
and read widely.[20]

[19] Judith H. Cohen, "Geniuses at Work," *Journal of Reading*, 13:4 (Jan., 1970),
p. 275.
[20] Nicholas P. Criscuolo, "A Multimedia Program for Reluctant Readers," *Journal
of Reading*, 13:3 (Dec., 1969), p. 212.

Mad magazine makes better readers of her remedial students, says Betty Sanders of San Jose, California.[21] Its use results in good class discussion and also, she says, in better understanding of poetry.

Another teacher uses for "The Recalcitrants" a plan by which for six weeks they may read any three books they wish—without reporting on them. Even more innovative is her plan to supply each student with earphones so that he may listen to a performance of *Alice's Restaurant* as he reads the play.[22]

Lawrence L. Hardman's slow juniors in Alexandria, Virginia, spent their time reading paperbacks and reporting orally to the teacher. There were no other assignments or discussion, no failing grades to students who read 1,800 pages or more per quarter; there was a chance for everyone to earn an A. Reading test scores, says Hardman, went up quickly.[23]

And maybe this is a vision of the future: "We watch as Johnny begins to read *The Pearl*—a shot of a Mexican village appears and music plays over the earphones, helping to set a mood. Scenes and music change as he progresses in his reading and equivalent pages flash before him. He determines his reading rate by operating a manual speed control." [24]

Thinking and Talking About What Was Read

In the discussion and other activities that follow the reading of a selection, the students concentrate their attention upon the selection and related items. But the teacher has an eye on the future reading of the students, and uses the present selection as a base for future operations. That is, he uses it to develop skills that the students will find useful in later reading in the course and in reading they may do throughout their lives.

The points and methods of attack will differ according to the needs of the class. With some groups the steady emphasis will have to be upon simple comprehension and relation of each selection to the students' lives. With other students the stress may be upon some

[21] "*MAD* Magazine in the Remedial English Class," *English Journal*, LIX (Feb., 1970), 266.

[22] Norma Wilson, "The Recalcitrants," *English Journal*, LIX (Jan., 1970), 105.

[23] *English Journal*, LVII (March, 1968), 405. See "They Read All Period" in the Idea Box, p. 116, for another account of a similar experiment.

[24] Joseph Auriello, "On Using Computers in English," *English Journal*, LVII (May, 1968), 650.

of the more advanced skills—"depth reading," as one teacher has
called it. Here is a brief discussion of a few of the reading-improvement techniques that have been proved workable.

Understanding Details. The study of details may best be related to finding answers to fairly general questions. For instance,
if a class has read excerpts from *Robinson Crusoe,* a before-reading
question may have been, "If a person is shipwrecked on an island,
what problems will he face, and how can he solve those problems?"
After reading, the question is "What problems did Robinson Crusoe
face, and how did he solve them?" The questions become more and
more specific: "How did Crusoe 'plow' his land?" "How and why
did he build a fence?" "What troubles did he encounter in making
utensils?" "How did he keep track of time?" "How would you
have coped with these same problems?" "Are there any problems
that Defoe seems to have overlooked?" The advantages of this
method are first, that it does not stress details for the details' sake;
second, that it gives purpose and therefore adds interest to the
search; and third, that it makes the details easier to remember, because they are placed in a framework.

Paraphrasing. When a selection seems rather difficult for students, a small amount of paraphrasing may be necessary. (Paraphrasing is discussed at greater length in Chapters 5, 6, and 7.)
Suppose, for instance, that the class has read Wilfrid Gibson's poem
"The Ice-Cart." Although this is not a difficult piece, some slow
students may not understand it. A brief summary by one of the
students, perhaps like the following, may help. "The narrator,
working in a hot office, sees a man delivering ice and imagines that
he himself is suddenly transported to a polar region, where he sees
white bears, swims with seals, and then lies on an ice floe while
gentle snow falls upon him, covering him deeper and deeper as he
sleeps peacefully. Suddenly the iceman cracks his whip, and the
narrator awakes in the grimy heat." More detailed paraphrase may
be used to clarify particular lines or groups of lines. For instance,

> . . . I was swimming, too,
> Among the seal-pack, young and hale,
> And thrusting on with threshing tail. . . .

may require paraphrase to make clear the point that the narrator
dreams that he himself actually *is* a seal.

Mastering New Words. The words chosen for class discussion will vary with the class. The principle behind the choice is this: Which of the probably unfamiliar words in this selection will be of particular use to the students in this group? For instance, in the long first paragraph of Lamb's rather well-liked "Dissertation upon Roast Pig," these words may be unknown to many students: *obscurely, Mundane Mutations, designates, mast* (i.e., nuts and acorns), *lubberly, Younkers, conflagration, antediluvian, new-farrowed, utmost, consternation, negligence, premonitory, nether, retributory, cudgel, callous,* and *ensued.* Instead of spending most of the class hour in defining all these words, it may be more profitable to pick out three or four (perhaps *obscurely, utmost, negligence,* and *ensued*), discuss their meanings, and have students construct original sentences with them. Some of the words (*Mundane Mutations, mast, lubberly,* and *Younkers*) your students may never encounter again and never need.

As often as possible, meanings should be figured out by the students, using contextual clues. "The following dialogue ensued" easily reveals the meaning of *ensued.* "His nether lip" is obviously either his upper or his lower lip, and, since moisture overflowed it, it must be the lower. Students are more likely to remember words whose meanings they have deciphered for themselves than they are those that have been defined for them by teacher or dictionary.

Students should be encouraged to ask questions about word meanings, word relationships, word peculiarities. "Are there any words in the paragraph that you do not understand?" is a good opening. And perhaps it need not be mentioned that the teacher should not discourage questions by making every question the occasion for student labor: "Look it up in the dictionary, George." Dictionary use is of course important, but too often teachers have unintentionally employed the dictionary as an apparent punishment for curiosity. And curiosity is the most vital ingredient in motivation.

Understanding Allusions and Figures of Speech. Teen-agers often have difficulties with allusions and figurative language. To many of them, one teacher reported, such expressions as "Herculean effort," "crossed his Rubicon," "built a better mousetrap," "old schooltie," and "the shot heard round the world" are meaningless. Daniel Webster's "brow like a mountain" doesn't denote intelligence to them; "As soon as she left, she was the life of the party" doesn't seem funny; "clippership clouds" are commercial planes; "mahogany-faced sea captains" are only red-faced; and "His nose was a topographical error" has not even one meaning, let alone two or three.

The teaching of figurative language may be somewhat more difficult than it once was, because, although the basic rhetorical figures remain the same, their possible content has been infinitely enlarged. Many of our students tend to be extremely literal-minded, perhaps because much in their environment encourages literalness: constant emphasis upon the tangibles of science, matter-of-fact newspaper accounts, prosaic television dramas, and endless analysis of sentences in English classes. It seems important, though, to teach what the basic figures are and to talk about them when some of their more interesting examples appear. (See also Chapters 7 and 12.)

The teaching of allusions becomes much more difficult every year, and no systematic approach appears feasible. Even a hundred years ago human knowledge was much less than it is now, and the possible content of allusions was consequently much less. It has been estimated that the sum total of human knowledge is now doubling every ten years. Think, then, of how many more things a modern author may allude to. Only an omniscient person could unfailingly grasp allusions.

If we define allusions more narrowly—perhaps restricting them to classical and Biblical—we can study myths in school and the Bible in church school, and thus familiarize students with Orpheus and Lazarus. Otherwise we must content ourselves with examining the content of each allusion as it appears.

Finding Main Ideas. Authors and editors are usually rather generous in supplying aids to understanding. Titles, chapter titles, headings, subheadings; paragraphing, transitions, "arrow words" (such as "especially significant"); use of additional space for important points; heightened style; mechanical devices (such as italic or boldface type)—these are some of the helps offered to the reader. But many high school students, and adults too, remain largely unaware of such bounty.

Helps to Teachers

Particularly when dealing with expository material, the teacher may seize the opportunity to point out some of these aids. Simple questions are useful: "What do you suppose the author will discuss under this heading?" "Why does he use three paragraphs to discuss this topic?" "Why is this sentence italicized?"

Also of value in helping students to find main ideas is calling for one-sentence summaries of paragraphs, then one-sentence summaries

★ good

of groups of related paragraphs, and then one-sentence summaries of entire expository selections. Class discussion of why one summary is better than another is useful.

Drawing Conclusions. Nobody can write everything about anything. If it were possible, it wouldn't be artistic. Something has to be left to the reader, who works with the writer to draw from words their threads of thought. An artistic writer does not insult his reader by telling too much. He seldom says, "The moral of all this, dear reader, is that. . . ." He makes clear and explicit what he must, and leaves implicit what the reader presumably already knows or can deduce for himself.

Unaided, few children are adept at between-the-lines reading. They see what the author sets before them, and no more, just as they see cornflakes on the breakfast table without awareness of farmers, tractors, marching rows of corn, dinosaur-necked corn pickers, trucks, elevators, trains, dietitians, ovens, packaging machines. To help them see more than words on a page requires patience, skillful questioning, tolerance of differing opinions—and a teacher who himself can read beneath the surface.

What, for instance, is Thurber driving at in "The Secret Life of Walter Mitty"? A student said, "Mitty's wife henpecked him so much that she drove him crazy, that's all." "Is he crazy?" the teacher asked. "No," said some students, "he's just a dreamer." "Do you ever dream of being a great athlete, a great doctor, a great actor, or anything else?" "Yes, of course, maybe we all dream a little," the students admit. "Does Thurber seem to like Walter Mitty?" "Yes, but he seems a little contemptuous of him, too." "Does Thurber think it's bad to daydream?" "No, only if it's overdone." And out of such inductive discussion, such Socratic questioning, the students conclude that Thurber is saying that it is human nature to dream great dreams, to imagine that we are someone else, and that dreaming is not bad unless it is carried to such an extreme that it becomes madness—that it is less bad to dream you are a dozen great men than it is to be sure you are Napoleon.

Often, especially in non-fiction, it is desirable to have students draw conclusions about the attitude and the purpose of the author, or even about his probable honesty. This is often called critical reading. For instance, in an article on a political question, the students may find as much as possible about the author, try to discover whether he would have any reason to weight his arguments unfairly, and examine the arguments carefully to see whether any important considerations have been omitted.   *Intellectual depth*

The Profundity Scale.   Oliver Andresen has described the use of a "profundity scale" by means of which students estimate, or at least talk about, the amount of profundity or depth in a selection.[25] This *5 levels* scale recognizes five possible interpretational levels or planes: physical, mental, moral, psychological, and philosophical. Although admittedly almost every piece of literature exists simultaneously on all five planes, there are some stories that stress physical action—event after event after event, with little intellectualizing. In others, intellectual activity (not just hitting someone in the nose) is involved in solving the character's problems. "Some more profound stories are meaningful at the moral and psychological levels, while a few can be shown to have universal philosophical meanings relating to essential problems such as the nature of man, of life or of history." Discussion of these levels may be of assistance to the student who tends to observe only the physical happenings.

Understanding Human Beings.   An important segment of drawing conclusions is drawing conclusions about human beings. One of the virtues of wide and intelligent reading is that it can introduce us to a much greater variety of persons than we are ever likely to know in real life. But authors do not tell us about all these actual and fictitious beings. Instead they show them to us, and from the persons' actions and their words we must try to understand them; from such understanding may come truths that we can apply to our own lives, our own relationships with others.

In *Giants in the Earth*, Rölvaag shows Per Hansa, Norwegian pioneer in the Dakota territory, and Beret, his wife. He shows Per Hansa performing brave acts, but he does not tell us that Per Hansa is brave. He lets us observe Per Hansa talking to the land and the land talking to him, but Rölvaag does not say, "This man is a poet." He lets us know that Per Hansa is disgusted because Hans Olsa does not get up and work despite his frozen legs, but Rölvaag does not say that Per Hansa is not really cruel—that it is just difficult for him to realize that many are less strong than he. Beret weeps and worries and makes dire predictions and indulges in mystic fancies; Rölvaag does not tell us that she is basically kind and delicate and loving but obsessed with terrible fears of an unfamiliar world. The reader

[25] "Evaluating Profundity in Literature," *Journal of Reading*, 8:9 (May, 1965).

must live with Per Hansa and Beret in the book and learn about them as he would in real life, draw conclusions about them as he would if he shared their roof. He may or may not come to admire and love them, but if he lives with them he will attain much understanding of them, of others like them who drove their oxen toward the sunset, of his own ancestors, of himself, of his friends who have strengths and failings like those of Per Hansa and Beret.

Understanding Literary Devices. In addition to reading for meaning, all classes to some extent—and able classes in particular—may be led to an understanding of certain literary forms and formalities. In poetry, for instance, they may note that a sentence does not necessarily end with the line, but they may see also the musical effects of rhyme and alliteration and assonance, the purpose of repetition, the reasons for and the effects of the great condensation characteristic of much poetry. In short stories they may observe the author's technique in plotting, the way he flashes bits of the setting on our mental screen, the things he does *not* say.

Special Problems in Reading

At convenient and appropriate times in the regular English classroom, the teacher and class may work on special ways of improving reading. Three of these ways are varying speed according to difficulty, locating information quickly, and scanning and skimming.

All three of these may be taught as matters of efficiency. It is not efficient to spend five minutes reading a page of easy material, although it may be efficient to spend twenty minutes reading a one-page poem or a complicated problem in mathematics. A reader who races through everything at 500 WPM may be no better than one who always slogs along at 100.

The library catalog and the table of contents and the index of a book represent wasted space to many students. Yet their efficiency as readers may be considerably improved if they learn to use these tools. Sometimes even college students thumb through a whole book to see whether it says anything about toadstools, when in thirty seconds they could find the answer in the index. Housewives may spend fifteen minutes in hunting percolators in the mail-order catalog.

To locate information, students need to know the alphabet, know it thoroughly. In addition, they need to know what kinds of information the cards in the library catalog contain, and what the difference is between a table of contents and an index. Then they need much practice, including some plain drill exercises, in using these three valuable tools.

For the teaching of scanning (i.e., searching quickly for a specific bit of information), the following procedure is generally effective: The teacher asks the students to bring to English class a textbook used in their history or science class. In one chapter the teacher finds the answer to a certain question, and he asks that question: "How close is Mercury to the sun? Find the answer in Chapter 4." The students who locate the information most quickly are asked how they did it. They will usually refer to the headings and subheadings, which show them where to read more carefully. They may also mention that the first sentence of each paragraph generally contains valuable clues.

In skimming, the technique is somewhat different. Skimming enables a student to discover quickly what a whole article or book is about. For instance, a student may wonder whether he wants to read a certain novel. He may skim by glancing through the first few pages to discover vocabulary difficulty and approximate setting, skip a number of pages and read quickly a paragraph or two, and repeat this process until he has made up his mind.

READING OUTSIDE THE CLASSROOM

Guided Free Reading

According to a famous statement by John C. Dana, the twelve rules for improving reading are the following: "(1) Read. (2) Read. (3) Read some more. (4) Read anything. (5) Read about everything. (6) Read enjoyable things. (7) Read things you yourself enjoy. (8) Read, and talk about it. (9) Read very carefully, some things. (10) Read on the run, most things. (11) Don't think about reading, but (12) Just read."

As teachers we are less interested in turning out graduates who have read than we are in turning out graduates who read. But students won't keep reading unless reading brings satisfaction. That means that during the school years we must cultivate in our students the habit of reading by giving them the opportunity to read widely in materials they can enjoy.

In some schools, extensive reading is completely free; that is, students may read anything and in any amount they desire. In others, it is almost completely guided, with the teacher making the selections. The happy medium is apparently "guided free reading," in which students choose from a long but carefully selected list representing various types and levels of difficulty. The teacher and librarian may both offer specific suggestions to individual students. They steadily recommend books just a little above the level of those the student is now reading, and encourage him to avoid restricting himself to one kind of subject matter.

Methods of conducting guided free reading vary. The most nearly typical procedure seems to be to set aside part of each class hour, or part of a week or other period of time, in which the students read whatever they select from the books and magazines that have been made available. In some classes there is no follow-up; in others there is class or group discussion regarding any topics of interest. For such a reading program to be successful the students must be surrounded by appropriate books and magazines, they must be led to read because reading is fun, and they must be taught by a person who is himself well read, quick to offer suggestions, but willing to slip unobtrusively into the background as the young people explore the variegated joys of reading.

Also frequently employed is the procedure of relating both in-class and out-of-class reading to the unit being studied. In some ways this is preferable, especially because the reading is likely to be purposeful and because subsequent class discussions will have unity and afford opportunities for all to participate.

Providing Materials for Extensive Reading

In a decreasing number of schools, the English teacher simply tells his students, "Go to the library and pick out a book for your next book report." Modern schools leave less to chance. They encourage reading in class but also set aside an occasional class period for reading in the library. During library periods, many different procedures may be followed: permitting browsing, having students spend only five minutes with a single book, spending periods with different types of books, giving library instruction, suggesting books, conferring with some students while others browse, etc.

Classroom libraries are assuming increased importance. The books, perhaps 50 to 200 in number, are changed at rather frequent intervals and may be "advertised" in various ways such as those suggested in The Idea Box, page 117. These books may be borrowed by the teacher from the school library or, if sufficient funds are available, may be purchased for classroom use and circulated from room to room. The paperbacks, if wisely chosen, are a boon to schools with little money; publishers of these books are now making an effort to print more titles that teachers want and students enjoy. Some schools collect a fee of a dollar or so per year from each student and buy classroom books and magazines with the money; the wisdom of this practice is at best debatable. Interest in the classroom collections may be built up by having students suggest many of the titles.

Checking on Outside Reading

"Book-report days" are still among the most detested in those schools where students make written or oral reports according to old, creaking formulas. But, since some teachers want records to help in guidance and to pass on to the teacher who will have the class next year, they feel a compulsion to continue the system of reports.

It is not necessary, however, to follow any dull routine pattern for reports. Here are a few tested devices (others are listed in The Idea Box, pages 118–19:

1. A small group of students reads the same book. The chairman and teacher prepare a list of thought questions to be answered independently before the class. Differences of opinion may lead to discussion, and create class interest in the book.

2. ". . . a bright-eyed bookworm with wide reading experiences might be asked for a careful statement of theme, a high-level analysis of some character's motivation, a discussion of some structural aspect of the author's craftsmanship, or a comparison with another piece of literature. Most important, reporting must not be a case of either this or that for an entire class." [26]

3. Students who have read books on similar topics (occupations, animals, history, etc.) exchange information about their books before the class.

[26] Stephen Dunning, "Everybody's Doing It—But Why?" *English Journal,* XLVIII (Jan., 1958), 33. Mr. Dunning stresses the need to have book reports reflect "common purposes that both teacher and student can hold as honest, valuable, and realistic."

4. A student tries to "sell" a book to another student, who believes that he would not like it.

5. "Conversation circles" with student chairmen discuss books on similar topics.

6. The class prepares a "newspaper" with stories based upon books read.

7. On a spindle, each student places the name of a book he has read. By the next day, the teacher has added a pertinent specific question concerning the book. In class, the student answers the question.

8. Students may work out dialogs, monologs, pantomimes, short plays, or television dramatizations, pertaining to the book read.[27]

9. Students prepare appropriate book jackets including "blurbs." Advanced students write reviews, criticisms, and evaluations.

10. "Tell the story again from the viewpoint of another character in the story." "Show how color or key words or ideas run through the story. Discuss their purpose and effectiveness." "Place yourself in the protagonist's position and relate how plot would have been affected with you as the hero." "Imagine the character in the book in a different setting. . . . Change mood, time, or setting and show how it affects characters and plot." "Imagine an eighteenth century schoolboy, accustomed to reading Shakespeare, Milton, Addison, etc., reading your book. What would be his reactions?" "Write a letter in the style, with the feeling, in the character of the subject of the biography, e.g., Thoreau writes to President Nixon." "What characteristics of the main character are present in all successful men and women? What are his or her unique characteristics?" [28]

11. One of the simplest and best methods of providing a motivated check on reading is to have the students record whatever reading they do, together with a brief comment. The Cumulative Reading Record (NCTE) is ideal for this purpose. The teacher encourages the students to bring into class discussions references to their reading, just as adults do. Since the teacher notes carefully what each student has been reading, he may frequently address to a student a question upon which his recent reading should throw some light. The class soon learns to expect and welcome such casual questions, and reads more carefully because of them. At the same time, students are learning that their outside reading may be related to many topics of discussion. They thus gradually acquire a more adult view of reading than they may gain from some other devices.

---

[27] For details on scripts, see Donald Noble, "Television Script Book Reports," *English Journal,* XLIX (April, 1960), 259–61.

[28] These and other suggestions are taken from Howard S. Rowland, "Alternatives for the Book Report, *English Journal,* LI (Feb., 1962), 106–13.

THE IDEA BOX

We Must Be Doing Something Right

According to a Gallup Poll in 1969, the amount of book reading by young adults had increased significantly since 1958. In 1969, 26 per cent reported having read a book in the past month; the 1958 percentage was 21. How can we increase the rate of gain?

Three Kinds of Reading

Reading may be: (1) literal, what an author says; (2) interpretive, what an author means; (3) applied, relationship of what an author says to the reader's own experience. Although a good reader may perform all three acts simultaneously, less experienced readers need to be taken through the steps in order.

Save Their Lives

It is useful for very poor readers to be taught to read quickly the signs that they must sometimes read for preservation of self or others: SLOW, CURVE, LANE ENDS, MERGING TRAFFIC, NO LEFT TURN, EXTERNAL USE ONLY, and GENTLEMEN(!) Corlett T. Wilson lists 226 essential words and phrases in *The Reading Teacher* (Nov., 1963).

Developmental vs. Remedial Reading

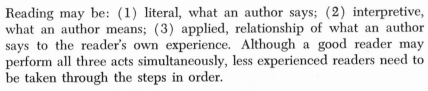

Developmental reading assumes continuous and steady progress toward reading goals, while remedial reading implies serious interference with such growth. Continuous instruction is the keynote of developmental reading: special attention to specific reading difficulties is characteristic of remedial reading. So says Robert Karlin, *Reading Forum* (Spring, 1962).

What Is Reading in Depth?

"When a high-school student has read a work in depth, he has, in the first place, simply understood the words; he has translated the imagery into lively sensory impressions; he has participated vicariously in the feelings of the characters; he has explored the work for its ethical or social or psychological outlook, which he has evaluated for its truth; and, most importantly if he is to continue reading, he has enjoyed himself," Bruce E. Miller says in the *English Record* (December, 1963).

Rank Order of Reading Difficulties

When 827 college students and adults were asked to rank their reading difficulties in order of importance, this was the result: (1) word-by-word reading, (2) vocalizing, (3) backtracking, (4) daydreaming, (5) monotonous plodding (not changing speed), (6) rereading, (7) word blocking (unfamiliar words), (8) clue-blindness (ignoring headings, key phrases, etc.), (9) finger following, (10) word analysis (giving a word more meaning than context necessitates), (11) head swinging, (12) number attraction (being stopped by a number). John W. Purcell, "Poor Reading Habits: Their Rank Order," *The Reading Teacher*, XVI (March, 1963), 353.

Newspaper Headlines

"From newspapers select short, interesting items with better than ordinary headlines. Number the headlines and corresponding articles for purposes of identification, cut off the headlines, and distribute the articles, giving easiest reading matter to poorest students. Headlines are kept at the teacher's desk. Each student reads his article and writes an original headline for it. As the teacher calls numbers, each student reads his article and the headline he has written. Then the teacher reads the one which was in the newspaper. The class compares them and makes comments. Students seem to enjoy a lesson of this type and do good work with it." (Mary Halloran, Braintree, Mass.)

Additional Techniques in Teaching Reading Skills

1. If any of your students move lips or tongue while reading, help them to understand that doing so retards their reading. Tell them of the student who had difficulty in breaking himself of moving his lips and tongue. He finally put a piece of tape across his lips and rigidly held his tongue against the roof of his mouth. After a few days he was able to dispense with the tape; his reading speed was nearly doubled.

2. Usually tests of reading speed should be accompanied by tests of comprehension, since speed without adequate understanding has no merit. However, at monthly or bimonthly intervals, students may time themselves in reading selections of comparable difficulty (selections chosen by the teacher). They may thus discover whether their reading is becoming more rapid. The teacher may, if he wishes, have the class answer questions to test comprehension.

3. Some reading teachers use flash cards to teach phrase reading.

4. Alan Robinson suggests emphasis on three comprehensional skills: finding key words in a sentence, finding key sentence in a paragraph, and finding the main thought in a paragraph that contains no topic sentence. "A Cluster of Skills: Especially for Junior High Schools," *Reading Teacher*, 15 (Sept., 1961), 25.

5. Asking questions as one reads is probably the best way to remember, suggests Delwyn G. Schubert. A quick survey of a chapter before SQ3R reading may help one to perceive relationships that otherwise would be missed. Giving oneself a quiz after reading is also helpful.

6. A student's ability to read humor understandingly is a good guide to his level of comprehension and general maturity.

7. Students are given paragraphs of simple instructions for doing something that may be performed in the classroom. Each does exactly what his instructions tell him.

8. Students read an untitled paragraph. Each suggests an appropriate title.

9. To assist visualization, students may draw or describe suitable pictures to accompany certain scenes in fiction.

10. Direct experience helps to clarify meaning. Thus, one class visited a newspaper plant and then read articles on how newspapers, magazines, and books are printed. The material was comprehensible because the students had something tangible to which to relate the words on the page.

11. To clarify sentence meaning, one student may read a sentence, and two others may restate its idea in two different ways.

12. To increase power to understand details, students may read a passage that contains many sensory images, and find words or phrases suggesting pictures, odors, sounds, tastes, or feelings.

13. For the same purpose, the teacher may supply a paragraph and three or four questions, one of which is not answered in the paragraph.

14. Students should frequently answer thought questions, not merely factual questions, based on paragraphs or articles.

15. Students may read two short articles about different inventions (or people, countries, etc.) and then decide how they are alike and how they differ.

16. The teacher prepares short paragraphs describing a person's actions. Students decide the person's purpose in acting thus. For instance, Ralph was invited to a dance. He washed his father's car, volunteered to help his mother, and remarked to his father that he wished he could take Jane to the dance. Why did Ralph do these things?

17. Students read a fable and then decide what familiar proverb it illustrates.

18. From a few clues in a paragraph, students decide what the setting is, or who the chief character is, or the approximate date of the incident.

19. In one column are several half-sentences; in a second column are the half-sentences needed to complete the first ones. Students are to find in the second column the words that logically complete each sentence.

20. Important tools in reading are the library catalog and *Reader's Guide to Periodical Literature*. Perhaps the best way to teach their use is to employ teacher-made or student-made problems, such as "Where can you find information about skin diving?"

21. To improve skill in locating information, the teacher prepares specific questions answered in various reference books. Students use the indexes, tables of contents, etc., and find the answers as quickly as possible. If the teacher desires, the class may be divided into teams for an information-finding contest.

22. To improve skill in scanning and skimming, students are given a limited amount of time to find in a magazine a specified item of information, or to prepare for writing a brief summary that will give the central idea and chief supporting points. The length of time permitted may gradually be shortened.

23. Have students rapidly examine a chapter in any one of their texts, preferably a chapter with subheadings. Ask them to list six to ten questions that they believe the chapter would answer. At another time you may have them draw up a skeleton outline of a chapter, and perhaps fill in the outline with the most important details.

24. Using a chapter with subheadings, ask students to indicate what is probably the chief question answered under each subheading. Then have them find and write the answer to that question.

25. Students read a paragraph, write an already familiar fact or idea related to the paragraph, and then point out how the two are related.

26. Some schools are experimenting with the plan of three different textbooks in each subject. Students are not segregated by ability but are given easy, average, or difficult texts. The plan has been both praised and severely criticized.

27. Useful films and filmstrips on reading, using the library, and similar topics are available from Coronet, Encyclopaedia Britannica, Inc., and other sources.

28. To improve students' ability to read critically, try constructing some relevance tests. Write a statement about any topic, and below it write three to five other statements. Students are to decide which of these statements are relevant to the first one. Similarly, to improve

use of the card catalog, *Reader's Guide,* and indexes, you may write a statement and then ask under which of several suggested topics the students would look to find further information, or students may prepare such items.

29. Critical reading may also be improved by asking questions concerning plausibility: "Does _____ seem to be a real person such as you might meet?" "Could this event have happened?" "Would it be probable?"

Unorthodoxy in Teaching Reading

At the University of Colorado Extension Center in Denver, poor readers have been encouraged to chew gum to reduce lip movement. "Classic" comic books were often read. Music was played while students read.

Reading Lounges

New Haven, Conn., elementary and secondary schools are establishing reading lounges—with comfortable chairs. They also have paperback book stores, managed by the students.

Linguistics and Reading

In recent years the possible application of linguistic principles to reading has attracted much attention. The key book (though it is mainly concerned with elementary reading) is C. C. Fries' *Linguistics and Reading* (Holt, Rinehart & Winston, 1963). Fries recognizes three stages of reading: "transfer," when the child learns to recognize the relationships between spoken language and that in print; "productive," involving response "to the meanings that are signalled without the use of the signals themselves"; and "vivid imaginative realization," which permits vicarious experience. Most students, but not all, in junior high school have passed the transfer stage; the emphasis in instruction, however, must be related to the stage in which each student is.

Skills That Can Be Taught Separately

Frederick B. Davis has identified the following reading skills that can be given separate emphasis: (1) recalling word meanings; (2) finding answers to questions; (3) drawing inferences from the content; (4) recognizing a writer's purpose, attitude, tone, and mood; and (5) following the structure of a passage. *Reading Research Quarterly* (Summer, 1968).

Oral Reading Helps Reading

In the "old days," children learned to read by reading aloud, but more recently oral reading has become less common. Walter Pauk of Cornell, in *Reading Improvement* (Winter, 1968) says that poor readers in high school may become much more proficient if they will agree to practice oral reading at home for fifteen minutes a day.

Eye Movements and Eye Span

According to Dr. George Spache, writing in the *Journal of Developmental Reading* (Autumn, 1963), eye movements cannot be controlled by the reader nor can eye span be appreciably widened. Speed reading "experts" who claim to be able to teach such things are in error, according to Dr. Spache.

Factors in Reading Power

Research by Jack A. Holmes and Harry Singler at the University of California at Berkeley found that the following elements account for 55 per cent of differences in *speed* of reading: visual verbal meaning, understanding of spoken English, knowledge of homonyms, inductive reasoning, and literary interest. The following elements accounted for 75 per cent of the differences in reading *power:* verbal analysis, understanding of spoken English, vocabulary in context, vocabulary in isolation, visual verbal meaning, tone intensity, and effective study planning. (Summary by Sue M. Brett.) The high rank of understanding of spoken English in both lists suggests that considerable class talk (the British method) may indeed be of significant help.

Preferences of Junior High Boys and Girls

Lorene Novotny summarizes likes and dislikes of 128 seventh graders: "In fiction, the boys preferred stories of frontier heroes, wars of our country, the jungle, western adventure and Indians. Girls preferred stories of teenage romance, adventures of girls, funny stories, and pioneer life. Least attractive to boys were modern sea stories, modern travel stories, teenage romance, and adventures of girls. Least attractive to girls were sea stories of the past, football stories, and stories of jet planes." *Kansas Studies in Education* (Feb., 1960).

"Best- and Least-Liked Stories in Junior High School"

A research study by Ray H. Simpson and Anthony Soares revealed that junior high students liked stories with a main character who was well delineated, that obscure authors were generally preferred to famous ones, and that plot, conflict, suspense, unifying effect, and concrete, clear language were important. *English Journal*, LIV (Feb., 1965), 108.

Vive la Difference – *multiple copies in Resource Center*

G. Robert Carlsen's *Books and the Teen-Age Reader.* (Harper and Row, 1967) is a valuable survey of student readers' likes and dislikes. Boys, says Carlsen, like an expansive book, with lots of elbowroom; girls like a confined book. Boys like emphasis on incident; girls like to read about interrelationships of people.

"Skimming Practice"

Irwin Weiss uses *Reader's Digest* articles to provide practice in skimming. The title, first sentence in paragraphs, and concluding paragraphs are especially important. *English Journal*, LVI (Jan., 1967), 135.

Book List for the Disadvantaged

See the *Journal of Reading*, May, 1967, for 101 titles of books of particular interest to disadvantaged Puerto Rican and black children.

"Using the School Magazine with Retarded Readers"

Poor readers may improve both their reading and their writing when they use the school magazine in which their contributions are welcome. They read it much more willingly than they do anthologies. Alice B. Conroy provides details. *English Journal*, LIII (Nov., 1964), 624.

"Easy-to-Read Adult Books for Senior High School Students"

A useful list of about a hundred rather modern books is contained in this article by Marjorie R. Empacher and Katherine W. Trickey, *English Journal*, LVII (Feb., 1968), 193.

Tailor-Made Books for the Inner City

In Los Angeles a number of literature books have been specially written for inner city young people, particularly those with reading difficulties. First reports were enthusiastic. A. C. Brocki tells of the experiment in "New Literature for Inner-City Students," *English Journal*, LIX (Nov., 1969), 1151.

Book Preferences of Juniors and Seniors

Karen Saterlee, librarian at Burris Laboratory School of Ball State University, has found that juniors and seniors prefer adult books to those supposedly on their age level. Such subjects as war, education, sex, narcotics, politics, and racism rank high with them.

What's New in the Library?

Students in Norwalk, California, High School prepare a little quarterly magazine called "A Look at Your Library," listing and annotating new acquisitions and giving brief biographies of authors.

Book Cafeterias

More and more schools are installing small bookstores especially for sale of paperbound books. The stores may be staffed by students under faculty supervision and should be open regularly at stated hours. Profits may be used for classroom libraries or other commendable purposes. Only books should be sold—not candy, etc. Titles should be faculty approved but may be student-suggested. Prices should be publishers' list prices. Titles displayed should be changed frequently.

An Example of Guided Free Reading

In an inner-city school, on "reading days," students in Lorraine Goldman's classes choose freely (and noisily) from the extensive classroom library. The book report system is for each student to answer in writing one thought-provoking question about his book. "Reading and Reporting," *English Journal*, LIX (Feb., 1969), 236.

Book Sampling

When students are choosing a book to read, David Sohn recommends that they examine the cover, read the blurbs, read pages 1, 50, and 100 (or 1, 100, and 200), and then, if still interested, take the "thirty-page chance" by reading the first thirty pages. They may reject the book after any step. *Media and Methods* (Feb., 1968).

They Read All Period

For six weeks Ann W. Ackerman's non-academic seniors did almost nothing but read—any books they wanted. Thirty-four students read 253 books; 13 said, "I'll probably read more than in the past," and 7 said,

"I have learned to enjoy reading for the first time (or again)." Thirty-three said "yes" to "Do you think six weeks of reading each year would be a good idea for Grades 9 through 12?" "Reading for Pleasure and Profit," *English Journal*, LVIII (Oct., 1969), 1042.

Motivating Outside Reading

1. "At the beginning of the semester, a junior boy says, 'Do you have any stories about sports? That's all I'm interested in.' I recommend *All-Conference Tackle, Career Coach*, or *Goal to Go*—not classics, I admit, but at least these books serve their purpose because upon finishing them this boy will say, 'Do you have any more like those?' I now have the motivation I have been striving for—an aroused interest in reading. I must be especially careful not to violate his trust by suggesting a book that, according to literary standards, is a classic, but according to his standards is difficult and boring. He is not ready for such a selection, and insistence on specific books to be read for credit is no procedure to follow if we are attempting to teach the student to like to read. Gradually, though, his reading horizon can be broadened to include far-away places, various professions, means of communication, etc." (Eleanor Vossler, Osawatomie, Kan.)

2. Raise the question, "What are the adventure zones in our world?" Get answers referring to things other than places. Then encourage reading in these zones.

3. "A touch of comedy may go further than a casual suggestion from a teacher. Post a large 'Bugs Bunny' poster which reads 'How about a Good Book, Doc?' Cards describing good books can be inserted in a window in the poster. Or one might have the cartooned figure of a diver (Gay Nineties suit); above it, 'Thinking of Taking the Plunge? Try Poetry.' Post below it some titles of quickly read poems." (Elaine Charles, Central High School, Grand Rapids, Mich.)

4. On the bulletin board put book reviews, pictures, and newspaper clippings referring to books. Better, let students do so.

5. "I post on the bulletin board 'best sellers' (not necessarily current books) that I recommend for the particular age group." (Marguerite Chamberlain, Franklin, N. H.)

6. The teacher's reading of brief, carefully selected excerpts from a book may make young readers eager to read it for themselves.

7. After reading books about various countries, Ruth Raymond's students in Keene, New Hampshire, hold discussions on such topics as Interesting People We Meet in Books, Problems Solved, Description of a Scene, Maxims and Aphorisms, Humorous and Witty Lines, Customs of the Countries.

More Suggestions for Book Reports

1. Let students consult *Book Review Digest* to discover what can be told about a book besides its story.

2. Often the form of a book report may be predetermined by the reason for reading the book. If, for example, a student reads a book about electronics in order to learn about electronics, shouldn't his report tell of some of the important things he had not known before?

3. In lieu of a report, allow a student to make a poster to advertise a book he has liked.

4. Have students prepare an advertisement for a book, such as a book club might use. (Esther Urie, Hartford, Vt.)

5. A week in advance of the date when reading reports are due, ask for titles of books being read. On the due date, select four or five somewhat related books for reports. The other students simply record their reading, but all must read, since they do not know who will be called upon. (Marguerite Chamberlain, Franklin, N. H.)

6. For a short oral or written report on fiction, have each student state the main character's big problem and its outcome. (Anna Haig, Bronxville, N. Y.)

7. Let students give oral or written reports, not summarizing the story but presenting their ideas concerning the author's motives and methods. (Paul Hassett and Harold R. Hansen, Menomonie, Wis.)

8. "Let students print titles of books read beside their names on wall charts; indicate the subject, e.g., aviation or careers or history, so that pupils will be encouraged to build a varied reading experience." (Iowa City Junior High School.)

✳ 9. Have a "Talk-About-Books Day" once a month. (Iowa City Junior High School.)

10. In El Cerrito, California, junior high school students hold "Book-of-the-Week-Club" panels. Five students review books they have read, and the class chooses the one most adequately presented as its book of the week.

11. Donald Noble, of Alvin, Texas, has his students write parts of the script of a television play as a book report. For detailed instructions, see *English Journal*, XLIX (April, 1960), 259.

12. Many variations of a point-credit system are in use. Instead of stipulating that a student read a certain number of books, this plan requires earning a certain number of points. Long, difficult books carry more points than short, easy ones. Defects of this plan, however, are numerous, as in any plan that makes a quantitative prescription for all students.

13. Have each student keep a diary of his reading, with titles and comments. Collect the diaries a few at a time, and read excerpts to the class.

14. Encourage summer reading by allowing students to check out books before the end of the school term. Get parents' signatures to ensure that the books will be returned.

15. Be sure to keep a permanent record of each student's outside reading.

16. Students may write a paragraph on each of two topics, choosing from six presented: (1) the character I'd like as a friend; (2) with specific reference to incidents, characters, or theme of this book, why I'd like to read another book by this author; (3) what makes the ending of the story satisfactory; (4) referring to at least two ideas in the book, why other students would find it helpful and not just entertaining; (5) comparison of the setting with my own environment; (6) permanent impression left upon me by the author's insights into human nature. Christine Yoder, *High Points* (Nov., 1961), p. 16.

17. The day before a book review is to be written, Elizabeth S. Sloat, Nazareth, Pennsylvania, puts on the board three or four general, thought-provoking questions, which are changed for each review. She thus leads students to search in their books for more than the superficial.

18. Brief reports, written in class and following specific instructions devoted to a single literary concept (theme, setting, point of view, etc.) work best for Mark Twomey of Minnesota. "A New Twist to the Book Report," *English Journal*, LVII (Dec., 1968), 1321.

19. Jane Rozsnafsby supplies lead sentences for book reports. E.g., "Paul Morel's family life as a child had a great effect on his mature state of mind in *Sons and Lovers*, by D. H. Lawrence." The student may then write only what supports this central idea. "Teaching Unity in Composition," *English Journal*, LV (Nov., 1966), 1073.

20. Let a student who has obviously understood a book write five good questions (and answers). Other students who report on the book later can be asked these questions. So A. H. Wolfington suggests in *Missouri English Teacher* (Oct., 1964).

State-Wide Emphasis on Reading

Connecticut is representative of the states that have embarked on statewide programs to improve reading of all students from kindergarten through high school. The aims, according to a 1970 release, are ". . . (1) to help each pupil acquire—within the limits of his capacity

—the skills necessary for fluent, easy, thoughtful reading, and (2) to persuade him that printed materials have a contribution to make to his success and happiness.[27] The Connecticut State Department of Education has developed "Criteria for Assessing School Reading Programs," an instrument to be used by all schools in analyzing what they are doing and should be doing to improve their instruction in reading.

Paperbound Books in Print

This quarterly catalog, published by the R. R. Bowker Company, lists most paperbound books (of American publishers) currently in print. It is essential for any school library and useful in making selections for classroom libraries. Other books from the same company include *Textbooks in Print* (annual) and *The Literary Marketplace* (concise information about publishers, annual).

Your Own Reading Record

After reading a book, article, or story that they may wish sometime to call to the attention of a student or students, some efficient teachers spend five minutes in writing pertinent bibliographical information on a 4" by 6" card, along with a brief summary or interpretive comment. A collection of such cards can be invaluable.

Useful Articles on Reading Research

The *English Journal* for March, April, May, and September, 1969, carried a series of articles under the general title "What Does Research in Reading Reveal?" Although both elementary and secondary schools are covered, these eight articles provide an authoritative summary very useful to the junior or senior high school teacher who has not had much training in teaching reading.

...s a consequence of instruction students will "approach" English materials, not avoid them.

Literature: Approach Responses and Avoidance Responses

5

DARTMOUTH CONFEREES AND OTHERS

Experimental British Schools

Americans who think of the British as staid conservatives should spend time in some of Her Majesty's secondary schools. Certainly the label does not apply to most teachers and students in large numbers of schools where experimentation is going on. (One of my colleagues, when we were visiting British schools, was engaged by a class in an informal question–answer session. A girl aged about thirteen piped up, "Do you have the Pill in America?" Though a bit nonplussed, he said "Yes." She came back, "Does your wife use them?")

Nor does the label "conservative" apply to literary content and methodology. In British schools one finds no thick anthologies and no elaborate courses of study. Thin little volumes or paperbacks substitute for the anthologies, and magazines and newspapers are frequently used. A course of study may consist of one to three pages of suggestions typed up by the department head. It may hint that the fourth form, say, might do well to read a play by Shakespeare or some Keats or Shelley, or it may be even less directive than that.

For the British teacher's classroom is his castle. With possibly a few exceptions, he makes the decisions about what, when, and how to teach. He bases those decisions upon what the students seem to need or seem ready for, upon what he has previously enjoyed teaching or found successful, perhaps upon some current news event, or sometimes just upon a whim or an idiosyncrasy.

But, if he is a modern British teacher, he strives to get his students "engaged," that is, personally involved in the literature. Engagement seldom comes, in his opinion, from reading *about* literature, or from analyzing it to discover the source of its effectiveness. It comes rather from getting the student inside literature and getting literature inside the student. That means much dramatizing, lively discussions of the people in the work, a great deal of talk.

And it means relating literature to other media, such as music. In a paper prepared for the NCTE Commission on Composition, Priscilla Tyler has written:

> The students frequently role-play, pantomime and put on class-made plays. On window-sills and tables stand models and artifacts the students have created to go with the stories they have written and acted out. Music, also, is often a part of the English class. For example, at Priesthorpe School near Leeds, I observed a group of over a hundred pupils as, first, they listened to a story told them with a symphony recording accompaniment; then as, in groups of three, they pantomimed the story, listening this time only to the music. The large room in which they assembled seethed with moving groups as each child acted out his role in accordance with the way he half-imagined, half-heard it in the beat and melody of the music. Such an activity ensured that any later wording of this happening would be made with an awareness of its underlying rhythm and imagery. Wording is empty, these British teachers feel, without an imagined, rhythmic experience as its source, and the imagined, rhythmic experience is empty, in another sense, without a wording of it to serve as its objective emblem.

Professor Tyler also comments that "films, television, radio, newspapers, magazines, advertisements [are] a special kind of living subject matter imaginatively coined by this century for the delight of English teachers and their classes."

In an all-girls school in a London slum, my first visit was to a class of eleven- or twelve-year olds. For a while I thought I was in bedlam. The girls were shouting, arguing, parading around the room, riding horse-back on one another. After twenty minutes or so, the young and pretty teacher rapped on her desk, and relative quiet descended. "Group 1," she said. A half-dozen girls disengaged themselves from the others and put on a pantomimed story about a girl horse that had fallen in love with a boy horse. After a minute or two of discussion and clarification, Group 2 presented its panto-mime, and so on. The teacher told me afterward that the class had become much interested in reading stories about horses and were now creating and pantomiming horse stories of their own.

I went next to a class of twelve- or thirteen-year old girls. The procedure was much the same, but the noise level was a little lower. These girls had been reading myths, and were producing improvised versions—with words, not just pantomime—of the Golden Fleece story.

In the next class, another year older, the girls had been bored by their study of Spanish with another teacher. Hoping to come to the rescue, the English teacher had introduced translations of Spanish poems filled with señoritas, balconies, and bull fights. Now the girls were writing their own poems about similar subjects, reading them chorally in small groups into a tape recorder, playing back the record-ing, and revising either the poems or the reading or both.

Near the end of the day I sat in a class of sixth-form girls (about eighteen years old) taught by the headmistress. The young ladies sat demurely (or as demurely as their mini-skirts permitted) in a semicircle, and quietly and intelligently discussed the characters and the structure of one of the Canterbury Tales. After class I rather hesitantly asked the headmistress, "Were these girls—were these girls once like the ones I saw riding horseback?" She smiled and replied softly, "Of course."

Perhaps what American teachers can learn profitably from the British is the emphasis upon engagement. Literature should turn students on, not off. Maybe many American teachers are so eager to have students learn facts about literature ("Who is the speaker?" "What is the rhyme scheme?" "When did Wordsworth live?") that many students never really become personally involved in the lit-erature.

On the other hand, maybe the British treatment of literature is too superficial. Critics of the British method (or nonmethod, if you prefer) say that until British children are at least fifteen or sixteen, literature is used mainly to titillate nerve ends. It creates an emo-tional rather than an intellectual reaction. Many children leave school at fifteen without ever having a "serious" encounter with a piece of literature. Only those who stay on into the fifth and sixth forms learn much about how a poem means, how a play is structured, or how characteristics of literature have changed through the centuries.

The Dartmouth Conference

In the summer of 1966, about fifty prominent educators from Great Britain, Canada, and the United States participated for a month in the Anglo-American Seminar on the Teaching of English, generally now referred to as the Dartmouth Conference. Elementary and secondary teachers, professors of English and Education and Speech, and officers of national organizations took part in "the first large-scale international conference on this basic subject."

The Dartmouth Conference has caught the fancy of American teachers, and the extent of its effects is still to be determined. The two major reports on this conference should be read thoughtfully by every English teacher.[1]

The unsophisticated would have guessed that the Americans would represent a liberal point of view, the British a conservative one. But the reverse was true. As Professor Muller explains,

> The British were reacting violently against an authoritarian tradition in schooling symbolized by stereotyped, nationwide examinations that rigidified the curriculum [and that now are being greatly reduced in importance]. . . . Americans, on the other hand, were reacting against the slackness and confusion dating from the excesses of the progressive movement in the last generation, symbolized by the statement "We don't teach a subject, we teach the whole child." This movement broke up the old habits of teaching and learning by rote, but it also encouraged a watering down of the curriculum and the introduction of "slops" that are mistaken for English.[2]

The British out-talked and out-maneuvered the Americans, who found themselves giving ground constantly and often being won over to a British point of view. The British, for instance, were wittily pugnacious in their attacks on what they referred to derogatorily as "lit crit" and "lit hist" (literary criticism and literary history). The Americans were forced to admit that lit crit and lit hist are often incomprehensible or boring to a high proportion of students.

---

[1] John Dixon, *Growth Through English* (Reading, England: National Association for the Teaching of English, 1967). Herbert J. Muller, *The Uses of English* (New York: Holt, Rinehart and Winston, Inc., 1967). Both publications may be purchased from the NCTE.

[2] Muller, *op. cit.*, pp. 12–13.

The British boasted that English people read more books per capita than Americans do (though the Americans might have retorted that the British adults who read all these books were brought up under the old, rigid system rather than the free-wheeling one now advocated). To quote Professor Muller again,

In one of the basic papers for discussion a British writer stated: "English has no content; there are virtually no facts to transmit." Americans at once began objecting that it did have a positive content of its own, in both language and literature. Soon it appeared that the British "content" had the disagreeable connotations of system, a set program, or a package of contents to be graded. Americans could then agree on the danger of a rigid program, but mostly they still argued for the importance of basic subject matter, the need of a definite syllabus, and the greater danger of turning a lot of mediocre teachers loose on the subject. The British typically wanted the utmost possible freedom of choice for both teachers and students. In the teaching of literature they shied away from any emphasis on "knowledge," which to them implied a body of inert facts; they deplored the tendency to present a body of historical or critical knowledge about literature, instead wanting to concentrate on the understanding and appreciation of particular literary works. Similarly they disliked the word "instruct," which for them connotes drilling, lecturing, or talking down. As Frank Whitehead put it, the teacher should "nudge" the young along the path of their natural development instead of instructing them in prescribed subject matter.[3]

The British argued strongly for an approach to literature that consists mainly of talk and dramatic activity. Literature, they said, cannot be taught by a direct approach; lectures on literature, for instance, "kill a personal response." Literature should not be studied, but should be experienced.

. . . *study* of literature is an ambiguous and often deceiving term, which often deflects the energies of teachers from what many of them now consider to be their primary concern. The term suggests, perhaps necessarily, that in the classroom experience with literary works, pupils and teachers should be seeking regularities and similarities, treating works as data or the source of data for establishing or testing general statements about classes of literary works, their parts, their authors, or the circumstances of their composition; or should be composing rather closed formulations of the probable causes in works of assorted effects in readers. On the other hand, *response* is a word that reminds the teacher that the experience of art is a thing of our making, an activity in which we are our own interpretative artist. The dryness of schematic analysis of imagery, symbols, myth, structural relations, *et al.* should be avoided passionately at school and often at college. It is literature, not literary criticism, which is the subject. It is vividly plain that it is much easier to teach literary criticism than to teach literature, just as it is much easier to teach children to write according to abstract models of correctness than it is to teach them to use their own voices.[4]

[3] *Ibid.*, p. 12.
[4] Dixon, *op. cit.*, p. 60.

The response, or involvement, that the British seek is exemplified thus by Dixon:

Interpretation however implicit should mean bringing our living experience to bear. Sometimes, it is not so much the line as the whole situation that demands this. If we look at Portia before the assassination (in *Julius Caesar* —II, iv), we see in part what it is for a woman to suffer while the man acts; a group would do well to improvise this scene, to engage for themselves in the struggle to contain oneself, passive in the moment of crisis. It is a beautiful scene for what is not said, but implied. Without an inner awareness of this, the lines mean little.[5]

Regardless of whether any American teachers begin to teach literature as many modern British teachers do, the Dartmouth Conference made it necessary for every teacher to take a hard look at his procedures, asking himself such questions as these:

Am I too rigid in my selection of literature? in my structure of the class? in my methods?

Do my students learn *about* literature instead of having experiences *with* literature? Do my students really get involved in what they read?

Do I dare try for a few weeks or a semester the British method of pantomime, improvisation, dramatization?

The Dartmouth Conference clarified for many teachers what they already knew instinctively: we want to create approach responses to literature rather than avoidance responses. In other words, we want students to enjoy literature and to read voluntarily, not to regard its reading as a task to be avoided if at all possible.

The remainder of this chapter and all of the next two chapters are written in this light, but with the assumption that the British way is not the only way to attain interest and involvement, although it is one very good one.

Three Reasons for Reading Literature

Why do we teach what we teach? That question might be phrased differently as "Why should we teach what we should teach?" or "How can we determine what we should teach?" It is related, obviously, to the even more basic question, "Why read literature?"

Let us consider that question, "Why read literature?" and then see how our conclusions may guide us in selecting literature for high school teaching and also in determining what we do with that literature.

[5] *Ibid.*, 61.

We read literature for three interrelated and overlapping reasons: for pleasure, for information of a kind not available in an encyclopedia, and for a means of sharing in our cultural heritage. We cannot separate these three with definite partitions, but, nevertheless, we can try to look at each in turn. (The British emphasize the first, pay some attention to the second, and generally ignore the third.)

Pleasure. We get our pleasure from different things, and the most truly educated persons are probably those who are most versatile in their joys. Such persons may turn in succession to a book, an art museum, a science exhibit, a kitchen stove or a jigsaw, a fishing rod or a set of golf clubs, a baseball game, a lecture, and the late late show on television.

He who knows how to read well enough can obtain a variety of pleasures vicariously. Though a baseball story by Ring Lardner should not be substituted for an afternoon in Yankee Stadium, the Lardner story may make the next baseball game a more vivid experience. The players on the field emerge as human beings; the Lardner reader is a better baseball fan because he realizes that baseball uniforms cover players who in background and temperament are themselves far from uniform.

Vicariously one could travel under the sea with Jules Verne decades before the first submarine was built. Vicariously one can visit lands that one may never see even with today's jet travel. Vicariously one can go back into the past and live as one's ancestors lived. Much of the pleasure of literature comes from such vicarious experiences. They help to create a versatility of pleasure.

Part of the pleasure for one who knows how to read well comes from a conscious recognition of artistry. We applaud what is done well, whether the act is one of juggling, painting a picture, playing the piano, or arranging words. The literary artist, though perhaps depicting "what oft was thought," chooses his words so that we may add "but ne'er so well express'd." We derive pleasure from the artful simplicity of Housman or Frost or Hemingway, from the resonant voice of Milton, from the dilettante extravagances and metrical experimentation of Swinburne, from the barbed satirical mastery of Swift or the gentleness of the remonstrances of Addison. The musics of Poe and Lanier have their beauty, and so has Millay's cry of exultation, "Oh world, I cannot hold thee close enough!" and so has Robinson Jeffers' bitter anguish.

Some years ago an advertiser ran a series of ads using the slogan "It's fun to be fooled, but it's more fun to know." It is fun to read literature even though one does not recognize the writer's techniques, but it is more fun when we do know what the writer has done to move us. If we can note how he has assembled the parts of a plot, how in a poem he has blended together rhythm and words to suit his purpose, how in a play he has characterized in only a few sentences, our appreciation is heightened. This does not mean that we have to count all the similes or scan all the lines, but it does mean that we analyze enough to identify the key aspects of the writer's craft. But as the British warn, too much analysis can be deadening.

Other parts of the pleasure can be identified. There is, for example, the pleasure of the puzzle, comparable to that of solving the Chinese box or ring puzzle; we attain this pleasure when we outguess the detective in a mystery story, or we attain it when we extract the essential kernel from a difficult lyric poem. There is also the pleasure of satisfying our curiosity about people, of comparing them with ourselves, of identifying ourselves with some of them, and of observing how they will react when they are thrust into changed surroundings or faced with unaccustomed obstacles. This is related, no doubt, to the pleasure obtained from discovering how things turn out—the age-old love of a story, which has its incipience in curiosity. Then there is the pleasure of intellectual stimulation—the stimulation that comes from new ideas and insights, thinking about these insights, and formulation of one's own conclusions.

Information. The pleasure of intellectual stimulation is related to the second reason for reading literature: It gives information of a kind not available in encyclopedias. If we want facts, we go to reference books. But, if we want insights different from those afforded by facts, we go to literature.

Dr. Sterling M. McMurrin, former United States Commissioner of Education, speaking on "Education for Freedom in a Free Society," said,

> One of the major deficiencies in our national effort to meet the challenges before us is the almost complete failure of the American people to recognize that the strength of a nation lies in its art and music and literature, and in its philosophical sophistication and the quality of its social sciences, just as much as in its physics and chemistry or its electrical engineering. When we raise the question of the survival of our Nation it is a question of proximate range of statesmanship and machinery. But when we speak of the decline or rise of our culture and the strength of the Nation for the long haul ahead, it is a question of the full cultivation of our spiritual, artistic, moral, and intellectual resources. Those who suppose that great music or great poetry or a knowledge

of classical literature is not essential to not only the quality but even the survival of a nation and its culture are quite unaware of the lessons of the past.

The insights that are deeper than mere facts are so numerous and varied that they can only be illustrated. In Crane's *Red Badge of Courage* is a portrayal of fear and self-finding more revealing than any of the studies made by psychologists. In Jonathan Swift's satire is a revelation of human weakness; it is a warning; it is a sermon. We recognize that we are the Lilliputians who will go to war over which end of an egg should be cracked first; we recognize that we are sometimes the Yahoos, with their repulsive habits; we recognize some twentieth-century scientists in the eighteenth-century scientists ridiculed by Swift. (Maybe the greatest need of this century is a reincarnation of Jonathan Swift.)

From the poetry of Robert Frost we learn once more the value of elemental things. The greatest accomplishment of the hired man in Frost's poem was his ability to load a hay rick tall and secure, every forkful in its place. The hired man reminds us of the bootmaker in John Galsworthy's short story "Quality," who made such good shoes that it took years to wear them out. We contrast the work of the hired man and the bootmaker with the shoddy workmanship, the built-in obsolescence, of so many items we buy today, and we wonder why we have lost what we have lost, and what the consequences may be, and what we may do to regain integrity and the pride that was once ours in a job well done.

From books like Mark Twain's *Life on the Mississippi* or O. E. Rölvaag's *Giants in the Earth* we can learn more than the history books tell us about the lives our ancestors lived. These are not glamorized, sleek presentations. Mark Twain's Mississippi is not just a broad, beautiful river with picturesque scenery along both banks; it has sand bars and mud, rough and sometimes violent men, sweat and confusion. Rölvaag's pioneers are both brave and fearful; in Beret, the pioneer wife who lacked the strength and the balance needed in a new land, we have one of the most sensitive portraits in all literature.

The humorous writers give us insights, too. Ogden Nash's famous four-line parody of "Trees," in which he laments that unless the billboards fall he'll never be able to see a tree, is more eloquent than most hour-long speakers on the conservation of natural resources. A drive along U.S. 1 in the East reveals the truth of Nash's lines.

"Literature is not a body of knowledge to be learned," insists James E. Miller, past president of the NCTE. Its function is to provide "a confrontation with life." Exploration of literature has lasting meaning "only if it leads to personal discovery." [6] Literature does contain information, Miller is saying, but that information should be experienced, thought about, and made a part of one's being—not just memorized for an examination.

Cultural Heritage. History classes bring parts of our cultural heritage to students; so do classes in science, mathematics, art, music, and so on. Can we in English identify as basic to our common heritage a number of literary selections that every American should know? Once the colleges, through their entrance examinations, in effect determined such a canon, including works like "The Bunker Hill Oration," Burke's "Speech on Conciliation," "Evangeline," "Idylls of the King," *Hamlet,* and *Macbeth.* After the turn of the century such dictation was rightly opposed. But the net result has been that we Americans have so little reading in common—on any academic level—that the late Professor William R. Parker of Indiana University asserted that even among his graduate students in English he could not count upon all of them to know any given work of literature.

It seems unfortunate that television rather than literature provides a common bond among most Americans. The man on the street or the woman at the bridge party can refer to any of a dozen currently popular television programs with fair assurance that the others present will understand the reference. Next week new programs, new allusions; next year many or most of this year's programs will be off the air, supplanted by something else. Without hostility to television one can justify the statement that it is ephemeral, it lacks roots, and it provides but a transitory bond. Literature could provide a permanent bond for us.

The NCTE's *National Interest and the Teaching of English* makes the case for literature in our cultural heritage in this way:

> The young who study our language and literature come into the best contact possible with the dreams, hopes, and aspirations, as well as with the roots of our culture. The rich texture of myth and folklore of lumbering, pioneering, and railroading stimulates the imagination and is a vehicle for the perpetual transmission of the American heritage. Only through the imagination do the complex natures of our various regions—Down East, the Old South, the prairie,

[6] In *Professional Growth for Teachers,* Third Quarter, 1967–68.

the corn belt, and the mining town—become ingrained in our rising generations. Many of the books our youth read suggest the richness which we define as our heritage—*Our Town, Huckleberry Finn,* "The Devil and Daniel Webster," "The Death of the Hired Man," *Abe Lincoln in Illinois, The Scarlet Letter, Moby Dick.* These stories are founded upon an older and wider tradition, but one still ours—*David Copperfield,* "The Ancient Mariner," "The Deserted Village," "Elegy Written in a Country Churchyard," *Robinson Crusoe, Macbeth.* And this literature depends upon and blends with an even older tradition—the temptations of Faust, the mystic Bluebird, the penetrating humor of Don Quixote, the wanderings of Ulysses, the heroic figures of Greek and Roman myth, the just and overseeing God of the Bible. The base of the heritage is as broad as the humanistic tradition.[7]

SELECTING

On the basis of valid reasons for reading and teaching literature, it is possible to answer some of the questions often asked about choosing the literature to be taught.

Should Only Classics Be Assigned?

College entrance examinations decades ago demanded familiarity with prescribed classics; even if they had not, the typical English teacher of 1910 would have cringed at the suggestion that that vulgar upstart Jack London be taught. William Lyon Phelps early in the century was regarded as dangerously radical when he encouraged his Yale students to read Stevenson.

But the old order changeth. London and Stevenson have attained respectability and have made the going easier for such of their descendants as Ernest Hemingway and C. S. Forester. Out the window have gone Burke's "Conciliation," Halleck's "Marco Bozzaris," and Landor's "Iphigenia and Agamemnon." Less attention is paid to Alexander Pope, and the name of Carlyle is never uttered in most classrooms. Most teachers today try to select for study only those pieces that have something clearly worth saying to today's young people and that say it well; these teachers realize that some of the old and some of the new meet this requirement.

Extremists exist on both sides, of course, though they are relatively few. Battling for an almost exclusive diet of classics are some teachers who argue that little contemporary literature is as good as what has stood the test of time; that the classics, because they are so well presented, can have even more appeal for adolescents than do materials whose chief virtue is contemporaneity; and that, if students are not exposed to the world's finest writing in high school, many of them will never read a line of it. On the other side are some teachers who assert that most classics are too difficult for teen-agers, difficult not just in language but also in conception and scope; only mature minds, these teachers say, can grasp what Shakespeare is really talking about or what Milton is saying about the ways of God.

A middle ground seems to be best. We must face the fact that most of the reading our students do after graduation will be taken from contemporary materials—newspapers, magazines, books-of-the-month, etc. As teachers we need to make this reading more discriminating than it would have been if we had never existed. We can teach discrimination only by introducing to our classes many varieties of reading and by helping students to understand the similarities and differences among those varieties. We need to present Homer, Chaucer, Hawthorne, and others, with sufficient skill that our students will not only see what has made these writers live but will also be able to use them as touchstones for the evaluation of other literature. The classics should be taught as samples of the best thinking and writing that man has yet achieved, and as expressions of the sensitivity of unusually perceptive human beings. Those children who are intellectually able to realize the mental and emotional penetration of great writers will have as a permanent possession the desire to find in other literature that which is no less evocative.

When a teacher is considering a selection, he should give it a high mark if it is readable by his class and if it will introduce students to some of the personalities who ought to be known to almost everyone. Somewhere in their high school careers students should become acquainted with Apollo, Minerva, and other mythological characters; with such semilegendary figures as Horatius, King Arthur, Marco Polo, and William Tell; and with such literary immortals as Oedipus, Sinbad, Chaucer's Knight, Cervantes' Don Quixote, Swift's Gulliver, Addison's Sir Roger, and Irving's Rip Van Winkle. It is doubtful that a modern American can be called truly "cultured" or even "educated" if such names are meaningless to him. Students in junior high school are usually ready for the myths of Greece, Rome, and Scandinavia, and for simple versions of the Round Table stories and other legends. But greater maturity—the near maturity of high school upperclassmen—is essential for an understanding of the Knight and other Chaucerian characters, Sir Roger, and Oedipus or Antigone.

The contemporary has its virtues, too, if it is carefully chosen. Some of today's contemporary literature will be tomorrow's classics. The first teacher to introduce O'Neill, Wilder, Hemingway, Steinbeck, Faulkner, or Frost to his students was departing from the classical canon, but today we realize that he chose well. The important point to remember is that, while modern writers of first rank are worth including, little class time should be spent on the tenth raters —or even the third.

In espousing the cause of contemporary literature, Edward R. Ducharme says, "The only disadvantage—if it is one—lies with the teacher. He is without his trusty literary guides and must, along with the students, think through the book extremely carefully and come up with intelligent positions supported from the text. Such an approach is difficult, demanding, and most worthwhile." [8]

How Difficult Should the Literature Be?

It is impossible to assess literary difficulty with exactitude. Formulas have been devised in the attempt, but, since they involve counting polysyllables and measuring sentence length yet cannot provide a yardstick to the difficulty of conceptions, they are hardly satisfactory. Readability formulas show, for example, that *Tom Sawyer* and *Huckleberry Finn* are equally difficult books, but anyone who has read and understood both stories realizes that Huckleberry Finn is infinitely more complex, multilayered, harder to grasp. Edgar Dale illustrates clearly how simplicity of words may conceal depth of meaning:

> In Dostoevsky's novel *The Brothers Karamazov*, Father Zossima asks: "What is hell?" and answers, ". . . it is the suffering of being unable to love." A fifth grader can pronounce these words, recognize them perceptually, but can he *read* them? He can't get the meaning because he is conceptually immature. [9]

But how can a student's conceptions mature if he is constantly exposed to immature conceptions? There is a way out of the apparent dilemma. The principle of pleasure that we have discussed implies that what we teach should be capable of bringing pleasure to

[8] "The Door Must Open," *English Journal*, LIII (Dec., 1964), 670.
[9] *Newsletter*, October, 1962, p. 2.

our students at the intellectual or maturational level they have attained at that time. In other words, a selection should not be so far beyond the understanding of students that there is no possibility of pleasure. Yet often it should be slightly beyond their full comprehension. Robert Browning provides the justification:

> Ah, but a man's reach should exceed his grasp
> Or what's a heaven for?

A well-chosen literary selection should stretch the student slightly; it should make him extend himself. If it does not stretch him, it provides no new challenges; he might as well spend his time before the TV set. But, if it is so far out of his reach that even utmost stretching will not bring him close, he will give up in despair.

Fortunately, many pieces of literature are comprehensible in part to most students, more fully comprehensible to others. Consider the analogy of an apple tree, laden with fruit. By stretching, every student in the class can reach the apples on the lowest boughs. Other students, by stretching, can reach apples on higher branches. Perhaps the ladders supplied by college and maturity will be necessary before any of the students can reach the apples at the top of the tree. But the other apples, some of them reachable by all students, are worth the picking.

As Robert Miles says in "Literature for the Average Student," ". . . the literature should be intelligible," it "should be enjoyable— not just tolerable, but actually pleasurable," and it "should be emotionally and intellectually significant to the student—not just stimulating to his superficial interests as a 'teen-ager,' but vital to his concerns as a young human being." [10]

Must Only Literature with a Capital L Be Assigned?

Perhaps no one can define exactly the line a writer must cross in order to be an author of literature. It may be helpful, though, to recall Van Dyke's definition of "literature": "Literature consists of those writings which interpret the meanings of nature and life, in words of clearness and power, touched with the personality of the author, in artistic forms of permanent interest." A sale bill seldom possesses any of these characteristics, nor, usually, does a news story about yesterday's murder or last night's basketball game. The purpose of the sale bill or the news story is utilitarian—to give informa-

[10] *English Journal*, LV (Feb., 1966), 172.

tion. But a non-utilitarian selection such as a story in a pulp magazine is not necessarily literature.

For practical purposes, as a rough guide only, the line between "mere reading" and "literature" might be drawn thus:

"Mere Reading"	*"Literature"*
1. May be utilitarian or affective (emotional)	1. Is always affective [11]
2. If utilitarian, has primary purpose of informing	2. Gives an author's personalized interpretation of life
3. If affective, lacks one or more of the last three qualities listed under "Literature"	3. Is clearly, strikingly written
	4. Is in an artistic form of lasting interest

Briefly, the question to consider is this: Should any material that is not literature be admitted to the high school English course?

The answer appears to be a qualified "yes." In their lives after graduation, many students will have more occasion to do utilitarian reading than affective. They will, for example, read recipes to find out how to bake a cake, timetables to discover when they will arrive in Denver, and newspaper and magazine articles to get information and form opinions. The English department has not done its duty if its students are graduated without knowing a great deal about how to read various kinds of utilitarian materials.

But, although the inclusion of some utilitarian reading is highly desirable in each year of the junior and senior high school, there is seldom a strong reason for including any affective material that lacks one or more of the qualities of literature. Outside the school's jurisdiction, students will sometimes read comic strips and *True Romances*. In class, however, they may read with profit selections that are of no less interest but are of satisfactory quality. Eventually, through the teacher's guidance, most (but not all) will search in their reading for qualities the poorer comics and the trashy magazines do not possess.

The "yes" may be qualified further by adding that most of the abilities requisite for reading utilitarian material should be developed in the elementary grades and junior high school. Many seventh, eighth, and ninth grade textbooks offer material of the sort needed to help the student in his work reading, and the resources

[11] It must be noted, though, that some utilitarian selections are on the borderline between "mere reading" and "literature." For example, some of Ruskin's prose dealing with art or with the dignity of labor is utilitarian in that it strives to inform, but it also possesses the characteristics listed here under "Literature."

objective

available in newspapers and magazines are nearly limitless. In the senior high school, the English teacher needs to help each student develop further his skill in reading utilitarian materials. A considerably larger proportion of the time, however, should be devoted to literature than to "mere reading." [12]

You will recall that one of the reasons for reading is to obtain information that transcends the factual. It is, therefore, wise to ask about almost every selection, "Will it provide insights valuable to today's students?" Ruled out, then, will be an article about fighting forest fires, if it provides nothing more than information about how to fight them. Ruled in will be an article or story on the same topic, if it sheds light on human nature and on the age-old conflict between man and nature. Novels by George R. Stewart, for example, might do this—*Fire* deals with forest fires and the men who combat them; *Storm* concerns the human effects of a fierce storm that sweeps from the Pacific across the western part of our country. Ruled out will be stories of conflict for conflict's sake—the bang–bang stories with little motivation, little probing of character: stories that hardly rise above children's backyard play-fights against the "bad guys." Ruled in will be stories of conflict that show why men fight, that show conflicts that may be more internal than external. *No* to Zane Grey; maybe *yes* to Walter Van Tilburg Clark, Conrad Richter, A. B. Guthrie, Jack Schaefer, Oliver La Farge.

Should the Whole Class Read the Same Literature?

The diagram on page 137 shows a desirable reading plan for a class.

Common cultural heritage

The material read by the whole class helps to provide for the common cultural heritage discussed on pages 130–31. In addition it makes possible some instruction in close reading, analysis of style, discussion of what to look for in literature, explanations of how each part contributes to the whole, and examination of the author's purpose. It assists students in relating literature to life, in distinguishing one type of literature from another, in learning the special techniques to apply to each type, and sometimes in seeing how literature grows not only from the author's experiences but also from the age in which he lives. Class reading may be regarded as an ideal form of the kind of reading it is hoped each student will do

[12] Some work in the reading of newspapers and in the reading of magazines is desirable, probably in the sophomore and junior years.

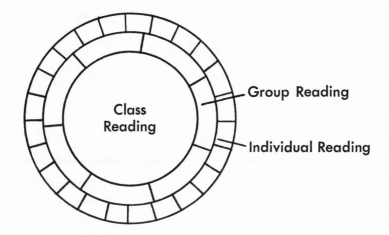

later on his own, alone with a book he has chosen, a book that he
has no obligation to discuss with a teacher or anyone else.

Group reading, used especially in thematic units but possible also
in other arrangements, involves reading of the same or very similar
material by several students in a class. They discuss within the
group, perhaps with the aid of questions or in a framework prepared
by the teacher, and they usually find some way to share their reactions with the class, maybe through panel discussions, reports, or
dramatizations. The material read by a group is teacher-approved,
although students may assist in the choices and sometimes select
their group on the basis of what is to be read in it. Groups of good
readers may read more material and more advanced material than
groups of poorer readers. Hence the groups provide for differentiation on two grounds: the nature of the material and the abilities
of the students.

In individual reading, perhaps no two students in the class are
reading the same book. Some of the choices should be perfectly
free; some may be free within prescribed limits such as those of a
literary type or a list of books on the same or varied subjects; some
should be chosen in conference between teacher and student. The
amount of individual reading should be larger than the amount of
class or group reading. In many schools, supervised individual reading has become the heart of the reading program. It should never
replace class and group reading, however, because those have values
not otherwise attainable.

ARRANGING AND APPROACHING

Arranging the Course in Literature

Four principles of arrangement are widely used in planning the reading for a course:

1. In chronological order.
2. According to types of literature.
3. In units based on central themes.
4. Around students' experience (sometimes overlaps no. 3).

In addition, teachers occasionally employ various combinations of the above arrangements, or modifications of them. For instance, a variation of the chronological approach is the "culture-epoch" plan, in which each unit is centered upon the literature and other cultural elements of the Colonial Period, the Revolutionary War Period, etc. Less frequent is the organization of a course with a few authors or a few classics as centers of interest or points of departure. The "guided free reading" mentioned earlier might also be called a method of arrangement. Correlation with history or some other subject is a plan followed in some schools. A few teachers, it seems, follow no plan of arrangement but merely teach whatever they want to whenever they want to. Other teachers, especially in British schools, simply follow up on clues from the class—deciding on the basis of students' reactions whether to introduce another play or some lyric poetry, or a short story with a particular theme, or something else.

Special mention should be made of humanities courses, which have grown in popularity in recent years. There is no neat definition for such courses; apparently no two are alike. Some of them attempt to relate literature to movies, television, and other media. Others combine literature with art, music, architecture, philosophy, history, or religion, or with any two or more of these. Some are team-taught by teachers from different departments; others are taught by English teachers with special interest in and knowledge of the related fields. Often these courses follow the "culture-epoch" plan, showing for instance the similarities in Romantic literature, art, and music and perhaps contrasting them with the more formalized cultural arts of the preceding century. A major virtue of humanities courses is that they take literature out of a vacuum by showing its often surprisingly close relationship to other arts. Drawbacks include the fact that few teachers are adequately prepared to offer such instruction, plus the fact that all aspects of the course, including the literature, may be treated superficially.[13]

Each method of arrangement has its good qualities and its drawbacks. The major pro's and con's of some of the arrangements are as follows:

ARRANGEMENT BY CHRONOLOGY

Pro's

1. Chronology, since it follows the inexorable calendar, affords the most orderly plan of procedure.
2. Students learn the pattern of development of literature.
3. Students learn some of the relationships between literature and history.
4. Students do not stay with one type long enough to become bored with it.

Con's

1. Learning to enjoy literature is much more important than learning who wrote what when.
2. The literature that students usually find least interesting is *True* presented first.
3. When time runs short, modern literature is likely to be neglected.
4. Sometimes the chronological course in literature degenerates into a course in literary history.

ARRANGEMENT BY TYPES

Pro's

1. Students learn to distinguish literary forms.
2. Comparison of work of different authors who used the same medium is facilitated.
3. Students learn how writing of each type has changed.
4. Students who like one type may be stimulated to further reading in that type.
5. It is easy to combine this arrangement with some other.

Con's

1. It does students little real good to be able to identify a type of literature.
2. Too much stress is put upon distinctions that are not always clear-cut (e.g., between short story and essay, or novelette and novel).
3. Students acquire no idea of the whole pattern of development of literature.
4. If much time is devoted to a type that some students dislike, that part of the course is a desert for them.
5. The selections often have no continuity or similarity other than being of the same type.

[13] The March, 1965, issue of the *English Journal* is devoted mainly to a critical analysis of humanities courses. Though now somewhat outdated, this is still useful. Sheila Schwartz has edited a fine collection of readings on humanities programs: *Teaching the Humanities* (The Macmillan Company, 1970); the readings are grouped under the headings "Definition of the Humanities," "The Humanities and the Contemporary Scene," "Humanities in the Secondary School," "Humanities in the Elementary School," "Teacher Education and the Humanities," and "Humanities and the Disadvantaged."

Arrangement by Units and Themes

Pro's	*Con's*
1. The reading is related to general topics (adventure, science, etc.) in which students are usually interested.	1. Sometimes selections are chosen not because of their quality but because they pertain to the theme.
2. Selections from different countries and different centuries may be introduced in the same unit.	2. Students acquire no idea of the whole pattern of development of literature.
3. Students do not stay with one type long enough to become bored with it.	3. Some students may not be interested in the general topic of the entire unit.
4. Students may readily be stimulated to do additional reading on a topic that they enjoy.	4. Regular use of this arrangement becomes tiresome.
5. Differences in authors' points of view may be studied.	5. There is danger that sociology and history may be stressed too much, literature too little.

Arrangement Around Student Experiences

Pro's	*Con's*
1. This arrangement emphasizes not the literature but the experiences that students can obtain with and through literature.	1. The material read may sometimes be of inferior quality.
2. Students' problems may be the focus; thus, students get help in regulating their own lives.	2. Independent work is difficult to grade.
3. Students are urged to do more independent reading than in other arrangements.	3. Students' laziness often makes independent work slipshod.
4. Individual differences create less of a problem in this arrangement than in others.	4. Students acquire no idea of the whole pattern of development of literature.

The fact that no one method of arrangement emerges as superior to all the others should cause no particular surprise or alarm. It has previously been remarked that there are no panaceas in teaching. If someone could find a plan of arrangement that has no weaknesses . . . but that is only utopian dreaming. It is necessary to take what is available, improve it if possible, but use it effectively.

Arrangements by themes and around student experiences have been found most satisfactory in the seventh, eighth, ninth, and tenth grades. Fine distinctions among types usually make little impression on students in those grades. Likewise, their sense of chronology is as a rule insufficiently developed to make a chronological organization meaningful; the year 1880 to most fourteen-year-olds sounds no nearer in time than 1680, and not much nearer than 1492. But the seventh-to-tenth graders can profitably study a number of selections about pets, holidays, pioneers, the sea, the mountains, Latin America, etc. Or they can read, with enjoyment and benefit, poems that emphasize rhythm, varied selections that add to their experience of city or country life, stories that give them vicarious experiences, etc.

Arrangements by types or chronology is better suited to the eleventh and twelfth grades, although even in these years long-continued exposure to lyrics or essays should probably be avoided. (Lyric poetry is so intense that few persons read much of it at one sitting. Lyrics are on the spice shelf of literature; none of us would make a meal of cloves.) The average sixteen-year-old, according to some psychologists, has reached or passed the average mental age of the whole population. If he will ever be able to learn about the types and the chronology of literature, and if these things are worth teaching, then the ages of sixteen and seventeen would seem to be the logical time to present them.

There are various ways of attaining a little variety in arrangement. Among possible variations of the above procedures are these:

1. Use the chronological order, but begin with modern literature. After a while, raise the question, "How did our literature get to be this way?" Then go back to early literature and work forward, keeping the question uppermost and drawing many comparisons between past and present writings.
2. Within the chronological order, have several units based on types or experiences; for instance, war in Elizabethan literature, the eighteenth-century essay in English, love of home in modern literature.
3. Teach a classic and then a similar modern work, or vice versa, for example, *Treasure Island* and *Mutiny on the Bounty*.
4. In the type organization, use several illustrations of one type to develop the same theme.

An especially interesting variation for the tenth, eleventh, and twelfth grades for able students is the one developed at the English Curriculum Center of Carnegie-Mellon University. They diagram and explain it as follows: [14]

[14] *A Senior High School Curriculum in English for Able College-Bound Students.* Volume I: The Tenth Grade (Carnegie-Mellon University, 1965), p. 3.

Oregon Curriculum   *does this too*

10th Grade	Universal concerns of men		M ——	L ——
11th Grade American Literature	U ——	Modification by culture pattern		L ——
12th Grade English Literature	U ——	M ——	Literary art forms; genres; techniques	

Good ideas

 Thus the tenth-grade course gives primary emphasis to the universal concerns of man as they appear in world literature (in translation)—such concerns as love, heroism, human weakness, portraits of social conditions or practices, and the search for wisdom. The eleventh-grade course consists of American literature which demonstrates how universal concerns are modified by the American culture pattern from Puritan times to the present. The approach to the American literature chosen is roughly historical, but looks nothing like the traditional survey. Rather, the course focuses on important aspects of the American character as they are revealed in our literature—such aspects as American Puritanism, the American desire to get ahead in the world, American optimism, and the American social conscience. The twelfth-grade course is primarily made up of English literature, and it gives major attention to the most sophisticated perceptions of the nature of literature, those implied in our definition by the phrase "verbal art forms." Once again, the treatment of literature is roughly historical; but this time the focal points are the various literary art forms: tale, tragedy, epic, satire, novel, and drama of social criticism.

Usual course content

 This arrangement, it will be noted, combines the chronological, types, and themes approaches, and may also incorporate student experiences. Particularly noteworthy is its emphasis upon the universal concerns of man, as modified by different cultural patterns. Certainly that is what literature is mainly about.

The Six Basic Approaches

 In recent years more and more attention has been given to students' responses to literature. To oversimplify, much earlier teaching was concerned in large measure with knowledge (cognition); today the emphasis is moving toward the affective domain—what the student thinks and feels about the literature he reads. In current educational jargon, today's tendencies are to emphasize output rather than input. However, it is obvious that there must always be some kind of input before there can be "outgo."

 Several contributory causes of this change in focus may be mentioned. One is the steadily increasing interest in behavioral objectives, which are always stated in terms of the "behavior" expected or hoped for from the student. Another is the aftermath of the Dartmouth Conference, whose British members largely concerned themselves with students' interactions with what they read, see, hear, or experience in any other way. Several publications have also spurred interest in student response. Two especially important ones are the revised edition of Louise Rosenblatt's *Literature as Exploration*,[15] which emphasizes "the literary experience in its totality," and *Elements of Writing about a Literary Work: A Study of Response to Literature*, by Alan C. Purves with Victoria Rippere,[16] which classifies under four headings the kinds of responses that students from four countries actually make when they are writing about literature. These elements are engagement-involvement ("the various ways by which the writer indicates his surrender to the literary work"), perception ("the ways in which a person looks at the work as an object distinct from himself"), interpretation ("the attempt to find meaning in the work, to generalize about it, to draw inferences from it, to find analogues to it in the universe that the writer inhabits"), and evaluation ("the statements about why the writer thinks the work good or bad").[17]

Previous editions of the book you are now reading have described in detail six widely used approaches to a literary work. That categorization still seems sound, and is still used in this edition, but the techniques suggested for each approach have been modified in light of the present trend toward enhancing student responsiveness. Only generalizations are given here; details appear in later chapters.

The Historical Approach. The historical approach emphasizes the biography of the writer and the literary and historical events of the age in which he lived. Overuse of this approach makes literature appear secondary to the history and biography, but if employed skillfully it can help the student to see literature as a changing, developing art. Perhaps more important, it can help him to place *himself* in the calendar of man's development. Although on the surface this approach appears to stress input, since most of its material is new to students, it can also encourage thoughtful reaction, especially from relatively mature and able students; it may aid both perception and interpretation.

[15] New York: Noble and Noble, 1968.
[16] Champaign, Ill.: National Council of Teachers of English, 1968.
[17] *Ibid.*, pp. 6–8.

The Sociopsychological Approach. The purpose of the socio-psychological approach is threefold. The teacher attempts to help students increase their knowledge of people, add to their understanding of the age in which the literature was written, and apply this knowledge and understanding to current living. The sociopsychological approach of necessity overlaps the historical but differs in that flesh is restored to the bones exhumed by the archeologist; it differs also in that an attempt is made to compare the flesh and nerves of the there and then with the flesh and nerves of here and now. The chief weakness of the sociopsychological approach is that it may lead to neglect of some of the qualities considered especially "literary." Its compensating virtue is that it demonstrates that people were people in the fourteenth century, and that people are still people; it helps to define people. Since most students are interested in people and in their social interactions, this approach is one that they especially like, and it gives them considerable opportunity to respond to literature in the light of their own knowledge of human beings, themselves included.

The Emotive Approach. In its inferior form, the emotive approach degenerates into gushing: "Isn't this pretty? . . . Isn't that a lovely metaphor? . . . What a thought-provoking statement!" In its more praiseworthy form, it helps students to realize much of the pleasure that literature can afford. It encourages both their emotional and their intellectual responses; it helps to engage them in literature.

The Didactic Approach. McGuffey readers of the nineteenth century customarily attached a conveniently labeled "moral" at the end of each selection. Many students are pleased to find a significant idea, a memorable thought capsule, in what they read, even though they dislike such obvious preachiness as McGuffey's. The didactic approach involves studying and reacting to the author's purpose, his observations on life, and the assumptions or truths that underlie his work. Students frequently interpret in hortatory fashion: "Conrad wants us to learn that civilization is only a veneer" or "The story urges us to beware the inroads of Fascism." [18] Frequent use of this approach may enhance engagement, perception, and interpretation, and may assist students as each searches for his own philosophy of life.

18 Purves, *op. cit.*, p. 40.

The Paraphrastic Approach.   In the paraphrastic approach, teacher and class restate in their own words what the author has said, the intention being to uncover the exact meaning lurking behind each of the author's sentences, paragraphs, or stanzas.   The usual objection to paraphrasing, however, is that it involves stating only the approximate meaning, since "saying the same thing in different words" is very seldom saying actually the same thing.   Paraphrasing is valuable, however, in the interpretation of abstruse literature; even though the connotations of some of the author's words will elude the paraphraser, he and his classmates may come near enough to the meaning to make the effort worthwhile.   Note that this approach does not evolve a reaction to what is read, but only an understanding.   Understanding, obviously, is prerequisite to reaction.

The Analytical Approach.   The last approach may be called the analytical, although this term is too restricted.   The analytical approach involves examining the ideas, the imagery, the mechanics, and the tone of writing in order to discover what each contributes to the total impression.   It is thus the "lit crit" system deplored by many modern British teachers but beloved by the followers of Brooks and Warren or Northrop Frye and other specialists in literary criticism.   It contributes particularly to evaluative responses, but may support others.   The constant aim, especially in the high school, is to help the student to see the selection as a whole, by assisting him to see the function of each part.   For example, students discover that the repeated references to sleep in *Macbeth* serve purposes of characterization and assist in the development of the theme.   In other words, the goal of the analytical approach is synthesis through analysis.   The weakness of the approach is that in distorted form it becomes what students call "picking to pieces."   Its value is that, through its use, students can discover that true literature does not just happen but results from careful planning, selection and rejection of details, and painstaking workmanship.   An even greater value is that, if the teacher uses the analytical approach competently, the students improve in their reading ability by learning to distinguish tree from grove in whatever they read.

These six approaches may not seem, on the surface, to be all-inclusive, but a little pondering will show either that other so-called approaches are subdivisions of these six or that they are not truly approaches at all.   The use of audiovisual aids, for example, does not constitute an approach, for such aids are tools or vehicles that may be used in any of the six basic approaches. The same comment applies to games and other special devices used by many teachers: they are actually vehicles.

Choosing the Approaches

The constant use of any one of the six approaches is objectionable on at least two counts: loss of interest and failure to show the versatile attractiveness of literature. Obviously, day-after-day repetition may lead to boredom for both students and teacher. If students are given the impression that authors write only that their works may be analyzed, or if they are led to believe that knowing literature means merely knowing literary history, they are likely to say, "Literature! Nobody cares about that stuff except English teachers, and they wouldn't either if they didn't get paid for it!" Not one "pure" approach but, rather, a multiple approach is best in the teaching of literature.

Since literature is many-sided, any one approach will reveal only a few of its attractions. A poem, an essay, or a novel is a castle, located deep in a forest. One person, the historian, explores its surroundings and says, "Now I know all about this castle." The sociopsychologist collars a couple of the inhabitants of the castle, puts them behind glass, and says, "If we observe how these inhabitants act, we shall know not only about this castle called Literature but also about Living." The emoter stands at the edge of the clearing, looks at the castle, and says, "Isn't it just darling, and aren't we having fun!" The moralizer looks up at one of the spires and says, "Atop that shining spire is a gem of wisdom for all of us. Let us ascend and grasp it." The paraphraser walks slowly around the castle, pausing to examine the surface of each stone with a magnifying glass. Upon completing the circuit, he says, "After careful inspection, I conclude that the intention of the builder of this castle was so and so." The analyzer studies the architecture, noting what each wall, each buttress, each arch contributes to the building; then he says, "Now I know all about the castle that is worth knowing." But like Saxe's six blind men, each "prates about an Elephant not one of them has seen." Each has acquired part of the truth about the castle, but a merging of all of the observations would give a much better understanding of the whole edifice.

If, then, no single approach is to be used, what should the teacher do? Should every literary selection be historified, socialized, glorified, moralized, paraphrased, and analyzed? Obviously not. The hourglass would run dry; human patience would not endure; and possibly the selection would become thin and frazzled. But sometimes two or three different approaches may be used with the same work or within the same hour. And all six approaches may be used at different times with different selections. Within a unit, probably only two or three approaches would be used, but, with a new unit, the approaches might well be changed.

The choice of approach should be made in the light of the objectives of the study, the characteristics of the literature, and the knowledge, ability, and interests of the class.

For example, a junior class is to read some of Whitman's poems including "I Hear America Singing," "When I Heard the Learn'd Astronomer," and three or four of the war poems. The teacher's immediate objectives are to interest the students in poems with no rhyme and little rhythm, and to help the students to realize that Whitman's poetry is still alive and vigorous a century after it was written. Most of the members of the class are also enrolled in American history, in which they have been studying the Civil War. The class is slightly above average in ability.

Any one or any combination of the six approaches *could* be used in these circumstances, but some would seem more desirable than others. The poetry is not so difficult as to justify the paraphrastic approach, and only a confirmed emoter or moralizer would be likely to insist that either the emotive or the didactic approach is peculiarly valuable in the study of Whitman. The historical might be employed to a slight extent, in order to relate Whitman to American history, and also, through a brief biographical sketch, to show that Whitman knew what he was writing about. But the sociopsychological and analytical approaches would be best.

Using the sociopsychological approach to (for example) "I Hear America Singing," the teacher and the students could compare the occupations of Whitman's time with those of today, and could discuss the role that singing played—and still plays—in people's lives. Wars, unfortunately, are not yet ended; students can realize that "Come Up from the Fields, Father" is an extremely human and even timely poem. Certainly there is no better way to show that a poem is alive than to show that it lives. The analytical approach will help the students to see that poetry may be poetry even though it does not rhyme and does not possess a da-dum da-dum da-dum rhythm. The slow-moving, burdensome opening lines of the "Learn'd Astronomer" give way to shorter, more direct lines as the narrator leaves the lecture room; the long lines are appropriate for the Ciceronian periods of the lecturer, and the short lines equally appropriate for the almost wordless thoughts of the stargazer. Whitman's words such as "gliding" and "mystical moist night air," may be shown to be exactly the ones essential to his purpose. The contrast between the lecture "with much applause" and the "perfect silence" in which the narrator looks at the stars ties the poem together. The analytical approach, that is, synthesis through analysis, will show the students the whole poem, will show them that it *is* a poem.

A different set of circumstances warrants a different approach. The teacher of an eighth grade class reading its first play probably uses the emotive this-is-fun approach. Markham's "Man with the Hoe" usually demands the sociopsychological approach. Bacon's essays are clarified by paraphrasing. During the Christmas season, a class profitably and enjoyably expands the "moral" of O. Henry's "Gift of the Magi." The careful construction of Galsworthy's "Quality" and of dozens of other selections justifies frequent use of the analytical approach. In Latin American literature, if the teacher wishes to emphasize the basic similarities between Latin Americans and other Americans, he uses and reuses the sociopsychological approach. Since Wordsworth's life colored everything he wrote, the historical approach to his poetry is a promising one. These are only examples and do not take into consideration specific classes or specific objectives as the teacher must do when deciding which approach or approaches to use with a given piece of writing.

The Need for Variety in Teaching Literature

A high school junior said, "I like English this year. Got a good teacher. She makes it interesting, doesn't kill it off the way some of 'em do."

"How does she make it interesting?" he was asked.

"Oh, I don't know. I never thought about how she does it. I imagine it's variety, though. We do lots of different things in class and read lots of different kinds of things. Other years we just repeated the same kind of thing over and over—for instance, last year, when we had to pick all the literature to pieces. It got awful dry, like—well, like just practicing shooting free throws in basketball would be. I like basketball, and I know that free throws are important, but, if there wasn't anything to basketball except standing in the same spot and doing the same thing over and over, I'd quit."

THE IDEA BOX

Test Your Own Taste

Stephen Dunning offers two short stories for teachers to test their own tastes, but warns that with some classes the poorer story would be the more suitable. "I Really Liked It," *English Journal*, LVII (May, 1968), 670.

How Can Kids Decide What a "Good" Book Is?

Pearl Aldrich and her class devised a checklist to differentiate a serious from a superficial book. Among the points: The serious book presents a universal truth about life, but the purpose of the superficial book is to make the reader's dreams come true. In a serious book, personality changes are slow and often painful, but in a superficial book they are quick and easy. "A New Method of Evaluating Fiction," *English Journal*, LIV (Nov., 1965), 744.

Don't Grow Up!

"The successful teacher of literature is the one who has never quite grown up, but lives in that eternal half-land of sunshine and shadow that is not geographical really but borders and wavers somewhere between adolescence and adulthood," says Edward Bruell in *Illinois Education* (March, 1964).

"Two Basic Convictions About Teaching Literature"

Anthony Tovatt supports these convictions: ". . . with the teacher rests the final responsibility for making choices that are governed by his best assessment of what a particular class needs"; ". . . literature must always be meaningful for the student in the *present* if it is to be meaningful for him in the *future*." *English Journal*, XLIX, 1960), 528.

"Stages of Growth in Literary Appreciation"

Margaret Early discusses the stages of (1) unconscious enjoyment, when the reader "knows what he likes but doesn't know why"; (2) self-conscious enjoyment, when he "gradually moves away from a simple interest in what happened" and toward interest in character, emotions, and literary interpretation; and (3) conscious delight, when the reader "responds with delight, knows why, chooses discriminately, and relies on his own judgment." "Among the readers who achieve this final stage we do not expect to find many high school students or even many university students." *English Journal,* XLIX (March, 1960), 161.

Motivation by Local Analogy

Often a local analogy will make a work more real to students. For example, Jerome Carlin of New York City introduces Frost's "Mending Wall" by having his students suppose that a battered fence separates their house from a neighbor's. Should the fathers pay $150 to get it repaired, or tear it down to give children more room to play? "A Pattern for Teaching Literature," *English Journal,* LV (March, 1966), 291.

General to Specialized

One curricular plan in literature for grades 7–12: Start with broad coverage as an introduction, including easy examples of all genres and nonliterary types as well. Move gradually into specialties: drama, short story, narrative poetry, film as literature, etc., perhaps through a large number of elective modules.

A Unified Literary Curriculum

Garfield Schools in Garrettsville, Ohio, have used "Man's Search for Guiding Principles in His Life" as the over-all theme for grades 7–12. It is subdivided as follows: 7—Sources of Power in People; 8—The Ingredients of Personality; 9—Heroic Ideals; 10—The Spirit of American Man; 11—Man's Outward Reach; 12—Man's Continuing Search for Truth. Prudence Dyer gives details in "An Expression, a Possession, and a Dream," *English Journal,* LIII (Sept., 1954), 442.

"Folklore Is Fun"

"This year by the last week in October, our classroom looked like a colorful international bazaar, as the students exhibited more than 100 articles from 16 different ethnic backgrounds in Madera." Later, Emily Wogaman's students in Madera, Calif., wrote plot outlines based on a part of the display, reported on unusual beliefs or customs, put on a TV program, did research on "Madera's own lore," conducted interviews, compiled a book, and sponsored an open house complete with a jumping frog contest. *English Journal,* LV (Feb., 1966), 208.

"In Defense of Trash"

"A book is good if it gives the student a meaningful emotional experience," says John Rouse, *Education Digest* (Dec., 1966). Such experience is more likely to come from some books considered trash than from most "classics." At any rate, he argues, books in the modern idiom have the best chance to turn kids on.

Content in American Literature

"Our courses in American literature and history must correct the imbalance in attitudes, point of view, knowledge, materials, emphases that has existed far too long. No longer can anyone justify offering pupils books, other materials, and assumptions representing almost entirely a white, middle class world. English courses should include points of view, materials representing a wide cross-section of artistic achievements by various groups comprising our pluralistic society." (From a convention speech by Alfred H. Grommon, past-president of NCTE.)

"The Idea of Coverage in the Teaching of Literature"

Teach a few things well, not many inadequately, argues George H. Henry of the University of Delaware. Colleges prefer students who have read and thought deeply, not necessarily widely. ". . . a perfect matching of authors and titles cannot sustain half-baked ideas about democracy, transcendentalism, sin, Puritanism, nature, progress, tragedy, and so on." *English Journal*, LIV (Sept., 1964), 475

"Good Books for 'Lower-Class' Students"

Instead of the "classics," Harvey R. Granite recommends *The Citadel, Cry, the Beloved Country, Fail-Safe, Sister Carrie, An American Tragedy, Of Mice and Men, The Pearl, A Single Pebble, The Old Man and the Sea, Raisin in the Sun, R.U.R.,* and *Our Town. English Journal*, LIV (Oct., 1965), 585.

"Science and English: A Rapprochement Through Literature"

Arguing for interdisciplinary scholarship, Edward R. Fagan of Penn State asserts that useful to the study of literature are such scientific concepts as ecology, entropy, field, indeterminacy, observer viewpoint, positioning, relativity, sets, and simultaneity. (Professor Fagan's *Field: A Process for Teaching Literature* elaborates upon the use of an interdisciplinary approach.) *English Journal*, LIV (May, 1965), 357.

Literature Isn't Science

We must never forget that literature belongs to the humanities and that "humanities" by definition refers to that which is *human*. If the study of literature is permitted to degenerate into analysis and classification, or even into mere explication of pattern and imagery, it becomes less human, more scientific, more mechanical.

Why World Literature?

In addition to the usual values of literary study, world literature introduces students to other cultures and shows that people of other lands wrestle with essentially the same concerns as the British and Americans do; thus it makes a contribution to the slow realization of the essential brotherhood of man. So James E. Warren argues, *Journal of Secondary Education* (March, 1965).

Teaching World Literature

1. Mark Van Doren says that teaching literature of another land is similar to teaching our own, in that what really matters is the work itself—what light does it throw upon the human predicament? He has this specific warning: "It is easier to lecture about the time and place of the book, the culture that produced it, its reputation in its own country or religion, its difference from any Western book—in other words, its unintelligibility." "Great Books—East and West," in *Approaches to Oriental Classics,* William T. DeBary, ed. (New York: Columbia University Press, 1959), p. 7.

2. A rich source of information and ideas is "Teaching World Literature in High School," *Illinois English Bulletin,* Dec., 1961, produced by a committee chaired by Mrs. Enid Olson. Among its many specific suggestions are these if a thematic arrangement is used: For a theme like "Search for a Better World," use parts of Plato's *Republic,* Bacon's *New Atlantis,* More's *Utopia,* Swift's *Gulliver's Travels,* and Hilton's *Lost Horizon.* For satire, try *Til Eulenspiegel, Reynard the Fox,* selections from Rabelais' *Gargantua* and from Voltaire's *Candide,* and Orwell's *Animal Farm.* For "Understanding Others," *Stories of Russian Life* by Chekhov, *Out of Africa* by Isak Dinesen, *My Country and My People* by Lin Yutang.

3. In teaching the literature of foreign countries, stress the similarities of people's basic needs, hopes, and characteristics; the differences are relatively minor and serve to add spice to life. How dull living would be if everyone were alike! Remember that the United Nations'

publications avoid terms like *odd, strange, exotic, inferior,* and *superior* with respect to people and their customs.

4. "The study of world literature developed a sense of 'one-world-ness' in my students." (Mary Hart Finley, Madisonville, Ky.)

In Defense of Humor

Howard Storm, afraid that "American students are becoming sober-sides," pleads for the inclusion of "serious" humor in the literature we teach. "Shut up, I Explained," *English Journal,* LVI (Feb., 1967), 208.

Junior Great Books

Initiated in Louisville, Kentucky, and spread to schools scattered throughout the country is a Junior Great Books Program in which children from the fifth through the twelfth grades are exposed system-atically to the ideas, attitudes, and values of great boks. The technique of Socratic dialog is usually stressed.

Why Study the Classics?

"Through the classics we can emphasize the best of nations, and unite pupils with the past to show them that man—no matter of what era or nationality—has always been basically the same, has always sought for himself answers to the great questions that men even today seek—What is life? What is love? What should a man do? What is good? What is bad? Why am I here? Where am I going? How should I live? What is worth living for? What is worth dying for? and the greatest, superseding all others, Who am I?" Clarence Hach, "The Universal in the Classics," *Illinois English Bulletin* (Oct., 1958).

Classics Too Soon

We teach some classics too soon, Arthur Daigon of the University of Connecticut argues. "Imagine, if you will, thirteen-year-old Johnny, crying over being ignored by the girls at the dance, worrying about his pimples and the contour of his hairdo, caviling with his parents about a fifty-cents-a-week increase in his allowance, imagine Johnny and T. S. Eliot (just the two of them) or Johnny and Shakespeare." "Literature and the Schools," *English Journal,* LIX (Jan., 1969), 30.

The Defects of Adapted Classics

Ruth Stein of the University of Minnesota made a careful study of five adaptations or condensations of *Huckleberry Finn.* Her conclusion:

". . . they present really only the skeletal structure . . . the heart and soul are gone. These simplified tales are so watered down and distorted, much of what made them great stories [is] lost. How they can teach youngsters a love of books in the vapid style is debatable and unmeasurable." "The ABC's of Counterfeit Classics," *English Journal*, LV (Dec., 1966), 1160.

A Great Books Club

1. In Merrill, Michigan, Edgar Madden organized a voluntary Great Books Club, whose student members bought, read, and discussed such books as Anne Frank's *Diary of a Young Girl*, Heyerdahl's *Aku-Aku*, and Hilton's *Lost Horizon*. The account is in "Popularizing Reading in the Small High School," *English Journal*, LII (Jan., 1963), 46.

2. It's a sought-after honor to be invited to join the Great Books Club in Denby High School, Detroit. Only able juniors and seniors who read ten or more books from a selective list may join and take part in the afterschool discussions of Homer, Dickens, Emerson, Thoreau, Shaw, etc.

Black Culture

Dorothy Sterling presents an extensive list of writings on various aspects of black culture in "What's Black and White and Read All Over?" *English Journal*, LVIII (Sept., 1969), 817.

Black Literature

"The legitimate demand for black literature . . . must not be allowed to undermine traditional literary values." There is plenty of good black literature available, including some from the 1890's that hasn't yet been sorted out. Robert Bone, "Negro Literature in the Secondary Schools," *English Journal*, LIX (April, 1969), 510. For an annotated bibliography relevant to the subject, see the NCTE/ERIC "Negro Literature for Secondary English and Humanities Courses," by Robert Denby, *English Journal*, LIX (May, 1969), 767. Especially recommended is Barbara Dodds' guide for teachers, *Negro Literature for High School Students,* a book published in 1968 by NCTE.

General to Specific

In an important article, Alan Purves says, "The first principle is to start with the response to the whole poem. Rather than attempt to move from an examination of the individual words and lines to a generalization, he should begin with the generalization or the establishing of the context and then see how the parts are related to it. . . . The focus of instruction should not be simply the text but the consciousness that is dealing with the text. . . . The teacher's function is to help the student to become more fully cognizant of what it is that shapes his responses and how his response depends not only on the literary work but on him." Be sure to read all of "You Can't Teach Hamlet, He's Dead," *English Journal*, LVII (Sept., 1968), 832.

The Right-Answer Fallacy

"The student's refusal to become involved and his inability to react with conviction may both stem from the assumption that the study of literature requires finding one's way toward a predetermined 'answer' defined by the teacher. The 'right answer' fallacy comes between the student and literature." (Bryant Fillion, University of Illinois)

The Perils of Censorship

Edward J. Gordon claims that because of censorship, writers like Hawthorne, Thoreau, Whitman, Twain, Hemingway, Steinbeck, Sherwood Anderson, and Arthur Miller are either ignored or read in their safest work—the ones in which they say the least. New England *Leaflet* (May, 1969).

Holden and the Censor

Wayne Booth says that a "good censor" will not draw any conclusions from any elements taken out of context, will not be satisfied with one reading, and will not confuse the "true values" of a work with "the expressed values of any one character." A would-be censor who honestly applies these tests to a book like *Catcher in the Rye* will abstain from censorship. A helpful article supplementing the NCTE's *Students' Right to Read*. "Censorship and the Values of Fiction," *English Journal*, LIII (March, 1964), 155.

"Challenging the Censor: Some Responsibilities of the English Department"

One of the best articles on the topic. Bibliography. By Kenneth Donelson. *English Journal*, LIX (Sept., 1969), 869.

The Transcendentalists As Hippies

"Henry Thoreau, doing his thing at Walden Pond; Ralph Emerson, the guru; and Walt Whitman, tripping out on grass. Irreverent? Perhaps, but not irrelevant. Thoreau's retreat to Walden is not significantly different from the hippies' dropping out; both are seeking a reasonable alternative to the stultifying demands of conventional life." Paul Wild, "Flower Power," *English Journal*, LIX (Jan., 1969), 62.

Multi-Media

"At Clark senior high school in New Orleans, Mrs. Consuela Provost's Trans-Love creative writing club produced 'Soul Images,' a multi-media show in which students read their own poetry while others sketched their impressions of the poems in pastels. Some of the readings were also accompanied by student dancers and appropriate background recordings by artists like Ray Charles and Nina Simone." Charles Suhor, New Orleans *Clarion Herald* (Aug. 15, 1968).

A Student Multi-Media Project

In Belmont, Mass., individuals and small groups of students produced multi-media projects to illustrate themes or moods. They synchronized poems, original writing, photographs, drawings, slides, and music. Muriel E. Morrissey, "To Illustrate a Mood, Creatively," New England *Leaflet*, LVIII (Feb., 1969), 39.

"A Course in Twentieth-Century American Literature"

Literature of this century is often neglected in American literature classes. As a remedy, Garden City, N.Y., offers seniors a course with emphasis on Sinclair, Hemingway, Fitzgerald, Lewis, various short stories, and various poems. William C. Boring and Charlotte Reppert, *English Journal*, LVII (May, 1968), 665.

"Asian Literature in the High School"

Elizabeth B. Stambolian lists many Asian books and authors, most of whom are seldom taught in American high schools, in *English Journal*, LIX (Jan., 1970), 27.

The Historical Approach: A Defense

An eloquent plea for the historical approach is Robert E. Spiller's "Is Literary History Obsolete?" *College English*, XXIV (Feb., 1963). Professor Spiller argues that teachers should "start with the work of art as the analytical critics demand, but move outward to the context . . . Remember that American literature is the expression of the civilization of the United States, English literature is the voice of the British people, and Greek literature speaks for Athens; but also remember that a good tragedy is a fine drama and a bad one is melodrama whenever or wherever or by whomsoever it was written. The two ways of considering literature are supplementary, not mutually exclusive."

Establishing a Time Sense

Time charts prepared by the class may help to clarify some time relationships. In a beginning study of American literature, for example, a stretch of chalkboard may be reserved. Ask the class to name a few great Americans, including authors, whom they remember. Arrange a chart with the names they suggest, putting each person in the period when he flourished:

1750–1800	1800–1850	1850–1900	1900–1950	Your Birth	This Year
Washington	Irving	Lincoln	London	Frost	
Franklin	Poe	Whitman	Cather	Steinbeck	
	Hawthorne	Twain	O'Neill		

Add other important names to the chart as study progresses. If space permits, a more elaborate chart may also list major historical events. In English literature a chart may go back to about A.D. 1000; in world literature, still earlier.

Social Implications of Literature

"I start from the premise that we all work for the betterment of our personal selves. Then I try to show students that their personal selves are bettered when other people are bettered. I utilize Tennyson's 'Flower in the Crannied Wall' to show that all things are interrelated. This is a new idea for most of them. It causes violent discussion and disagreement. When they finally realize clearly that their every action influences society in some way, some of them, at least, tend to adjust their conduct accordingly." (Robert L. Stevens, Flagstaff, Ariz.)

Understanding a Character

Select several short speeches of a character, and ask the class to suppose that all they know of the character is found in those speeches. What conclusions about him can they draw? For example, Middleton in Cooper's The Prairie: "God in Heaven protect us! There is no time to lose, old man; each instant is a day; let us fly." "Let us mount and ride; is life not worth a struggle?" "We will ride into the centre of the whole tribe, and put their manhood to the test." "This resignation is maddening! But we are men, and we will make a struggle for our lives."

Behind the Didactic Approach

The didactic approach is not intended "to bring values to kids but to bring kids to values." (Lillian Lahti, University of Illinois) But whose values? Two studies reported in the *Journal of Educational Research*, April, 1962, showed that grades given students were correlated highly with the extent to which they shared the teacher's values. In a comment, Peter K. Gurau, *Educational Technology*, May 15, 1968, said, ". . . the ability to guess [the teacher's values] correctly is dependent upon the degree of similarity of background and value structure between the teacher and a given student. In effect, teachers have a hidden agenda."

"So Who Needs Analysis"

Protesting against excessive critical analysis of literature, Virginia Joki says, "we are teachers of English, not puzzle-solvers . . . Instead of so much analytic criticism, I would like to see us go back to more humanistic criticism by showing how literature communicates ideas, attitudes, perceptions, and emotions that we must understand if we are to achieve responsible maturity." *English Journal*, LVII (March, 1968), 569.

How an Author Attains His Effects

John M. Nagle of the University of Pittsburgh advocates more attention to the word choice and sentence structure employed by authors in attaining their effects. As prime examples he uses *The Old Man and the Sea* and *The Pearl*. "A View of Literature Too Often Neglected," *English Journal*, LVIII (March, 1969), 399.

How Does a Writer Surprise?

Thomas E. Gaston asserts, "Style consists of purposeful and patterned violations of expectations, violations that approach but never exceed predetermined limits." *English Journal*, LIX (Jan., 1970), 65.

How Authors Name Their Characters

Phyllis E. Nelson's students like to play "The Name Game," and decide early that Ichabod (which means "inglorious") won't win the girl. They study original meanings of people's names, suitability or irony of names authors choose, famous people with this name, how the name aids understanding of the character, and how authors choose names for their characters. *English Journal*, LVI (March, 1967), 439.

"Style *Is* Content"

"When we turn to prose, say the short story, we emphasize character, plot, setting, and theme, but we rarely pay much attention to style, except perhaps to point out a felicitous phrase here and there. And yet, we know that style is an integral part of art, and it follows that unless we teach style as part of literature, we really are not teaching literature adequately." Milton A. Kaplan, *English Journal*, LVII (Dec., 1968), 1330.

Paperbacks at Nova

At Fort Lauderdale's experimental Nova School, "No assigned anthology for any literature class. Basic texts for study in the novel or the short story or plays—all in paperback. This is the heart of the program. Students buy paperbacks, underscore them, marginally annotate them, and then save them as the nucleus of their home libraries. Suggested readings, which grow out of classroom study and small group interest, are readily available in the school bookstore." Marta U. Gordon, "Ten in a Tote Bag," *English Journal*, LVII (Sept., 1968), 837.

Does Reading About Sex Hurt Anybody?

Sanford Clarke, in the *New Jersey English Leaflet* (Winter, 1966) says that 174 psychiatrists and psychologists were asked whether they had ever had any patients who were "provoked into antisocial behavior primarily as a result of exposure to sexually oriented literature." Ten answered *yes;* one hundred sixty-four said *no.*

If You Were an Artist

Sometimes ask students to imagine that they are artists employed by a magazine to illustrate stories or poems. Have them describe the picture they would draw or paint to illustrate an especially significant part of a literary work read by the class.

Literary "Trip"

good

"We begin our English literature course by taking a 'trip' to England. This involves writing letters to travel bureaus, keeping a diary, reading background materials, compiling a bibliography, using reference tools, listening to records such as 'White Cliffs of Dover,' making a scrapbook of pictures and articles from periodicals, and finally presenting a travel talk." (Hortense Finch, Davenport, Iowa.)

"An Exercise in Comparison"

Detailed comparison of two literary treatments of the same topic are often helpful. Richard Stonesifer, for example, has his students compare Sandburg's familiar "Grass" with several paragraphs about grass in Jesse Stuart's *The Year of My Rebirth*. "An Exercise in Comparison," *Exercise Exchange*, IV, No. 3 (Feb., 1957), 8. Socrates A. Lagios does something similar with Hemingway's 1932 one-paragraph version of *The Old Man and the Sea* and the expanded 1952 version. "The Old Man and The Sea, 1932 and 1952," *ibid.*, X, No. 2 (March, 1963), 12.

Literary Maps

1. Let students make their own. In American literature, a literary map of their own state or region is stimulating. Several state associations of English teachers have prepared printed maps, most of which may be purchased from the NCTE. (See the list by Ben W. Fuson, *English Journal*, LIX [Jan., 1970] 87.) A student in Dallas prepared such a good map for *Pilgrim's Progress* that the Dallas English Council printed it and it was distributed nationally by the NCTE.

2. If a literary map of your state exists, its chief value may be to dispel students' notion that famous authors have always lived far away. A literary map of the United States helps students to associate authors and their works with their locales. A literary map of the British Isles is perhaps most valuable of all, since British place names mean little to American students, many of whom do not even know whether London is in the northern or the southern part of England. A collection of literary maps adds both color and informativeness to a classroom and may be referred to frequently for specific points.

"Proverbs: The Seeds of Literature"

Useful in the didactic approach, and useful also for literary background (since literature often is an expansion of a proverb), is the study and classification of proverbs. Elizabeth C. Hood gives details for a twelve-day study. *English Journal*, LVI (Oct., 1967), 970.

Group Work

In an increasing number of schools, students spend part of their time working in groups, sometimes on subjects assigned to the groups, sometimes on projects devised by themselves.

Verifying a Generalization

As a step toward more connected writing about literature, each student is asked to write a general statement about an author, a work, a character, the plot, the setting, the style, or a concept. Then he finds and copies a short passage proving or at least illustrating the generalization, or he draws from the work some other kind of relevant evidence.

"Charlie Brown Goes to School"

Marylin Miner's junior high students not only enjoy "Peanuts" books but find in them lessons in faith, hope, charity, and other virtues. *English Journal,* LIX (Nov., 1969), 1183.

"Cartoons in the Classroom"

Cartoons may be used to teach such concepts as satire, symbol, irony, and caricature, say Lurene Brown and Helen B. Wachs, *English Journal,* LVII (May, 1968), 662.

Do-It-Yourself Filmstrips

Vermont teacher Doris P. Miller tells how she, though inexperienced, made sound filmstrips to accompany literature, and offers many useful suggestions. (Question: For some purposes, can't students make their own filmstrips?) "Adventure in Educational Media," *English Journal,* LVII (Feb., 1968), 223.

Sources of Recording

The NCTE sells numerous literary recording, which members may buy at substantially reduced prices. Commercial catalogs include those of Schwann, available at most record shops, and Libraphone, Inc., Long Branch, N. J.

The Professional Theater in the School

Other large cities might well emulate New York and Pittsburgh, which use small professional casts to perform suitable plays on a regular schedule during school hours in secondary schools. Thus, *Romeo and Juliet* was presented in 154 New York schools in one year; a program offering a condensed history of the theater attracted over 100,000 students in a year.

For Extensive Book Lists

Purchase from the NCTE the inexpensive pamphlets "Your Reading" and "Books for You." They contain annotated lists of hundreds of books suitable for junior and senior high schools. Also valuable: various booklists from the American Library Association, Chicago.

National Book Week

Use National Book Week (instituted in 1919) as an occasion for furthering interest in books. A book fair, art, exhibits on a particular theme, talks, contests, and community participation may be included. Cooperate with your librarian and principal on the project.

Building an Interest in Books T A B

1. Encourage students to start their personal libraries now. In a PTA talk, you might suggest that parents buy books as presents, and give specific criteria for selecting them. Let parents know that you are willing to give advice concerning books suitable for Johnny or Susie.

2. If you are a teacher–librarian, let students help to select new books for the library. They can write for publishers' catalogs, read advertisements and reviews, and discuss the most suitable books to be bought with limited funds.

Relevant Questions

Through the right kind of questioning, students can be led to learn much about life. Underlying a question about literature there should often be an implied question about our own lives. Examples based on *Death of a Salesman:* What is unhealthy about Willy's inability to face reality? Why was it wrong for Biff to quit trying after he surprised Willy in the hotel in Boston? What does Arthur Miller say about the American business world? James H. Norton, "A Matter of Life and English," *English Journal,* LV (Dec., 1966), 1221.

On the Advantages of *Why* and *How* Questions

Who, what, when, and *where* questions about literature are usually superficial. Try stressing *why* and *how* questions to encourage greater understanding and thought. Not "Who is Polonius?" or "What does Polonius tell Laertes?" but "Why is Polonius often considered a foolish person?" or "How does Shakespeare reveal what kind of person Polonius is?"

A Question of Values

Instead of factual questions or concept questions, ask "value" questions, Sidney Simson and Merrill Harmin urge. E.g., "Part of *Hamlet* is about the obligation of a son to seek revenge for his father. Where do you stand on that kind of act?" *Educational Leadership* (Oct., 1968).

The Art of Questioning

Examples of poor and good questions based on Poe's "The Cask of Amontillado":
Poor: Montresor was a hypocrite, wasn't he?
Good: How do we know that Montresor was a hypocrite?

Poor: What happens at the end of the story?
Good: What word in the second paragraph foreshadows the end of the story?

Poor: Who is Luchresi?
Good: How does Montresor use the name of Luchresi to entice Fortunato into the vaults?

Poor: What were the motto and the coat of arms of the Montresors?
Good: How were the Montresors' motto and coat of arms appropriate?

"The 'Class Answer' As a Teaching Device"

Lawrence Rosinger of Detroit dittoes excerpts from various students' good answers to questions about a play, and then shows the depth of insight revealed in the answer as a whole. *English Journal,* LVII (Oct., 1968), 1032.

Devices for Reviewing

1. Try a "Stump the Experts" contest, with students asking questions of class "experts" who volunteer.

2. Let students make up questions involving recognition of stories they have read. For example, "In what story are combs, a watch chain, and a woman's beautiful hair significant?"

3. In junior high, try a variation of TV quiz contests, with play money.

4. Original plays may be used to review and clinch the subject matter of a unit.

5. Upperclassmen may learn a little about literary criticism through

this method of review: Each student selects three or four of the important selections or authors studied, and in literary histories or critical works he finds two or three pertinent and specific sentences concerning each. He copies these and brings them to class, leaving out the names to be identified. The other students use the clues to name the work or the author.

6. Useful with either under- or upperclassmen is the game of five clues. Each student prepares several sets of five clues for different works studied by the class. The first four clues are moderately difficult, though reasonable; the fifth is so easy that it almost gives away the answer. Classmates attempt to identify the work. For example, for "To Althea, from Prison": (a) "This building has known more of evil than of good." (b) "Yet sometimes good men and women have unwillingly spent time there." (c) "Once a poet dwelt for a time in this building, and was not especially unhappy there." (d) "In fact, he wrote, 'The birds that wanton in the air/ Know no such liberty.'" (e) "The poet was Richard Lovelace, who wrote a poem to Althea from this building."

7. Students may also construct *who, what, when, where, why* and *how* questions for their classmates' review, with each student responsible for one or two questions in each category. Caution the class to ask important questions, not minor ones such as "When did Tennyson write 'Ulysses'?"

Tests on Literature

1. Try asking some questions that probe for facts, some that require interpretation, some that necessitate relating a selection to other literature or to life.

2. For variety, give occasionally a short open-book test.

3. Help your students to learn to organize their answers.

4. On some occasions, let each student make out a set of final-examination questions that he thinks would be fair. Choose the questions from those submitted.

5. Before a short surprise test, allow two or three minutes for reviewing notes. This procedure encourages careful, methodical notetaking.

6. Dwight Burton suggests these methods of evaluation, in addition to objective and essay tests: observation by the teacher; records of voluntary reading; interest inventories, questionnaires, and attitude scales; performance in book reports or activities following reading; group discussion; small-group reports; and individual reports. *Literature Study in High Schools* (New York: Holt, Rinehart & Winston, 1960), Chapt. 12.

6

Teaching Fiction
and Drama

WHY DO PEOPLE READ NOVELS, SHORT STORIES, AND PLAYS?

"Fiction carries a greater amount of truth in solution than the volume which purports to be all true," said William Makepeace Thackeray. In that sentence the key words are "in solution." A book of non-fiction says, "Here are facts, and facts, and facts." But in fiction the facts and the deeper truths that underlie facts are hidden, in solution. It is possible to read an entire novel, enjoy its story, and almost completely miss the "truth in solution."

The thoughtful reader of good fiction finds insights into human nature that may have eluded him in a score of books devoted to psychology, sociology, or anthropology. Fiction dramatizes; the psychology text merely explains. The dramatizing brings abstract principles to life and, in so doing, entertains through appealing to the universal love of a good story. "It is the first duty of the novelist to let himself be read—anything else that he gives you is a bonus, a trimming, a dessert," as George Saintsbury once wrote. It is to the combination, then, of readable story and underlying significance that the superior novel or short story owes its ability to hold the attention of a reader.

Fiction provides partial answers to age-old questions. "Who am I?" "Why was I born?" "Is life purposeless?" "Are people merely accidental excrescences on a planet that is but an atom in the universe?" Since no author is omniscient, the reader knows that he will never find complete answers to his metaphysical queries. But he knows also that from a clue here and there he can piece together a philosophy of life which will serve him, or that he can amend his existing philosophy.

It may seem contradictory to say that fiction also provides an escape from life, but so it does, and in that way it is closely akin to drama. "The world is too much with us"; it is often too humdrum, too tearful, or too frightening. The little boy escapes it by putting on a space helmet; the little girl bosses her family of dolls, anticipating the time when she can really give orders instead of obeying them; the adult, like Miniver Cheevy, may escape to the Medici or to the bottle, or to the book or to the theater.

The drama, of course, also reveals truths about life, but it is especially successful (at least on the stage, its intended habitat) in carrying us out of ourselves. Studying plays in school is an artificial activity, taking them from their medium, the stage, and exposing them only to visual rather than both auditory and visual scrutiny. Modern teachers, however, try to make play-reading more than just reading, in ways that we shall note in parts of this chapter.

SOME OFTEN-ASKED QUESTIONS

The answers to these frequent questions are no doubt too arbitrary, but let's risk them; they may provoke worthwhile discussion.

Q. How should we select the novels we teach?

A. That depends on your students, your purposes, and the overall emphasis and plan for your course. In general, choose relatively short and "easy" novels for junior high, longer and "harder" ones for senior high. But ruthlessly reject any novel that you cannot respect for its literary quality. Your time and students' time shouldn't be wasted on trash.

Q. Does this mean concentrating on *Silas Marner* and *Tale of Two Cities*?

A. Who said there aren't other novels of high quality? With a junior high class, Annixter's *Swiftwater*, Forbes' *Johnny Tremaine*,

Stevenson's *Treasure Island,* or any of a number of other books is fine. With a senior high class, the choice is much wider. Other novels by George Eliot or Charles Dickens may be better for some classes than the traditionally taught ones. See The Idea Box after this chapter for titles of a score of different novels and articles on teaching them. And look again at some of your own favorites to see how suitable they may be for your students.

Q.   Should all members of a class read the same novel?

A.   Not necessarily, though some reading in common is desirable. Sometimes try having three or four groups reading different novels, perhaps relating to the same theme. Use panel discussions, along with class discussions of questions all the novels can illuminate, to bring the class together. With able classes, sometimes each student may read a different book, and report to the class on what it seems to say about certain important questions.

Q.   How long should we spend on a novel?

A.   Seldom more than three or four weeks, often less. Frequently, potential enjoyment has been killed by prolonged study.

Q.   How much should be assigned at a time?

A.   If the novel is not too difficult and if the class is fairly able, it is good to have the whole novel read (with the help of a few guiding questions) before any discussion. But, with long or difficult novels, a series of perhaps ten or fifteen assignments may be necessary. It is important, though, to reserve some time for discussion of the whole novel, so as not to leave an impression that it is only a number of vaguely related episodes.

Q.   What kinds of questions should we ask?

A.   With young or slow students, stress *who* and *what* questions. With older or brighter students, ask *why* and *how* much more often. For example, "Why is Huck usually afraid to approach strangers?" "How does Clemens employ irony in the chapter where Huck dresses as a girl?" (The most overused question in the teaching of fiction and drama is "What happened next?")

Q.   What about "dirty books"?

A.   Obviously you won't teach pornography, the book that is dirty for the sake of being dirty and that has little or no social or literary value. But in general you should feel free to teach any other book that has something to say to your students and that you can respect for its literary qualities. Some communities, though, are more straitlaced than others and are unwilling to have their children read in school what they can readily buy at the drugstore or see portrayed in movies or on television. If you are teaching in such a community, your department should have an approved plan of procedure in case challenges arise. The NCTE pamphlet "The Student's Right to Read" offers concrete suggestions for such a plan.

note

Q.   What plays should we teach?

A.   Choose high-quality one-act plays for the junior high years. Move on, as your classes' abilities permit, to Maxwell Anderson, James M. Barrie, Rudolph Besier, John Galsworthy, Oliver Goldsmith, Kaufman and Hart, Sidney Howard, Lindsay and Crouse, Arthur Miller, Eugene O'Neill, Edmond Rostand, William Shakespeare, George Bernard Shaw, Robert E. Sherwood, and Thornton Wilder, or carefully selected more recent plays. With able students, Sophocles, Euripides, Aeschylus, Ibsen, and the like are possible.

Q.   Which plays by Shakespeare?

A.   You'll not confine yourself to Shakespeare, of course. Today the most popular choice, by far, is *Macbeth*. Others frequently taught are *Julius Caesar* (especially with sophomores) and *Hamlet* (generally seniors). *As You Like It* and *Merchant of Venice* seem to be slipping. *Taming of the Shrew* and *Twelfth Night* appear to be gaining favor. *A Midsummer Night's Dream* is a good opener. *Henry V* and *Romeo and Juliet* perhaps deserve more attention, as does *Henry IV*, Part I.

Q.   How should we teach a play?

A.   Remember that it is a play. Use much reading aloud, as well as considerable prepared (but not memorized) and some impromptu dramatization. British teachers tend to plunge students immediately into such dramatization, without any preliminaries about, for example, the Globe Theater or Shakespeare's biography. Help students to visualize the action as stage action, for example, to be aware of what other persons are doing while one is speaking. Stress characters and characterization. Discuss theme and underlying meanings, especially with advanced students. Three weeks is usually enough time for a full-length play, though the range may be from a few days to four or five weeks.

Q. To what extent should composition and the study of language be related to fiction and drama?

A. Increasingly, good schools are asking students to write on literature-oriented topics, especially in the junior and senior years. It would be unwise, however, to devote *all* compositions to literature, because students need to learn to write on other topics also, to be successful in college and in various occupations. The study of language is often profitable in connection with literature. Such topics as these may be considered: How does Shakespeare's language differ from ours and from Chaucer's? What peculiarities of sentence structure and diction mark the stories of Hawthorne, Irving, Poe, Cooper, Hemingway, etc.? How does stage conversation differ from actual conversation?

Q. Which of the six basic approaches should be used with fiction and drama?

A. All, at different times. Often two, three, or more will be used with a single work. The choice depends upon the needs of the class, the purpose of the study, and the characteristics of the literature being studied. Details about the use of each approach follow.

THE HISTORICAL APPROACH

The historical approach has greater value for juniors and seniors than for younger students, although driblets of literary history and background may well be offered throughout the high school years. The teacher's intentions in using this approach are to present authors as human beings and to clarify time relationships—to show that people for many years have been much like us, and to give the students some understanding of the continuity of literature and the relationship between history and literature. Adults who lack such understanding are likely to carry distorted mental pictures like those of a character in Dos Passos' *Manhattan Transfer:* "I always think of history as lithographs in a schoolbook, generals making proclamations, little tiny figures running across fields with their arms spread out, facsimiles of signatures."

Traditionally, the historical approach has meant study of the history of American and English literature. At its worst, this study has degenerated into the memorization of names and dates: "In what year did Dickens die?" "Give the titles and dates of three novels by

Thackeray." "What happened in 1881?" At its best, it has brought recognition that each writer is an outgrowth of his age, that his characteristics were shaped by the time in which he lived. The historical approach disagrees with the theme of such a book as *Shakespeare Apart,* whose author declared that Shakespeare was apart from, different from, and superior to, everything else in his age; the historical approach says that Shakespeare and every other author is not *apart* but *a part.*

For a doctoral dissertation at the University of Illinois, Edward Wingler in 1970 queried teachers of teachers concerning their attitudes toward many aspects of teaching secondary school English. The respondents were among the leaders in English teaching, and although there was never complete agreement on anything, their responses are worth serious consideration. Here are a few of those responses; others will be mentioned later.

In literature, secondary students should be required to acquire a knowledge of literary periods, the conventions of literary forms, and biographical information about important literary figures.

    Agree or Strongly Agree—108   *Disagree or Strongly Disagree*—46

(We have noted earlier, though, that British leaders are opposed to "lit hist" as well as to "lit crit.")

Requiring acquisition of a knowledge of literary history and our cultural heritage is part of any sensible secondary English curriculum.

    Agree or Strongly Agree—65   *Disagree or Strongly Disagree*—78

The construction of an historical, biographical, and/or geographical frame of reference for literature makes personal, affective response by students unlikely.

    Agree or Strongly Agree—53   *Disagree or Strongly Disagree*—90

A possible interpretation of these somewhat conflicting responses is that English educators tend to believe that there is value in a historical-biographical approach but that they have reservations about it, fearing that a rigid framework would make difficult the students' "personal, affective response." In the second item, the presence of the word *any* probably influenced the decision; English educators would be likely to argue that especially for slow or immature students there should be little stress on literary history and the cultural heritage.

For the more mature and more able students, however, the historical approach can be useful. The usefulness lies in the fact that the basic concerns of man have always been essentially the same (*e.g.,* survival, relationships with others), and we can learn about these concerns by observing how our ancestors coped with them. The past, that is, enlightens the present. Anyone who is unaware of the mistakes of the past is doomed to repeat many of those mistakes in the present. Anyone who is unaware of the achievements of the past is uninformed about what he may hope to emulate; he does not know the step on the ladder that man has already reached and beyond which he may be able to climb. Study of the past is unimportant if it merely attempts to recreate the past, but it is of momentous significance if it relates the past to the present and to the potential of the future. Never look back to regret, to deplore, to envy. Never look back to yesterday—except to learn what it is important for today to know.

The following paragraphs offer suggestions of ways to recreate past eras vividly enough to allow those eras to speak to the present.

Wide Reading Pertaining to the Period. One story or one book should often lead to more reading of similar material. How one book may enrich another is obvious: Bret Harte and Edward Eggleston throw light on Mark Twain and his America; Ross Lockridge's *Raintree County* adds depth to understanding of Whitman's poetry or Crane's *Red Badge of Courage;* Jane Austen, Charlotte Brontë, George Eliot, and even Thomas Hardy make Dickens' England seem more real; the writings of Defoe's contemporaries bring early eighteenth century England alive. The student just introduced to Latin American literature may read about ancient Peru in Victor Von Hagen's *Highway to the Sun* before reading about more recent Peruvians in Thornton Wilder's *Bridge of San Luis Rey.* Books about the period of World War II help to recreate the time when your students' parents were children and may assist in bridging the generation gap by acquainting students with the world their parents once knew. Books such as Frederick L. Allen's *Only Yesterday* and *Since Yesterday* and Mark Sullivan's *Our Times* interpret earlier years of twentieth century America, and *The Long Week-End, A Social History of Great Britain,* 1918-1939, by Robert Graves and Alan Hodge, describes entertainingly the period between wars.

Not all students will do the same supplementary reading, of course, but you should use every opportunity to let students share with the class the additional knowledge they have gained as individuals.

A teacher points out another value of studying the background of the age, with special reference to drama:

The program of study . . . should emphasize . . . the causes for the emergence of particular dramatic forms and theaters during different historical periods. For example, students better perceive the intentions of tragedy once they realize that it has been the product not of disillusioned, depressed cultures, but of societies, like those during the times of Sophocles and Shakespeare, which have prized individual resourcefulness, personal freedom, and human happiness. . . . Similarly the comedy of manners or satirical drama should be seen in the context of the Restoration Period, broken loose from a decade of Puritan austerity, or of the eighteenth century, with its surface proprieties, material concerns, and inflexible class distinctions inviting the playwright's mocking or witty scrutiny.[1]

Clues from the Literature Itself.   The best way to learn about a past age is to read the fiction and drama of that age.   In Shakespeare one senses the exuberance of the Elizabethans, but also becomes aware of their worries, their class distinctions, their independence combined with habitual obeisance to royalty and nobility.   Fielding's *Tom Jones* paints a sprawling panorama filled with earthy, often bawdy men and women driven by desires as strong today as they were in the eighteenth century.   The novels of Dickens show a grimily picturesque London with its multitudinous small shops, its streets and alleys, its one-of-a-kind Englishmen.   Mark Twain's writings show the nineteenth century American small town, the robust Mississippi River men and those of farther west, and a concern with man's continuing inhumanity to men.   O. Henry depicts the New York of the early twentieth century.   Such writers as Chekhov and de Maupassant reveal that Russians, Frenchmen, and people from other nations are not basically different from Americans or Englishmen.

The forces that drove people, the roots of human conflict, and the ideas of goodness, truth, and beauty are portrayed in the fiction and drama of the past.   Those forces, those roots, and those ideas and ideals have changed superficially in this age of technology, but basically they are the same; fiction and drama dramatize both the superficial differences and the basic identity.   They help students to define what *human* means and what for centuries or millenniums it has meant.

Visual Aids.   Maps, drawings, pictures, slides, filmstrips, videotapes, and motion pictures have considerable value in the historical and other approaches.   With such a work as *A Tale of Two Cities*, for example, one of the teacher's problems is to re-create a world

[1] Gladys Veidemanis, "Drama in the English Classroom," *English Journal,* LI (Nov., 1962), 544–45.

without automobiles or television, with living conditions different in many other ways from our own, and with its own particular kinds of conflict and turmoil. At least a partial solution is offered by a movie version, which familiarizes the students with the clothing, modes of transportation, etc., of the late eighteenth century. For another example, when there is no opportunity for students to see Shakespeare on the stage, good films (even short excerpts) can help students to visualize the characters and action and to realize that what they are reading really *is* a play.

Reports on the Period. For years, a favorite device of teachers has been to ask students to give reports on the backgrounds of authors and selections. Such reports are most worthwhile when the topics are carefully chosen and when there is opportunity for the class to ask questions and to provide supplementary details. The reports need not be limited to history, geography, and famous names but may pertain to music, athletics, art, clothing, medicine, superstitions, schools, etc. A student prepares carefully when he has a topic that interests him and when he knows that he may be subject afterward to questioning by the class.

Newspapers. By preparing "newspapers" relating to a literary selection, students improve both their ability to write and their understanding of literature. High school classics such as *A Tale of Two Cities* and *Silas Marner* are especially suitable for journalistic enterprises.

A *Raveloe Gazette* or a *Roman Bugle* may contain news stories, sports stories, editorials, advertisements, etc., related to *Silas Marner* or *Julius Caesar.* In such an activity, students find it necessary to carry themselves back mentally to an earlier day, which they try to re-create.

Radio and Television Programs. Some radio and TV programs, especially on educational channels, dramatize famous historical events. Students should be encouraged to view such broadcasts and to talk about them in class, especially when the programs are related in some way to literature the class has read or is reading. Some excellent kinescopes and tapes are also available, and have the advantage that they can be shown when they are most appropriate.

In addition, students enjoy preparing a simulated broadcast of their own. An interesting method of presenting a historical incident with literary overtones is to produce a program called "＿ ＿ H.S. Was There" (using the initials of your high school).

Some schools that are given radio time by a local station prepare programs of this kind for actual broadcasts. Others present the programs before the assembly or before younger classes.

Time Charts. Textbooks often include time charts that show the chronological relationship between history and literature, or among the literatures of different countries. Unless students have these charts called to their attention, and unless they are asked occasional questions that can be answered only by reference to the charts, the students are likely to ignore them.

A few teachers, on the ground that people learn more by doing than by reading, have students prepare their own time charts. Some of these are elaborate, with pictures or drawings to illustrate the chief events.

Correlation and Integration. In some schools, history and literature are integrated, sometimes to the extent that students enrol in a two-period-a-day course which carries credit for both history and English. The theory is that the history throws light on the literature, and vice versa. American history and American literature are the courses most often combined in this way. The strengths of this procedure are that it does demonstrate that literature is inevitably an outgrowth of the social, economic, and political climate and that it does make history seem real—not merely "little tiny figures running across fields with their arms stretched out." One weakness is that it works well only for America, since courses in the history of England, of Europe, or of the Orient are seldom included in high school offerings. A second weakness is that some important periods of history produced little literature of merit; in America the periods of exploration, colonization, and the Revolutionary War are of great significance historically, but not much genuine literature was written. (This weakness may be overcome, however, by choice of literature written later but descriptive of these periods.) A third possible weakness is that the integrated course demands either a team of teachers or one teacher who is well prepared in both history and English, and about equally interested in each.

Even without such complete integration, however, it is possible to relate literature to the most significant events of the period. Thus fiction of the Civil War period (e.g., *Gone With the Wind*) may be tied in, through films and reports, with the historical events.

Still another kind of correlation is between literature and language. The English language in America as illustrated in Irving was different in many ways from the language as illustrated in Hemingway or other moderns. When the literature is studied, its linguistic characteristics may also be studied—e.g., the early predilection for long sentences, for a fairly high degree of formality, or for certain usages now obsolete may be compared with present tendencies. Similarly, in the study of British literature the language of Chaucer, Shakespeare, and other writers may profitably be compared with modern English.

In recent years the growing interest in humanities has led some teachers to an even broader kind of articulation, sometimes including in a single course literature, art, music, architecture, social history, and even simplified philosophy. Such courses are often team-taught, since no one teacher is likely to be sufficiently well-informed in all these subjects. Even when the "humanities" designation has not been used, though, some teachers have found it worth while to show art reproductions from the historical period under consideration or to play some of its music, since tendencies in literature, art, and music are generally related. Thus the differences between neo-classicism and romanticism appear not only in the literature of the two periods but also in the music and the art.

THE SOCIOPSYCHOLOGICAL APPROACH

The historical approach, as we have noted, has been attacked by leading British teachers of English and is regarded with some reservation by a fair number of American leaders. Many of its opponents would replace it with a sociopsychological approach, designed to use literature to increase students' awareness of how people act and react in various circumstances, why they react as they do, and how they interact with other people.

An early proponent of this approach, Professor Louise Rosenblatt, wrote:

Through literature the individual may develop the habit of sensing the subtle interactions of temperament upon temperament; he may come to understand the needs and aspirations of others; and he may thus make more successful adjustments in his daily relations with them.

. . . all the student's knowledge about literary history, about authors and periods and literary types will be so much useless baggage if the student has not been led primarily to seek from literature a vital personal experience.[2]

2 Louise M. Rosenblatt, *Literature as Exploration* (New York: Appleton-Century-Crofts, 1938), pp. 3, 218. Thirty years later, in the second edition of her valuable book, Dr. Rosenblatt reinforced and updated her position.

In the Wingler study previously cited, English educators displayed considerable enthusiasm for the sociopsychological approach, as these responses suggest:

If literature is to be of value in shaping students' lives the teacher must constantly relate life as it is represented in literature to real experiences.

Agree or strongly agree—133   Disagree or strongly disagree—17

The competent teacher can bridge the distances between a good book and the immaturity of his students; that is, in fact, his primary duty as a teacher of literature.

Agree or strongly agree—86   Disagree or strongly disagree—53

Methods of Employing This Approach. Even without any conscious effort on the part of the teacher, students inevitably learn about human characteristics when they read. Shakespeare's *Julius Caesar* illustrates the strength of emotions and the constancy of human conflict; Goldsmith's *She Stoops to Conquer* shows that eighteenth-century ideas of what is funny differed little from our own; Poe's "Gold Bug" demonstrates human ingenuity; Garland's "Under the Lion's Paw" exemplifies the misuse of power; Wilder's *Our Town* shows how people may get along with one another in a small town; Salinger's *Catcher in the Rye* develops an understanding of a sensitive young person whose good instincts are thwarted both by society and by his own shortcomings; Golding's *Lord of the Flies*, Knowles' *A Separate Peace*, and all of Kurt Vonnegut's novels probe underlying human drives; the novels of Ellison, Baldwin, and Wright are among many of recent decades that have analyzed the problems and revealed the mental and emotional reactions of black people. Whether the teacher wills it or not, students learn many social and psychological truths from the mere act of reading.

But the teacher can and should expedite the learning of these truths. He can do so through the kinds of assignments he makes, through class discussion and written work, and through what he emphasizes in examination questions and other means of measurement.

Any assignment, of course, should be carefully planned and carefully made—whether determined by the teacher alone or by the teacher and class together. The assignment mentioned casually at any odd moment during the hour or shouted at the backs of students leaving the classroom seldom brings good results. Neither does the vague assignment ("Read the first twenty-five pages of *To Kill a Mockingbird* for tomorrow"). The good assignment provides a reason for doing the work, specific information concerning what the objectives are, and suggestions for accomplishing it efficiently. Mimeographed thought questions often have considerable merit. In some schools, students are given questions and suggested activities for an entire unit; these may be changed or supplemented as need arises.

Class discussions—whether teacher-led or student-led—should never be aimless. Although class members may often bring up points not thought of by the leader (and should be encouraged to do so), and although it is sometimes desirable to follow a worthwhile tangent for some distance, a discussion should generally center upon certain predetermined points. Often there are no definitely right and wrong answers to discussion questions, but such questions nevertheless have value in stimulating thought and in helping students to see more than one side of controversial issues and to draw at least tentative conclusions from the evidence.

Discussions involving the sociopsychological approach can be especially lively, since they focus upon people—and most people would rather talk about people than about anything else. Here is a list of questions representative of the kinds that may profitably be considered by a class at various itmes. (Some of these may need simplification for some classes; examples are often helpful.)

UNDERSTANDING A CHARACTER

1. What kind of person is _____? What is your evidence?
2. If _____ were living today, what kind of clothes would he choose? What books, magazines, movies, and music would he like?
3. What is there in _____'s character that makes him disliked (or liked, feared, laughed at, etc.)?
4. What would _____ do if he found himself in (a certain hypothetical situation)? How does this differ from what you would do?
5. Does _____ usually reason out what he should do, or does he merely react emotionally? Your evidence?
6. Is _____ actually true to life, or is he only a stereotype? (Teaching the recognition of stereotyped characters is one of the best services that a teacher can perform, since too many persons think in terms of the "typical" Negro, Jew, Mexican, Frenchman, Russian, etc.)
7. Are any of _____'s actions surprising to you? Can they be accounted for by anything in the story? Are there any inexplicable developments (such as an abrupt reformation, as in As You Like It)?
8. How and why does _____ change in the course of the story?

Understanding the Character's Relation to His Environment

1. Why do you suppose _____ is the kind of person he is? What clues concerning his background are included in the story? How has his background contributed to making him what he is?
2. If _____ had lived in a different century, would he have been the same kind of person?
3. If _____ had lived in such and such a country, how would his thoughts and actions have differed?
4. If _____ had been of the opposite sex, how would his (or her) decisions and actions have varied? Would he (or she) then have faced the same problems?
5. How does _____'s economic status affect his attitudes and his actions?
6. How has _____'s occupation affected his life?
7. If _____ had been of a different race, how might his behavior have differed?
8. Is _____ entirely responsible for what happens to him, or do outside circumstances beyond his control determine his fate?
9. Could this story have happened in the same way in a country with a different form of government?
10. If you were a native of another country and read this story, which customs would seem strange to you?

Understanding the Interaction of Characters

1. Which of these characters would you rather have as a close friend? A parent? A teacher? A brother or sister? An uncle or aunt? A companion on a desert island? A wife or husband? Which would you like least? Why?
2. What does the selection show about family relationships? About the way people get along in a neighborhood? About racial attitudes?
3. What is _____'s attitude toward the opposite sex?
4. Is it fitting that _____ should be married to _____? What are some of the factors that determine whether a couple are well matched?
5. What is the real cause of the conflict between _____ and _____? Could it have been prevented?
6. Why do _____ and _____ react toward one another as they do? How does _____ influence _____?

Understanding General Principles of Human Behavior

1. What similar incidents have you experienced or heard or read about? What historical incidents are parallel?

2. Is the ending of the story in harmony with the portrayal of the characters?
3. Ten years after the end of the story, what has probably happened to the chief characters? What makes you think so?
4. What evidence is presented in the story to show that a group of people who share a difficulty tend to cooperate better than they otherwise would? (This question is only a sample of many of the same kind to help the students understand the theme or social implications of a selection.)
5. Who are usually responsible for human progress—people who try to be exactly like everyone else or people who dare to be somewhat "different"? Your evidence? May "differentness" be carried too far? (These are examples of dozens of general thought questions that may bring stimulating discussion.)
6. What are some of the major problems faced by all human beings? What are some of the problems peculiar to people of the twentieth century? Of twentieth-century America?
7. What are some important concerns and motivations of all human beings? (E.g., food, clothing, shelter, power, the need to be needed.) Which of these are prime concerns of _____? Your evidence?

This rather long list is by no means exhaustive but is intended only to be representative of discussion questions using the socio-psychological approach. Examinations may often contain similar thought-questions.

Phyllis Miletich describes use of a study of characterization to build an understanding of theme. Her students follow a four-step procedure: (1) They copy characterizing details and interpret each. (2) They group the characters in "teams" representing opposite sides. (3) They find what common elements are represented in each team; these are the elements involved in the conflict. (4) They synthesize these elements to show in a few words what generalization applies: Individual man vs. society, Man vs. nature, etc.[3]

THE EMOTIVE APPROACH

Both teacher and students should enjoy the process of reading and talking about a piece of literature. The best-loved teacher of literature at the University of Illinois, the late Professor Paul Landis —a man whose classrooms were always filled to the windows, a man

[3] *English Journal,* March, 1966.

about whose teaching his students spoke, years later, with enthusiasm tinged with near reverence—used to say, "My only object is to help the youngsters have fun with reading. If they do that, everything else will follow." A whole philosophy of education is in those sentences.

Part of the fun, of course, comes from understanding. The baseball fan who understands the technicalities of the game enjoys it more than the one who sees only a man hitting a ball and running over to stand on a dirty sack. Likewise, the reader who knows something about fictional or dramatic techniques and technicalities reads with more pleasure than the one who sees only that boy gets girl. But the weakness of much teaching of literature has been that knowledge of intricacies has been considered as an end and not as a means. Thus personification, irony, symbolism, paradox, and intentional ambiguity have sometimes been taught as if knowledge of them was the goal, whereas actually they are of importance as they contribute to the accomplishment of the author's purpose and to the emotional and intellectual reactions of the reader. The technicalities should be taught not for themselves but for what they offer to understanding, which in turn leads to enjoyment.

Another part of the fun comes from cheerful, democratic discussions of topics both significant and less significant. Questions like those mentioned under the sociopsychological approach may lead to enjoyable and informative discussion. Sometimes the teacher may be the chairman; more often, one of the students should be. Usually the whole class will be involved, but sometimes a student panel may assume responsibility. The teacher does not take the attitude that he knows all the answers. The author Jesse Stuart, who also has been a teacher, once wrote,

> [My students] will tell me that I am wrong about this or that. I never was able to tell my teacher that he was wrong; he was right, always right, definitely right. I listen to the student, often agreeing with him, for I know that I have him where I want him when I get him interested. Interest will bring about love for any subject. Lazy boys get interested in my classes. All of my students get interested. They do not take the textbook for everything. They go to the library of their own accord and look up material. Tho our library is small, it is one of the most widely used in this state.[4]

And some of the fun comes from activities related to the literature. Generally there should be a choice of activities—not just a

[4] Jesse Stuart, "Teaching the Short Story," *NEA Journal*, XXII (Jan., 1943), p. 24.

required one.[5] Any activities genuinely in the spirit of the literature may be adopted, provided that they have intrinsic worth for the students. One teacher, whose class was reading *As You Like It*, asked each student to be responsible for a contribution that should grow out of the play and in no way violate its spirit. As a result, two boys made puppets and used them to act out scenes of the play; a girl with musical talent composed melodies for the lyrics and sang them; some students drew scenes on a long scroll, which they unrolled to present the story; several built model stages; some drew cartoons; and some wrote imaginary letters from Shakespeare, accounts of a visit to an Elizabethan theater, Elizabethan diaries, character sketches, or short plays of the same type. Did they learn anything about Shakespeare or drama? Probably, because they had enjoyed what they associated with Shakespeare and because they had to read carefully in order to make their contributions.

Plays, as has been remarked, were written to be acted, not to be studied. Since that is true, one of the best activities to employ when a play has been assigned is to act it out. Students will take most of the parts, but the teacher should not be simply a spectator. Before doing any acting, the class must understand the events and the chief characteristics of each role, just as professional actors must. In *Twelfth Night*, for instance, they must recognize that Orsino is lovesick; Maria, frisky; Andrew, cowardly; Toby, jolly and drunken; the singing fool, plaintive. Parts of the room, one teacher suggests, may be marked—Duke's throne, Olivia's palace, etc.; each of the players may be given a simple identifying token—Olivia, a veil; the clown, a dunce cap; Maria, an apron; Malvolio, a yellow cross-gartering made of crepe paper. Action must accompany reading of the parts —students bow or curtsy to the Duke, crouch behind imaginary trees, and laugh at Malvolio. Undignified? Perhaps, though not unduly. Shakespeare was a great dramatist partially because he knew when to unbend. His serious scenes owe much of their effectiveness to the contrast with the hilarious ones. May not we teachers follow the lead of this author whom we revere?

Another teacher who advocates much acting believes in releasing students' bodies as well as their thoughts—letting wiggling freshmen

---

[5] The author still recalls with chagrin his mistake in requiring all his tenth graders to make soap carvings related to *Julius Caesar;* the waste of time must have amounted to at least 200 man-hours, and the waste of soap, it was said, caused a temporary shortage in the community.

learn while wiggling, through wiggling. She makes much use of pantomime; in a study of myths, small groups of ninth graders volunteer to pantomime a myth of their choice, with the rest of the class to guess the story. An accelerated group writes plays of its own based upon class reading, and acts them out. Old Testament narratives are also acted: the discovery of baby Moses—a foot ruler in a dictionary; the plague of frogs—with everyone wanting to be a frog. Reviewing in June, someone giggles and says, "We ought to remember that. Don't you remember what we did . . . ?"

Paul T. McCalib describes a variant method of dramatizing.[6] His students read only to a pre-selected point in a story or a play. Then some of them role-play what they believe would happen or be said next.

Many British teachers stress such dramatic activities, not only with plays but also with fiction. A class that has read a short story, for instance, may improvise missing conversation or may remake the story as a play, divided where necessary into brief scenes. Episodes from novels may be treated similarly.

A valuable book concerning classroom dramatization is James Hoetker's *Dramatics and the Teaching of Literature.*[7] It should be a part of your own professional library.

Respondents to the Wingler questionnaire agreed that there is an additional value in dramatization:

For adolescents, dramatic enactment (through improvisation, role-playing, etc.) is a valuable way of developing control of a wide range of language behaviors.

Agree or strongly agree— 140   *Disagree or strongly disagree*— 9

What the respondents probably had in mind is that in dramatization the student necessarily must put himself into the situation of a different person. To do so, one thing that he must strive for is an appropriate variety of language. If, for example, the role is that of a pompous ass, the student must try to talk as he believes a pompous ass talks.

Note that the teacher who uses the emotive approach does not lecture about how beautiful or how exciting the literature is. He does not gush. Instead, by having students participate actively in dramatization and discussion, he allows them to react emotionally as well as intellectually to the literature.

[6] *English Journal,* Jan., 1968.
[7] NCTE, 1969.

THE DIDACTIC APPROACH

On page 128 you were reminded that one of the reasons for reading literature is to garner knowledge of the sort that one is unlikely to find in completely factual articles like those in encyclopedias. This is the sort of knowledge stressed by teachers at the times when they use a didactic approach.

Such knowledge often embodies truths, supposed truths, or observations about human nature and human conduct. Thus it is similar to—sometimes almost indistinguishable from—the sociopsychological approach. It differs, though, in that the sociopsychological approach is largely descriptive, whereas the didactic approach is intended to serve as a possible guide to decision-making and to behavior. To oversimplify, the sociopsychologist says, "This person has such and such characteristics because of such and such influences upon him." The didacticist says instead, "I should (or should not) act like this person because of such and such possible consequences."

Old-fashioned elementary school readers were very boldly didactic, supplying after each story a "moral" for students to carry away. No one can say to what extent these morals served later as guides to their readers. Today we tend to rely less on direct preachments; we doubt whether anyone became an honorable man or woman because of memorizing morals in English 9A. And we realize that morals, like proverbs, may be contradictory. Should we believe "Look before you leap" or "Nothing ventured, nothing gained"?

Nevertheless, many people agree with what Clayton Hamilton wrote in *The Art of Fiction:* "The purpose of fiction is to embody certain truths of human life in a series of imagined facts." These truths may be ethical principles, or they may not. Even when they aren't, they may offer insights into what it is wise or unwise for human beings to do, or may portray attitudes that it seems wise or unwise to share.

For example, a war story like Stephen Crane's *Red Badge of Courage* or William March's "Fourteen Men from Company K" may influence students' thinking about war. Discussion may include consideration of such questions as "Is war ever justified?" "What are conscientious objectors?" "What should an opponent of war do if his country is attacked?"

For other examples, Pearl Buck's "The Enemy" suggests that American principles become embedded in people who spend even a few years in the United States; Poe's "Cask of Amontillado" shows to what lengths a warped mind will go for revenge; Galsworthy's "Quality" has relevance as a protest against sleazy, slipshod manufacture that seems to be increasingly characteristic of much American goods. Such stories increase students' understanding of life and assist in the development of attitudes.

Much modern literature, students feel, is "so pessimistic . . . so tragic . . . so hopeless . . . so negative . . . filled with violence and cruelty and hatred . . . and frustration and degradation . . . and death." [8] Are such viewpoints the ones we hope students will carry away, especially at a time when many of them are trying to awaken the world to a new idealism, a renewal of hope? Faced with such a question, Charles Clerc compiled a list of works that are more affirmative than most. Included in his list are Lewis's *Arrowsmith*, Hersey's *A Bell for Adano*, Silone's *Bread and Wine*, Paton's *Cry, the Beloved Country*, Malamud's *The Fixer*, Tolkien's *Lord of the Rings*, Kim's *The Martyred*, Warnke's *A Pursuit of Furies*, Kaufman's *Up the Down Staircase*, Fry's *The Lady's Not for Burning*, Saroyan's *The Time of Your Life*, and some twenty more novels and plays published between 1921 and 1966.

Ray Bradbury's *Fahrenheit 451* is a science fiction story that can get students excited over worthwhile things. It describes a future where, as Charles F. Hamblen says, "Happiness is the end, conformity and continuous entertainment the means to that end. Original thought is outlawed; the possession of books is a crime against the state." [9] Discussion of such ideas can contribute to the shaping of students' philosophies of life.

Sometimes students are disappointed when a comedy, such as one of Shakespeare's, doesn't seem really funny. They need to be shown that comedy is critical of human hypocrisy and pretense. "It laughs as much at the spirit as at the flesh," as Michael L. Lasser explains.[10]

In using the didactic approach, the teacher asks three basic questions: "What does the author show about life?" "How does he show

[8] Charles Clerc, "On Spirit Booster Literature," *English Journal,* LVI (Dec., 1967), 1255.
[9] *English Journal,* Sept., 1968.
[10] *The English Record,* Dec., 1969.

it?" "Why do you agree or disagree?" These questions should be supplemented by others, involving a discussion of incidents in the story and similar incidents familiar to the class. The students need not accept, of course, the implications of the story: their own conclusions, based on knowledge from other sources, may sometimes directly contradict what the author implies.

The merits of the didactic approach are these: It teaches the student to read between the lines; it makes him think; and it contributes to the building of his personal philosophy of life. An author seldom makes a bald statement of his purposes or beliefs; the student must put clues together to discover them, and often must attempt to differentiate between an author's point of view and those of his characters. So the student must read thoughtfully, attending not just to the events of the story or play, and he must relate what he reads to other bits of his knowledge. From wide reading and much thinking and discussion, he eventually formulates a philosophy that may serve him in the manifold events and decisions of his present and later life.

THE PARAPHRASTIC APPROACH

Particularly useful in the study of difficult selections is the paraphrastic approach, which is essentially an exercise in reading. It requires the translation of sentences, paragraphs, or longer passages into language that the student comprehends.

This approach has serious disadvantages, but at times may be necessary. One disadvantage is that constant repetition of the question "What does this mean?" may lead to boredom. Another may be that the candle lighted by the explanation doesn't always reveal anything very significant; the amount of understanding may not be worth the effort. Respondents to the Wingler study suggested a third disadvantage:

An ever-present danger of the cognitive-analytical-academic approach to English is that students may become "emotionally" disadvantaged, unable to respond fully to literature or life.

   Agree or Strongly Agree—107   *Disagree or Strongly Disagree*—34

The majority of these respondents seem to be saying that both the paraphrastic and the analytical approaches endanger the sensitivity of students to what is really important in literature.

Nevertheless, at times brief use of the paraphrastic approach may be essential to the understanding that must precede discussion of underlying significance. A passage from *The Merchant of Venice* may illustrate the procedure useful with a class not previously exposed to Shakespeare:

> SOLANIO. Believe me, sir, had I such venture forth,
> The better part of my affections would
> Be with my hopes abroad. I should be still
> Plucking the grass, to know where sits the wind;
> Peering in maps for ports, and piers, and roads;
> And every object that might make me fear
> Misfortune to my ventures, out of doubt,
> Would make me sad.

In this passage, students' difficulties arise chiefly from failure to understand the situation, the use of words in unfamiliar ways, peculiarities of sentence structure, and incomplete development of one or two thoughts. In other passages, the troubles might come from figures of speech or unknown words or allusions.

Let us examine the quoted passage carefully in order to find the specific sources of difficulty. In the first place, the student must have a picture of the scene. Antonio, Salarino, and Solanio are standing talking on a street in Venice (not floating in a gondola as one student thought). Antonio has complained of being sad—he does not know why—and Salarino and Solanio are suggesting that the reason is that he is worried about his ships at sea. Therefore the "sir" in the first line refers to Antonio; it suggests also the respect that Solanio has for the merchant.

When the student comes to "had I such venture forth," he may be temporarily baffled. For one thing, the clause is not constructed as we usually would construct it today. Recall to the class that we do sometimes say "had I known" or "had I been there" instead of using the "if" construction. "Venture forth" may be misinterpreted for two reasons: The words have meanings strange to us, and "venture" is here a noun and not a verb. Solanio therefore means "if I had such an investment at stake" or, in other words, "if I had so much merchandise at sea."

"The better part of my affections would/Be with my hopes abroad" causes little trouble except for the word "affections," which here refers to thoughts rather than love. Solanio is saying, "Most of my thoughts would be about the ships carrying my fortune." Some students may need to be shown that the sentence does not end

with "would." Many students, in both silent and oral reading of
poetry, stop completely at the end of each line.

"I should be still/Plucking the grass, to know where sits the wind"
contains two difficult words and one undeveloped thought. "Still"
has the old meaning of "constantly" or "always"; yet a student may
think that "be still" means "be quiet." "Sits" refers to the direction
from which the wind blows. But why does Solanio say that he
would be plucking grass? Someone will probably realize that he
means that he would toss blades of grass into the air in order to
discover the direction of the wind.

"Peering in maps for ports, and piers, and roads" goes along with
"I should be still." Solanio says that he would be constantly engaged
in plucking grass and looking at maps. The word "roads" does not
mean highways, but anchorages.

"And every object that might make me fear/Misfortune to my
ventures, out of doubt,/Would make me sad" needs a little elaboration and requires explanation of "out of doubt." Students may suggest objects that might appear to Solanio, who is on dry land, that
could make him fear the loss of his ships. "Out of doubt" is mis-
leading until it is translated as "beyond doubt" or "surely."

The entire passage, then, would be paraphrased in some such
way as this: "Believe me, Antonio, if I had such a large investment
at stake, most of my thoughts would be about the ships that carry
my fortune. I should be constantly picking blades of grass and
throwing them into the air in order to find the direction of the wind,
or examining maps to locate ports, piers, and anchorages where my
ships might be. Every sign I happened to observe that would make
me fear the loss of my ships would surely make me sad."

This passage has been analyzed at some length because it exemplifies several of the difficulties that students often encounter. Students, because of limited experience, do make absurd misinterpretations. A near-classic example was given by the late C. H. Ward,
who told of a boy's explanation of

> The stag at eve had drunk his fill
> Where danced the moon on Monan's rill . . .
> With one brave bound the copse he cleared.

To the boy, a stag is "when a fellow hasn't got any girl." This stag
had been drinking one night at Monan's roadhouse (grill?) and,
presumably when he was about to be arrested for intoxication, had
jumped over the policemen (copse) and escaped.

Impossible? Ward assured us that it was true, and any experienced teacher can cite instances of misconceptions equally absurd but perhaps less funny. The late Reed Smith summarized a study showing that Masefield could not be identified by a single college freshman in a group of 44, that Malvolio was known to 4 of the 44, that Canterbury was known to 23, and the Koran to 14. Euripides was identified as "higher mathematics" or "a river in Asia Minor"; Falstaff was "a musical term"; the Koran was "the ruler of Japan." One of my students confidently assumed that Macbeth's command "Be large in mirth" meant the same thing as "Laugh and grow fat."

Sometimes only single lines or parts of lines need to be paraphrased, as Alfred T. Vogel demonstrated.[11] He used as illustrations "Take this from this" (*Hamlet*) and "take thee that too" (*Macbeth*), in which the reference of the pronouns must be clarified for understanding.

Variations from normal wording or sentence structure often puzzle students. An intelligent girl once pointed out what she called a "misprint" in a British story: "The time was come"; to her, "was come" seemed an error. Hawthorne's "what with telling the news . . . Dominicus was delayed" baffles a youngster who has not previously encountered the "what with" construction. Some students may become lost in a sentence no more complicated than this from Bret Harte:

> Of their married felicity but little is known, perhaps for the reason that Tennessee, then living with his partner, one day took occasion to say something to the bride on his own account, at which, it is said, she smiled not unkindly and chastely retreated—this time as far as Maryville, where Tennessee followed her.

Often an entire passage does not need paraphrasing, but only a word or two requires explanation. It is best if a student can supply the information; otherwise the teacher should try to do so. If the teacher cannot (and he may take comfort from the fact that there are numerous passages in Shakespeare and other authors concerning which scholars disagree), he, of course, should avoid bluffing, although he may hazard an intelligent guess. But his guesses need not be numerous, if he foresees students' probable difficulties and decides how to attack them.

The paraphrastic approach is not necessarily dull, although it is more susceptible to dullness than any other. If it is used only when

11 *English Journal,* Dec., 1968.

needed, and if the presentation is enlivened with illustrations, this approach may be as interesting as its results are valuable.

THE ANALYTICAL APPROACH

In the 1950's and much of the 1960's the analytical approach to literature was probably the most widely used, often in combination with the sociopsychological. Most college English courses, strongly influenced by the unfortunately named "New Critics," concentrated on such things as literary structure, imagery, and symbolism, regarding each work as an entity isolated from history and from society, or else, influenced by other critical schools, sought energetically for archetypes or regarded each work as an opportunity for in-depth psychological searching. *Explication de texte* (which combined paraphrastic and analytical methods) was in vogue. High school teachers took such courses as undergraduates or graduates, and tended to use similar methodology in their high school classes.

Of late, however, antagonism toward preoccupation with the analytical approach has been growing. Among the identifiable reasons is the feeling that only the top fourth or fifth of students gain much from constant analysis, and that it tends to turn less able students away from literature rather than toward it. The widely publicized Dartmouth Conference, whose British participants were almost violently opposed to "lit crit," brought focus to this feeling.

Respondents to the Wingler study in 1970 indicated the trend clearly:

Teaching literature essentially means teaching students the tools of literary criticism and their use.

Agree or Strongly Agree—13   *Disagree or Strongly Disagree*—137

A curriculum based upon the principles of the structure of literature is likely to be more arbitrarily ordered than truly sequential.

Agree or Strongly Agree—120   *Disagree or Strongly Disagree*—21

Most of what a teacher can teach and a student can learn about literature is form—the rhetorical and structural means by which literature achieves its ends.

Agree or Strongly Agree—24   *Disagree or Strongly Disagree*—122

In teaching drama an approach which assumes the pupil's ability to experience the play and so moves straight from a "reading" of the text to impersonal literary comment is overacademic and not valuable.

Agree or Strongly Agree—105   *Disagree or Strongly Disagree*—35

The analytical approach is the most "literary" of all. It entails an analysis of literary characteristics, an examination of the ways by which an author achieves his effects.

But why consider this approach at all, given the currently growing antipathy for it? It does have value, I believe, if it is employed frequently but not constantly, and if the stress is not upon abstruse literary terminology but rather upon broad description of the author's techniques. Such study may (1) increase the attainment of what we vaguely call "appreciation," (2) help the student to differentiate between inferior and superior pieces of literature, (3) make him more ready for college classes in which analysis is still often stressed, and (4) sometimes help him in his own writing.

Particularly important is investigation of the interrelationships among (1) setting, (2) style, (3) characterization, and (4) plot. Also involved is study of the effect of each of these upon theme, and some consideration of other literary qualities such as imagery, symbolism, irony, paradox, and voice.

Setting. The setting of most modern fiction and drama usually is a determining factor in theme, characterization, and plot. This was not always true; in the "once upon a time" stories the setting is almost anywhere and anytime. Today's authors realize, as Clayton Hamilton reminds us, "that any given story can happen only in a given set of circumstances, and that if the setting be changed, the action must be altered and the characters be differently drawn." The stories in Kipling's *Plain Tales from the Hills,* for example, would be considerably different if the setting were not India in Queen Victoria's time; tales about China, or even tales about India as it was in Queen Anne's time, would of necessity differ markedly from those that Kipling has given us.

Setting is a matter not only of place but also of time and "moral environment," to use a phrase of Burges Johnson. A story about Chicago in 1970 differs from one about Chicago in 1920, and differs still more from a story about Fort Dearborn in 1820. Moral environment similarly varies with both place and time. For example, in some lands it is still immoral for a woman to leave her house without wearing a veil; in the United States our attitudes toward such matters as divorce, dress, and woman suffrage are considerably different from those of 100 or even 50 years ago.

James Hoetker has addressed an essay to students, which you may want to reproduce, describing his emphasis on helping students to visualize setting and action; [12] he provides hints that, if followed, can be very useful.

Some questions that will make your students more aware of the significance of environment have been listed on pages 177–79. Here the special concern is with teaching the literary techniques employed in presenting the setting.

A writer of fiction may show the setting in either of two basic ways: cataloging and suggesting. Sir Walter Scott and many of his contemporaries illustrate the catalog method, writing long paragraphs of description, offering details and more details, describing almost every tree in the grove. Modern writers sometimes use the catalog technique, but tend more often to choose only a few representative details that suggest the rest of the picture. They have adapted the poet's technique of selecting and pruning. Thus, in Marjorie Kinnan Rawlings' short story "A Crop of Beans," in which the setting has importance as a motivation of the action, a few phrases and sentences like these set the stage: "live oaks and palmettos," "blinding blue of the Florida afternoon," "swaying palms, precise and formal against a turquoise sky," " 'Floridy don't make none o' her own troubles,' she grumbled. 'They all comes in from some-'eres else. Wind from the south an' cold from Texas,' " "a small melodeon . . . the sole ornament of the main room."

The dramatist's problem is different. Since plays are to be acted, not read, the spectators see the setting, or at least part of it, and do not need a description. Therefore, the dramatist merely gives some technical details concerning placement of exits and furnishings. Occasionally he may suggest or call special attention to a detail, or to something not visible on the stage, but primarily he presents only brief stage directions.

Teacher and class should now and then talk about points like those just discussed. Students may note the method that an author employs to portray the setting, and discuss the reason for including some details and excluding others. Often elements of the setting are tied closely to the action and the characters, as in the play *Emperor Jones* or in the novels *Return of the Native* or *Notre Dame*. Since this is true, questions that may be asked frequently are "What does [a certain part of the setting] show about [a certain character]?" and "What effect does [the setting, or part of it] have upon [a character]?"

[12] *English Journal,* Nov., 1968.

When the class is occupied with a play, diagrams or pictures of the stage are often helpful. In a presentation before the class, a few lettered labels and some suggestions of furnishings are useful. Settings of Shakespearean plays, with their many changes of scene, require more visualization than do most others, although Shakespeare helped by letting his characters comment upon their surroundings. Thus King Duncan, before Macbeth's castle, remarks about the "pleasant seat" and the "sweet" and "nimble" air, while Banquo observes the "jutty, frieze, buttress [and] coign of vantage"; in *As You Like It*, much of Act II, Scene 1 serves to paint the Forest of Arden.

In summary, teacher and class will try to visualize the setting of each novel and play, and will try to decide why the author uses that setting, how he presents it, and what effect it has upon the characters or the action.

Style. Matters of style should be touched rather lightly in the high school years. Unlike setting, style is elusive and abstract. Even scholars and critics have failed to reach agreement on its definition. Such ingredients as choice and arrangement of words, sentence structure and sentence length, and tricks of expression are commonly recognized, but over and above all these is the mysterious element of personality that led Buffon to state, "*Le style est de l'homme même.*"

Some of the less subtle distinctions in authors' styles even an average class can discover. They can quickly become aware that Hemingway does not write like Poe, that Somerset Maugham's quietly dramatic sentences have no resemblance to Dorothy Parker's barbs, that O'Neill's characters do not talk like Goldsmith's, that Barrie's stage directions are distinguishable from Maxwell Anderson's. Further, they can learn to identify some of the causes of disparity, such things as Hemingway's terse tough-man-to-tough-man sentences, Poe's love of polysyllables and his use of mood-creating words, and Barrie's amiable chitchat.

An average class sometimes may profitably analyze the ways in which an author achieves a particular effect. They read, perhaps, Chekhov's "Grief," the account of the driver of a horsedrawn cab who can find no one to listen to his lamentations over the death of his son. They read the concluding sentence: "Iona's feelings are too much for him, and he tells the little horse the whole story." They note the simplicity of that sentence, its shortness, its restraint; they see that a less competent author would have gone on and spoiled the effect. They wonder about the use of the present tense throughout the story, and comment upon how the use of that tense makes the action seem nearer and more real. Little things, they discover, make the difference between a good story and a great one—the selection of a word, the sound of a sentence, the emotional burden of a phrase, the color of a clause. A useful teaching device is to translate a "just right" sentence into a drab, feebly wandering one, or to substitute an abstract noun or a sickly verb for a vigorous word, and have the students note the loss; the power of the original is made apparent by the contrast.

Capable students may be led further. These are the students who like to write or who want to know the "how" of everything. Their curiosity is high. Use them as leaders of class discussions on matters of style. Ask them pointed questions about why an author chooses a particular word, why he uses short sentences in one place and long ones in another, how he builds up a feeling of tension or hatred or longing. These students will welcome such questions and dig deep for the answers.

Characterization. Now let us turn to the matter of characterization. When one has finished reading a story or a play, how does one know that a character is noble, cranky, whimsical, fickle, or something else? One has learned from the author's use of one or more of the nine basic methods of revealing a character:

1. Telling what kind of person he is.
2. Describing the person, his clothing, and his environment.
3. Showing his actions.
4. Letting him talk.
5. Relating his thoughts.
6. Showing how other people talk to him.
7. Showing what other people say about him.
8. Showing how other people react because of him.
9. Showing how he reacts to others.

Most elementary of these methods is the first. An unskilled writer says, "Fred was a grouchy old man," but an experienced author knows that showing is superior to telling and therefore uses one of the other devices.[13] Dickens frequently employs the second method,

[13] For a detailed treatment of authors' methods of presenting characters and point of view, see Wayne Booth's *The Rhetoric of Fiction* (University of Chicago Press, 1961), one of the most scholarly treatments of the role of the author in the writing of fiction. Booth defends "telling" more vigorously than do most fiction theorists.

taking his reader down the streets and alleys of London to a black old gateway, or into a vast hall with massive but cobweb-covered furniture; there he meets someone whose person and accouterments Dickens sweeps before the reader's eyes by giving a single impression and then filling in details. Almost inevitably, authors employ the third and fourth methods to reveal character. For example, when Huck Finn disguises himself as a girl, Mrs. Judith Loftus readily penetrates his incognito but, thinking he is a runaway apprentice, aids rather than hinders his flight. These actions reveal both her quick intelligence and her kindliness. Further, almost every sentence that she speaks tells something about her. She says, "You do a girl tolerable poor, but you might fool men, maybe," and the reader knows from that one sentence that she is blunt, good-natured, not well educated, and slightly contemptuous of masculine acumen.

Since what a person thinks is often more significant than what he says, authors often take the reader inside characters' minds. A Shakespearean soliloquy does that, and so does O'Neill's device in *Strange Interlude*, where the characters not only talk to one another but also speak their true thoughts for the audience to hear. Novelists, of course, when they use the omniscient point of view, often recount what their characters are thinking. The last four methods of revealing character may be illustrated in almost any story or play.

Composition teachers today express much concern with the "voice" used by the author. Gary Taylor, of Blytheville, Arkansas, argues that "voice" is important in the study of literature, too, and that students can learn about characters by observing how the author creates the voice of each. He says, "An awareness of the possibilities of characterization through diction, word-length, sentence-length, punctuation, stress, and syntax should bring to the student a keener appreciation of the craft of the fiction artist." [14] Clearly, though, such study should be only a sometime thing: if every story were so anatomized, boredom would be inevitable.

In classroom consideration of characters, the analytical and the sociopsychological approaches are likely to overlap. The distinction, though, is that the sociopsychological approach emphasizes human beings and their interrelationships, whereas the analytical stresses the author's technique. Very desirable is a combination of the approaches, founded upon two basic questions: "What kind of person is ———?" and "How do we know that he is?"

[14] *English Journal*, Oct., 1968.

Plot.   In a story or play, the characters are usually involved in a series of events called the "action" or "plot." (Some modern short stories, of course, are virtually plotless.) A plot is a more or less artificial tying together of incidents involving the same character or characters and leading to a solution of a conflict. The artificiality arises from the fact that the loose ends, common in real life, are concealed in the story, and only those persons and events essential to bringing the story to a conclusion are retained. In life, much conversation and many actions are aimless, but in a play or story the author generally reports only conversation and incidents that have a bearing upon the outcome; thus Shakespeare time after time plunges into the heart of a scene, ignoring the "Hello, nice weather we're having," etc. that would be typical of actuality. In life, dozens of big and little things happen every day, but, in a story, the author selects only those that move the narrative forward.

Basic to plot is conflict. One force opposes another force. Generally a character has a goal, but there are obstacles (conflicting forces) that may make it impossible for him to reach that goal. A story is usually just an account of the battle between a character (or group of characters) and the forces that make the goal hard to attain. In Skaneateles, New York, Carl Sandell had his students identify the kinds of foes they could find recurring in fiction. They came up with these: man vs. man, man vs. society, man vs. self, man vs. nature, and man vs. God (or conscience). In some stories more than one of these pairings may be present.[15]

The easiest narrative structural unit to make clear to a class is the short story. Unaided, students will say only that the plot of a story tells what happens; prompted further, they will add that it involves moving forward in time. In your classes, you may try to show them that an author does more than move his characters forward, that he presents a series of closely linked episodes. Each episode is related to each other episode. Thus, in the familiar "boy meets girl" story, the very first episode generally suggests why he may love her, why he may lose her, why he may win her. The four episodes in such a story may be diagrammed as below. Each part of the story is related to every other part. Each incident grows naturally out of the preceding incidents. Each one, after the first, happens because of one or more of the others.

[15] "The Architecture of Walter Mitty's Secret Life," *English Journal*, LVI (Dec., 1967), 1284.

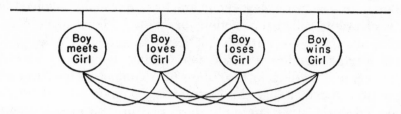

."We frequently speak of 'weaving' a plot," you remind the class. "By looking at the lower part of the diagram, you can begin to see what is meant by that expression; some of the lines cross one another, forming the beginning of a web. Naturally, the more episodes we have, the more interwoven the plot will be. That is, each episode introduces some complication and makes the plot more intricate, like this:" (and you show the following diagram).

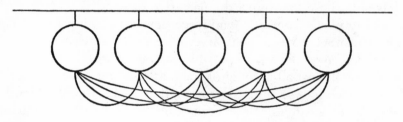

"The important thing to remember is that each part of the well-plotted story is related to every other part, is either the cause or the effect of one or more of the other parts. There are no unrelated segments. Each complication is present—at least potentially present —from the beginning, and each is solved at the end."

The diagrams of most stories are fairly easily evolved by a class (perhaps not by individuals) on the principles just explained. The value, of course, lies not in the diagraming but in the understanding of story technique and character relationships that results.

Nine short stories out of ten are constructed similarly. So are most novels and dramas, although in these the episodes, and hence the complications of the web, are more numerous, and digressions more frequent. Nevertheless, once the students have grasped the fundamental principles of plot, they have little difficulty in seeing how a novel or play, as well as a short story, is put together.

Understanding of principles of construction can add tremendously to anyone's enjoyment. Although the class should not be made to analyze painstakingly the plot of every story or play assigned, enough such analyses should be made to help the students see that stories do not "happen" but are built by an author who cleverly weaves together a number of essential and related episodes.

Setting, style, characterization, plot, and the relationship of each of these to the central idea—all of these are involved in the analytical approach. Like any of the other approaches, it is good if not overdone, if not allowed to degenerate into "picking to pieces." Just as a visit to an automotive assembly line gives one more complete knowledge of automobiles, and perhaps more interest in them, so an investigation of the assembly technique used by an author makes a story or a play more understandable and more enjoyable.

COMBINING THE APPROACHES[16]

A small boy had a bow and arrow—one arrow. He stood in the back yard, aimed at a target about twenty feet away, shot his arrow, retrieved it, smoothed the feathers, and walked back to repeat the process. Over and over he aimed, shot, and retrieved. It was a monotonous procedure. After a while, he got tired of shooting his one arrow.

Later, his father bought him some more arrows, and the two of them rigged up more targets, constructed just like the first but requiring the boy to shoot part of the time at a different angle. A little variety thus being added to his archery practice, his enjoyment was renewed. And, since he spent less time in retracing his steps and in refeathering his one arrow, his marksmanship improved more rapidly than before.

The scene was a classroom. "In what year was Robert Browning born, James?" "What do you know about his school days, Mildred?" "What was the title of his first important poem, Pauline? *You* should certainly know that." "Name three other long poems by Browning, Wilbur." "Where was he buried, Marcella?" "We shall now hear George's report on the years the Brownings spent in Italy."

The scene was another classroom. The class was studying *Julius Caesar*. The teacher said, "Ronald, read the first two speeches in this scene aloud and tell us what they mean." Then, "Lucille, read the next two speeches and tell us the meaning." So the hour crawled

[16] The following paragraphs are adapted from the author's article, "The Multiple Approach in Teaching Literature," in *They Will Read Literature* (NCTE, 1955).

by. The following week the class was studying an essay. "Daniel, read the first two sentences and tell us what they mean."

One-arrow teachers they apparently were. They aimed, shot, retrieved, smoothed the feathers, and aimed again. Over and over their classes did the same thing, relieving their boredom only by horseplay or by raucous laughter at something not really funny.

The plea in this chapter has been that every teacher of English should have and use more than one arrow. The literature teacher is hunting big game for his class. Not tigers or elephants, but pleasure, and understanding of literature as a key to life, and understanding of literature as an influence upon life. No tiger was ever so large or so formidable or so much worth capturing as any one of these quarries.

Six arrows have been described. One should be used now, another tomorrow. Two or even three may be used almost concurrently. But no one arrow should be worn out. The teacher with six arrows is much more likely to hit the target than the teacher with only one.

THE IDEA BOX

"Epitome: How To Begin a Book"

Leonard Solo of New York starts discussion of a book by having students discuss a key scene, or passage: "Chapter I of *The Scarlet Letter;* the squirrel incident in *The Red Badge of Courage;* the turtle scene in *The Grapes of Wrath;* the tired warbler scene in *The Old Man and the Sea;* . . . the First Witch's story of the sailor and his wife in *Macbeth;* . . . Gatsby's walk in the moonlight with Daisy in *The Great Gatsby.* . . ." *English Journal,* LVI (Oct., 1967), 1023.

Choosing a Novel for Class Reading

If enough copies are available, you may use the "loaded deck" method. Name several worthy novels, tell a little about each, and let the class choose the one they would like to read.

Opposing Forces

In the study of a play or novel, analysis of the forces working for and against the protagonist—perhaps writing them in parallel columns —adds to the understanding. (Norman, Okla., High School.)

"Teaching Meaning Through Structure"

A good opening question in discussion of structure is "If you were to divide the story into three parts [or some other number], where would you make the division?" Bernard E. Peltzie illustrates with Saki's "The Open Window" and Katherine Mansfield's "The Fly." *English Journal*, LV (Sept., 1966), 703.

Introducing a Book

A class that has studied a novel or a play may prepare a short program to introduce the book interestingly to next year's class.

Progression in the Short Story

Helvi Lansu of Los Angeles recommends plot stories first (e.g., Richard Connell's "The Most Dangerous Game"); then stories that stress character, setting, tone, symbol, and ambiguity. This appears to be a good formula to follow as students mature. "The Shape of Literature," *English Journal*, LIV (Sept., 1965), 520.

For Variety in Teaching Fiction

1. If a story is told in the first person, discuss how it would have differed if another character had been telling it.

2. Try a "Mr. Anthony" program, in which two students representing fictional characters who are in conflict in a book present their stories to an arbiter.

What Is the Story About

The late Professor Randall Stewart, of Vanderbilt, recommended asking the apparently simple question "What is the story about?" But the student who starts to recount the events should be stopped. "No, that's the story, but what is it *about?*" With enough prodding, students name the main topic: idealism, justice, etc.

Authors Once Went to High School

. . . but students seldom think about that, and biographers generally pay little attention to school days. Your class may be interested in what Hemingway was like as a high school student. Daniel P. Reichard, of Oak Park, Ill. ("Ernie's" home town) tells about it in "None Are to Be Found More Clever than Ernie," *English Journal*, LVIII (May, 969), 668.

Puppets

English and art may sometimes be combined in junior high school classes. Students make puppets and use them to present original plays or plays studied in class.

If the Comic Books Bother You

1. Don't give them the sweetness of forbidden fruit by banning or confiscating them. Some teachers have been able to use comics as steppingstones to *Treasure Island, Sherlock Holmes, Paul Bunyan*, etc.

2. Beryl Sullivan's junior high school students read and reported on whatever they wished for a week. Many read comics. The comic stories were so similar that even their avid followers noticed their monotony.

3. In class, let students examine a number of comic books from the point of view of their truth to life.

Understanding Through Comparison

Bright freshmen compared *Lord of the Flies* and *Animal Farm*, finding nine parallels and contrasts: social implications, man-to-pig and pig-to-man, reactions to freedom, key incidents leading to breakdown, dissension, "right hand men," one character with mystic insight, use of comparable symbols, and use of irony. See Suzanne Gulbin, "Parallels and Contrasts," *English Journal*, LV (Jan., 1966), 86.

Understanding Flashbacks

In dealing with a story using flashbacks, ask the students to rearrange the events, putting them into strict chronological order. Then discuss what was probably the author's reason for altering this sequence and what the story gained or lost as a result.

Examples of Fictional Scenes that May Be Dramatized

1. Godfrey Cass and Silas Marner discuss the custody of Eppie.
2. Long John Silver is given the Black Spot.
3. Trial of Charles Darnay.

Teaching Short Stories

It is good, for motivation, to have some before-reading discussion of a question related to the story. For instance, for "The Necklace": "What would you do if you had borrowed some expensive bit of jewelry to wear to a party and had lost it?"

"Baseball in American Fiction"

Maybe one way to interest some boys in literature is through baseball stories. Ralph S. Graber of Muhlenberg College describes a large number of baseball books that have some literary merit, including stories by Malamud, J. T. Farrell, Thomas Wolfe, Ring Lardner, and J. D. Wallop. *English Journal*, LVI (Nov., 1967), 1107.

Teaching Science Fiction

For suggestions about books arranged in ladder style, as well as a list of goals (e.g., "To understand that any science fiction work is based on, and circumscribed by, one or more scientific hypotheses"), see Alan L. Madsen, "That Starlit Corridor," *English Journal*, LIII (Sept., 1964) 405.

"How To Read a Victorian Novel"

The pace of much older literature is that of walking, not of riding in a car, Betty M. Bivins tells her students. Therefore, as in walking, one sees more details, pauses to look in store windows, etc. Given this parallel, students are less impatient with Dickens, Eliot, and Thackeray. *English Journal*, LIV (Nov., 1965), 741.

"Teaching Point of View from *David Copperfield*"

Iva B. Byers' Philadelphia students examine ways that Dickens characterizes: through what the narrator (David) sees at the time of the story, through what he sees in later life as he writes the story, and through Dickens' own version as revealed by facts, choice of details, and direct quotations. A similar plan can work with other novels, to clarify concepts of point of view and to add depth to understanding of character. *English Journal*, LVI (Dec., 1967), 1273.

"*The Scarlet Letter* and Student Verse"

Advanced Placement students were asked to think of themselves as a character in Hawthorne's novel, to try to experience that character's emotions, and to write a sonnet expressing their feelings as that character. Albert K. Ridout, *English Journal*, LV (Oct., 1966), 885.

If You Teach *Huckleberry Finn*

Despite the thousands of pages of commentary, the best statement made about *Huckleberry Finn* is still Mark Twain's own: "A book of mine in which a sound mind and a deformed conscience come into conflict and conscience loses." The novel may well be taught from that point of view, with emphasis upon Huck's "sound mind" and the way that his upbringing ("deformed conscience") has affected his thinking.

"Proportioning in Fiction: *The Pearl* and *Silas Marner*"

Students may better understand a novel if they note "the amount of space allocated to various episodes, characters, and themes," asserts Roland Bartel of the University of Oregon. He analyzes *The Pearl* and *Silas Marner* to illustrate. *English Journal,* LVI (April, 1967), 542.

"The Contemporary American Novella"

Gary Steinley argues that the novella is an ideal length of fiction for high school reading. He describes his system for teaching William E. Barrett's *Lilies of the Field,* John Steinbeck's *The Pearl,* James Jones' *The Pistol,* Ernest Hemingway's *The Old Man and the Sea,* and William Styron's *The Long March. English Journal,* LIX (Jan., 1970), 52.

"The Screen and the Book"

Frank Manchel, *English Journal,* LIII (Mar., 1964), suggests that the following books may be taught effectively to slow learners who also see the movie:

Arsenic and Old Lace
Goodbye, Mr. Chips
The Ox-Bow Incident
Abe Lincoln in Illinois
Light in the Forest
Tale of Two Cities
Pride and Prejudice
Cyrano de Bergerac
The Old Man and the Sea
To Kill a Mockingbird
1984

Lost Horizon
Dr. Jekyll and Mr. Hyde
The Bad Seed
Gentleman's Agreement
The Red Badge of Courage
Johnny Tremain
Robinson Crusoe
All Quiet on the Western Front
Hunchback of Notre Dame
The Grapes of Wrath
Shane

"Introducing the Faust Legend"

From relatively simple works like "The Devil and Tom Walker" and "The Devil and Daniel Webster," students may trace the devil legends to Marlowe's *Dr. Faustus,* Melville's *Moby Dick,* Frankenstein, *Paradise Lost,* Greek myth, and even to Adam, "who wanted to be like God, knowing good and evil." Mildred Frederiksen, *English Journal,* LV (Oct., 1966), 875.

A Semester of Drama

For a semester course in drama, students may study three modern plays and six by Shakespeare (*Macbeth, Hamlet, Romeo and Juliet, As You Like It, Twelfth Night,* and *Taming of the Shrew*). Recordings, films, a Shakespearean bulletin board, paraphrasing, seeing stage plays, and a term paper may be included.

Our Town

For an excellent critical analysis of this popular play, see Arthur H. Ballet's "In Our Living and in Our Dying," *English Journal,* XLV (May, 1956), 243.

"So You're Going to Teach Shakespeare?"

According to Frank Hook, a good teacher of Shakespeare needs to be well informed about the historical background, the intellectual background, the social background, the history of the theater, the text, the biography, and the sources of the plays—even though he may seldom teach any of these things. "Show me the teacher who manages to convey everything he knows to his class, and I'll show you an intellectual lightweight—and a not very good teacher." Obviously, no teacher can ever know too much—about anything. *English Journal,* LVI (Nov., 1967), 1120.

"Shakespeare in the Boondocks"

John S. Simmons recommends some study of Early Modern English, preliminary reading of simpler plays than Shakespeare, discussion of incidents and ideas, attention to unfamiliar words, oral reading, summaries of long and important speeches, use of AV materials, and frequently asking "What do you think will happen next?" *English Journal,* LVII (Oct., 1968), 972.

Group Work with Shakespeare

Gwen Buck divides her Illinois students into groups of four. Each group is responsible for detailed characterization of one person in the play, with passages to be cited as evidence. One member presents the findings to the class, for its reactions.

Shakespeare and Modern Events

In studying *Julius Caesar,* the students of Elizabeth Deur, in Kalamazoo, Michigan, cut out political cartoons from newspapers and find appropriate Shakespearean lines as captions.

Introducing Shakespeare

Some teachers employ recordings to introduce Shakespeare. Excellent is the Caedmon record "Shakespeare: Soul of an Age," with Sir Michael Redgrave and Sir Ralph Richardson. It includes biographical information and short selections from about a dozen plays.

"A Groundling's Approach to Shakespeare"

Imagine that you are a groundling in the Globe Theater. What do you see? How do you act? What problems do you cause the actors? Are there groundlings today (e.g., at sports events)? Richard J. Mueller's students enjoy the groundling's point of view, which enriches their understanding of Elizabethan staging. *English Journal*, LIII (Nov., 1964), 584.

Who's Who in Shakespeare

"Who's who" questions may serve as the basis for either a game or a quick quiz, and may help students to recall essential facts. For example, ask who is referred to in "He doth bestride the narrow world like a Colossus" and "Yond _____ has a lean and hungry look;/He thinks too much; such men are dangerous," from Act I of *Julius Caesar*.

How Would a Journalist Tell It?

Occasionally a scene from Shakespeare (or some other author) may be rewritten by students in the style of a modern journalist. Examples would be the assassination of Caesar, or Macbeth's victories (Act I). Comparing the original with the journalistic account, even though the news story is well done, may help students to understand and appreciate the original writer's artistry.

Re-creating the Past Through Drama

1. In the study of such a play as *Julius Caesar*, let the students imagine that they are twentieth-century people carried back to ancient Rome by a time machine; they write letters to their twentieth-century friends.

2. Prepare news stories or TV programs describing the events of the play.

Writing Stage Directions

Students may add to their understanding of a Shakespearean play if they write some detailed—perhaps Barrie-like—stage directions for it.

Shakespeare Festival

The Academy of St. Catherine, Ventura, California, culminates a four-week, schoolwide study of Shakespeare. Sister Mary Helen, C.S.C., lists scenes that the girls especially like to perform. "Living Shakespeare," *English Journal*, LIV (Jan., 1965), 48.

The Dilemma of Brutus

As an approach to understanding Brutus in *Julius Caesar*, James Hoetker has his students consider and dramatize a comparable dilemma of a high school student, "Bruce," an intelligent quarterback whose football teammates want him to steal some test questions for them. The exercise helps Hoetker's students gain awareness of the kind of emotional anguish that Brutus endured. *An Introduction to Theatre*, Vol. 2 (Central Midwestern Regional Educational Laboratory).

"*Romeo and Juliet* and the Disadvantaged"

Inspired by an NCTE conference, Jeannette D. Hanke of Kirkwood, Missouri, had her disadvantaged students try dramatizing *Romeo and Juliet* act by act, criticizing and grading their own performances. Even though one girl said "Romeo, Romeo, where ya at, Romeo?" and even though two boys got into a fistfight over the interpretation of a line (student involvement!), the class was more than usually successful. For a moving account, see *English Journal*, LIX (Feb., 1970), 273.

"An Annotated Guide to Audio-Visual Materials for Teaching Shakespeare"

Richard N. Albert has compiled a useful guide to scores of films, film-strips, and recordings. *English Journal*, LIV (Nov., 1965) 704.

Some *Don'ts* in Teaching Shakespeare

Avoid: (1) "too much time on unrelated art and history projects," (2) "overexhaustive study of a single play," (3) "too much attention to footnotes, criticism, emendations," (4) "too much 'rapture,'" (5) too much teacher explication, too little student reading, (6) use of comic book or other cheapened versions, (7) "pushing Shakespeare on students who are too immature to handle it or are incapable." Gladys Veidemanis, "Shakespeare in the High School Classroom," *English Journal*, LIII (April, 1964), 240. This article also includes many positive suggestions. Other articles in the same quadricentennial issue also consider Shakespeare.

Shakespeare Isn't Dead

Teacher and class may gather from current magazines and newspapers allusions to Shakespeare or his characters.

Sidewalk Drama

"Students can become conscious of sidewalk drama and even classroom drama in their own everyday lives, and make comparisons with that which they read." (Alma W. Roberts, Abbeville, Ala.)

The Theater of the Absurd

Though seldom taught in high school, the Theater of the Absurd (e.g., Edward Albee, Samuel Beckett, and Eugene Ionesco) is worth trying. George Smith and Gay Sauer tell of success with juniors at Bernardsville, N.J., in "Who Is Afraid of Godot?" *English Journal,* LVII (Jan., 1968), 17.

Two other articles on teaching this sort of drama are in the April, 1969, *English Journal,* written by Peter J. Sheehan and Lenore Mussoff.

Using Professional Theater

Professional companies in a number of cities present plays in high schools. For one account, see Shirley Trusty, "Teaching Drama the Way It Is," *English Journal,* LVII (Nov., 1968), 1187.

When Students Read Different Plays

John Sweet suggests topics like these for essays when students have not all read the same play. Each student relates his play to the topic. "In a good play, the ending follows naturally and inevitably from the beginning." "At the heart of every drama is the success or the failure of an attitude towards life." "In every drama we see an individual at the end of his tether." "Notes on the Teaching of Drama," *English Journal,* LIII (Nov., 1964), 589.

Thinking About Staging

Students may consider how a particular scene, or a whole play, could be most effectively staged. "This has good results in stimulating what otherwise may be dormant imagination." (Harold R. Hansen, Menomonie, Wis.)

Drama and Other Talk

In a pamphlet-outgrowth of the Dartmouth Conference, *Drama in the Classroom* (NCTE, 1968), Douglas Barnes of the University of

Leeds writes: "Drama . . . differs from other talk in three ways: movement and gesture play a larger part in the expression of meaning; a group working together upon an improvisation needs more deliberately and consciously to cooperate; the narrative framework allows for repetition and provides a unity that enables the action more easily to take on symbolic status—to have meaning beyond the immediate situation in which it occurs." (p. 8) The appendix on "Principles and Methods" for classroom drama, improvisation, etc., is particularly useful.

A Caution About Drama in the Classroom

". . . the teacher who too often imposes his authority, or who conceives of drama as a kind of inductive method for arriving at preordained correct answers [about literature], will certainly vitiate the developmental values of drama and possibly its educational values as well." James Hoetker, *Dramatics and the Teaching of Literature* (NCTE, 1969), p. 28. Hoetker's book offers a useful overview of the use of drama as a learning method in British and American schools.

Useful Articles on Specific Novels, Short Stories, and Plays

The following articles offer helpful teaching suggestions or literary analyses useful in the classroom. Except for those marked *CE* (*College English*), all are in the *English Journal*.

All the King's Men (Warren), LVIII (Nov., 1969), 1169.
April Morning (Fast), LVIII (Nov., 1969), 1186.
Black Boy (Wright), LVII (Nov., 1968), 1140.
Brave New World (Huxley), LVII (Sept., 1968), 820.
"The Bride Comes to Yellow Sky" (Crane), LIV (April, 1965), 314.
"The Cask of Amontillado" (Poe), LVI (March, 1967), 461.
Catcher in the Rye (Salinger), LVII (Oct., 1968), 977.
A Christmas Carol (Dickens), XLVIII (Dec., 1959), 537.
The Crucible (Miller), L (March, 1961), 183.
Cry, the Beloved Country (Paton), LI (Dec., 1962), 609; LIII (Dec., 1964), 658.
Darkness at Noon (Koestler), L (Sept., 1961), 416.
David Copperfield (Dickens), LIV (Dec., 1965), 789.
The Education of H*Y*M*A*N*K*A*P*L*A*N (Ross), LVII (March, 1968), 334.
An Enemy of the People (Ibsen), LIV (Dec., 1965), 626.
Ethan Frome (Wharton), LVII (Sept., 1968), 818; LIX (Feb., 1970), 201.
A Farewell to Arms (Hemingway), LI (Nov., 1962), 527.
Gilbert and Sullivan, LI (March, 1962), 203.

"First Confession" (O'Connor), LIX (Jan., 1970), 48.

The Glass Menagerie (Williams), LVII (Feb., 1968), 109.

Great Expectations (Dickens) *CE*, XXIII (Nov., 1961), 118; *CE*, XXIII (Nov., 1961), 122; *CE*, XVI (Oct., 1954), 9.

The Great Gatsby (Fitzgerald) LV (Oct., 1966), 853.

Hard Times (Dickens), LVIII (Feb., 1969), 212.

The Hobbit (Tolkien), LVIII (Nov., 1969), 1175.

Huckleberry Finn (Twain), L (Jan., 1961), 1; *CE*, XXII (Dec., 1960), 178; *CE*, XXII (Dec., 1960), 172.

The Invisible Man (Ellison), LV (Nov., 1966), 1019; LVIII (Sept., 1969), 833.

Julius Caesar (Shakespeare), L (Oct., 1961), 451; XLIX (Dec., 1960), 632; LII (Sept., 1963), 411; XLVII (Jan., 1958), 1.

The King Must Die (Renault), LVIII (Dec., 1969), 1335.

"The Leader of the People" (Steinbeck), XLVII (Nov., 1958), 449.

The Light in the Forest (Richter), LV (March, 1966), 298.

Lord Jim (Conrad), XLIX (Oct., 1960), 447; LV (Nov., 1966), 1039.

Lord of the Flies (Golding), LIII (Nov., 1964), 569; LIII (Nov., 1964), 575; LVIII (March, 1969), 408; LVIII (Dec., 1969), 1316.

The Lord of the Rings (Tolkien), LV (Oct., 1966), 841.

Macbeth (Shakespeare), XLVIII (May, 1959), 254; XLVII (Feb., 1958), 90; XLVII (Feb., 1958), 90.

Main Street (Lewis), LVII (Oct., 1968), 985.

A Man for All Seasons (Bolt), LV (Nov., 1966), 1006.

The Nigger of the Narcissus (Conrad), LVI (Jan., 1967), 45.

1984 (Orwell), *CE*, XXII (Jan., 1961), 235.

The Old Man and the Sea (Hemingway), LI (Oct., 1962), 459.

The Pearl (Steinbeck), XLVIII (March, 1959), 149.

Portrait of the Artist as a Young Man (Joyce), LVII (Feb., 1968), 200.

The Red Badge of Courage (Crane), L (Nov., 1961), 534; LVII (Jan., 1968), 24.

"Rip Van Winkle" (Irving), LIII (Dec., 1964), 643.

Romeo and Juliet (Shakespeare), LI (Oct., 1962), 484.

The Scarlet Letter (Hawthorne), *CE*, XIX (Oct., 1957), 11; LI (Oct., 1962), 449; LIII (Oct., 1964), 528.

"The Secret Life of Walter Mitty" (Thurber), LIV (April, 1965), 310.

The Secret Sharer (Conrad), LVI (Jan., 1967), 49.

A Separate Peace (Knowles), LIV (Dec., 1965), 795; LVIII (Dec., 1969), 1322.

"Spotted Horses" (Faulkner), LVIII (May, 1968), 700.

To Kill a Mockingbird (Lee), LIII (Dec., 1964), 658.

A Tale of Two Cities (Dickens), XLVIII (Jan., 1959), 31.

Tom Sawyer (Twain), LI (Jan., 1962), 51; XLVIII (Nov., 1959), 443.

Victory (Conrad), XVIII (Jan., 1969), 40.

Wuthering Heights (Brontë), XLVIII (April, 1959), 175.

The Zoo Story (Albee), LVII (Jan., 1968), 21.

7

Teaching Poetry and Non-Fiction

POETRY

Why Read Poetry?

Reasons given for reading poetry are varied in emphasis and convincingness. Stephen Dunning, whose anthologies are generally enjoyed by students, lists four reasons: ". . . poems, especially short poems, offer the unique opportunity of bringing complete works of art into focus." ". . . poetry tends to be richer, linguistically, than any other genre." ". . . it is an exotic form [and] poems give young readers a chance for objectivity." ". . . when students are taught poetry successfully, they are given high-caliber ammunition for their battles against conformity and faddism." [1] The last of these reasons is the most unusual, but may suggest a means of motivation too seldom tried.

Dame Edith Sitwell prefaced *The Outcasts*, published on her seventy-fifth birthday, in 1962, with this comment: "It is as unseeing to ask what is the *use* of poetry as it would be to ask what is the use of religion. . . . Poetry is the deification of reality, and one of its purposes, amongst others, is to show that the dimensions of man are,

[1] "Why Poetry?" *English Journal*, LV (Feb., 1966), 158.

as Sir Arthur Eddington said, 'half way between those of an atom and a star.' "

In *The Powers of Poetry* [2] Gilbert Highet suggests more pedestrianly that poetry appeals for these reasons: It gives "the pleasure of following a pattern of sound," as music also does; because of its heightened language it is sometimes better than prose for telling a story; poetry is easier to remember than is prose (e.g., "Thirty days hath September,/April, June, and November" is easier to recall than "The months that have thirty days are April, June, September, and November"); poetry "can express general experience—can say what many men and women have thought and felt"; and, conversely, it can say what few of us have ever thought or felt, and thus broaden our experiences memorably.

These are good reasons, surely, and Highet skirts the pitfall of attempting to justify the reading of poetry by utilitarian reasons. Few persons make a living from poetry, and students should look dubious if a teacher suggests that knowing about Keats will ever put a dime into their pockets. The best reason for reading poetry is strictly non-utilitarian: It is the same as the reason for listening to music, watching ballet, or looking at a painting; that is, poetry can be enjoyable.

The more one knows about music, ballet, or painting, the greater may be one's pleasure. The more one knows about poetry, the more one may enjoy it. But many students are reluctant to do what is necessary to increase enjoyment. They claim (and rightly) that poetry is artificial, that people don't really talk like that. Some feel that, once they understand a poem, the result is not worth the effort. Some have become antagonistic because teachers have gushed too much about poetic beauties or have dismembered every line. Most of the objections, though, are to the difficulties of reading poetry. A poem is by its nature highly compressed; a single reading will seldom reveal many of its secrets.

The objections to poetry may best be met in terms of the main purpose for reading poetry: pleasure. Enjoying rhythm, treating the comprehension of compressed language as the solving of a puzzle, and discussing the broadly applicable human truths or the individual insights and emotions—these are representative of the kinds of pleasure we shall discuss in connection with the six fundamental approaches.

[2] Fair Lawn, N.J.: Oxford University Press, 1960.

In discussing the principle that literature should be read for pleasure, Professor Fred H. Stocking objects to reading literature for moral awareness and improved ethics, "because I have known so many good people who read literature badly and as many bad people who read literature well."[3] He also objects to the use of literature to promote psychological health, because

I cannot fully respect the conception of literature as a kind of psychological medicine. In fact, I dislike all arguments which make literature a slave to something else. . . . We too often act as though pleasure were something shameful, at least in a school building constructed with taxpayers' money. . . . I like to think of literature as a great compendium of celebrations. All literary works say that life is full of wonder, that life deserves our admiring attention.

One of the complicating factors in teaching poetry is that not all students are ready for the same kind of pleasure at the same time. Wittick, in 1960, described five levels of appreciation: The first, which is evident in preschool children and may remain for a lifetime, is "conscious pleasure in strong rhythm and rhyme, even with nonsense syllables"; the second, which characterizes many upper elementary and junior high pupils, is a liking for limericks and other "fun poems"; third is the emotional and story appeal of narrative verse; fourth comes lyric verse in conventional patterns; and finally there is the "sometimes baffling pleasure of considering modern, experimental forms."[4] An implication of the Wittick classification is that there is some poetry that will appeal to any child, but not every child can be expected to like every poem, partly because he has not reached a sufficiently advanced stage of development. A second implication may be that the poetry selected for class discussion should ordinarily be on, or slightly above, the level presently attained by most members of the class, with a few "fun poems" or narratives interspersed for the slower students and a few relatively advanced poems for the advanced students.

The Historical Approach

Under the influence of the "new critics," who say that only the poem matters and not the circumstances of its composition, the historical approach has fallen into disfavor. It is certainly true that this approach may be abused—that it may, for example, become largely

[3] "The Two Jobs of English Teachers," *English Journal*, L (March, 1961), 165.
[4] Summarized in "Developing Tastes in Literature in the Elementary Grades," *Elementary English*, XXXIX (Dec., 1962), 783.

a matter of emphasizing unimportant biographical facts, dates, and the like. But the historical approach is justified in high school teaching when knowledge of the circumstances of writing will help to clarify the poem, when the poem sheds light upon the age in which it was written or which it describes, or when the poem relates to a historical subject.

No true poem, of course, has ever been written that did not grow from the author's current thinking and feeling. Some poems, however, illustrate his thoughts and emotions better than others. Here are three examples.

Bryant's "To a Waterfowl" developed from a personal experience. Twenty-one years old—not the gray-bearded, bald-headed old man pictured in the anthologies—Bryant was walking the seven miles from his home to Plainfield, Massachusetts. He was worried, uncertain. Because of lack of money he had not been able to complete his college work. He wanted to write and had written, but he knew that his writing could not yet support him. He had passed his bar examination, but had no law office, no chance to practice. On this day, a chilly one in December, 1815, he was going to explore the possibility of opening a law office in Plainfield. But the future was doubtful and dreary. The sun seemed to be setting on his bright youthful hopes just as it had already disappeared in the west. Then, also in the west, Bryant saw a lone wild duck, flying rapidly southward. The young man noted the assurance of the bird, the straightness of its course. Certainly a higher Being was guiding it. And if that Being cared for this wild creature, need he, the poet, fear anything?

> He who, from zone to zone,
> Guides through the boundless sky thy certain flight,
> In the long way that I must tread alone,
> Will lead my steps aright.

Without an explanation like this, "To a Waterfowl" is just another poem. With the background, however, it achieves visible significance.

Poe's "Annabel Lee" has a less specific story attached to it than has "To a Waterfowl," but to appreciate it a class must be familiar with the story of Poe's tender love for his child-wife, Virginia, who had died three years before. They must know of her delicate loveliness, her singing ability, her lingering illness that often threatened death before it actually arrived. They should know that she had already inspired some of Poe's best work such as "Ulalume" and "The Raven." It is also helpful for them to realize that there is at least figurative truth in the line "She was a child and I was a child," because Poe never "grew up" to the conservatism and subdued emotionality that usually accompany adulthood. And the class should know, too, that "Annabel Lee" was probably the last poem that Poe wrote—that memory of his dead wife remained sharp within him up to the time he died.

Quite different is the background of Siegfried Sassoon's "Suicide in the Trenches" or any other of his bitter antiwar poems:

> In winter trenches, cowed and glum,
> With crumps and lice and lack of rum,
> He put a bullet through his brain.
> No one spoke of him again.

At twenty-eight, Sassoon himself had gone to war. He knew its filth, its heartlessness, its blood. Twice wounded, he was awarded the Military Cross for rescuing injured soldiers under fire, and he threw the decoration into the sea. Later he declined the D.S.O. because he had learned that war is completely futile. In his poem—indeed in his whole life after World War I—his chief aim was to fight war:

> You smug-faced crowds with kindling eye
> Who cheer when soldier lads march by,
> Sneak home and pray you'll never know
> The hell where youth and laughter go.

These illustrations should make it plain how knowledge of the poet may clarify some poems and make them vivid experiences, not dull words. Similarly, knowledge of the age in which a poet lived may often remove a poem from the realm of the abstract.

Chaucer's "Prologue" may serve as the example here. To us, who know medieval history and who are familiar with H. O. Taylor's *Medieval Mind*, R. L. Poole's *Medieval Thought and Learning*, and G. G. Coulton's *Medieval Panorama*, the knights, squires, yeomen, monks, friars, franklins, clerks, reeves, summoners, and manciples seem at least as distinct as next-door neighbors on a foggy day. But between our students and these characters is a brick wall in which we must make a few chinks if we cannot tear it down.

Consider, for instance, the Clerk:

> A Clerk ther was of Oxenford also,
> That unto logyk hadde longe ygo.

As leene was his hors as is a rake,
And he nas nat right fat, I undertake,
But loked holwe, and therto soberly.
Full thredbare was his overeste courtepy,
For he hadde geten him yet no benefice,
Ne was so worldly for to have office.
For him was levere have at his beddes heed
Twenty bokes, clad in blak or reed,
Of Aristotle and his philosophye,
Than robes riche, or fithele, or gay sautrye.

A combination of the paraphrastic and the historical approaches seems essential here: the paraphrastic to clarify word meanings and sentence structure, and the historical to add facts essential to understanding and appreciation. Unaided, some students will assume that the clerk sold groceries; Oxenford and Oxford they will suppose to be two different places; "nas nat" will be meaningless; and so on. The second line opens the way to a little discussion of medieval education. The line does not mean "Who'd turned to getting knowledge long ago" (as translated in one modern version) but means, rather, that the clerk had long since been familiarized with the "trivium" (grammar, rhetoric, and logic) and was probably studying the "quadrivium" (arithmetic, geometry, astronomy, and music); in other words, he was an advanced student. Line 6 offers opportunity to show some pictures of medieval costumes. Lines 7 and 8 point out that a more worldly scholar than the clerk might abandon his desire to become a priest in order to accept a position as secretary to some rich man or government official. Line 10 provides an opening for a discussion of what books were like before the invention of printing, and how costly twenty books would be. Line 11 might well be passed over quickly with only a mention of Aristotle's doctrine of the "golden mean" for the few students who might be interested. Pictures of medieval musical instruments would illustrate line 12, and a musically inclined student might find here a good subject for a report.

Not all the "Prologue," of course, is crammed with so many reflections of the fourteenth century as these lines are, but, nevertheless, this poem and many others have sufficient historical connections to make such study worthwhile and interesting. The poetry suggests the social history, and the social history enlightens the poetry.

Political history also has often been tied closely to poetry. Obvious examples are Emerson's "Concord Hymn" and Whitman's "O

Captain! My Captain!" To teach these without reference to their historical background would be not only pointless but almost impossible. Somewhat less obvious examples are Longfellow's "Skeleton in Armor," which might be related to the puzzle of who really discovered the New World; ballads, both English and American, some of which have a historical foundation; "London, 1802," which demands an understanding of the England that Wordsworth described as "a fen of stagnant waters"; and Tennyson's "Locksley Hall," published in 1842 but foreseeing aviation, gigantic aerial wars, the steady advance of science, and a "Federation of the world" that has not yet been attained.

As a final and somewhat different example of the usefulness of the historical approach, consider Keats's "Ode on a Grecian Urn." Obviously, it is desirable in teaching this poem to comment upon Greek art and pagan religious rituals. But why does Keats say that the urn carries two quite different scenes, the one depicting love and pursuit and near frenzy, the other a sedate procession of pious persons on their way to perform an act of worship? The dichotomy is not characteristic of classical Greek art. As Gilbert Highet says, "The sculptor or painter who decorated a vase would not think of mingling half-naked bacchantes with decently dressed churchgoers, any more than we should put voodoo drums into a Bach choral prelude and fugue." But Keats knew that the Greeks were somewhat schizophrenic persons, in constant conflict within themselves. To quote Professor Highet again, "The conflict was a struggle between the life of reason, for which they were uniquely gifted, and the dark forces of the passions, to which they were terribly sensitive." Apollo, the god of reason, and Bacchus, lord of revelry, warred within them. Keats was sufficiently informed about the Greeks to recognize this conflict and to dramatize it in his poem.

When one of these close connections exists:

    poem ← → the poet's life
    poem ← → the poet's time
    poem ← → the time depicted in the poem

the historical approach is justified. It removes the poem from the pages of a book and places it in its proper context—in physical surroundings that may be made familiar, and among real people with fears, tears, joys, and aspirations not unlike our own.

The Sociopsychological Approach

Still more may the sociopsychological approach give vitality to a poem. In this approach, even more than in any of the others, lively discussion is desirable and essential. Many questions like those listed on pages 177–79 are as appropriate for poetry as for fiction and drama.

"I think," says Henry I. Christ, "the teacher's job is to broaden experience, to help students find more and more materials they can read with excitement, to lead the students on to ever more complex experiences so that their responses may become more varied . . . in short, to find more poems that turn students on." [5] Human-interest poems, like human-interest stories in newspapers and magazines, are the most likely to turn them on.

Most adolescents are keenly interested in people. They want to know how people act, why they act that way, what might cause them to act differently. Social relationships concern them deeply. Boy–girl and family relationships provide much of their conversational diet, but not infrequently they talk with utter seriousness about solutions of national and international social problems that most of us adults hardly dare to face squarely. Recently, for example, a fifteen-year-old boy was proposing answers to the problems of racial integration—a boy with ordinary ability and the usual interests in athletics, airplanes, and automobiles. He was thinking seriously of an important matter, thinking with a fairness and an unselfishness that adults might envy. One could not help wishing that the fine idealism and the high seriousness that he shares with millions of other adolescents would not be worn away in a few short years. And one could not help wondering whether we might not come nearer to solving our biggest social problems if through education we could provide practical knowledge of humanity that might modify but not debilitate the idealism of youth. The idealist proposes solutions that often ignore reality; the realist—at least in one of his more extreme guises—scorns ideals and accepts the status quo as almost immutable. Somewhere between the two must lie a space where idealism and realism overlap. The Founding Fathers apparently located it. They knew people well; they were neither excessively idealistic nor excessively insistent upon maintaining the status quo. Our Constitution

[5] *English Journal*, Oct., 1968.

—indeed the whole basis of American democracy—lies in neither idealism nor jaded realism but in an awareness of rough reality and an equal awareness that a beautiful Thule may lie beyond the horizon. Today's students are tomorrow's Founding Fathers. As teachers, we can say "Well done" to ourselves if we can help them to blend practical knowledge with ideals.

Poetry offers endless opportunity for adding to knowledge of human beings. It offers, too, tentative conclusions—guesses to be weighed and modified. The poet, even though he may be what Shelley called him, the legislator of mankind, does not know all the answers. But he does raise many questions and he does supply clues to help answer them.

The sociopsychological approach inevitably helps students to relate poetry to their own experiences. Robert C. Pooley has pointed out both the difficulties and the promises of doing so:

Let us face the fact honestly that the experiences in life which produced great poetry are not in many cases the experiences of junior high school students today, or at least are externally different. The moon shines feebly on a street filled with neon signs, the trees of Central Park are not the Forest of Arden, the ocean at Miami Beach would probably not awaken another "Dover Beach," the factories and shops of Detroit do not suggest, "O world, I cannot hold thee close enough! Thy winds, thy wide grey skies!" Yet the world of our young people is full of experiences whose emotional content is parallel to the impact of the poems I have suggested. Our task is to help them find this emotional content and to experience in their own lives the kind of responses to people and settings which aroused the poetry of earlier times.[6]

In the following paragraphs we shall consider some familiar poems to illustrate the use of the sociopsychological approach. In the first group are poems about individuals; those in the second are about the relationships between two or more persons; those in the third refer to large groups.

Poems About Individuals. "Richard Cory." In considering Edwin Arlington Robinson's poem, the class would discuss the kind of man that Cory was—rich, handsome, courteous, and envied by all. But why did such a man commit suicide? What may have been lacking in his life? What really are the ingredients of a rich, full life? Other character sketches by Robinson, such as "Miniver Cheevy" and "Mr. Flood's Party," offer equally good material for consideration of the individual.

[6] Quoted in *Ideas for Teaching English,* Ruth E. Reeves, ed. (Champaign: NCTE, 1966), p. 208.

"Lucinda Matlock." Edgar Lee Masters has portrayed a woman who possessed the secret that Richard Cory apparently lacked: "It takes life to love life." Cory was all superficiality; "he glittered when he walked." But Lucinda did not glitter; there was a depth in her that Cory could never have. She worked hard, gave birth to twelve children of whom eight died young, nursed the sick, wandered through the fields,

> Shouting to the wooded hills, singing to the green valleys.
> At ninety-six I had lived enough, that is all—
> And passed to a sweet repose.

The teacher might ask the class why Lucinda was happy, whom they have known comparable to her, what are the ingredients of happiness. Masters' *Spoon River Anthology* and *New Spoon River* are filled with additional sketches, many of them suitable for class discussion.

"The Haunted Palace." Poe's poem is not about a palace but about "a mind haunted by phantoms—a disordered brain," as he himself explained. In dealing with this poem, the teacher would probably combine the paraphrastic and sociopsychological approaches, having the class explain first what the poem says about the palace and then translating it into what it implies about a human mind. The class would also supply its own illustrations. What, for instance, may have been the "evil things, in robes of sorrow, [that] assailed the monarch's high estate"?

"Ozymandias." What did Ozymandias look like? What did his appearance show about his character? What does the inscription on the pedestal show about him? Would you have liked to be one of his subjects? Can you think of two or three modern men who were like Ozymandias and shared his fate? If being a "king of kings" will not enable a person to be long remembered, what will? By asking such questions, the teacher will do more than clarify the character of the king in Shelley's poem; he will help the class to see that mere possessions and power do not insure immortality in the hearts of men.

"Excelsior." Like Poe's "Haunted Palace," Longfellow's poem has a double meaning. Ostensibly it is the story of a headstrong youth who perished while climbing a mountain. Actually it tells of an intelligent, fearless young man who was not satisfied with things as they are but ever strove to rise higher. Longfellow's summary should suggest appropriate questions for class discussion:

His motto is "Excelsior,"—"higher." He passes through the Alpine village—through the rough, cold paths of the world,—where the peasants cannot understand him, and where the watchword is "an unknown tongue." He disregards the happiness of domestic peace and sees the glaciers—his fate—before him. He disregards the warnings of the old man's wisdom and the fascinations of woman's love. He answers to all, "Higher yet!" The monks of St. Bernard are the representatives of religious forms and ceremonies, and with their oft-repeated prayer mingles the sound of his voice, telling them there is something higher than forms and ceremonies. Filled with these aspirations, he perishes, without having reached the perfection he longed for; and the voice heard in the air is the promise of immortality and progress ever upward.

A word of warning is in order here, however. Not every poem is like "Excelsior"; not every poem has a double meaning. Yet some teachers have spoiled a potential liking for poetry by insisting that students always read between the lines and locate things that simply are not there. Finding a double meaning in every couplet of Whittier's "Snow-Bound," for instance, is absurrd. Other poets comparatively seldom introduced a multiplicity of meaning. (For a comment on modern poetry, see page 229.)

Poems About Two or More Persons. "The Cotter's Saturday Night." Poetry that clarifies family relationships has especial value in this age, when some persons fear that the family unit is disintegrating. A poem like this one by Burns affords a splendid opportunity to consider what family life was formerly like, how and why it has changed, whether the changes have resulted in improvement or loss, and what the future of the family unit seems to be. Involved in such a discussion would be a consideration of how much authority parents should exert; what assistance, advice, and cooperation a child has a right to expect from his parents; whether parents should interefere in their children's choice of friends; what parents have a right to expect of their children; whether grown children should contribute to meeting the household expenses; and so on.

"Forbearance." Emerson names only one quality for which he would value a friend, but suggests several others. As students enjoy talking about friendship, a teacher may use a poem like this as an entrance to a free discussion of the qualities that a genuine friend should possess.

"Maid of Athens," "The Indian Serenade," etc. To many high

school students, especially juniors and seniors, love is real and love is earnest. They—at least the boys—may sneer at a Byronic or a Shelleyan effusion, but, nevertheless, some of them are themselves feeling, mayhap in a diluted form, the ecstasy and the pain described by a thousand thousand poets and poetasters. A certain amount of love poetry is therefore not inappropriate. The teacher probably should touch these poems lightly; he needs to make sure that meanings of phrases like "champak odours" are cleared up, but after that he may merely let the poems do their own work.

Sonnets from the Portuguese, "Maud Muller," "My Last Duchess," etc. We sometimes forget that our juniors and seniors are physiologically mature, or almost so; we forget that in other centuries or in other lands those who seem children to us would probably be husbands and wives and even parents; we ignore the steadily increasing number of teen-age marriages in the United States; we conveniently ignore the fact that tens of thousands of girls now in American classrooms will mother illegitimate children. What has this to do with literature? Only that young people need to know more about human relationships, and that literature helps to clarify such relationships. We cannot continue to dodge our responsibility; if people did not need to be educated, we should not need educators. And education is much more than dates and charts and the spelling of *psychology*. It is a provision of the knowledge and a strengthening of the abilities requisite to satisfactory living in a complex world.

Selections like some of Mrs. Browning's *Sonnets from the Portuguese* portray the beauty of married love, and stress—without stating—that such love between a well-matched couple is worth waiting for. Whittier's "Maud Muller," read superficially, suggests that the Judge and the rustic Maud would have been happy if they had married; but pondering raises the question of whether this is true, whether they were suited for one another, what qualities a well-matched couple hold in common. (Bret Harte's pointed parody "Mrs. Judge Jenkins" mercilessly reveals Whittier's sentimentality.) Browning's "My Last Duchess" indicates how the pride and the jealousy of one of the partners may bring a marriage to a tragic end. Abundant are other poems, as well as short stories, novels, and plays, pertaining to different aspects of married life, although unfortunately most high school anthologies contain too few such selections.

Poems About Groups. "I Hear America Singing," "The Man with the Hoe," "The Cry of the Children." Much poetry enlightens the relationships not of a few people but of vast groups of people. Whitman's "I Hear America Singing" should lead to a discussion of means of earning a livelihood, of ways of enjoying one's work, and of methods of choosing a lifework; it might lead to a discussion of other selections pertaining to the building of skyscrapers, the life of a doctor or nurse, the work of a pilot, etc. Markham's "The Man with the Hoe" (read, of course, with a copy of Millet's painting before the class) may be introduced as the theme song of the early twentieth century, when laborers in America began to make spectacular gains. Mrs. Browning, in "The Cry of the Children," along with Dickens in his novel *Oliver Twist*, was partially responsible for the reduction of child-labor abuses in nineteenth-century England. Through selections like these, a class can learn that literature is indissolubly mixed with life—indeed, that literature may help to change and improve life.

"Come Up from the Fields, Father," "The Man He Killed." War and hunger, according to historian Carl Becker, are man's two greatest enemies, and either may extinguish the human race. It is usually not pleasant to read about war, but it is interesting to note that something—perhaps prolonged experience with war and prolonged reading about its horrors—has changed human attitudes toward it. Savage tribes and even the otherwise admirable Greeks apparently fought largely for the joy of fighting, killed for the pleasure of killing. Today most of us look upon war as something hateful, a childish way of settling disputes that man must outgrow if he is to survive. This modern attitude can be strengthened in our schools. Poems like Whitman's "Come Up from the Fields, Father," depicting a family which receives the news that its son and brother has been killed, and Hardy's "The Man He Killed," suggesting that the enemy is human also, are only examples of the many that accentuate man's greatest folly.

"Chicago," "Clean Curtains," "Mamie." In our increasingly urbanized life, writers frequently emphasize the problems inherent in dwelling within congested areas. Sandburg sees both the glory and the gloom of city life; he hears Chicago laugh "the stormy, husky, brawling laughter of youth," but he knows, too, that in Chicago is Mamie, from a little Indiana town, underpaid Mamie who has always dreamed and still dreams of "romance and big things off somewhere." In the city also are the new neighbors who put up clean curtains, but:

> Dust and the thundering trucks won—the barrages
> of the street wheels and the lawless wind took their way—

Writers, it seems, tend to stress the undeniable squalor of the cities and to ignore the equally undeniable advantages of urban life. A good class discussion will consider both sides—what is good and what should and can be bettered.

Poems by and about members of minority groups. Probably poems by members of minority groups should not be singled out for special comment. That a Jew should write a poem is no more remarkable than that a Methodist or a Catholic should; that a Negro or Japanese or Mexican can write beautifully should excite no more surprise than the fact that an Englishman can. It is better to take each poem for whatever it happens to offer, regardless of who wrote it. Yet at the same time one must realize that we cannot bury our heads and thus conceal the presence of minority problems (or are they *majority* problems?). Therefore, when a class comes across a selection bearing directly upon such issues, the poem should be discussed as frankly as a poem about war or city life or country life or anything else. The students in today's classes are tomorrow's lawmakers, tomorrow's citizens who must live together. If the teacher can do anything to build in them a spirit of live-and-let-live, he should be more than pleased.

"The Building of the Ship," "Old Glory." Many students still like poems of patriotism, even though they increasingly question some of the decisions made by the nation's leaders. The greatness of one's own land is a topic that most people never tire of extolling.

> Breathes there the man with soul so dead
> Who never to himself hath said
> "This is my own, my native land"?

The teaching of patriotism, however, is swinging slowly away from a narrow, chauvinistic variety to a broader type that interests itself in the possible contributions of a nation to world peace and world advancement. A poem like the conclusion of Longfellow's "Building of the Ship" and especially a more modern poem like Russell Davenport's "Old Glory" may illustrate what has been called "the higher patriotism":

> Old Glory! Guard the hopeful and the good,
> And lead us onward, unconfusedly,
> That in our freedom others may be free!

"The World Is Too Much with Us." Wordsworth's sonnet may serve as an illustration of many poems that help students to ponder some of the big and possibly abstract questions concerning human conduct and human relationships. Do we devote too much of our time to "getting and spending"? "What else does life offer? Wordsworth advocates paying more attention to nature. Is he right? What could we gain from following his advice? What besides nature may make our lives truly rich?

For many more poems like those mentioned—poems that shed light upon individuals, upon the interrelationships among a few individuals, or upon the possibilities of rapport within large groups— the sociopsychological approach is invaluable if not indispensable.

The Emotive Approach

Robert Frost, teacher and poet, once said,

> I don't want to analyze authors. I want to enjoy them. I want the boys in the class to enjoy their books because of what's in them. Here again, perhaps, I am old-fashioned. Youth, I believe, should not analyze its enjoyments. It should live. It doesn't matter what they think Hazlitt thought or tried to do in his works; what matters is the work, the story, the series of incidents. Criticism is the province of age, not youth. They'll get to that soon enough. Let them build up a friendship with the writing world first. One can't compare until one knows.[7]

And a state superintendent of schools who visited Frost's class said of him later, "He was neither raising his voice nor cutting up any pedagogical monkeyshines but rather talking to them as he might talk to a group of friends around his own fireside." [8]

The ghost of Amy Lowell is represented as saying (in a delightful article by Genevieve Quigley) [9] "Remember, the object of reading poetry is to enjoy it and to have our sense of beauty prodded in new and ever fresher ways. Teach your students to read poetry with a sense of recognition and discovery of what they were really aware of all the time."

If one had to follow a single principle in teaching poetry, that principle would be easy to choose: Poetry should be enjoyed. Enjoyment is intrinsic in the emotive approach, but it should never be

[7] Quoted in Robert Newdick's "Robert Frost as Teacher of Literature and Composition," *English Journal*, XV (Oct., 1936), 632.

[8] *Ibid.*

[9] *English Journal*, Jan., 1965.

divorced from the other approaches. That is, the teacher should never say, in effect, "Since I'm going to use the historical approach with this poem, we won't have any fun today." Both pleasure and worthwhileness should be a part of every approach.

The emotive approach stresses the pleasure more than the others do, however. This pleasure is inherent in the language, rhythm, story, emotional intensity, and pictorial qualities of poems. It may come also from the oral reading and other activities that may be associated with poetry.

The old but still useful *An Experience Curriculum in English* mentions a number of units in which enjoyment is to be the primary objective. Some of these, with titles of representative poems, are as follows:

1. To enjoy poems of delight in physical nature and in bodily activity. Carman's "Vagabond Song," Whittier's "Barefoot Boy," Emerson's "Snow Storm," Beeching's "Bicycling Song," Untermeyer's "Swimmers."
2. To enjoy poems of the merely ludicrous. Lear's "Owl and the Pussy Cat," Daly's "Mia Carlotta," Service's "Cremation of Sam McGee," limericks.
3. To enjoy poems in which rhythm or (and) onomatopoeia are prominent. Tennyson's "Brook," Lanier's "Song of the Chattahoochee," Shelley's "Cloud," Browning's "How They Brought the Good News from Ghent to Aix."
4. To share in expressions of friendship, tenderness for pets, friends, family. Bang's "My Dog," Tennyson's "Sweet and Low," Burns's "To a Mouse," Teasdale's "Grace Before Sleep."
5. To enjoy poems in which vivid sensory images are especially prominent. Wylie's "Velvet Shoes," Lanier's "Tampa Robins," Brooke's "The Great Lover," Southey's "How the Water Comes Down at Lodore."
6. To enjoy poems in which suggestion is predominant. Guiterman's "Hills," Field's "Little Boy Blue," Sarett's "Four Little Foxes."
7. To enjoy poems of subtle humor or of humor mingled with other emotions or accompanied by didactic purpose. Robinson's "Miniver Cheevy," Holmes's "Last Leaf," parodies.
8. To share delight in intellectual experiences or poetic contemplation. Frost's "Stopping by Woods," Wordsworth's "My Heart Leaps Up," Milton's "Il Penseroso," Arnold's "Dover Beach."
9. To delight in poems with more intricate or more varied music, including free verse. Masefield's "Sea Fever," Poe's "Bells," Amy Lowell's "Patterns," Sandburg's "Fog."
10. To enjoy poems in which much of the charm is due to elaborate,

exotic, or fanciful imagery. Frost's "Birches," Shelley's "To a Sky-lark," Teasdale's "Barter."

11. To enjoy poetic expressions of romantic love. Whittier's "School Days," Burns's "My Love Is Like a Red, Red Rose," Jonson's "Drink to Me Only with Thine Eyes," Byron's "She Walks in Beauty."

12. To enjoy poetic fantasies, in which beauty and imagination predominate. Coleridge's "Kubla Khan," "Christabel," Yeats's "The Lake Isle of Innisfree," Tennyson's "Lady of Shalott." [10]

Poetry offers the sources of enjoyment suggested by these objectives, and offers many more besides. We teachers know that, but how can we get our students to know it?

The solution seems to lie in doing many things with poetry—not just one thing again and again. One of the attractions of sports is that there are many types of plays in each game, not the same play repeated ad infinitum. Poetry can have the same appeal. Teacher and class can (1) read aloud, (2) dramatize, (3) present choral readings, (4) sing, (5) discuss, (6) compare, (7) write about, (8) emulate or imitate, (9) illustrate with words, (10) illustrate with pictures, (11) listen to recordings of, (12) laugh about, (13) memorize (voluntarily), (14) collect favorite poems or passages, and (15) with modern poetry, serve as a cocreator. These methods of employing the emotive approach are discussed in the following paragraphs.

Oral Reading. That the teacher ought to read aloud with effectiveness goes without saying. Constant application of only one rule leads to good oral reading: The voice should "do the thing shall breed the thought." That implies, of course, that the reader must understand what he is reading—its mood as well as its ideas. Then he makes his voice convey the mood at the same time that he is presenting the thought. When he is reading a serious passage, his voice suggests the seriousness; for a light passage, his voice is lilting; in an exciting passage, his voice becomes tense, his breathing more rapid. This may sound difficult, but, if one really understands and *feels* a poem, the voice tends to adjust itself with little conscious effort by the reader. It is easy because it is natural; when one talks, he naturally adjusts his delivery to what he is saying. Good poetry is natural enough that one can read it without becoming pompous, oratorical, or even silky smooth or sickeningly sweet. Natural de-

[10] Abridged from *An Experience Curriculum in English* (New York: Appleton-Century-Crofts, Inc., 1935), pp. 53–62.

necessarily at the end of each line) and of avoiding excessive stress upon the accent, rhythm, or rhyme. Practice is essential, of course; but, if a college senior preparing to teach English devotes ten minutes a day through the school year to oral reading of various kinds of poetry, and keeps the above rule constantly in mind, his reading at the end of the year should be satisfactory. This is almost certain to be true if he has the opportunity to hear a few recordings of his livery has the advantages of placing pauses where they belong (not reading, made periodically during the year.

Not all or most of the reading aloud should be done by the teacher, though. Some teachers unwisely distrust students' reading, saying that poor reading will spoil the poem for others. But how can students ever learn to read aloud well if they have no chance to practice?

The best of teachers manage to have a short poem read three or four times in the course of an hour—the first time by themselves, while students follow in the text, the subsequent times usually by students, when questions of interpretation invite rereadings. At best, these subsequent readings are prompted by differences of opinion, with one student after another reading aloud in order to argue his point about tone, emphasis, or meaning. Finally . . . teachers often end by reading through once more, so that the poem is heard with all its meanings "in".[11]

Dramatizing. Classes enjoy dramatization of poetry. A ballad such as "Get Up and Bar the Door" may be dramatized with little time-consuming preparation, as it falls readily into dramatic form. Two capable boys may work out a dramatization of "Sohrab and Rustum" that will help to clarify the action and the speeches. Some poems may be pantomimed effectively by one student while another reads. Reading of parts in such a poem as Poe's "Raven"— with a narrator, a speaker, and a hoarse raven—assists visualization and understanding.

Readers' Theater, discussed on page 507, is sometimes as suitable for poetry as for drama or fiction. Excerpts from narrative poems, like Benet's *John Brown's Body* or *Western Star*, are especially appropriate.

Choral Reading. Choral reading has been made the subject of several books, and cannot be adequately discussed here. The proficient choral group attains majestic organ-like effects, but these

[11] James Knapton and Bertrand Evans, *Teaching a Literature-Centered English Program* (New York: Random House, Inc., 1967), p. 115.

are usually beyond the attainment of an English class, where choral reading is only one activity among many. Simpler effects, though, may be obtained rather easily. For example, in "Lord Randal" the girls may read the mother's questions, and the boys Lord Randal's replies. Other poems divide themselves naturally into three parts or four parts, or into parts suitable for a solo and a chorus. Junior high school youngsters, in particular, enjoy choral reading, although many senior high groups also like it.

"Since it is a social activity, the students will benefit most if they take the responsibility for selecting their material on the basis of criteria decided upon in earlier discussions of types of poetry. Students should also take responsibility for arranging the poem for group reading and for directing the performance." So says Ruth Paller, and among selections she has found well-received are Psalm XXIII, "The Apple Orchard," "The Ballad of the Oysterman," "Lochinvar," "Gunga Din," "The Highwayman," "Silver," and "The Charge of the Light Brigade." [12]

Singing. Much poetry was written to be sung. Then why not sing it? If the teacher cannot lead the singing, there is usually a student who can. Ballads, perhaps one or two of the roisterous American folk ballads or cowboy songs like "The Old Chisholm Trail," make a good entering wedge. Later, lyrics by Shakespeare, Jonson, Burns, and others may be sung. Ballads should be "sung, acted, danced to, and made up jointly," says Rachel Potter of Sheffield, England. [13]

Discussing and Comparing. Discussions of poems should be lively and interesting. A good discussion inevitably involves more than one of the approaches. Comparisons between poems or between poets (e.g., Frost and Wordsworth, the rhythm of Chesterton's "Lepanto" and the rhythm of Lindsay's "The Congo") are invaluable.

Writing. Written work in connection with poetry seldom adds to the enjoyment. Sometimes, though, the members of a class, or a few students, become sufficiently excited over something they have found in a poem to want to put down their excitement on paper. This effect is unlikely to be reached often, but when it does it should certainly not be stifled. Also, a few students like to write verse of their own, verse possibly inspired by or modeled on something they

[12] *English Journal,* Feb., 1965.
[13] *English Journal,* Oct., 1968.

have read. To get all students to engage in such an activity, some teachers use the group poem technique and find that classes that have written group poems tend to be more appreciative of the efforts of professional poets.[14] The author has taken a class for a walk around a city block or past part of a lake, asking them to be perfectly silent and to keep all their sensory organs alert. After returning, the students write on the board words and phrases indicating what they have seen, heard, smelled, and felt. (Young people tend to express themselves much more picturesquely than older ones; with a class of adults, the phrases obtained are generally trite ones like "rippling water," "swaying grass," etc.) Then they find some element that seems to tie most of the phrases together—usually a dominant impression. The last step is assembling the pertinent phrases in coherent order and applying a little polish to make the result reasonably like free verse.

Illustrating. Since a poem is highly compressed, a class often profits from expansion of its meaning through illustration. The illustrations may be in words: examples of what the poet was saying, or experiences or scenes comparable to those the poet presented. Or they may be pictorial: photographs, drawings, or paintings supplied by both teacher and class to assist visualization.

Playing Recordings. Numerous recordings of favorite poems are available, some of them made by the poets themselves. A recording may be played before or after the class has read a poem, or both before and after. Perhaps the best source of such recordings is the National Council of Teachers of English, which will send a descriptive folder upon request.

Enjoying Humor. Shared laughter means shared enjoyment. A fairly large proportion of the poetry read should be light and amusing. Limericks, parodies, and some poems by Holmes, Field, Lear, Gilbert, Daly, and Nash are examples of appropriate light verse. Many collections of humorous poetry are available.

Memorizing. Memorization should be encouraged but not required. In too many instances, forced memorization has caused dislike,[15] and, in too many instances, the student, told that he must

[14] The poet Countee Cullen had his class write the first stanza of a Mother's Day poem; then individuals supplied additional stanzas. He also encouraged the writing of limericks and parodies, and got good results from an exercise called "How Would a Poet Say This?" ("Snow is nature's salt." "Winds are violent songs in motion.") *High Points*, XXV, No. 7 (Sept., 1943), p. 26.

[15] It is probably now unnecessary to remind any teacher that memorization of a poem should *never* be used as punishment.

learn twenty-five or fifty lines, has chosen his lines solely on the basis of their brevity. Three suggestions on memorization: (1) If poetry is taught effectively enough, students will *want* to tuck away certain lines and brief passages. (2) Choral reading and dramatization tend to fix certain lines without the student's conscious effort. (3) If the teacher himself occasionally quotes a few lines pertinent to the topic being discussed, some students will be motivated to emulate him.

Collecting. Adolescents love to collect stamps, coins, matchbooks, records, and so on. Why not have them collect poems? As individuals or as a class they may make notebooks of favorite poems. In one small school, each senior class prepares a book of its favorites for presentation to the library; the books prepared by earlier classes are eagerly read and compared with what the present class is doing. In other schools, classes have collected poems on topics of particular interest to them: nature, city life, poetry to be sung, patriotism, heroism, etc. One all-boy class objected to reading poetry until the teacher commented that many other boys were similar to them in attitude and that this class might perform a real service by making a collection of poems that boys really like.

Creative Reading. Professor Marshall McLuhan has made an observation about modern poetry that may result in its having considerably greater appeal for your upperclassmen. According to McLuhan, most modern poets do not spell out a meaning as did their predecessors. Indeed, there is often no single meaning, but instead a large variety of possible meanings. Earlier poets expected their readers to be only consumers; modern poets tend to think of their readers as cocreators. A poem, then, presents a stimulus for creative thought on the part of the reader, and two readers of the same poem may emerge with widely different creative responses. For a high school class the significance of McLuhan's thesis appears to be that modern poetry provides an opportunity for a type of enjoyable intellectual activity that in the past has infrequently penetrated into classrooms. Freed from the requirement of saying that T. S. Eliot "means" so and so, students may find in his verse a rare richness of suggestion.

One caution is necessary, though, lest the McLuhan hypothesis be considered a sanction for "anything goes." Although more than a single interpretation of a poem may often be possible, complete freedom of interpreting is not. Lawrence Perrine says wisely that the best interpretation is:

. . . that which most fully explains the details of the poem without itself being contradicted by any detail. If more than one interpretation satisfactorily accounts for all the details of the poem, the best is that which is most economical, i.e., which relies on the fewest assumptions not grounded in the poem itself.[16]

The authors of *The Dimensions of Poetry* say that a poem may be looked at as a physical object and as a process. The physical object is the lines, shape, scenes, and words of the poem; the process is

. . . the experience—what the reader *does,* and what happens to him when all the elements of the poem come alive in him. . . . The process is both exciting and demanding: The reader can set off an explosion from the chemicals the poet provides, making a carnival of stars out of a few plain words. But he must also approach the creation of a poem, through his own craft of imaginative reading, with the same close awareness, attention, and practiced skill that a pianist gives to music, or a skier to motion in sky and snow.[17]

The same authors quote from Walt Whitman:

The reader will always have his or her part to do, just as much as I have had mine. I seek less to state or display any theme or thought, and more to bring you, reader, into the atmosphere of the theme or thought—there to pursue your own flight.

It is not *only* the moderns, then, whose poems can be cocreated by the reader.

Psychedelic Poetry Units. Rita Jean Childress says,[18] ". . . take the old concepts underlying the study of poetry and give them a mod presentation" via close examination of familiar objects, art, music, words, clippings, posters, montages. Move gradually into Tagore, Sandburg, Williams, Li Po, and Yukihara. Bruce Appleby of Southern Illinois University employs simultaneously record players, projectors for movies, slides, and transparencies, and anything else useful in creating the effects he wants—a real three-ring circus, or in more modern terms, a real "happening." [19]

Some of these methods of employing the emotive approach will work better than others in your classes. You may wish to give each of them a brief trial and thereafter emphasize the six or seven that bring the best results in your school. The next-to-last one, creative reading, may well become one of your stand-bys.

[16] "The Nature of Proof in the Interpretation of Poetry," *English Journal,* LI (Sept., 1962), 393. Be sure to read all of this extraordinarily helpful article.

[17] James E. Miller, Jr., and Bernice Slote, *The Dimensions of Poetry* (New York: Dodd, Mead & Co., 1962), p. 5.

[18] *English Journal,* Dec., 1968.

[19] Other *English Journal* articles on multi-media include Louise F. Dellone's "The 'Link' Is the Thing," May, 1968, and Steven Schwartz's "Snowball Throwers Last Forever," November, 1967.

The Didactic Approach

With the didactic approach, teacher and class find and discuss the author's viewpoint toward his subject. They may or may not accept that viewpoint. "Poetry does not demand our belief; it invites us to experience," as Miller and Slote say. The students examine the viewpoint from several sides, compare it with other viewpoints, and evaluate it in light of their own experience. Four poems will be discussed to exemplify this approach.

"Miracles." Whitman calls all commonplace things "miracles"—houses, bees, fish, rocks, food, companionship, the new moon. Is he right? A "miracle" is defined as a wonderful thing. What is wonderful about a honeybee? About a rock? How does Whitman's definition of "miracles" differ from yours? What are some things that you consider miracles?

"Mending Wall." Frost's poem has been taught as an argument between an internationalist and an isolationist, with the latter having the last word. Such an interpretation is not necessarily far-fetched, because one of the pleasures of poetry is that it can be given wide application. There is danger, however, in saying that Frost *intended* to convey any such idea, a danger of reading into a poem something that was not written into it. To apply the thought of a poem to something outside it is one thing, but to say that the "something outside" is really inside is perverting the poem. Frost merely says that two neighbors, of unlike temperaments, each spring mend the stone wall between their fields; one is opposed to the mending because he sees no need for walls, but the other, moving in the darkness of time-worn beliefs, insists that "Good fences make good neighbors." Without referring to international implications at all, a class can ponder the questions of why the two men were different, whether it is true that good fences make good neighbors, what kinds of fences we put up between ourselves besides physical ones, and whether people still tend to repeat the ideas learned in their childhood. Then, if someone sees that fences between neighbors are like fences between nations—good, but it should not be said that the fences-between-nations idea is in the poem itself.

"I Saw a Man." Stephen Crane's little poem is a good introduction to symbolism:

> I saw a man pursuing the horizon;
> Round and round they sped.

> I was disturbed at this;
> I accosted the man.
> "It is futile," I said,
> "You can never"—
> "You lie," he cried,
> And ran on.

A hint from the teacher will give the key that the horizon symbolizes ideals. The discussion then may center upon whether it is futile and senseless to pursue ideals that can never be reached. Who is right, the speaker or the pursuer of the horizon? What have men gained from seeking the ideal means of transportation, the ideal means of communication, the ideal form of government? Who is more likely to leave his "footprints on the sands of time"—the one who says "You can't" or the one who says "I can try"?

"Mother to Son." The mother in Langston Hughes's poem tells her son,

> Life for me ain't been no crystal stair . . .
> But all the time
> I'se been a-climbin' on.

One young lad, catching the significance at once, remarked, "My dad was climbing up the ladder of success but came to a place where a couple of rungs were missing, and he fell through and had to start all over." Class discussion may profitably expand the metaphors. What are the tacks, splinters, boards torn up, and bare places in life's stairway? Does everybody find them? Is life for anyone a crystal stair? Wouldn't crystal stairs become tiresome after a while?

Howard Kirschenbaum and Sidney B. Simon advocate a frontal attack in teaching values. For example, in connection with Donne's "No Man Is an Island" and Simon and Garfunkel's "I Am a Rock (I Am an Island)" they ask students what they would do if they saw a woman being choked, a deformed girl being teased, a three-year-old being taught to hate a minority.[20]

Use of the didactic approach, then, gives opportunity to explore authors' opinions, to elaborate upon them, and to agree or take issue with them. It is an approach useful in teaching students to think straight, and in developing their philosophies of life.

The Paraphrastic Approach

Several years ago a teacher pointed out some of the vocabulary difficulties that students encounter in Milton's minor poems. *Cloister*

[20] "Teaching English with a Focus on Values," *English Journal*, Oct., 1969.

they confuse with *cluster*, *furrow* with *furrier* or *burrow*, *dame* with *Dane* or *dam*, *hamlet* with *hammock*, and *haycock* with "a bird that lives in the hay." Such students may read "The upland hamlets will invite" and get a mental picture of someone being lured by a slanting hammock; "the tanned haycock" is a sunburned bird; and "the studious cloister's pale" is a cluster of pale, overworked students. It is almost beyond the imagination to guess how students may interpret "sable stole of cypress lawn," "daisies pied," "country messes," and "Jonson's learned sock."

Then, besides the traps of vocabulary, there are the pits of allusion. In the first twenty lines of "L'Allegro" are at least ten allusions that will mean little or nothing to the average high school senior—words like *Cerberus*, *Stygian*, etc.

Morasses of sentence structure also abound. One example will suffice:

> Straight mine eye hath caught new pleasures,
> Whilst the landskip round it measures.

Even though a student knows that *straight* means "straightway" or "at once," *whilst* means "while," *landskip* means "landscape," and *measures* means "examines," the couplet is still unintelligible unless he also knows that *it* refers to "eye" and is the subject of the clause. If he does not realize this, he interprets the second line to mean that the landscape is examining something; but, if he does realize it, he can see that the couplet means, "Immediately my eye has seen new pleasures while it examines the surrounding landscape."

Although these poems set more toils for the unwary than do most of the others that are taught in high school, similar perils lurk in many non-Miltonic poems. Sometimes textbook annotations suffice to clear the way; textbook editors have become more and more helpful during the twentieth century. But, even with the annotations, some students will continue to misinterpret unless the class is guided by a capable and conscientious teacher.

It is to prevent gross misinterpretations that the paraphrastic approach is employed. It is not a lively approach and cannot employ a variety of techniques as the others can. But it does have value in clarifying meaning. Often it may be used as a preliminary to some other approach. Students must understand the words and the sentences in "My Last Duchess," for instance, before they can discuss it as a social document.

Miller and Slote, in *The Dimensions of Poetry*, point out that a poem may be summarized, paraphrased, or explicated, while they emphasize that the result of any one of these processes is by no means the same as the poem itself. A summary "captures and preserves only the bare substance of what is said in the poem, its nonpoetic part." They illustrate with a summary of this poem by Emily Dickinson:

> The Bustle in a House
> The Morning after Death
> Is solemnest of industries
> Enacted upon Earth,—
>
> The Sweeping up the Heart,
> And putting Love away
> We shall not want to use again
> Until Eternity.[21]

Their summary, "One of the most difficult of all tasks in life is the emotional adjustment following the loss through death of someone close," is, they say, "like the bruised rind of an orange from which all the golden juices have been squeezed." A paraphrase, in contrast, is longer, follows the original closely, and attempts to convey the full meaning: "On the day after the death of a beloved relative, the soberest activity in the home (the soberest, in fact, in the world) is the disposition of the affections which have lost their object and which will be superfluous until a spiritual reunion outside time is effected." Such a paraphrase is "like a black-and-white photograph of a brilliant masterpiece of art."

An explication, however, is less inclusive than either a summary or a paraphrase. It attempts to answer the hard questions about meaning, to show relationships among parts not obviously related. In the Dickinson poem, for example, why is the word "industries" used? Why "enacted"? How does one sweep up the heart? How can love be put away?

A series of penetrating questions, requiring close reading and close thinking, may bring the same results as a paraphrase. Sister Mary de Lourdes Muench, R.D.C., illustrates such questions in her article "Taking the Duchess off the Wall." [22]

[21] Reprinted by permission of the publishers from Thomas H. Johnson, ed., *The Poems of Emily Dickinson* (Cambridge, Mass.: The Belknap Press of Harvard University Press, copyright 1951, 1955, by the President and Fellows of Harvard College).

[22] *English Journal*, Feb., 1968.

The point of all this, the point that the teacher must always re-member in paraphrasing, summarizing, or explicating, is that the poem is an entity that cannot be replaced by something else. The paraphrastic approach (broadly enough defined to include summary and explication) may help to make clear, but the result must not be said to equal the poem itself.

The Analytical Approach

Just how much knowledge of poetic theory and terminology should be taught to high school students has long been a moot ques-tion. Is the architecture of the poem the important thing, or is it only incidental to something more important—the meaning and implications? Can meaning and implications be adequately taught if there is no understanding of the architecture? Some teachers expose students to every literary term that they themselves know, hoping that at least a few will stick; at the other extreme are a smaller number of teachers who call a poem a "story" and point out none of its distinguishing characteristics. And, in the middle, the majority of teachers introduce students to the poetical theory and terminology that seem to them most likely to be valuable.

Here the majority is probably right. The student must know something about poetic architecture in order to understand and appreciate, just as he can better appreciate the beauty of a cathedral if he knows something about naves, transepts, arches, and keystones. But minute metrical analysis is more the province of the professional poet or scholar than it is of the high school student who may soon be driving a truck or working in a laundry.

It is the whole poem that demands attention. Diction, figures of speech and other devices, sentence structure, and verse form are of significance only because of what they contribute to the whole. A "good" poem represents a happy blend of the thought and the poetic devices. The wrong device—inappropriate verse form, for instance, or an unwisely chosen simile—may spoil a poem. If Homer some-times nodded, his descendants often do. Shelley, for example, wrote a serious poem about death, beginning,

> Death is here and death is there;
> Death is busy everywhere.

It is a bad poem because the meter does not fit the thought; if the subject were a rambling wreck from Georgia Tech the verse form would be more appropriate and the poem might be better. Words-worth's occasional infelicities are notorious. In a poem about the curse laid upon a young man by a poverty-stricken old woman—a theme that Coleridge might have handled with consummate skill—Wordsworth begins,

> Oh! what's the matter? what's the matter?
> What is't that ails young Harry Gill?
> That evermore his teeth they chatter,
> Chatter, chatter, chatter still!

The prosaic "what's the matter?" is hardly fitting in a serious poem about a curse; the feminine rhyme, as in *matter* and *chatter*, gives a humorous effect of the sort that Byron often intentionally attained and that we associate with Ogden Nash in our day; the repetition of *chatter* belongs in Tennyson's "Brook" but is out of place here; and the verse form no more fits the subject than does that of Shelley's poem on death.

A teacher should find these negative observations meaningful in his instruction because he ought to teach that a good poem is a unit in which all elements are in harmony. The metrical form, the similes, etc., are not merely surface decoration; they are intrinsic. A poet does not write a rough draft of a poem and then say to himself, "I'll add a few similes to increase the attractiveness." The similes are, instead, natural outgrowths of the idea or emotion that the poet is expressing. Neither does a true poet choose a particular word because it is euphonious or because it is the first one that comes to mind; he selects it because it is the one that best reveals the meaning and best conveys the mood.

In using the analytical approach, then, one does not pick to pieces, but one notes the contribution of each piece to the whole pattern. Students learn definitions of technical terms almost in-cidentally, through the class discussions. A student who has mem-orized the words "A metaphor is a figure of speech in which a term is applied to something to which it is not literally applicable" does not necessarily know what a metaphor is, but the student who has often talked about such expressions as "The wind was a torrent of darkness" and "The fog comes on little cat feet" probably does. This second student has examined the contribution of metaphors to indi-vidual poems and has understood the work that they do; he has recognized that they are implied comparisons; his experience with poetry has probably been much happier than that of the lad who was told to memorize dry definitions, or the one who was told to find and copy fifty metaphors from *Julius Caesar,* or the one who was left with the impression that poets sprinkle metaphors over their poems as a soda jerk sprinkles nuts over a sundae.

In a book that for decades has been read by British teachers of English, *English for the English,*[23] George Sampson warns against breaking into the mood of a poem by analyzing its parts:

> What pleasure should we get from a performance of the C minor symphony if the conductor stopped the orchestra at every occurrence of the main theme to expatiate upon the wonderful significance with which Beethoven can invest a simple rhythmic phrase, or from a performance of the B minor mass if a choir were silenced while someone explained the harmonic effects that make the hushed close of the *Crucifixus* such a wonderful moment? It is delightful to have these beauties of musical language pointed out to us; but not while we are on the emotional plane of a performance.

If Sampson is right, a three-stage study of many poems would seem desirable. The first stage would involve one or two readings (at least one aloud) for the pleasure the poem can afford. Then would come any necessary paraphrasing, possibly a discussion of historical background, possibly some discussion of the author's purpose or point of view, and some analysis of the poetic techniques employed. After that, through one or two additional readings, the poem would be reassembled, so to speak; these new readings, with the light added by the second stage, should result in greater enjoyment than the first ones.

Comparisons of authors' techniques is also often useful in analysis. For example, Linda J. Clifton tells of her success in having her students compare the Simon and Garfunkel song "Richard Cory" with E. A. Robinson's poem.[24]

For further clarification of the matter of studying the architecture of a poem, in the second stage of the process just described, several aspects of "The Rime of the Ancient Mariner" may be briefly considered.

In the first place, the basic verse form used by Coleridge is the ballad stanza. For this poem, the ballad stanza is appropriate because the subject matter is akin to that of the Middle English ballads, which often stressed the supernatural. (It is probable that this stanza was widely used in late medieval times because it is versatile

[23] London: Cambridge University Press, 1921.
[24] "The Two Corys: A Sample of Inductive Teaching," *English Journal,* March, 1969.

and because it is an easy form to compose, to learn, and to sing.) Sometimes, though, Coleridge departed from the pattern and included stanzas of five, six, or more lines. The reason is that the longer stanzas prevent the monotony that might result from constant employment of the ballad stanza in a lengthy poem.

The archaic diction of Coleridge's poem also contributes to the total effect. The ship leaves an unnamed country; the story takes place at an indefinite, unknown time. The language, therefore, should not suggest the here and now, but instead a vague "there" and an indefinite "then." Words like *stoppeth, eftsoons, swound,* and *grammercy* remove the poem from 1798 and carry the reader backward two centuries, three centuries, or more.

The frequent repetition is deliberate and appropriate. You recall that when the ship was becalmed,

> There passed a weary time. Each throat
> Was parched, and glazed each eye.
> A weary time! a weary time!
> How glazed each weary eye.

Coleridge wanted to stress the weariness. How could it be better stressed than by repeating the word *weary*? Or how could the Mariner's loneliness be better emphasized than in

> Alone, alone, all, all alone,
> Alone on a wide wide sea!

Coleridge used alliteration for an equally specific purpose. As the south wind pushed the ship rapidly along,

> The fair breeze blew, the white foam flew,
> The furrow followed free.

The alliteration is more than "pretty"; it serves to hasten the line, to accentuate the speed of the ship. Consonantal alliteration often does this, whereas vocalic alliteration (as in "Alone, alone, all, all alone") tends to make a line move more slowly.

Personification—the sun as *he*, the moon as *she*, the storm blast as *tyrannous*, Death and Life-in-Death, the articulate spirits of the sea, etc.—is more appropriate in this poem than in most. The setting is a vague period reminiscent of the Dark Ages, when many people believed that the physical forces of the world were conscious beings, often hostile to man. Moreover, it is human nature to employ a sort of reverse empathy and transfer our feelings to inanimate things; without thinking, we employ figurative expressions like "biting wind," "cruel sea," and "relentless sun." Shipwrecked men have been known to curse the sea as if it had plotted against them; travelers on a desert have looked upon the sun as a personal and implacable enemy. Coleridge's use of personification, then, is intrinsic in the situation he describes.

The similes and metaphors serve to clarify, to picture, to make the unreal seem real. "Mast-high" and "as green as emerald" show us the ice; the seamen's hailing of the albatross "as if it had been a Christian soul" demonstrates how happy the men were to see any living thing but suggests also the mysterious power of the albatross and the cruelty of killing it; "as idle as a painted ship upon a painted ocean" dramatizes the ship's complete lack of movement. Hardly can a more ghastly picture than that of Life-in-Death be imagined; yet the picture is composed largely of figures of speech:

> Her lips were red, her looks were free,
> Her locks were yellow as gold:
> Her skin was white as leprosy,
> The Night-mare Life-in-Death was she,
> Who thicks man's blood with cold.

In teaching "The Ancient Mariner," then, or any other poem in which it seems desirable to refer to poetic devices, it is desirable to help the students to understand the appropriateness of the meter, the diction, and the figures. Sometimes it is wise to talk about the organization of the whole poem, how each part fits, why each part is where it is. If students can be led to regard a poem as a unit to which each part contributes, their appreciation will be considerably increased.

In an extraordinarily useful article,[25] Howard Creed says, "The framework is significant: the guest, next of kin to the bridegroom, is on his way to celebrate a ceremony that fuses two people into one; but he is stopped to be taught that there is a more universal unity than that of an isolated marriage, that all the world is one." In discussing imagery, Creed states,

I see no reason why an alert class, after being reminded that the Romantic imagination works best by moonlight, shouldn't be able to discover for itself which events in the poem happen under the moon, which under the sun, and whether or not any particular pattern of moon-sun imagery seems to be used. A simpler analysis, and one easily fitted into the fusion of the natural and the supernatural, can be made of the sequence of the vivid images as the voyage

25 "'The Rime of the Ancient Mariner': A Rereading," *English Journal*, XLIX (Jan., 1960), 215.

progresses: the natural images of the harbour (kirk, hill, lighthouse) giving way to the supernatural images of the polar sea (the skeleton ship, for instance) and then returning (lighthouse, hill, kirk).

Perhaps no two teachers would agree exactly concerning which technical terms ought to be introduced during the study of poetry. It would seem, though, that any technical term that is innate to the poem being discussed is appropriate, but that no term should be dragged in simply because the teacher happens to know it. Further, it seems reasonable to assume that a simile or an anapaestic foot is of no importance in itself, but attains significance only because of the part it plays in the structure of the poem.

In other words, no teacher should do what one teacher actually did: She could never remember the distinction between metonymy and synecdoche, but knew that both are figures of speech. Therefore, once each year she relearned their definitions and required her class to memorize them!

The analytical approach (which could as well be named the synthesizing approach) has merit when it is used to help students understand clearly how a poem is constructed, what function each constituent part performs. But, if it becomes merely a process of disassembly, it is almost valueless. As a participant in the Dartmouth Conference said, "The dryness of schematic analysis of imagery, symbols, myth, structural relation *et al.* should be avoided passionately at school and often at college. It is literature, not literary criticism, which is the subject. It is vividly plain that it is much easier to teach literary criticism than to teach literature, just as it is much easier to teach children to write according to abstract models of correctness than it is to teach them to use their own voices." [26]

NON-FICTION

No extended discussion of the use of the six approaches with non-fiction is necessary; the teacher need only observe the principles already illustrated in considering fiction, drama, and poetry. Biographies clearly lend themselves to the historical approach, as do certain essays such as the *Tatler* and *Spectator* papers. Steele and Addison also provide splendid material for the sociopsychological approach, since they, along with Goldsmith, humanize the eight-

[26] Quoted in John Dixon, *Growth Through English*, p. 60.

eenth century perhaps more than do any other writers. Elsie E. Ringler uses the sociopsychological approach in a unique way: Four students serve as Thoreau's "mediums," answering class questions about application of his ideas to modern questions, such as "Would you support the Hippie movement?" or "Don't you consider love between a man and woman, marriage, and children essential for a fulfilled life?" The panel bolsters its answers with relevant quotations from *Walden* or "Civil Disobedience."[27] Essays such as the perennial favorite, Lamb's "Dissertation upon Roast Pig," and travel accounts such as Stevenson's *Travels with a Donkey* or some of Harry Franck's *Vagabonding* stories lend themselves to the emotive approach. Almost any personal essay or biography may justify occasional use of the didactic approach. Francis Bacon, Benjamin Franklin, and possibly Thomas Huxley and a few others whose writings are sometimes taught in high school need to have their essays partially paraphrased before students can do much else with them. The analytical approach may be employed in the comparison of styles and techniques of various non-fiction writers; the personal essay, for example, may be used to demonstrate that the typical pattern is the reporting of observation and then the reporting of speculation upon what was observed.

The examples mentioned are all classics or near classics. For several reasons it is desirable to expose students to a number of these works of unquestioned merit. In the first place, the classics often have historical significance and thus help us to understand ourselves by clarifying our backgrounds. Second, they usually possess high literary merit. Third (to adduce an old argument), everyone should have an opportunity to share knowledge of our common cultural heritage—to know something about the best that has been thought and said. Fourth, superior students, at least, may use the classics as Matthew Arnold advised: as "touchstones" by means of which other pieces of writing may be judged.

But it is true that the non-fiction diet should not consist exclusively of classics. Teachers have the responsibility of paving the way for the reading their students will do as adults. A classroom contact with Bacon and Addison may influence youthful tastes somewhat, but as adults their chief non-fiction reading will probably be today's newspaper, this week's news magazine, and this

[27] "Thoreau: The Medium and His Message," *English Journal*, LVII (Nov., 1968), 1138.

month's digest or other popular magazine—not Bacon's essays or the *Spectator.*

Newspapers vary widely; some are ultrasensational, others ultra-conservative, and the majority in between. Some are much more likely than others to contribute to the good of humanity. We may or may not agree precisely on the dividing line between good and bad periodicals, but the places where we draw our respective lines will probably not be far apart. Our students, however, may not have that critical knowledge unless we instill it in them. Because adults—somebody's former students—do not know or do not care, the sensationalizing newspapers and the most lurid of the cheap magazines flourish.

A partial solution is the teaching of a unit on newspapers and another unit, perhaps in a different year, on magazines. For this the sophomore and junior years appear most satisfactory, because the students on these levels are better able to read a large variety of materials and judge them with more discrimination than are their younger brothers and sisters. Some teachers, though, have successfully taught such units in the junior high school.[28]

The usual procedure is to provide a number of newspapers or magazines, varying in quality from worst to best. By reading and by making detailed comparisons, students learn the strengths and the weaknesses of the various periodicals. No teacher can expect to convert an entire class to a sincere love of *The New York Times* and *Harper's,* but he can expect to bring each student to a place somewhat above his original level. And, if a student comes to a clear realization that in an inferior newspaper he pays for distortion of facts, emphasis upon the trivial, and omission of significant news, he is more likely when he becomes an adult to purchase a fairly good newspaper. Likewise, the student who by his own comparison has convinced himself that the lurid magazines are repetitious and in-accurate is likely to buy something a little better at the newsstand.

In one unit of this sort, the teacher asked each student to bring to class his favorite newspaper. The class discussed the points that they believed intelligent people ought to know about newspapers and made notes of the "Canons of Journalism" as named in Edgar Dale's *How To Read a Newspaper:* responsibility, freedom of the press, independence, sincerity, truthfulness, accuracy, impartiality, fair play, and decency. The students evaluated the various news-

[28] Newspaper and magazine articles may often add enrichment to any unit, of course.

papers in the light of these canons, and compared them with *The New York Times* and *Christian Science Monitor*. They noted and deplored the dearth of "pitchers" and "jokes" and sports news in the latter two but were impressed by the number of important national and international news stories that were omitted from the papers they usually read. The teacher says that, although she has no proof that any of the students became confirmed in wise newspaper reading habits, she does know that they began to have a new conception of the meaning of a newspaper, and to consider newspapers critically.

Roberta Monteith recommends these objectives for newspaper study: (1) To show how language can be used to sway people. (2) To gain an understanding of the scope of a newspaper. (3) To learn to compare the treatment of news. (4) To become aware of slanted news. (5) To differentiate between lurid, limited, objective, and general news. (6) To judge the logic of editorials. (7) To read newspapers that have national recognition. (8) To interest students in reading some newspapers daily.[29]

A magazine unit may be handled in a similar manner. An ingenious variation, which brought satisfactory results when an Illinois teacher tried it with a group of sophomores, involves emphasis upon the advertising. Students are shown that most magazines are simply media for advertisers and that each advertiser aims at what he believes to be the mental level and the interests of the readers. Nothing more clearly demonstrates the low caliber of some magazines than their advertisements; just as a man is known by the company he keeps, so a magazine is known by the advertisements it keeps. These sophomores quickly saw how gullible people would be who would believe that they could "have a physique like mine in 90 days," "learn to throw your voice into a trunk," "play the piano in one month," "get a high school education in three months," "solve this easy puzzle and win $1,000." Since the sophomores did not want to be classified on such a low mental level, they agreed that these magazines were not for them.

Some teachers have planned units on travel books and modern biography, as parallels to units on newspapers and magazines. "Round-the-world trips," with each student responsible for one of the countries on the itinerary, have proved popular, as have units on "The Lands of Our Ancestors," "Europe Today," "Europe Yesterday," "Flying Carpets," "From Here to There in Fourteen Days," etc. A

[29] "Newspapers Aid in Teaching Logical Thinking," *English Journal*, LV (March, 1966), 348.

Missouri class studied biographies of nineteenth- and twentieth-century personages; separate committees specialized on scientists, statemen, etc.; each student prepared an interesting report on some one person; there was a "Guess Who" program with five carefully prepared clues concerning each biographee; radio skits were presented to dramatize highlights; and the class tried to find concerning these great men and women "the source of their dynamic living" and "what they have discovered about life."

Some teachers, interested in a didactic approach, employ biographies in hopes that students may absorb moral values. Thus Lois Taylor says that she emphasizes questions like these: "What qualities have these people that make their lives remarkable? In what ways did they go along with the pattern of life set by their society? In what ways did they break away? Were they just different, or did they actually and actively oppose the society in which they lived? What difficulties and discouragements did they surmount? What goals did they set and how did they achieve them or change them? What standards do they reveal in their relationships to others?" [30]

In many schools today the Bible is being studied as a literary document. The Indiana University Curriculum Study Center has developed a useful small book, *On Teaching the Bible as Literature*, edited for Indiana University Press in 1967 by James S. Ackerman and Jane Stouder Hawley, which provides historical background for the teacher, specific guidelines for teaching various biblical narratives, and an annotated bibliography.

The brevity of this treatment of non-fiction should not suggest that essays, travel books, biographies, and other non-fictional materials ought to be slighted. They deserve a fairly large proportion of the class time because they are informative and stimulating and may possess high literary value. Only a few pages are here devoted to them, because the techniques of teaching them are essentially the same as those for other types of literature.

THE IDEA BOX

Anti-Vivisection

"I spent an afternoon helping a student who marveled at Kahlil Gibran to see how it was that the poet achieved his effects. At the time, I

[30] *Reading Improvement*, Spring, 1965.

believed I was being helpful; now the student no longer marvels at Gibran, no longer enjoys the sound, the imagery, the pleasant leaps of imagination Gibran once meant to him." James A. Mecklenburger, "The Poetry Pickle," *English Journal*, LIX (Feb., 1970), 263.

"Who Killed Poetry?"

Mark Neville says that excessive emphasis on metrics and on prosodic (or prosaic!) analysis has given many students a distaste for poetry. The remedy: "Enjoyment, admiration, and sympathy are the stuff of appreciation." *English Journal*, XLVII (March, 1958) 133.

What Is Poetry?

Erwin Steinberg suggests that students may decide inductively that poetry often has rhyme (well integrated with rhythm), rhythm appropriate to the subject, and frequent, compact, and specific images. He uses Countee Cullen's "Heritage" as an example. "Toward a Definition of Poetry," *English Journal*, LVI (Sept., 1967), 834.

Poems for Pleasure

Herman Ward of Trenton State College believes that teachers make poetry laborious instead of fun. To counteract this tendency he has published an anthology called *Poems for Pleasure*. Whether you use this book or another, the principle is a sound one. Robert C. Pooley, in a speech in 1968, echoed the principle, saying that we need a "pleasure-meter" for literature.

Stating Themes

A comparison of two or more statements of the theme of a work may lead to understanding. One statement is accurate; the others, flawed. For example, for Browning's "My Last Duchess": "Fra Pandolf captured the grace and beauty of my last Duchess; although I regret her death, I shall now be honored to have the Count's daughter marry me." "My last Duchess showed too little respect for me and was not formal enough with others; now, if the dowry is sufficient, I shall honor the Count's daughter with my hand."

Understanding Metaphor

If you say "He has two strikes against him" when you are not talking about baseball, or when you call a person a skunk, you are using metaphors and symbols in essentially the way that a poet does. Building on this idea, with several sports and several animals, Edward T. Hubert shows his students that they themselves use metaphors frequently. "On the Teaching of Poetry," *English Journal,* LIV (April, 1965), p. 334.

"Poetry: Denotation and Connotation"

"[The poet] cannot possibly reckon on the reactions his words may evoke from readers whose experiences go beyond his own. When this happens, when a reader applies the language of the poet to his own sense of life, he makes the poem his own. It no longer belongs to the poet alone." D. Bruce Lockerbie, *English Journal,* LIII (Dec., 1964), 691.

Coleridge's Plan

Some teachers use Coleridge's critical plan of finding the author's purpose, noting the methods used to achieve that purpose, and judging the success.

Pictures in Poetry

Read to your junior high school students a short descriptive poem, and ask them to draw something that they "see" in it. If some of them say that they can't draw, let them write a word picture.

Providing Added Examples

Students' understanding of some poems may be enhanced if they add other examples to those chosen by the poet. For instance, in "Each and All" Emerson says that the sparrow, the sea shells, and the girl became less attractive when removed from their natural surroundings. What other examples might he have used?

Poets Struggle for Definitions

Often poets attempt to sharpen our awareness of a word's meaning. Students may study some poems from this point of view. E.g., how do Donne, Wordsworth, Millay, and Ransom define death differently? Students may also attempt their own metaphoric definitions. For details, see Harvey S. Wiener, "Poetry for Creative Definitions," *English Journal,* LVI (Sept., 1967), 845.

Teaching Imagery

The haiku is an excellent way to teach imagery, because the haiku almost always is basically an image. Phyllis Rose Thompson elaborates in "The 'Haiku Question' and the Reading of Images," *English Journal*, LVI (April, 1967), 547.

Do You Write Poetry?

If you do, do you dare submit one of your poems for your students' criticism? What can they learn about poetry from your struggles to find the perfect image, the precise word? Edward G. Eberhard describes his procedure in "An Upside-Down Thing," *English Journal*, LVIII (Nov., 1969), 1192.

Teaching Poetry with a Computer

Arthur Daigon, in "Pictures, Punchcards, and Poetry," describes how "The Man He Killed" could be taught by a computer, using pictures and thought-questions, and making an assignment at the end. It's a good lesson, but there's no reason why a teacher couldn't do as well as the machine. *English Journal*, LVIII (Oct., 1969), 1033.

Do You Know a Young Poet?

The Poetry Center at San Francisco State College brings in published youngs poets to talk with classes. Students ask questions like "Why did you write that line?" "Does poetry mean anything else besides just poetry?" If you know of a young poet, your own class might like to meet him, say John W. Marlowe and Francisc J. Hosman. "If Someone Can Begin," *English Journal*, LVII (Feb., 1968), 206.

"Hearing Poetry"

An excellent poem for teaching the relationship between sound and sense is W. S. Merwin's "Leviathan," says Paul H. Wild. *English Journal*, LVI (Oct., 1967), 954.

Poetry Set to Music

Robert E. Morgan offers a short list of recordings of English poetry of various centuries, set to music in the modern manner. "More Avant-Rock in the Classroom," *English Journal*, LIX (Nov., 1969), 1238.

Folk Songs and Ballads

In "An Approach to Poetry," Frederick E. Danker describes his use in a sophomore class of his compilation of eighty pages of American folk songs and ballads. Advantages of this type of verse: strong rhymes and rhythms, dialog, simple stanza forms, and concentration. *English Journal*, L (April, 1961), 274.

If You Don't Like Electric Guitars

Some modern songs are rich in metaphor. Read the lyrics (even if you may not like the music). "Cultural anxieties that may preclude caring for electric guitars should not keep us from making reasonable critical judgments about the imagery of, say, Dylan's 'Mr. Tambourine Man' or the Beatles' 'Lonely People.'" Paul D. McGlynn, *MLA Newsletter* (Oct., 1969).

More on Poetry and Music

Good culminating activity for poetry unit [handwritten annotation]

Students love this [handwritten annotation in margin]

1. You might devote an hour to a ballad party, with phonograph records, class singing, and possibly the presentation of an original ballad or two.

2. Anna Haig, Bronxville, New York, recommends having students find music and a painting that express the same mood as some poem. The student names the mood, describes the painting brieflly, copies a few bars of the music, and quotes from the poem. In Cheraw, South Carolina, students keep a "poetry-picture" scrapbook, with appropriate pictures to accompany poems or excerpts from poems.

3. "I use the theory that the first poetry was sung and that great poetry has the same elements as great music. I show how poetry is set to music and what patterns of rhythm are most readily adapted to music. I show how parodies are written. I read 'Boots' by Kipling to show the accented syllables. I read a few lines that I have written." (Elizabeth B. Barton, Clanton, Ala.)

4. Harold P. Simonson, in Puyallup, Washington, spends a week playing records and reading related poetry. Some of his pairings include Tschaikovsky's "None but the Lonely Heart" with Wilde's "Requiescat," Debussy's *"La Mer"* with Byron's apostrophe to the ocean in *Childe Harold*, Debussy's "Clair de Lune" with De la Mare's "Silver," Grofé's "Sunrise" from the *Grand Canyon Suite* and Grieg's "Sunrise" from *Peer Gynt* with Dickinson's "I'll Tell You How the Sun Rose" and G. B. Hoover's "Mountain Dawn." See "Music as an Approach to Poetry," *English Journal*, XLIII (Jan., 1954), 19.

6. Use a drum in the classroom to show the beat in "The Congo" and others poems with a marked rhythm. (Marguerite Chamberlain, Franklin, N.H.)

From Songs to Poetry

One way to introduce poetry to junior high students is to start with the lyrics of songs they like and bring to class. They talk about what they enjoy in these songs and then search for similar qualities in poems. For further suggestions, see "On Teaching Poetry," by Rachael N. Perkins, *English Journal*, LV (Jan., 1966), 91.

The First Poem

In any unit containing a number of poems, it is especially important that the first poem be one that will interest and stimulate the class. This first happy experience will make discussion of the later poems easier and more satisfying.

Sandburg As a Door Opener

Though Carl Sandburg is not dramatic or philosophical or even lyric, his non-conformity appeals to the eternal—and inevitable and desirable —rebelliousness of youth and, hence, makes him a door opener to poetry. Michael Yatron, "Carl Sandburg: The Poet as Non-conformist," *English Journal*, XLVIII (Dec., 1959), 524.

A Junior High Discovers Poetry

Eric W. Johnson's junior high students, in Germantown Friends School, arrive at these characteristics of poetry: "(1) rhyme (not always) (2) rhythm (almost always)—meter (3) form—verses; rhyme and meter a part of form (4) emotion—expresses feeling usually (5) concentration—says a lot in a few words (6) figurative language—comparison." Mr. Johnson finds Robert Nathan's "Dunkirk" a good opener, follows it with W. R. Benét's "Skater of Ghost Lake," then a group of poems with students assigned to discuss meaning, form, sound, feelings created, and memorable lines. Students also write limericks, couplets, and a poem each, and learn principles of oral reading. *English Journal*, L (Nov., 1961), 546.

"Poetry for Ninth-Graders"

August Franza and his ninth graders asked these basic questions about poems studied: "First of all, what is the 'sense' of a poem? What does the poem say? What does it tell us about? Secondly, what is the 'feeling' of the poem? What moods and emotions are conveyed to the reader? Thirdly, what is the 'theme' of the poem (if one can be determined)? What ideas is the author trying to get across? What is the significance of his poem? Finally, what is the 'form' of the poem? . . . Then we asked general questions. Does the poem make us aware of something we did not know before? Does it make us 'see' more clearly commonplace things we have taken for granted? Does it help us understand the complexities of human behavior? Has it introduced a new thought, idea, or vision we have never before considered?" *English Journal,* XLVII (Dec., 1958), 575.

Students and Romantics: The Common Bond

William E. Lucas, De Kalb, Illinois, emphasizes what the romantic poets and high school students have in common: a rebellious spirit, idealism, susceptibility to religious and philosophical influences, and interest in the natural world.

Which Moderns?

Sister M. Bernetta Quinn, O.S.F., recommends selected poems by these poets as especially suitable for reading by able high school students: Frost, Eliot, Yeats, Cummings, Sandburg, W. C. Williams, H. Crane, W. Stevens, Jarrell, Nims, Larkin, Thomas, Spender, Auden. "Modern Poetry and the Classroom," *English Journal,* L (Dec., 1961), 590.

"Introducing Homer's *Odyssey* in High School"

Enid Olson describes these materials and methods used with the *Odyssey:* Tennyson's "Ulysses"; a student map of the eastern Mediterranean; individual reports on the *Iliad* and the Trojan War; guest lecture by a teacher who has visited the Mediterranean; committee reports on the people and the mythology of ancient Greece; filmstrips of Athens and of the story of Ulysses; much reading aloud from the story. *Illinois English Bulletin* (Nov., 1957).

Uses of Literary Recordings

1. Occasionally play the recording of a poem or a part of a play before the class reads it, especially for a "mood piece," in which emotion or mood should be understood from the beginning.

2. Sometimes students may read silently, following the text while the record plays. Thus eye and ear reinforce each other.

3. Oral reading by the class, in unison with the record, is good for descriptive or mood poetry.

4. Often study should precede the playing. As the class listens, it may watch for the reader's interpretation of particular passages to discover previously unsuspected meanings or to help settle possibly controversial points.

5. Sometimes a record should be played for sheer enjoyment, without class study of the selection. "Easy" verse or brief dramatic selections are particularly suitable. Seasonal poetry is often appropriate.

6. "Sing-along sessions" (especially ballads and folk songs) are good fun.

7. Musical recordings related to literature (e.g., Tschaikovsky's "Overture" to *Romeo and Juliet*) may help to show links between two arts. Some historical records also provide good background (e.g., "The London Story: A Sound Portrait of London through the Ages," London LL839, with scenes from the time of Elizabeth I, the Great Fire of 1666, the Age of Victoria, the Blitz of 1940, voices of Churchill and Elizabeth II, etc.).

8. Caution: Always listen to a record before playing it for a class. Some ostensibly suitable selections may prove undesirable because of the quality of the recording, faulty interpretation, or excessive frankness of language.

Which Did the Poet Write?

To help students observe a poet's careful choice of words and the probable reasons for his choices, Robert L. Stevens of Northern Arizona University suggests giving a class slightly garbled lines of a poem along with the original. If the lines are intermixed, as in the passage from Pope's "Essay on Criticism" below, students can decide which lines are the author's:

True ease in writing comes from learning, not chance
As those move best who have learned to dance.
'Tis not enough no harshness gives offense,
The sound must seem an echo of the sense:
Mild is the mood when Zephyr lightly blows,
And the smooth stream in smoother numbers flows;
But when loud surges lave the sounding shore,
The hoarse, rough verse should like the torrent roar;
When Ajax strives some rock's vast weight to throw,
The line too labours, and the words move slow.

True ease in writing comes from art, not chance
As those move easiest who have learned to dance.
'Tis not enough that no harshness gives offense,
The sound must seem a mirror of the sense:
Soft is the strain when Zephyr gently blows,
And the smooth stream in matching meter flows;
But when loud surges lash the sounding shore,
The howling verse should like the torrent roar;
When Ajax tries some heavy rock to throw,
The rhythm alters, and the words move slow.

Problems in meter, diction, auditory appeal, alliteration, context, and total effect may be discussed through these few lines. (Pope wrote lines 3, 4, 6, 8, 9, 10 in the first column, and lines 1, 2, 5, 7 in the second.)

Meter

If you want to teach names of metrical feet, use names of your students to illustrate (e.g., iamb, Laverne; trochee, Wilbur; dactyl, Dorothy; anapaest, Antoinette; amphibrach, Louisa).

On the Uses of Bad Poetry

Harvey Firari uses verses by Edgar A. Guest, by a local rhymester, and by himself in introducing poetry to his Culver, Indiana, classes of boys. Finding the flaws (while the teacher mildly defends these "poems") makes the boys more ready to applaud the truly poetic they encounter in better writers. *English Journal*, XLVIII (May, 1959), 262.

Chaucer in Modern Dress

In addition to writing parodies of parts of the "Prologue" to the *Canterbury Tales*, with modern characters replacing Chaucer's, students may enjoy preparing modern versions of some of the tales. For example, "The Pardoner's Tale" is the story of three hoodlums who hijack a liquor truck and, when each attempts to secure the profits for himself, all three are killed.

Poems About the City

A good collection of poems about the city has been compiled by Nancy Larrick: *On City Streets: An Anthology of Poetry* (published by M. Evans and Co., Inc.).

Alliteration in Old English Poetry

To show their understanding of alliteration in Old English poetry, students at Bay City, Mich., parody more recent poets, showing how those poets might have written a thousand years ago. E.g., for Emily Dickinson:

> The sky is somber, the clouds severe;
> An infant flake of newformed snow
> Blows 'cross a barn or barren field
> Debating its descent this autumn day.

Poetic Structure Via the Overhead Projector

Robert S. Moore teaches the structure of a sonnet by using a series of transparencies. The first depicts the limitation of space, the second the fourteen lines, the third the iambic pentameter rhythm, the fourth the rhyme scheme, and the fifth the sonnet itself. The procedure might also be useful for other verse forms. "A Wedge Toward Willingness," *English Journal*, LVI (Feb., 1967), 293.

"On Reading *Paradise Lost* in High School"

If the teacher plans carefully and encourages varying activities, *Paradise Lost* may be taught successfully to superior high school seniors, claims Nancy M. Cooper of Palo Alto. Book I requires intensive study "to obviate an initial impasse with the verse." Other books are read less intensively, and some portions are skipped. *English Journal*, LV (March, 1966), 320.

"Substitution in the Teaching of Poetry"

Get the class to talking about the change of effect if a poet had expressed a line differently. E.g., suppose that Sandburg had written "The fog comes/on little dog feet" or "The fog appears" or "The stealthy fog comes/ on the velvet feet of a cat." Milton A. Kaplan, *English Journal*, LVI (Sept., 1967), 842.

Showing Why Form Is Important

Marjorie Elvove wrote a limerick about the death of a boy in a mine. The class quickly grasped the inappropriateness of the form for such a subject. In her "Teaching How a Poem Means," Miss Elvove also discusses form in E. E. Cummings. *English Journal*, LVI (Dec., 1967), 1290.

"Questions That Have No Answers"

Although there may be "wrong" answers about what a poem "means," "there is no single [right] answer." Often poems, through their intentional ambiguity, mean only that "there is no single answer to the mystery of life and movement." So argues Dorothy Petitt, *English Journal*, LIV (May, 1965), 382.

Teaching "Kubla Khan"?

You may want to read Richard M. Rothman's "A Re-examination of 'Kubla Khan,'" *English Journal*, LV (Feb., 1966), 169.

"The Eve of St. Agnes"

C. F. Burgess tells how he coordinates technique, structure, and theme by emphasizing the contrasts Keats uses: youth and age, love and hate, the spirit and the flesh, chill and warmth, the real and the unreal. *English Journal*, LIV (May, 1965), 889.

"Longfellow and the Modern Reader"

Despite the prevalent modern attitude that Longfellow is an inferior poet, Richard Ruland of Yale argues that much of his work is worth teaching, especially "The Courtship of Miles Standish," "Paul Revere's Ride," and some of the sonnets. *English Journal*, LV (Sept., 1966), 661.

T. S. Eliot on Teaching the Moderns

In "The Appreciation of Poetry" T. S. Eliot warned against excessive analysis of modern poetry and against examinations based on such poetry. He suggested, though, that students may listen twice to a recorded poem and then write their interpretation of it and about the feelings or impressions it left with them. *The Critic*, XVIII (April–May, 1960) 78.

"Values and the Poems of Marianne Moore"

Students write their beliefs about truth, love, courage, duty, independence, etc., and then compare their attitudes with those of Marianne Moore. Constance H. Edsall illustrates this use of the didactic approach. *English Journal*, LVIII (April, 1964), 516.

Is Frost Too Simple?

There are depths in Robert Frost's poetry that students can learn to penetrate, and simultaneously they can learn to find their way beneath the surface of other "easy" poems. Charles R. Hands illustrates with "For Once, Then, Something," "Stopping by Woods," "The Runaway," and "Desert Places." "The Hidden Terror of Robert Frost," *English Journal*, LVIII (Nov., 1969), 1162. "The Wood-Pile" is explicated by Robert Narveson, *English Journal*, LVII (Jan., 1968), 39.

"A Man Named Robert Frost"

Your class may enjoy reading this warm personal account by a man who several times met one of America's greatest poets. Harry L. Walen, *English Journal*, LV (Oct., 1966), 860.

Analysis of "Fern Hill"

Mary C. Davidow analyzes the imagery of Dylan Thomas' "Fern Hill" and suggests discussion questions. "Journey from Apple Orchard . . . ," *English Journal*, LVIII (Jan., 1969), 78. Another article on the same poem: "How Green Is 'Fern Hill'?" by Jack L. Jenkins, *English Journal*, LV (Dec., 1965), 1180.

Archy to the Rescue

Don Marquis's literary cockroach, archy, may clarify for a class what a poet is like. After all, cockroaches have a 200,000,000 year view of history, and poets tend too toward long-range views. An archy-enthusiast is Mary-Jo Powell of Edmonton, Alberta, author of "War on Poetry-phobia," *English Journal*, LV (Oct., 1966), 887.

Ferlinghetti for High Schools!?

Poetry doesn't have to be "pretty." Brother Russell O'Neill, S.M., found that the frank, rough poetry of social protest aroused intense reactions among the boys in his junior classes. "A Fling with Ferlinghetti," *English Journal*, LVIII (Oct., 1969), 1025.

Helps in Teaching Specific Poets

These articles (in the *English Journal* except where the designation *CE,* for *College English,* appears) provide insights useful in teaching some major poets:

Matthew Arnold. Friedrich, Gerhard, "A Teaching Approach to Poetry," XLIX (Feb., 1960), 75. (Especially on "Dover Beach.")
William Blake. Gleckner, Robert, "'The Lamb' and 'The Tyger': How Far with Blake?" LI (Nov., 1962), 536.
Robert Burns. Fisher, Mary C., "Ayr Lines, Ceiling Unlimited," XLIX (Jan., 1960), 39.
John Ciardi. Southworth, J. G., "The Poetry of John Ciardi," L (Dec., 1961), 583.
S. T. Coleridge. Owen, C. A., Jr., "Structure in 'The Ancient Mariner,'" CE, XXIII (Jan., 1962), 261.
E. E. Cummings. Mills, Ralph J., Jr., "Poetry of Innocence," XLVIII (Nov., 1959), 433; and Ray, David, "The Irony of E. E. Cummings," CE, XXIII (Jan., 1962), 282.
T. S. Eliot. Smith, Grover, Jr., "Getting Used to T. S. Eliot," XLIX (Jan., 1960), 1.
Robert Frost. Cook, R. L., "The Stand of Robert Frost, Early and Late," XLVIII (May, 1959), 233.
John Keats. Slote, Bernice, "Of Chapman's Homer and Other Books," CE, XXIII (Jan., 1962), 256.
Karl Shapiro. Southworth, J. G., "The Poetry of Karl Shapiro," LI (March, 1962), 159.

Wallace Stevens.   Doggett, Frank, "Wallace Stevens and the World We Know," XLVIII (Oct., 1959), 365.

Analyses of Specific Poems

Over a period of time the NCTE Committee on the Reading and Study of Poetry in the High School published in the *English Journal* analyses and teaching suggestions for a number of poems, recent as well as old. You may find the articles on the following poems helpful.

Arnold, Matthew, "Dover Beach." LIV (May, 1965), 446.
Auden, W. H., "O What Is That Sound?" LI (Dec., 1962), 656.
Bishop, Elizabeth, "Jeronimo's Horse." LII (March, 1963), 221.
Cummings, E. E., "what if a much of a which of a wind." LV (March, 1966), 352.
Eberhart, Richard, "The Groundhog." LII (April, 1963), 229.
Frost, Robert, "Carpe Diem." LIV (Feb., 1965), 135.
    "Neither Out Far Nor in Deep." LIII (March, 1969), 214.
    "Nothing Gold Can Stay" and "Stopping by Woods." LV (May, 1966), 621 and 624.
Gibson, W. W., "The Ice-Cart." LV (Jan., 1966), 98.
Hopkins, G. M., "God's Grandeur." LIII (April, 1964), 285.
    "Spring and Fall." LI (Nov., 1962), 584.
Jeffers, Robinson, "Hurt Hawks." LI (Sept., 1962), 439.
Johnson, James W., "The Creation." LII (Nov., 1963), 643.
Moore, Marianne, "The Monkeys." LII (Jan., 1963), 65.
Owen, Wilfred, "Disabled." LI (Oct., 1962), 494.
Shakespeare, William, Sonnet 90. LIII (Sept., 1964), 459.
Shapiro, Karl, "Auto Wreck." LIII (Nov., 1964), 630.
Stevens, Wallace, "The Poems of Our Climate." LIV (Nov., 1965), 762.
Swenson, May, "Cat and the Weather." LV (Feb., 1966), 221.
Thomas, Edward, "The Sign-Post." LIV (Sept., 1965), 568.
Wilbur, Richard, "The Juggler." LIV (Dec., 1965), 879.
    "To an American Poet Just Dead." LII (May, 1963), 376.
Yeats, W. B., "Red Hanrahan's Song about Ireland." LIV (May, 1965), 448.

Mythology in Modern Life

Mercury automobiles, Atlas tires, Jupiter and Thor missiles, Venus pencils, and the like may help students to see that remnants of Greek and Roman mythology still exist.

"Teaching the Analysis of Expository Prose"

Richard L. Larson of Hawaii believes that high school English should pay considerable attention to study of the sort of expository prose students are likely to encounter in college, in quality magazines, etc. He offers detailed suggestions for such teaching. *English Journal,* LVII (Nov., 1968), 1156.

To Build an Interest in Biography

1. Start with biographies of living men and women. Then pick comparable figures of the past.
2. Allow considerable freedom in the choice of biographies.
3. Let students compare problems faced by famous people with their own problems.
4. After discussing a number of biographies, help to straighten out chronology by playing the game "Who could have known whom?" For example, could Washington have known Lincoln?
5. Study famous friends (David and Jonathan, Damon and Pythias, Tennyson and Hallam, etc.).

"A Small Success with the Slow"

Betty Giltinan recommends the biographical *Cheaper by the Dozen* as a book for slow ninth-graders. *English Journal,* LVII (March, 1968), 402.

Friends From Non-Fiction

"At the beginning of the study of a nonfiction unit I like to gather all available books and turn the class loose. At first there is a tendency to change books frequently, but soon they settle to concentrated reading. Ten minutes of each period is used to exchange ideas from and enthusiasms for books. At the end of the wide reading time we make lists of new friends we've met through reading. Sometimes this résumé takes the form of one student's introducing a newly acquired friend-through-reading to the class as though the subject of the biography were to address the group." (Esther Urie, Hartford, Vt.)

Organization of Non-Fiction Articles

Nelly Doherty, Las Vegas, New Mexico, High School, gives her students outlines of difficult articles to be read by the class. This procedure helps their reading and also assists them to see the value of organization.

Why Not Try *Walden?*

In "*Walden,* Neglected American Classic," Leo A. Bressler argues that, because Thoreau was a rebellious spirit, he has built-in appeal for able young people. *English Journal,* LI (Jan., 1962), 14.

Satire

For lucid interpretations of the satire in *Gulliver's Travels* and the works of Dr. Bernard Mandeville, see two articles by James A. Preu: "The Case of the Mysterious Manuscript," *English Journal*, LII (Nov., 1963), 579; and "Private Vices—Public Benefits," *Ibid.* (Dec., 1963), 653.

Utopias A-Plenty

Paul Wild and his fellow teachers in Shaker Heights, Ohio, find a unit on utopias appealing to tenth-grade students. Included for basic reading are *Looking Backward, 1984, Brave New World,* with optional reading in such classical utopias as those of Plato, More, and Bacon, plus modern ones like those of James Hilton (*Lost Horizon*), William Morris (*News from Nowhere*), H. G. Wells (*A Modern Utopia*), and B. F. Skinner (*Walden Two*). "Teaching Utopia," *English Journal*, LV (March, 1966), 335.

"We Study the Bible as Literature"

In Massillon, Ohio, Bible study begins with a short overview on the origin and history of the Bible. Readings include the first four chapters of Genesis, the books of Ruth, Esther, and Job, selected Psalms and Proverbs, the Sermon on the Mount, and a few parables. Various translations are used. R. Paul Hildebrand, *English Journal*, LV (Nov., 1966), 1022.

"This I Believe—About the Essay"

Jerome Carlin answers four objections to teaching the essay: It's dull. It's difficult. It's archaic. Its form is hard to analyze. He makes a convincing case for more teaching of essays. *English Journal*, LI (Sept., 1962), 403.

"Essay Study on a Single Theme"

Richard M. Keller recommends that students study a number of essays on a single theme, such as the Pocket Book *Great Essays in Science*. *English Journal*, LIII (Mar., 1964), 205.

In an Essay, What Keeps the Idea Aloft?

Montaigne defined an essay as a trial flight of an idea and of a mind. Don L. Cook recommends, after initial discussion of the idea, that a class discuss "What keeps it aloft? What prevents its descending into banality, dullness, or obscurity? What powers its flight and gives it buoyancy?" Such discussion not only develops initial sense but may help the student as writer. Edward B. Jenkinson and Jane S. Hawley, eds., *On Teaching Literature* (Indiana University Press, 1967), 150.

Orwell As Essayist

Kenneth Keskinen finds George Orwell's essays highly teachable. He tells why in "Shooting an Elephant: An Essay to Teach," *English Journal*, LV (Sept., 1966), 669.

Magazines

1. To arouse interest in magazine articles, some teachers ask their students to prepare signed bulletin-board lists of articles they recommend, with brief annotations. Individuals or groups may make a careful study of certain magazines. The teacher and members of the class may occasionally read aloud excerpts from articles they have especially liked.

2. Have students examine a number of magazines to determine which ones they would like to have later in their own homes.

3. In Greenwich, Connecticut, Hardy Finch's students learn to read magazine articles critically by (1) reading a controversial article and then having a panel find and present the arguments on the side not favored by the author, (2) examining the editorial policies of a magazine, (3) studying the author's competence to write authoritatively on the subject he has chosen.

4. Ruth Hughson's Princeton, West Virginia, sophomores spend about three weeks in reading digest-type articles, writing summaries of some they like, giving talks based on the articles, and (in connection with a study of punctuation) discovering that punctuation "rules" are really only generalizations summarizing how authors really punctuate.

5. Maybe magazines won't help students to cover the ground of a traditional English course, Edgar Dale says in *The News Letter* of Ohio State University, Nov., 1965, but they can help students to uncover new ground. Which is more important?

"The Ten-Cent Journalism Workbook"

Use copies of daily newspapers in studying journalistic techniques, Norman Crampton recommends. Among the exercises: Teacher scrambles the facts of a story and dictates them; students write the story and compare their versions with those in the paper. Or teacher poses as someone in the news; students interview him as a group of reporters might, and write the account. Or students compare a news story with an editorial on the same subject, or try to write better headlines than the professional ones. *English Journal,* LIV (Dec., 1965), 864.

Newspapers

1. Have students compare a newspaper such as *The New York Times, Christian Science Monitor,* or *St. Louis Post-Dispatch* with one of the scandal-sheet sort, answering such questions as: "What is emphasized in headlines and major news stories?" "Are stories biased?" "What do the editorials emphasize?" "What kinds of feature stories are included?" "Does the paper appeal more to emotions or to reason?" Criteria for judging newspapers should result.

2. A helpful book: Edgar Dale's *How To Read a Newspaper.*

"Five Dozen Ideas for Teaching the Newspaper Unit"

Howard F. Decker uses newspaper study to build vocabulary, improve reading ability, assist writing, and provide material for class discussion and special projects. His useful article is in *English Journal,* LIX (Feb., 1970), 288.

A Test on Newspaper Reading

The American Newspaper Publishers Association Foundation has assisted in developing a test of newspaper reading, which includes questions based on simulated newspapers. Available from Educational Testing Service, Princeton, N.J.

8

The Process of Composing

Underlying Theory

The use of language consists of employing increasingly complex sets of associations and differentiations. It is thus a reflection of the thought-process, or perhaps *is* the thought-process, which basically is composed of associating and differentiating.

Before the very young child learns his first word, he has begun learning to associate sounds with things. A tiny infant quickly realizes that crying often brings a desired action: Mama changes his diaper or feeds him. Unwittingly he may begin to alter his cry according to circumstances, and Mama comes to recognize a "hungry cry," "sleepy cry," "wet cry," "hurt cry," and so on. When he makes a cooing sound, he evokes a pleasant reaction, and he may coo again to have the reaction repeated. He learns to respond to his name, perhaps by smiling or by raising his arms. He may smile also when he hears his mother's or his father's gentle voice, and cry when they talk loudly or angrily. These preliminary associations and differentiations are essential to the learning of words.

The child's first word is usually "Mama" or some approximation. Among the oft-repeated sounds that babies make, there is likely to be a frequent "muh-muh-muh." This is not yet the "word" *Mama:* wordship is attained only when the child comes to associate the word

261

with the specific person. The mother often helps the process along. She repeats his "muh-muh-muh," says "Muh-muh is coming," "Here's Mama," "Mama loves you." When it is quite apparent that through his experiences the child has completed the link between the person and the sound, he has his first word, and the door to speech and writing is ajar.

Let us use T (meaning *Thing*) to stand for *mama, daddy, doggie, ball*—for each of the things in the child's world. To the child, probably every word he learns to use represents a T. Thus *go* represents the act of going, or *big* represents an observable physical quality. He learns such words as he learns *mama*, through experience that involves association and differentiation. In all, he may have a vocabulary of a hundred or two hundred or more words of various kinds—all representing "things" for him—before he begins putting two or more words together.

Now let us use E (meaning *Experience*) to stand for the child's experience with the T. Not until he has experiences with a ball will the word *ball* enter his vocabulary. The thing must not only exist but must exist in the child's world—be capable of being experienced through his vision, his touch, his hearing, his sense of taste, his sense of smell, or some combination of these.

Finally, let us use Sy (meaning *Symbol*) to mean the sound that the child uses to represent the T with which he has had E. This Sy has no physical relationship to the thing it names; it is only a set of sound waves arbitrarily chosen by users of a language long ago to stand for a given thing.

For every word, then, the child establishes a neural linkage that can be represented thus:

$$T \longleftrightarrow E \longleftrightarrow Sy$$

Mothers are quite right when they excitedly write Baby's first word in his Baby Book, because Baby has demonstrated mastery of a difficult relationship by means of which through his experience he can tie together a thing and the linguistic symbol for that thing.

While the child is making associations, he is also making differentiations. These, too, are part of his experience. At first all animals may be "doggies" and all motor vehicles "cars," but later he learns to narrow *doggie* and *car* to one kind of animal or vehicle, and to use as appropriate *cat, cow, pig, truck,* or *bus.*

On another day worthy of Baby Book recognition, the child combines words for the first time in a way recognizable by adults as a sentence. It's usually just two words, such as "Baw pwetty" or "Dah bweak" (Doll break). This act represents another huge step forward, which can be represented like this:

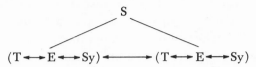

To say "Baw pwetty" the child must have had (1) enough experience with balls to recognize the object, (2) recognition that the sound of "baw" is the symbol of the thing he sees (and he of course must have the ability to utter the sound-combination), (3) enough experience with "prettiness" to be aware of that "thing," and (4) recognition that the sound of "pwetty" that he can make is its symbol. Further, and this is where the big step exists, he must realize in some dim way that ball and prettiness can be related to each other.

Three-component sentences come a little later: "Daddy bweak bwoon" (Daddy break balloon). Somewhat later still are four-component sentences like "Daddy give me candy," and possibly much later are four-component sentences of the type "Candy make me sticky." The three- and four-component sentences are obviously further steps up toward sentence maturity.

I'll not take the space to discuss in detail how some of the sentence refinements get in, such as determiners, the use of negatives, or the formation of questions. Most such refinements involve transformations that translate deep structure into surface structure. The development of the compound sentence, though, may be used to illustrate the increasing complexity of the child's language:

I saw a airplane, and it was great big. The number of T ↔ E ↔ Sy relationships has obviously grown substantially, but something else has happened, which can be represented in this way:

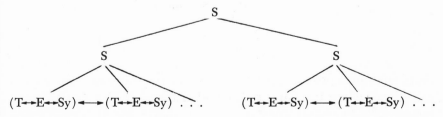

The child has now recognized an association between two sentences, which themselves comprise a number of associations. The child who can put together a sentence like the example is on his way toward making a speech, writing a school composition, or perhaps writing a novel.

Although the steps differ, the child quickly learns other types of sentence-combining besides the one just illustrated. "I see a tree" and "The tree is tall" he learns to combine as "I see a tall tree." "I heard a noise" and "The noise came from the basement" he combines as "I heard a noise from the basement." And so on.

The composing of a unit of discourse longer than a single sentence is a further elaboration of the same process. Say that a sentence represents an idea (e.g., a piece of information, a hypothesis, or a question). Then the idea expressed in the speaker's or writer's next sentence should be associated with the first one. The third should be associated with the second. So a series of sentences on a given topic can be represented by

$$S \longleftrightarrow S \longleftrightarrow S \qquad (\text{or } I[\text{idea}] \longleftrightarrow I \longleftrightarrow I)$$

In written discourse, ordinarily a few consecutive sentences, all bearing some relationship to one another, constitute a paragraph. The diagram looks like this:

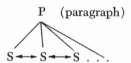

P   (paragraph)

One further step is putting together several paragraphs—the kind of exercise frequently required in secondary schools, and the kind of task imposed upon many adults who must prepare business or technical reports and the like. Consecutive paragraphs, like the consecutive sentences within a paragraph or the consecutive words within a sentence, must be associated with one another in accordance with some principle. Our now-familiar diagram reveals this:

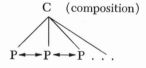

C   (composition)

This diagram represents one more step in the ladder of association that began when the child put T and E together and spoke the Sy "mama."

Learning to put together the parts of a speech, an essay, or a story, then, simply represents a building upon the basic linguistic process of association and differentiation. A sentence is a combination, in an order established by the language, of the symbols which through experience the child has learned to associate with things. A paragraph is a combination of sentences; this combination results from association and differentiation of the ideas represented by the individual sentences. And a longer composition is a combination of paragraphs associated with and differentiated from one another.

Translating Theory into Practice

Assuming the truth of the theory that has been presented, what are its implications for the teaching of composition? Here are some of them:

1. *Increasing experiences adds to the number of associations and differentiations that can be made.* The infant confined mainly to a single room and to the company of only one or two untalkative people is less likely to build a sizable vocabulary and form the associations requisite for sentences than is the infant with rich and varied experiences. Similarly the student with limited experiences is less likely to write content-rich compositions than is the one who in his living and in his observing and reading (which are vicarious forms of living) has ranged widely. The explanation is simple and obvious: if one student has twenty experiences upon which to draw and another has two hundred, the second has a much greater number of possible associations; or if (to choose more likely figures) the first student has ten thousand experiences and the second has a hundred thousand, the second can develop infinitely more than ten times the number of associations that the first can.

Robert Frost once said, "All there is to writing is having ideas." But ideas, as we have seen, are based upon the symbols drawn from experiences.

The implication for teaching is clear. School should be a place that will vastly enlarge the student's store of experience. One reason for the success of many British elementary schools is that the children are constantly doing things—a variety of things, including painting, hammering, dancing, molding, reading, writing, drawing, figuring, playing in sand, conversing, playing games, and much more. Other kids, who have to sit for hours in hard chairs and do nothing but work on textbook exercises and listen to a teacher and to each other, are cheated.

The English teacher in junior or senior high school will obviously not have his students playing in the sand, but he does have an opportunity to enrich their experiences constantly. "Read, write, and recite" has for too long been the accepted formula. Reading and writing are fine, but other roads to experience are also valuable. Conversing, pantomiming, improvising, and dramatizing are among the possibilities. So are viewing films and videotapes and filmstrips and television, planning and making films, making a collage, drawing or other art work, planning a program, doing choral reading, choreographing a poem or a playlet, taking field trips, seeing a stage play. . . . The list can go on and on.

The literature that students read can obviously broaden their experience. In each of the approaches to literature, discussed in earlier chapters, I have recommended putting things together—associating things. The historical approach puts together a selection and relevant background; the sociopsychological, a selection and human characteristics; the emotive, a selection and emotional reactions; the didactic, a selection and the author's purpose; the paraphrastic, a selection and other ways of expressing its ideas; the analytical, a selection and the author's techniques. I have not said "Memorize facts." I have not said, "Forget everything else you know, and look at this story as a discrete entity." Instead I have said "Associate. Compare. Contrast. Agree or disagree. Tell why. Reason. Think."

In teaching literature we ask students to consider the thoughts, emotions, and experiences of other people. In teaching composition we ask them to deal with their own thoughts, emotions, and experiences. Many or most of these, of course, are derivative, secondhand; but they in some way have become the students' own. We ask students to put together parts of their background—be it observation, reading, daydreaming, venture, or adventure. In composition they associate the parts and draw conclusions about the meaning of the pairing, the assemblage, the concatenation.

2. *Frequent opportunities to talk assist students in creating the associations essential for composition.* As linguists have for years reminded us, language is basically oral; the written or printed language is a derived one, a visual symbol of an oral symbol, and hence twice-removed from reality. But "Silence" has long been a school motto: "Speak only when the teacher asks you a question." And

some teachers (emulating their university professors, perhaps) have talked so much that students have little chance to talk at all; the people who don't need practice get it, and those who need it don't get it.

So in up-to-date schools a change has been made. Teachers talk less, students talk more; teachers do fewer things, students do more things. Discussions replace lectures; dramatizations often substitute for explications; small-group work is more frequent; students conduct interviews, make plans, assume responsibility.

3. *Frequent practice in putting things together is another essential for composition.* Able teachers help students to be *homo cogitans* and not merely *homo sapiens.* They do so in large part by asking questions that require reflection, not regurgitation of facts. The thought questions are not huge and amorphous, like "What seem to have been the trends in English literature for the past three hundred years?" Rather, they are pointed questions that guide thinking, like "Besides the love of nature, what do these two poems by Frost and Wordsworth have in common?" or "Why is *because* better than *and* in this sentence?"

Constantly, then, minute after minute and hour after hour, good teachers are reinforcing the process that students began learning when they were infants: sorting out, putting parts of their experience together, saying that *a* is like *b* in this way and that, and that *c* is unlike *a* and *b* in this way and that. The comparisons are often far-ranging: between Holden Caulfield and Hamlet, between romanticism in literature and romanticism in music and art, between man and the lower animals, between the lyrics of a popular song and the theme of a metaphysical poem, between the student in the 1970's and prehistoric man and Cain and Abel and Moses and Jesus and Mohammed and Buddha and Abraham Lincoln and Nicolai Lenin and a drug addict, between idealism and realism (and whether the twain can ever meet), between today and yesterday or today and tomorrow. What kind of world would you like to live in? Why? What do literature and history point out as obstacles in the way of attaining such a world? How can those obstacles ever be surmounted? What can you do about them?

The teachers don't, or shouldn't, ask all the questions, or envision all the similarities and differences. A class properly brought up is full of questions, full of observations—and it doesn't have to be a "fast" class to be so. Some of the questions and comments may be irrelevant, because the process of learning to sort out is still going on (and ought to go on all through a person's life; the know-it-all whose sorting-out was completed years ago is mentally dead). Students may often work together in small groups on a problem.

Part of the sorting out involves distinguishing emotion from reason. The word *Republican* causes some persons to emit sparks of fury; the word *Democrat* can hardly be spoken by others without an implied "damn." *Poetry* to some students connotes effeminacy. To city students, *rural* refers to "hayseeds and hicks," and to some rural students, city people may be "dudes" or "smart alecks." Mere bigness often seems a virtue. Since Bigg High has a larger enrolment than Possum Trot High, Bigg must be a "better" school; since *Luscious Lucifera* is a best-seller, it must be a "great" book. Emotional reactions have their roots in prejudice, and although they can't ever and shouldn't ever be eliminated, they need to be tempered by facts and by logic.

4. Composition is not just writing something on paper. Every time a person speaks the parts of a sentence, like "The sky is blue," he is composing, putting together. Every time he expresses a relationship (as he does in every sentence), he is composing. Whenever he puts two or three or five sentences together, he is composing on a larger scale.

But he sometimes composes also in media other than words. It is no accident that we speak of "musical compositions" or of "composition" in painting and sculpture. When a student makes a collage, he is composing, and perhaps through the medium of the concrete he can grasp principles of organization—can see relationships—that would remain hidden to him if he used only the symbolic medium of words. When he makes a scrapbook, he is composing. When a class makes a film (as more and more classes do today), the students are putting pieces together, are associating and differentiating, are composing.

The end-product of composition, then, is not necessarily words on paper, though that should be one of the end-products. Students who through their school years have had varied experiences in composing are more likely to write in unified and coherent fashion because they have had many chances to put things together in a variety of forms and to visualize relationships of which they might otherwise never have been aware.

WHAT SHOULD STUDENTS WRITE ABOUT?

"This I Believe"

On the basis of his experiences, everyone draws tentative conclusions: about himself, about life, about polar bears, about racial discrimination, about Rip Van Winkle, about everything that has become part of his being. He fits each experience into a context, using in infinite repetition his faculties for associating and differentiating. The process goes on daily, hourly, minutely. As he puts together parts of his experience, but often without actually verbalizing, he forms connections that tell him things like "Polar bears are in danger of extinction" or "Like Rip Van Winkle, I wish I could sleep for twenty years and see what the world would be like when I awoke."

Whatever a student writes should reflect part of his credo. In effect, he should be encouraged to say again and again, "This is what I now believe concerning. . . ." If what he writes about is as simple as an explanation of how a ball-point pen works, he is saying "I believe that a ball-point pen works like this." Or if he is writing a comparison of *Brave New World* and *Nineteen Eighty-Four*, he is saying, "I believe that these two books have these similarities and these differences."

Each composition, then, is today's statement about a developing human being. It is an attempt on the student's part to define one segment—tiny or large—of what he believes about life, about humanity, about inanimate objects, about himself. It is no mere exercise in copying or in mechanically making squiggles on paper; it is no mere exercise in well-formed sentences or in punctuation.

But not enough student writing is regarded as a credo. Too often it is only a rather random amalgamation of facts or observations, and it is bad writing because that is true. Several years ago Professor Bertrand Evans of the University of California described an all-too-typical theme by an entering freshman.[1] The student is writing about "My Home Town." Systematic and dutiful, he outlines his composition: Introduction—Name, Location, Size; II. Recreational facilities—Skiing, Swimming, Fishing, Hunting; III. Educational facilities: Grade Schools, High School, Libraries; IV. Sources of income: Farming, Industry, Business; V. Conclusion. He writes the

[1] "Writing and Composing," *English Journal*, XLVIII (Jan., 1959), 12.

paper, with a sentence or two on each of the subtopics, and hands it in.

So what's wrong? The student has written, but he has not composed, Professor Evans would reply. He has reached into his mind, pulled out these snippets of information from the compartment labeled "home town," and hung them up on a line where they flutter meaninglessly. The student had a *topic*, but he didn't have a *subject*. A topic is the name of something, anything: hobbies, Aunt Sara, atomic energy, bricklaying, my home town. A subject, in contrast, says something, states a belief: Hobbies are overrated; Aunt Sara is a miser; atomic energy may yet solve our transportation problems; bricklaying requires special skills; my home town is an exciting place in which to live.

A subject, then, demands thinking—putting together. It requires more than a listing of facts. It necessitates a selection of facts, an interpretation of them, a stateemnt of this-I-believe about them. The writer puts things together and tries to see what they mean.

Another way of saying this is to say that a subject demands proof or at least evidence. The student writing about his home town wasn't proving anything. The writer of an article in your favorite magazine, in contrast, gives evidence in favor of something that he believes: movies are worse than ever; jet planes are polluting the stratosphere; etc. Even description attempts to prove something; for instance, that the "beautiful blue Danube" is now neither blue nor beautiful, or that a room is tastefully decorated. Narration tries to prove something: An adventuress (Becky Sharp) may bring much grief to good but relatively simple persons.

The statement of subject involves a word or expression that may be called either "ambiguous" or "controversial." The italicized words in these sentences are examples:

> Making a willow whistle is *easy*.
> Automobiles are *safer than ever*.
> My cousin is a *mathematical genius*.
> My home town is an *exciting* place to live in.

Adequate development requires that the ambiguity be clarified, or that the weight on one side of the controversy be chosen to exceed that on the other. What, for example, is a mathematical genius? What does my cousin do that shows he is one? Some persons believe that my home town is dull. What is the proof that it is really exciting?

Teachers normally suggest, assign, or lead students toward topics, not subjects. That is as it should be, for a student should find his own point of view rather than accept a hand-me-down from his teacher or anyone else. But teachers should help students to see how they can transform a topic into a subject. The way to do it is this: "Ask yourself, 'What do I believe about this subject? What do I want to prove about it?' Put your belief into the form of a short simple sentence. Check the sentence to make sure that it includes one expression that means different things to different people [like *easy* or *genius*] or that can be argued about [like *safer than ever*]. It is this expression on which you will focus your attention in most or all of your composition. You now have a subject."

Compositions written about subjects rather than about topics are inevitably idea-centered, thought-provoking, or sometimes just provoking. The teacher and classmates may disagree with what a student attempts to prove, may not share his belief because their experiences have been different from his. Sometimes his evidence may be demonstrably incorrect, derived from the experience of hearsay rather than from personal observation or from authority. Sometimes there are clearly flaws in his reasoning, caused by flaws in association and differentiation. If frank discussion is customary in the classroom (as it should be—frank but kind and constructive), there will be statements of appreciation of good illustrations and strong arguments as well as suggestions about possibly better illustrations and attacks on weak arguments.

Students *do* have something to say. They *do* have beliefs, even though those will and should change as they grow older. Each student has had experiences, has read a little, has heard and seen much, and has formed opinions worthy of expression and careful scrutiny. But many students have never learned that they can find something to say that will interest someone else, and hence their compositions too frequently have been pointless exercises that bore their writers or even torture them.

Suitable Topics for Student Writing

Topics, then, are to be converted to subjects before students write. But what kinds of topics? [2]

2 Teachers find very useful the hundreds of specific suggestions in *Composition Situations,* edited by Grace E. Wilson (NCTE, 1966). They appear in groups under the headings "Personal Experiences," "Language Study," "Mass Media," "Analysis and Communication of Ideas," and "Literature."

No definitive answers exist. Some teachers argue in favor of personal topics; some, in favor of literary topics; others say that anything related to the current unit is appropriate. Some advocate expository topics only, but others like description, narration, argumentation. Short stories and poetry are considered suitable by some teachers, not by others. Disagreement exists about the desirability of the so-called research paper, journalistic topics, current events, papers related to the work of other courses. In some schools students choose most of their own topics; in others, printed lists are used. Some schools insist on a planned sequence, but others pay little attention to sequence.

Despite such differences, however, it seems that in recent years the amount of emphasis on personal writing has been increasing, especially in grades 7–9. Included are letters or other accounts based on personal experiences, descriptions of things students have seen or experienced in other ways, free responses to literature, and considerable imaginative narrative, as well as occasional practice in exposition. For grades 10–12, the amount of writing on literary topics is comparatively larger than in the earlier years of school, stressing especially the people and the ideas in literature. In addition, there is still much writing on topics of personal interest, some practice in extended definition and in answering examination questions, and some attempts at persuasive writing. The shift, then, as students get older, is from mainly personal topics to a balance between personal with literary and others.[3]

The kind of personal writing that for want of a better name is usually called "creative" merits special mention. Until the late 1920's most high school writing tended to be factual and interpretive essays. Then the pendulum swung, aided by a big push from two influential volumes by Hughes Mearns, *Creative Youth* and *Creative Power*, which contained many excellent examples of picturesque, imaginative writing by children of secondary school age. The creative-writing fad lasted into the 1940's, when many college instructors began to complain that some of their freshmen wrote excessively

[3] Describing the writing programs in high schools reputed for excellence, James R. Squire and Roger K. Applebee say, "At all levels students are required to write narration, description, exposition, and argumentation, though in the ninth grade there is likely to be a greater emphasis on narration and description, and in the twelfth, greater concern with more complex and subtle forms of exposition and argumentation." *High School English Instruction Today* (New York: Appleton-Century-Crofts, 1968), p. 131.

flowery language and that many of them could not organize an exposition that demanded any arrangement other than chronological. The pressures of science and of education for science seemed to demean the importance of creative writing. Many school administrators were not interested in it. Demands for more attention to the three R's filled newspaper columns, written by men who assumed that "correctness" was more likely to result from factual and interpretive reporting than from the writing of poetry and short stories.

So for a number of years creative writing was largely ignored, despite protesting voices that insisted, for instance, that such writing "requires planning, and form, and emphasis—in fact, all and more than is required in expository writing. I would not abolish expository writing, to be sure, but I plead for more attention being returned to the 'creative' approach." [4] When the Dartmouth Conference in 1966 called American attention to the emphasis in many British schools on the writing of plays, short stories, poems, and other evocative sorts of writing, large numbers of teachers began changing from their almost exclusive attention to exposition. The precision of diction characteristic of good creative writing, the lightning flash of its imagery, its economy in words, and its human quality make it useful in sharpening and brightening any kind of composition.

PUTTING THE INGREDIENTS TOGETHER

Starting Points

Where do student compositions start? From a specific teacher-made assignment, or as a natural outgrowth of other classwork, or as the result of a student's overpowering urge to communicate with others by organizing his thoughts on paper?

Ideally, all writing would grow from the third impulse, but unfortunately most students feel only infrequent overpowering urges to write and perhaps the majority of teachers are not skilled enough to create such urges with much regularity. The specific teacher-made assignments are generally the least ideal, on the other hand, partly because teachers often fail to choose topics that students can get excited about and partly because the topics for weekly or biweekly themes frequently may bear little relationship to anything else going on in the course.

[4] R. Stanley Peterson, "Once More to the Well: Another Look at Creative Writing," *English Journal*, L (Dec., 1961), 612.

Practically, then, often the most satisfactory starting point is in the material being read and the other things being done in the course. Since much of the time in English classes is devoted to literatuure, considerable writing can have literature as a base or at least as a point of departure. This does *not* mean that it should often be a retelling of a story or some sort of critical analysis. Rather, it should more frequently be a reaction to the ideas of the literature or a reaction to people in the literature. Such writing has great value in developing the associations and differentiations discussed in the first part of this chapter; it helps students to grasp literature as something real, as relevant to their own lives. Examples:

(After reading Miller's *The Crucible*) What kinds of "witches" do we hunt today? Are you a "witch" to anyone? Who are your "witches"? Must society have "witches"?

(After reading poems from Masters' *Spoon River Anthology*) How are Fiddler Jones and Doc Hill alike and different? Tell the story of someone you know about who resembles a certain Spoon River resident.

(After reading a book about the future) What is most alarming about the future world as described by this author? Why? What would you like best in that world? Why? If you were building your own utopia, what is one thing you would insist upon? Why? What is there in twentieth-century life that causes so many writers to predict an unhappy future for mankind? How can such an unhappy fate be prevented?

Not only in literature, though, are the starting points to be found. They exist in the films that students see, in often-spontaneous class discussions of some controversial topic of current interest, and in the study of the English language. There are scores of starting points, for instance, in dialects (where they come from, how they differ, whether they're good or bad), in history of the language (why some of our spellings are "odd," how places or people get their names, how American English and British English differ), in semantics (how words can hurt people, why "the map is not the country," how meanings differ from person to person), even in usage (the long controversy over *ain't*, the rightness or wrongness of social pressure to use "standard" English).

Some starting points, though, may be less closely related to regular classwork. Often a current happening rouses much interest: a student is shot on a college campus nearby, changes in military draft regulations are contemplated, there's a new international tension building; or, closer home, the school's Student Council is seeking new powers, a popular teacher is threatened with dismissal for teaching James Baldwin, our team's chances for the basketball championship are jeopardized by a change in policy on eligibility. The more controversial the topic, and the more it hits students where they live, the more likely it is to stir their thinking, to make them reach some kind of conclusion, and to be eager to support that conclusion.

Not every starting point, of course, must be controversial. There should be a chance for the girl who likes flower-arranging to tell about her hobby, or for the mathematician to clarify the working of the computer. There should be plenty of opportunity for explosions of free creation, sometimes but not always set off by a teacher–spark. Examples of sparks:

> "You are walking home from school and you find a letter in the street. It is unopened. It is not to you. . . . Who is it from? . . . It might be a love letter. . . . It might have been sent in 1890 and just now arriving due to bad postal facilities. It might have anything inside. Write the letter."

> "So the kids launch into writing about how awful air pollution is, but only after I explain that they'll also have to write something telling how great air pollution is, how healthy it is, how beautiful, how wonderful, etc. Some protests: that's not true! But I remind them of the Lie Poem. Oh, yes, this is poetry, so we can lie. They go to work."

> "This week I expanded the idea of voice by asking them to write in a narrative voice other than their own. I told them that it was important for writers to be able to get inside someone else's skin, inside his head, show what his character was like from the way he talked and told a story. As a quick example I read them a passage from Ring Lardner's 'Haircut.' "

> "I whipped on Varese's POEME ELECTRONIQUE, a piece about 8 or 10 minutes long. I instructed them to close their eyes and imagine whatever the music told them to." [5]

First Steps

Each student needs to find the writing process that can most generally be successful for him. Professional writers themselves have

---

[5] All four examples are from *Teachers & Writers Collaborative* (Jan., 1970), a newsletter concerning experiences of New York City writers who try their hands at teaching. These tactics were used by Ron Padgett and Phillip Lopate.

quite different work habits, as a glance through the two volumes of *Paris Review* interviews with professionals will quickly reveal. Some writers, for example, work very methodically, planning and outlining in considerable detail before they write, but others improvise upon the bare, unassembled bones of an idea to see what may fit together. Some do most of their revising as they go along, but others may go through several drafts plus a final revision. Many do their best work in certain surroundings: H. L. Mencken, for example, could write in Baltimore but not in New York.

Nevertheless it is possible to describe and illustrate several steps that work well for many people. Students may need to experiment by omitting some steps, combining steps, or adding steps as needed. The teacher ordinarily ought not to insist that every student try to follow exactly the same process.

After a topic has been chosen, the writer needs to decide what he believes about the topic. Thus he translates it into a subject. Sometimes he will not know what he believes when he starts: many people find that out only when they put words on paper.

So the student—let's call him *Tom*—looks at his topic, starts making some jottings and some doodlings. Say that the topic is "Lady Macbeth." Tom writes down *cruel, greedy, ambitious, heartless,* and a few other words. He thinks then about the pathos of the hand-washing scene, and feels a surge of sympathy for the woman whose conscience was troubling her, whose husband had outstripped her in cruelty and now paid little attention to her, a woman haunted by a dark night in her past, perhaps a woman whose reason was tottering. He wonders, "Was she really such an evil person?"

Can any excuse be found for her inciting her husband to commit murder? Did she do so because of her love for him, her wish to help him 'succeed'? Tom tries to phrase his belief: "Lady Macbeth wasn't quite as bad as she seems," and perhaps a tentative title emerges, such as "A Defense of Lady Macbeth."

Note that in arriving at his subject, Tom is also narrowing it. He is not going to write everything about Lady Macbeth; he is going to consider only those things that are relevant to a defense of her.

Next he adds to his evidence. Already he knows that he can build sympathy for Lady Macbeth through the sleepwalking scene, but what else is available? He rereads the pertinent passages in Act I. Obviously there's nothing there that makes her appear very lovable. He wouldn't like to have her as his mother, he decides. But she loved her husband, was ambitious for him, would do anything for him. She does not think of the jewels and the fine clothes that she might have, but only of "the golden round" for his head. She is kind to the messenger: "Give him tending." She is shrewd: "Look like the innocent flower/But be the serpent under't." She is strong in determination: "But screw your courage to the sticking-place/And we'll not fail." And in Act II a softer part of her nature is revealed: "Had he not resembled/My father as he slept, I had done't." And she is bold: "Give me the daggers. . . . If he do bleed,/I'll gild the faces of the grooms withal."

Tom thinks some more about his evidence. Lady Macbeth has many qualities generally praised, even though she misuses them: love of her mate, ambition, kindness, shrewdness, strength, tenderness toward those she loves, boldness. If there is a chance, he talks with classmates or the teacher about his idea, which he is still willing to modify. He clearly can't honestly present Lady Macbeth as an ideal woman. He plays again with an earlier idea. Maybe that should be his focus: "I Wouldn't Want Lady Macbeth for My Mother, But . . ."

Next Steps

For whom is Tom writing? In his class, students often share their compositions with their classmates, and their teacher has told them that they should ordinarily try to interest, inform, convince, and possibly amuse their fellow-students—not necessarily the teacher. (In other situations, students may be asked for practice to address hypothetical readers: school officials or political leaders, for instance; or real readers outside the school: television broadcasters or people who read letters to the editor. What they write and the way they write are influenced by the characteristics of the expected readers.)

What is an appropriate tone? If Tom could honestly support the idea that Lady Macbeth was an admirable woman, he would obviously write with complete seriousness. But since he can't do that, he decides to be semi-serious, writing with his tongue aimed toward his cheek. "Mothers should be strong, affectionate, tender, self-sacrificing, resourceful. Lady Macbeth was all of these. What more could anyone want?" [6]

[6] Tone is related to "voice," a term increasingly used in recent years to indicate the persona or the point of view from which a student is writing. Usually, as Tom is doing, a student writes as a student, addressing other student. But occasionally he may adopt other voices, e.g., as an older student explaining or describing or telling something for young children, as an expert on a particular subject, as a person who wants to move others to action, or as a character in a story.

Remaining Steps

How should the parts be arranged? Being a fairly methodical student, Tom jots down a few words to suggest each of the parts that he may include, and then puts a number or a notation after each part to indicate where it might fit. His list looks like this:

What good mothers are like	(1—introduction)
Why I wouldn't want LM as my mother, though I admire her	(3)
Her good qualities:	(2—several paragraphs)
strength	(2–b)
deep love	(2–a)
resourcefulnes, shrewdness	(2–d—relate to strength)
ambition	(2–c—relate to strength)
tenderness	(2–a—combine with deep love)
conscience	(2–f—sleepwalking scene)
self-sacrifice	(2–e—tie back to deep love)
Misdirection of her excellent qualities	(tie in with 3; use as conclusion)

Having gone this far in his planning, Tom finds the writing rather easy. He does not need to stare blankly at blank paper, nor does he make a number of ineffectual starts destined for the wastebasket.

As he writes, with his copy of *Macbeth* before him, he refers often to the play for specific examples; often he copies brief passages as evidence. (An even more methodical writer would have made notations in the rough outline to show which passages to use as references, but few students and perhaps not many professionals are quite so methodical as that.)

Tom, unlike many writers, is a reviser-as-you-go-along. So he scratches out a word here or there, writes substituted words between lines, modifies his punctuation, checks a spelling, draws an arrow to show a transposition, and so on.

When he finishes, he rereads and makes a few more changes. If time permits, he sets the composition aside for a day or two, so that he can reread it again, with a fresh mind, and perhaps make a few more changes.

Finally he makes a clean copy to submit to his classmates and teacher.[7]

---

[7] Excellent discussions of the process of writing, with illustrations developed for different kinds of topics, may be found in Edward B. Jenkinson and Donald A. Seybold, *Writing as a Process of Discovery* (Indiana University Press, 1970). The chapter titles suggest the coverage: "Examining the Familiar," "From Subjectivity to Objectivity," "Two Ways of Looking at People," "The Audience Responds," "Examining Events," "Defining Words," "Controlling Tone."

Variations

Tom's procedure won't work equally well for everyone, but it is basically sound and has often enough proved successful to warrant such a detailed description.

James Thurber didn't write that way. He once asserted that he never knew what any of his characters would say until they said it. Nevertheless, he thought endlessly about whatever he was writing, even though he did not plan very methodically. At cocktail parties, when his wife saw him standing abstracted, she would sometimes whisper, "James, you're composing again!"

Through improvisation, through one word or idea leading to another, the Thurbers write best. They feel chained if they must prepare and follow an outline; it makes their writing mechanical and often dull.

Other writers know their main headings—and hence the general pattern—but no more. They combine rough planning with improvisation, but plan less specifically than Tom did.

Some writers, including many students, whet their minds by discussing with their friends whatever they are writing. Often ideas or examples from such discussion find their way into the product. Other writers, though, especially many young professionals, find that talking much about their book hinders their writing, dulls their pen, reduces their imagination; if they "talk out" a book or a story, they may never get it down on paper.

Practices in revision, too, vary. Some professionals write draft after draft, but in contrast the late Jack Kerouac simply put a long roll of paper into his typewriter and typed and typed and typed, folded up the resulting manuscript, and sent it off to a publisher. Shakespeare, to the displeasure of Ben Jonson, who was an inveterate reviser, is reported never to have "blotted a line."

Circumstances also necessarily influence procedures. If Tom had had only an hour of class time to do his paper, or if he had been faced in an examination with a ten-minute question, "Characterize Lady Macbeth," he obviously would have had to modify the process drastically by some short-circuiting. Or if he had been writing his paper for a group that had not read *Macbeth*, it would have been necessary for him to fill in enough about the story to make his explanation comprehensible.

To summarize, although it is useful for all students to have practice in following a procedure like that which Tom used in "I Wouldn't

Like Lady Macbeth as a Mother, But . . . ," no teacher should insist that this is the only "correct" way to write. There is no correct way, but many possible ways, and each writer needs to discover the way or ways that best fit his temperament.

THE IMPORTANCE OF THE PARAGRAPH

Reasons for Emphasizing Paragraph Construction

An analogy exists between teaching composition and teaching woodworking. The shop instructor in junior high school generally chooses for student projects whatnots, magazine racks, and other medium-sized articles, not jewel boxes or dining room tables. The polished sentence, like the skillfully made jewel box, requires much practice and experience. The long composition, like the table, is too large for much experimentation and revision. But the paragraph is neither too large nor too small, and it may be fairly well constructed even though there are flaws in the component sentences.

Therefore much writing in the junior high school may be in the form of single paragraphs. These paragraphs, if well constructed, require the writers to practice association and differentiation, and to learn about and decide upon methods of development and organization. There may, of course, when a topic demands it, be some compositions in which several paragraphs are banded together, and some junior high students may occasionally write rather extensive narratives consisting of many paragraphs of a somewhat different kind from those used in exposition.

In the senior high, there is likely to be less writing of isolated paragraphs, since more mature students should be able to develop their subjects more fully. Nevertheless, especially for slower students, some practice in the writing of isolated paragraphs can still be valuable. For other students, paragraphs should be treated as building blocks in a composition. Each block makes its contribution to the structure, and a defective block can weaken that structure.

The Structure of the Paragraph

In the October, 1965, issue of *College Composition and Communication,* Francis Christensen made an important contribution to understanding of the paragraph in an article called "A Generative Rhetoric of the Paragraph," which has been much discussed and frequently reprinted. The remarks that follow here are based largely upon Professor Christensen's article.

Earlier, in writing about the structure of the sentence, Christensen had stated that a sentence typically consists of a base clause to which various additions are made. It is the additions that give each sentence its individuality and that carry a large part of its freight of meaning. For example, the base clause "Children were playing" may be amplified to

Several children, six or eight years old, dressed in ragged shorts and no shirts on either the boys or the girls, were playing lackadaisically on the muddy edge of the stream, their skinny bodies grimy and their long hair matted with dirt.

Were it not for the additions, "Children were playing" might convey to the reader a very different picture based on his stereotype of clean, happy children shouting as they run gaily about; or it might convey only a vague, blurry picture with no details.

Like a developed sentence, according to Christensen, a developed paragraph has a base idea to which other information is added. This base idea, usually called the topic sentence, almost always comes first, although sometimes a transitional or introductory sentence or two may precede it.

In connected writing, the topic sentence varies greatly in how explicit it is in designating the thesis of the paragraph. Sometimes it is quite explicit; sometimes it is a mere sign pointing to the turn the new paragraph is going to take. Sometimes it is the shortest sentence of the paragraph; sometimes it is not even a grammatically complete sentence. It seems to me that these differences are irrelevant, provided only that the reader gets the signal and the writer remembers the signal he has called.[8]

The additions may be of two sorts, coordinate and subordinate. Coordinate additions are equal to one another in importance, but a subordinate addition is of a lower rank than the addition above. Coordinate additions may be illustrated in this brief paragraph:

1   Several flaws existed in older descriptions of paragraph structure.
    2   One was the statement that the topic sentence is likely to occur almost anywhere, whereas in reality professional writers generally begin their paragraphs with it.
    2   Another was the statement that each paragraph generally follows a single method of development; the truth is that two or more methods often appear in a paragraph.
    2   Still another flaw was. . . .

[8] Christensen, *op. cit.*, p. 146.

Note that each of the second-level sentences bears the same kind of relationship to the first-level, or topic, sentence. That is, the second 2 is not subordinate to the first 2. In contrast, note the subordinations in this paragraph quoted by Christensen from J. Bronowski, *The Common Sense of Science* (Vintage), p. 111:

1 The process of learning is essential to our lives.
   2 All higher animals seek it deliberately.
      3 They are inquisitive and they experiment.
         4 An experiment is a sort of harmless trial run of some action which we shall have to make in the real world; and this, whether it is made in the laboratory by scientists or by fox-cubs outside their earth.
            5 The scientist explores and the cub plays; both are learning to correct their errors of judgment in a setting in which errors are not fatal.
               6 Perhaps this is what gives them both their air of happiness and freedom in these activities.

As you can readily see, 2 is subordinate logically to 1, 3 to 2, and so on. "There is no theoretic limit to the number of levels," Christensen says, although there is a practical limit, because if the writer takes the reader too far down the ladder of subordination, the reader may forget the basic idea, the topic sentence, and thus lose sight of what the paragraph is really about.

A mixed sequence—some coordinate and some subordinate additions—is by far the most common. Christensen includes several long paragraphs as examples. In one of these, sentences are numbered by levels as follows: 1, 2, 2, 2, 2, 3, 4, 2, 3, 3, 4. Here the 2's are all coordinate; the first 3 is an example of the fourth 2; the 4's are subordinate to the 3's; the second and third 3's are coordinate subdivisions of the fifth 2. Another paragraph has the sequence 1, 2, 3, 4, 4, 5, 5, 6, 7, 7, 7.

Christensen grants that some paragraphs have no topic sentences, and therefore no level 1. Such sentences are most frequent in narrative writing, but may appear also in exposition or argumentation when the main idea is readily inferred.

Some Implications of the Christensen Analysis

The Christensen article has been fairly well accepted as a reasonably accurate description of paragraph structure, and has been somewhat amplified and modified by Paul Rodgers.[9] It has been attacked, however, by Leo Rockas,[10] who believes that "you can justify an indentation before almost any sentence of sophisticated prose." Also, many teachers have argued that Christensen's method does not represent a useful teaching device; they say that if students have to worry about coordinating and subordinating their ideas, they will have even more trouble in writing then they now have—that they will resemble the centipede who became immobile when he tried to decide which leg to move first.

Certainly students can become like that centipede. Excessive emphasis on the leg movements—or on the machinery, if you prefer that metaphor—can result in immobility or in what Ken Macrorie has described as "A feel-nothing, say-nothing language, dead like Latin, devoid of the rhythms of contemporary speech." [11] Macrorie, however, has suggested (in a book that should be required reading for every English teacher from kindergarten through college) that it is possible for students to "operate with freedom and discipline. They are given real choices and encouraged to learn the way of experts." [12]

Macrorie rightly stresses the preeminent importance of content— something to say—and of language—saying it vividly, memorably, often movingly. And Christensen rightly stresses the fact that the way the parts are put together can clarify the content and can contribute to the intellectual and emotional impact of that content. The two points of view are not antithetical, although some teachers have so regarded them.

The clue to teaching a Christensen-like understanding of a paragraph lies in the quotation from Macrorie ". . . learn the way of experts." Through examination of a number of expository paragraphs, students can discover for themselves the ways that professional writers assemble their ideas in paragraph form. Paragraphs in contemporary magazines of high quality are good for this purpose, as are paragraphs in current books of nonfiction. Narrative paragraphs are less useful, since often they lack topic sentences or

9 "The Stadium of Discourse," *College Composition and Communication*, XVIII (Oct., 1967), 178. See also "Symposium on the Paragraph," *CCC*, May, 1966, for brief articles by five writers.

10 "Further Comments on the Paragraph," *College Composition and Communication*, VII (Oct., 1966), 148.

11 *Uptaught* (New York: Hayden Book Company, 1970), 18.

12 *Ibid.*, p. 27.

consist only of quotation. Newspaper paragraphs should also be avoided for this purpose, since newspaper editors generally employ only very short paragraphs, somewhat randomly split off.

After a number of such analyses—say in grade nine or ten—students may work with scrambled paragraphs. The teacher may prepare such paragraphs by copying in mixed order the sentences of paragraphs using only two-level (coordinate) development, other paragraphs using three level, still others where each sentence is subordinate to the one before (like the example from Bronowski, page 282), and others that employ both coordination and subordination. Students may also prepare or copy a scrambled paragraph for their classmates to unscramble.

Following such exercises, students may practice writing paragraphs of their own using coordinate, two-level structure, and then more complex modes. For this purpose, topics that involve classification and examples are easiest and most useful. Such writing ought to be presented honestly for what it is—an exercise designed to clarify a method of procedure that will be useful in much subsequent writing.

Understanding the Christensen analysis, and being able to use its principles in their writing, has the important value that it helps students to grasp relationships between ideas. It assists them in seeing, for instance, that three examples are parallel to (coordinate with) one another, and that all three are subordinate to a general statement. It thus helps them in the lifelong process of associating and differentiating, the basis of clear thinking and clear expression.

The Paragraph in Narrative Writing

The narrative paragraph deserves separate consideration because its characteristics are different from those of exposition, argumentation, and description. It is less likely, for instance, to have a topic sentence, though such a summary as "Tuesday morning was hectic" is possible. It may rely more on action words than other paragraphs do. And, by virtue of being narrative, it is almost always chronological in organization. Some fiction writers such as William Faulkner and Robert Penn Warren wrote long paragraphs; others, like Hemingway, prefer short ones.

Some students erroneously conclude, however, that no rules at all exist for narrative paragraphs. It is wise, therefore, to teach that a new narrative paragraph is usually required in these circumstances:

1. With each change of speaker.
2. At the end of each significant bit of action.
3. When attention is switched from one character to another.
4. When an important new character, setting, or emphasis is introduced.
5. If the material differs in some way from its context (e.g., several · sentences of description inserted in a story).
6. If the particular type of reader being addressed may need the psychological relief of a break on the page (e.g., a young reader needs more breaks than a sophisticated adult).
7. If dramatic effect will be heightened (i.e., short paragraphs, if not used excessively, tend to be more dramatic than long ones).[13]

These observations show that narrative paragraphs possess a degree of unity. Coherence may be illustrated through examining their steady chronological progression; and emphasis, through noting points that are stressed and the writer's choice of language.

PUTTING PARAGRAPHS TOGETHER

Similarity of Paragraph and Composition

If the paragraph is emphasized as a basic unit in the teaching of writing, the task of helping students with longer compositions is not difficult. The whole composition differs from the paragraph mainly in being larger. If a paragraph develops an idea, then a whole composition develops a larger idea. To say it a different way, the whole composition develops an idea, and each paragraph develops one phase of that idea.

It may be helpful to recall here the theoretical presentation that opened this chapter. An individual sentence involves the interrelation of symbols standing for one's experiences with things:

$$(T \leftrightarrow E \leftrightarrow Sy) \qquad (T \leftrightarrow E \leftrightarrow Sy) \ldots = S$$

A paragraph is composed of interrelated sentences:

$$S \leftrightarrow S \leftrightarrow S \ldots = P$$

A composition is composed of interrelated paragraphs:

$$P \leftrightarrow P \leftrightarrow P \ldots = C$$

[13] Adapted from J. N. Hook, *Hook's Guide to Good Writing: Grammar, Style, Usage* (New York: The Ronald Press Company, 1962), p. 315.

Just as a paragraph has a controlling idea, usually expressed as a topic sentence, so the whole composition has its controlling idea, which is often expressed at the beginning, or may be built up to as a conclusion, or in some instances is only implied.

How Many Themes?

Despite the similarity of paragraph and composition, students do need practice in writing longer compositions, partly because greater space is essential for expressing some ideas and partly because practice is essential for the successful interlocking of paragraphs.

The guidance and evaluation of extensive written work, though, if carefully performed, require much time and thought. For that reason, the NCTE, Dr. James B. Conant, and various state and local organizations of English teachers have recommended that administrators and school boards work toward an English class load of no more than four classes per teacher and a maximum of twenty-five students per class. Many school systems have reached this goal, but others, hampered by inadequate funds, large enrolments, and a shortage of classrooms, have not been able to do so. English teachers, nevertheless, should without whining keep before the public the fact that they cannot do their best work if they are so heavily loaded that their work week is fifty or sixty hours; the constructive evaluation of large numbers of student-written compositions may require fifteen or more hours per week.

A considerable amount of practice in writing is needed if most students are to learn to write well. However, it is not essential, as many teachers once believed, to require a rather long composition every week. Fewer compositions, carefully planned and carefully written (as Tom wrote his on Lady Macbeth), are much more valuable than a large number of thoughtless, hurried, and sloppy pieces of writing.

No specific number of themes, then, can be stipulated for each year. The more formal compositions can be supplemented, as in many British schools, by a small amount of daily free writing in a journal, which is scanned rapidly by the teacher every two or three weeks and unmarked except for occasional positive comments like "Good" or "Exciting" or "Worth developing later" or "You might like to read such and such on this topic." For more formal writing, students in junior high schools should each year write many compositions of one paragraph and a few of two, three, or more paragraphs. Sophomores and juniors should also write a number of one-paragraph themes and perhaps a dozen to eighteen longer ones, as well as some "finger-exercises" that can be checked over by the students themselves in small groups. Seniors should write somewhat more compositions of a few hundred words, and at least one library theme or other "research" paper of 1,500 or more words. (The requirement of the "research" paper has been hotly debated but still seems to me to be valuable, especially for the college-bound students.) Each piece of writing needs to be adequately motivated; students' problems need to be anticipated; and the finished product needs to be carefully analyzed.

The Need for Prevision

Grading of composition work is time-consuming, undeniably. It is one of the biggest of the chores that fall to the English teacher. The grading may not be painful, however, under certain conditions. If the teacher has helped the students to plan, and if he has attentively overseen their labor, the result need not be a mass of red when he returns it. That in itself may give some slight pleasure. But the real glow of happiness and pride comes when he sees proof that Dick is at last using his head, that Marilyn has thought one subject through, that scatterbrain Harold has for once put the horse before the cart, that shy Pearl has dropped her shyness long enough to defend a positive belief. Two or three such discoveries in one evening afford deeper pleasure than almost any movie.

The late Lucia Mirrielees used the term *prevision* for a process that may make such moments of pleasure more numerous. Prevision refers to the very desirable practice of helping students with their compositions before they write them and to some extent while they are writing them. Through prevision, teachers can make sure that students are ready to write a particular kind of theme, can anticipate many of their difficulties, and can partially supervise the writing.

Prevision involves choice of subject, motivation, and help in removing obstacles.

Choice of subject has already been discussed (pages 269–71). It is especially important that students do have subjects, not just topics, on which to write. A dramatic improvement in content sometimes results from simple insistence upon this distinction.

Motivation is increased, too, if subjects are carefully selected. There must be a reason for each assignment, and students should be helped to see the reason. A teacher of English should never teach anything that he himself does not consider valuable, and he should never teach anything without letting students see at least part of the value that it has.

Choosing theme subjects becomes somewhat easier if one keeps the preceding sentence in mind. It automatically excludes such a topic as "Pea Green" (which a teacher once did actually assign—500 words on "Pea Green"!). The teacher asks himself the question, "Would this subject have demonstrable value for this particular class?"

The words "demonstrable value" imply that the subjects chosen should require purposeful writing. A theme is not to be written for the sake of writing a theme. It is to be written to convey connected thoughts to interested readers. In a September class a teacher asks students to write about themselves so that he may best plan the course to meet their needs. In October classes students are writing to inform one another, to exchange information about their reading, their ideas. In November and later classes they may be writing to have opinions evalued, arguments weighed. Sometimes they write to entertain (a perfectly valid purpose). They write letters—real letters to be mailed, if at all possible. They write answers to examination questions so that the practice will help them next week to clarify for themselves and their classmates some of the material being studied in a unit. They write a poem to search for economy and precision in words or to express a striking image.

When composition subjects do not grow from a class unit, one good plan is to specify a certain kind of topic but to let the student make his own choice within the given area. For example, there may be a good reason for having a class write "How to . . ." themes. Not everyone should be asked to write on "How To Make a Kite"; each student may choose for himself the process he wants to explain. Before the writing, teacher and class will discuss the pattern of organization, the use of transitions, and anything else that the majority of students may need.

Sometimes the entire class may cooperate on a writing project. In a high school where I taught, the sophomore class wanted to find out as much as it could about the birds of the area. Committees set to work and apportioned the tasks. Everyone did some of the searching and writing, one committee served as editors, more artistic students provided illustrations and a binding, and typing students typed the edited copy. The result was an attractive book, proudly presented to the library. At the end of the year, one of the students remarked, "I learned more from working on the bird book than I did from all the rest of the course."

One quality that students need to develop is accurate observation. Stevenson, in his *New Arabian Nights*, has a character exclaim, "I would have [observation] a piece of education in all schools! . . . Where is the use of eyesight and articulate speech if a man cannot observe and recollect? . . . Cultivate this art in future. . . . You may find it of momentous service." The teacher sometimes asks the question "Why do we have eyes?" and then issues a challenge, "How well do you observe? Can you see anything so clearly that you can put it down on paper exactly? If you roll a piece of paper into the shape of a tube and look through it out the window at one spot for thirty seconds, can you write down exactly what you have seen without looking again? Your eye is like a camera, and words are like film. Can you make a word snapshot?"

For the same purpose, I once borrowed a technique often used by psychologists. I asked two senior girls to learn to act out a prepared script. At a prearranged time, while the junior class was in session, the two seniors burst into the classroom, rushed over to a wire basket containing some papers, seized a letter, and began arguing and almost fighting over it. I finally quieted them and ushered them out of the room. Then I explained to the juniors that the incident had been staged to test their powers of observation. Each was to write an account of exactly what had occurred, including the conversation. Needless to say, when they compared their accounts with the copy of the script followed by the two girls, they were amazed at the discrepancies. This incident paved the way for several fruitful assignments.

In general, when theme subjects have once been chosen and when students clearly understand what they are to do and why, the teacher still needs to remove as many obstacles as he can. For instance, if the theme will probably entail the use of conversation, he may review quotation marks. If certain words will almost certainly appear, he may make sure that everyone can spell those words. If a particular method of organization is most probable, he discusses that method. If the theme will require note taking, he talks about the qualities of good notes. If footnotes are needed in the senior research theme, he illustrates their uses and form. In other words, he tries to anticipate the problems the students will encounter and to demonstrate the solutions. The students thus learn and apply. The learning is itself motivated because it is put into meaningful context.

Work with transitions may require special attention in prevision. With young students the term *bridge* may be preferable to *transition,* since it helps them to visualize the connecting function. The employment of bridges is an aid to clear thinking. It trains students to get into the habit of asking themselves, "Just how is this statement (or this paragraph) related to the preceding one? Is it an added illustration; is it an apparent contradiction; is it related in time; or what?" They then choose the appropriate transition: "in addition," "on the other hand," "next," "while this was going on," "because he was unhappy after his father's death," etc. Sometimes the teacher may offer some rather dramatic examples of the need for transitions. For instance, "Jess is a star football player. He scored five baskets last night." With transitional elements added, these sentences make sense: "Jess is a star football player. He showed that he is versatile, though, by scoring five baskets in the basketball game last night."

Still another help in prevision is having much of the actual writing done in the classroom. There the students will have access to dictionaries and other reference books, and will be able to avail themselves of the teacher's aid. In some schools, in fact, nearly all writing is done in this laboratory fashion.

Finally, practice in proofreading is important for prevision. Geneva Hanna suggests these steps:

1. To learn to attend to what is actually written, not to what the author intended to say—
   A. *Hear* (verbalize) wrong words, omission of words.
   B. Read word for word.
   C. See stops and pauses and misspelled words.
2. To learn to listen for meaning, as a stranger listens—
   A. First, be sure the meaning is there.
   B. Second, if the meaning is not there, revise the material.[14]

[14] "Proofreading, a Panacea," *English Journal,* LI (Oct., 1962), 482.

As a goal for all students, though realizing that its full attainment will be possible for only a limited number, teachers may keep in mind (and perhaps share with students) the following description of good student writing, published in the Advanced Program Syllabus of the College Entrance Examination Board in 1958:

> The core of training in composition is . . . the frequent writing and careful revision of substantial themes on subjects sufficiently mature to challenge both thought and linguistic powers. These themes should be distinguished by superior command of *substance*, thoughtfully and interestingly presented.
> A good student writer will demonstrate a high level of proficiency in *organization*, combining clear sentences in well-shaped paragraphs and arranging these in an order clear to the reader as well as to himself. . . .
> However, a neat pattern of paragraphs is not in itself proof of, and can never be a substitute for, sound and compelling *logic*. . . . [The student] is careful to support general statements with specific proofs; he distinguishes between causes and effects, between subjective reactions and objective judgments; and he has cultivated the ability to select fresh rather than hackneyed illustrations.
> A good composition exhibits a feeling for style, displaying both *precision* and *fluency*. An able student will make use of the varieties of English sentence structure. . . . His vocabulary will be distinguished not so much by its extent as by its exactness and appropriateness.
> It should go without saying that a student in an advanced course will have mastered the *mechanics* of writing. His command of the conventions of spelling, capitalization, and punctuation will be firm; his syntax will be clear and accurate.

Outlining

When we observed Tom writing his paper about Lady Macbeth (pages 276–80), we noticed that he planned by jotting down points he wanted to include, numbering them to show what seemed to him the best order. Tom was really preparing a simple, informal outline. Such an outline is enough for most purposes; it is what I use, for instance, in planning each chapter and chapter section of this book.

Some teachers, however, argue in favor of a more elaborate outline. In their favor it may be said that a detailed outline can help students to see the relative level of importance of each point—to see clearly, for example, that point A is subordinate to point I. In general, though, most students detest making formal outlines, and if they are required to hand one in with a composition, many admit that they prepare it *after* the composition is written—somewhat like preparing a floor plan after the house is built.

If you believe that some work in formal outlining is desirable, you can tie it in with the Christensen-based work on paragraph structure. A good outline reveals clearly the levels of coordination and subordination. The following partial outline is faulty:

I. George Washington was born in 1732.
   A. He was born in Virginia.
   B. He went to elementary schools.
     1. Then his brother got him a job as surveyor.
   C. His young manhood was filled with adventurous exploits.
   D. One of these was his defeat of the French at Fort Duquesne.
     1. Another was his serving as commander of Virginia's forces.

Most students can readily see that I does not summarize the points below, that B.1 is not actually subordinate to B; that A is not equal in importance to B and C; and that D and D.1 should both be subordinated to C.

Such hodgepodges may best be prevented by working out sample outlines as a class. Content should be stressed more than form. Since competent outlining requires a considerable ability to grasp abstractions, only advanced and able classes should be exposed to a discussion of the more subtle points.

Evaluating

The teacher faces a stack of compositions written by his students. What should be his goal in evaluating them?

Not just to attach a grade, certainly. Not to locate mistakes that he can pounce upon.

Rather, the goal should be to find something to say to the writer that will help him to move from his present stage of development, whatever that may be, toward the next higher stage. Sometimes a suggestion on technique. Sometimes only a word of encouragement or praise. Sometimes a hint about organization. Sometimes a plea for going deeper into the subject. Usually more emphasis on content than on mechanics.

Shouldn't, then, the "errors" be marked? Well, some the teacher marks; others, he ignores for the time being. He marks errors that have been adequately discussed in class; points that have not yet been taken up he usually does not check. In a paper filled with errors, he marks only the most serious, those that should be eliminated first. To show Cedric (IQ 86) all his infractions at one time would be to leave him feeling helpless and beaten, but to show him exactly what his gravest faults are (and a way to correct them) would be to give him hope. Cedric must learn only one or two things at a time. Paul, a bright boy, makes no elementary errors. Should the teacher, then, leave Paul's paper entirely free of red and give him the feeling that it is perfect? No, because his writing can be improved. Therefore the teacher makes some specific suggestions to him—suggestions that Cedric could not even understand. These suggestions pertain to matters that have not been discussed in class, that may not be discussed until next year. When the teacher reads Paul's composition, he thinks, "This is excellent. What does it lack, though, that an ideal article on the subject would possess? What would a professional author do that Paul has not done? How much of this shall I tell Paul?" The teacher helps Paul to use profitably the intelligence that he has; he does not hold him to Cedric's pace.

In other words, as the teacher sits with pencil in hand, he has one of his best opportunities to provide for individual differences. All students in the beginning have the same needs in composition, but some master the minimum essentials more quickly than others. At present, Cedric needs especially to work on the minima, Paul on something else, Wilma on something else. Each paper is part of a growing mind. The teacher wants to help each mind to grow as straight and as strong as it can. What he is doing with his pencil is much more than marking misplaced commas, fragmentary sentences, misspelled words, and incoherent paragraphs. He is feeding minds, shaping minds.

There is a wise philosophy of grading expressed many years ago in this comment by Luella Cook:

In recent years the marking of papers with red pencil has become for me chiefly a memorandum for myself. Less and less am I troubled by the errors that I find—these are already committed—and more and more concerned with what lies behind them and how one may forestall them in future writing. And so I have come to make a distinction between errors that are a careless failure to put into operation what one already knows and errors that arise from lack of knowledge or imperfect control over meaning. The first can be handled with a minimum of teacher effort. Students can be taught to edit their own and their neighbor's papers for careless errors, checking their finished copy against a "check list" made up of items agreed upon by class and teacher as understood. And teachers can refuse to accept a paper which has not been edited or edited carelessly. On this level, accuracy is merely a matter of discipline. . . . The second type of error can best be handled, I think, by making each set of papers the basis for a study of sentence structure and correct usage [and straight thinking, it may be added].[15]

[15] "Fundamentals in the Teaching of Composition," *English Journal*, XXX (May, 1941), 360.

William J. Dusel has analyzed four methods of evaluating compositions.[16] The first, and least time-consuming, consists of marking a few of the most obvious mechanical errors and affixing a grade. The second, which requires a little more time, involves marking all mechanical errors, writing one or two negative comments such as "Weak opening sentence," and giving a grade. The third has the teacher himself writing in all the corrections he thinks desirable, attaching a grade, and writing "Recopy this and turn it in on Friday"; this takes about as much time as the second method. The fourth—the procedure that Dusel recommends—requires about two and a half times as many minutes per paper as the first method. It involves attending to ideas and not only to mechanics, commenting on something good in the paper, making suggestions for improvement, and giving a grade. Dusel correctly points out that students whose papers are evaluated by any of the first three methods are likely to learn comparatively little.

Some teachers favor two grades, one for content and one for mechanics, but there is no overwhelming evidence that two grades are better than one. Whether the teacher gives one grade or two, he has to consider these items on the debit and credit sides:

Debits	Credits
Below-ordinary content	Reasonably stimulating and fresh content
Lack of unity, coherence, or emphasis (crooked thinking)	Unity, coherence, and emphasis (straight thinking)
Infelicitous diction	Reasonably apt use of words
Errors in sentence structure, grammar, spelling, and mechanics (only those previously studied)	Some especially good sentences; accuracy in grammar, spelling, and mechanics
Failure to keep the intended reader in mind	Success in adjusting content and style to the intended reader

As the teacher balances the books, an especially large debit item may more than equal two credits, but, on the other hand, a large credit may cancel two debits. The A theme usually possesses, to a fair degree, all the elements on the credit side; the B theme may lack one of these but have no very noticeable debits; the C theme has a fairly even balance; the D theme has little to recommend it; and the F theme is weak in several respects and not very strong in any.

These debits and credits are, of course, composed of relative

16 "Determining an Efficient Teaching Load in English," *Illinois English Bulletin*, Oct., 1955, pp. 6–13.

terms. "Reasonably stimulating and fresh content" in a senior theme is not the same as "reasonably stimulating and fresh content" in a freshman theme. The instructor expects a maturity in the senior paper that he could hardy hope for in one written by a freshman. Likewise, he excuses in a freshman theme certain errors that he would consider serious in a senior paper.

A somewhat different check list for evaluation has been suggested by the NCTE Committee on High School—College Articulation:

Content—Is the idea worth writing about? Does the student know what he's writing about?

Structure—Is there a clear statement of thesis? Does the theme follow an appropriate logical pattern? Is there adequate evidence to support the thesis? Is each paragraph clearly related to the thesis? Is there adequate transition within and between paragraphs? Is the ending adequate? Are the main points emphasized and the minor points subordinated by proper sentence and paragraph structure?

Diction—Is the level of language appropriate to the subject, the audience, and the writer? Is the wording exact and free from clichés, jargon, and deadwood? Is there a proper balance between denotation and connotation? Is the wording concrete? [17]

When the grade has been written, the teacher still must affix a comment—not merely "Good" or "Poor." Ida Jewett has stated that every comment should be measured by the "five S's: Sound, Significant, Stimulating, Specific, Suggestive." [18] Ponder those five words for a few moments. If comments possess those five qualities, they will be genuinely helpful. Most comments will have the five S's if they follow a simple formula—singling out one or two things for praise and then making one or two suggestions for improvement. Please note the phrasing: "suggestions for improvement," not "adverse criticisms."

After a student has had his paper returned to him, he should be expected to revise it. If he does not do so, he will glance casually at the grade and the comment, throw the paper into the wastebasket, and in his next composition make exactly the same mistakes. Careful revision, when it involves an understanding of why each correction is made, can prevent later repetition of the same errors. This fact should be made clear to the class, who otherwise will look upon revision as a penalty rather than an opportunity.

---

[17] *English Journal*, L (Sept., 1961), 410–11.

[18] Miss Jewett also suggests that teachers who put marks like "Gr," "P," etc., on students' papers should in addition use some symbols of praise such as "Ilt" = I like this.

Revision consists only of writing the necessary corrections, either between the lines or on the back of the page. It is perhaps not necessary to have a student rewrite a whole composition unless it is so poor in organization that the student will profit from thinking through the subject again and writing a new version.

If an English teacher has such a large number of students that he cannot give as much personal attention to evaluation as he would like, he may make some use of student help. Groups of three or four students may occasionally work together, reading and discussing and suggesting ways of improving themes that they themselves have written or that students in another group have written; each member of the class will be in one of these groups, which may meet simultaneously. Unless the class has had experience in group work, the teacher must make careful preparation. The first time, relatively simple tasks will be given each group, but the tasks may gradually grow more complex and the responsibilities, greater. It is most important that the groups understand precisely what is expected of them.[19]

A number of schools now use lay readers to evaluate many student-written compositions. These readers are usually college-educated housewives who are interested in working with student writing and who can pass appropriate tests. Arguments for and against use of lay readers are presented in articles listed in The Idea Box (page 326). Most English teachers agree that, ideally, class load should be small enough to permit each teacher to grade his own students' papers but that, if such a situation does not exist, carefully selected lay readers usually do a good job and make possible the requirement of larger amounts of writing than would otherwise be feasible.

Conclusion

This chapter has offered the view that composition writing affords systematic practice in stating relationships—in depicting the likenesses and differences that lie at the base of human thought and communication. It thus far transcends mere "correctness," although

[19] For details, see Loren V. Grisson, "Student Leadership in Evaluating Compositions," *English Journal*, XLVIII (Sept., 1959), 338. For additional suggestions on evaluation, see Eric W. Johnson, "Avoiding Martyrdom in Teaching Writing: Some Shortcuts," *English Journal*, LI (Sept., 1962), 399. For more on the theoretical basis of evaluation, see T. A. Koclanes, "Can We Evaluate Compositions?" *English Journal*, L (April, 1961), 252.

because society values "correctness," that quality cannot be completely ignored.

Composition writing enables the student to put his ideas together in a coherent fashion that reveals his grasp of himself, as he writes on varied topics that are all part of the same big topic: "This I Believe."

THE IDEA BOX

Unity, Coherence, Emphasis

These three characteristics of good writing, stressed in earlier editions of this book, have not been abandoned but are implicit in the chapter. "Unity" refers to the need to have one controlling idea in each paragraph or composition. "Coherence" refers to interrelating the parts accurately and clearly. And "emphasis" shows an awareness of proportion through calling attention most forcefully to whatever is most important.

Composition for What?

At a time when we are moving closer to teaching the mechanics of writing by programing, Edward Lueders says we should try to teach "order, power, beauty, play, wonder, honesty, responsibility." "Teaching Writing Today," *English Journal*, LVI (Jan., 1967), 103.

Beyond Errors

". . . error-free and well organized writing is but a beginning. We must work for improvement in quality." To do so, Alexander Frazier would stress relatedness of ideas within a sentence, richness of detail, precision of vocabulary, variety of structure, and cohesiveness. "The Teaching of Writing as Writing," *English Journal*, LIII (Sept., 1964, 435.

Honesty

Honesty in writing is meaning what you say, which is no less important than saying what you mean. "We cannot teach the student to compose honestly merely by teaching him about paragraphs, or organization, or transition." Bryant Fillion, "The Case for Freedom in Composition and Literature." *English Journal*, LVII (Jan., 1968), 52.

"The Four Freedoms of the Student Writer"

William F. Irmscher advocates these freedoms: (1) freedom to think and feel and say; (2) freedom to choose and to go wrong; (3) freedom from interruption; and (4) freedom from fear. *Oregon Council Newsletter* (Spring, 1968).

Frustration

Carl Wonnberger, on the basis of thirty-two years of secondary teaching, says that even slow students can learn to write: "The trouble . . . is that too many students are frustrated in their English study and begin to think of English as a formal discipline instead of a functional tool for man and the aspirations of man, that they get lost in verbal calisthenics, identification of 'speech parts,' the memorization of definitions that do not define, the filling in of blanks in workbooks, diagraming, and doing all manner of things that have no possible justification in the study of language and the development of sound language habits." *Michigan English Teacher* (March, 1961).

Why Do Some Students Write Badly?

"We believe that much of the bad writing in the schools is a result of the student's failure to understand what is expected of him when he is asked to write and his lack of a basic knowledge of language that goes beyond syntax and usage. Therefore, we attempt to help the student understand exactly what he is to do, how he goes about achieving his purpose, and how he asks questions to help him gather information, find precise words to communicate that information, and put it all together for a designated reader." (From the Introduction to Edward B. Jenkinson and Donald A. Seybold, *Writing as a Process of Discovery,* Indiana University Press, 1970.)

The Class As Workshop

"The teacher needs to supply time for the students to collect materials and to talk about what they have found, time for them to rough out their ideas (not necessarily on paper or in outline form), time for them to share ideas before they are forced to commit themselves to paper, time for them to read one another's drafts, and time for them simply to stare out the window when the act of writing becomes insufferable." For an unusually penetrating look at the *learning* of writing, see Stephen Judy's "The Search for Structures in the Teaching of Composition," *English Journal,* LIX (Feb., 1970), 213.

A Fresh Look at Teaching Structure

The basis of organization is the kind of sorting that even a small child can do. Thus

can readily be grouped as

In building upon this basic point, Virginia Ireland goes into clock faces, jigsaw puzzles, a collection of student paintings, and other devices. Read the delightful "Give Junior a Frostie," *English Journal*, LIV (April, 1965), 317.

Misapplied Energy

"The pupils could parse and construe sentences and point out the various parts of speech with great facility, repeating the rules of grammar in each case, yet they were utterly unable to put this theoretical knowledge to any practical use, as they showed when called upon to write an ordinary English letter." (From a report to the Quincy, Mass., school board in 1873.)

Thirty Ideas for Writing

In an article that every teacher of composition should read, Ken Macrorie develops thirty ideas to elicit readable writing, ranging from "Ask for honesty" (rather than affectation) to "Try word play in journals." "To Be Read," *English Journal*, LVII (May, 1968), 686.

"Some Notes for Student Writers"

"Make yourself see. . . . Release your feelings. . . . Don't apologize. Take sides. . . . Don't tell, show." These are among the pieces of advice given his students by John Sweet of Chappaqua, N.Y. *English Journal*, LVI (Feb., 1967), 257.

Students on the Left Write

According to a study at Swift Academy on Long Island, students who are radically inclined tend to write better than others, and when a student becomes radical his writing improves. Gerard Onisa describes the study in *Media and Methods* (March, 1969). One reason may be that people with convictions write better. Another may be that the radicals try to write well in order to convert others. In contrast, though, a reader of College Bound themes considers the writers "a surprisingly conservative lot," maybe because they fear that honest expression of opinions will keep them out of college. F. B. Maynard, *The New Republic* (May 20, 1967).

In Watts

After the Watts disturbances, author Budd Schulberg worked with teachers there. They said, in effect, to the students, "Write about what's bugging you. Let it all come out. . . . Write a hell of a piece, and you may find a hearing, an audience beyond your imaginations." Schulberg tells teachers to reduce their emphasis on conformity, on correctness.

In a House of Ill-Repute

Suppose that a boy hands in a paper describing graphically his visit to a house of ill-fame with his older brother. It's the only paper he has handed in all year. What do you do? Do you show it to the principal, who may suspend the student? How do you get him to write more papers (on other subjects)? Donna Geyer discusses this and other questions in "Teaching Composition to the Disadvantaged," *English Journal,* LIX (Sept., 1969), 900.

Keeping the Reader in Mind

Students may be asked to designate what specific readers they have in mind for a composition and then determine what strategies are most likely to work best for those readers. Many other suggestions for practical employment of rhetorical principles are in Richard L. Larson's "Teaching Rhetoric in the High School: Some Proposals," *English Journal,* LV (Nov., 1966), 1058.

Ten Suggestions for Theme Beginnings

(1) Definition of a key word or phrase, (2) brief, vivid history of the subject, (3) direct statement of your position on an issue, (4) statement of major divisions in your paper, (5) description of topic without naming it, (6) a relevant anecdote, (7) general statistics relevant to the reader's interests, (8) contrast of two opposing views, (9) question or questions to be answered, (10 brief narrative. Lawrence E. Nelson, "In the Beginning," *English Journal,* LV (March, 1966), 342.

Teaching Specificity

On a transparency, show a student's composition like this one: "*The Secret Life of Walter Mitty* tells about a man's daydreams. His wife nags him, and he begins to dream. In his dreams he is a hero who has many adventures, such as a pilot and a doctor. In real life he is a very ordinary person. . . ." Get from students answers to the questions "What isn't specific enough? How can it be made more so?" So James M. McCrimmon advises in "A Cumulative Sequence in Composition," *English Journal*, LV (April, 1966), 425. He also discusses the meaning of class names (semantics), paragraph structure, comparison and contrast, and classification.

Get-Acquainted Writing

1. In "Anecdotal Autobiographies," Robert Lambert and Dorothy Mack explain how they enliven autobiographies by insisting on a central point of view, limited coverage, and development by appropriate anecdotes. *English Journal*, XLVIII (Dec., 1959), 528.

2. "Students write one-paragraph themes, each student describing some other member of the class. When themes are read, everyone tries to guess which student is being described." (Elaine Clark, Central High School, Grand Rapids, Mich.)

"Using Models for Improving Composition"

Paragraphs, carefully selected from professional writing, may serve as models of sentence structure or paragraph organization. Students imitate the structures, but write about different subject matter. James F. McCampbell says that use of such models may allow some students "to write acceptable sentences for the first time." More able students may be introduced to patterns they have not previously tried. *English Journal*, LV (Sept., 1966), 772.

"Practice Without Pain: The In-Class Journal"

Linda W. Wagner reads a controversial or at least topically interesting paragraph or two to her students, who then write a paragraph or two of reaction in their journals. They also do journal writing on their own time. Journals are looked at but not graded by the teacher; a good one can raise a student's composition mark. *English Journal*, LVII (Feb., 1968), 221.

"Generating a Composition"

Oscar Bouise of Southern University describes a three-step process in writing: a parent idea, which is a general topic like *parents* or *dogs* or *people;* a topic idea, like *people with problems;* and a theme statement, like *People with seemingly insoluble problems need more than sympathy; they need help. English Journal,* LVI (Oct., 1967), 1011.

"The Speaking Voice Approach"

Spurred by the writings of Walker Gibson, many teachers have begun stressing the "voice" of the writer. In which of his many life roles is the student writing—as an athlete, a son, a rebellious student, an expert on a particular subject, a humorist, or what? Voice is often a major determinant of style. One article about it is by D. Bruce Lockerbie, *English Journal,* LVI (March, 1967), 411.

"A Free and Untrammeled Unit"

"There were no specifications, boundaries, restrictions, taboos, or expectations. There was to be no grading for content or mechanics. The results were amazing," Paul S. Redding says of the writing of his California juniors. For evidence see *English Journal,* LVII (Sept., 1968), 846.

Human Hands

In *Teaching Strategies for the Disadvantaged* (Rand McNally, 1966), Hilda Taba and Deborah Elkins suggest having students discuss and write about "Important Things My Hands Can Do." Then for a while longer they observe and discuss hands some more. Finally the students (sixth and seventh grade disadvantaged) write some more and put together a booklet "Observation of Hands."

Unfinished Stories

Grace Ashenfelter of Urbana, Illinois, suggests reading stories to junior high children, stopping at the climax. Each student writes his own conclusion, and students compare their versions. A very effective story for the purpose, this teacher says, is Shirley Jackson's "Charles."

Story Starters

To generate somewhat unconventional personal narratives, Fred E. H. Schroeder suggests use of *New Yorker* covers, stop-action pictures, the writers' various "careers" as high-heel wearers or trout-fly tiers, etc., and looking back at one's sixth birthday or other remote personal event. *English Journal*, LVII (Jan., 1968), 79. In the same issue, p. 93, Rollyn Osterweis tells how he used pictures from Edward Steichen's *The Family of Man* to inspire mainly Negro classes. And on p. 113, Janet M. Thorpe advocates catchy phrases: "worth $575," "he threatened," "if I were," "Loneliness is," etc.

"Slow Learners: Stop, Look, and Listen"

After describing simple classroom incidents (dropping a book, turning out the lights, etc.) slow learners are asked to observe as carefully when they walk to class along the corridor. They are provided the opening sentence, "I stop in the middle of the hall to look and listen." Marilyn L. Lindsay, *English Journal*, LVII (Sept., 1968), 866.

Unusual Assignments

Clifford J. Walker specializes in unusual assignments. E.g., What is the opposite of a tree? A mother of eight cannot love each child as the mother of one loves hers. Can God make a rock so big that He cannot lift it? "The Opposite of a Tree," *English Journal*, LV (April, 1966), 450.

Composition As Process

As an example of class preparation for writing, Milton A. Kaplan tells of reading Christopher Morley's "On Unanswering Letters," then having students discuss how they procrastinate about doing homework, and then assigning "a composition in the same tone as the Morley essay, in which you excuse yourself for not doing something you really know you should do." "Compositions: Assigned or Developed?" *English Journal*, LVIII (Nov., 1969), 1194.

Unusual Composition Topics

Students in Donald Nemanich's advanced composition class at the University of Illinois suggested these as "fun" topics: (1) What from today's world would you put into a time-capsule? (2) What aren't you? (3) For a class period everybody snubs and discriminates against everyone in class who has blue eyes (or blond hair, or what have you). The next period, each student writes his reactions to the way he was treated or the treatment he gave. (4) Each student draws a small item from a paper bag and then writes about it in a genre prescribed by the teacher: fairy tale, adventure skit, etc. (5) An advertisement for an imaginary product.

" 'Make a Town' Makes Better Themes"

An unusual plan for a long series of single-focus themes is described by George Reinfeld. Students create an imaginary town, write descriptions of parts of it and of its citizens, explain its government and its problems, publish an edition of its newspaper, design its educational system and a recreational program, print a public relations brochure, etc. *English Journal,* LIV (March, 1965), 214.

Impromptu Themes

In college most students will have to do considerable writing in class, under pressure. It is kind to give them some practice in the upper high school years.

"Composition Number One, Or the Same Old September Song"

Robert F. Blake works with his students on data sheets for use in viewing TV premieres in September, and their first compositions report their reactions to one of these shows. *English Journal,* LVII (Sept., 1968), 843.

Yale's "Daily Themes"

In the famous "Daily Themes" course at Yale ("daily" means Monday through Friday) seven slogans, introduced one by one at intervals of some weeks, lead to improvement in description, narration, and characterization: (1) Individualize by specific detail. (2) Vivify by range of sensory appeal. (3) Clarify by point of view. (4) Use the indirect method (i.e., show, don't tell). (5) Characterize by speech and gesture. (6) Use words for their connotations. (7) Unify by a single expression. (Richard B. Sewall, Yale University.)

Précis Writing

In many schools, especially in the upper forms of British schools, précis writing is employed to help teach organization. The theory is that a careful précis will not only aid students to understand difficult material but will also show them how the author organized it. Then they may employ similar organizational patterns.

Why Avoid *I*?

Emerson, Franklin, Thoreau, Jefferson, Montaigne, and Gandhi often used first person in their essays. Why, then, do some teachers insist on avoiding *I*? William C. Dell, *Peabody Journal of Education* (Nov., 1963), thinks that the use of *I* helps a student "to preserve his individuality."

Teaching of Style

Style involves making choices among alternatives, says Stephen Judy. There are different ways of writing anything, and the choices a writer makes determine his style. Analysis of different ways that professional writers might have written their sentences can affect students' styles. "Style and the Teaching of Literature and Composition," *English Journal,* LVI (Feb., 1967), 281.

A Contrast of Styles

Able students may enjoy writing the same thing in contrasting styles of diction, says Priscilla Tyler, University of Missouri at Kansas City. E.g., Latinate and Anglo-Saxon: "Will the cosmonauts of tomorrow traverse interstellar space in solitary crews—audacious, infinitely peripatetic?" "Tomorrow will skyfarers sail from star to star in lonely crews—fearless, boundless wanderers?"

Legitimate Borrowing

Shakespeare borrowed his plots. Students may borrow theirs, too, or their ideas for poems. They should change the time to the present, the setting to one the student knows, and then make the adaptations that are inevitably necessary. So Donald J. Dunning argues in "A Derivational Approach to Creative Writing," *English Journal,* LIV (Dec., 1965), 845.

Developing the Five Senses

Mary Ann Eichenberg describes many activities to encourage students to use their senses in their writing. E.g., finding words to describe *ocean,* finding substitutes for *walk* in specific situations, describing a food, describing an object such as a hair roller or a snippet of silk, writing about a bakery or a barber shop, etc. "Bringing a Class to Its Senses," *English Journal,* LIV (Sept., 1965), 515.

"Senior English—Business Emphasis"

Seniors in San Mateo, Calif., may take either a college prep course or one with business emphasis—business letters, sentence study, paragraphing, and a research paper on a business topic. Jacquelyn B. Carr, *English Journal,* LIII (Nov., 1964), 614.

Journalism Via the Class Newspaper

Studying and discussing a series of prepared transparencies, Vermont teacher Marjorie Dundas's eighth graders learn to write leads, news stories, sports stories, editorials, etc., for a once-a-year class newspaper." "A Good Project: A Class Newspaper," *English Journal,* LVI (Feb., 1967), 269.

Manuscript Preparation

If your school does not have definite rules for manuscript preparation, you and your classes may work out a set to be followed in English work.

"Keeping a Journal"

Student-written journals are frequently used today. Dorothy Lambert says, "A journal may be many things: a treasury, a storehouse, a collector's cabinet, a snapshot album, a laboratory, a wardrobe, a drafting board, a psychoanalyst's couch, a tape recorder, a history, a travelogue, a mystical exercise, a letter to oneself." If any of these metaphors are too enigmatic, see her article in *English Journal,* LVI (Feb., 1967), 286.

Six Lessons in Exposition

In the tenth grade, Anna Lou Klein gets results with this series of compositions: (1) Explaining by writing a concrete illustration. (2) Describing by use of detail. (3) Achieving unity by choosing important details. (4) Making a point by comparison or contrast. (5) Convincing by means of logical argument. (6) Using imagination to explain, delight, convince, embroider, or lengthen the paper without wordiness. "Expository Writing for Amateurs," *English Journal,* LIII (Jan., 1964), 16.

Drawings Based on Descriptions

Students in one class describe a real object that is before them (e.g., a wheel puller for a Model-T or the sounding tubes of a xylophone. Students in another class make drawings based on these descriptions, and write criticisms of what is unclear. Then roles are reversed. See Bruce Reeves, "The Object Lesson," *English Journal,* LV (March, 1966), 328.

Student Folder

Many teachers keep folders of student writing, for their own reference and that of students. Some permit inclusion of only carefully revised work. Some use the folder as a motivating device, with no writing to be filed except that which teacher and student have agreed is especially good. Shirley Carriar, in the March, 1961, *English Journal,* recommends having students take home their folders near the end of the year, for parental inspection.

"Ideaform" Theme Paper

This theme paper, prepared and sold by the NCTE for student use, features a useful check list to make easier and more effective evaluation.

Laboratory Period

Some schools use a laboratory period for individual and group guidance in improving writing.

In Barrington, New Jersey, a voluntary laboratory gives help to those requesting it. Small groups, especially of college-bound or foreign-born, write there almost daily and secure special aid. See Grayce F. Salerno, "An English Laboratory in Action," *English Journal,* LII (Jan., 1963), 37.

Concluding a Composition

Lila Chalpin offers these suggestions for effective conclusions: (1) End with a speculation about the future of your subject. (2) End with alternate suggestions on how to handle or interpret your subject. (3) End with the major solution to the problem. (4) End with a by-product or after-effect of an issue which has just been analyzed. (5) End with the meaning that the theme of a literary work has to contemporary man. (6) End with the major effect of the issue or theme of the literary work. "On Ending with a Bang Not a Whimper," *English Journal,* LIII (Jan., 1964), 46.

Drugstore For Sentence Ailments

In a small high school, Jane Z. Carroll has a file of "phamaceuticals," which are exercises to be completed by students who have committed specific errors in compositions. For details, see "A Plan for Meeting

Individual Differences in Composition and Reading," *English Journal,* XLVIII (Nov., 1959), 466. *Individualized English,* sets of materials available from the Follett Publishing Company, provides such exercises.

"Needed: Sequences in Composition"

In November, 1960, Clarence Hach of Evanston, Ill., described in the *English Journal* a sequential plan for compositions. Eight years later, he wrote, "Ideally, we should have as many sequences as we have pupils because all of us know that pupils have various needs and they progress at various rates." He then describes possible sequences for students of various abilities. *English Journal,* LVII (Jan., 1968), 69.

Speaking Precedes Writing

Sometimes the best way to improve students' writing may be to give them many opportunities to talk, argue, discuss, describe, etc., orally. "If the ideas a child expresses orally are meager, immature, and lacking in clarity, his writing will exhibit all these problems in even greater measure." Ruth Strickland, "Evaluating Children's Composition," *Elementary English,* XXXVII (May, 1960), 321.

No Kinesics

"The trouble with the written word is that it comes to us without kinesics—no voicebox, no eyebrows. And the writer's task is to surround his words with other words on the paper so that his reader may infer the quality of the desired speaking voice. That is an art at all levels of writing." A useful concept for both literary study and composition work. Walker Gibson, "The Speaking Voice and the Teaching of Composition," *English Leaflet* (Winter, 1963).

The *Why-Because* Approach

"Why do you believe such and such?" Vivian Buchan asks her Iowa students. Their "becauses" pour out. "Write them down, a paragraph for each *because,* and you'll have a composition," she tells them. "Priming the Pump and Controlling the Flow," *English Journal,* LVI (Jan., 1967), 109.

"Tape Recorders and Writing"

In Indianapolis high schools, students may dictate compositions sentence by sentence into a tape recorder, hear how they sound, and make revisions. The well-equipped laboratory has a tape recorder for each student, writing carrels, a transparency-making machine, and an over-head projector. Stuart L. Sheeley describes the details in *English Journal*, LVII (May, 1968), 637. The work is based on research done at Ball State University and described by A. Tovatt and E. Miller, "The Sound of Writing," *Research in the Teaching of English*, I (Fall, 1967), 176.

Friendly and Business Letters

1. Classes may enjoy writing Christmas letters of appreciation to their parents—possibly *before* Christmas.

2. Some teachers have students write a letter to parents, telling what they have learned during the semester.

3. The Junior Red Cross will help teachers locate other teachers whose students want correspondents. The International Friendship League in Boston will supply foreign addresses.

4. Students in Natchez, Mississippi, wrote to students in other towns along the river. This plan may be varied according to local conditions. For instance, Danville, Virginia, may write to Danville, Illinois, or students in mountainous territory may write to students on the plains.

5. As sauce for the gander, one teacher writes an error-filled letter to be corrected by the class.

6. One teacher collects advertisements about free or inexpensive materials. Students write for any that they want.

7. Some teachers have students write letters to television stations or networks, praising good programs, criticizing bad ones.

8. A Massachusetts teacher prepares slips outlining situations for letters. Boys draw slips from one pile; girls, from another. Each student writes the letter called for by his slip, for example, "Ernest Nash, your good friend, has just received permission to invite you for a week's visit to the family camp in the White Mountains." Betty Leach, "Assignment—Social Letter," *English Journal*, XLVIII (Sept., 1959), 336.

9. Letters of appreciation to prominent persons or organizations (national, state, or local) make a good assignment. Each letter should be specific—not just "I like you."

10. The "five C's" of business letters: "Clear, Courteous, Concise, Complete, and Correct."

11. The biggest problem in letter writing in school is that of motivation. Try to make each assignment as realistic as possible.

More About Thinking

Give students occasional exercises in "balancing the books." For instance, propose the problem of the student who wonders whether he should take a job after school hours; have the class members make needed assumptions, line up in parallel columns the arguments pro and con, weigh the importance of each, and reach a conclusion.

Exercises in Logic

1. Help students to differentiate opinion from fact. For this purpose, discuss statements like these: (a) Our basketball team lost twenty games and won five this seaon. (b) Our basketball team had a poor season. (c) Our coach is not a good coach. (d) Lack of student support cost us several victories.

2. Statements of opinion may be accepted if agreement is reached on the meaning of key terms and if those terms are measurable. For instance, in (b) above, if everyone agrees that "poor" refers to losing over half the games, the opinion may be accepted. But what if preseason predictions were that the team would win no games at all? Help students to see that some statements of opinion cannot be proved, for example, "Chocolate cake tastes better than angel food."

3. Have students distinguish between hypothesis and reality. If an engine stops, the hypothesis may be that it is out of gas. But the flat statement "The engine is out of gas" does not represent reality; the engine may have stopped for another reason.

4. Discuss inductive thinking: reaching a conclusion or generalization on the basis of a number of bits of evidence. The classic example: Came home at night. Flipped light switch—no light. Another—no light. Other houses dark. Clock is stopped. What has happened?

5. Discuss deductive thinking: applying a generalization to a specific instance and reaching a conclusion. For example, test "He's an Italian, so he must like spaghetti" by the syllogism "All Italians like spaghetti. He is an Italian. He likes spaghetti." (The first statement, the major premise, is probably not true.)

Consider the Generalization

1. Discuss with students such hasty generalizations as "I knew I couldn't pass algebra. I failed in the very first test." "Plane travel is unsafe. Every few days you read about a crash." "Let's pick some mushrooms. The Smiths pick them every spring and never get sick from them."

2. Louis Zahner illustrates the pitfalls of generalizations with a student's sentence, "Long books are dull." He asks the student: "On what specific firsthand particulars is the generalization based? Are there enough? How does this statement differ from 'This book is rectangular in shape'? Upon what grounds may value judgments (*dull*) be based? How long, exactly, is *long*?" May 'long' refer to the way a book seems,

not just the number of pages?" After such discussion, the student re-writes: "The longest story I ever tried to read was X, and it didn't in-terest me. I didn't finish it." E. J. Gordon and E. E. Noyes, eds., *Essays on the Teaching of English* (New York: Appleton-Century-Crofts, 1960), p. 13.

Organization

1. Ask students to write single sentences explaining what their pur-pose might be if they were writing on specified topics. For example, Advice to a Practical Joker: "My purpose would be, through presenting an account of a joke that caused an injury, to discourage practical jokes that may be harmful."

2. To keep students reminded of the need for a plan, some teachers ask them to indicate at the end of a composition what type of organiza-tion they used.

3. "We can clarify thinking on the relationship of sub-topics and main topics if we insist upon a more specific statement than 'The sub-topic is *related* to the main topic.' Pupils should understand that the sub-topic is *part* of the main topic. When they have had many illus-trations of this relationship they can see why a certain sub-topic is illogical and can correct the error." (Margaret Mosher, Roosevelt H.S., Chicago.)

4. Help the students to see that a good topic sentence does not merely name the topic, but also suggests how the topic is developed. Poor: Pinochle is the game I wish to discuss. Better: Pinochle is an easy game to learn but a difficult one to play well.

5. Mimeograph pairs of paragraphs. One paragraph in each pair will be notably deficient in unity, coherence, or emphasis; the other, on the same or a similar subject, will be especially strong. Ask students to compare the two and to analyze the weaknesses and strengths.

For Clarity of Exposition

1. Have each student write a paragraph explaining to a "greenhorn" how to perform a simple task that can be demonstrated in class; for example, how to tie a shoelace or how to put on lipstick. The student reads his paper slowly while a volunteer greenhorn attempts to follow instructions, being careful not to do anything not included in the para-graph. If the instructions are inadequate, they must be revised.

2. As a variation, students prepare instructions for drawing a simple, unnamed object such as a fork, spoon, table, or chair. While one stu-dent reads, others, at the board, try to draw according to his directions.

3. Another variation, especially good for oral explanations, is to have

several students prepare moderately intricate diagrams, comparable to this:

A student takes a diagram prepared by another and tells a third student, who is at the board, how to draw the diagram.

4. Have students explain, as to a complete stranger, how to get from the school to various places in the community. The class may object to inaccuracies or to anything that would puzzle the stranger.

Against Research Papers

"The research paper is of no value in the high-school English class, because reasonably correct and creative writing—the goal of instruction in composition—cannot be developed by teaching students to regurgitate the thoughts of others." Thomas E. Taylor, "Let's Get Rid of Research Papers," *English Journal,* LIV (Feb., 1965), 126.

The Point of a Research Paper

A biography of Washington or a description of the Grand Canyon is not a research paper, which must make a point, take a side, argue a thesis. So says Beth S. Newman of Cincinnati, in a useful article, "A Handbook for the Teaching of the Research Paper," *English Journal,* LVI (Feb., 1967), 262.

Let Them Research Themselves

The Oregon Curriculum Study Center recommends as the focus of junior research papers "The American High School Student Today." Students may choose, for instance, to write about causes of dropouts, rebelliousness, drugs, pregnancies, college plans, etc. Glen Love and Michael Payne give details in "The Research Paper," *English Journal,* LVI (May, 1967), 739.

Ideas For Research Papers

1. Sister M. Christina of Rochester, N.Y., gets better results with several short papers rather than one long one. Some are based on

"research-within-the-book," perhaps a novel or a play the class is reading and for which each student chooses a topic. Or, with such a play
as *A Man for All Seasons,* a student may examine part of the historical
background. Other papers, on non-literary topics, may be in the form
of magazine articles. "Training for Research Writing," *English Journal,*
LIII (Nov., 1964), 610.

2. A Chicago teacher recommends as a subject "The Historical Basis
for Characterization of _____ in _____." His example is
characterization in *Abe Lincoln in Illinois,* but the topic could be
adapted to other literary works based on history. Carlisle L. Rast, "The
Beginning Research Paper," *English Journal,* L (Oct., 1961), 469.

3. Some teachers help students select "research" questions answer-
able by intense scrutiny of only one literary work, for instance, for
Hamlet, "Why Hamlet Delays in Killing Claudius." For description of
one example of this approach, see Doris Benardete, "An Experiment in
Primary Research," *English Journal,* LI (Oct., 1962), 487.

4. Librarian Evelyn Cornish offers helpful suggestions for teachers
whose students will write term papers. Among them: (1) Make sure
that material for approved topics is available. (2) Help students to
limit topics. (3) Teach note taking. (4) Require handing in of rough
draft and notes before the finished paper. (5) Stress the content, not
fancy covers, clipped illustrations, etc. *Clearing House,* XXXV (Jan.,
1961), 287.

5. The choice of subject is of major importance. A subject is good
if (1) it interests the student, (2) material from at least four or five
sources is available, and (3) it is not too large and general and vague.
"Aviation" is a poor subject; "Before the Wright Brothers Flew" is better. See Robert L. Coard, "The First Research Paper," *Clearing House,*
XXX (Nov., 1955), 140.

6. To reduce plagiarism, discuss and illustrate proper use of sources
and quotations. Some teachers have students' notes handed in with
the themes.

7. Emphasize that an encyclopedia is only a starting point.

8. With upperclassmen, at least one theme should have all the para-
phernalia: working bibliography cards, note cards, footnotes, bibliography.

9. Able upperclassmen in Porvay, California, may take an English
Research Seminar that meets three times a week, with emphasis on a
large "research" project for each student. The purpose: to build the
self-sufficiency necessary for college study. For details, see Harry E.
Pike, "Survival Kit for the Gifted Student," *English Journal,* LIV (Oct.,
1965), 640.

"Learning to Think and to Write"

Says S. I. Hayakawa, "The way to get students to think is to treat them as if they were capable of independent thought. The self-fulfilling prophecy will operate, and the students will start thinking." Hayakawa also recommends frequent periods in which students write rapidly and continuously for fifteen or twenty minutes, "without pausing, without taking thought, without taking pen from paper. If the student runs out of things to say, he is to write the last words he wrote over and over again over and over again over and over again until he can find other things to say. The paper is to be turned in unsigned—unless the student feels like signing it. . . . [There] will be tremendous improvement with about the third or fourth exercise." *College Composition and Communication* (Feb., 1962), 6 and 8.

Subjects for Written Work

1. Usually, the closer the subject, the better the result. Sometimes let students write about historical incidents, landmarks, or houses of their town.

2. Have students jot down their ideas for themes in a part of their notebook reserved for that purpose.

3. The majority of theme subjects should ordinarily be related to other work of the course. According to Robert Pooley, these subjects should arise from genuine needs or interests of the students—topics that stimulate them to thought and feeling.

4. Occasionally have students write explanations of how a story made them change their minds, how environment made the characters what they were, how a fictional portrayal helped teach an understanding of living people, or how a personal problem may be solved by finding a parallel in fiction.

5. Albuquerque, N.M., High School uses subject matter of other departments for theme subjects in English, whenever practicable.

6. Students' own problems, ideas, hopes, fears, experiences are inevitably the basic stuff for their writing. Let them write what they know and occasionally go outside that to what they imagine.

7. After juniors in Charles Reich's class in Port Washington, New York, have read the four stories in Steinbeck's *The Red Pony,* in which the unifying theme is Jody's learning of basic, universal things, they are given this writing assignment: "Look back into your earlier years to discover an incident or moment when you first became aware of some basic truth—the more staggering, the better. The discovery may be of a factual or a philosophical nature. Emulate the Steinbeck style

in a composition by using as much vivid, sensory, connotative detail as possible to describe your discovery." "Study Questions for *The Red Pony," Exercise Exchange* (April, 1962), 4.

Descriptive Writing: A Planned Sequence

Sister David Marie, Burlington, Wisconsin, suggests a sequence for description, in "Specific Objectives in Composition," *Wisconsin English Journal,* V (Oct., 1962), 17. The major steps:
  1. Informative description, an objective report (e.g., describing for the cleaners a dress for which the claim check is lost).
  2. Somewhat more imaginative description, written from a single physical point of view (e.g., a flower garden or the inside of a room).
  3. Description requiring change of physical point of view (e.g., outside and inside of a house, or going around on a Ferris wheel).
  4. Description with a dominant impression (e.g., loneliness, peace, drabness, gaiety, fear, or disorder).
  5. Description of the physical appearance of a person.
  6. Development of one basic character trait.
  7. Blending of external and internal characteristics of a person ("A loud, brazen individual and a reserved, retiring person would probably not dress alike.").
  8. Suggesting character rather than stating it (may be combined with 7).
  9. Using setting to reveal character (e.g., a girl's room or even a loose-leaf notebook).
  10. Describing from several mental points of view (e.g., "Describe the prom from the point of view of a girl who is going, of one who hasn't been asked, of the mother of a girl who hasn't been asked, of a faculty member, of the janitor."

Literary Writing

1. What the child writes is less important than what the writing does for the child.

2. In the teacher's file should be a gradually growing accumulation of the best writing done by his students. A student who is asked to make a copy for the file is motivated to do still better work. The teacher may choose appropriate material to read to his classes or may keep the file open for their browsing.

3. Each student keeps a journal of his observations, thoughts, emotional reactions, etc. They are not graded, not read by other students, but are read frequently by the teacher.

4. The British author of *Creative English*, Gordon Taylor, offers this advice about describing places: "(1) Select the dominant feature. (2) Be clear about the time, weather and season. (3) Express as indirectly as you can the effect the place has on you. The *indirectly* is important. Present your sense data, and allow it to produce its own effect on the reader."

5. Barbara Hadley's juniors studied main ideas of American short stories, and each drafted a main idea for his own story; studied characterization and wrote character sketches; studied plot and outlined his own; and then spent five days writing stories. "Short Story Writing in Senior High," *English Journal*, LI (Jan., 1962), 49.

6. Virginia Craig suggests having students write "omitted" chapters to accompany books they have read. For example, for *Treasure Island*, the first interview between the doctor and Ben Gunn; for *Ivanhoe*, a new first chapter, "Father and Son," introducing Cedric and Ivanhoe.

7. During the year, each student may make a "magazine" containing his various writings.

8. Let your class, if it wishes, prepare an anthology of original verse or fiction.

9. In a unit involving reading *King Arthur and His Knights*, *The Once and Future King*, and *A Connecticut Yankee*, eighth graders each chose one Arthurian character and wrote an adventure for him consistent with the sort of person he was. Eleanor K. Friedman, "Studying King Arthur in the Eighth Grade," *English Journal*, LI (March, 1962), 200.

10. A systematic program in creative writing is described by Lois Josephs, *English Journal*, LI (Oct., 1962), 468. Students write first objective descriptions, then subjective descriptions, creative exposition, a research paper, character sketches, simple accounts of personal experiences, and finally a short story.

11. Euclid Junior High School in Ohio has a schoolwide haiku contest each year. In the seventh grade it is used to introduce the idea of form in literature. (In the eighth grade, the "blues form" is taught, and able students also experiment with tankas, cinquains, triolets, and free verse.)

12. In writing poetry, start with the image or the emotion or the idea, then search for the form that will best express it. Every poem and every part of a poem is a picture; the form is the canvas and the paint, the medium for transmitting the picture.

13. To observe how poets make use of "sense words," Oakland's budding versifiers read de la Mare's "Silver" for sense of sight, Poe's "Bells" for sound, Morley's "Smells" for smell, and Elinor Wylie's "Velvet Shoes" for touch, B. Jo Kinnick reports. "Creative Writing," *English Journal*, XLVI (Feb., 1957), 86.

14. Paintings may sometimes be the inspiration for students' short stories. They tell the imaginary story behind the painting, or the story of one of the persons or objects portrayed.

15. Selma Bishop says that good creative writers often have IQ's of 95 to 106, are dreamers, aren't good in spelling and mechanics, and are sometimes called "dumb" by other teachers. "What I've Learned About Creative Writers," *Clearing House*, XXV (Oct., 1950), 89.

16. Students may be asked to clip a news story concerning a large number of people, for example, "Thousands Homeless as Floods Strike." The assignment: Pick out one person involved, and build a story on what happened to him.

17. Marianne Marshall's seventh graders use inconspicuous little newspaper stories as the starting points of narratives, or sometimes a concrete object (an apple for every student!), pictures, music, or a story begun but not finished by the teacher. "Helping Seventh Graders To Spot Plots," *English Journal*, XLVII (Nov., 1958), 507.

18. In *Julius Caesar*, what might have happened had Brutus stayed for Antony's oration? Donald Noble advocates having students write on such "iffy" questions. "Rewriting the Great Plots," *English Journal*, L (Dec., 1961), 628.

What Can They Write About Literature?

Will C. Jumper, *Iowa English Yearbook* for 1966, suggests eleven kinds of literature-based compositions. Among them: imitation of a writer's devices, argument of a question of values, argument of a question of policy, persuasion in connection with a course of action, comparison of two selections, an analogy with non-literary materials.

In Favor of Creative Writing

A study by Nita M. Wyatt, reported in *The University of Kansas Bulletin of Education*, XVI (Nov., 1961), 13, and in *Educational Leadership*, XIX (Feb., 1962), 307, revealed that sixth grade children "wrote sentences of greater length and used a greater variety of vocabulary in compositions based on derived [i.e., imaginary] experience than they did in compositions based on real experience."

Creative Writing As Interpretation

"Creative writing must be rooted in the individual's experiences. . . . A student's writing should be an interpretation of what he knows and understands . . . written in such a way that the reader can feel the personal warmth and electricity of the writer." Kenneth D. Jenkins, "Towards a New Awareness of Creative Writing," *English Journal*, LIV (Jan., 1965), 21.

"Verse Writing in an English Class"

Students often write best about common, everyday things they know well. Rupert Brooke's list of "These I have loved" in "The Great Lover" offers something that students can emulate. School buses, trees in winter, dismissal bells . . . the subjects for poetry are all around, says Milton A. Kaplan, *English Journal*, LV (Oct., 1966).

"Concrete Poetry: Creative Writing for *All* Students"

Concrete poetry may be classified as general, found, and a–b–c. The first consists of typographical artistry, the second of miscellany from advertising, etc., and a–b–c poems may consist of words in a–b–c order. Such poetry, says Lavonne Mueller, is "consistent with the visual world of the adolescent." *English Journal*, LVIII (Oct., 1969), 1053.

Word Cinquains

Line 1—one word names topic. *Line 2*—two words define or describe topic. *Line 3*—three words express action. *Line 4*—four words express personal attitude. *Line 5*—one word gives synonym for the topic. E.g., this verse by a seventh-grade class:

Halloween
Inky, gripping
Deceiving, terrifying, haunting
Dancing spirits roaming freely
Mystery

Sister Junette Morgan moves from word cinquains to syllable cinquains, haiku, tanka, Korean sijo, and rhymed poetry. "Writing Poetry in Junior High," *English Journal*, LVII (Oct., 1968), 1009.

"Teaching Students to Write Poetry"

After reading a number of poems, students write tanka, then blank verse, then a stanzaic form, and then anything they choose. Joseph J. Feeney, S.J., *English Journal*, LIV (May, 1965), 395.

"Prelude to the Making of a Poem: Finger Exercises"

Charles Rathbone suggests dozens of finger exercises; e.g., lists of onomatopoetic words, alliterative brand names, a sentence catching the sound of a subway train coming into a station, a rhythmical monolog for a circus barker, a plain and a fancy menu, "animal metaphors" like "Anticipation is a twitching poodle." *English Journal*, LIV (Dec., 1965), 851.

After *Spoon River*

Try having students write poems from the beyond, after they have read in Edgar Lee Masters' *Spoon River Anthology*, suggests Howard F. Decker. "Poetry-Writing," *English Journal*, LVII (Sept., 1968), 849.

Trial Scenes

Students may enjoy converting into trial scenes some appropriate episodes from literature. For example, suppose that Macbeth had been brought to trial shortly after Duncan's death. The defense could contend that there were no witnesses, and of course a wife need not testify against her husband. Ted Gordon edits one such scene in *Clearing House* (Feb., 1968).

Not a Utopia but a Dystopia

Richard Lederer gets some exciting creative writing from his Concord, N.H., students by having them project a present trend into a rather horrifying future. E.g., city buildings get painted over with op art, and thousands of people die of art attacks; or young people take over the world and their leader dies, gasping, "There was nothing, nothing, nothing to protest." "Shaping the Dystopian Nightmare," *English Journal*, LVI (Nov., 1967), 1132.

Creative Satire on Criticism

"The assignment [for honors students] is simply this: 'Being sure to explicate the portmanteau words, write a critical analysis of "Jabberwocky" so that in content and tone your interpretation will satirize the structural analyses of poetry and other genres done earlier in the year.'" Margaret A. Nicholson, "On the Track of the Jabberwock," *English Journal*, LIV (Jan., 1965), 45.

Creative Writing Contest

Beaver Creek High School, in West Jefferson, N.C., holds an annual creative writing contest. Managed by students, who secure an outside judge, the contest has increased the esteem in which writing is held. Elizabeth S. Borlow gives details in *North Carolina English Teacher* (Oct., 1966).

An Anthology of Student Writing

Among eighteen good suggestions for creative writing, William C. Dell suggests "The Ditto Anthology" of student writing; students write critiques on their own and other students' contributions. "Creative Writing in the English Classroom," *English Journal*, LIII (Oct., 1964), 500.

"Patterns by Students"

Schools in Castleton-on-Hudson, N.Y., print a hundred-page collection of student writing each year, illustrative of various kinds of writing, simple and complex, poetry and prose. The collection is used for models during the ensuing year. Richard E. Bamberger, *English Journal*, LVI (March, 1967), 422.

"Writers on Learning to Write"

Be sure to read Lee Frank Lowe's article, reporting what fourteen prominent modern writers say about how they learned to write. Some surprises here! *English Journal*, LIII (Oct., 1964), 488.

Robert Graves on Good Writing

"The craft of good writing is based on a single principle: never to lose the reader's attention. Since the most obvious ways of losing it are to offend, confuse, or bore him, good writing can be reduced simply to the principle of active care for his sensibilities." (From a speech at the 1966 NCTE convention.)

Tips From the Pros

1. Saul Pett, Associated Press feature writer, offers advice most students need (*Illinois English Bulletin*, Nov., 1960):

"Without a viewpoint, the writer's separate little facts, his quotable quotes, his stubborn statistics, his bouncy biographical data, his clever alliterations, his flashy touches are all so much trivia, strung together without purpose, without shape, without effect.

"Don't tease me unless you can deliver, baby. Don't tell me the situation was dramatic and expect me to take your word for it. Show me how it was dramatic and I'll supply the adjective. You say this character is unpredictable? When, where, how? Give me the evidence, not just the chapter headings."

2. Margery Allingham, English novelist, says, "I write every paragraph four times: once to get my meaning down, once to put in everything I left out, once to take out everything that seems unnecessary and once to make the whole thing sound as if I had only just thought of it."

3. Chapter 16, "Work Habits of Professional Writers," in J. N. Hook, *Writing Creatively* (Boston: D. C. Heath, 1966), provides additional information.

Creating Characters

According to novelist James Yaffe, who teaches courses in the writing of fiction at Colorado College, the central part of writing fiction is the creation of characters. Construction, language, and all other elements are important only in terms of their success in bringing characters to life. A student naturally begins by making himself the main character, but he can gradually be moved into putting himself inside other people's skins.

Teaching Tone and Point of View

To teach tone, Sherry Zivley has students write paragraphs in serious, light, angry, and satirically understated manner. To teach point of view, she has her students write about a school problem as it would be seen by a new sophomore, a sophisticated senior, a parent, and a teacher. "Sugar-Coated Tone and Point of View," *English Journal*, LIII (Sept., 1964), 439.

Point of View Again

Auto crash: Boy and girl in each car. Police officer. An observant witness. Write an account of the crash from each of these six points of view.

Practice in Writing Description

H. C. Brashers suggests that students write the same descriptive paragraph from the viewpoints of three different personae (e.g., dark clouds as seen by a would-be picnicker, a drouth-stricken farmer, and a fan at a baseball game whose team is ahead 8–0 in the fourth). A second exercise is to write a description of the same thing for different audiences (e.g., for a child, a foreigner, a grandmother). "Teaching Descriptive Style," *Journal of English Teaching Techniques* (Spring, 1968).

On Paragraphs

Richard A. Meade and Geiger Ellis studied the paragraphing in *Saturday Review*, *English Journal*, and letters to the editor. Fifty-six per cent of the paragraphs did not follow procedures prescribed in standard textbooks. Of the forty-four per cent that did, development by examples ranked first, with development by reasons, chronology, contrast, repetition, cause-effect, definition, and description trailing far behind. Of the non-textbook methods, a combination of procedures ranked first, followed by "additional comment," "two themes," "one-sentence paragraphs," "opposition," and "question." This useful survey is reported in "Paragraph Development in the Modern Age of Rhetoric," *English Journal*, LIX (Feb., 1970), 219.

Developing a Paragraph

1. In Pittsburgh's Schenley High School some teachers follow the practice of taking a couple of student-written paragraphs that are unnecessarily general and then rewriting them with enough detail to make them vivid. The contrasting paragraphs are then examined by the class, so that students learn how they can expand and brighten a generalized, dull statement.

2. Useful in teaching paragraph development are exercises in which students merely list all the details they might include if they were writing a paragraph. Give them such topic sentences as these: "Christmas morning is a hectic time at our house." "No cats are better than one cat." "Washing a car is easy if one prepares for the job."

A second step may consist of deleting the items that do not harmonize with the others.

The Kellogg Hunt Study

A synopsis of the research which won the 1964 NCTE Distinguished Research Award is presented in the April, 1965, *English Journal*, pp. 300–309. Professor Hunt shows the significant growth in "T-unit" length from grade 4 to grade 12. A T-unit is a group of words that can be terminated grammatically between a capital letter and a period. Older students have learned to cram much more information into each T-unit.

"The Overhead Projector—Aid to the Composition Program"

"I use transparencies to teach subordination, proper parallelism, logical transitions, effective punctuation. When working on the longer literary paper . . . , there are visuals for teaching outlining, note-taking, documenting the information." Gloria Erwin, *English Journal*, LIII (Jan., 1964), 48.

"About Those Sentence Fragments"

Conclusion of an article writen entirely in fragments: "The conclusion being that effective writing often contains many sentence fragments, that these fragments are a must for today's professional writers. But, with a warning that most any composition may become ineffective if sentence fragments are overused. Right?" C. T. Shades, *English Journal*, LIX (Nov., 1969), 1223.

The Teacher's Comments

When marginal comments already show, for instance, that a student's punctuation is shaky, a comment at the end like "You need to work on punctuation" is rather pointless. Instead, argues James L. Green, the comment should chiefly concern the extent to which the student has developed his controlling generalization by following out whatever it has suggested he is going to do. *English Journal*, LVII (Feb., 1968) 215. In March, 1968, p. 372, Virginia FitzPatrick discusses the use of the tape recorder to present comments to each student.

Let's Play Editor

Gordon R. Wood, of the University of Chattanooga, points out that, though it is the students who need practice in editing their writing, in actuality it is the teachers who get this practice. Insruction in what an editor looks at and how he works may help students to edit their own work. A copy editor from a local newspaper may be willing to present a lecture.

How Many Themes?

Research at Florida State suggests that writing ability is not related directly to the number of compositions written. Nevertheless, at Murray State College it was found that the majority of students placed in remedial classes had done little writing in high school. Although there is nothing sacred about a theme a week, considerable practice in writing (like considerable practice at the piano) seems essential for success.

Comments Do Help

In a controlled experiment, Dr. Ellis B. Page found that greatest average improvement was made by students whose teachers commented rather specifically on test papers; next largest improvement, by students whose papers carried such comments as "Excellent!" or "Let's raise this grade!"; and smallest improvement, by students who received only a grade with no comment.

Guide to Revision

Henry Fitts, of Winchester, Massachusetts, provides for his students a list of about thirty questions that they should try to answer as they revise the first draft of a composition. The questions are grouped under the headings of "looking over the job as a whole" (e.g., are the points in the best order?), vocabulary (e.g., is every word the best word for the job it is doing?), sentence structure (e.g., is the meaning of every sentence absolutely clear?), and style (e.g., are there any clichés that should be removed?).

"Teach Revision—It Works!"

Howard A. Van Dyk of San Mateo, Calif., recommends this exercise in revision: *Step I:* Write a six-sentence paragraph of description. *Step II:* Improve the verbs. *Step III:* Improve the nouns and modifiers. *Step IV:* Eliminate the deadwood. *Step V:* Copy and proofread. *English Journal,* LVI (May, 1967), 756.

Student Reactions to Writing

West Virginia high school students were polled to get their reactions to the way theme writing was taught them. They advocated more writing (!), definite directions, choice of topics, understanding of grading system, use of models, much writing in class, help in writing poetry, chance to read classmates' themes. Among their dislikes: lack of explanation of a grade, failure to recognize plagiarism, overemphasis on serious subjects, lack of discussion of what makes a good theme. A valuable article. Lorena A. Anderson, "Ways and Means in the Teaching of Writing," *English Journal,* LI (Dec., 1962), 621.

Plagiarism

Clues to possible plagiarism, but not definite proof, are these, says Richard Braddock (*Iowa English Bulletin,* Dec., 1959): (1) Much better than usual writing; (2) smooth writing with careless spelling, punctuation, or omissions; (3) content with which the writer probably would not be familiar; (4) writing that does not match the assignment.

To forestall plagiarism, Braddock recommends (1) frequent writing assignments, with about half done in class; (2) requiring submission of a rough draft with the finished out-of-class paper; (3) avoiding assignment of the same topics year after year; (4) clarifying what plagiarism is and why independent writing is important. (*N.B.:* The most frequent plagiarism probably involves copying from the encyclopedia or a similar source. Teach students how to copy honestly, giving credit as professionals do.)

Gimmicks in Grading

1. Sometimes, try for a month or so to mark only *good* things in student writing, ignoring all errors, bad sentences, etc.

2. Have a class or a group evaluate some papers by listing in parallel columns for each theme "Strong Points" and "Weak Points."

3. As a once-a-year device, have "state's attorneys" and "defense lawyers" analyze papers.

4. Don't be afraid of humor in your written comments, but beware of satire, irony, sarcasm. Don't be afraid to praise, but avoid overuse of that colorless word "interesting."

5. Bar or line graphs may show students' progress in selected phases of writing. Time-consuming to construct, though, unless you teach students to keep their own graphs up to date.

6. Since a teacher tends to become either more or less liberal as he proceeds, it is wise to grade answers to question 1 in A–Z order, question 2 in Z–A order, etc.

Grading Trading

In 1902 Gardiner, Kittredge, and Arnold recommended trading of sets of papers between classes "of equal rank" in different schools, with all papers written on the same subject. Each class evaluates the other's compositions in detail. Seventy years later the idea still seems good.

Group Evaluation

Students write single paragraphs. They develop a brief list of superficial things to look for in evaluation (margins, neatness, spelling, capitalization, punctuation). In groups of four or five they comment on each paper from their groups—in regard to these criteria only. Each paper is then rewritten. A little later, one more criterion, such as unity, is added, and the process is repeated. Then other criteria— always one at a time. Joseph P. Fotos, "Teaching the Paragraph in the Junior High School," *English Journal,* LV (Nov., 1966), 1071.

"The Student-Centered Theme Series"

Students spend a week evaluating and discussing a group of themes written by their class. Lively discussion results, and genuine learning.

Teacher stays in the background. Linda W. Wagner, *English Journal,* LIII (Dec., 1964), 689.

"Evaluation of Writing: A Three-Part Program"

(1) Papers containing errors that the class agrees are thoroughly understood are not accepted and must be corrected. (2) Laboratory sessions consider paragraphing and organization of students' themes. (3) Teacher-student conferences concentrate on content. Sister Miriam Bernadette, SNJM, *English Journal,* LIV (Jan., 1965), 23.

Dictation of Comments

For a few suggestions about use of dictating equipment for recording comments about students' themes, see Bernard Tanner, "Teacher to Disc to Student," *English Journal,* LIII (May, 1964), 362.

Lay Readers

In Princeton, N.J., one day a week is reserved for lay readers to confer with students whose papers they have evaluated. Eugene N. Doherty, "The Princeton Township Lay-Corrector Program," *English Journal,* LIII (Apr., 1964), 273.

Students As Lay Readers

Coral Gables, Florida, has experimented with using senior honors students as lay readers.

If Your School Has Lay Readers

(1) Select readers with care. (2) Don't insist that teachers must use readers. (3) Let students regard the reader as "another audience." (4) Use guidelines for the program. (5) Make the program teacher-oriented. (6) Evaluate the program regularly. So says Charles Blondino, "Looking at a Theme Reader Program," *English Journal,* LVII (Oct., 1968), 1028. Guidelines that he recommends are in Leonard Freyman's *Improving English Composition* (National Educational Association, 1965).

How Should Non-Academic Writing Be Evaluated?

Marjorie X. Schwartz recommends evaluation of (1) intention (issue clear; assertion narrowed, qualified, defensible; purpose sustained throughout); (2) reasoning (generalities supported with particulars; organized sensibly; free of contradiction and free of proof or comment which is irrelevant; free of fallacies); (3) word choice (free of vague, careless references; free of terms which over-generalize). She quotes several compositions as examples. "Non-Academic Writing," *English Journal*, LV (April, 1966), 468.

Rating Scales for Compositions

In "An Investigation of the Reliability of Five Procedures for Grading English Themes," *Research in the Teaching of English*, I, No. 2 (Fall, 1967), 190, John C. Follman and James A. Anderson describe these rating scales, with subpoints not included here:

CALIFORNIA ESSAY SCALE
   I. Content
  II. Organization
 III. Style and Mechanics

CLEVELAND COMPOSITION RATING SCALE
  A. Content—50%

Convincing	Unconvincing
Organized	Jumbled
Thoughtful	Superficial
Broad	Limited
Specific	Vague

  B. Style—30%

Fluent	Restricted
Cultivated	Awkward
Strong	Weak

  C. Conventions—20%

Correct Writing Form	Incorrect Form
Conventional Grammar	Substandard

DIEDERICH RATING SCALE

	Low		Middle		High
Ideas	2	4	6	8	10
Organization	2	4	6	8	10
Wording	1	2	3	4	5
Flavor	1	2	3	4	5
Usage	1	2	3	4	5
Punctuation	1	2	3	4	5
Spelling	1	2	3	4	5
Handwriting	1	2	3	4	5

FOLLMAN ENGLISH MECHANICS GUIDE
    Reference
    Spelling

    Punctuation
    Sentence Structure
    Paragraphs
    Diction
    Word Usage

What Joy?

"English teachers seem to talk much about the joy of writing, though they seem in fact to write little. . . . An English teacher who does not occasionally write for publication has *no* business teaching writing. The blind lead the blind too often already. English teachers need not compound the error," says Kenneth L. Donelson, *Arizona English Bulletin* (April, 1968). Similar is "The Case for Pop Scholarship," by Charles Suhor, *English Journal*, LIX (Jan., 1970), 116, who urges teachers to write popularized articles for newspapers and magazines.

9

The English Language

THE NEED FOR BREADTH

Past Narrowness and the Reaction Against It

For many years, in many classrooms, instruction in the English language was characterized chiefly by its poverty. Typically it emphasized only grammar and usage. Instruction in grammar was mainly a matter of labeling: underline the complete predicate, encircle the direct object, define a pronoun, diagram a sentence. Instruction in usage was too often just a matter of distinguishing "incorrect" from "correct," filling in blanks with the words approved by textbook writer and teacher. In these classrooms recall was stressed more than reason, rigidity was emphasized more than flexibility, analysis outweighed creativeness, linguistic pains and perils were greater than linguistic pleasures and promises. Teachers and students alike regarded the study of language as the dullest part of the English course; it seemed useful but necessarily painful and dry.

A reaction was bound to come eventually. It was triggered in part by teacher and student unhappiness with the arid content, in part by research which demonstrated that the multitudinous hours of instruction were not bringing the hoped-for results, and in part by the "new grammars," which revealed inaccuracies and inadequacies in traditional school grammar and which attacked the extreme prescriptivism of traditional usage.

As so often happens, however, reaction became over-reaction. In some schools, the study of the English language was virtually abandoned, the time saved being added to the literature component. Whereas about fifty per cent of instructional time had in many places been used for work on grammar and usage, one national study in the mid-sixties showed that time given to the English language had dwindled to about fifteen per cent.

Almost unquestionably, fifty per cent of class time on grammar and usage was too much. Almost equally certain is that fifteen per cent of class time is too little for the English language, broadly conceived.

Facets of the Language

The English language, you see, is much more than grammar and usage. It encompasses not only those two segments, but also history of the language, dialectology, and lexicology, each of which has subdivisions. One possible outline showing major subdivisions is as follows:

I. English grammar
   A. Phonology
   B. Morphology
   C. Syntax
   D. Lexicon
II. Usage
   A. Principles
   B. Specific questions of usage
III. History of the language
   A. Relationship of English to other languages
   B. The English language in America: vocabulary development, pronunciation, spelling, etc.
   C. The English language in England and other countries
IV. Dialectology
   A. American dialects
   B. British dialects and those of other English-speaking countries
V. Lexicology
   A. Lexicography
   B. Semantics
   C. Word origins and historical development

Like any outline, this shows only bare bones. It does not hint at the wealth, the fascination, inherent in some or all of the items. In the following sections, and in Chapter 12 (which concentrates on lexicology), we'll look at the beautiful flesh.

Why a Broad Conception Is Desirable

But first we should consider why the study of the English language should be broadly conceived. I've already suggested one reason: the old exclusive emphasis on grammar and usage turned students off, not on; it failed to arouse in many of them a keen interest in the language and its effective use. Also, in theory this study was expected to make students "better" writers and "more correct" writers, but it was by no means uniformly successful in doing so. Further, it told only partial truths because grammar and usage were not taught in the context of language as an exciting human activity, the context of language as a developing thing that changes as human experiences change, the context of language not of constraint but of an avenue to freedom.

The broader emphasis that now seems more appropriate does not ignore grammar and usage but places them in this context. Children learn that "right" and "wrong" are relative terms; linguistically what is "right" in one century or in one situation may be "wrong" in another. They explore the sociology of language: what people do with language and what language does with, to, and for people. They consider why people don't all talk alike and they come to realize that the use of a "different" dialect is no sign of inferiority or superiority as a human being. They learn that the English language has changed through the centuries, that it is still changing, and that throughout their lives it will continue to change. They play with the language, experiment with it, become familiar with the richness of its resources, and learn more about its potential than about its perils.

TEACHING GRAMMAR

Traditional Grammar

A grammar of any language is a systematic description of that language. There have been many such descriptions of English, some varying only in details, some basically unlike the others.

The major descriptions are those labeled traditional, historical, structural, and transformational. The last few years have witnessed the emergence of still other descriptions, such as tagmemic, sectoral, and stratificational, but these have not yet had great impact upon instruction.

Traditional grammar treats English as if it were Latin or at least Latin-derived; it may be traced back to the Latin grammarian Priscian of Constantinople, about A.D. 500, who strongly influenced Ben Jonson and other early English grammarians, and whose eighteenth-century followers such as the British Joseph Priestley and Robert Lowth and the American Lindley Murray adopted in large measure his classifications. They used Latin terminology and tended to regard Latin as an ideal language of which English represents a debased form. One of the functions of a grammarian, they believed, is to prescribe ways in which English may come closer to "purity." Through the exercise of his reason, a grammarian should evaluate each construction, determining whether it is "correct" or "incorrect." Then he should lay down rules for all users of the language to follow.

Traditional grammar has provided the basis for most instruction in the language for the past two centuries. Such instruction involves classifying words as parts of speech; classifying groups of words as phrases, dependent clauses, or independent clauses; and judging the rightness or wrongness of each locution or syntactical structure.

The strengths of traditional grammar are that it is a fairly complete system and that it has the advantages of tenure; it has been around long enough that many people know something about it. Its chief weaknesses are these: (1) It does not explain important differences in superficially similar sentences like those used as examples by Noam Chomsky: *John is eager to please* and *John is easy to please*. (2) English is a Teutonic language, and its grammar is Teutonic, not Latin. To try to force one language into the mold of a quite different language is as unwise as to try to bake an angel food cake in a pie pan. (3) Anyone who is familiar with the history of language knows that absolute rights and wrongs do not exist in language. What is regarded as right in one century or one language may be regarded as wrong in another; for example, Chaucer and his contemporaries regularly employed double negatives, and the French language still uses two negative words (*ne . . . pas*) to express one negative idea, but modern English considers *don't have none* incorrect. The prescriptive traditionalists flatly decreed that each construction was absolutely right or absolutely wrong. (4) The definitions by traditionalists were often questionable. "A sentence is a group of words expressing a complete thought," for instance, is untrue because a sentence is not necessarily a group of words and because a whole paragraph, chapter, or book may be needed to express a complete thought—if such an expression is even possible. For another example, if an adjective is "a word that modifies a noun or pronoun," then *upstairs* and *here* in *the man upstairs* and *the man here* must be adjectives, as must *brick* and *rose* in *brick house* and *rose garden.*

Historical Grammar

Historical grammar concerns itself with the history of English and its relations to other languages. Many nineteenth-century grammarians, especially in Germany, explored Middle English, Old English, the related Teutonic tongues, and eventually the other members of the vast Indo-European family of languages, of which English is but one of a few dozen descendants of an ancestral tongue. Modern English, these grammarians found, is a sister of German, Dutch, and the Scandinavian languages, and a cousin (in one degree or another) of the Romance languages, Russian, Iranian, and a number of others. The work of the historical grammarian was brought to a climax by the great Danish scholar Otto Jespersen, whose huge grammar (1914) is based upon sound historical scholarship and corrects many of the misconceptions of the traditionalists.

Historical grammar has had little impact upon instruction, except in scattered places. Here and there a unit has been taught on the history of English, or a brief lecture has been given on the relationships of English and other languages. But in general the work of the historical grammarians, when known to teachers at all, has been accorded respect but not put to use. On pages 343–49 are some suggestions for employment of historical background.

Structural Grammar

Structural grammar derives from the twentieth-century work of Leonard Bloomfield, of anthropologists such as Edward Sapir, and of various others such as C. C. Fries, Bernard Bloch and George L. Trager, and Henry Lee Smith. Their first assumption is that study of the spoken language is especially important, since written language is based upon spoken. Secondly, they believe that it is desirable to separate form from meaning in describing language, and to concentrate on form. Thus it is possible to analyze grammatically "The wolders adeled a tadful poggy" even though four of the words are unknown; it is good to do so because connotations and idiomatic problems do not get in the way. Thirdly, the structure of a sentence can be revealed by an analysis of its "immediate constituents," which always come in pairs. For instance, the nonsense sentence above consists of *The wolders/adeled a tadful poggy*; the constituents of the part to the left of the slash are *the* and *wolders*; the part to the right is *adeled/a tadful poggy*, and so on. Fourth, English sentences are constructed according to a few basic patterns (as described, for instance, in Paul Roberts' high school text of the mid-fifties, *Patterns of English*). Fifth, structural grammarians directly oppose the prescriptivism of the traditionalists. They argue that the grammarians' function is to describe the language, not to prescribe or to label "right" or "wrong"; a scientist, they say, studies horseflies without judging the rightness or wrongness of horseflies' behavior. (This does not mean that structural grammarians advocate *ain't*; they certainly do not use it in their articles. But they find that *ain't* exists, and therefore they have a responsibility to describe the conditions in which it exists.)

A number of teachers, especially in the fifties and early sixties, made some use of structural grammar in their classrooms. But it did not sweep the country. One reason is that teachers brought up on traditional grammar did not feel comfortable with structural. Another is that the structuralists antagonized some teachers by unnecessarily vicious attacks upon what those teachers had been teaching. A third is that the structuralists went off in various directions, often disagreeing among themselves on basic questions as well as on details. A tradition-oriented teacher would ask, "How can I teach something in such a state of uncertainty and flux?" Fourth, teachers who taught a great deal about phonology and immediate constituents were often not convinced of the value of this instruction to their students. And fifth, the extreme emphasis upon form divorced from meaning alienated many teachers, who felt that the separation was artificial and unwarranted.

Transformational Grammar

The pioneers of transformational grammar were Noam Chomsky and Zellig Harris, with Robert Lees, Robert Stockwell, Owen Thomas, and Paul Roberts among the many who have made notable contributions to theory or popularization. Whereas structuralists are interested in scientific ways to describe sentences and sentence parts, transformational-generative grammarians concern themselves with the ways by which we generate new sentences. Early transformationalists said that we employ a limited number of "kernel" sentences, which are in the active voice, are positive rather than negative, are declarative, and are very simple in structure. By means of various kinds of "transformations" these kernels can be changed to passive voice, to negative, or to interrogative, modifiers may be added, and by a combining transformation a simple sentence may be made compound or complex. An an example of the transformation from active to passive, Chomsky gives a formula for changing a sentence like "John admires sincerity" to "Sincerity is admired by John": $NP_1 - V - NP_2 \rightarrow NP_2 - \text{is} + V_{en} - by + NP_1$.[1] Essentially this says that to form the passive the nominal *sincerity* (NP_2) is moved to the front of the sentence, *is* and the past participle *admired* (V_{en}) are used, and the nominal *John* (NP_1) is moved to the end of the sentence and placed after an inserted *by*. This formula will account for any passive voice sentence.

Since 1957, transformational theory has been developing rapidly, although disagreements among its proponents are frequent. Today these grammarians seldom mention kernel sentences, but talk instead about the "deep structure" of sentences. The sentence "Sincerity is admired by John" represents surface structure only. The deep structure (in simplified form) would be $John + O_2 + \text{Pres} + be + en + admire + by + \text{Passive} + sincerity + O_2$. This reveals the underlying structures that result in "Sincerity is admired by John."

Several studies have offered evidence that transformational grammar is a useful teaching tool. At Ohio State, Bateman and Zidonis conducted a study of ninth graders which showed that ninth and tenth graders exposed to such instruction wrote a higher proportion of "well-formed sentences" than did comparable students in control groups.[2] In a Harvard doctoral dissertation John Mellon described teaching that emphasized the use of combining transformations with seventh graders; his conclusion was that such instruction resulted in the writing of more mature sentences.[3]

[1] *Syntactic Structures* (The Hague: Mouton & Co., 1957), 43.
[2] Donald Bateman and Frank Zidonis, *The Effect of a Study of Transformational Grammar on the Writing of Ninth and Tenth Graders* (Champaign: NCTE, 1966).
[3] John C. Mellon, *Transformational Sentence-Combining: A Method for Enhancing the Development of Syntactic Fluency in English Composition* (Harvard University, 1967).

Many teachers, however, have been rather frightened by the transformational formulas, which often remind them of mathematics or chemistry. They have been no less frightened by the "sentence trees" that transformationalists employ in an attempt to visualize linguistic operations. For example, Owen Thomas uses this tree to illustrate the deep structure of the passive sentence "The car has been bought by the boy": [4]

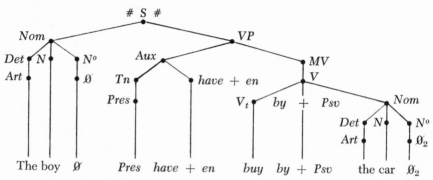

Fearful that they themselves do not understand the intricacies, even after a course or two in college, some teachers have been understandably reluctant to teach transformational grammar to students in junior and senior high schools.

A Modern Pedagogical Grammar

Told that traditional grammar is full of holes, and not really at home with structural or transformational grammar, too many teachers, as we have already noted, have given up entirely on the teaching of grammar—any kind of grammar.

It is a mistake to abandon grammar, just as it would be a mistake to go back to the days when fifty per cent of English class time was devoted to grammar and usage. A pedagogical grammar for the secondary schools should not be the detailed sort that you may have encountered in college linguistics courses. Scholars rightly study the details and thus contribute to the sum of human knowledge; one doctoral dissertation, for instance, was devoted solely to the use of the expression *do so*. A pedagogical grammar, however, may not even mention *do so*, and it need not stress the elaborate formulas or

[4] Owen Thomas, *Transformational Grammar and the Teacher of English* (New York: Holt, Rinehart and Winston, Inc., 1965), p. 193. Reprinted by permission of Holt, Rinehart and Winston, Inc.

the sentence trees, although simplified formulas and trees are useful teaching devices.

What pedagogical grammar ought to do is to stress and clarify the systematic nature of the English sentence. A sentence is not a random collection of words. If the preceding sentence had been phrased *Not words sentence a a collection of random is,* you would not have understood at all what I was saying. Small children learn a language as quickly as they do because every language is a systematic thing, a patterned thing. Children learn the basic patterns, along with the less advanced transformations, at a very early age. They also learn, and continue throughout their lives to learn, words and more words that can fit into the various slots of a sentence. If there were no patterns, no slots, the learning of a language would be much more difficult or even impossible; in fact, any communications except the simplest could probably not be made.

But why should students be taught the description of a system that they already follow fairly capably? One reason is just to help them see that it is a system. Students often feel that they live in a chaotic, unpredictable world, a world without system. That which is regular may comfort them, whether it be the constant and predictable orbiting of the planets around the sun, the constant presence of a mountain on the horizon, or something so apparently unimportant as the methodical working of the English sentence. Another reason for teaching about the system of the sentence is that many students gain confidence in themselves when they realize that in large degree they have already mastered the operation; it takes a reasonable amount of intelligence to follow the system for putting a sentence together, but they do it (at least in speaking) hundreds of times a day, so therefore they are reasonably intelligent. Further, as the Bateman-Zidonis and Mellon studies revealed, an understanding of the basic system may lead to more extensive use of sentence combinations, a decrease in babyish sentences, a growth toward maturity in sentence construction.

Twentieth-century grammarians have done much to clarify the syntactic system of English—to help us understand how the English sentence works. Even though no one of their descriptions may be completely satisfactory for schoolroom use, a grasp of these descriptions enables a teacher to select pieces that fit together as a reasonably coherent whole. In the following explanation I shall ignore phonology (the study of sounds) and morphology (the study of word form) and shall emphasize syntax (the way that parts of a sentence are put together). And even though modern transformationalists do not talk about kernel sentences, I shall retain the term as one useful for pedagogical purposes.

When we put a sentence together, basically what we are doing is assembling two or more concepts in a form that shows a relationship. For example, if you say "Water evaporates," you are saying in effect, "The thing that is composed of hydrogen and oxygen and that is designated in the English language by the symbol *water* [concept 1] performs either now or as a characteristic mode of behavior the action designated in English by the symbol *evaporates* [concept 2]." More elaborate sentences may bring together a substantial number of concepts. The words used in each sentence (except possibly for a few "function words" like *or* or *the*) are in effect shorthand symbols that stand for possibly huge concepts with many ramifications, like *love* or *democracy*. These words are assembled in a highly systematic fashion so that an approximation of the relation between symbols as it exists in one person's mind may be conveyed to the mind of another.

The number of basic relationships is relatively small, although no complete agreement exists about how many there are; it may be four or nine or ten or seventeen or some other number, but certainly not an infinite number. In an article that I once wrote for a Japanese magazine,[5] I chose nine. If some other number seems better to you or to your textbook author, it doesn't matter. The important point is to let students see that we repeat a small number of patterns, or kernels, again and again.

Here are illustrations of the nine patterns, together with the formula for each. In these formulas, *NP* stands for "noun phrase," which may be any kind of nominal, one word or more; *Vi* stands for intransitive verb and *Vt* stands for transitive verb; *ADJ* stands for adjective; *ADVp* for adverb of place. *Be* refers to any form of *be*, such as *is* or *were* or *has been; seem, become, remain, give*, and *make* or *consider* are symbols which also stand for other verbs that behave in the same way.

1. SOMEBODY OR SOMETHING IS IDENTIFIABLE OR CLASSIFIABLE AS SOMEBODY OR SOMETHING. E.g., *George is a fireman. My sisters were actresses. Eagles are birds. Spinach is a vegetable.* The formula is

[5] "The Nine Things That Everybody Says." *Taishukan: The English Teachers' Magazine*, XVII, No. 2 (1968), 56–58.

NP¹ *be* NP¹. (The raised 1 indicates that both NP's refer to the same person or thing.)

2. SOMEBODY OR SOMETHING IS DESCRIBABLE IN A CERTAIN WAY. E.g., *Mary is beautiful. Henry is handsome. Melons are delicious. Those grapes are sour.* The formula is NP *be* ADJ.

3. SOMEBODY OR SOMETHING IS LOCATED. E.g.,*Visitors are downstairs. The children are here. Fog was everywhere.* The formula is NP *be* ADVp.

4. SOMEBODY OR SOMETHING SEEMS TO BE DESCRIBABLE IN A CERTAIN WAY. This is slightly different from 2. In 2 we say boldly that *Mary is beautiful* and that *Melons are delicious.* In 4 we are a little less positive, saying *Mary sems beautiful* and *Melons taste delicious.* In addition to *seem, appear* and the verbs of the senses (*taste, smell, feel, look, and sound*) are often used—verbs often called "linking." The formula is NP *seem* ADJ.

5. SOMEBODY OR SOMETHING BECOMES OR REMAINS SOMEBODY OR SOMETHING, OR DESCRIBABLE IN A CERTAIN WAY. E.g. *Jeff became a policeman. Henry remained a student. The boy grew tall. The weather turned cold. The weather stayed cold.* As the last three examples indicated, synonyms may replace *become* or *remain.* The formula is NP¹ *become* or   NP¹ or
   remain   ADJ

6. SOMEBODY OR SOMETHING PERFORMS AN ACTION. E.g., *Louise hurries. Fish swim. Water evaporates.* Thousands of verbs may fit into the second slot. The formula is NP   Vi.

7. SOMEBODY OR SOMETHING PERFORMS AN ACTION UPON SOMEBODY ELSE OR SOMETHING ELSE. *Marge invited Helen. Charles burned his fingers. A landslide demolished the house.* The formula is NP¹ Vt NP². (The raised 1 and 2 indicate that the nominals do not refer to the same person or thing. An exception is the *-self* or *-selves* words, as in *Charles hurt himself.*) The NP² in traditional grammar is called the "direct object."

8. SOMEBODY OR SOMETHING GIVES (TO) SOMEBODY ELSE OR SOMETHING ELSE SOMEBODY ELSE OR SOMETHING ELSE. E.g., *Louise gave her husband a child. Robert told his son a story. Whiskey gives Jerry heartburn.* The formula is NP¹ Vt-*give* NP² NP³. The NP² in traditional grammar is called the "indirect object," and this time the NP³ is the direct object.

9. SOMEBODY OR SOMETHING MAKES OR CONSIDERS SOMEBODY ELSE OR SOMETHING ELSE SOMEBODY ELSE OR SOMETHING ELSE. E.g., *Hunger made him a savage. The voters elected Nixon President. We consider Reginald an upstart.* The formula is NP¹ Vt- *make* or NP² NP².
   consider

Note that the second NP² refers to the same person or thing as the the first NP². (A variation of this pattern is NP¹ Vt- *make* or
   consider

NP^2 or ADJ. E.g., *His reading made him wise. Her friends consider her beautiful.*)

Notice that the verb in the first three of these patterns is always a form of *be*. In the fourth and fifth it is a linking verb like *seem, become,* or *remain*. In the sixth it is an intransitive verb. And in the last three it is a transitive verb, which necessitates the presence of at least one following *NP*, a direct object. Thus the nine patterns fall into four basic types, depending upon the kind of verb employed.

To any of the nine patterns, an adverbial modifier may be added at any place where it makes sense. The modifier, then, does not occupy a specifically designated slot, as the other items do. For instance, the pattern 5 sentence *The weather turned cold* may include the adverb *suddenly* in any one of three places: (Suddenly) the weather (suddenly) turned cold (suddenly). Transformational grammarians show this possibility by adding (ADV) at the end of each formula. The parentheses indicate that the addition is optional.

Techniques for Teaching a Modern Pedagogical Grammar

In showing that the English language is systematic, you may well begin with instruction in the sentence patterns. The procedure may be largely inductive. For instance, a student may be asked to speak a very short sentence about someone or something in the room. He may perhaps say "Our teacher is Mrs. Lively." You put the sentence on the board, and work with the class until they see that the underlying statement is SOMEBODY IS SOMEBODY. Later, with a sentence like "Desks are furniture," this statement is expanded to SOMEBODY OR SOMETHING IS SOMEBODY OR SOMETHING. After working with several sentences of different patterns, the class recognizes that each basic sentence starts with SOMEBODY OR SOMETHING. Since this expression is rather awkward, you suggest an abbreviation or symbol; for this, *NP* may be used, although some teachers prefer *NOM* (for *nominal*). Later, other symbols (*be*, ADJ, etc.) are used for the other slot-fillers. Eventually the class will arrive at all nine patterns, although for some the teacher may need to provide specific leads, such as "Let's use *seem* or *seems* in our next sentences."

Another procedure, after some preliminary work on one type of sentence such as the three patterns that use *be*, is to place a number of cards in small boxes labeled *NP* (or *NOM*), *be*, ADJ, ADVp, and

NP again. In the twenty or so cards in each *NP* box are various nominals with words like *a, an, the,* or *some* prefixed when necessary: *shoes, a student, some salt,* etc. The *be* box contains *am, is, are, was, were, must be, has been, is being,* etc., with some form of *be* always as the main verb. The *ADJ* box has some adjectives that can describe the nominals used: *red, interesting, dry,* and so on. The *ADVp* box contains words or phrases indicating place: *here, downstairs, in the street,* etc. A student draws a card from the first *NP* box, then one from the *be* box, and then one from one of the remaining boxes. He may be lucky enough to come up the first time with a sentence that makes sense, such as *A student is here.* But sometimes he may come up with nonsense like *A student were furniture.* When this happens, he keeps his first *NP* but draws other cards from the other boxes until he brings out a meaningful sentence.

In constructing sentences, the mind works in a way analogous to what the students have just done, except that the mind has a much greater supply of words in its "boxes," with each word representing a concept. A speaker or writer chooses the *NOM* representing the concept that he wants to say something about, chooses the *be* or other verb that fits with it and that will help him say what he wants to, and then selects from another "box" the word representing the concept to be tied in with the others. The mind performs this operation at amazing speed, comparable to that of a computer. It almost instantaneously makes its choices, and out comes a sentence. As I have already said, a student may gain respect for himself and his mind when he comes to realize that he performs this computer-like operation hundreds of times each day.

Later the class learns how through transformations the mind creates negatives, interrogatives, commands, and passives, as well as sentences much more complex than the kernels. For example, students learn how adjectives are "embedded." Say that a speaker has in his mind the concepts underlying *Mike is a boy* and *Mike is strong.* Because of his familiarity with the language, the speaker instantly combines these sentences as *Mike is a strong boy.* The procedure for the transformation may be illustrated in this way:

MATRIX: | Mike is a boy |

INSERT: Mike is strong

When the insert is moved into the matrix, the repetitious *Mike is* is deleted. One idea, as you see, is combined with another. A highly involved sentence combines a large number of ideas according to a regular system.

For a slightly more complicated example, consider how the mind combines sentences like these:

Matilda straightened the picture.
Matilda is a meticulous girl.
The picture was on the wall.

MATRIX: Matilda straightened the picture.

INSERT 1:   Matilda is a meticulous girl

INSERT 2:   The picture was on the wall

If we use the relative clause transformation, we come out with *Matilda, who is a meticulous girl, straightened the picture on the wall.* The appositive transformation is a little shorter: *Matilda, a meticulous girl, straightened the picture on the wall.*

The "parts of speech" of traditional grammar are implied in the patterns. Nouns and pronouns occupy the *NP* slots, as do phrases or clauses used as nouns. Verbs are always in the second slot. Adjectives and adverbs of place (as well as other *NP's*) are in the third or sometimes the fourth slot; other adverbs, as we have seen, may be put wherever they make sense. Conjunctions appear in certain transformations that combine sentences. Prepositions may precede nominals; the prepositional phrases are then used as substitutes for one-word adjectives or adverbs.

It is not possible here to go into additional detail about this method of grammatical description, which draws upon traditional, structural, transformational, and tagmemic grammar.[6]

Whatever kind of grammar you teach, you will get best results by encouraging the student to think rather than to memorize. Basically you are asking them to analyze and describe the processes that they themselves use in constructing sentences, and gradually to add to these processes by writing sentences of kinds they do not ordinarily write—perhaps employing transformations they do not frequently use. As an example of such adding we may consider the appositive.

---

[6] Some features of this kind of grammar may be found in two books by Paul Roberts, *Patterns of English* and *English Sentences* (published by Harcourt, Brace and World in 1956 and 1962); the first is more structural in its emphasis, the second more transformational. Roberts' widely-used series of language books is also eclectic. *Modern English Grammar for Teachers,* by J. N. Hook and Michael Crowell (Ronald Press, 1970), is a more sophisticated and theoretical treatment.

This is a relatively mature construction that is found infrequently in the speech or writing of young children. Through showing how we combine sentences like *My father is an ardent golfer* and *My father shot a hole-in-one last week* into *My father, an ardent golfer, shot a hole-in-one last week*, and through providing ample practice, you can add this useful construction to a student's linguistic repertoire. Similarly you can increase the use and precision of relative clauses, adverbial modifiers, participial and other phrases, nominative absolutes, and other valuable structures. The method, to repeat, is to place little emphasis on definition and on picking out these constructions in professional writers' work, and to place more stress on thinking about how the structure is inserted in sentences and on giving creative practice in its use.

The procedures described here differ in two important ways from traditional ones. The first difference is that students compose many sentences instead of spending most of their time on analysis. The second is that the teacher steadily uses inductive tactics. The deductive approach, in contrast, begins with telling the students what the rule or principle is and then continues by having them dissect illustrative sentences. *The English Language Arts in the Secondary School* says:

> The inductive method (discovery of a generalization through the study of many specific illustrations) should for the most part be used in introducing a new grammatical point. Although there is nothing wrong with stating a grammatical point first and then illustrating it, a more effective procedure, usually, is to have the student find for himself from the analysis of a number of carefully prepared sentences the principle for which he has need. The important point here and elsewhere in the teaching of grammar is that the student shall not be tempted to memorize a statement instead of developing a clear concept.[7]

TEACHING THE HISTORY OF THE ENGLISH LANGUAGE

Why Teach Language History?

In recent years a number of schools have incorporated instruction in the history of the English language. Sometimes the instruction is only casual and incidental, as for instance when the teacher and class note differences between Shakespeare's language and that of today, or when they look up the meaning of an unfamiliar word. Sometimes it is more methodical, in the form of a planned unit or two.

[7] New York: Appleton-Century-Crofts, Inc., 1956, pp. 376–77.

There is room for both kinds: the casual instruction can create an appetite for the more formal, and has the advantage of relating language history to other parts of the program; a well-developed unit provides a coherent view of language growth over the span of centuries.

Why this increasing interest in teaching history of the language? Here are a few of the reasons:

Such study builds an awareness that language is not a fixed thing, but that it changes in relation to historical events and social change, that it responds to the needs and interests of people. Thus it ties language to history and sociology. The language is changing steadily even today, and will continue to change as long as anyone uses it.

Knowledge of the characteristics of language of a bygone day makes it easier for students to read the literature of that period. The language barriers to Chaucer, Shakespeare, Milton, Swift, and even to some nineteenth-century writers, are considerable, but can be reduced by historical study.

In the history of the language are found explanations of why people speak in different dialects. Patterns of settlement reveal, for instance, why New England, the Midlands, and the South have different dialects.

Similarly, historical study explains many of the differences in usage, often showing that forms currently in bad repute (e.g., *have wrote, ain't*) were once widely accepted.

Knowledge of language history also clarifies many oddities of the English language, such as the spellings of *doubt* and *colonel* or the use of plural *were* with the singular subject *you*.

Historical knowledge makes clear how words enter a language, how the huge English vocabulary developed, and what may happen to a word after it is entrenched in the language. Thus it may increase students' interest in words.

Study of language history shows how English is related to many other languages of the world.

Teaching the History

In connection with the final point above, you may want to work out with the class a chart tracing the languages descended from the Indo-European spoken several millenniums ago, probably in northeastern Europe but gradually spreading to almost all of Europe and to much of Asia. The chart will show that English has a sibling relationship to other Germanic languages (High and Low German,

Dutch, Flemish, Norwegian, Icelandic, Danish, and Swedish), has a first-cousin relationship to Latin-descended languages (Spanish, Portuguese, Romanian, French, and Italian) and a similar relationship to Greek, Scots Gaelic, and Irish Gaelic, and has a second-cousin relationship to Balto-Slavic languages (Lettish, Lithuanian, Bulgarian, Slovenian, Serbo-Croatian, Polish, Czecho-Slovak, and Russian) and a similar relationship to Iranic and Indic languages (Persian, Hindi, Bengali, Romany).

One way to illustrate the closeness of relationship of English to other Germanic languages is to show students how to count to ten in several of those languages. In contrast, a less closely related language like French shows fewer similarities, and an unrelated language like Japanese shows none.

English	Dutch	German	Danish	French	Japanese
one	een	eins	en	un	ichi
two	twee	zwei	to	deux	ni
three	drie	drei	tre	trois	san
four	vier	vier	fire	quatre	shi
five	vijf	fünf	fem	cinq	go
six	zes	sechs	seks	six	roku
seven	zeven	sieben	syv	sept	shichi
eight	acht	acht	otte	huit	hachi
nine	negen	neun	ni	neuf	ku
ten	tien	zehn	ti	dix	ju

A unit on American English is especially suitable in conjunction with the study of American literature. It may be presented either all at one time or scattered appropriately throughout the year. Among topics suitable for inclusion are these:

The language of American Indians; Indian words surviving in Modern English.
How early settlers named unfamiliar things (e.g., *skunk, catbird, Jack-in-the-pulpit*)
French and Spanish influences on American English; the influence of other languages
How American places got their names
Sources of people's surnames (e.g., names chosen by blacks after emancipation)
Similarities and differences between British and American English; criticisms of American English by British writers
The influence of independence on American English
Syntactic and stylistic changes in American English from 1600 to the present; the trend toward shorter sentences; language experimenta-

tion in American writing (e.g., Whitman, Cummings)
American spelling
Changes in American pronunciation
Historical reasons for dialects; dialect in literature; American dialects today (See the next section of this chapter.)

✳ Growth of the American vocabulary; sources of new words; some recent coinages; words for the Space Age
American slang; rapidity of change in slang; up-to-date slang in your school

In the study of British English, a chronological approach is probably best. One method is to start with examples of British writings from the past and to make comparisons with Modern English. For example, consider this Old English version of the Lord's Prayer:

Father our, thou that   art in   heaven,   be thy name hallowed.
Faeder ure,   u   e   eart on heofonum, si   in   nama gehalgod.

Come   thy kingdom. Be done thy will   on earth   as   in
To becume   in   rice.   Gewur e   in willa on eor an swa swa on

heaven.   Our   daily   bread   give us today.   And forgive
heofonum. Urne ged eghwamlican hlaf syle us to d eg. And forgyf

us our debts   as   we   forgive   our debtors.   And not   lead
us ure gyltas, swa swa we forgyfa   urum gyltendum. And ne gel ed

thou us into temptation, but deliver us from evil.   Amen.)
 u   us on   costnunge, ac alys   us of   yfele. So lice.

The purpose of study of such a passage is not to teach students to read Old English (graduate courses in universities do that), but only to give them some familiarity with an older form of the language and thereby to get a better understanding of its modern development. Among the points that can be observed in the example are these:

1. Although there have been changes in pronunciation, some Mod E words have the same written form as in OE (*on, and, we, us*).
2. Other words, though they have changed in spelling and pronunciation, are still similar to their OE forms (*f eder, ure, u, eart, heofonum*, etc.)
3. Some Mod E words are derived from OE words that look very different (e.g., *daily* represents a considerable shortening of *ged eghwamlican; loaf* comes from *hlaf*).
4. Some words have been lost from the language and replaced by others (*gewur e, costnunge, alys*). In some instances, a form related to an OE word survives in German (as *rice* is a cognate of German *Reich*).

5. OE words more often have inflectional endings than do Mod E words, since OE was a more highly inflected language (e.g., *ure, urne,* and *urum* for *our, forgyf* and *forgyfa* for *forgive,* inflectional endings on *heofonum* and *eor an*).

6. OE word order often differs from that of Mod E (e.g., *Faeder ure, To becume in rice, urne ged eghwamlican hlaf syle us*).

Similarly, passages in Chaucer and later writers may be examined to compare them with Mod E.

Here are some other suggestions for activities in connection with the study of older forms of the language.

1. To show the contributions of other languages to English, the class draws a river with Anglo-Saxon as the source. Into this river flow tributaries as follows: Celtic (small), early Latin borrowings (small), Danish (small), Norman French (large), Latin in Renaissance times (large), Greek in Renaissance times (medium), later French (large), Italian (medium), Spanish (medium), and then a number of small or medium tributaries that in the last few centuries have contributed to English, including German, Greek and Latin again, French again, Chinese, Japanese, African languages, American Indian, Russian, etc.

2. Choose a somewhat longer OE passage than the Lord's Prayer (above). A selection from the writings of King Alfred, such as his account of the voyage of Ohthere, is suitable. With the class, scrutinize it carefully, as we did the Lord's Prayer.

3. Trace the spellings of a few words from OE to the present. E.g., *all, home, it, few, summer, how, sail* (verb), *might* (verb), *they.* Note that spelling did not become very systematized until after the invention of printing; discuss why this was so.

4. Devote some attention to the pronunciation of older forms of the language, noting especially how several vowel sounds changed in a regular pattern, as illustrated by *ham home, hus house, swete sweet, ridan ride, etc.* A student might report on the Great Vowel Shift, which gave to English vowels values different from those in Continental languages.

5. Compare the forms of OE nouns, verbs, and adjectives with their modern equivalents, noting the numerous inflectional endings on the former and the comparatively few such endings in Mod E. How does Mod E get along with so few inflections?

6. Study the Normal Conquest and its influence on the language: class distinctions, contributions to vocabulary, expediting of the loss of inflections, gradual merging of English and Norman French (with English predominant).

7. Besides looking at the language of Chaucer, examine some other passages in Middle English. Parts of Layamon's *Brut* (c. 1205) may illustrate the transition from OE to ME. Students will also

find interesting passages from *The Travels of Sir John Mandeville* (translated into English c. 1377). Verses from Wycliffe's Bible, translated in Chaucer's time, may be compared with later versions.

8. As an example of the language just before Shakespeare flourished, the class may look at a scene from *Gammer Gurton's Needle*, which uses a southwestern dialect instead of the London dialect that was soon to become preeminent. Then, in looking at the language of Shakespeare, the class may observe not only vocabulary differences from Mod E but also word order, the manner of phrasing questions and negatives, forms of verbs and nouns and adjectives (e.g., *most unkindest*). The *do*-transformation, now used in questions like *Did he respond?* and negatives like *He did not respond,* was just coming into being. Shakespeare used both it and older forms like *Responded he?* and *He responded not.*

9. Compare sentence length in the prose of Milton, Swift's and Johnson's essays, and nineteenth-century prose with sentence length today. Discuss any advantages or disadvantages that today's relatively short sentences may have.

10. Compare conversational style as reflected in one of Sheridan's or Goldsmith's eighteenth-century plays with modern conversational style.

11. Find out and give examples of how words may enter the language (by borrowing, compounding, use of affixes, functional shift, onomatopoiea, back-formation, acronyms, blending). Find out and give examples of what may happen to words once they are in (degeneration, elevation, generalization, specialization, radiation, shortening, lengthening, metathesis, shifts in pronunciation and spelling).

12. In light of the historical study, list some of the outstanding characteristics of Mod E, such as huge vocabulary, few inflections, tendency toward short sentences, existence of various dialects, rather fixed sentences, extensive use of transformations, single "accepted" spellings for most words.

A number of compact textbooks suitable for high school students' study of English language history are now coming on the market, most of them containing a wealth of useful exercises. For the teacher's reference, two books by Thomas Pyles are especially useful: *Words and Ways of American English* (Random House, 1952), and *The Origins and Development of the English Language* (Harcourt, Brace and World, 1971). Other fairly recent and good books are Margaret Bryant's *Modern English and Its Heritage* (Macmillan, 1962), Morton W. Bloomfield and Leonard Newmark's *A Linguistic Introduction to the English Language* (Knopf, 1963), and L. M. Myers' very readable *Roots of Modern English* (Little, Brown, 1966).

Many excellent collections of readings also exist; among them are C. Merton Babcock's *The Ordeal of American English* (Houghton Mifflin, 1961); Donald W. Lee's *English Language Reader* (Dodd, Mead, 1967); Elizabeth M. Kerr and Ralph M. Aderman's *Aspects of American English* (Harcourt, Brace and World, 1963); Gary Jennings' *Personalities of Language* (Crowell, 1965); and W. L. Anderson and N. C. Stageberg's *Introductory Readings on Language* (Holt, Rinehart and Winston, 1966). For a broad view, suggested by the title, Robert F. Hogan's collection called *The English Language in the School Program* (NCTE, 1966) is valuable. The great source for detailed information about American English is H. L. Mencken's three-volume *The American Language* (Knopf, 1936–48), which has since been abridged and updated by Raven McDavid (Knopf, 1963).

DEALING WITH DIALECT

Dialectal Variations

When the Angles, Saxons, and Jutes came from northern Europe to the British Isles in the fifth and sixth centuries A.D., they spoke slightly different versions of their common Germanic tongue. The Jutes settled mainly in the southeastern area, the Saxons in the southwestern, and the Angles in the middle and the north. As a result, Old English had several major dialects: the Kentish where the Jutes lived, the West Saxon where the Saxons were, and two divisions of the dialect of the Angles, Mercian in the middle area and Northumbrian to the north. In Middle English, Kentish and West Saxon merged as the Southern dialect, Mercian became known as the Midland dialect, and Northumbrian became the Northern. East Midland, the major dialect of London, was a variety of Midland and was eventually to become "standard" British English; Southern differed from it in many respects, as did the dialects in the shires to the west of London; and Northern differed (and still does) in other ways. Today as one travels through the British Isles he notes very substantial dialect variations.

Patterns of settlement thus contributed to the growth of divergent British dialects. They contributed no less to the growth of American dialects, although the pattern of distribution is less neat because American immigrants came from many countries and often moved from one area to another. Nevertheless, dialect geographers can describe with considerable accuracy the characteristic differences in the dialects of, say, Philadelphia and Boston and New York, or northern Illinois and southern Illinois. An expert can talk for a few minutes with a person and can then make a comment like "You must have grown up in the area of Charleston, South Carolina, but probably spent some time in Milwaukee, Wisconsin, since I notice a Milwaukee overlay."

The point is that everyone's speech is influenced by that of the area where he lives, especially in his childhood and youth. Dialects differ in pronunciation (e.g., *creek, orange, tomato, tire, greasy*), in vocabulary (e.g., *skillet* or *frying pan* or *spider, corn on the cob* or *roasting ears* or *sweet corn, levis* or *jeans* or *blue jeans* or *overalls*), and in grammar or usage (e.g., *dived* or *dove, sick to* or *at* or *in* or *on* or *with my stomach, this is theirs* or *theirn*). Although education may alter some forms to others, everyone tends to retain at least some of the dialect characteristics he learned in the place where he grew up.

The dialectal variations we have discussed so far are geographical, the results of patterns of settlement. But there are also social or socioeconomic variations. Men don't talk exactly like women in the same region, nor do the old and the young talk just alike, or the poorly educated and the well-educated, or the rural and the urban, or the people with one occupation and those with another. The social and economic circumstances of one's life inevitably affect one's speech.

Note that there is nothing inborn in all this. If a baby is taken from one environment and placed in a quite different one, he acquires the linguistic coloration of his new environment. Mark Twain's *Pudd'nhead Wilson* dramatizes this fact. A white infant and one with some black ancestry are successfully interchanged by the mother of the part-Negro child. The one with Negro blood is brought up as the scion of a well-to-do family and is given a good education. In manhood he talks like this:

It couldn't be helped, uncle. If I had known you were going to challenge him I should have felt obliged to sacrifice my pledged word in order to stop it, but Wilson couldn't be expected to do otherwise than keep silent.

The all-white child, brought up as a Negro slave, talks like his putative mother, whose speech is like this:

You done it. Gwine out to cle'r yo' brain! In de fust place you ain't got none to cle'r, en in de second place yo' ornery eye tole on you. You's de low-downest hound dat ever—but I done tole you you dat befor'.

Had the children not been interchanged, the dialect patterns of the two would have been reversed. Socioeconomic environment, then, not racial or other heritage, and in this instance not geography, accounts for such dialectal variations.

The Sins of the Past

Before much was known about dialectology, teachers assumed that people shouldn't speak a dialect. Everybody should speak "correct English," and most teachers believed they knew what correct English was. It usually meant the language that they themselves spoke natively or that they had laboriously learned in school and college. A dialect used wrong pronunciations, wrong words, wrong grammatical forms. A dialect was a bad thing that should be extirpated.

These teachers were unaware that everyone speaks a dialect. No two persons' dialects are exactly alike. Each has an "idiolect," his own personal manner of expression. Although each idiolect is necessarily colored by the speaker's geographical area and his socioeconomic environment, it shows at least small variations from other idiolects. But teachers who did not know this tried to make everyone speak alike, though the attempt was in vain.

The constant attacks upon dialectal differences sometimes had a blighting effect on students. They were made to feel that their language and that of their parents and friends was inferior, something to be ashamed of. Some of them did their best to eliminate the variation between their speech and that which teacher and textbook said was correct. Others merely did the exercises and emerged unaffected. Still others—the ones adversely affected—concluded that here was only one more piece of evidence showing the unreality and the uselessness of school; they were penalized because they didn't learn to "talk like a book," and often these penalties, along with others in the school, made them decide to drop out at the earliest possible time.

Lack of knowledge about dialectology had another harmful effect as well. Say that a Southern boy moved into a Northern community (or vice versa). He talked differently from the natives. They ridiculed his speech and imitated it derisively. Unless he was strong and agile enough to beat up his tormentors, or unless he had skill in football or some other activity prized by the community, the torture might last a long time. But if the children had known some of the facts about language variation, they might have accepted him a little more readily.

The Present Attitude

Today enlightened English teachers try to avoid the errors of their predecessors. For one thing, they build understanding that everyone speaks a dialect and that dialectal variations are interesting. Life would be monotonous if every human being were blonde, blue-eyed, and five feet eight inches tall, and also if every human being possessed the same skills and the same temperament. We don't expect all people to be exactly alike, and we'd be bored if they were. Language variation can add its own spice to living and to our appreciation and enjoyment of our fellows. This attitude of interest in and acceptance of dialects is easier to inculcate than it would have been fifty years ago, because radio and television have exposed today's students to many dialects, people today travel more than they once did, and Americans move to other communities more often than was formerly true. Therefore there is ever-increasing opportunity to hear dialects other than one's own and to realize that a person who speaks differently may nevertheless be worth knowing.

One step in teaching about dialects lies in familiarizing students with the chief reasons for the existence of dialects. Geographical dialects exist, as we have seen, mainly because of patterns of settlement. Thus French influence is evident in parts of Canada, German in parts of Pennsylvania, Elizabethan English in isolated pockets in the South, Spanish in the Southwest. Within a given community the speech patterns of today may still reflect the coming of Finns, Norwegians, Italians, Irish, or some other group a century ago.

Another reason for the existence of geographical dialects is physical barriers—mountains, rivers, large lakes, etc. Even though settlers on the two sides of a barrier may have similar language backgrounds, they gradually diverge in language if they do not communicate steadily. Perhaps the most dramatic example of this is the growth of the Romance languages from the parental Latin. As there was little mingling across the Pyrenees or the Alps, the Latin in what we call Spain, France, and Italy became more and more divergent until eventually what started out as only small dialectal differences became different languages.

The influence of a leader may also sometimes affect the language in an area. For example, it is said that the lisped Spanish *c*, as in *Barcelona*, exists because a Spanish king lisped. He said "Barthelona," etc., his courtiers who wanted to be like him said the words in the same way, and the common people later imitated the courtiers. Today the influence of a leader may be less potent, but historically it probably was the cause of a number of variations.

Imitation

It is more difficult to locate the ultimate sources of social dialects. Certainly differences in speech have for thousands of years gone along with differences in social rank. There are hints of this in ancient drama, and anthropologists have described tribes in which use of one set of language forms was the prerogative of chiefs only, or in which men and women spoke essentially different languages. The language of medieval serfs was apparently highly unlike that of their masters. Shakespeare reflected the difference a few centuries later by the artifice of having his "inferior" characters speak in prose (the Porter in *Macbeth*, Bottom and his fellows in *MND*) while his dukes and kings and other such worthies spoke a blank verse that in reality would have been far beyond their powers.

Social dialects

If we could with assurance explain why social dialects exist, we would no doubt have to draw upon such historical bases. In countries where class distinctions have been openly made, the lower classes were uneducated and were restricted to menial tasks. Though many lower class individuals were unquestionably as intelligent as their social superiors, their lack of advantages made them tend to be less articulate, to be more repetitive in their speech, to make less use of abstractions, and to be less concerned with "refinement" of their speech since refinement of any sort had little relevance in their lives.

In America's supposedly classless society, millions of people still get poor education, live in ghettos or rural shacks, and speak a language that the snobbish regard as inferior and incorrect. Others, especially those climbing out of poverty, still employ the language of their childhood homes or modify it by attempting to use some of the forms they hear in the school or office or factory or on television. Each person, in fact, tries to use a language appropriate to his surroundings. The change to a different type of language, however,

Note! sometimes results in problems when the speaker returns to his family or childhood friends.[8]

Teachers know, though, that society being what it is, users of non-standard dialects may be penalized for its use; front doors open and good jobs are available to the speaker of a standard dialect, but the front doors close and a "No Vacancy" sign may go up when a non-standard speaker appears.

So teachers have a dilemma. They know that there is nothing inherently inferior in expressions like "I's heah" or "She don' wan' none," and that the users of such expressions may be as capable as other persons. But they know also that society values "I'm here" and "She doesn't want any" and has its own ways to reward persons who use them, its own ways to punish those who do not.

Teacher's task Faced with this dilemma, modern teachers spend quite a bit of time teaching facts and attitudes about dialects. They start with geographical variants, about which people are less sensitive. When they come to social variants, they make clear that nobody's language is wrong or inferior. One kind of language, called standard, is however more highly regarded by many influential people of all races. This prestige dialect is thus introduced as one of the variants. Children are given opportunity to learn about it, to practice it, and to decide eventually for themselves whether they want to use it when it seems appropriate to do so. In other words, there is no condemnation of the child's present language and that of his parents, nor is there forced use of the prestige dialect. But the instruction is there, and the student can decide for himself how much use he wants to make of it.

Eldonna L. Evertts, former assistant executive secretary of NCTE, has stated the point in this way:

> Certainly there need be no concentrated effort to demand that all persons speak alike. Differences in language can be recognized and appreciated. It is not derogatory that a person's idiolect reflects his personal background. When, however, a pupil uses a variety of language which places economic, social, or academic limitations upon him, the teacher should help the pupil gain access to another more generally accepted dialect—without expecting him to abandon his former patterns, as there will be times when these patterns will serve him well.[9]

[8] This theme is one of those developed in a British book, *The Uses of Literacy,* by Richard Hoggart (Pelican edition, 1958). Hoggart tells of the difficulties encountered at home by a young man who is the first in his family to get a college education.

[9] Dimensions of Dialect (Champaign: National Council of Teachers of English, 1967), Introduction.

Note "without expecting him to abandon his former patterns." The old attempt was to replace one dialect with another. The modern attempt is to add, for those who don't have it, another dialect and to encourage the student to switch from one to the other as situations demand. Some such switching is already done by almost everyone, students may be reminded. They themselves don't use quite the same kind of language in talking to a small child, to a grandmother, to the minister, and to the principal of the school. Similarly they may find it valuable to use "home" language at home, "school" language in school or in employment, switching from one to the other.

Some Techniques for Teaching

The Board of Education of the City of New York has produced a pamphlet called *Nonstandard Dialect* (1967; available from NCTE). Among its many suggested activities designed to teach standard English to speakers of nonstandard English are these:

1. Use a regional map to present major American dialects.
2. Use recordings to show that recent prominent Americans spoke different dialects: Roosevelt, Kennedy, Johnson, King, Humphrey, television performers, etc. (The point could again be emphasized here that there are geographical variations in standard dialect.)
3. Use pronunciations of key words such as *penny, Mary, office,* and *park* in class committee preparation of a chart showing dialect variations existing among students and faculty members.
4. To show how language changes with time, play recordings of early English.
5. Play and discuss a recording of *My Fair Lady;* more advanced students may substitute *Pygmalion.*
6. Make extensive use of oral pattern-practice drills to make students more at home with sentences containing verb forms and other standard forms not customarily used by the student: *He's a tall boy, Does she sing,* etc.
7. Play "Toss a Word." Team members "toss" a nonstandard word at the opposition, who give as many standard synonyms as they can think of.
8. Relate appropriate language to appropriate dress.
9. Use role-playing to show switching of dialects according to the situation.
10. Read poetry illustrating effective use of both standard and nonstandard dialect: Langston Hughes, Countee Cullen, Gwendolyn Brooks, etc.

11. Discuss and drill on "The Magic of S," which is frequently omitted in nonstandard speech (*he walk, two desk,* etc.).
12. Provide drill on *t, d,* and *l* at the ends of words.

Thirty-two maps from linguistic atlases are reproduced in Carroll E. Reed's *Dialects of American English* (World, 1967). Through their use, students may learn about dialect areas, isoglosses, and dialect geographers' methods of indicating frequency of use of such synonyms as *cottage cheese, Dutch cheese,* and *smearcase.* The small book also has useful information about colonial English and regional variations.

Roger Shuy's *Discovering American Dialects* (NCTE, 1967), in addition to providing many examples of geographical differences, makes suggestions for dialect "fieldwork" that students can do. E.g., study local history to find out where early settlers came from and what changes in population have since occurred; fiind the origin of local place names; conduct a questionnaire study to discover local residents' names for various things. Shuy also recommends study of dialect in various literary works, such as *The Yearling, I Remember Mama, Giants in the Earth, Papa Is All, My Antonia, The Education of Hyman Kaplan, Mr. Dooley Says, In the Tennessee Mountains, Huckleberry Finn,* and *Gentle Persuasion.*

Raven McDavid makes this helpful general recommendation about social dialects of minority groups:

> Forms, words, pronunciations which are obviously characteristic of a minority group and which produce unfavorable reactions among members of the dominant culture should be the systematic target of the early programs in the schools. The emphasis should not be negative, or error-chasing exercises, but positive, or habit-forming drill.[10]

Later in the same article McDavid offers this advice:

> . . . Too many students, too many teachers even, shy away from alien varieties of English as from the plague; they feel that any variety different from their own is *ipso facto* inferior. In Detroit, even superior students have been brainwashed in courses in "corrective speech" if their pronunciation has been that of Oklahoma. But once the problem of social dialects is honestly faced it should be possible to explain that differences arise not from mental or moral inferiority but from differences in cultural experience—and that the most divergent dialect, however poorly suited for educated middle-class conversation, has a dignity of its own. Faced in this way, the social dialects of a metropolitan area become not a liability but an asset—a positive contribution to

[10] "Dialect Differences and Social Differences in an Urban Society," in Robert F. Hogan, ed., *The English Language in the School Program* (Champaign: NCTE, 1966), p. 194.

educating our students to an understanding of the variety of experience that enriches a democratic society.

PROBLEMS IN SYNTAX

Talking about Sentences

Study of grammar somewhat like that described on pages 336–42 will enable students to understand the system of the English sentence and perhaps to add a few structures to their syntacticon (their repertory of syntactic structures). Particularly effective, as was suggested, is the building of sentences rather than mere analysis.

Much talking about sentences and their structure is also useful. Sometimes, for instance, a group of words may be found that does not resemble any of the usual sentence patterns. Suppose that Frances, a girl in your class, encounters "Along the highway sped the black Cadillac." Frances observes that something seems wrong, or at least different, about the structure. You say a word of praise, and with the class take a closer look at the sentence, noting that word order has been shifted from the conventional "The black Cadillac sped along the highway." Instead of *Nom + Vi (+ Adv)*, Frances' sentence uses inverted order: *(Adv) + Vi + Nom*. The class notes that this is an optional kind of transformation; writers sometimes use it for special effects. Students may construct other examples: *Next came the band*, or *To this goal were all his efforts directed*. Then or later they may look at other kinds of inverted sentences, such as those starting with *nor* (e.g., *Nor did his injury keep him out of the game*) or with an adjective (e.g., the palindrome *Able was I ere I saw Elba*). Many questions, they recall, are inversions of statements: *Is he?* is the inverted form of *He is*.

Suppose that at another time Larry finds a sentence fragment such as "Never again" or "On the contrary." These represent a different kind of transformation, one in which deletions have occurred. Usually the context will suggest at least approximately what has been chopped out. For instance, Larry's "On the contrary" may occur in this context: "You may suppose that the twins learned their lesson. On the contrary. The next day they were once more climbing the same tree." The fragment is shortened from something longer such as "On the contrary, the twins did not learn their lesson." The short form was used to prevent unneeded and perhaps boring repetition.

The class notes also that fragments are frequent in conversation:

"Where to?"
"Gym."
"Why?"
"Big game today."

The class observes that such fragments (really deletion transformations) are a kind of shorthand. In the rush of conversation, more than in writing, we often leave out parts of sentences that our listeners can readily supply for themselves. Without the deletion transformations the conversation above might have gone like this:

"Where are you off to?"
"I am going to the gymnasium?"
"Why are you going to the gymnasium?"
"A big game is being played today."

Fragments, if the deleted elements are readily recoverable, are useful in speeding up conversation. And if the listener does not understand, he can ask for clarification. When something is written or printed, though, there is usually no opportunity to ask questions. For that reason—to assure clear communication—fragments are relatively rare in writing.

The point of all this is that much talking about sentences is beneficial. It can shed light on rather rare constructions, such as inversion after an adverb, and on the virtues and limitations of other structures such as the fragment. Such open discussion gets much better results than, say, a flat, unreasoned, and unrealistic demand that students must never use fragments.

Diagraming

The beloved Columbia professor the late Allan Abbott used to tell his classes that he had learned so well in secondary school how to diagram sentences that he could construct a diagram of the sixteen-line opening sentence of *Paradise Lost*. But, he said, "the chief adverse criticism of the themes I wrote in college freshman English was 'faulty sentence structure.'" Although some teachers and textbooks still employ their own variations of the nineteenth-century Reed–Kellogg system, there is hardly an iota of evidence that such instruction leads to improved student-written sentences. Students who already "know their grammar" may enjoy diagraming as a men-

True.

tal activity, but few students who do not already understand syntax
learn much about it through their attempts at schematic picturing.

Very simple diagrams like those showing matrices (page 341)
may be used in class to clarify some elements of structure. An arrow
or a brace to show what goes with what, may be helpful. But complicated diagrams, like the ones that Professor Abbott learned as a
boy, have little value.

The sentence trees of the transformationalists are another kind of
diagram. At the risk of alienating my transformational friends, I
have to state that tall sentence trees with a multitude of branches
appear to be no more useful as pedagogical tools than Reed-Kellogg
diagrams were. The teacher or even a student may occasionally
draw a compact little tree or one branch of a tree, to illustrate a
particular point, but when branches and twigs and leaves spread all
over the blackboard, students often can't see the sentence because of
the trees.

Programed and Computerized Instruction

A number of programs have been published, intended to teach
principles of sentence structure or to combat specific structural weaknesses in students' sentences. With such programs, students work
independently, at their own speed, on series of "frames" that build
toward mastery of a concept. Linear programs move methodically,
frame by frame, from something like "Birds fly" to much more difficult structures. Branching programs, rarer and more complicated
than linear ones, send the student to elementary explanatory frames
when he makes a mistake.

Computer-aided instruction, which relies heavily on programed
materials, is being increasingly advocated by educational technologists. In the form that its proponents consider ideal—a form not yet
fully realized—it would consist of these elements: (1) detailed diagnostic tests, with results marked and recorded by computer; (2) a
varied wealth of teaching materials, including programed offerings
(perhaps "teaching machines" or book or card format), slides, transparencies, films, recordings, microfilm or microfiche readers, individual small-screen television sets, and the like; (3) a system by which
the computer makes individual assignments in these materials, on
the basis of the diagnostic texts; (4) continuous evaluation by means
of frequent computer-analyzed mastery tests; (5) further assign-

ments (or repetition of assignments when needed), based on results of the mastery tests.

Some English teachers look with horror upon such mechanization as a forerunner of a dehumanized "brave new world." Carried to the extremes that some technologists appear to desire, it could indeed become that, with each student strapped in his cubicle and with little or no opportunity for discussion and other humanizing activities. School might become a place where socializing would be confined largely to the gymnasium. (Technologists have not yet learned to develop physical fitness in a cubicle.)

But without going to such extremes, a teacher can make some use of programed instruction. If, for instance, only a few students in a class need help with a particular transformation or with the use of quotation marks, it would be wasteful of class time to repeat this material with the entire class. Instead, the students needing this instruction could be assigned appropriate programed material while others worked on things that they as individuals needed.

Not all programs are equally good, however, just as all textbooks are not equally good. Some of the first programs devised for English merely stressed identification and were not at all superior to the conventional workbook. Now, however, some programs do stress sentence building or attacks upon particular sentence weaknesses. The choice must be made with care, and assignments made in accordance with what will most profit each student.

The Honest Approach to Sentence Improvement

Improvement in sentence structure and a closer approach to standard usage (about which more will be said in the next chapter) will come only if the student *wants* to improve. As Professor Allen F. Hubbell has said,

> An individual's linguistic usage is among other things the outward sign of his most deep-seated group loyalties. If the usage of the group or groups with which he identifies himself is not that of Standard English, the schools are not likely to have much effect on his practice. For the blunt fact is that only if his loyalties shift will his grammar change. In a democratic society, the schools have an obligation to make a knowledge of the standard language available to everyone. And teachers have an obligation to make the instruction as interesting and meaningful as possible. They should not be surprised, however, if the nonstandard forms of English continue to flourish. They are hardy growths and will be with us for a long time to come.[11]

[11] "Multiple Negation," *Inside the ACD*, X, No. 1 (Oct., 1957), 3.

The time-dishonored method of having students memorize rules may as well be forgotten. No more successful has been the constant use of the labels "wrong" or "incorrect" or the admonition "Watch your grammar."

Some classes and some students are eager to bring their sentence forms and their usage into closer conformity with what we smugly call "standard." These are usually the students with cultured parents or with parents who wish they were cultured. Less frequently they are intelligent students who are eager to surmount what they have come to recognize as handicaps of their environment.

But thousands of students have never been convinced (and perhaps can't be) that the language you encourage them to practice is a language they should learn. They will not be convinced by such essentially dishonest statements as "This is the only right way to say it" and "Successful people are always careful of their language." [12]

The honest approach to a don't-care class takes some such form as this: "I'm not going to pretend that using 'good English' will make you rich and successful. I know a hundred persons whose English seems worse to me than my own does but who have a lot more money than I'll ever have. And I'm not going to pretend to you that one way of saying something is always right and that other ways are always wrong. We'll look a little at history of the language and discover that ideas of right and wrong in English have changed from century to century. I can't tell you that people won't know what you mean if you say 'I ain't got nothin'.'"

"But I can say this to you: Sometimes it will be important to you to make your meaning so clear that nobody can possibly misunderstand you. Sometimes you will write letters that will affect your future. Sometimes you will talk with people who will be sizing you up for a job that is important to you. Some of you will go to college where it is simply taken for granted that you use language in the ways that happen to be socially approved in this century; if you don't, out you go, even though these colleges may be using a poor reason for getting rid of you.

"So what we're doing is learning about the language that many of today's leaders, in all kinds of work, consider most clear and most

---

[12] At the annual business meeting of the National Council of Teachers of English in 1968, there was serious and heated floor discussion concerning a resolution that in effect would have asked employers to disregard as a hiring criterion the quality of a prospective employee's language.

acceptable. It is something that will be useful for you to know and that *may* make a difference in your future, though I can't say for sure. I'll not say that 'haven't any' is better than 'ain't got none,' but many important people today *think* it is better, and for that reason I'll say you should have it available as one of your styles of speech."

Individualizing Instruction

One method of individualizing instruction in syntax, as well as other elements of language, has already been mentioned: the use of carefully chosen programed learning materials. Another exists in relation to marking of compositions. If Ellen writes too many *and* . . . *and* sentences, give her some appropriate work. If Ron has a penchant for dangling modifiers, try having him make up some intentional danglers that produce a ludicrous effect; he may learn more from doing that than from correcting a workbook exercise.

The small-group plan may also be used. Four to five students have the same kind of problem in sentence structure. Let them meet with Beverly, for whom the problem does not exist, so that she can provide the necessary help. Simultaneously, other groups may work on other problems.

Sometimes a large part of a class, but not all, needs work on a stumbling block. Instead of wasting the time of students who you are sure do not need this instruction, allow them to read or to do some other constructive work.

Individual conferences are extremely valuable, and are possible for those teachers whose course load is not too heavy. Often a little personal encouragement and individual help bring big returns.

Combating the Most Persistent Errors in Syntax

When the word *error* is used with regard to language, it is usually defined in this book as a construction or a usage that results in a reduction of clarity, and occasionally as a construction or usage that deviates enough from standard English that in some situations its user may be penalized.

Some British teachers, like those at the Dartmouth Conference, argue that errors should be largely ignored save for an occasional question like "Would it be clearer if you . . . ?" It is certainly true that Americans have overemphasized, often pettily, the attack on errors. But until American society becomes as permissive about sentences as it has become about sex, teachers will have to continue their attempts to overcome student use of sentences that are unclear or well outside the pale of standard practice.

The sentence errors that are most difficult to eradicate are the undesirable fragment, the run-on sentence and the related comma fault, excessive coordination, faulty subordination, dangling modifiers, faulty word order, faulty parallelism, and pronounced incoherence or lack of logic. Each of these will be discussed briefly.

The Undesirable Sentence Fragment. Some fragments, as was shown on page 357, are useful, and are employed by professional writers. The undesirable one is that which is unintentional and that results from confusion with a complete sentence.

The best way to prevent fragments is to teach what a sentence is. A class that has mastered sentence patterns realizes that every sentence has at least two slots, one for the subject and one for the verb. The two most common kinds of unacceptable sentence fragments are 1. the dependent clause punctuated as a sentence and 2. a group of words with a participle instead of a finite verb. For example:

1. Because the water in the canteen was almost gone.
2. The sand stretching endlessly before us.

In some contexts, even such fragments can be defended, but ordinarily they cannot. A student who has learned that such constructions are the result of transformations used in sentence-combining is more likely than not to combine them with other sentences or to change them so that combination is not necessary. For example:

1. Because the water in the canteen was almost gone, we realized that thirst would become a real danger. (*or*) The water in the canteen was almost gone. That made us realize. . . .
2. The sand stretching endlessly before us was beautiful but terrifying. (*or*) The sand stretched endlessly before us. It was. . . .

Students can be shown, repeatedly if necessary, how a clause or a phrase can be attached to a related sentence. A reminder that a participle needs a helping verb is also pertinent. Ask the class, "Would you say, 'I running'?"

In an article filled with specific suggestions, Kellogg W. Hunt suggests substituting nonsense words to make clear that a fragment is a fragment:

In years later after the foons wamped it can stand as the answer to a question or the beginning of a statement, but students quickly see that it is only a fragment. Whether or not it is a complete thought, it is an incomplete structure. The students' original was *In years later when the Italians conquered it.*[13]

Some rather bright student will probably ask the old question, "Why can't we use sentence fragments? Professional writers do." You may give the old answer that professional writers sometimes consciously use sentence fragments for special effects. It is the unconscious use that is to be condemned. If a student, or a whole class, has consistently demonstrated mature ability in sentence construction, encouragement may indeed be given to stylistic experimentation, including use of fragments. For less mature students it may be appropriate to ask them to put a star in the margin opposite a fragment to show that the use is intentional.

The Run-on Sentence and the Comma Fault. The run-on sentence consists of two or more sentences run together without punctuation, e.g., "I arrived home late the door was locked." The comma fault or comma splice is the same, except that a feeble comma tries in vain to hold the sentences apart: "I arrived home late, the door was locked." These mistakes, like the undesirable sentence fragment, may be basically attacked through instruction in sentence patterns and through much practice in building sentences with proper terminal punctuation. It is also useful to show that a reader's task is increased when sentences are run together; e.g., "I found the ring on the floor beside it was a note." (The comma fault is discussed further in Chapter 10.)

Excessive Coordination. This is the *and . . . and* or the *so . . . so* sentence, in which ideas are strung together as if they were beads of equal size: "I talked with Sam, and he is my older brother, and he is very smart, and he advised me to call the police, so I did." Instruction and practice in sentence-combining through the use of subordinate clauses and appositives can help a student to write more sentences like "I talked with Sam, my very smart older brother, who advised me to call the police. I did so at once."

Faulty Subordination. The complex sentence has pitfalls of its own. Used effectively, it can make writing precise. When in a given context one idea is clearly more important than another, the less important one should be subordinated. Suppose that a student wants to say that lightning struck his house and that the time was

---

[13] "Improving Sentence Structure," *English Journal,* XLVII (April, 1958), 209. The entire article is worth studying. See especially the discussion of the use of nonsense words in attacking run-on sentences, on pages 209–10.

about eight o'clock.   In all likelihood, unless there is a special reason for stressing the time, it would be unwise to combine the two ideas as "It was about eight o'clock when lightning struck our house."   The concept of the matrix (page 341), which consists of a sentence stating the main idea, is useful here.   After deciding what the matrix is, the student determines how he can insert supporting details.

A second pitfall is the "house-that-Jack-built" construction.   This usually consists of a string of adjective clauses each modifying a noun in the preceding clause: "This is the dog that worried the cat that killed the rat that. . . ."   It may also consist of a string of loosely related adverbial clauses: "Dad agreed because he wanted me to go because he thought I needed the experience because. . . ."   The name "house-that-Jack-built" may help both to clarify the nature of the problem and to laugh it out of existence.   Assisting the student to see the underlying relationships of the parts may lead to a satisfactory revision.   Sometimes a long sentence of this kind may need to be divided into two or three sentences.

Student-written sentences illustrating either excessive coordination or faulty subordination may afford excellent material for class discussion and for the sentence manipulation that is often highly productive.   Duplicate the sentences, write them on the chalkboard, or show them with an overhead projector.

Dangling Modifiers.   Sometimes the dangling modifier is a "howler," as the British occasionally call it: "After failing in geometry, the principal had a talk with Stuart."   "Standing on the peak and looking into the valley below, his heart pounded at the beauty of the scene."   Usually, though, it is more prosaic: "By getting tickets early, good seats will be available."

When you find a dangling modifier in student writing, remark that it reminds you of a sentence you once read.   On the board write a "howler."   (A few gems are in the Idea Box, page 381.   You should have a rather extensive collection.)   Show the class why the howler does not clearly make sense, and then show them that the sentence under discussion fits a similar pattern, even though it may not be funny.   Get the class to make corrections.   Show them that there is usually more than one way to place modifiers for clarity but that sometimes, for reasons of logic, a modifier can be in only one place in a particular sentence.   Write down some more howlers or look at some examples in the textbook.   The class corrects these.   To clinch the point, you write a few verbal phrases like these:

Upsetting the bucket,
While living in Spokane,
To make a kite,

Ask the students to finish each of these sentences. Have them test each sentence by noting whether the modifier has something that it can logically modify. Someone is almost sure to write, "While living in Spokane, it was very rainy." Let the class help the writer of the sentence see that "it" was not living in Spokane.

Kellogg W. Hunt, in the article previously cited, makes this suggestion:

> I can give them this: *Puffing and panting, the womble was woobled at last.* In place of the first nonsense word, students will substitute words for people, for animals, for a number of things than can puff and pant. But when I substitute what a student wrote, they reject it with a laugh. I write on the blackboard, *Puffing and panting, the top of the hill was reached at last.* They see that tops of hills don't really puff and pant even when they are being reached. They see this far more clearly when I substitute nonsense syllables than when I lecture to them on dangling modifiers.

The use of matrix and insert may also be helpful. e.g.,

MATRIX	The play delighted the audience
INSERT	The audience was laughing uproariously.

The class can find several ways to make the combination: "The play delighted the audience, which was laughing uproariously," "Laughing uproariously, the audience was obviously delighted by the play," but not, "Laughing uproariously, the play delighted the audience."

Faulty Word Order. In English, more than in most other languages, word order is important. The reason is that most English words do not have distinctive endings to show how they are used in the sentence. Consider, for example, "The dog killed the rat." In some other languages—Latin, for instance—the word order in that sentence could be changed somewhat without affecting the meaning. But in English, if we say "The rat killed the dog," the meaning is entirely different; or, if we say "Killed dog the rat the," there is no meaning.

Most problems in word order arise in the placement of modifiers. It is well to admit to the class that some sentences are very difficult to write. For example, try straightening these out: "Seated in front of her were several men whose heads only she could see." "Carol is the girl in the hallway with blue shorts." When one happens upon such a sentence, often the best solution is to start the sentence in an entirely different way.

Students, however, often write sentences in which only a shift in word order is needed for clarity. As always, stress the fact that in writing and speaking we are trying to express our thoughts clearly, so that others can understand us. Perhaps your students have written sentences like these: "I pulled the heavy fishing line up on the bank on which I found only a tin can filled with mud." "Sally encouraged him vigorously to fight back." "Ted was arrested before his intended crime was committed by the police chief." Using terms like *attributive adjectives, appositional adjectives,* and *squinting modifiers,* you could talk for hours about the placement of adverbial and adjectival modifiers. The results will probably be better, though, if you have the class apply simple logic: "Where was the tin can that was filled with mud? . . . How can we make the sentence say that?"

Faulty parallelism. Not at all rare, but difficult to overcome, is the habit of writing sentences in which grammatically equivalent elements are stated in different grammatical forms. For example, a student may write, "The dictionary shows us how to pronounce a word, its meaning, and where it originated." Though such a sentence may be considered excellent if written by a young or a slow student, an average eleventh or twelfth grader ought to be able to do better.

There are four main situations in which parallelism is needed: (1) in a series, (2) in comparisons, (3) with *be* and the linking verbs like *seem,* and (4) with correlative conjunctions. The last two cause little difficulty and may be ignored in high schools. But a faulty series, like the illustration above, and a faulty comparison such as "I like baseball better than to run races" demand attention.

Concentrate first on the series. Write, "The dictionary shows us the . . . of a word." Ask, "What does the dictionary show us about a word?" Someone says, "Pronunciation." The class tests that in the blank and sees that it will fit. But the next person says, "How to spell it." Testing that, the class sees that "The dictionary shows us the how to spell it of a word" does not make sense, and changes the insert to "spelling." Other inserts will be other nouns, like "meaning," "history," or "part of speech." Get the class to construct sentences with other series of nouns, then with series of adjectives, clauses, gerunds, and infinitives.

At some time later, consider parallelism in comparisons. Write, "I like *baseball* better than *track*." "I like *to play baseball* better than *to run races*." "I like *playing baseball* better than *running races*." Help the students to see that the italicized parts are the things being compared and that within the same sentence they are stated in the same form. From the class get other comparisons requiring parallel construction.

Able students will enjoy observing how master craftsmen employ parallelism for special effects. The novels of Alan Paton offer especially good examples.

Pronounced Incoherence or Lack of Logic. An experienced teacher recognizes this error, even though its forms are myriad and even though it is usually accompanied by all the other errors in the book. Here is an example from an examination paper of a sophomore: "Juluis Cesar went forum and soothsayer sayed be wear of Idies of March he didn't and died (got killed." This student needs almost everything, though even he can be commended on content.

With as poor a student as this, you may as well face the fact that sentence polish is for him eternally impossible. Indeed, you may feel like adopting the traditional tactics of a coach whose team loses most of its games—work on building character. (Not a bad idea, really.) Although he may be a sophomore or junior, your goal is to bring him up to a sixth grader's level. Praise him when he writes a five-word sentence that is clear. Let pairs of students sometimes revise their papers together; this boy, and others, will profit from the experience. Help the boy to see that careless omission of words is like careless omission of clothing or careless assembly of a motor. Show him how easy it is to misread something like "Julius Caesar went forum."

You will have succeeded with such a student if he becomes a respectable adult citizen who can write sentences like these: "Please send me one claw hammer. The catalog no. is X1905. I enclose four dollars ($4.00)."

THE IDEA BOX

"American Traditions of Language Use"

Michael G. Crowell traces the history of American attitudes toward language, from the neoclassical (prescriptive) through the romantic (like Whitman's) to the present scientific. Useful for a teacher's background. *English Journal,* LIX (Jan., 1970), 189.

What a Speaker Reveals

In his useful "Language-Learning Objectives: A Checklist," Arnold Lazarus includes this item: "To understand that whenever a speaker in literature or life makes an utterance, he always reveals one or more of the following: his historical era, his geographical stance (country, region, locality), his age (infancy, childhood, adolescence, adulthood, senility), his sex (male, female, effeminate, tomboyish), the age and sex of his audience, the size of his audience (from intimate to public), his formal education (lack of education, half-education, 'prestige' dialects), his socioeconomic status . . . , his cultural milieu's values, sports, and pastimes." *Word Study* (Feb., 1965). This objective suggests the value of occasionally asking the question, "What does this speech, considered only by itself, reveal about this character?" The question is especially useful when a character is first met in a story or play.

The Evanston Language Plan

Evanston, Ill., Township High School organizes its language work like this: "for the ninth-graders, a fairly long, linguistically-oriented language unit which gives them some exposure to lexicology-lexicography, dialectology, and the history of the language, all of which, excepting the grammar, they will study in more detail as they go through school. The sophomores have a two-week unit in lexicology-lexicography; the juniors concentrate on dialectology, and the seniors study the history of the language." Dorothy M. Griffin, "Dialects and Democracy," *English Journal,* LIX (April, 1970), 551.

Eight Functions of Language

Teachers may want to acquaint students with the eight functions of language listed by John C. Condon, Jr., in *Semantics and Communication* (Macmillan, 1966): (1) Phatic—inconsequential remarks, e.g., "Nice day," to show attitude. (2) Prevention of communication—"Oh, really?" (3) Recording-transmitting—"It's starting to rain." (4) Instrumental—causing something to happen, e.g., "Shut the door." (5) Affective—expression of emotion. (6) Catharsis—expressing pain or frustration, e.g., swearing. (7) Magical powers—avoiding a word for fear of evil results. (8) Ritual—for building feeling of amity, e.g., prayer.

Linguistics Is for People

Neil Postman declares that linguistics should be taught "as the rigorous study of language situations." Thus he would study the purposes, tone, symbols, audience-relationships, social values, metaphors, and standards of various kinds of language—in advertising, news reporting, politics, religion, science, etc. Thoughtful and useful. "Linguistics and the Pursuit of Relevance," *English Journal*, LVI (Nov., 1967), 1160.

An Overview of Grammars

John Algeo offers an informative brief history of English grammars and asserts that no linguistic Messiah has yet appeared. Excellent for a teacher's background. "Linguistics: Where Do We Go From Here?" *English Journal*, LVIII (Jan., 1969), 102.

Inductive Teaching of Linguistics

In "Linguistics in Junior High School: Principles and Difficulties," Sister Philomene Schiller stresses the triumphs resultings from having students make their own classifications of words and sentence patterns. *English Journal*, LVII (May, 1968), 705. W. Wilbur Hatfield illustrates inductive teaching very specifically in "Helping Students See Their Language Working," *English Journal*, LVI (Jan., 1967), 67.

"A Language Unit in the Junior High School"

Among fifteen assignment suggested by Thomas E. Melchior are examination of the language of advertising (using *The Hidden Persuaders*), building a scrapbook of affective language, using highly connotative words, examining fictional language of teen-agers, and noting variations in TV language according to sex, age, education, etc. *English Journal*, LVI (Sept., 1967), 858.

British vs. American English

Benjamin J. Novak describes British and American differences in spelling, vocabulary, and usage, and illustrates differences in terms for food, transportation, clothing, and general conversation. *English Journal*, LIII (May, 1964), 360.

Where Do Words Come from, Teach?

R. C. Simonini, Jr., describes fifteen sources of new words, as distinguished from native or borrowed words: (1) Idiomatic compounds *(egghead, iron curtain).* (2) Greek and Latin combining forms *(astronaut, demography).* (3) Derivatives *(belittle, bizonal).* (4) Semantic change *(bologna, bug* for *microphone).* (5) Self-explaining compounds *(supermarket, ballpoint pen).* (6) Acronyms *(Texaco, NASA).* (7) Blends *(chortle, cinemonster).* (8) Functional change words *(know-how,* the plane was *missiled).* (9) Pure root creations *(kodak, dacron).* (10) Shortening *(bus, bra).* (11) Reduplication *(wishy-washy, hush-hush).* (12) Echoism *(ack-ack, zipper).* (13) Back formation *(baby-sit, fact find).* (14) Sound symbolism *(sweetie, sneeze).* (15) Mistaken *-s* singulars *(specie, pea).* "Word-making in Present-Day English," *English Journal,* LV (Sept., 1966), 752.

Seven Categories of Language Instruction

John Bushman, of Ottawa, Kans., University, recommends attention to these seven categories of language study: (1) Exploring the Nature of Language. (2) Exploring the Structure of Language. (3) Exploring Usage in Language. (4) Exploring Language Heritage. (5) Exploring Geographical and Social Dialects. (6) Exploring Semantics. (7) Exploring the "Silent Language." "The Power of Language," *English Journal,* LIX (Nov., 1970), 1091.

"Down Giantwife: The Uses of Etymology"

Charlton Laird discusses (fascinatingly) how students' vocabularies may be enriched as they become increasingly aware of word etymologies and interrelationships. For example, did you know that all these words have a common source: *much, mickle, megaton* (and dozens of other *mega-* words), *maharajah, mahatma, magistrate, master, magnitude* (and other *magn-* words), *maximum, maxim, major, majority, mayor, majesty? English Journal,* LIX (Nov., 1970), 1106.

Teaching English in Junior High with *Beowulf*

Junior high students may learn much about the characteristics of English by reading the exciting story of *Beowulf;* Bruce Robinson declares that they enjoy it. "Beowulf's English," *English Journal,* LV (Feb., 1966), 180.

"Language and the Culturally Different"

William D. Green makes a thoughtful survey of ways to make the language of the culturally different conform more closely to "standard" English without diminishing students' self-respect. Thus his position is opposite to that of James Sledd, who would not attempt to make any changes. See the *English Journal*, LIV (Nov., 1965), 724, for Green, and p. 698 in the same issue for Sledd, who asserted his position even more strongly in the Dec., 1969, *English Journal*.

"Disadvantaged Student? or Disadvantaged Teacher?"

In this article, which every English teacher should read, San-su C. Lin (a native of Taiwan who teaches in predominantly black American schools) offers many suggestions for teaching students whose own language is not standard English. E.g., "Rich language experience can . . . include the use of both standard English and the child's dialect; one need not be rejected in favor of the other." *English Journal*, LVI (May, 1967), 751.

Is Nonstandard English Illogical?

No, answers William Labov. "They mine" for "They are mine" may be different but is not illogical, since such languages as Hebrew, Hungarian, and Russian also lack a present copula. Labov's book, *The Study of Nonstandard English* (NCTE, 1970) should be on every teacher's bookshelf because it dispels a number of old myths.

Second Dialect

At St. Mary's Dominican College, New Orleans, "Business Speech" is the title given to a course for those who need to master a second dialect (standard English) for use in business or a profession. This term avoids the pejorative connotations of other titles, and does not suggest that this variety of speech need be used in the home.

Regional Dialects

Evelyn Gott's "Teaching Regional Dialects in Junior High School" concerns regional pronunciations, dialect areas, and British vs. American English. *English Journal*, LIII (May, 1964), 342.

"Old English Survival in Mountain Speech"

In Ozark speech, Jewell K. Fitzhugh found not only color but also many survivals from Old or Middle English. Excellent for use in a unit on dialects. *English Journal*, LIX (Nov., 1969), 1224.

"Effecting Dialect Change Through Oral Drill"

William R. Slager gives detailed suggestions for oral drills involving repetition of the same sentence, substitutions in parts of a sentence, completion of sentences, transformation to questions, combining two sentences. *English Journal,* LVI (Nov., 1967), 1166.

Regional Dialects Again

". . . no single local or regional standard exists in any absolute form which has prestige over all others, and . . . dialects or regional types other than the one to which, by accident, the student was born have much of interest to offer—interest as contributing to communication, to literary characterization and portraiture, to imaginative expression, to language and its growth." So says Professor Frederic G. Cassidy, in describing the projected *Dictionary of American Regional English,* which will be a valuable tool for dialect teaching. "American Regionalisms in the Classrooms," *English Journal,* LVII (March, 1968), 375.

Teaching Dialects

Annabel T. Ashley offers useful suggestions for teaching American dialects in "Using *Dialects—U.S.A.* in High School Classes," *English Journal,* LIII (April, 1964), 256. Maps, cartoons, themes, etc., are recommended.

English Around the World

An interesting project for a group of able students is to examine the extent and the variety of use of English around the world—not just in English-speaking countries but in Japan, Russia, Malaysia, Africa, South America, etc.

Motivation

1. A text formerly used at West Point pointed out that an order not written with perfect clarity or an order misinterpreted might cost lives.

2. During World War II, Secretary of the Navy Knox stated: "I would go so far as to say that the ability to use clear, concise, and forceful English underlies and reinforces efficiency in any and all branches of the Naval Service." And Secretary of War Stimson declared, "In war, as in peace, the ability to report facts and to express ideas clearly is an important attribute of the leader in every field of action."

3. Joseph W. McGovern, lawyer and a member of the New York State Board of Regents, has said, "A lawyer should not merely be logical and orderly in his thinking but he must be precise in his use of language. . . . To the extent that the lawyer achieves clarity and accuracy in [his] work of setting down the thoughts of other persons, he succeeds; otherwise he fails." *English Record,* XIII, No. 1 (1962), 3.

4. "An English teacher should be as enthusiastic over things in which the student is naturally interested as he is in the subject in which he is trying to interest the student. The boy who is interested in wrestling has much more respect for the nonrestrictive clause or transistive verb if his English teacher can appreciate the scissors hold or the half-nelson." (Harold R. Hansen, Menomonie, Wis.)

A Day's English

To provide motivation, some teachers have students list all the uses they make of language in one day, from hearing Mother's "Time to get up" to the last "Good night." Presence of both formal and informal English may be noted.

"Show 'em and Let 'em Copy"

In wartime an ververbal teacher was trying to tell a recruit the principles for adjusting the barrel of a machine gun. No success. A combat veteran took over. "Look, Mac, this way," he demonstrated. The recruit understood at once. Said the combat veteran to the teacher, "If we tried to explain *how* everything works, we'd never win a war. Show 'em and let 'em copy." A group of New England teachers point out that people learn most of their grammar and usage by imitation, too. E. J. Gordon and E. S. Noyes, eds., "What About Grammar?" *Essays on the Teaching of English* (New York: Appleton-Century-Crofts, 1960), 35.

The Role of Grammar in the Classroom

Robert C. Pooley presents an exceptionally clear history of the teaching of grammar to 1957, along with a specific discussion of grammar's present and potential role in the English classroom. This book, as well as Pooley's earlier *Teaching English Usage* (New York: Appleton-Century-Crofts, 1946), must have a place on your bookshelf. *Teaching English Grammar* (New York: Appleton-Century-Crofts, 1957).

Facts Are Not Enough

Professor William Paulk, West Carolina College, says that he is happy when a student can tell him facts about Whitman's life or about the metrical scheme of a sonnet but that he is disturbed when a student cannot understand "Out of the Cradle Endlessly Rocking" because he does not comprehend the grammatical structure. Hence he pleads for more attention to poets' use of inverted patterns, elliptical sentences, and the like. *North Carolina English Teacher* (April, 1960).

Grammar in College Placement Tests

Many teachers still hold misconceptions about college placement tests. Neither College Entrance Examination Board tests nor the tests given by individual institutions place emphasis on the ability to classify grammatical constructions. What they *do* stress is ability to distinguish poor constructions from good ones; those institutions that require compositions also emphasize the ability to compose coherent sentences in thoughtful, coherent paragraphs.

"Spatial and Temporal Grammar"

A sentence, says Arthur A. Stern, may be described spatially (identifying its parts) or temporally (showing where each part probably came from). Stern illustrates the latter by showing the five sentences underlying "The old man who lives next door was chased by a ferocious brown dog." *English Journal*, LVII (Sept., 1968), 880.

Grammar Is a Map

"The professional grammarian is the mapmaker who charts all the known roads of the English language; grammar is the map; the teacher is the driving instructor who chooses the most useful roads recorded on the map and teaches them to his students. Ultimately the students develop their own judgment and read the map for themselves. The mapmaker does not say . . . , 'You must use this road and no other.' He says, 'Here is the map of the roads,' and he may, by the red and black lines on his map, indicate which are most used and which are in best condition." E. J. Gordon and E. S. Noyes, eds., "What About Grammar?" *Essays on the Teaching of English* (New York: Appleton-Century-Crofts, 1960), 44-45.

In Defense of Traditionalism

A. M. Tibbetts ridicules the "New Grammars" and attacks Webster III in a controversial article. "Real Issues in the Great Language Controversy," *English Journal*, LV (Jan., 1966), 28. Another defense of the old is Don M. Wolfe's "Grammar and Linguistics," *English Journal*, LIII (Feb., 1964), 73.

Any Prescriptive Grammar?

Albert Marckwardt, though a "modern" grammarian, says that as long as we must teach large numbers of students from homes in which "standard" English is an unknown tongue, "we shall have to employ prescriptive grammar to a degree. We must see to it that we use it in as enlightened a manner as possible." "Grammar and Linguistics in the Teaching of English," *Illinois English Bulletin* (Oct., 1958), 4. Perhaps this means that we should not equate the double negative, for example, with sin or even with crime but only with a social misdemeanor that, like other social blunders, may be expensive.

The "Why" of Parts of Speech

Have students try to write a story, using only nouns and verbs. Then they see the reason for other parts of speech.

Playlet on Sentence Parts

Donald F. Mortland offers a playlet in which words in a sentence discuss and argue about their roles. A junior high school class might enjoy writing a similar play for themselves. "The Sentence," *English Journal,* LIV (Feb., 1965), 95.

The Student Expert

Donald Zimmerman, writing in *Education* (Feb., 1965), tells of using individual ninth-graders as "experts" on pronouns, capitalization, troublesome verbs, spelling, singular–plural, etc. When a student encounters difficulty in one of these areas, he consults the appropriate expert.

Sentence Patterns

After unscrambling a number of sentences like "crawls baby a" or "eats elephant daisies the," junior high students determine what the usual English sentence patterns are. Later, they enjoy a "pattern hunt" to find examples of these patterns in newspaper or magazine articles. (Grace Ashenfelter, Urbana, Ill.)

Games for Junior High

1. The baseball game is a favorite. Have two teams. A right answer to a question on grammar (or something else) is a single; a wrong answer is an out.

2. In the old game of adverbs, one student (It) is sent out of the room. Others decide upon an adverb to act out. When It returns, class members do what It says, for example, "Go to the blackboard in the manner of the adverb," "Make a face that suggests the adverb," etc.

Improvement of Style

Verna Newsome's "Expansions and Transformations to Improve Sentences" "demonstrate certain procedures used either in transformational grammar or in structural grammar" contributing to style in writing. *English Journal*, LIII (May, 1964), 327.

Tense Study

Ellen Newman takes a sentence like "Yesterday I washed my sweater" and substitutes *tomorrow* for *yesterday*. Students realize that another change is then needed. They try again with *today*, etc. "An Experiment in Oral Language," in *The Disadvantaged Learner*, S. W. Webster (ed.), (San Francisco: Chandler Publishing Co., 1966), 513.

"A Boinger Has Boingized the Boingians"

Through close scrutiny of nonsense sentences, Peter Youmans' students learn a great deal about form classes and about which forms may appear in each sentence slot. "Practicing Linguistics," *English Journal*, LIV (April, 1965), 331.

Sentence Patterns in Structural Terms

Michael Grady has his students construct sentences, and expand them, using seven basic patterns from structural grammar. "Structural Structuralism," *English Journal*, LIV (Oct., 1965), 633.

Feature Analysis

It helps students' understanding of how language works if they can identify word features. E.g., *boy* is animate, masculine, human, young, and count. For details, see Keith Schap, "The Feature System in the Classroom," *English Journal*, LVI (Jan., 1967), 74.

"Applied Linguistics in the Seventh Grade"

James W. Ney tells how through oral and written drills, with emphasis on sentence combining, his seventh-graders learned to use more complex sentence structures in their writing. *English Journal*, LV (Oct., 1966), 895.

"Sentence Building and Transformational Grammar"

Eileen J. McGuire breaks down effective sentences by professional writers into their components, and has students come as close as they can to reconstructing the original. *English Journal*, LVI (May, 1967), 747.

"On Identifying the Parts of Speech"

Falk S. Johnson argues that young students should be taught to identify parts of speech by looking at their typical forms, that older students may consider their positions in sentences, and that still more mature students may consider both, noting the transformations that may be employed. *English Journal*, LV (Sept., 1966), 747.

"Written English Is a 'Second Language'"

Robert L. Allen points to differences between spoken and written English—e.g., in possessives, spelling, written substitutes for intonation, indicators of paragraphing—and suggests the need for a grammar truly descriptive of written language. Thoughtful, valuable. *English Journal*, LV (Sept., 1966), 739.

Useful Structures in Written English

Andrew MacLeish analyzes eight structures fairly common in written English but not in spoken: (1) Pre-junctural adjective or participle (*Confused,* he sat down); (2) Pre-junctural infinitive (*To make the team,* he practiced every day); (3) Pre-junctural absolute (*His friends* having left, John went to bed); (4) Nominal that-clause as subject (*That they would not come* was the problem); (5) Infinitive and infinitive phrase as subject (*To see* his father was his greatest wish); (6) Non-restrictive relative clause (She has a large hat *which is red and woolly*); (7) Non-restrictive appositive (Joe, *the star of the team,* made the touchdown); (8) Conjunction *for* (She closed the door, *for* it was raining). "Some Structures for Written English," *English Journal*, LVIII (Sept., 1969), 877.

Movable Modifiers

Dorothy Dakin, in the Puget Sound Council *English Notes*, suggests using cards on a flannel board. Print on cards the parts of a sentence such as *"The leaves of the trees rustle/when the wind blows/in the forest."* Move the parts around to note possible positions of modifiers and resulting changes in meaning or emphasis.

Usage: Opinions of Teachers and Others

In 1967 Robert C. Pooley found Wisconsin English teachers still rather conservative in such usage items as *who–whom,* the split infinitive, *dove–dived,* etc. "Teaching Usage Today and Tomorrow," *English*

Journal, LVI (May, 1967), 742. In a 1971 doctoral dissertation at the University of Illinois, Raymond D. Crisp found that in judging matters of usage, language specialists are most liberal or permissive, followed in order by members of the American Dialect Society, elementary section members of NCTE, college section members of NCTE, members of the Conference on English Education, members of the Conference on College Composition and Communication, secondary section members of NCTE (high school teachers), editors of publishing houses, members of the Journalism Education Association, members of the Speech Communication Association, representatives of the news media, contemporary authors, members of MLA, leading businessmen, editors of newspapers, editors of magazines.

The Problem Isn't New

A grammar published in Boston in 1817, Daniel Adams' *The Thorough Scholar,* cites this sentence as an example of the importance of punctuation and spelling: "A man having gone to see his wife, desires the prayers of the Congregation." The intended meaning: "A man having gone to sea, his wife desires the prayers of the Congregation." (Quoted in *Purdue English Notes,* Feb., 1961.)

"On With *Up*"

You may want to read to your class Marian Gleason's short article on the modern ubiquitousness of *up,* and have them try their hands in writing a similar article about some other commonly used word. *English Journal,* LV (Nov., 1966), 1087. (An article on *-wise* is Donald Houghton's "Humor as a Factor in Language Change," *English Journal,* LVII [Nov., 1968], 1178.)

Levels of Usage

1. Draw up groups of sentences like these: "She has an appointment with James to attend the dance." "She has a dance date with Jimmy." "She's gonna cut a rug with Jimmy-boy." Ask the class to discuss which sentence they would probably use, which they might use in certain circumstances, which they would never use seriously, and what alternative version they might prefer.

2. An exercise involving reader's point of view as well as levels of usage is to ask students to write three versions of the same letter; for instance, "You have been involved in a minor automobile mishap. Write about it to the insurance company, to your father or mother, and to your closest friend." Other possibilities: an autobiography to go

with an application to a college, and an autobiography for a new pen pal; instructions for making something, addressed to a child and addressed to a how-to-do-it magazine.

The Useful Double Negative

Not all double negatives are undesirable. There's one in the preceding sentence. For another example, this bakery commercial: "Everybody doesn't like something, but nobody doesn't like Sara Lee." Or this: "I didn't want to not wear them," which isn't quite the same as "I wanted to wear them."

But May I Start a Sentence with *But?*

Herman R. Struck analyzes the persistent myth that a sentence should not start with *and* or *but*. "The Myth about Initial Conjunctions," *English Journal*, LIV (Jan., 1965), 42. Paul C. Rodgers adds historical depth to the discussion in "The Two Hundred Years' War," *English Journal*, LV (Jan., 1966), 69.

Mentally Retarded Teachers

If you teach mentally retarded children, should you be called a "mentally retarded teacher"? Norman Stageberg analyzes some of the causes of ambiguity in writing in "Structural Ambiguity: Some Sources," *English Journal*, LV (May, 1966), 588. You may want to discuss with your classes some of his delightful examples. Other examples are in Stageberg's earlier article in the *English Journal*, XLVII (Nov., 1958), 479.

Department of Slight Confusion

Students may enjoy collecting slightly confusing sentences from ads, newspaper stories, or other sources, and posting them. E.g., an announcement by an airline stewardess, "When the seat belt sign is turned off, we suggest that you still keep it loosely fastened."

The Uses of Language History

Edwin A. Hoey, in "History Might Help," suggests a few of the rich insights that students may attain through study of language history: understanding of language change, the impossibility of purism, the interactions of language and society, the development of dialects, and the ways that "rules" were formulated. *English Journal*, LVII (Oct., 1968), 1041.

Poster Display

Try cartoons, stick figures, or other posters stressing the elimination of certain common errors. Student-made cartoons usually arouse most interest.

Pruning

"A considerable part of revision is basically a matter of sentence pruning. Developing an alertness for unnecessary words will therefore automatically teach correct usage. A group of common faulty expressions (in sentence setting), can be economically studied as a unit. E.g., this (here), have (got), sort of (a), (had) ought, (in) back of, could (not) hardly, off (of), made (out) of, opposite (to), (on) last Sunday, take (a) hold, started (in), amount (up) to." (Braintree, Massachusetts, High School.)

Howlers

Use sentences like these to show your students how ridiculous a dangling modifier may be: "Sitting around the campfire, he told us the story of his life." "Standing on my tiptoes, the horse was barely visible." "After ringing violently for a couple of minutes, the door finally opened." "While laughing aloud, his teeth fell out." "Sailing toward the plate, the batter said that the ball looked as big as a balloon."

Which Sentence Is Better?

"School spirit is when somebody gives up something he wants to do to cheer at an unimportant football game." "School spirit is loyalty to the highest ideals of the institution." Louis Zahner prefers the first, because "The content is the precious cargo; start with it, find and teach its appropriate form. . . . Our job is to wed form and content." So, says Zahner, we praise the fullness of an idea, condemn the empty words of a platitude, and thus we build the desire to say well what is worth saying. You'll not want to overlook "The Teaching of Language," *English Journal* (Nov., 1955), 443.

Student Observation

Students can learn much about usage by observing conventions in the articles they read and in the speech of television announcers, assembly speakers, etc. Each member of a class may be asked to make notes for a week on a particular item—"It was he" vs. "It was him," "went" and "gone," etc. Then he prepares an oral or written report, giving examples and drawing conclusions.

Making a Dictionary of Slang

Students listed slang words they knew, gathered citations, and in editorial committees worked on definitions, etymology, pronunciation, spelling, and areas of grammar. Useful to build understanding of lexicography. See "Junior High Lexicographers," by L. Lakota Brown, *English Journal*, LV (Oct., 1966), 909.

Parallel Construction

Margaret Lamon, of Siena High School, Chicago, demonstrates parallel construction and introduces students to this useful rhetoric device by writing a speech of Brutus *(Julius Caesar)* in this way:

"Romans
countrymen
and lovers!
hear me
for my cause,
believe me
for my honor,
censure me
in your wisdom."

A more elaborate example of this procedure, based on Alan Paton, is in J. N. Hook, *Hook's Guide to Good Writing: Grammar, Style, Usage* (New York: The Ronald Press Co., 1962).

Should We Write As We Speak?

To attain fluency in writing some students should be encouraged to write approximately as they speak, including details they would normally include in conversation. However, Gordon R. Wood, University of Chattanooga, has advanced the hypothesis that some college freshmen write too much as they talk. He says that the written expository paragraph conforms to the principles of oratory. Hence he recommends discussion of essential differences between informal and formal presentations, paralleling differences between conversation and oratory.

"A Teacher's Adventures in Programland"

"Programming by itself is no panacea. It is one more teaching device to be used when and where it does the job best. For teaching grammar and rhetoric, a well-conceived and well-taught program has proved to be the most effective device I have ever used." Grace L. Graham, *English Journal*, LVIII (Feb., 1969), 261.

Individualized Study

Individualized English provides a method by means of which each student can learn to overcome his own problems in usage, sentence structure, punctuation, and mechanics of writing. Thus, the whole class need not be retaught something that only a few students need. *Individualized English*, consisting of specially designed program cards, along with diagnostic and mastery tests, is published by the Follett Publishing Co., Chicago.

Wordless Communication

Edward T. Hall's *The Silent Language*, a paperbound Premier Book, discusses such things as gestures and facial expressions as devices of communication. Since these differ from culture to culture (e.g., clapping hands is not universally a symbol of approval), this kind of knowledge is of value to a traveler. Moreover, it helps students to understand more clearly that spoken language too is tied to the mores of a people.

Stylistics

Detailed linguistic analysis of a few sentences may help superior students to become more clearly aware of principles of style. Yakira H. Frank illustrates with Irving and Hemingway in "Stylistics in the Classroom," *English Journal*, LV (Nov., 1966), 1051.

Grammar in Relation to Rhetoric

Philip H. Cook describes how he used grammatical principles in teaching the application of Francis Christensen's method of describing sentences. He began with sentences lacking the element to be taught, then added and discussed the element, gave practice in its use, and finally attached its name. "Putting Grammar to Work: The Generative Grammar in the Generative Rhetoric," *English Journal*, LVII (Nov., 1968), 1168.

Applying Linguistics to Literature

E. E. Cummings often dropped verbs into noun slots ("sowed their isn't," "went their came"). D. H. Lawrence used different syntactic patterns for expressing different moods. These are two of the discoveries made by Sallie Isaacs' classes when they applied linguistics to literature. "From Language to Linguistic Criticism," *English Journal*, LVII (Jan., 1968), 47.

10

Important Dots and Curls

WHY BOTHER ABOUT PUNCTUATION?

A Brief History of Punctuation

When written communication was still in its infancy, neither spaces nor marks separated words or sentences. The result was comparable to this:

NEITHERSPACESNORMARKSSEPARATEDWORDSORSENTENCES
THERESULTWASCOMPARABLETOTHIS

After some centuries, great benefactors of the race (unfortunately unknown, so that we cannot pay them the homage they deserve) began using spaces between sentences; still later, other ingenious men put spaces between words.

In ancient Greece the practice began of using a very few marks as added signals to the reader, usually telling him that he had reached the end of a thought. The Romans continued the practice. Medieval scribes developed ornamental letters that became our capitals, and they used dots or lines that became our periods.

The man chiefly responsible for systematizing punctuation (has he a statue anywhere?) was Aldus Manutius (1450–1515). An Italian, he founded the famous Aldine Press, edited Greek manuscripts, and invented italic type. But his greatest contribution was the formulation of principles upon which sentences and parts of sentences may be marked off for clarity—principles that writer and reader both interpret in the same way. Most of our uses of commas, periods, question marks, semicolons, and colons follow his precepts.

There have been changes since Manutius, and even today punctuation cannot be regarded as permanently fixed. The nineteenth century sprinkled punctuation marks like black pepper on a page. The twentieth century tends increasingly toward few marks and insists that each be clearly justifiable. The eighteenth and nineteenth centuries were periods of much oral reading; numerous commas and other marks suggested desirable vocal pauses. Today little material is read aloud, and a multiplicity of punctuation marks would slow down the silent reader.

No Aldus Manutius has yet completely clarified the principles for modern Americans. Some marks such as the period at the end of a complete statement are obligatory. Others such as the comma before "and" in a series are optional. As teachers we need to insist upon the obligatory and to discuss the pros and cons of each option, realizing that usages in punctuation, like usages in words, can never be pinned down to simple and permanent codification as right or wrong.

Five Axioms

To teach punctuation intelligently, a teacher should understand five things about it.

Axiom 1. The purpose of punctuation is to help a reader understand a writer's meaning. When writer and reader both understand that ! shows strong feeling (almost a shout), writer uses the mark to help to indicate the feeling, and reader sees it and says to himself, in effect, "Aha! Strong feeling! This is almost a shout!" Similarly with the other marks. "Men work together," says Robert Frost, "whether they work together or apart." Writer and reader work together even though miles and years separate them.

You will recall that, when Bottom and his fellows present "Pyramus and Thisbe" in *Midsummer Night's Dream,* Quince mangles the prologue by putting periods in the wrong places:

. . . All for your delight
We are not here. That you should here repent you,
The actors are at hand. . . .

Theseus comments, "This fellow doth not stand upon points." Lysander elaborates, "He hath rid his prologue like a rough colt; he knows not the stop. A good moral, my lord: it is not enough to speak, but to speak true."

Quinces are not merely sixteenth-century phenomena. Joe Quince and Marjorie Quince are in every American high school classroom. They know not the stop, and as a result they often do not speak or write true.

To help them, lead them to see what happens if punctuation is lacking or is out of harmony with the principles generally accepted in our age. Have them imagine, for instance, that no punctuation marks or capital letters existed. (Capitals have a function similar to that of punctuation marks.) Give them a little paragraph like that following, and ask them to time themselves to find how long it takes each of them to understand it thoroughly.

i am enjoying my stay in st petersburg where i have a room one with a glorious view of the bay in the grandvilla hotel where did you tell me that you stayed when you were here in the manor house was it that is where louella and i ate dinner friday morning and noon meals we usually take in our own hotel

After the students have timed themselves, have them insert the needed capitals and punctuation and time themselves again. Most students' time will be cut at least in half.

Then raise the question "Suppose each of us punctuated to suit himself; what would the effect be?" Hand out another paragraph without capitals or punctuation, and ask each to punctuate it, not according to rules he has already learned, but letting his imagination roam. He may use X's, for instance, or circles, or check marks, or anything else he chooses; he may capitalize at random. Let the completed papers circulate for a few minutes, so that students can see what would happen if we had no common agreements about what punctuation to use where.

Axiom 2. Most punctuation marks are written substitutes for intonation. When we speak, the things we do with the voice tell a listener a great deal. He hears that one group of words is a statement, another an exclamation, another a question; that a phrase is attached to a preceding part of a sentence rather than to a following part; that the White House (the President's mansion) is meant and not just any white house. He has unknowingly learned in childhood the principles of juncture and intonation that linguists have described scientifically, and he uses these principles in interpreting the spoken word.

The reader, however, does not hear a speaking voice. Hence, he must rely upon the visual symbols that have been developed as substitutes. The symbols are less than perfect, but, if they were nearly enough complete to reflect all that the voice does, they would be too complex to learn with any degree of ease.

Frank C. Church [1] recommends study of the oral stress-patterns of structural grammarians, so that students may become aware of the relationship between the ways we say things and the ways we punctuate them. For example, natural oral reading of "a short, jolly, chubby young man" shows that two commas but not three are needed.

Not all marks are substitutes for intonation. Some, such as the punctuation in the formal parts of a letter, are simple matters of convention.

Axiom 3. Variations in the punctuation of a sentence may result in difference of meaning, lack of meaning, or difference in emphasis.

Here are examples of difference of meaning:

> Henry said his teacher was ill.
> Henry, said his teacher, was ill.
>
> She brought thirty-five dollar bills.
> She brought thirty five-dollar bills.

Too much punctuation, too little punctuation, or misplaced marks may make a sentence almost meaningless. Examples: "When, after the first, snowfall—of the season, he brought out his, old, pair of skis; his lovely, worshipful, bride, was lost (in admiration), because, he could move, at all, on those, clumsy things." (Only two marks are needed.) "Old elephants like old men, cherish memories, and relive their days of glory." (Insert a comma after *elephants* and delete the comma after *memories.*)

Differences in emphasis are revealed in these sentences: "The candidate spoke well, but he carefully avoided local issues." "The candidate spoke well. But he carefully avoided local issues." (The second version puts more stress on the second idea.)

Axiom 4. A rule of punctuation is only a statement about what at present is customary practice. "Right" or "wrong," then, means only that a mark in a particular context is or is not used in accord-

[1] *English Journal*, March, 1967.

ance with current custom, or that it aids or reduces clarity and the smooth flow of a sentence.

The misuse of a mark, therefore, may be only a social blunder like using the wrong spoon. Yet, like other social blunders, it may have both social and economic consequences. No one can say how many carelessly written social letters have caused misunderstanding, heartache, and the cooling of friendship. No one can say how many persons have failed to get or keep positions they wanted, or to gain advancement in their chosen professions, because their writing was sloppy in spelling, punctuation, or other mechanics. No one knows how many legal cases have depended on the interpretation of a clause that would have meant something quite different if a comma had been inserted or omitted.

Nor can anyone estimate the dollars-and-cents cost of faulty punctuation. The story is told of a father who wired what he intended as a refusal of his daughter's request for a fur coat: NO AMOUNT IS TOO MUCH. The lack of a stop after NO cost him several hundred dollars. The federal government once passed a bill saying that "all foreign fruit, plants" should be admitted duty-free. The intention was to say, "all foreign fruit-plants." Before the error could be corrected, two million dollars in duty had been lost. In July, 1962, the federal space agency sent its first probe toward Venus. It failed, at a cost of eighteen million dollars. The reason for the failure: a hyphen missing from an equation.

In summary, a writer's and a reader's mutual understanding of current conventions of punctuation may lead to clear communication and sometimes may save money.

Axiom 5. Punctuation cannot make a bad sentence good. Some students appear to believe that they can correct almost any writing fault by slipping in an extra comma or two. Thus, one student wrote, "Flying just beneath the low-hanging clouds I saw a V of wild geese." He tried, unsuccessfully of course, to remedy the faulty structure by placing a comma after *clouds*. The only cure possible for that sentence was redrafting.

OBLIGATORY AND OPTIONAL PUNCTUATION

Obligatory Punctuation

Some principles of punctuation afford virtually no choice. These should be taught as established conventions followed by all careful modern writers. The following list includes the chief of these, exclusive of certain formularized practices in letters, footnotes, bibliographies, and other writing not involving complete sentences.

Terminal Punctuation

1. Period after a sentence making a statement
2. Period after a command or a request, even though phrased as a question ("Will you please close the door.")
3. Question mark after a direct question
4. Exclamation mark after a sentence expressing strong feeling
5. Comma after a sentence quoted within a sentence, unless a question mark or exclamation mark is required ("That is all," she said. "Is that all?" she asked.)

Divisional Punctuation

1. Semicolon to separate complete statements within a sentence when *and, but, for, or, nor, yet,* or *so* is not used
2. Colon to separate a formal list from the rest of a sentence
3. Quotation marks around quoted sentences or parts of sentences; comma after *he said,* or colon if the statement is very formal
4. Single quotation marks around a quotation within a quotation
5. Comma to prevent momentary confusion ("Whatever is, is right.")
6. Comma to separate consecutive modifiers of the same type ("The angry, snarling dog pursued him relentlessly, endlessly.")
7. Comma to separate pairs of items ("His meal consisted only of bread and milk, and tea and lemon.")
8. Comma to separate items in a sequence ("Refer to Act 1, scene i, line 14.")
9. Comma or dash to separate words used for effect ("Long, long ago he should have decided—decided to make the climb.")
10. Dash to signal an abrupt change in structure ("When he was— Don't drive so fast!")

Parenthetical Punctuation

1. Comma to enclose non-essential clauses ("Grady Blue, who played left tackle, was injured.")
2. Commas to enclose non-essential phrases if clarity will be enhanced ("A bookcase, laid flat on the floor, occupied one corner.")
3. Commas to enclose non-essential appositives
4. Dashes or parentheses to enclose strongly interruptive elements
5. Brackets to enclose interpolations in quoted material

Optional Punctuation

The University of Chicago's *A Manual of Style* says of the comma, "There are a few rules governing its use that have become almost obligatory. Aside from these, the use of the comma is mainly a matter of good judgment, with ease in reading as the end in view." What is true of the comma is true in varying degree of the other marks also. Punctuation is an art and not a science.

In a number of situations, of which the most important are listed below, a writer may choose between one mark and another or between one mark and none. Sometimes clarity will dictate one choice or the other, or sometimes the emphasis will be changed by the presence or absence of marks, but often the choice is completely free. It seems wise to indicate and permit this freedom to students; if they follow the obligatory usages, they should not be condemned if they depart from the teacher's or the textbook writer's preferences in the optional ones, although they should be consistent in their own choices. (Some preferences of the author of this book are indicated later.)

1. Comma optional before *and* in an *a, b,* and *c* series ("The flag is red, white, and blue." Or ". . . red, white and blue.")
2. Commas optional in an *a* and *b* and *c* series ("The ground was hard and cracked and sun-parched." Perhaps more emphatic: ". . . hard, and cracked, and sun-parched.")
3. Commas or question marks in separating two or more parallel questions in the same sentence ("When will she have time for shopping, for cooking, for keeping house?" Or ". . . for shopping? for cooking? . . .")
4. Comma optional before *and, but, for, or, nor, yet* or *so* in a compound sentence
5. Comma optional to set off an introductory adverbial clause
6. Comma optional to set off an introductory word or phrase
7. Commas, dashes, parentheses, or sometimes no marks, with interpolated phrases ("He may, or may not, win the election." "He may— or may not—win the election." "He may (or may not) win the election." "He may or may not win the election.")
8. Comma optional to indicate omission of one or more words ("Hyperbole refers to exaggeration; litotes, to the opposite." Or ". . . . litotes to the opposite.")

Two Modes of Presentation

The usual method of teaching punctuation is to devote some lessons to terminal punctuation, some to the comma, one or two to the semicolon, and so on. This procedure has the advantage of affording a systematic overview of the specific uses of each mark.

A second method is to teach punctuation along with sentence structure. When the class is studying the compound sentence, for example, the teacher helps students to learn the ways in which varying forms of the sentence should be punctuated. This instruction is timely and useful; it has the special merit of permitting the class members to practice the usage as they compose sentences requiring it.

Both of these procedures are to be commended, and both should be used at one time or another. Each may reinforce the other. The second procedure should always be followed when a particular structure is being introduced. The first is valuable for review or to tie loose ends.

The remainder of this discussion will consider the marks one by one, concentrating on chief uses and major trouble spots. It might with equal logic, though, consider the various structures that require punctuation and the obligatory or optional usages with each.

The Period

The most important of punctuation marks is the period. High school students seldom omit periods except through carelessness. As motivation this old jingle may be used; when capital letters and periods are properly inserted, it makes some degree of sense:

> A funny old man told this to me
> I fell in a snowdrift in June said he
> I went to a ball game out in the sea
> I saw a jellyfish float up in a tree
> I saw some gum in a cup of tea
> I stirred my cream with a big brass key
> I opened my door on my bended knee
> I beg your pardon for this said he
> But tis true when told as it ought to be
> Tis a puzzle in punctuation you see.

In junior high school, students usually get the idea that a comma is a versatile mark of punctuation. In fact, they consider it so versatile that they often substitute it for a period. Thus is born the hated comma splice, also called the comma fault and the run-on sentence. It is actually a failure to use a period. This error often persists through the senior high school and appears in thousands of papers written by college freshmen and even in those by upperclassmen.

Juliet to the contrary, there is something in a name. As long as one teacher called the error a comma fault or comma splice, he could not eradicate it. In the hazy way that all of us sometimes think, students apparently believed that a "comma fault" was a failure to use enough commas; as a result, commas and comma faults both increased remarkably, despite the teacher's hours of work. When he began to use the term "run-on sentence" for the same error, its frequency decreased somewhat. Then, somewhere, he discovered the name "Siamese sentence" for this unnaturally joined construction. The students, sharing the universal interest in so-called Siamese twins, grasped the meaning of "Siamese sentence" at once, and came to look upon such a sentence as a linguistic monstrosity. In a short time no more than one Siamese sentence appeared where ten comma faults had flourished. If you have students who put commas where periods belong, you may try referring to Siamese sentences.

A teacher in a Champaign, Illinois, junior high school uses a different device to help students determine whether a comma, semicolon, or period is the right mark. She tells them, "When you are writing a sentence, pretend that you are a sign-maker and that the reader is driving a car. You put up a comma sign to tell him to drive slowly, a semicolon sign to say that there is a spot where he must almost stop, and a period sign to represent a stop." This device is, of course, only an inadequate rule of thumb, but it has the positive merit of reminding the writer that he is always responsible for helping the reader.

Some students use not too few periods but too many. They write, "Silas was very lonely. Although he enjoyed counting his gold every night." Correcting the habit of punctuating sentence fragments as sentences is not easy. Here, punctuation and knowledge of sentence structure are closely linked. The student who really knows what a sentence is does not write graceless, unintentional sentence fragments. The cure for this error is not to preach punctuation but to teach sentence structure.

Classes that learn about juncture in structural linguistics can use that knowledge in determining whether a comma will suffice or a semicolon or period is needed. Plus juncture / + / helps a listener to recognize where one word ends and the next begins; the classic examples are *ice* / + / *cream* and *I* / + / *scream*. Single bar juncture / | / comes at the end of a group of words at a place where there is a slight pause but no change in pitch; it usually comes just after an accented word, for example, *The men in the barn* / | / *were* . . . Double bar juncture / || / involves a slightly longer pause and a slight rise in pitch; for example, *My uncle* / || / *who lived in*

Nebraska / ||| / *was* . . . . Finally, double cross juncture / # / sig-
nifies a still longer pause and generally a slight fall in pitch; for
example, *The crowd left quietly* / # / *The surprising defeat had
left nothing for them to say* / # /.

Usually plus and single bar junctures require no punctuation.
The double bar normally indicates a comma. The double cross generally signifies a semicolon or a period. Students who have learned
to distinguish the double bar juncture from the double cross juncture may apply that knowledge directly to the punctuation of their
own sentences.

The Question Mark

In high school most omissions of needed question marks arise
from carelessness. Sometimes, though, a student will use unnecessary question marks, as in "I wondered whether I should run now?"
or "After our warm(?) trek through Maine last December . . ."
The first error is caused by unawareness of what an indirect question
is and may require five or ten minutes of instruction. The second
is probably written by the same student who writes "Ha ha" or
"Laugh now" after a joke; he is trying to make sure that his humor
or irony is not overlooked. Tell him that, although the question
mark is sometimes used to indicate uncertainty ("Chaucer, Geoffrey,
b. 1340?"), it is not used to show that the writer is trying to be
funny.

The Exclamation Point

Perhaps least troublesome of the punctuation marks is that denot-
ing exclamation. Two cautions, though, must sometimes be given
individual students: (1) Despite the practice of comic-strip artists,
one exclamation point is sufficient after any ejaculation. Two or
more exclamation points shout deafeningly in the reader's ear. (2)
Like any other device for securing emphasis, exclamation points
should not be overused. A long series of exclamatory statements
tires out the reader; besides, the third or fourth exclamation is not
nearly so emphatic as the first.

The Comma

The text that the senior class used had a section of thirty-five or
forty pages devoted to comma uses. Most of the section consisted
of rules and illustrations. The volumes used by the other classes

contained the same section in abridged and slightly varied form. The then-inexperienced teacher [2] tried manfully to get his students to master all the rules, but it seemed that when they learned to set off non-restrictive appositives they forgot about transitional words, and when they remembered transitional words they forgot names in direct address. They did not learn very much about using commas, even though they could state the rules. One sophomore girl wrote, "Use commas to separate members of a series and use them also to set off non-restrictive elements because those are not really needed and use them between clauses in a compound sentence."

The fault was the teacher's. He did two things that were entirely wrong. In the first place, he falsely assumed that knowing the rules and being able to apply them were synonymous. The result was mere verbalism; the students could parrot the rules but could not punctuate a sentence. In the second place, he taught each rule as an entity. He pointed out no similarities among the rules; indeed, he may not have seen any similarities. Each rule was there in its own little shell. The teacher was attempting to teach technical differences between herrings and sardines to students who did not yet know the differences between fish and mammals.

After that first painfully inadequate teaching, he gradually developed a simplified plan of teaching comma usage. He borrowed ideas from so many places that he cannot say for sure that any part of the plan is original. But he found that it does work.

The heart of the plan is a reduction in the number of comma rules. The rules may be reached inductively, and should certainly be taught inductively in the high school class.

What do the following sentences have in common?

Just opposite a tall building was in flames.
To cope with these people must be energetic.
Mary Howard was here, but he has gone.
Her crying spell over the girl went home.
If James is sure there can be no mistake.

In each of these sentences, a comma is needed to prevent momentary misreading. Insert commas after *opposite, these, Mary, over,* and *sure.*

Comma rule number 1: *A comma may be used to prevent a pos-*

---

[2] His name: J. N. Hook.

sible misreading. If a sentence is poorly constructed, of course, punctuation alone cannot make it clear.

Now to develop the second comma rule. Once more, what quality do all these sentences share?

> Oh, I didn't know that.
> The lesson being finished, Sandra was happy.
> He insists, I should warn you, that his employees be punctual.
> Yes, I agree.
> After that, Mother, we went to a show.
> Helen, above all, is meticulous.
> In March, 1968, he announced his candidacy.
> Portland, Oregon, has a splendid school system.
> "You see," he said, "I was once wealthy."
> Dorothy, who is my sister, was at the station.
> Dorothy, my sister, was at the station.
> These five answers, however, possess varying degrees of correctness.

In each of these twelve sentences is one element that is not essential. The element may add interesting or relevant information, but it is not really needed. If you read any of the sentences without the part set off by commas, the meaning of the sentence may be reduced, but it is not changed. For example, *I agree,* means the same as *Yes, I agree. Dorothy was at the station* means the same thing as *Dorothy, my sister, was at the station.*

Thus comma rule number 2: *A non-essential part of a sentence should be set off with one comma if it comes first or last in the sentence and with two commas if it comes anywhere else.*

You notice that this rule does not make a separate issue of restrictive and non-restrictive clauses. It seems that the term *restrictive* is never completely clarified for any except the brighter students. The others can echo definitions and attain 90 per cent success in workbook exercises involving identification of restrictive and non-restrictive elements, but their own punctuation of such elements remains shaky. Therefore, non-restrictive clauses may simply be called non-essential clauses. They thus fall into the same category as *however, oh,* words in address, and other non-essential elements. When students write a sentence such as "Henry, who is two years older than I am, led the way," they recognize that the clause is not essential and set it off with commas. When they write a sentence such as "People who lack loyalty are traitors," they see that the clause is needed and, therefore, omit commas.

Now, to develop comma rule number 3. What do the following sentences have in common?

The tall, straight soldier entered.
The soldier was tall, straight, and young.
We hunted pheasants in the cornfields, in the patches of long grass, and near the pond.
The old man asked who we were, what we wanted, and why we had knocked on his door.
Helena started to answer the question, but Hermia interrupted her.

Each comma in these sentences separates adjoining ideas that are stated in the same form and that serve the same purpose. In sentence 1, *tall* and *straight* are both adjectives describing the soldier. In 2, *tall, straight,* and *young* are adjectives modifying *soldier.* Sentence 3 has three prepositional phrases used as adverbs modifying *hunted.* Sentence 4 contains three noun clauses used as objects of the verb. The last sentence consists of two equal clauses.

Comma rule number 3 might be stated thus: *When two or more words or groups of words are similar in form and function, they should be separated by commas.* If students are sufficiently advanced to understand the expression "coordinate elements," the rule might be stated like this: *Use commas to separate coordinate elements within the sentence.*

There are two corollaries to this rule. One is that, in an *a, b,* and *c* series, the comma before *and* is optional. It seems preferable to have it there, but, since many reputable publications omit it, one cannot insist upon it. The chief reason for preferring the comma before *and* is that some sentences may be misread if it is left out; for example, "Charlotte, Lucille and Alice called today." It is difficult to say whether that sentence means that two persons called or three. A comma after *Lucille* would make it clear that three persons called. A second reason for the preference is that the comma distinguishes a true series from a false one:

That tall, ugly, and unpainted house is my home. (True series; comma before *and.*)
That tall, green and white house is my home. (False series; no comma before *and.*)

The teacher's personal preference, however, should not carry much weight. If students still omit the comma before *and* in a series, it should not be considered an error unless the class has agreed to consider it incorrect.

The second corollary is that sometimes words appear to be the same in form and function when they actually are not. For instance, consider *four tall trees*. *Tall* modifies *trees,* but *four* modifies *tall trees;* it does not tell how many trees there were, but how many tall trees. Similar expressions not requiring commas are *large brick building, the first heavy snowfall,* and *blue silk dress.* Show students that they can usually test whether or not they need a comma between two such words by inserting *and* between the words. If the *and* makes sense and seems a natural expression, a comma is required; if it does not, a comma should not be used. *Four and tall trees* would be almost meaningless; therefore, no comma. *Tall and straight soldier* makes sense, therefore, *tall, straight soldier.* A second test is to invert the order of modifiers. *Brick large building* is un-English; so is *silk blue dress.* But *straight, tall* soldier is satisfactory. When the modifiers survive the test of inversion, they are truly coordinate and should be separated by a comma. Structural linguists, by classifying *four* and *first* as determiners, *tall, large, heavy,* and *blue* as adjectives, and *brick* and *silk* as nouns or noun adjuncts, show an accurate grammatical reason for the needed punctuation. Coordinate adjectives (*tall, straight soldier*) are separated by commas, but determiners and adjectives (*four tall trees*) or adjectives and noun adjuncts (*large brick house*) are not.

These three comma rules summarize the multitudinous rules sometimes found in textbooks, except for those dealing with such formalized matters as the punctuation of parts of a letter. They are statements of general principle; they use no difficult terminology. A student need not know forty definitions or memorize twenty rules.

You may have a legitimate complaint at this point. "The text we use doesn't simplify rules like this. Won't it be confusing to students to tell them one thing in class but have them read something different outside of class?"

Although reduction of the number of rules is a feature of many present-day texts, let us suppose that your text cites thirty rules for the comma. Instead of having the students learn the thirty rules, let them see that all thirty are simply subdivisions of the three basic principles. Teach the thirty as specific illustrations, and insist only that the students understand thoroughly the big three. Thus, when your sophomores read the rule that a non-restrictive appositive should be set off by commas, help them to see that *the Father of Waters* is non-essential in "The Mississippi, the Father of Waters, flows past St. Louis." It thus comes under the second principle. Students may study the other examples of the non-restrictive appositive and see that they fall into the same category. They contrast these non-essential words or phrases with "Mark Twain's novel *Huckleberry Finn* is more profound than his *Tom Sawyer*," noting that *Huckleberry Finn* is not set off, because it is essential rather than non-essential; the sentence would lose its meaning without those two words.

One of the curses in the teaching of punctuation, especially the teaching of commas, has been excessive verbalization. Teachers have insisted that students learn rules by the bookful, and have given them good grades if they could repeat the words. But the parroting of words is by no means proof of comprehension or of ability to apply. Punctuation may be taught much more effectively if every teacher emphasizes (1) that a writer should always have a reader in mind, asking himself, "How can I punctuate this so that even a stupid or willfully stubborn reader will understand?" (2) that a small number of rules, thoroughly mastered, will be enough to guide the writer to punctuate almost any sentence, and (3) that where legitimate options exist, students may be permitted at least whatever freedom the editor of the *Atlantic* would grant them.

Quotation Marks

Junior high school students readily grasp the fundamentals of using quotation marks but seldom are mature enough to understand and remember the intricacies. As with any other mark of punctuation, the first step in teaching is to let the students see why quotation marks are used. Trick sentences may be employed to advantage:

> The author said the reader was an ignoramus.
> "The author," said the reader, "was an ignoramus." [3]

Paragraphs that are confusing until quotation marks are inserted will also be valuable.

Most junior high school students can learn to use a separate paragraph for each speaker, put quotation marks around what each

[3] *English Journal*, XXXXIII, 560.

speaker actually says, and indicate the break around such inserted elements as *he said.*

The intricacies such as the punctuation of several paragraphs spoken by the same person and the punctuation of a quotation within a quotation may best be left until the sophomore year or later, except when a class or some bright students ask questions about such intricacies or show that they have mastered the more fundamental processes. Always it is best to teach technicalities in response to a need felt by the students themselves. For example, the students may be preparing to write a composition that is almost certain to include considerable dialog. Before they write, they may be shown what is standard practice in using quotation marks in various situations.

Let your students know that the relative placement of closing quotation marks and other marks of punctuation is simply a matter of convention. Americans have adopted one set of conventions; the British, a different set—just as Americans refer to *truck, hood,* and *gasoline,* while the British say *lorry, bonnet,* and *petrol.* We Americans place periods and commas inside closing quotation marks, and colons and semicolons outside. But we let logic, not an arbitrary rule, determine whether the question mark and the exclamation point go inside or outside. The British usually let logic determine the placement. Examples of American usage follow.

> "I agree," said she.
> Steinbeck wrote "The Red Pony"; he did not write "The White Rabbit."
> He recited a couple of lines from "To a Mouse": "The best laid plans of mice and men/Gang aft agley."
> "Who's there?" he asked.
> Did he say, "Five more"?
> "Watch out!" she shouted.
> What a "concobberation"!

The Semicolon

Although bright youngsters in junior high school may master the chief use of the semicolon—to separate two rather closely related ideas each expressed in sentence form—usually the tenth grade is the best time to put emphasis on this useful mark, with review and much additional practice in the eleventh and twelfth grades.

Miss Eunice Helmkamp has described an excellent inductive procedure.[4] She asks her students to bring to class six sentences con-

4 "Semicolons in Action," *English Journal,* XLII (Oct., 1953), 391.

taining semicolons. The sentences are to be taken from contemporary printed material, but not from advertising, poetry, headlines, and the like. Each sentence is to be written or pasted on a 3- by 5-inch card. In class she tells the students that a semicolon is sometimes like a "weak" period, sometimes like a "strong" comma, and she reads examples to illustrate what she means. The students examine their own sentences to see how the semicolons are employed. They discuss their sentences in groups or with the class, copying some of them on the chalkboard to clarify various points. As a class, they attempt to formulate their own rules. One class came up with these:

A. Use a semicolon when the ideas in sentences are so closely related that a period would make too distinct a break between them. Sometimes the second sentence may contain a word which states the relationship between the two ideas. Typical relationship words: *besides, nevertheless, similarly, also, then, furthermore, instead, however.*

B. Use a semicolon between items in a series if the items contain commas, or if they are long and complicated.

C. Use a semicolon before the conjunctions *and, but, for, nor* in a compound sentence if the sentence is long and involved, or if there are other punctuation marks within the sentence, or if you wish to give special emphasis to the last part.

The students' examples on the cards are tacked under A, B, and C on the bulletin board. When one of the students comes up with a sentence that does not appear to follow one of these rules, such as "Broadway has its Lunts; London its Oliviers," the class and teacher examine it. They find, for the example given, that the second half is a complete sentence with a verb implied and that, hence, it fits under Rule A.

The advantage of such a procedure is that it shows students that semicolons are not just things they study in school. Their "research" and their active thinking will enable them to remember much more easily than if they had just listened to a lecture by the teacher or studied a textbook discussion. Textbook practice exercises may clinch the understanding.

One caution is necessary. Some college freshmen who have half-learned the use of the semicolon write, "Although it was raining hard, we decided to drive on; since we were already late." Pressed for an explanation, these students say, "In high school the teacher said that, when there was some other punctuation, we should use a semicolon between clauses." The caution, then, is this: Stress the fact that the basic use of the semicolon is to separate clauses that could stand alone as sentences. The clause *since we were already late* cannot. If a sentence has a long and involved series, especially if the elements in the series contain commas, then a semicolon is justified between the elements, as in this example: "We spent spring weekends at Aunt Jane's, either in her town house or at the lake; long summer days with Uncle Judd, who owned a small farm; fall Saturdays, which seemed much less pleasant, at home." The semicolon is primarily a mark to be used in compound or compound-complex sentences; simple or complex sentences almost never need it unless a series is involved.

The Colon

The colon is not a troublesome mark. In junior high school, its use after the salutation of a business letter should be taught. Mention that this use is only a matter of etiquette, like shaking hands. Everyone expects it of us, and we are considered queer if we do not follow the general practice. Ninth graders may also learn that the colon is used before a formal list. Tenth graders may learn the other uses of the colon: before a formal quotation, between biblical chapter and verse, and between hours and minutes (8:24 A.M.). Your bright seniors can understand how a colon may introduce a follow-up statement for which a preceding independent clause has made the preparation: "A novelette is not a small novel: it is an art form with characteristics all its own."

You may want to tell students that the colon is a very formal mark of punctuation, that you associate him with white ties and tails, and that he is never found in boisterous surroundings. And when someone asks why a semicolon is not half a colon, since *semi-* means half, you may answer simply that the word *semicolon* is now a misnomer and that in present American usage there is no relationship between the colon and the semicolon, although originally the semicolon was intended to indicate a shorter pause than that shown by the colon.

The Apostrophe

Perhaps the apostrophe and the hyphen should be treated in the chapter on spelling, since both are spelling devices, used in single words, rather than punctuation marks, which separate parts of sentences. Convention, however, places these marks with punctuation. It might be interesting to experiment in order to see whether any improvement would be noticeable if all misuses of apostrophes and hyphens were marked *sp* instead of *P*.

After reading a good many reams of student themes, I have come to the conclusion that the number of times the apostrophe is omitted just about balances the number of times it is used unnecessarily. If we could only teach students to put apostrophes in the right places. . . .

Here is what some of them do: They omit apostrophes in possessives, misplace them in contractions, insert them to form possessives of personal pronouns (especially *it's for its*), and insert them to form all sorts of plurals. Many of the errors are due to students' carelessness; others are caused by poor teaching.[5]

The first step is to let students see that apostrophes are too important to be neglected. Have them pronounce these words:

shed were wed shell well hell as is

Then insert an apostrophe in each word, and have someone pronounce them again:

she'd we're we'd she'll we'll he'll a's i's

Motivation, all-important motivation, consists often only of letting them see why!

Junior high school students should learn and practice the two most common uses of the apostrophe. With the students' help, build on the blackboard a rather long list of words in which apostrophes are used to show omission of letters. The words above (except *a's* and *i's*) will be included, and also words like *o'clock* and numbers like '71 (meaning 1971). Be sure to stress that the apostrophe always goes into the place where the omitted letter or letters were taken out. By emphasizing that fact, you can prevent monstrosities like *were'nt* and *ar'ent*.

Tell the seventh, eighth, or ninth graders that the second use of the apostrophe is related to the first. Several hundred years ago some people believed that the proper way to show possession was to use the noun with the pronoun *his*. Instead of writing *Henry's*

---

[5] There is a little agitation, especially in England and in avant-garde American writing, to do away with the apostrophe as an unnecessary mark. However, in some contexts, at least momentary confusion arises when it is omitted.

shoes these people wrote *Henry his shoes;* likewise, they wrote *the king his crown,* etc. When they pronounced *Henry his shoes* rapidly, however, the *hi* could hardly be heard (let the class try it); the result sounded like *Henrys shoes. The king his crown* sounded like *the kings crown.* So, many people wrote *the kings crown.* Here they ran into difficulty, because *kings* might mean two kings, or it might indicate possession. Someone then got the idea of using an apostrophe to show that the *hi* had (supposedly) been left out. In that way the form for the possessive originated.

It seems best to teach possessives by having students write the words in phrases—*king's crown, woman's hat, Edward's watch,* etc. Doing so may prevent the tendency to use the apostrophe in such a sentence as "Two kings fought for the crown." It is also best to be sure that students master singular possessives before they go on to plural possessives. Many a ninth grader has been confused because he was told about *kings' subjects* before he had really learned *king's subjects.*

In teaching plural possessives, teachers have found the following procedure successful: Start with simple plurals. Ask the students to spell the plurals of such words as *dog, raven, lady.* Put these in one column, and for a second column have students spell the plurals of irregular words such as *man, woman, ox.* (With advanced classes, words like *sister-in-law* and *alumnus* may be included.) Then, after each plural noun, write, with class help, the name of something that noun might possess, as *dogs noses.* Ask the students how the possession could be made clear. Someone in the class will say that an apostrophe should be used after the *s* in *dogs.* Go down the first column, inserting an apostrophe after each final *s.* Have the students copy the list of phrases in their notebooks, because the act of writing will tend to make the principle stick.

Then turn to the second column. The problem is different here, because these plurals do not end in *s.* Show the students that these irregular plural possessives are formed by adding an apostrophe and *s.* Have them copy this second list.

The next day, dictate a number of phrases from both lists, and add a few others for additional practice. Repeat a few days later, and repeat after that until perfection has been attained. Vary the phrases sufficiently that rote memory will not suffice; it is the application of the principle, not a memory of a few phrases, that you want.

Students who make two perfect scores in succession may be excused from later drills.

Possessives of words like *Jones* cause particular trouble. Unless a student asks the question, probably Mr. Jones should be ignored until the sophomore or junior year. Teach *dog's nose* and, sometime later, *dogs' noses,* but let Mr. Jones take care of himself. When he finally demands your attention, tell the class that *Jones* (*Dickens, Burns*) is a regular noun; let them use *Jones's* as the singular possessive, just as they would write *Smith's.* (Actually, either *Jones'* or *Jones's* is acceptable; what you want to avoid is *Jone's.*) The plural may also be taught as a regular plural, like *churches.* If your juniors learn to write *the Joneses' automobiles,* you have done a good job of teaching this matter.

Students tend also to write *her's, your's, our's, their's,* by analogy with *dog's,* etc. Some teachers, after their students have made such an error, review the forms of the personal pronoun, stressing that *hers, yours, ours,* and *theirs* are personal pronouns. "No personal pronoun," they say, "ever takes an apostrophe. Nobody would write *m'y* for *my,* or *hi's* for *his.* There is no more reason for apostrophes in any other personal pronouns." The same reasoning applies to the possessive *its,* although that word is used as a possessive adjective rather than as a pronoun. A simple injunction: "Never write *it's* unless you can substitute *it is* or *it has;* the possessive form is always *its.*"

The Hyphen

Junior high school students should learn the use of the hyphen to divide a word between syllables at the end of a line and to separate compound numbers. Show them that the hyphen at the end of a line prevents misreading in such a sentence as this:

> . . . He climbed up the flag
staff.

Let them see also that there is a reason for the hyphen in compound numbers. Call their attention to the sentence already cited on page 387: "She brought thirty five dollar bills." Help them to see that the placement of the hyphen makes a difference of $115.

Encourage the use of the dictionary when students must divide a word at the end of a line. Show them that failure to divide between syllables sometimes leads to impossible or ridiculous pronunciations: flagst-aff, packthr-ead, thoro-ugh, etc.

In the senior high school, when you come to the matter of hyphenation of compound adjectives and nouns, you will need to explain that the practice of hyphenation changes. Tell them about *basketball*. When Dr. Naismith invented the game, he called it *basket ball* because a ball was thrown into a peach basket. As the game became better known, the two words were felt to be closely associated, and were written with a hyphen. Today we consider the two words as a unit—*basketball*. The same thing has happened in *football* and *baseball*. That is, a word may be written as two words in one period of time and with a hyphen in another; it may be written with a hyphen in one decade and solid in another. Advise students to refer to the dictionary when they are in doubt whether a compound noun should be hyphenated (although dicitonaries frequently do not agree). Tell them about the expensive hyphens mentioned on page 388.

Let them see that words linked together to form single adjectives need to be hyphenated except when the dictionary indicates that they are written solid. Call to their attention the difference between *strange looking glass* and *strange-looking glass*, between *man made mistakes* and *man-made mistakes*, and between *man eating tiger* and *man-eating tiger*. Dictate a number of expressions such as a *never-to-be-forgotten moment, an old-time dance, a quick-as-a-flash retort.*

Parentheses

Juniors and seniors, and sometimes younger students, may be introduced to the mysteries of parentheses. These marks are used in rather formal writing to indicate the insertion of material that has no structural relation to the rest of the sentence. Teach inductively, using numerous examples. For instance,

> I am enclosing a check for three dollars and twenty-seven cents ($3.27).
> These questions (page 47) remain unanswered.
> William Shakespeare (1564-1616)
> His reply (it was delivered in a speech in New Haven) aroused much controversy.

College teachers are sometimes rightfully distressed because somebody, somewhere, has taught students to enclose in parentheses words or groups of words that are to be disregarded. Material in parentheses is *not* disregarded. If a student wants to show that something should be omitted, he should neatly draw a single line through it.

The Dash

Dashes are useful in writing that is not very formal, and are occasionally found even in formal writing. The teacher must not advocate frequent use of dashes, though, or some student may become a dashomaniac. Some college freshmen at the beginning of the year use no mark of punctuation except the dash. Reading the first page of their first compositions leaves the instructor completely breathless.

The chief use of the dash is to indicate an abrupt break in thought or construction. For example,

When I was—there's a skunk, George!
This machine—another one like it is over there—is a combine.

It may be used to indicate hesitation:

I—I doubt it. (Tell the students to put a dash right between the *I*'s.)

Finally, the dash may set off an introductory appositive or an appositive loosely attached at the end of a sentence:

Sympathy and willingness to make haste slowly—these are two requisites for any teacher.
He did possess something that was superior—his teeth.

It is advisable to have students use two short marks or one rather long mark for a dash, to distinguish it from a hyphen. In typing they must use two hyphens, as the standard typewriter keyboard has no dash.

The dash is not an important mark of punctuation. If your students do not know the more useful marks, do not spend time on the dash. You may want to explain its use to your more capable students, but you can let the others ignore its existence.

Brackets

If your seniors write a research paper, they may need to know about brackets. These marks have a more limited use than any others. Contrary to popular superstition, they are not alternative forms of parentheses. Brackets are used primarily to enclose one's personal comments or corrections when one is quoting from someone else:

> The senator continued: "Our state now leads the nation in production of butterfat. [Applause] We now . . ."
> "When Rhodes died in 1901 [actually 1902], he left six million pounds to the public."

A second use, very rare, is to represent parentheses within parentheses:

> The new state (the boundaries of which [see map, p. 647] had recently been ratified) still had no constitution.

Italics

It is conventional to underline titles of books, magazines, newspapers, plays, and motion pictures, and to place quotation marks around titles of short stories, poems, chapters, and articles. Nothing subtle or abstract is involved here. Junior high school students of even below-average intelligence may be led to follow this convention.

The other uses of underlining (italics) are less important; some, indeed, seem on the way to the discard pile. Although numerous texts still say that names of ships, trains, airplanes, and pullman cars should be italicized, not all editors of magazines and books, and probably no editors of newspapers, now follow this rule. Perhaps a casual mention of the principle might be made to the college-preparatory seniors, but the point is not worth stressing.

The use of italics to indicate a word referred to as a word, a letter referred to as a letter, etc., is more defensible than the preceding use and is more widely observed. "She left an *o* out of *sophomore*" may be slightly more clear than "She left an o out of sophomore." "He said that the *when* was misplaced" is easier to read than "He said that the when was misplaced." Therefore, unless there are more fundamental things to present, this use of italics should be taught. (An alternative is to enclose in quotation marks any word referred to as a word, with the exception of technical terms, which are italicized.)

Caution is necessary in teaching the use of underlining for emphasis. Too many students make a vice of underlining. Some seem to reason that, if one underlining creates emphasis, two underlinings should create more. In the paper of one student some words were underlined five times, and an applicant for a secretarial position once double-underlined every sentence in her letter of application because she wanted the letter to be emphatic. (She did not get the job). The sane approach is to tell—and show—the students that a little underlining goes a long way and that too much underlining for emphasis detracts from a piece of writing.

Students like to know the relationship between underlining and typesetting. When a printer sets copy, he will set in italic type anything underlined once, in small caps anything underlined twice, in capitals anything underlined three times, and in boldface anything underlined with a wavy line.

Capitalization

As remarked at the beginning of this chapter, capitalization is closely related to punctuation. It is a signal to the reader, just as a punctuation mark is. It tells the reader, "Here is the beginning of a new sentence, or here is a proper noun or something comparable to a proper noun, or here is some kind of title."

The seventh grader will already know that he needs a capital to start a sentence, that he should capitalize the pronoun *I*, and that he should capitalize names of persons and places. Beyond these things, his knowledge of capitals will probably be sketchy. More than likely he will use too many capitals rather than too few. Some high school compositions have a slightly German look because most of the nouns are capitalized.

A week spent on capitalization in any grade is likely to be three days wasted. A few of the principles will stick, but, since there are twenty or more capitalization rules, many will be forgotten. A better technique is to take up individual questions about capitalization at the time when the need is present. Learning thus becomes purposeful.

For example, suppose that the students are going to write a paper on the football prospects of their school. The teacher will anticipate the kinds of capitalization they will need and talk over the matter with the class. The composition will have a title. Which words do we capitalize in titles? There will be references to this high school and perhaps to other schools. When do we write *High School* and when do we write *high school?* Teacher and class will provide illustrations, and the principles will probably be remembered because they are presented at a time when the students feel a need for them.

Similarly, when one writes a letter, one usually refers to one's relatives. So, before the students write a letter, they talk over the question of when we capitalize *Mother, Aunt,* etc., and when we do not.

The capitalization errors most frequently made by students are in names of relatives, seasons, directions, and school subjects. Difficulty is the reason; students' stupidity is not. To the young student, capitalization looks hit and miss. Sometimes people do capitalize *Uncle, South,* and *Algebra,* and sometimes they do not; but whichever he chooses, it seems, is wrong. Poets get by with capitalizing *Winter,* but Miss Demeanor tells him that he must not do so. The apparent contradictions do not make sense.

Statistics on the "holding power" of schools are often interesting, but they do not reveal enough. It would be interesting if statistics were available to show how many students drop out of school because capitalization or the federal judiciary system or quadratic equations do not make sense. It would be equally interesting if other statistics were available to show how many students stay in school because one teacher can explain things so that they seem reasonable and understandable and worth knowing.

Why are *Uncle, South,* and *Algebra* capitalized part of the time? There is the key: Why? Consider these sentences:

But, James, I haven't any money.
But, Uncle, I haven't any money.

He lives in Alabama.
He lives in the South.

I am taking Algebra I.

In the first pair of sentences, *Uncle* is used as a proper noun, the equivalent of *James.* In the second pair, *South* is a proper name, including Alabama and other states. In the last sentence, Algebra I is a proper name; it does not refer to algebra in general but to this particular algebra course.

But sometimes these words are not used as substitutes for proper names:

My uncle came for a visit.
We walked south two blocks.
He enjoys studying algebra.

In these sentences, *uncle, south,* and *algebra* do not refer to proper names. That can be proved, at least in the first two, by trying to substitute a proper name. Most persons would not write:

My James came for a visit.
We walked Alabama two blocks.

Let them see why! If one teaching technique is of greater importance than any other, it is probably that one—let them see why.

FOR TALL PEOPLE ONLY

When the young man began teaching, very fresh from a year of graduate school, he was taller than he is now—much taller. He was so tall that he had his head in the clouds.

A wise old professor had told him and others in his class that getting educated consists of learning limitations, their own limitations and those of others. The young man did not believe it. He rather doubted that he had any serious personal limitations, and he was reasonably sure that humanity was on the verge of a more golden Golden Age. He knew what his contribution to that age would be. He was going to make all his students into Lovers of Literature; he was going to imbue them with a desire for nothing less than the Good Life; he was going to inspire them to write sentences filled with Rhetorical Fire. He gave little thought to such trivialities as commas, semicolons, capital letters, and spelling. His eyes were above cloud level.

The first papers that his students wrote reduced his stature considerably. From a typical freshman came, "I like to go Swimming and to hunt Frogs with my Father in the Summer that is of corse." And from, alas, an almost typical senior, "My father is engaged in the profession of Dentisty, someday I hope to become a dentist too." Rhetorical Fire, he decided, would have to wait.

During the rest of the first year, his stature continued to shrink. The juniors did not share, and apparently could not be induced to share, his enthusiasm for Melville. How, he wondered, could they become Lovers of Literature if they were not Lovers of Melville? The sophomores got lost in the fourth act of *Julius Caesar.* The Good Life, fortunately, seemed to be faring reasonably well, although he found himself becoming a little less certain of its ingredients.

He went back to the wise old professor and told him his troubles. "That is what often happens to English teachers," the professor said.

"During the first year they discover that they and everyone else have limitations. You have found that in nine months you cannot turn a hundred or so average boys and girls into polished writers or into worshipers of Santayana. This is a crucial time for you. Like every English teacher who becomes disillusioned during the first year, you have an important decision to make. You may go on teaching 'the finer things' exclusively, in the hope that something you teach will make an impression. Some English teachers choose that alternative. Or you may start at the level where each class is—or even where each student is—and try to help the students grow, try to help them get ready for 'the finer things.' Some of them will grow so much that eventually they may outstrip you or me. Others, because of their limitations, will never be able to comprehend the more esoteric uses of punctuation, will never be able to write a coherent compound-complex sentence, and will never feel at home even with a Sinclair Lewis novel.

"I hope that you choose the second alternative, that of helping the students to grow," the professor went on. "Patience is what you need, patience to let nature work, patience to irrigate and to cultivate. People grow slowly, like oaks. Asparagus grows quickly, but soon goes to seed. We want human oaks, not human asparagus."

"But the things many of these youngsters need seem so petty, so insignificant," the young man said. "I feel as if I'm wasting my time and theirs when I spend so long on these minutiae. Why, I'd have to spend hours on teaching elementary reading and on spelling and capital letters and commas and writing of simple sentences. It would take hours, months, years."

"Precisely," said the wise old professor.

THE IDEA BOX

Importance of Punctuation

1. Legend has it that the Czarina of Russia saw on the desk of Alexander III a note: "Pardon impossible; to be sent to Siberia." She changed the punctuation: "Pardon; impossible to be sent to Siberia."

2. As a motivating device, occasionally write on the board a tricky sentence for students to punctuate. For example, write, without punctuation or capitals, "Bill, where Henry had had 'had,' had had 'had had.' 'Had had' had had the examiner's approval." Or, "That that is, is; that that is not, is not. Is not that it? It is."

3. Here are some old favorite examples, showing how punctuation may affect meaning:

> Woman! Without her, man would be a savage.
> Woman without her man would be a savage.

> Louise thinks her employer is attractive.
> Louise, thinks her employer, is attractive.

> Mr. Rice, the superintendent came in.
> Mr. Rice, the superintendent, came in.

> "Bill," called Ralph. "Come here!"
> Bill called, "Ralph, come here!"

> The tight-rope walker almost fell.
> The tight rope-walker almost fell.

> The net was made of four wire cables.
> The net was made of four-wire cables.

> She is there now.
> She is there now!

> No man can be happy.
> No. Man can be happy.

The following make sense if properly punctuated:

The Indian Toti went off by himself to eat the rattlesnakes and the lizards squirming uneasily in the fragile box at my elbow rather spoiled my appetite.

Lord Wellington entered on his head a helmet on his feet a pair of well polished boots on his brow a cloud in his hand his favorite walking stick in his eye fire

The fight over the boys came home

While I was dressing my little brother came in

4. In *Ralph Roister Doister* (*ca.* 1553) Ralph had a scrivener pen this epistle to the wealthy lady he was courting:

> Sweete mistresse, where as I love you, nothing at all
> Regarding your substance and richnesse; chiefe of all
> For your personage, beautie, demeanour, and wit
> I commende me unto you: Never a whitte
> Sorie to heare reporte of your good welfare.

His false friend, Merygreek, transmitted the message like this:

> Sweete mistresse, where as I love you nothing at all,
> Regarding your substance and richesse chiefe of all,
> For your personage, beautie, demeanour and wit,
> I commende me unto you never a whitte.
> Sorie to heare reporte of your good welfare.

5. Encourage your students to collect sentences in which mispunctuation would cause comic misreading.

"Punctuating the Compound Sentence"

J. C. Gray teaches this formula: ; = (, + cc). (The cc means coordinating conjunction.) *English Journal,* LI (Nov., 1962), 573.

Intelligence and Punctuation

Although it can hardly be argued that poor punctuation and poor capitalization are signs of intelligence, a study by Nita M. Wyatt, reported in "Research in Creative Writing," *Educational Leadership,* XIX (Feb., 1962), 307, shows that bright sixth graders try more experiments, for example, in writing conversations or in writing complex sentence structures, and hence make more errors than do their classmates who are content with sentences like "I saw a woodpecker." Perhaps this suggests the unwisdom of simply counting errors in determining a grade. A student cannot fairly be penalized for a mistake in a construction not yet studied.

Blackboard Reminder

In some classes, part of the blackboard is reserved for reference purposes. Principles of punctuation, etc., that are needed most are kept there as convenient reminders for students.

Distributing Punctuation Marks

Some teachers in junior high school occasionally pass out sentences with all necessary punctuation marks at the end. Students put the marks where they belong.

Eliminating "Siamese Sentences"

Lou LaBrant suggests that the "comma splice" is caused by a student's failure to supply the word necessary to relate the two clauses, and recommends helping him to supply that word. For example, "He breathed rapidly, he was nervous" needs a *because.* "Teaching High-School Students To Write," *English Journal,* XXXV (March, 1946), 123.

Punctuation in Business Letters

Madeleine Sparks, in Westbury, New York, has her business seniors study punctuation in real business letters, analyzing the reason for each mark and checking their analyses against textbook rules. In groups of five, the students present their findings to the class. "A Practical Approach to Punctuation," *English Journal*, XLII (March, 1953), 158.

Punctuation Chart

Here is a convenient summary of the most widely followed punctuation practices. You may want to prepare and post a chart based upon it or to duplicate copies for individual student reference. The amount of grammatical terminology has purposely been kept small.

A SIMPLE GUIDE TO BASIC PUNCTUATION

Pattern	*Usual Punctuation*	*Example*
1. A statement	Period at end	He went home.
2. A question	Question mark at end	Did he go home?
3. An exclamation	Exclamation mark at end	Run for your lives!
4. Any construction that may be misread without punctuation	Usually a comma	To overcome this, work is essential.
5. A series of grammatically equal items	Usually a comma or commas	(a) She writes novels, plays, and poems. (b) . . . a scrawny, underfed kitten.
6. Two complete statements connected by *and, but, for, or, nor, yet, so*	Usually a comma; sometimes a semicolon if there is much other internal punctuation	(a) Man proposes, but God disposes. (b) Although the day was cold, she felt warm, cheerful, and optimistic; but Harvey, who walked with her, was grouchy.
7. Two complete statements not connected by *and, but, for, or, nor, yet, so*	If written as one sentence, a semicolon between the statements	The squirrel scurried along the ice-coated wire; beneath it ran a dog, barking hopefully.
8. Introductory clause (not used as the subject) followed by a complete statement	Usually a comma after the clause; now tending increasingly to be omitted	While she played the organ, he washed the dishes.
9. At beginning of a sentence, words not necessary to basic meaning	Usually followed by a comma	Well, I can find time if I must.
10. Within a sentence, words not necessary to basic meaning	Usually a comma on each side; less often dashes, parentheses, or brackets	My father, who objected to cigar smoke, thought that a bit of snuff was all right.
11. At end of a sentence, words not necessary to basic meaning	Usually preceded by a comma	He made a poor impression on my father, who objected to cigar smoke.

12. After such words as *as follows* or their equivalent	Usually a colon	He ordered the following merchandise: one gross horsecollars, one dozen . . .
13. With quoted words	Double quotation marks around the exact words quoted	Helen exclaimed, "He was never in Ithaca!"
14. Preceding a quotation	Usually a comma	(See 13 and 15.)
15. Quotation within a quotation	Single quotation marks	Bert asked, "Who said, 'Whatever is, is right'?"
16. Titles of short literary works, etc.	Quotation marks	Poe's "The Raven"
17. Titles of books, plays, etc.	Underlining	*For Whom the Bell Tolls*

Can They Get Rid of Technical Errors?

William M. Thomas, *School Review* (Summer, 1963), reports that seniors who still write run-ons and undesirable fragments and make other technical errors can through intensive work halve the number of errors but cannot eliminate them all.

11

Spelling: Trial and Terror

WHY ENGLISH SPELLINGS LACK CONSISTENCY

Before the invention of printing, most users of English were illiterate. Those who could write were free to spell as they chose, for there were no dictionaries, no spelling books, few schools, and no widely held belief that a single "correct" way exists for the spelling of each word. Among Chaucer and his fourteenth century contemporaries one may find, for example, as many as a dozen different spellings for such a simple word as *day;* Chaucer himself often spelled the same word differently.

After Caxton introduced the printing press into England, however, pressures toward uniformity of spelling began to mount. Printshops, anticipating the stylebooks of today's publishing houses, began making arbitrary decisions about spellings; they prepared lists for the guidance of their compositors so that whatever came off their presses would be orthographically consistent. The lists were often in disagreement; even today dictionaries include hundreds of variant spellings and differ in their judgments of which is preferred.[1] The fact that the early printers were not highly literate did not help English spelling during the period of standardization. Neither did the fact that English was simultaneously undergoing the Great Vowel

[1] Every teacher may be enlightened by the NCTE pamphlet *Variant Spellings in Modern American Dictionaries,* by Donald Emery, which includes an annotated list. Articles by James A. Preu and G. R. Turner in the September and November, 1966, *English Journal* argue that teachers should accept any spellings listed in standard dictionaries; e.g., *rime, paralyse, judgement, accidently, propellor, indispensible.*

416

Shift, by which English pronunciation of vowels became different from the Continental pronunciations (the sounds now represented by *a, e, i, o, u* in English are very different from the sounds of the same vowels in French or German, for example). A further complication was added by Renaissance scholars who tried to make English spelling conform to Latin: They insisted on the *b* in *debt* and *doubt,* for instance, even though the letter was silent even then, because *b* appears in the Latin ancestor; and, thinking mistakenly that the English *iland* came from the Latin *insula,* they demanded that printers insert an *s,* making the word *island.* Words ending in *-ation* and others equally out of accord with phonetic principles multiplied during these years of the fifteenth and sixteenth centuries.

As Englishmen increasingly wandered over the globe and transacted business hither and yon, words from more and more foreign languages were borrowed. Sometimes they were anglicized; sometimes they retained their original forms. The resulting problem is illustrated by Eva M. Tappan with reference to place names borrowed from Indian tongues:

> For they fastened a name to every nook,
> And every boy with a spelling-book
> Will have to toil till his hair turns gray
> Before he can spell them the proper way.

In brief, English spelling is inconsistent in two ways: (1) We represent a number of sounds by a single letter, and (2) we use a number of letters to represent the same sound. Thus, the letter *a,* according to Merriam-Webster, represents different sounds in *ale, chaotic, care, add, account, arm, ask,* and *sofa.* The sound called "long i" is represented by sixteen different letters or letter combinations in *aisle, bayou, aye, stein, geyser, eye, isle, choir, kind, lie, sigh, coyote, guide, buy, sly,* and *lye.* In some other languages such as Finnish, Spanish, and Russian a single letter usually represents a single sound; conversely, when one makes a sound, one knows what letter or letter combination to use in writing it. It has been estimated that the Russian language, which has 36 symbols for 34 basic sounds, is about 90 per cent efficient in its sound-letter relationships and that English, which has 379 symbols for 40–44 basic sounds, is about 20 per cent efficient. Such a disparity has implications for the teaching of reading as well as for the teaching of spelling. A Russian child may learn to read much more quickly than an English or American child because he need only sound out the letters to recognize a word. But an American child faced with *pneumonia* or *colonel* finds sounding of little avail.   And, when he has to spell *psychology,* an ear-justified spelling like *sikoloje* is red-penciled or even ridiculed.

Correct spelling, the mastery of inconsistencies, has become a status symbol of sorts.   In nineteenth-century America, spelling bees flourished; the man or woman who could spell *syzygy* could win a prize.even if he thought that syzygies were porcupines or petunias. Thorstein Veblen, in *The Theory of the Leisure Class* (1899), commented,

As felicitous an instance of futile classicism as can well be found is the conventional spelling of the English language. English orthography satisfies all the requirements of the canons of reputability under the law of conspicuous waste.   It is archaic, cumbrous, and ineffective; its acquisition consumes much time and effort; failure to acquire it is easy of detection.

Today a person misspells at his own peril.   Spelling errors in a letter of application or an important report may result in unemployment. Employers seldom complain about a secretary's faulty sentences, which may not be very easy to detect, but they are loud in their wails about faulty spelling.

Through the centuries many persons have tried to reform our chaotic spelling.   As early as 1573, John Barrett suggested simplifying by elimination of the letter *q* and of the letter *c* except in *ch* combinations.   Two centuries later, Benjamin Franklin recommended a new alphabet.   Noah Webster achieved some simplification, notably in reforming such words as *honour, centre, musick,* and *plough,* but he was defeated in his plea for *farewel, crum, wo, ake,* and *soop.* Late in the nineteenth century the philological associations of Great Britain and the United States vainly sought a basis for simplifying. Andrew Carnegie proved, to his regret, that wealth could not effect the needed changes.   When Theodore Roosevelt wanted to use simplified spelling in his White House correspondence, Congress threatened to withhold his appropriation.   Slowly a few shortened spellings like *gram, catalog, quartet,* and *traveled* have become accepted. Some newspapers have entered the campaign for simplified spelling. Groups of scholars and laymen have worked in various directions: some to simplify the spelling of only a few especially unphonetic words, some to respell virtually all words, and some to employ a new alphabet with a different letter for each of the forty-odd sounds of English.   In his will, George Bernard Shaw provided funds for the development of a new alphabet; the winning entrant in the subse-

quent competition has gone almost unnoticed. Upton Sinclair wrote
an impassioned plea to President John F. Kennedy. Bills for reforming spelling have been introduced in Congress, and in 1949 the
British Parliament narrowly defeated one such measure. In the
early 1960's the British, followed by some Americans, experimented
with the teaching of reading, using what they call the Augmented
Roman Alphabet. Chicago businessmen are helping to support the
Foundation for a Consistent and Compatible Alphabet, partly on the
ground that a revised alphabet and mode of spelling would possess
great economic value. The publisher of *Parents' Magazine* begs repeatedly for reform. The examples could go on and on.

The future of simplified spelling will not be bright unless three
unlikely events are brought to pass: A workable basis for simplification must be found, powerful backing must be obtained, and human
inertia must be overcome.

English teachers and their students, then, must go on making the
best of a bad bargain. English spelling may be a poor thing, but 'tis
our own. Maybe we can learn to chuckle at its idiosyncrasies, love
it with its faults, even take pride in its uniqueness and unpredict-
ability. Men have learned to do that with women.

MOTIVATION FOR SPELLING

You have heard the saying that one must be cautious in deciding
what one wants, because one is likely to get it. If a student decides
that he really wants to learn to spell, he is likely to learn to spell.

Here are several suggestions for motivation. None are infallible,
but one will work with some students, another with others. A combination of the five should effect a wholesome desire to improve and
to continue improving.

Building an Interest in Words

Help students to see that words are like people. Words have personalities—drab, shy, aggressive, colorful, scary, etc. Like people,
too, they often belong to families: the Antes, Antis, Ocracies, Ations,
and so on. The English language has been a melting pot for words
as America has been a melting pot for people; just as it is sometimes
interesting to find out a person's ancestry, so it is often interesting
and informative to discover the ancestry of a word. (See Chapter
12 for further discussion of building interest in words.)

Demonstrating Why Spelling Has Become Standardized

You might have each of your students write three or four sentences on any subject. Tell the class that each is to spell all he words in any way that he wishes—the more original the spelling, the better. Write something like the following as an example:

> Hwenn thuh Innngglissh lannggwidge wuzz jungrr, itt wuzz vehree dyf-fruhnt phrumn thuh lannggwidge ovv 2da.

Have the students exchange papers and try to read what their classmates have written. The time will not be wasted, for they will prove to their own satisfaction that, if each person spelled to suit himself, confusion and loss of effort would result.

Showing that Employers Value Correct Spelling

If you have the opportunity to find out what a few employers in your community think about spelling, make use of it, because nothing will impress students more than the point of view of influential local people. Collect a few pertinent real-life anecdotes about a stenographer who couldn't spell (and one who could), the mechanic's trouble with *gas kit* and *gasket,* the farmer who ordered clover because he couldn't spell *alfalfa,* etc.

Making Correct Spelling a Challenge

Unless a student is determined to learn to spell, he will not do so. For some students the greatest challenge may come from awareness that bad spelling may cause failure at a job or in college. (Some evidence suggests that the greatest weakness of students placed in remedial English in college is poor spelling.) For other students the challenge may be to pride: "You aren't going to let twenty-six little letters get you down, are you?" One teacher made a friendly wager with a class, betting that the class could not make an average score of 95 per cent on a semester test. At stake were some special (and legitimate) privileges that the class wanted. The poor spellers were so much hounded and helped by their classmates that the average was 98 per cent.

Continuing Motivation by Praising Improvement

Graphs or charts to show individual or class improvement are often helpful. Praise of the student who has just overcome his habit of confusing *their, there,* and *they're* is beneficial, even though he still misspells a dozen other words in one paper. To tell a class that it is improving in its spelling brings better results than to say, "Your spelling is worse than that of any other class I've ever taught."

SELECTING THE WORDS TO BE TAUGHT

Word counts have revealed that about 1,000 words constitute the basic vocabulary of English. Many of these are used over and over: *a, an, the, you, of, with,* etc. If one were to take random passages of English writing totaling 100,000 words, one would find that about 90,000 of the words were these basic 1,000 employed again and again.

Common sense, then, dictates that these 1,000 words are the ones everyone should know how to spell. The spelling bee of Grandfather's day placed stress instead upon long, difficult, and seldom used words. Sometimes the spellers learned the orthography of words they could not define or use. Today we emphasize spelling for use. Since few students will ever have occasion to write *catachresis,* that word is not taught, but, since all will probably need *coming, certain,* and *choose,* these are taught.

But, of the 1,000 or 2,000 or 3,000 most common words, not all cause spelling problems, at least for high school students. Words like *with, sand, window,* and *understand* are almost never misspelled except through rank carelessness. It is wasteful to spend time on words already mastered. However, some of the frequently employed words do cause trouble. These are the "demon" words, like *its, than,* and *too.* For instance, a group of twenty-five students who had just been graduated from high school, in writing that totaled about 110,000 words, misspelled 291. The only words misspelled more than once were *already* (2), *believe* (2), *convenience* (2), *doesn't* (3), *evidently* (2), *immensely* (2), *incidentally* (2), *indispensable* (2), *its* (5), *it's* (3), *nuisance* (2), *occasionally* (2), *preceding* (2), *receive* (3), *review* (2), *similar* (2), *strenuous* (2), *than* (4), *their* (4), *then* (2), *there* (3), *too* (9), *truly* (2), *woman* (2), and *writing* (2). For this particular group, then, 25 words accounted for almost a fourth of the errors. Mastery of a relatively small number of demons—100 or 200—may reasonably be expected to reduce spelling mistakes by half or more.

No two lists of demons are exactly alike. The 417 words in one list, compiled by Thomas C. Pollock, were found to account for 52.4

per cent of misspellings by college students.[2] Another list, prepared by Fred C. Ayer, is a composite based upon twelve spelling books.[3] The following list was compiled by Edna L. Furness and Gertrude A. Boyd on the basis of frequency of appearance on five carefully compiled lists including those by Pollock and Ayer. A student who can spell correctly all 231 of these words will not necessarily be a good speller, but he is unlikely to be a bad speller. Words which appear on two lists are unmarked; words which appear on three lists are marked by the number 3; those in four lists, by the number 4; and those on five lists, by the number 5.[4]

3 absence	bureau	3 deceive	extremely
3 accept	5 business	decided	3 familiar
accidentally	3 busy	definite	4 February
4 accommodate	cafeteria	3 definitely	3 finally
acquaintance	calendar	definition	3 foreign
across	campaign	describe	3 forty
advise	cancel	4 description	fourth
3 affect	capital	desert	freight
3 all right	captain	desirable	friend
already	3 cemetery	despair	3 fundamental
3 amateur	certain	dessert	generally
analyze	changeable	3 develop	genius
answer	3 chauffeur	development	3 government
anxious	3 choose	3 different	3 governor
apparatus	clothes	disappear	4 grammar
3 appearance	coarse	3 disappoint	guarantee
appreciate	3 column	disapprove	handsome
Arctic	3 coming	disastrous	3 height
3 argument	3 committee	3 discipline	humorous
arrangement	competent	divine	hungry
athletics	completely	3 doesn't	4 immediately
awkward	conceive	3 effect	3 independent
4 beginning	4 conscience	embarrass	interested
3 belief	conscientious	emphasize	interesting
4 believe	consistent	equipped	interfere
beneficial	convenience	especially	it's
3 benefit	corporation	exaggerated	3 its
3 benefited	course	3 excellent	knew
brilliant	courtesy	except	knowledge
Britain	criticism	4 experience	3 laboratory

2 "Spelling Report," available from the NCTE. The list has been reprinted, with trouble spots indicated and with an additional list of 583 words, in J. N. Hook, Hook's Guide to Good Writing: Grammar, Style, Usage (New York: The Ronald Press Co., 1962), pp. 427–31.

3 A Study of High School Spelling Vocabulary (Austin, Tex.: The Steck Co., 1945).

4 "231 Real Spelling Demons for High School Students, English Journal, XLVI (May, 1958), 269–70. Reprinted by permission of the NCTE.

laid
3 leisure
library
loose
3 lose
losing
magazine
maintenance
marriage
mathematics
meant
minute
mischievous
misspell
mortgage
naturally
5necessary
nickel
niece
ninety
3 noticeable
nuisance
occasion
4 occurred
occurring
omitted
opinion
3 opportunity

original
paid
pamphlet
3 parallel
parliament
pastime
peculiar
perhaps
permanent
persuade
physician
piece
3 planned
3 pleasant
possess
3 principal
3 principle
4 privilege
3 probably
professor
pronunciation
psychology
3 quiet
quite
realize
really
3 receipt
5 receive

received
recognize
4 recommend
recommendation
reference
referred
relieve
religious
3 repetition
respectfully
3 restaurant
sandwich
3 schedule
4 secretary
3 seize
5 separate
shining
3 similar
3 sincerely
3 sophomore
speech
straight
studying
succeed
success
sufficient
superintendent
surely

4 surprise
tariff
4 their
3 there
they're
5 thoroughly
3 to
together
3 too
3 tragedy
tried
tries
3 truly
Tuesday
3 two
typical
3 until
3 usually
valuable
vegetable
weather
3 Wednesday
4 whether
whose
woman
3 writing
4 written

If a limited list will cut spelling errors approximately in half, it is certainly worth teaching thoroughly. An English department may agree, for example, that a list like the one above will constitute the bulk of the spelling program for, say, the ninth or tenth grade, with perfection the goal for all students, and with each student to be excused from the basic spelling work once he has made a perfect score on the total list. (A tape recorder may pronounce the words, twenty-five or fifty in a group, and save the teacher's time.) In subsequent years, a small amount of review should be sufficient, and attention may be devoted to students' individual spelling problems that are unrelated to the common demons.

GROUP PROCEDURES

Although learning the spelling of a word is in the last analysis the result of individual effort, some group instruction may make that effort easier. In this section we shall look at what the teacher and class can do together; in the next, at what the student needs to be encouraged to do by himself.

Phonetics

You may have some students who do not know the usual sounds of letters. Although today's reading instruction in the elementary schools typically combines phonic and other approaches, some schools still exist in which students never learn to "sound out" words. A study made in Indiana revealed that students who have never learned phonetics have about a 50 per cent greater chance of being retarded in spelling than those who have received such instruction. Students who lack knowledge of basic sounds are likely to write some such curiosities as *brapoly* for *probably*, or *furtst* for *forest*.

If your students do need such training, spend a few minutes a day for several weeks with simple one-syllable words, grouping them as the "at" family (*bat, cat*, etc.), the "it" family, the "and" family, and so on. Give additional drill on the usual sounds of consonants, employing both real and nonsense words such as *bib, bob, bab, beb, bub*. Move on to simple combinations such as *batboy, hotrod*, etc. Teach the blends: *sl, sp, st, ch, sh*, and the like. Next may come clarification of the effects of a final *e* or of a doubled letter, as in *fad* and *fade*, *hug* and *huge*, *hoping* and *hopping*. All this is elementary work and is not very helpful with unphonetic spellings like *thought* and *psychology*, but it does prevent some of the more ridiculous misspellings.

One huge study conducted at Stanford University (the final report is 1,716 pages long!) has elaborated greatly on what has just been said, and holds promise for improved practices in teaching spelling in the future, although much remains to be done before the best ways are found to introduce the findings into pedagogy. The researchers summarize the results in this way:

A modern spelling program is possible today as a result of new research both in linguistics and in teaching-learning theories. Such a modern spelling program will (1) start from the child's possession of a large aural-oral vocabulary; (2) teach him how to break these words into component sounds; (3) lead him to discover the correspondences between the phonemes and the alphabetical letters that have come to represent these sounds in standard American-English spelling; (4) help him discover the influences that position, stress, and environment have in the choice of grapheme from among the several options; (5) guide him to go beyond the phonological analysis to examine the morphological elements such as compounding, affixation, or word families; (6)

teach him how to use all his sensorimotor equipment of ear-voice-eye-hand to reinforce each other in fixing the standard spelling in his neural system; and (7) help him build a cognitive-based spelling power that should make possible a writing vocabulary "unlimited" or limited only by the size of his spoken vocabulary.[5]

Pronunciation

Slovenly or otherwise inaccurate pronunciation may lead to misspelling. Class drill on frequently mispronounced words such as those in the following list may eliminate some spelling errors.

accidentally (Note AL.)
Arctic (Note C.)
athlete (Two syllables.)
attacked (Two syllables.)
barbarous (No I.)
cavalry (CAV.)
diphtheria (Note PH.)
diphthong (Note PH.)
drowned (One syllable.)
February (Two R's.)

film (One syllable.)
government (GoverN.)
jewelry (Not joolery.)
laboratory (LABOR.)
mischievous (Three syllables.)
perform (PER.)
perspiration (PER.)
probably (Three syllables.)
relevant (REL.)
remembrance (Lost E.)

sacrilegious (Cf. sacrilege.)
surprise (Two R's.)
temperature (TempER.)
tragedy (Not tradegy.)

Grouping of Words

Wise grouping of words seems desirable. Grouping means, for example, teaching several words ending in *ible* at one time, and words ending in *able* a few weeks or months later; *ent* words at one time and *ant* words at another; *prove, move,* and *lose* at one time but *smooth, booth,* and *loose* at another. Words with various common characteristics may also be grouped; for example,

define	imagine	sincerely	perform	already
definite	imaginable	merely	perforate	altogether
definition	imaginary	severely	perspective	almost
definitive	imagination		pertinent	
	imaginative			
	image			

Mnemonic Devices and Games

Associational devices in limited numbers may be helpful, but too many of them create more confusion than they dispel. The teacher may suggest to Tommy, who can never remember how to spell

---

[5] Paul R. Hanna, *et al., Phoneme-Grapheme Correspondences as Cues to Spelling Improvement* (Washington, D.C.: U. S. Government Printing Office, 1966), p. 116.

separate and *grammar*, that Pa is in one and Ma in the other. When Linda leaves out two letters in *laboratory*, she may be told that scientists *labor* there. Students may sometimes wish to originate their own mnemonic devices for a few words.

Games may occasionally be used for teaching spelling, but, when they are, they should be regarded just as educational fun and not as serious competition for grades. The old-fashioned spelling bee has little value except for good spellers. One variation of it, which partially overcomes this objection, is to have two teams standing. As soon as a player spells a word (or two words) correctly, he may sit down. The first team to have only three players standing is the winner. Another variation is to have everyone remain in the game, a point being given a team for each correct spelling. Words that someone has missed may be reintroduced later in the session, with two points awarded for the right spelling.

Prefixes and Suffixes

The spelling of words to which prefixes or suffixes are attached puzzles students rather often, giving them trouble especially in deciding whether or not to double a letter. Exercises like this are valuable:

dis	+ *agree*	= *disagree*
dis	+ *appoint*	= *disappoint*
dis	+ *satisfied*	= *dissatisfied*
smooth	+ *ness*	= *smoothness*
drunken	+ *ness*	= *drunkenness*
sudden	+ *ness*	= *suddenness*
immediate	+ *ly*	= *immediately*
final	+ *ly*	= *finally*
principal	+ *ly*	= *principally*

Inductive Teaching of Rules

The value of rules has been warmly denied and hotly defended. In the nineteenth century, some texts contained dozens of rules with hundreds of illustrations and scores of exceptions. At present, the consensus is that only a few rules are worth teaching and that those rules should be taught inductively.

Here is an illustration of teaching a rule inductively. The teacher writes on the board *hate, name, arrange, fate,* and *like.* He asks what all of these words have in common and gets the answer that each ends in a silent *e.* Then he asks students to spell *hateful, namely, arrangement, fateful,* and *likeness,* and he writes these words opposite the first list, underlining the suffixes. "What would happen if we didn't keep the *e* in *hateful?*" he inquires. The students explain that the *e* prevents confusion between *hateful* and *hatful* and between *fateful* and *fatful* and that one would tend to mispronounce *arrangement* if the *e* were not there. The teacher wonders whether the suffixes have anything in common and is told that each begins with a consonant. He calls for other words ending in silent *e;* the students find suffixes to add to words like *state, late, white,* etc., but they notice that many words such as *dice, while,* and *please* do not take suffixes beginning with consonants.

At this point the teacher may pause to have the class formulate a rule that says that, when a suffix beginning with a consonant is added to a word ending in silent *e,* the *e* is retained. He may, however, first go back to the original list and ask the class to spell *hating, naming, arranging, fatal,* and *likable,* which he writes in a third column. Here is something new, since the *e* has been dropped. A little judicious questioning reveals that the distinction between these words and the ones in the second column exists because here the suffix begins with a vowel. The teacher comments that there is a good reason for dropping the *e,* for, if one saw such a word as *fateal,* one might have trouble in pronouncing it. More illustrations and then on to the formulation of a rule something like this: In adding a suffix to a word ending in silent *e,* retain the *e* if the suffix begins with a consonant, but drop the *e* if the suffix begins with a vowel.

One more step remains—mentioning the most important exceptions. On the board the teacher writes *singe* and tells the class that, for a good reason, this word is an exception. He writes *singeing* and lets the class see that the *e* is retained here before a vowel. "Why?" he asks. Immediately someone sees that *singing* would be confusing. The teacher refers to *shoeing* and *hoeing,* commenting that *shoing* and *hoing* would look like names of Chinese provinces. He may mention a few other exceptions such as *dyeing, courageous, noticeable,* and *judgment.*

Later practice does not involve the restating of the rule except to verify a spelling. At subsequent class meetings, though, the teacher does give much practice in adding suffixes to many words ending in silent *e.* Without such practice, the rule will have little value.

Four other rules are of particular worth. They may be taught inductively, several weeks apart, by following procedures similar to the one just described. These are the rules:

1. Words of one syllable ending in a single consonant preceded by a single vowel double the final consonant before a suffix beginning with a vowel (*lag, lagging; plan, planned*).
2. Words of more than one syllable ending in a single consonant preceded by a single vowel double the final consonant before a suffix beginning with a vowel, if the syllable preceding the suffix is accented (*occur, occurred; prefer, preferring; repel, repellent;* but *travel, traveled, traveling; preference*).
3. Final *y* preceded by a consonant changes to *ie* before an *s* (*army, armies; fly, flies;* but *turkey, turkeys; attorney, attorneys*—because a vowel precedes the *y*).
4. In the *ei, ie* combinations pronounced *e* as in feel, *i* comes before *e* except after *c* (*believe, receive*). The most common exceptions are contained in this sentence: "Neither leisurely financier seized either weird species."

Teaching from Lists

In the junior high years some teachers devote part of each class period to spelling. The most common pattern is that of the weekly list of about twenty words. On Monday, a pretest is given, and students immediately study the words they missed. (If they miss none, they are excused from spelling for the week.) On Tuesday, they once more study the words they missed; Wednesday brings another test and more study; Thursday, more study; and Friday, a final test and study of any words still missed. The strong points of this procedure are that the test-study plan has been proved efficient and that each student works only on the words that he misses. Its weaknesses are those inherent in any plan in which the teacher uses the list approach; particularly, the words may not be the ones that these students need.

Ideally, each student should work each week on his own individualized list, but no teacher has time to draw up 100 or 150 tailor-made lists every few days. Here are some possible compromises:

1. Have each student keep a record of all words he misspells in any class. Each week he is required to add five of these words to the basic list assigned to the whole class. He studies these, and at testing time a spelling partner pronounces the five words for him.
2. Divide the class into two or three groups on the basis of spelling ability, and prepare separate lists. The poorest spellers concentrate

on demon words; the others, on other useful words encountered in their reading.
3. Prepare weekly lists, half the words from the demon group, half from recently studied literature.
4. Sometimes have each student draw up his own list of "Words I Should Learn to Spell." In testing sessions use spelling partners.

Able classes in the senior high school may need no work with lists, although some students may need help. Bright students may be made to feel completely responsible for the correctness of their own spelling.

INDIVIDUALIZED PROCEDURES

Discovering One's Own Road to Success

Individual differences exist in methods of learning. What works well for one person will not necessarily work well for another. Let your students know that a speller may recall a word mainly by motor, auditory, or visual means. Some persons, in a sense, have spelling at their fingertips; once they have written a word, say *existence*, a few times, they can write it automatically, without thinking. Others remember with their ears: "Ex-is-tence," they say, perhaps exaggerating the pronunciation to remind themselves of the *e* after *t*. Still others have camera vision; when they encounter a new word, they take a "snapshot" of it, and when they need the word again, it flashes on a "screen" inside their heads: They actually "see" the word. And some persons combine two or all three of the methods. Having students think about their own techniques for remembering may assist them in making best use of their strongest assets without ignoring the other means of remembering.

Harry Shefter, in a popular paperbound book, *Six Minutes a Day to Perfect Spelling* (Pocket Books, 1954), advocated a five-step procedure in learning a word. His steps included the three techniques just described, and added some others: "SEE THE WORD" (i.e., look at it carefully, spotting its peculiarities and possible trouble spots); "THINK THE WORD" (i.e., associate the word with something that may help you to remember it: "She screamed 'EEE!' as she passed the cEmEtEry."); "FEEL THE WORD" (i.e., pronounce it carefully); BUILD THE WORD (i.e., relate it to other forms or to similar words: *beauty, beautiful, beautify, beautifully, beautification*). Lawrence P. Shehan [6] varies Shefter's formula a little, emphasizing these six steps: See it! Say it! Hear it! Check it! Write it! Use it!

To increase independence in studying spelling among children in upper elementary grades, Howard Blake recommends giving them individual copies of questions they may find it useful to answer.[7] Blake's list consists of forty-three questions under the headings of phonetic analysis, structural analysis, meaning, and usage. Representative questions: "What other words can I write that begin like this word?" "What story, poem, announcement, report, letter, or instruction can I write using this word and others on the list?" Blake emphasizes that each child should select from the forty-three questions the ones that seem to him to be most helpful in studying.

An NCTE Committee recommends this procedure:

> In studying a word, a good procedure for a learner is, (1) to say each syllable distinctly and look at the syllable as he says it, (2) with eyes closed to think how the word looks, (3) to look at the word again to check his impression, (4) to write the word and check with the book, and (5) to repeat twice the writing and checking. If on any of these five trials he misspells the word, he should copy it in his spelling notebook. Finally, he should write the group of words studied as a parent, brother, sister, or friend pronounces them for him.[8]

From an assortment of suggestions such as these, a student should through a little experimenting find what works best for him.

Harold Blau suggests the use of a tape recorder, with earphones.[9] The student pronounces a word into the microphone and then copies it, pronounces another, and copies it, and so on; later, he writes (rather than copies) each word as his own tape-recorded voice pronounces. Blau also suggests writing with "magic markers" on white cards, perhaps with a different color for each syllable. "Changing the medium seems to help to change the mind set. Also, poor spellers seem to learn more easily from the words 'writ large.' "

Characteristics of Good Spellers

Good spelling is not necessarily a mark of high intelligence. Rather, it is likely to be the result of certain attitudes and habits. These are described by E. W. Dolch:

[6] *English Journal*, March, 1964.

[7] "Studying Spelling Independently," *Elementary English*, XXXVII (Jan., 1960), 29–32.

[8] *An Experience Curriculum in English*, p. 259.

[9] "First Aid for Extremely Poor Spellers," *English Journal*, LV (May, 1966), 583–84.

. . . the "good speller" (1) checks his guesses, (2) proofreads for spelling, and (3) studies the spelling of new words, which means (a) he gets the exact pronunciation of each new word, (b) he asks if this sounding tells the letters, and (c) where it does not, he finds a means of remembering the exact letters at the difficult spot. He makes this rapid check in all subjects, in English, in history, in science, or what not. He habitually makes this check, and does it in a few seconds only.[10]

Programed Instruction

Interest in machine teaching or other forms of programed instruction has extended to spelling, and a number of new programs are emerging. The ideal program first offers a number of diagnostic spelling tests, to be taken by all students. On the basis of this diagnosis, each student then does the programs indicated as best for meeting his deficiencies. Posttests reveal the extent of his gains, and periodic reviews help him to retain the correct spellings. Although more experimentation with programing is needed, it may be safely said that spelling is one subject in which its promise is considerable.

Marilyn Snydan, of the Pennsylvania State University's Center for Cooperative Research with Schools, reports that computer-assisted instruction helps students to spell better, partly because the computer can soon indicate what technique works best for each child.[11]

SUMMARY

Improvement in spelling most often results from proceeding in these ways:

1. Motivate spelling.
2. Teach the words that most students will need.
3. Encourage students to find and master their own demons.
4. Suggest a variety of attacks on spelling problems.
5. Encourage visualization.
6. Teach correct pronunciation.
7. Teach phonetics, if necessary.
8. Encourage tracing, writing in air, etc., to build the "feel" of a word.
9. When practicable, present words in related groups.
10. Use a few mnemonic devices.

[10] "Teaching Spelling," *Illinois English Bulletin*, XXX, No. 6 (March, 1943), 5.
[11] In *Education U.S.A.*, Oct. 28, 1968.

11. Teach the addition of prefixes and suffixes.
12. Teach only a few rules, always inductively.
13. When teaching a list, use the test-study procedure.
14. Use a few spelling games.
15. Give individual help when it is needed.
16. Encourage the dictionary habit for checking guesses.
17. Give plenty of practice in writing.
18. If possible, experiment with programed instruction.

THE IDEA BOX

What Do Teachers Think About Spelling?

Arnold Lazarus of Purdue polled 456 English teachers concerning their attitudes toward spelling and methods of teaching it. Among the results: (1) 88 per cent believe that use of arbitrary lists is not very helpful, and that teaching in context (e.g., the context of student writing) is preferable; (2) 99 per cent endorsed individualizing spelling as much as possible; (3) 75 per cent think spelling less important than other factors in writing, but 88 per cent said that spelling is "illiterate-looking"; (4) 99 per cent believe that other teachers share in the responsibility for teaching spelling.

Spelling As an Influence on Grades

Even when examination graders are asked to grade on content only, spelling errors result in their giving lower grades. D. P. Scannell and J. C. Marshall report the research on which this generalization is based in *American Educational Research Journal* (March, 1966).

"Don't Say Unkle"

This article by Mary Peavey and Nell Stillwagon, *English Journal*, XXXVIII (March, 1949), 150, recommends having students find pairs or groups of words that have similar trouble spots, for example, *sincerely, merely; perform, perforate; already, altogether.*

Spelling for Your Job

Students may construct their own spelling lists of words they will need to know in their own probable future jobs, and learn to spell these, sometimes working in pairs. This procedure may improve motivation for learning to spell other words.

Spelling Lessons Via Tape Recording

Teacher time may be saved by pronouncing spelling test words into a tape recorder. Each student may then use earphones and write his test words when he believes he is ready.

A Spelling Aid Called a Teacher

When students are writing in class, stopping to look up a spelling in a dictionary may break a chain of thought. You may want to let them improvise a spelling that can be checked later, or quickly supply the spelling needed.

"A Common-Sense Approach to Teaching Spelling"

This pamphlet, written at Ball State University, Muncie, Indiana, as a result of a study sponsored by the Eli Lilly Foundation, compares results of teaching spelling through the individualized approach, with each student concentrating on the words that trouble him most, and through a conventional use of word lists. Students following the individualized approach appeared to spell better at the end.

Anecdote for Motivation

A motorist was arrested for parking beside a sign that said "No stoping." He was freed when he proved that he had not been "stoping," that is, digging for ore.

Spelling "Must" List

Let students agree upon a short list of words that must never be misspelled. This list may gradually be enlarged.

Logical Analysis

Often a moment's thought will clarify a spelling; for example, "bookkeeper" has two *k*'s because it combines "book" and "keeper."

A Hard Look at the Word

One of the spelling techniques recommended by Sister Josephina, C.S.J., in "Spelling: The Responsibility of Every Teacher," *Clearing House*, XXXII (March, 1958), 393, is having students observe anything noteworthy in the meaning, root, prefix, or early history of each troublesome word.

Simplified Spelling

Minor simplification of spelling will do little good, yet a plan for a new alphabet such as George Bernard Shaw advocated would necessitate scrapping all our typewriters and linotypes, retraining their operators, and reteaching reading to everyone. We need a system in which each English sound will always be represented orthographically in the same way; with such a system, no teaching of spelling would be needed after the second grade, as is true in Finland even now. One workable (but not flawless) system was almost adopted in England in the late 1940's. Its characteristics are revealed in this verse from *The New York Times:*

> Mai hart iz sad fer litel wunz
> Hw uend dher uei tw skwl
> Tw lern dhe Inglish langgwidj
> Uith its totel lak ov rwl.

Mnemonic Devices

> "You wouldn't believe a lie for a minute,
> But the word *believe* has a *lie* right in it."

Harriet Johnson, *Word Study* (Oct., 1946).

Spelling Partners

Frank Dunn, Sayville, N.Y., Junior High School, has students work in pairs on their spelling chores. Mr. Dunn has three levels of spelling words for each grade, assigning to each student words on the level for which he is ready. "Multi-level Spelling Program," *New York State Education* (May, 1960), 22.

Homonym Down

To increase sensitivity to homonyms, Louise Swinney's tenth graders, in Elsinore, California, enjoy an occasional spelldown with homonyms. The teacher pronounces a homonym; a member of one team spells it; and then a member of the next team must spell another version of it. The student may be asked to use in a sentence the homonym he has spelled.

Proofreading

Proofreading exercises, requiring students to look carefully at every word, have some value. Even more valuable is insistence that students proofread their own written work. Sometimes their reading the work

slowly aloud will help them to catch spelling errors they would otherwise miss.

Trouble Spots

Since usually a word has only one bad trouble spot (e.g., the sixth
letter in *"existence"*), it is often useful to focus students' attention on
that spot. For an extensive list, see Arthur I. Gates, *A List of Spelling
Difficulties in 3876 Words* (New York: Teachers College, Columbia
University Bureau of Publications, 1937).

Games and Other Motivation

Robert L. Coard of Minot, North Dakota, lists for lowerclassmen the
words his seniors misspell and issues the challenge "Can you outspell
our seniors?" For other tactics, see Mr. Coard's "Spelling-Game Time,"
Clearing House, XXX (Sept., 1955), 9.

Excusing Good Spellers

Some of the best spellers may be excused from spelling work, with
the proviso that they may at any time be called upon to demonstrate
that they are maintaining their ability.

12

Words, Words, Words

BUILDING VOCABULARIES

The Cardinal Principles of Vocabulary Building

In Sherwood Anderson's *Winesburg, Ohio* appears a teacher advising one of her former students who wants to become a writer. "You will have to know life," she says. "If you are to become a writer you'll have to stop fooling with words. . . . You must not become a mere peddler of words."

Her advice is good not only for would-be professional writers but for all who use language. Accurate understanding of words comes from experiences with the things and ideas for which words stand. To a farm boy, *cow* is a rich and meaningful word because the boy knows what cows are and has had much experience with cattle. But *wombat* is probably only a fortuitous collection of letters, unless the child has happened to see a wombat in a zoo. To the city child, *subway* is replete with associations. *Silo*, however, if it means anything to him, is likely to suggest only a thumb-shaped projection that stands near farmers' barns; the city child knows nothing of silo filling, of the damp, green smell that silage has in midwinter, or of the way that silage is fed.

A word is nothing in itself. The word's power of suggesting is everything. Before a bomb hit Hiroshima, *atom* for most people was only a word encountered in a science class. But now *atom* suggests measureless energy, submarines, ships, interplanetary travel, destructiveness and human suffering, an unbounded source of good, the hope and the dread of mankind. A group of letters has assumed vivid meaning because all of us at least vicariously have had experiences in which that group of letters played a part.

Suppose that, instead of learning about *atom* as we did, we had been told in school that an atom is a minute particle consisting of a nucleus and a varying number of electrons. The richness of association would have been missing. We would have remembered *atom* long enough to define it in an examination and then perhaps would have forgotten it forever. Or we might have remembered the word and dragged it into the conversation some evening when chemistry was the topic of discussion; that is, we might have peddled the word, though for us it was empty of real meaning.

Word peddlers are persons like the one described by Sara A. Garratt in the New York *Sun:*

> I like the words *epitome,*
> *Digamma,* and *baleen.*
> I toss them off with nonchalance,
> But don't know what they mean.

Or they are like the high school senior girl who wrote,

In the celestial radiance of my maternal forebear's enigmatic smile, my *frater* and I puissantly and incessantly grew toward that apex of desiderata, adulthood as pleasurable as juvenility had been because of the incontrovertible fact of her existence.

(Teacher, puzzled, gave the girl an A.)

Word peddlers may be as harmless as this erstwhile senior probably is now. It is easy to picture her, a dozen years older, floridly introducing today's speaker to the Community Culture Club. But other word peddlers may be dangerous when they wrap little ideas in big words. They may be elected to Congress.

The long prevalent attitude toward vocabulary has been that the number of words learned is all-important. The slogan "Learn a new word every day" has too seldom been phrased, "Learn a useful new word every day" or "Learn what words really mean." In the merry or not so merry chase after new words, students have emerged with terms that not one in a thousand will ever need: *sphagnous, oxytone,* and *elasmobranch.* Perhaps to these same students, *overture, laxity,* and *corroborate* are unknown, and *culture* and *democracy* are words that they mouth with little comprehension.

All available evidence points to the belief that vocabulary grows as alert children and adults encounter new experiences. Words do not exist in a vacuum and are not learned in a vacuum. The weekly list of twenty randomly selected words is almost a vacuum; tests a couple of months later will usually reveal that only a small proportion of previously unfamiliar words from such a list will be remembered. A thing and the name for the thing impress themselves simultaneously. Vocabulary and a spirit of inquiry grow together. The crippled child of illiterate parents, living on an isolated farm, without electricity, back in the hills, almost certainly will possess a meager vocabulary even if he is highly intelligent. Another child, whose homelife and school life are filled with varied activity and whose teachers have stimulated an interest in words, is likely to attain a resourceful vocabulary.

Vocabularies, like fingerprints, are never identical. They vary, partly because of differing experiences, partly because of degrees of intelligence, and partly because of the way words are regarded by the child's parents, peers, and teachers. Two children may share an experience and still not receive the same word dividends. In a chemistry class, for example, one student may learn early in the semester the meaning of *reagent, catalyst,* and *osmosis,* but another for a long time may refer to "stuff that looks like water." After reading *Treasure Island,* one student may have vivid impressions of *schooner* and *coracle,* while another still uses no more definite words than "big boat" and "little boat." The difference arises in part from variation in intelligence; bright students learn new words quickly, just as they do most other things. But it may arise also from interest or lack of interest in words. To some students, a new word is a challenge, something to examine, taste, experiment with, and use; to others, it is a thing to ignore. Some will employ the word to express themselves with exactness; others, unless they can catch the same spirit, will remain content with "stuff" and "deal" and other woolly words.

The two cardinal principles of vocabulary building may be summarized thus:

1. Rich vocabularies result from rich experiences, firsthand or vicarious.
2. Precise diction results in part from intelligence and in part from a keen interest in words as symbols.

Adding to Students' Experiences

Despite the shortcomings of television, it brings our students experiences and consequent knowledge that they might never attain without it. A fad for westerns brings information about mesas, buttes, and saguaros; a fad for courtroom drama clarifies the meanings of *plaintiff, defendant, habeas corpus;* a fad for doctor stories dramatizes a score or two of medical terms. More offbeat programs add information on a wide range of subjects, and with the information comes the relevant vocabulary. Radio, newspapers, and magazines, accessible now in almost every home, provide still more information.

Within the schoolroom, the films, kinescopes, filmstrips, and recordings that are now available are rich resources. English field trips to libraries, colleges, newspaper plants, museums, theaters, government buildings, and places related to literature may directly broaden experience. Pictures, maps, bulletin boards, and chalkboards may supplement experiences. According to a report on a study by James I. Brown, who taught adults, "Visual aids, including programmed transparencies, reduced forgetting of technical terms from 72 percent, after fifteen months, to 22 percent." [1]

In short, more opportunities exist now than ever before for students to step outside the boundaries of home and school and to participate at least vicariously in the varied experiences of the human race. From these experiences are derived the words to describe them.

Alert teachers use such opportunities. Television, filmstrips, and the like are part of their teaching arsenal. So is a constant attempt to associate words with ideas, and ideas with things. Straight thinking involves accurate use of words. Through class discussion, students can have stimulating experience with ideas, particularly when the ideas are translated in terms of tangibles. Few students—indeed, few adults—can think in abstractions. Teachers can assist students to associate words, even abstract words, with things. In fact, if students do not make such associations, words will lack meaning. The child who can glibly quote the dictionary definition of *democracy* as "government by the people" knows less about the

[1] Reported in Walter T. Petty *et al., The State of Knowledge about the Teaching of Vocabulary* (Champaign: NCTE, 1968), p. 57.

word than the one who has examined a specimen ballot, attended a town meeting, taken part in a mock political convention, and participated in student government. If you tell a child that a symphony is "an instrumental composition in sonata form for a full orchestra," his understanding will be less than if you make it possible for him to hear even part of a symphony.

Alert teachers stress the rich experiences afforded by literature. Although no one lives long enough to participate personally in even one-millionth of the experiences that life offers, each, through books, can participate vicariously in multitudinous activities—sharing in the observation, thoughts, emotions, and acts of thousands of other people near or remote in time and place. Literature, chosen wisely and read well, opens the floodgate of experience.

Increasing Interest in Words

"Here is your list of useful words for this week. Look each one up in the dictionary, copy its definition, and write a sentence containing the word. We'll have our test on these words on Friday." That is the traditional method of vocabulary building, which still has its practitioners. It is not valueless, particularly if the words listed are useful. But it has its weaknesses. One is its puny motivation. Another is that a word out of context may be misunderstood. For instance, one youngster looked up *quaver* and found that it means "shake"; she had trouble in understanding why it is incorrect to say, "I quavered the tablecloth." Still another weakness is that most of the words are forgotten in a few months.

Better than the list approach or any other single approach is keeping an interest in words going constantly. This means that there is some talk about words in almost every class period—oblique references in discussion of literature, direct comment in study of composition, remarks about the language of a TV newscaster, and so on. It means that the teacher uses variety in his attack on the problem.

The trouble with much vocabulary building is that it is spasmodic, whereas it should be part of every day's work. It need not be labeled "vocabulary drill"; in fact, there will often be no drill involved. The teacher must be interested in, and well informed about, words. When questions arise that the teacher cannot answer, he and the class search for the answers. In a story, a class found a woman characterized as a *mimosa*. Neither teacher nor class knew the word. Upon looking it up, they discovered that it is another name for the "sensitive plant," which folds up when it is touched. When someone noticed that it is derived from the same word as *mimic* and *pantomime*, the class tried to guess at the connection. They returned to the story to find why the author had used this word, and uncovered examples of the character's sensitiveness. Had the teacher merely said, "Look up the word," the class would have missed a wealth of associations. *Mimosa* itself is not a particularly valuable word, but the class discussion that arose from it threw light upon the story, added the useful words *mimic* and *sensitivity* to several students' vocabularies, and increased interest in words. In this teacher's class, such study of words is common; yet it does not smack of "drill."

The following paragraphs discuss several devices, traditional and otherwise, used successfully by teachers to build interest in words and to increase verbal precision. Others are in The Idea Box, pages 466–75.

The Dictionary. Students need help in order to learn to use the dictionary efficiently. From unhappy experiences, some students have come to regard the dictionary as a foe rather than a friend. The chief trouble is that many students have not learned to find a word quickly. Using a desk dictionary, a student should be able to locate in about fifteen or twenty seconds any word that he can spell. (You, the teacher, should need no more than twelve seconds.) Teach students to know the alphabet thoroughly, to open the dictionary in about the right place, and to use the guide words. Give them numerous dictionary problems. Help them to analyze dictionary entries to see what a wealth of information each contains. (Most publishers of dictionaries supply free pamphlets containing dictionary exercises.)

Here are a few examples of worthwhile dictionary problems:

1. Why do Londoners sometimes call their policemen "bobbies"?
2. What three different kinds of animals are called "gophers"?
3. What is a corollary? How do the British pronounce the word?
4. Find definitions of *scale* referring to zoology, botany, metallurgy, and music. Use *scale* in sentences that will illustrate each definition.
5. How does the Gregorian calendar differ from the Julian?
6. What might you expect to see if you heard someone shout "Hoicks!" or "Yoicks!"?

7. Does your dictionary suggest that some meanings of *fix* are less formal than others?

Expansion of Meaning.   It has been said that it is not more words that make an educated man or woman, but more meanings. With this in mind, classes have explored all the meanings of common words such as *like, light, name, go, tie, fast, start, lie, dream,* and *beat.*   The result is at least a better understanding of the versatility of words.

Learning from Words Previously Known.   Sometimes it is possible to determine word meanings by associating them with other words.   Thus the word *micrometer* is composed of elements already familiar in *microscope* and *meter* or *metric.*   A bright student may be able to put the parts together and decide that a micrometer is something to measure small objects.   A valid criticism of this technique, though, is that the guesses may often be erroneous; the student may decide mistakenly that *micrometer* means a small measurement.   The chief value of association with other words seems to be that meanings once learned may more easily be retained because of an awareness of similarities.

At the heart of Frank C. Flowers' method for building understanding of words and dictionary use is the study of words in groups. For example, *organic, organically, organicism, organist, organizable, organization, organizational, organizationally, organize,* and *organizer.*   The contributions of base meaning and affixes are studied in detail.[2]

Learning from Context.   "Whenever you come to an unfamiliar word, look it up in the dictionary."   Too many teachers have given this advice, ignoring the fact that learning words via the dictionary is an artificial method.   The six-year-old child may have a vocabulary of 20,000 words, even though he has never touched a dictionary; he learned the words by hearing them in context.   The dictionary is valuable to verify a guess about a word or to define it when the meaning cannot be obtained from the context.   But anyone should attempt first to determine the meaning by noting the surroundings of the word.   For example, if a student does not know the meaning of *tractable* in the sentence "The children were more tractable than she had anticipated; in fact, only Joel was at all

---

[2] "Discovering Truth about Words," *English Journal,* LIX (Feb., 1970), 159.

stubborn," he should follow the contextual clues before referring to the dictionary.

High school students enjoy being "word detectives." The teacher gives them sentences with one or more unfamiliar words and is careful to include clues to their meanings. He lists four or five other words from which a synonym is to be chosen. The following types of clues are suggested in *The English Language Arts in the Secondary School:*

1. The experience clue, which enables the students to draw on their own experience; e.g., their experience with crows enables them to define *raucously* in "A pair of crows called raucously."
2. The comparison or contrast clue, as in the example of *tractable* above.
3. The synonym clue, in which the sentence contains a near-synonym.
4. The summary clue: "He was completely *disheveled*. His hair was mussed, his shirttail was out. . . ."
5. The association clue: "He was out of it in an instant with the *agility* of a pickpocket."
6. The reflection of a mood or situation clue, as with the word *melancholy* in the first sentence of "The Fall of the House of Usher."
7. The previous contact clue: students' knowledge of the Emancipation Proclamation should help them to understand *emancipate*.[3]

Notebooks. A favorite device is to have students record, define, and copy in context the new words that they have learned. One teacher suggests that only one new word be put on a page; below the word the student pastes a picture illustrating or suggested by the word; under the picture he puts a definition and a sentence using the word. *Relaxation,* for instance, may have a picture of a cat stretching lazily.[4] The value of the device is in the association of the word with something tangible.

Word Diaries. Some students may be encouraged to keep for a few weeks a word diary in which they record useful new words they hear or read, together with the context and an original sentence.

"The Word of the Day." Marilyn Hackett [5] says that her eighth-grade students enjoy dramatizing as they learn a useful new word

[3] *The English Language Arts in the Secondary School* (New York: Appleton-Century-Crofts, Inc., 1956), p. 170.
[4] Harold T. Eaton, "Timely Teaching Helps," *English Leaflet*, XLV (Dec., 1946), 138.
[5] *English Journal*, Dec., 1966.

each day. For example, to dramatize *foliage,* a boy drops erasers to represent a tree's shedding leaves.

Synonyms and Antonyms.   Able students enjoy discovering the fine distinctions that exist among near synonyms. *Distant, far,* and *remote,* they discover, do not mean exactly the same thing, nor do *decadence, deterioration,* and *degeneration,* or *dominant, domineering,* and *dominating.* Less able students often fail to see the distinguishing points involved in such words, but even they can profit from discussion of the numerous specific synonyms for such words as *go* and *say.* In French schools, teachers spend time in having students find the exact antonym of given words, the theory being that one does not actually know a word unless one also knows its opposite.[6]

Games.   Word games are fun and, with junior high school students, may be played as rewards. Some classes have vocabulary bees, comparable to spelling bees. The teacher keeps a list of interesting, useful words encountered in literature or employed only incidentally in class. Students use these words in sentences or define them, as they wish. The teacher or an elected student is the judge, and three students, equipped with dictionaries, may be a court of appeal for dubious meanings. Possible variations of this game are endless.

In teaching slow learners, Nancy J. Doemel of Columbus, Indiana, sometimes lets them play "Scrabble" and "hangman," or create trees showing families of words. Her students also discuss what they call "funny" words, and help one another with word choice in their compositions.[7] In other classes students bring words they have encountered in their reading, and challenge their classmates to define them; archaic, technical, and foreign words are barred.

In the game of "hanky-panky," a player says, for instance, "Large swine. Hank-pank." The response is "big pig." Or a player says

---

[6] It is interesting to note that, in learning a word, one first puts it into the class to which it belongs, and later one distinguishes it from other members of the same class. I once gave the word *erudite* in a multiple-choice text to eighty-seven recent high school graduates. Ten defined it as "rude," five as "rough," eleven as "polite," thirty-one as "well educated," and thirty as "ignorant." The last figure is the significant one, as these thirty students realized that the word referred to knowledge, but did not yet know whether it pertained to much knowledge or little. Even though they gave the opposite of the true meaning, they knew more about the word than did those who defined it as "rude," "rough," or "polite."

[7] "Vocabulary for Slow Learners," *English Journal,* LIX (Jan., 1970), 78.

"Humorous cottontail. Hanky-panky." The "hanky-panky" shows that the responses are rhyming two-syllable words: "funny bunny." Raymond J. Rundus says that the game teaches students useful things about rhyme, definitions, and spelling variations for the same sound.[8]

Units. Short units, closely related to other work in oral or written composition, may stress words. A teacher in a vocational high school taught one unit based on the origin of the last names of his students, another on geographical names, and others on military slang, baseball slang, and Hebrew derivatives. Especially enlightening was a unit called "One Word Led to Another." Starting with the word *kilometer*, the vocational students thought of two other words based upon either *kilo* or *meter*, then two words based upon each of these two new words, and so on. They thus learned much about root words and families of words.

Another teacher offered frequent short units on words. Students checked on words they thought might describe them or their personalities: *burly, ruddy, prim, prepossessing, swarthy, punctual, tactful, veracious, energetic,* etc. In other units students had fun with malapropisms or puns, studied the diction in advertising and in headlines, and made collections of picturesque speech.

Derivations. Many words have fascinating histories. A few examples are *lunatic, salary, supercilious, curfew, pecuniary, kindergarten, familiar,* and *boycott.* Students enjoy discovering that *lunatic* comes from the Latin word for "moon," and that it was once believed that lunacy arose from being too much in the moonlight. When they know the derivation of *salary*, they can see a connection with the expression "He's not worth his salt." Often they can learn words and history at the same time, as with the words *boycott* and *pecuniary.*[9]

World Words. The English language has borrowed from dozens of other languages. A teacher stimulated the interest of one sophomore class by placing a large map of the world on the bulletin board. The students tried to find English words taken from the languages of as many countries as possible. The words were typed and fas-

---

[8] "Hanky-panky in the Classroom," *English Journal*, LVI (March, 1967), 435.

[9] The G. and C. Merriam Company, Springfield, Mass., supplies free booklets giving interesting word histories. Another useful publication of this company (sent free to English teachers who request it) is *Word Watching*, a periodical pamphlet with short articles on words.

tened to the map in appropriate places. At the end of the month, few of the world's land areas were visible.

Roots and Affixes.   Knowledge of the meanings of forty or fifty Latin and Greek roots and affixes will enable some students to add hundreds of words to their vocabularies. More important, it will show them relationships between words and help them to use words with greater accuracy. From the Latin *audire* (to hear) come such words as *audibility, audible, audience, audile, audiometer, audition, auditive, auditor, auditorium,* and *auditory.* From the Greek *chronos* (time) are derived such words as *chronic, chronicle, chronogram, chronological, chronologist, chronology, chronometer,* and *synchronize.* Other especially useful roots are listed in The Idea Box (page 471).

Programed Instruction.   A number of experimental programs for individual learning are being developed, including some that involve computer-assisted instruction. They make it possible for a student to concentrate on groups of words least familiar to him. In the program, the student is given brief information about a root such as *spect.* Then he faces a number of multiple-choice problems such as "Retro*spect*ion means a. preparing for the future, b. becoming worse, c. a survey of past time." He keeps the answer column covered until he has chosen his response, which he may then check immediately. Following that, he faces a number of "frames" devoted to words he missed. The frame for "retrospection" explains the derivation of the word and requires the student to write the parts of the word in three different blanks.

History of the Language.   One of the best ways to build an interest in words is to refer frequently to details of the captivating history of the English language. Most people are more interested in life than in death. Life involves change and development; death is immutable. The English language is alive and has long been alive. It is still changing. Let the students know that it is alive, that changes in usage are still occurring, that words are dying, that new words are being born. One of the services that English teachers can render is to instil in students a wholesome, creative attitude toward language—the kind of attitude that existed in Elizabethan times.

Information about how words enter the language is interesting. The routes of entry, plus an example or two of each, are these:

1. Sheer invention (rare): *Kodak*
2. Compounding: *railroad, out-of-date, barn*
3. Addition of affixes or combining forms to existing words: *unknown, newness, cigarette*
4. Functional shift (use of a word as another part of speech): to *ink* a contract
5. Back formation: *editor edit*
6. Extension of meaning: the fifth *power* of a number
7. Figurative language: *lady's slipper, Red* (for Russian)
8. Use of initials (acronyms): *WAVE, CORE*
9. Conversion of proper nouns to common: *sandwich, volt*
10. Onomatopoeia: *fizz, pop, meow*
11. Telescoping: *brunch, electrocute*
12. Borrowing from other languages: *betatron, blitzkrieg* [10]

Study of what may happen to a word after it enters the language also deserves some time. Among a number of changes that may be considered are those in the following list, condensed from the same source as the above group:

1. Shortening: *taximeter cabriolet* became *taxicab* or *taxi* or *cab*.
2. Metathesis: *bird* was once spelled *brid; wasp* was *wæps*.
3. Generalization (broadening of meaning): *cupboard* was originally a board to hold cups.
4. Specialization: although *liquor* may still mean any liquid, it is generally specialized to refer to alcoholic beverages.
5. Elevation: *pastor* was once a shepherd.
6. Degeneration: *knave* (cf. German *Knabe*) once meant a boy; *hussy* was once any housewife.

Students also like to learn about how places and people get their names. (There is a magazine called *Names*.) Over half of our states have Indian names, some of which have been translated in various ways. Other places are named for persons (*Lincoln, Jonesboro*), are descriptive (*Mapleton, Wolf Point*), or are humorous (*Rabbit Hash, Git-Up-an'-Git*). Persons' names often indicate physical characteristics (*Longfellow, Brown*), are names of occupations or places (*Miller, Smith, York, Lake*), or are patronymics (*Johnson, Fitzgerald, O'Brien*). George R. Stewart's *American Place Names* and H. L. Mencken's *The American Language* are among many excellent sources of information.

[10] Condensed from J. N. Hook, *Hook's Guide to Good Writing: Grammar, Style, Usage* (New York: The Ronald Press Co., 1962), pp. 101–2.

Dialect Study. Many students are fascinated by regional differences in dialect, which often involve the use of different words for the same thing. Examples: *bag, poke, sack, toot; faucet, spicket, spigot, hydrant, tap; cantaloupe, mushmelon, muskmelon; green beans, sallet beans, snap beans, snaps, string beans.* Roger Shuy, in *Discovering American Dialects* (NCTE), lists fifteen different expressions meaning "to be absent from school"!

WORDS AND THOUGHTS

The Importance of Semantic Study

Ernest Hemingway is reported to have said in an interview that an essential possession of a great writer is "a built-in, shock-proof crap detector." Charles Weingartner argues that having such a detector is no less important to everyone else.[11] In fact, Weingartner would make semantics central to the English curriculum. He defines semantics as "examining language as a process in actual human contexts, rather than as an abstract taxonomy of signs and symbols to be ritualized into a series of prescriptions and proscriptions intended to preserve some arbitrary notion of 'correctness.'" He asserts that "the study of semantics can do more to help students become more perceptive and sophisticated users of language than any other form of language study."

Whether or not one accepts Weingartner's views completely, it must be granted that study of semantics has been too much neglected and that it is too valuable for such neglect to continue. All of us are engulfed daily, hourly, in a sea of words. Someone, somewhere, is constantly trying to convince us that we should do something, try something, believe something, act in a certain way. Each of these someones steadily uses words (often along with pictorial, musical, or other reinforcements) to convince and persuade. Many of the motives are or should be suspect: the persuader often has some sort of personal gain as the hidden reason for his persuasion. Semantic analysis often reveals or at least hints at the hidden reason, and the reader's or listener's response may be changed when that reason becomes apparent.

The persuaders often do not agree with one another. "Buy *my* product," says one. "*My* product is best," says another. "Elect *my*

---

[11] "Semantics: What and Why," *English Journal,* LVIII (Nov., 1969), 1214.

superb candidate," one person pleads. "The country will be in trouble unless *this* man is elected," another person threatens. The study of semantics can help people to weigh evidence, to make up their minds. The success of democracy depends in large measure upon citizens' ability to do these things—to choose the stronger candidate, to detect the "crap" in the statements of each candidate and to value more highly the candidate who uses less of it, to decide upon the relative degrees of desirability in the two or more sides of a controversial question.

Even in relatively small personal decisions an awareness of semantics can be helpful. What does the guarantee of a new refrigerator really guarantee? Who is our strongest candidate for Student Council representative? What was the minister actually driving at in his sermon? How shall I react to Tom when he again says, "If you really love me, you'll let me"? (What is Tom's definition of *love*? Is it the same as mine?)

Aldous Huxley described the power of words, for good and for evil, in this way:

Children should be taught that words are indispensable but also can be fatal—the only begetters of all civilization, all science, all consistency of high purpose, all angelic goodness, and the only begetters at the same time of all superstition, all collective madness and stupidity, all worse-than-bestial diabolism, all the dismal historical succession of crimes in the name of God, King, Nation, Party, Dogma.[12]

Huxley went on to explain, in part, the reason why semantics has been so little studied: such study can be dangerous to an Establishment:

Generals, clergymen, advertisers, and the rulers of totalitarian states—all have good reason for disliking the idea of universal education in the rational use of language. To the military, clerical, propagandist, and authoritarian mind such training seems (and rightly seems) profoundly subversive.[13]

S. I. Hayakawa added *parents* and *teachers* to the list of generals, etc.:

. . . we, as parents and teachers or both, rely profoundly on word-magic, the confusion of inferences and judgments with reports, and the authority of lofty and unexplained abstractions in our attempts to control our children. Until the anxious years of high school are over for our children, most of us would rather not put into their hands such critical instruments as would enable them

---

[12] "Education on the Non-Verbal Level," *Daedalus*, Spring, 1962. Quoted in Weingartner, *op. cit.*
[13] *Ibid.*

to expose as nonsense much of what we say to them. Hence, there cannot be much in the way of semantics . . . until . . . parents and teachers begin to be willing to treat the children as children no longer.[14]

To the extent that Hayakawa is right, children have been denied the opportunity to take a close look at the process of language, to examine truths, untruths, and half-truths and to distinguish one from 'another, to understand the use of language as both a tool and a weapon, to see how words divorced from reality have often shaped the destiny of a man or a nation or a large part of the world. There may indeed be dangers to an Establishment if everyone learns to be critical of language, but we have never really tested the hypothesis that it is better for people to be brought up on truths than on half-truths and lies. Perhaps those parts of an Establishment that are based upon less than truth deserve to be reformed.

Verbal Confusion

In the case of *Towney* v. *Eisner*, Justice Oliver Wendell Holmes stated, "A word is not a crystal, transparent and unchanging; it is the skin of a living thought, and may vary greatly in color and content according to the circumstances and time in which it is used."

Almost any word could be chosen to illustrate Holmes's statement. "Resolution" one normally thinks of as something praiseworthy, but New Year's *resolutions* one is likely to regard with contempt because they are often broken. "Clever boy!" may express approbation or sarcasm. Soil described as *fertile* in one region might be considered *poor* in another. In "The snail hurries," the meaning of the verb is not exactly the same as in "The rabbit hurries."

Because of such semantic difficulties, scrupulous writers and speakers often pause to define key terms, whereas unscrupulous or careless ones add disorder to confusion by adopting the tactics of Humpty-Dumpty, in *Alice in Wonderland*, whose words meant whatever he chose they should mean. Many arguments are caused not by difference of opinion but by difference of definition or by failure to define. Recently two reasonably well-schooled adults were discussing socialism. One contended that it is good; the other, that it is bad. As the discussion progressed, it became apparent

[14] *College Composition and Communication*, Feb., 1962.

that one was thinking of socialism as governmental ownership of utilities and that the other was thinking of complete governmental control of all production and distribution. Their discussion got no further than would an argument about the best way to grow grain, when one person was thinking about oats and the other about corn.

Some writers and speakers add still more to the confusion by hiding their thoughts in a fog of words. "Gobbledygook" is the picturesque name given to this kind of language by former Congressman Maury Maverick, who said that it sounds like the gobbledy-gobbling of a turkey cock, which usually ends in a gook. Here is an example from a field manual for quartermasters, most of whom no doubt rapidly become gray-haired:

Proper application of prescribed preventative maintenance measures must be a prime consideration in order to minimize replacements. Vehicle equipment of tactical organizations and that of administrative units and reserve pools should be interchangeable wherever possible in order that needed replacements for forward areas be cleared by inter-organization transfers to meet emergencies in which normal channels of supply would introduce delays.[15]

Connotation and Denotation

Words then, sometimes fail to convey thoughts adequately. Often, though, words convey more than their dictionary definitions. Professor Pooley illustrates this fact in his comment on these five sentences:

1. I think I'll hit the hay.
2. It's time for me to turn in.
3. I believe I'll go to bed.
4. I think it is time to retire.
5. I shall withdraw to seek repose.

. . . Sentence 1 is intentionally slangy, appropriate only to intimate circumstances when humor is the intent. Sentence 2 is still intimate, but less slangy; it would pass as appropriate usage in the close family circle. Sentence 3 is the simplest and most direct of the five forms; it is acceptable usage in almost any circumstances. Sentence 4 implies less intimate circumstances; the word *retire* is a polite substitute for the blunt "go to bed." This form would be appropriate to a guest in the home of relative strangers. Sentence 5 is stilted and artificial. The simple act of going to bed makes such elaborate wording slightly ridiculous. Yet there are people with a mistaken idea of elegance who would prefer sentence 5.[16]

[15] Quoted in H. L. Mencken, *The American Language: Supplement* I (New York: Alfred A. Knopf, Inc., 1945), p. 416.
[16] Robert Pooley, *Teaching English Usage* (New York: Appleton-Century-Crofts, 1946), p. 29.

In short, from the choice of words in sentences we infer not only a factual meaning but also some of the attendant circumstances and even the mood and character of the speaker.

Because words do carry connotation as well as denotation, they may cause emotional reactions. S. I. Hayakawa tells of two cities that in depression days gave aid to the needy. In one city, words like "relief," "poverty," "shiftlessness," "laziness," and "shame" accompanied the aid. The recipients became sullen, humiliated, and defeated; their children were ridiculed at school. The officials in the other city referred to the past services of those who were temporarily unemployed, spoke of the aid as a kind of insurance dividend, called giving the assistance a "straight business proposition," and referred to bright days ahead. The recipients squared their shoulders and set out energetically to seek work anew.[17]

By changing a single word, one may subtly move someone else to favor or oppose an action or idea. Suppose that a bill is before Congress. If one is neutral toward the bill, he says, "Congress intends to pass the bill." If one favors it, he says, "Congress promises to pass the bill." If one opposes it, he says, "Congress threatens to pass the bill." Likewise, if one favors something new, it is an improvement, but, if he dislikes it, it is an innovation. A judge who is one's friend sometimes receives gifts, but a judge whom one detests takes bribes. A statesman whom one likes is conservative, but a politician whom he dislikes is reactionary. Consciously or unconsciously, one allows the emotional overtones of words to affect his choice; usually unconsciously, listeners are influenced by these emotional overtones.

Two chief points are involved in the foregoing discussion. One is that a person often uses words inaccurately or unskillfully and therefore fails to convey the ideas present in his mind. The other is that one's words, through their connotations, may cause readers or hearers to react emotionally and to deduce from the statements more than the words actually say. In subjective writing (poetry, for instance) one consciously tries to rouse emotion, but in factual writing (such as a news story) one should use uncolored, neutral words. As Professor LaBrant has said, "There is immediate and

[17] *Language in Action* (New York: Harcourt Brace Jovanovich, Inc., 1941), Introduction. (This book and its revision, called *Language in Thought and Action* [1949], are perhaps the most readable on semantics.)

profound need for teaching the citizens in our schools the power for good or for ill which is in that greatest of man's inventions, language.[18]

Later her sister, Roberta Green, observed that some progress was apparently being made:

> In almost any adult discussion which involves opposing or dissimilar attitudes, we are likely to hear phrases that suggest a groping for clearer means of communication than are customarily used: "Define your terms"; "That's only a generalization"; "It's all a matter of semantics." Although they may do little more for the immediate discussion than indicate confusion, such phrases suggest a growing realization that there are better ways of thinking and talking than the general public or even those in high places use.[19]

Translating Semantic Principles into Practice

Knowledge of semantic principles has increased remarkably since 1930, as more and more teachers have realized the need for teaching not only dictionary meanings but also the emotional implications of words and the fact that speakers and writers can influence people not merely by what they say but also by how they say it. Some teachers have studied such basic books as those by Korzybski, and Ogden and Richards, and simpler ones like Chase's or Hayakawa's.[20] Others have found in the books by LaBrant and Thomas numerous ideas for teaching about what language does to us.[21]

Teachers may profitably employ pairs of related sentences in order to make students aware of differences in connotation. For instance,

---

[18] Lou LaBrant, "Control of Language: A Major Problem in Education," *Bulletin of the National Association of Secondary-School Principals*, XXX (Feb., 1946), 49.

[19] "Teaching How Language Works," *English Journal*, XLVII (Jan., 1958), 25.

[20] C. K. Ogden and I. A. Richards, *The Meaning of Meaning* (New York: Harcourt Brace Jovanovich, Inc., 1938); I. A. Richards, *Practical Criticism* (Harcourt Brace Jovanovich, Inc., 1938); Alfred Korzybski, *Science and Sanity*, 3rd ed. (Lakeville, Conn.: Institute of General Semantics, 1948); Stuart Chase, *The Tyranny of Words* (Harcourt Brace Jovanovich, Inc., 1938), and *The Power of Words* (Harcourt Brace Jovanovich, Inc., 1954); S. I. Hayakawa, *Language in Thought and Action* (Harcourt Brace Jovanovich, Inc., 1949). A good source of books, pamphlets, and periodicals on semantics is International Society for General Semantics, San Francisco, Calif.

[21] For example, Lou LaBrant, *We Teach English* (New York: Harcourt Brace Jovanovich, Inc., 1951); and Cleveland A. Thomas, *Language Power for Youth* (New York: Appleton-Century-Crofts, Inc., 1955). A convenient and useful summary of concepts to be taught is to be found in Dr. Thomas' article, "Semantic Concepts for Secondary School English," *English Journal*, XLIX (March, 1960).

He is one of the homeless unemployed. (This creates a feeling of pity and possibly a desire to help the poor unfortunate.)

He is a tramp. (The word "tramp" suggests dirt, shiftlessness, and a possible tendency toward criminality.)

He is generous. (Generosity is considered a virtue.)

He is a spendthrift. (We usually do not like people who waste money.)

He is a holder of uncommon views. (This suggests that he is praiseworthy because of his presumably original thinking.)

He is a crackpot. (He holds uncommon views we do not like.)

He sauntered down the lane. (He is a pleasant, carefree chap.)

He sneaked down the lane. (He is a deceitful person, afraid to be seen.)

Study of headlines may also be valuable, especially when two or more newspapers are available for comparison. One paper may head a story DEMOCRATS BLOCK TAX CUT; another, DEMOCRATS SUCCEED IN HOLDING TAX LINE; another, CONGRESS DEFEATS TAX SLASH.

A fun-game is that attributed to Bertrand Russell, involving comparisons like this: "I am firm. You are stubborn. He is a pigheaded fool." Other starters: "I am a genius." "I am intelligent." "I am relaxed." "I have a good time at parties." "I am athletic."

Students should certainly be familiarized with various questionable tactics commonly used to influence a course of action. (1) *Name calling:* using a bad label in order to make us oppose something or someone. "He is incompetent." "He is unprogressive." "He is a radical." "The plan is undemocratic." "He was involved in an underhand political deal." (2) *Glittering generality:* the reverse of name calling. "He fought bravely for his country." "She is a superior cook." "She was a ravishing beauty." "Old Dominion Virginia-cured ham is tops." (3) *Transfer:* connecting a person, idea, action, or thing with something highly regarded. "In the well-run home, Nomar is as necessary as soap and water." "Doctors use Antamine." "Strike for Harry and for England!" "Hollywood endorses Glamour Hour." "The soap that lovely women prefer." (4) *Plain folks:* following the theory that what is "common" is best. Using the plain-folks approach, office seekers sometimes plow corn, have their pictures taken while they are drying dishes, sing hillbilly songs, quote Edgar A. Guest, and repeat the commonplaces that "plain folks" supposedly like to hear. (5) *Band wagon:* urging others to follow the crowd. "More people smoke Dromedary cigarettes than any other brand." "Be sure that your vote is included in the landslide of ballots for Adams." "Most thinking people prefer the *Herald*."

The chief tests to apply to statements like these are two in number. Is there any evidence to support the statement? If the statement is true, does it matter? For example, consider "Hollywood endorses Purple Night perfume." Perhaps the advertisement names five actresses who have given or sold testimonials of the perfume's efficacy in hypnotizing men. Does that necessarily mean that "Hollywood endorses" the perfume? And even if it does, is Hollywood's endorsement a sufficient reason why Janet should use Purple Night?

Another teaching technique leading to straight thinking and to a correspondingly apt use of words is to make conscious attacks upon generalizations. "All generalizations are false—including this one" is more than an academic wisecrack; it points at the widespread tendency to generalize, to oversimplify. The validity of generalizations ("Women are fickle by nature." "All men are beasts.") can be weighed. Most students will unthinkingly accept such statements simply because they have heard them frequently. It is both provocative and wholesome, therefore, to have the class point out numerous exceptions that show that a generalization has only limited applicability. Once a pattern of attack has been established, students become less and less gullible in accepting statements of "allness." They begin to question whether all cowboys are noble and fun-loving, all gangsters ride in black sedans, all Swedes are big, blond, and stupid, all Jews are avaricious, all Europeans are musical, and so on. They may pursue the attack further to the point of definition. What is a Negro? If a man is one-thirty-second "colored," is he a Negro? In Sinclair Lewis' *Kingsblood Royal,* is Kingsblood, whose great-great-great-grandfather was black, a Negro? Is Kingsblood's daughter? In the light of recent studies concerning the races of mankind, is any narrow definition of race permissible? A highly desirable broad-mindedness may grow from such analysis. "Never accept statements using *never* or *always;* always reject them."

A variation of the approach is to analyze proverbs, which are, of course, generalizations. The purpose is not to prove that the proverbs are "wrong" but to show that exceptions do exist and that proverbs sometimes contradict one another. For example, "A stitch in time saves nine" is antithetical to "Don't cross the bridge before you come to it." Some teachers place two familiar proverbs side by side and have students decide whether they are similar in meaning, opposite, or unrelated.

Much of the work involving the study of language as symbols may be done incidentally, when the "felt need" appears. But some should be done directly. The purpose is to make students sharply aware of the nature of the language, its resources, its deficiencies, and the ways in which it can be employed effectively.

So that students may clearly understand that language is symbolic, some teachers write the word APPLE on the board.

> "What is that?"
> "Apple."
> "Can you take a bite out of it?"
> "No."
> "Why not?"
> "It isn't a real apple."
> "Then what is it?"
> "It's a word that means a kind of fruit."
> "A symbol?"
> "Yes."
> "What if everybody called it a 'glag' instead?"
> "Then 'glag' would be the symbol for the kind of fruit."
> "What if I called it a 'glag' and you called it an 'apple'?"
> "Then we'd have trouble understanding each other, because we'd not be using the same symbols."
> "What if I think that all apples are red and you know that some are yellow or green? Do we then understand the symbol 'apple' in the same way?"
> "No."
> "Can you think of any words that you and your parents don't always understand in the same way?"
> "Get home *early*." "Be *good*." "Do you really *need* the car?" "It's a *free* country."
> "Let's look at the word 'free' a little more. Do you think that words like *freedom* and *democracy* mean the same thing to everybody, both here and in other parts of the world?"

It is necessary also to draw a distinction between objective and subjective writing. A factual explanation of how to change a tire should normally employ uncolored, unfigurative words. So should an objective statement of a candidate's qualifications for a public office. But a poem, play, short story, or personal essay may—indeed, must—be subjective, because it offers an interpretation of a facet of life, not a photograph. Shelley's "To a Skylark" is not a scientific, unbiased description of a bird but a frankly personal statement of admiration.

Failure or unwillingness to recognize a difference between the two types of writing leads to a confusion between factual and emotional or persuasive presentations and may reveal itself in such things as editorialized news stories or prosy imaginative writing. When a teacher fails to see the difference, he is likely to praise only vivid writing, even when straightforward prose is more suitable for the purpose. Vivid writing has its place, but so has quiet presentation of facts. Both teacher and student should keep in mind the purpose of the writing, and choose words accordingly.

Objective writing presents verifiable facts: "Dr. Ladd's car is parked in front of the Jackson house." Subjective writing, in contrast, makes judgments, which may or may not be accurate and verifiable: "Someone in the Jackson house is sick." (That judgment is not necessarily true; maybe Mrs. Ladd drove the car, or maybe the doctor is making only a friendly visit, or maybe he entered the house across the street.) Exercises intended to help students distinguish facts from judgments can be useful throughout their lives.

In subjective as in objective writing, it is necessary to choose appropriate words. In addition, since subjective writing is often figurative, it is also essential to select fitting figures of speech. Characteristically, a poor or untrained writer uses figures that are either trite, far-fetched, or mixed: "The burning sun was hot as fire." "She tripped downstairs like a feather in the breeze." "That snake in the grass is barking up the wrong tree." Once a student combined all of the figurative vices by writing, "The sky was black as pitch, and it was raining pitchforks." It takes a creative mind (not necessarily an "educated" one) to originate an effective simile or metaphor, but even an ordinary mind can borrow someone else's tropes and use them effectively. The test of the quality of a figure of speech is always its appropriateness in the particular situation.

Students frequently have the impression that figures of speech are things that only authors employ, in order to vex and confuse readers. It is helpful to let them see that tropes, especially metaphors, abound and that there is good reason for their existence. When we refer to the arm or leg of a chair, the eyes of a potato, or the hands of a clock, we are speaking metaphorically. "Black looks," "a hangdog expression," "leaden sky," "carefree laughter," "raining cats and dogs"—hundreds of more or less common expressions are figurative. "Wheel" for "bicycle," "Washington says" for "government officials say," and "a volume of Wordsworth" are other examples of tropes in daily use. Slang is composed largely of figurative language.

Why use tropes? Primarily for picturesqueness, for persuasion, and .for clarification. "The moon was a glistening white balloon, released by a careless child" is picturesque, but it also portrays clearly the appearance of the moon on a particular night. "He is like Hitler in his lust for power" tends to persuade us to detest the person described. Thoreau's comparison of the shape of Cape Cod to "a bended arm" enables us to visualize the Cape. Students enjoy finding illustrations of the employment of tropes for all three of these purposes. One class, divided into committees, concentrated on metaphorical language in slang, advertising, cartoons and caricatures, songs, editorials, and sports writing. They learned that the use of figurative language is not restricted to long-haired poets.

A Unit in Semantics

In an article worth reading in its entirety, a Utah teacher, Solveig Torvik has described a unit taught to high school seniors.[22] I would argue for much semantic instruction well before the senior year, and Torvik's unit presents ideas usable on earlier levels of instruction.

Torvik emphasizes seven points in the unit, which is based on Hayakawa: symbol-thing confusion; generalizations; inferences, judgments, reports; classification; abstractions; directive, affective, informative uses of language; two-valued and multi-valued orientation. The following paragraphs offer only brief examples of the sort suggested by Torvik.

> 1. Symbol-thing confusion. A girl becomes ill when she sees a picture of a spider; another faints when she sees the word *snake*. These girls are confusing symbol with reality. An *A* on a report card is an inadequate symbol of the knowledge it supposedly represents. A swastika or an American flag is only a geometrical figure, but each is invested with emotional overtones that vary from person to person. "You think you think, but words structure your thinking for you."
> 2. Generalizations. Generalizations, says Torvik, are acceptable if one can find 100 per cent proof to support them; but one seldom can. In this part of the unit students learn to question words like *all, never, always, everybody.*

[22] "Teaching Semantics in High School," *English Journal,* LVIII (Dec., 1969), 1341.

3. Inferences, judgments, reports. Students examine groups of statements like these:

(Report): Mary Smith didn't get in until two o'clock last night.

(Inference): I bet she was out tearing around.

(Judgment): She's a worthless hussy. I never did like her looks.

Inferences and judgments, students learn, are often confused with reports (statements of fact).

4. Classification. Mother 1 is not Mother 2. Negro 1 is not Negro 2. Mary today is not Mary yesterday. Democracy in Russia is not democracy in the United States. American democracy 1976 is not American democracy 1776. Classifications shift, and differ with individuals, times, places, and other circumstances. What's "good" for A may be bad for B.

5. Abstractions. "The students can then be led to see that specific referents for such words as *justice, love, evil, patriotism, good,* and *moral* are essential in actually communicating what one means to say *in this instance.* 'For example' becomes a key phrase in writing and discussion."

6. Directive, affective, informative uses of language. Language is often used to direct or influence actions of other human beings. A directive may be defined as expected behavior rather than a report of facts or a universal truth: "Mothers love their children."

7. Two-valued and multi-valued orientation. The best answer to a question like "Do you love school or hate school?" is often "Sometimes one, sometimes the other." Two-valued orientation is either-or thinking; either this must be true or that must be. In reality a number of choices may exist. The search for *the* answer is often futile, for there may be several answers or more or many shades of a "right" answer.

Students exposed to imaginative, many-exampled study of semantics, like that used by Torvik, are less likely than others to accept statements uncritically. They learn much about the power of language to influence others and about their own need to examine language to see where it may be taking them.

LEVELS OF USAGE

Good English is appropriate English. At a baseball game, "Hit it over the fence, Joe" is better than "Smite the sphere vigorously, Joseph" simply because it is more appropriate. Yet, in countless classrooms the doctrine of appropriateness is ignored, and a mythical "correctness" is substituted—"correctness" usually meaning a pseudo-literary language.

Largely to blame for this misplacement of emphasis is the idea that levels of usage vary in desirability from literary English at the top to vulgarisms at the bottom. This ladder of levels—to which there are serious objections—looks something like this:

Literary English
Technical English
Formal English
Colloquial English
Localisms
Ungrammatical English
Vulgarism and illiteracies

Most English teachers are cognizant of the large amount of scholarly writing concerning such levels, and, being near perfectionists, many strive to teach literary English as the goal toward which all should aspire. In the classroom, students are generally acquiescent. If the teacher wants them (horrible thought) to write, "Smite the sphere vigorously, Joseph," that is what they write. But at the ball game, at home, in conversations, in the writing of friendly letters, and in most other circumstances, they revert to their old habits. They are justified in doing so, for only literary writing demands literary language.[23]

Actually, as Professor John S. Kenyon has pointed out, there are only two levels, standard and substandard. (The term *nonstandard* is now preferred, since *sub* suggests inferiority.) Kenyon does not mention slang, which, it would seem, is in a no-man's land between the two levels.

Standard English
Slang
Nonstandard English [24]

Let us start with the bottom rung.

---

[23] Professor Pooley (*op. cit.*, p. 24) says, "It is obvious that the literary level cannot be made a requirement for all students in schoolroom composition. It is too much the product of mental maturity and highly developed skill to be attainable by the average student, or indeed, by the average teacher. Therefore, while examples of beautiful prose should be given to pupils to study, and the few who are gifted should be encouraged to strive toward the development of a literary tone and style, the great body of school children should be expected to do no more than to cultivate the clear, direct English of communication, together with a feeling for the appropriateness of word and idiom to the purpose intended. Students in whom these perceptions have been engendered will always use 'correct,' adequate English."

[24] J. J. Lamberts suggests a different three levels: Hyperstandard, standard, and substandard. The hyperstandard label would be applied to usages that seem affected or unnecessarily elaborate, for example *desire* where *want* is sufficient, *ablutions* for *bath*, *domicile* for *home*, *mortician* for *undertaker*. "Another Look at Kenyon's Levels," *College English*, XXIV (Nov., 1962), 141–43.

Nonstandard English

Nonstandard English is that which is not idiomatic, is not in accord with the grammar and usage of cultivated people, or is limited to a particular geographical area. For instance, "I bought the dog off of Harvey" is unidiomatic. "We was," "this here dog," and "hadn't ought" would be used only jocosely by most people who consider themselves cultivated. "May I carry you to the dance, Lilybell?" is a localism or provincialism, as is "make a bed down" in contrast to the standard "make a bed."

Nonstandard English, then, is not appropriate except in reproducing the speech of people who use that level of language. In students' English, it is usually regarded as underbrush that needs to be cleared away to let the trees grow. To the educated ear, it is ugly and often indicative of incompetence. Only a small proportion of the American population would be likely to vote in a presidential election for a man who said, "Us Republicans is agonna clean up this here mess that the Democrats has gotten us in." Most people would feel that, as the candidate's degree of mastery of his native language was so pitifully small, his mastery of the country's economic and political problems would be even smaller.

V. Louise Higgins sums up the matter succinctly for her students like this:

> "If you speak this way, you go in the back door; if you speak *this* way, you go in the front door." I make it very clear that I neither built the house nor did I designate the doors. In this case, I am merely an agent showing off the real estate. I have the key to the front door, and once the student has the concept of usage levels I have given him the key. The back door is always ajar.[25]

Not everyone agrees with Miss Higgins, however. James Sledd, for instance, in a widely discussed article,[26] argues that although "making children who talk wrong get right with the world has traditionally been the work of English teachers," what those teachers are actually doing is providing "incessant drill on inessentials," reducing tolerance by indicating that only one kind of language is "right," and using language differences to perpetuate white racism. (Sledd ignores the fact, though, that the same kinds of "incessant

[25] "Approaching Usage in the Classroom," *English Journal*, XLIX (March, 1960), 185.
[26] "Bi-dialectalism: The Linguistics of White Supremacy," *English Journal*, LVIII (Dec., 1969), 1307.

drills" are used regardless of the children's color.) A somewhat different position is that children should be offered the possibility of choice, should be familiarized with standard forms and be given practice in their use, but should not be forced (e.g., by grades) to employ them. This position has these virtues: (1) It is realistic, for everyone in the long run will make his own choices anyway, regardless of what he is taught in school. (2) It is honest, because it says that some forms have greater social approval than others, even though no form is of itself either "right" or "wrong" but is only a reflection of custom. (3) It is democratic.

Actually, the number of nonstandard usages is not tremendous. It consists chiefly of pronoun case forms, irregular (strong) verbs, and forms of *be*. Familiarizing students with these items and giving opportunity at least to try out the standard forms are not huge tasks.

Slang

Slang has long been a controversial topic. In a study reported in 1925, the elimination of slang was listed as one of the chief goals of 193 teachers of English who answered a questionnaire. Since that time, though, the middle-of-the-road attitude of William Lyon Phelps has been widely accepted:

> Our slang's piquant as catsup. I decry it
> Not as a condiment, but as an entire diet.

More to the right of center are the *Oxford English Dictionary* definition and the comment of Greenough and Kittredge:

Slang. Language of a highly colloquial type, considered as below the level of standard educated speech, and consisting either of new words or current words employed in some special sense.
A peculiar kind of vagabond language, always hanging on the outskirts of legitimate speech, but continually straying or forcing its way into the most reputable company.

A slang expression may sometimes add picturesqueness to a sentence. Shakespeare, as is well known, frequently used Elizabethan slang, some of which has since become standard English. There is nothing inherently bad in slang.

Slang may be objectionable, however, on one or more of three counts. One is that it is a transitory language. Little of the slang prevalent in grandfather's day would be comprehensible to grand-

son. The "bop talk" of the early 1950's followed the "jive talk" of
the 1940's into obsolescence, and the slang of the "hippies" changes
constantly. How completely slang or cant disappears is shown by
H. L. Mencken, who quotes from the eighteenth century: "to fib the
cove's quarron in the rumpad for the lour in his bung" (which
means "to beat the fellow in the highway for the money in his
purse").[27]

The second objection, sometimes called a virtue by those who
like to mystify others, is that some people will fail to understand a
slangy sentence. The third is that constant use of slang expressions
(or any others) tends toward mental debilitation on the part of the
speaker and toward boredom on the part of the listener. A person
who calls everything either "swell" or "lousy" gradually loses whatever power of discrimination he may once have had.

Students of a California teacher, Dennis R. Dean, compiled a
dictionary of teen-age slang and reached two sorts of conclusions.
First, they and their teacher decided, slang can be interesting and
colorful, slang words are unusually difficult to define, and slang is
the language of an in-group. Second, slang should not be used:

—whenever any written record is meant to endure;
—whenever exact definition is necessary;
—whenever communication is with an adult, person in authority, or non-member
  of the group.
—whenever one wishes to use language that will command respect.[28]

Through analysis of current slang, Madison, Wisconsin, students
learn useful information about similes, metaphors, metonymy, synecdoche, onomatopoeia, reduplication, compounding, shortening,
functional shift, derivation, acronyms, hyperbole, and euphemism—
not just about slang.[29]

It is both impracticable and undesirable to attempt to eliminate
slang. It is desirable, however, to talk with students, as Mr. Dean
did, about both the good and the bad aspects of slang—its piquancy
and its weaknesses. The couplet by Professor Phelps quoted earlier
in this section may well be a teacher's theme song in dealing with
the problem of slang.

27 *The American Language: Supplement* I (New York: Alfred A. Knopf, Inc.,
1945), p. 158.
28 "Slang Is Language Too!" *English Journal,* LI (May, 1962), 324.
29 Ernest Heiman, "The Use of Slang in Teaching Linguistics," *English Journal,*
LVI (Feb., 1967), 249.

Standard English

The top rung of the English language ladder is the standard. Included in standard English are literary, technical, formal, and colloquial language. No one of these is always "better" than another. Each may be "better" in some circumstances. What must be understood is that colloquial English is as good as literary, technical, and formal, and that there are many more occasions for employing colloquial English than for employing the other three.

Literary English is that used in subjective writing for the primary purpose of conveying emotional reactions. Thus Tennyson used literary English in most of his poetry because he wanted his readers to share his feelings; William Thackeray in his novels and E. V. Lucas in his essays used it for the same reason. Technical English is that which is appropriate in scientific, unemotional writing, for example, in a treatise on the swordfish family or in a monograph on the preterit in Old Norse. Formal English is that used when one's subject is serious but not technical and when one is addressing groups composed mainly of people who are strangers and who will probably remain strangers. Colloquial English is that used in discussing any subject with people whom one knows or expects to know fairly well.

All of these varieties of standard English, then, are useful. One is not superior to another, except in a given set of circumstances. The teacher should clarify the distinctions and should help the students to use the kind of standard English most appropriate to the time and place.

In creative writing of the highly subjective type, the writings of a few students may possess a literary tone. The reference paper or papers written usually in the senior year may be somewhat technical. Contest writing, much newspaper writing, business letters, and public addresses and debates usually demand rather formal language. But, most of the time, colloquial English is particularly appropriate—in friendly letters, in conversations and class discussions, on the athletic field and in the shop, and with the family, the teacher, and one's other friends.

Colloquial English is the natural English to use in a friendly, familiar environment. It differs only slightly from the formal; it makes use of contractions, nicknames, and a few words and grammatical constructions that would not appear in formal English. Thus "I'm," "Johnny," "squelch," and "Who did he select?" are colloquial, whereas "I am," "John," "subdue," and "Whom did he select?" are formal. Kenyon stressed the fact that most words may be used either colloquially or formally and added,

Consequently, it is impossible to draw a strict dividing line between the colloquial and the literary or formal vocabulary—between colloquial diction and formal diction; the boundary consists rather of a very wide belt of words. The colloquial or formal character often depends as much on occasion and circumstances apart from the language as on the words themselves. Many whole sentences may be either colloquial or formal according to context and circumstances. . . . Sometimes only a slight sprinkling of words gives to a passage either its colloquial or its formal coloring.[30]

What brand of standard English should be taught in the classroom? "Unstiff formal" may be the best answer. V. Louise Higgins, in the article previously mentioned, makes the point by a useful discrimination between private and public language:

The hallmarks of private utterance are that it is definitely limited and that the emphasis is on content, nor form. It is language in most pragmatic form and we all use it with our families, our friends, in our note to the milkman. Public communication differs in that it is meant for a wider audience and that both form and content are considered. In our classrooms, we are dealing primarily with usage as it pertains to public utterances.

The "unstiff formal" usage is suitable for most of the public utterance likely ever to be required of your students. The few of them who become lawyers, scientists, writers, or the like will need later to make special adaptations of their language, but the "unstiff formal" provides an easy point of departure.

WORDS, WORDS, MERE WORDS

One of the masters of words, William Shakespeare, made some of the wisest remarks concerning these tools of mankind. Hamlet, buried in his grief, read only "words, words, words," because his troubles were much more intense than printed syllables. Claudius knew that unmeant, unfelt words are empty, that his prayers were vain because they were not sincere: "Words without thoughts never to heaven go." Troilus found in Cressida's letter "words, words,

---

[30] John S. Kenyon, "Levels of Speech and Colloquial English," *English Journal,* XXXVII (Jan., 1948), 25.

mere words, no matter from the heart." And Holofernes pointed at a general vice when he said, "He draweth out the thread of his verbosity finer than the staple of his argument."

Words, however pretty, however sonorous, can be no stronger than the thoughts behind them. We who teach words must always remember that fact, if we are not to divorce words from action. The Bible says, "A word spoken in due season, how good is it!" But it also asks, "Who is this that darkeneth counsel by words without knowledge?"

THE IDEA BOX

Magazine Articles for Vocabulary

Each week Hazel Cohen's students report briefly on two magazine articles; their reports include notes on new words or new expressions and phrasings they have found. Thus they learn words in context. *Clearing House* (March, 1969).

Vocabulary Building Through Word Analysis

Laura Dunklin describes a detailed plan including such exercises as this:

New word: "derision."
Sentences in which it appears: "This sports writer thinks the players deserved the derision of the crowd."
Analysis: *de*—down, *ris*—laugh, *ion*—act of.
Original sentence: Martha, discouraged by her classmates' derision, gave up trying to learn to swim.
Synonyms: ridicule, scorn, contempt.

"Developing Word Mastery," *High School Journal*, XXX (Jan., 1956), 233.

Other Vocabulary-Building Devices

Teacher writes a word like *signal* on the board. Students (slow junior high) choose a category (e.g., music, education, or food) and write down all the words they can think of in that category for each letter in the word *signal*. They profit from the exchange of words and discussion of the meanings. Synonym and antonym contests are also useful, says Grace Ashenfelter of Urbana, Ill.; in teams, students write as many synonyms or antonyms as they can discover for a given word.

Four Steps for Learning a Word

(1) Copy the sentence containing the word. (2) With help from the dictionary, learn to pronounce it. (3) Again with the help of the dictionary, write a one-sentence definition that fits the context. (4) Use the word in an original sentence. Virginia Ireland, "A Method of Vocabulary Study," *English Journal*, LV (Sept., 1966), 763.

Synonyms in Blanks

Give a definition and the first and last letters of a synonym; for example, unfriendly: h _ _ _ _ _ e.

Students as Word Coiners

Know what *geobios* is? Earth life, of course. How about *megamaniac*? Big nut. Jean L. Campbell's junior high students have fun coining words based on roots and affixes she helps them define. They try their hands at writing things like "One day as a decigenarian was autoporting himself to school, he was stopped by multimicroorganisms." See "Hydrozoology in the Microcosm," *English Journal*, LIV (Dec., 1965), 861.

Vocabulary Building and Semantics

Sidney Shanker's students pay particular attention to commonly used root words and to word histories as they develop their vocabularies. "Is Your Vocabulary Teaching Obsolete?" *English Journal*, LIII (Sept., 1964), 422.

Guessing Definitions from Context

Given several sentences in which the same unfamiliar word is used, students can learn to guess accurately or fairly accurately because of the context clues, says William B. Mullen, "Teaching Contextual Definition," *English Journal*, LIV (May, 1965), 419.

Activities for Word Power

These are listed by Verna Hoyman among forty-five activities, as part of a long article on the teaching of vocabulary (*Illinois English Bulletin*, Nov., 1961): (1) Finding color words that give clues to a mood; (2) finding substitutes for overworked words; (3) finding words based on Greek myths, for example, "chaotic" (chaos), "odyssey" (Odysseus), "vulcanize" (Vulcan); (4) finding in a magazine examples of trite subject matter, hackneyed words, poor diction; (5) pointing out words that are the expression of opinion in news stories; (6) writing a definition of an abstraction and developing it with a paragraph of concrete illustration; (7) appreciating the vivid language of the sports announcer; (8) choosing ten words that aptly describe the movements of animals; (9) writing an article, slanting it favorably, then rewriting, slanting it unfavorably.

Playbooks Needed

Our vocabulary textbooks (and language books in general) are overly serious, Edgar Dale of Ohio State once said in a lecture. We need more "playbooks," with puns, anagrams, word games of various sorts. If no such books are available, teacher and students can still do much playing with words in class. Professor Dale's *Techniques of Teaching Vocabulary* (Field Educational Publications, 1971) contains hundreds of useful exercises.

"Amelia Bedelia"

Peggy Parish's poem about a maid calls students' attention to facets of our confusing language; students enjoy adding other examples. E.g., told to dust the furniture, the maid put dust on it. "Draw the drapes." (She drew a picture.) "Put the lights out." (She hung the bulbs on a clothesline.) "Dress the chicken." (As a boy or as a girl?)

Manipulating New Words

For a word to become an active part of a student's vocabulary, it must be used. Among useful manipulative activities: (1) give the antonym of the word; (2) ask a question using the word (e.g., "Is it *inevitable* that the Yankees will win the pennant this year?"); (3) compare the meanings of words (e.g., "Is a person who is *vigilant* ever *cowardly?*"); (4) supply another form of the word (e.g., "imply," "implication"); (5) name contexts suitable for the use of the word (e.g., "marauders" could be used for pillaging soldiers, for pirates swooping down on a coastal village, for some of the Danish invaders of medieval England).

The Evil of Overwriting

A study of admittedly great non-fiction such as the best of Winston Churchill or of Rachel Carson may help both a teacher and his students to realize that the best prose is not flashy, not decorated with gingerbread, not cryptic, not flowery, and never—never—wordy.

The Exact Word

1. Say to someone in the class, "Your name is Wilbur, isn't it?" "No, it's Ralph." Turn to the class. "Is it right for me to call Ralph Wilbur? No? Then it isn't right to call a _____ a _____ is it?"

2. Tell students of trouble sometimes caused by failure to choose the right word, for example, the ambiguous sign "Fine for fishing." (Dilla Tucker, Nampa, Idaho.)

3. Remind students that noted authors have often had to struggle to find the precise word; for example, Elizabeth Browning used to put pyramids of words in the margin while she wrote, and then would select the most appropriate one. Conrad and Flaubert sometimes sought the right word for hours. Mark Twain said that the difference between the right word and the almost right one is as great as the difference between lightning and the lightning bug.

4. Write a paragraph with numbered blanks replacing certain words. Below, write the numbers, with four or five suggested words for each. Students are to pick the word that best fits the context.

5. Discuss with able students the shades of difference in words generally considered synonyms such as "wages," "salary," "fee," "stipend," "remuneration," "emolument," "honorarium," "dole." It is wise to have Webster's *Dictionary of Synonyms* available to check questionable distinctions.

6. Try a "Find a Better Word" exercise. Sentences illustrating misconceptions of words may be accumulated for the exercise, especially from students' themes, for example, "We should *mimic* noble men and women." "He *administers* a large restaurant."

Related Words

Mabel Lindner, in Latrobe, Pennsylvania, has her classes study groups of works related to menus, to medicine, to plays and ballets that the class sees, etc. Frederic Baxter's West Bend, Wisconsin, students improve their vocabularies through newspaper study, finding that words in headlines are often defined in the news stories and that even the comics and the advertisements may lead them to new words or new meanings. Edgar Logan's sports-minded Detroit students are interested in colorful words related to boxing and other sports and are encouraged to use these "physical" words in their writing, thus getting away from colorless abstractions.

Sophomores vs. "Said"

Martha Pence's sophomores in Kittanning, Pennsylvania, found in their reading 567 substitutes for "said." Perhaps their reading benefited as much as their vocabularies.

General to Specific

"Take a paragraph from a good writer and replace the specific words with general ones. Then let the students use colorful, vivid words to see how near they approach the writer's vocabulary." (Eva Frost, Roosevelt High School, Chicago.)

Encourage Use of the Dictionary

"I stimulate use of the dictionary by frequently using it myself, in class." (Elizabeth Barton, Clanton, Alabama.)

Metaphors

1. Talk about the difference between a "*black* cat" (literal) and a "*black* look" (figurative). Other examples: "warm hands," "warm heart"; "roaring lion," "roaring fire"; "break my leg," "break my heart" (or "my word"). Have students use words like these both literally and figuratively: *sea, root, anchor, hound, crown, tower, mountain, river.*

2. Talk about favorable and unfavorable metaphors applied to people; for example, a girl may be a peach, a lemon, the apple of someone's eye. A man may be a fox, a pig, a snake in the grass, a mule, a sheep, a lion in battle, a jackal, or a sly or gay dog.

Mrs. Clay's Freckles

"Mrs. Clay had freckles, and a projecting tooth," Jane Austen wrote. In eight words (or two brush strokes) she painted a portrait. Let your students try their hands at two-stroke portraiture.

A Few Words with Interesting Histories

abundance, accost, aftermath, aggravate, agony, ambition, assassin, astonish, ballot, bonfire, candidate, capital, congregation, curfew, deliberate, easel, enthrall, extravagant, fool, garret, halcyon, inaugurate, intoxicate, journey, milliner, panic, pedigree, prevaricate, remorse, tantalize, taxicab.

Word Origins

In a study of word origins, try giving students a short list of English words of Germanic origin for which they are to find English synonyms derived from Greek or Latin, and another list reversing the procedure. Among many possible pairs: *tongue, language; friend, companion; heavenly, celestial; red, vermilion; forgiveness, pardon.*

Useful Root Words

Besides knowing the means of the most common affixes, students will find it helpful to know the meanings of these roots: *aqua, audio, bene, corpus, credo, dominus, ego, facio, frater, jungo, locus, loquor, mater, mitto, multus, omnis, pater, pes, primus, pugno, scribo, socius, solus, totus, utilis, verto, video; aer, arche, autos, bios, chronos, cratos, grapho, homos, hydro, logos, metron, micro, orthos, pan, pathos, penta, philos, phone, polis, poly, pseudos, psyche, sophos, tele, theos.*

Prefixes, Suffixes, and Roots

1. Plan an exercise on this pattern:
   benignant, well disposed ___ ___ ___ *ignant*
   homogeneous, of the same kind ___ ___ ___ ___ ___ ___ *geneous*
Students are to supply beginnings to form antonyms of the words at the left.
   2. Another exercise:

Word	Prefix	Root or Stem	Suffix	Meaning of Word
amorphous	*a*, without	*morph*, form	*ous*, having	having no form, shapeless
implacable	*im*, not	*placare*, to quiet, to appease	*able*, capable of	not capable of being appeased

Choose words whose meanings are made rather clear by their component parts. In the first exercise of this sort, leave the last column blank for students to fill in. In later exercises, leave the last four columns blanks.
   3. James I. Brown, University of Minnesota, talks about the numerous technical terms that students encounter. He then gives a twenty-item vocabulary test, students putting their answers under *I:*

				I	II
1. aberrance	1. deviation 3. comprehen- sion	2. entrance 4. precision		1. ___	___
. . . . 20. endocarp	1. thick layer 3. outer layer	2. inner layer 4. middle layer		20. ___	___

Then he hands out a list that gives only the meaning of the prefixes or initial combining forms, for example, *ab-,* from; *endo-,* within. The students take the test again, putting their answers in column II. Since he has found that college upperclassmen average 66 on the first test and 92 on the second, his procedure dramatizes the importance of knowing the meanings of common prefixes and combining forms. *"Vocabulary Development," Exercise Exchange* (April, 1962), 12–13.

"Clever" Definitions

Occasionally let students try to make clever definitions like these: *Abuse:* "The refined substitute for fists when confronted by an argument which cannot be refuted." (George Dorsey) *Art:* "Usually what the most influential critics approve." (Charles Poore) *Elegance:* "A quality appropriate to the young man who presides at the button counter." (Elbert Hubbard) One class came up with these: *Home:* "Last resort." *Homework:* "Something to put off until you get done what you'd rather." *School bus:* "The only vehicle in which one can get run over while inside." *Pizza:* "A round dish, often used as a substitute for food." Carolyn K. Tuttle, "A Little Lexicography is *Not* a Dangerous Thing," *English Journal,* LI (Dec., 1962), 648.

Charged Words

Have students clip attractive advertisements and note the reason for their appeal. They should observe especially the copywriter's use of words that appeal to emotion.

Stylistic Parodies

Able students may sharpen their observation of style by attempting to imitate the sentence structure, typical word choice, and point of view of various authors. Let them try, for example, to write such a story as "Little Red Riding Hood" in the styles of Hemingway, Faulkner, Dickens, Addison.

Show; Don't Tell

Provide a number of sentences that simply tell something, for example, "Rollie made a fine catch in deep center field." Ask students to rewrite them, showing what happened, for example, "At the crack of the bat, Rollie turned his back to the infield and raced toward the center field wall. As he reached it, he spun around and sprang high into the air. The ball struck the fingers of his glove and plopped into his bare hand as he fell to the ground."

The Importance of Context

1. To dramatize for students the need for considering the meanings of words in context, have them compose sentences in which the context requires a specialized meaning, for example, "A goose is one bird from which you can get *down.*" Other words to suggest to the students who stare uncomprehendingly: *runner, fly, well, corn, boxer, ring, diamond, gridiron, flat, light, type, base.*

2. Discuss the prime meaning of certain words to various persons, for example, *pipe* to piper, plumber, organist, oil worker, Dad; *court* to a king, judge, tennis player, suitor; *log* to mathematician, sailor, woodsman.

Predescription

Two lessons precede Eric W. Johnson's assignment of a one-page description. One involves replacing certain words with "more interesting" and accurate words, for example, "The *nice* girl *went* into the *unpleasant* cellar." The other requires completion of comparisons or implied comparisons: "Their team came onto the field like_____" and "The strikers _____ into the stadium." Mr. Johnson helps students to see that *oozed* in the last blank implies a comparison, but that *went slowly* does not. "Stimulating and Improving Writing in the Junior High School," *English Journal*, XLVII (Feb., 1958), 68. (Read the whole article for excellent suggestions about teaching writing.)

What Is Effective English?

According to Louis Zahner, "English is most likely to be effective if it is appropriate in at least five directions: to the purpose; to the subject; to the occasion; to the receiver; and to the speaker or writer." (E. J. Gordon and E. S. Noyes, eds., *Essays on the Teaching of English* [New York: Appleton-Century-Crofts, 1960], 14.) Test Zahner's statement with a class by taking a sentence such as "Football is an athletic contest requiring strength, skill, stamina, speed, and mental and physical alertness." Is that sentence effective if the supposed speaker or receiver is a small child? an uneducated elderly person? a person opposed to football? May it be effective if the occasion is a party? a speech contest? a literary discussion? an exciting moment in a game? May it be effective if the subject of conversation has nothing to do with athletics? Is it effective as a defense of football? as part of a poem extolling athletics?

Slang

Classes enjoy analyzing current slang to find the implied comparisons that are almost always present.

Archaic to Modern

Copy some sentences with archaic words (from Shakespeare, Spenser, the Bible, etc.) and have students substitute appropriate modern words.

Word Autobiographies

Students may write autobiographies of words. As a variation, the class may guess the word described in the autobiography.

A Journalist's Advice

Sally Winfrey got good results from her Englewood, New Jersey, students by urging these rules of a journalist: (1) Make your sentences short. (2) Use the right word, especially the verb, to picture what you are telling. (3) Avoid weak words. If your sentences begin with strong words, you will save your reader time. (4) Avoid trite expressions as you would a puff adder.

The Fear of Ridicule

Sometimes students object to using the language that they learn is "correct." They say, "I'd get made fun of if I talked like that anywhere besides school." It is perhaps best to let such students know that you understand their dilemma, but to add that you are not urging them to use stilted, unnatural language; you are trying only to help them to learn to speak and write clearly and effectively. Tell them that, if they do not feel that they should use certain expressions in their homes and neighborhoods, they of course do not need to do so; but the knowledge is still worth having, because there will be times when they will be in different surroundings and will be writing or speaking to persons who will expect standard English.

Reducing Wordiness

Laurence Perrine, Southern Methodist University, suggests "padding" a well-written paragraph by inserting in it "a number of favorite student devices for wordiness." Students are asked to squeeze out the excess words. They may then compare their new version with the original well-written paragraph. "A Class Exercise in Paragraph Revision," *Exercise Exchange* (April, 1962), 6–7.

Motivating Vocabulary Buiding

Remind your students that civil service tests and promotion tests used by some big industries often stress vocabulary, as do most college entrance examinations.

True–False

Prepare some true–false statements. Students are to correct each false statement and tell why the correction was made. For example, *Levitation* results when something is funny.

Completion

Have students fill in a word that agrees with the thought expressed. For example, "The selection was played by a (group of five musicians)."

Vocabulary Game for Junior High School

Give a word such as *atrophy.* Students try to think of all possible words of a certain type beginning with each of the letters in that word. For example, they may think of verbs of action or abstract nouns, or names of plants, etc.

Television Commercials as Propaganda

Through television commercial slogans students may be taught to recognize name calling ("greasy kid stuff"), glittering generality, band wagon ("more people are switching to . . ."), card stacking, plain folks, testimonial, and transfer (picture of a doctor in a patent medicine ad). Mary Kay Murphy, "Propaganda—A Part of Students' Lives," *English Journal,* LIII (Sept., 1964), 445.

How Media Slant News

Students can have fun noting examples of slanting in magazines like *Time* or *Newsweek* or in broadcasts. E.g., "*Unhappily* this occurred." "He was *understandably* reluctant." "He said it was a debacle. *So it was.*" "The President, *of course,* will run again." (The last quote concerns Lyndon Johnson in 1968.)

Word Gradations

Have students supply word gradations, for example, "Freezing, _____, _____, boiling." "Amoeba, _____, _____, _____, man." "Sad, _____, _____, _____, happy."

Semanticists use similar ladders to show degrees of abstractness, for example, Hayakawa's "Bessie, Cow, _____, _____, _____, Wealth." They further show that the Bessie one person sees is not the same as the Bessie another sees.

Semantic Exercises

1. Have students rearrange items in a list, from most general to most specific, for example, animal, cat, organism, tiger; fiction, "The Gold Bug," prose, short story. As an oral exercise, give a general word such as "vegetation"; a student makes it more specific ("plant"); others make it still more specific ("flower," "lily," "Easter lily," "the Easter lily in Carter's window").

2. Have students make referents of abstract words clear by writing an original one-sentence definition followed by a one-sentence example; for instance, "*Freedom*" is the privilege of doing as one pleases, providing that one does not interfere with the privileges of others. I am free to drive down the highway but not down the middle of it."

3. Have students develop paragraphs of comparison and contrast, to show the similarities and differences in two words; for example, *famous, notorious; prudence, timidity; boldness, bravery.*

4. Discuss connotations of groups of words, for example, *acquaintance, chum, companion, friend, pal; antagonist, enemy, foe, opponent, rival; aroma, fragrance, odor, scent, smell, stench.*"

5. Discuss whether such words as *horse, steed, nag; liberal, leftwinger; farmer, agriculturist, hick;* and *wise, smart, crafty,* are neutral, favorable, or unfavorable in connotation. Have students compose pairs of sentences with the same basic meaning but different connotations; for example, "She gave us dinky little sandwiches." "She served delectable tea sandwiches."

6. Have students write paragraphs in which they explain the connotations that given words have for them; for example, *television, Saturday, football, courtroom, crash, mathematics, April.* Or ask for both the denotations and the connotations of words: *pig, date, average, childish, antique, tenement.*

7. Use semanticists' subscripts (e.g., democracy$_{USA}$, democracy$_{USSR}$, automobiles$_{1935}$, automobiles$_{1971}$). Ask students to point out common elements (if any) in the things being discussed, and also the differences. Relate the discussion to the dangers inherent in such words as *all, never, everybody, nobody, always.*

8. Let bright students try their hand at Bertrand Russell's game of formulating triads like these: I am slender; you are thin; she is skinny. I am firm; you are obstinate; he is a pig-headed fool.

9. Teachers at a Rhode Island College summer session suggested this team game for connotations: Students from each team take turns at the board. The teacher pronounces a word (e.g., *proud*) and then says either "Positive" or "Negative." For "Positive," the students try to think of a word with favorable connotations, like *self-confident;* for "Negative," a word like *haughty.* Other words for the teacher: *good, rude, radical, rural, bold, dull-witted, selfish, horse.*

10. Think of a specific house or piece of real estate. Write an advertisement intended to interest a possible buyer. Then write what an unscrupulous real estate dealer might tell a prospective purchaser if the dealer thought he could persuade him to buy a different, more expensive property.

Semanticists in Unesco

A report from a 1968 UNESCO conference says, "Terms such as 'tribe,' 'native,' 'savage,' 'primitive,' 'jungle,' 'pagan,' 'kaffir,' 'bushman,' 'backwood,' 'underdeveloped,' 'uncivilized,' 'vernacular,' 'Negro,' 'coloured,' and 'race,' *inter alia,* are so charged with emotional potential that their use, with or without conscious pejorative intent, to describe or characterize certain ethnic, social, or religious groups, generally [provokes] an adverse reaction on the part of these groups." The conference grants that occasionally there is no alternative to words like *race* or *tribe,* but insists that in such a case the word must be used "correctly." UNESCO prefers *inhabitant* to *native, developing countries* to *underdeveloped countries, wooded savanna* to *jungle.*

"Semantics and Thomas Hardy"

Henry I. Christ finds semantics of value in literary interpretation. For example, the characters in *Return of the Native* create false images of others: "the map is not the territory." *English Journal*, LIV (Nov., 1965), 738.

Books Your Classes Will Like

The Tree of Language, by Helene and Charlton Laird (Cleveland: World Publishing Co., 1957), is a delightful and yet scholarly book from which high school students can learn the story of their language, the reasons for its oddities, and the stories behind about 100 common words. *Words: Tricks and Traditions*, by M. Newton Friend (New York: Charles Scribner's Sons, 1957), is full of word games, puzzles, limericks, boners, palindromes, and the like.

Word Games and Puzzles

Word Ways is a quarterly magazine for adults interested in word play, but some of its games and puzzles are suitable for students. E.g., think of three homophones meaning respectively "summit," "glance," and "resentment." (*peak, peek, pique*). Now try "before," "successor," "to ventilate."

Note Taking

The South Molton School, Devon, England, early in the course stresses economy in words achieved through writing of telegrams, postcards, advertisements, headlines, and summaries of paragraphs. Later, its students practice taking notes that will capture the gist of an article. "There is nothing like note-making for dispelling foggy writing and foggy thinking," says A. Elliott-Cameron, *Times Educational Supplement* (December, 1958).

Attacking Stereotypes = Attacking Discrimination

Ask the class what an Englishman is like. An Italian. A Russian. A Chinese. The ready responses will be stereotypes. Then look at some literary selections that deny the stereotypes. This is a good way to attack discrimination, which often is rooted in stereotypes, says librarian Sarah Ryder, "The Librarian Goes to the Classroom," *English Journal*, LIV (Sept., 1965), 550.

13

Listening Creatively

When Daniel Boone strode along the faintly marked trails in the Kentucky woods, usually the only sounds he heard were the chirps of the birds and the rustle of leaves as a startled chipmunk scurried to safety. If Daniel or his contemporaries went into town, even there the sounds were subdued—the faint clop clop of horses on the dirt street, a few voices, perhaps a church bell.

But now sound engulfs us. Automobiles and trucks roar along a maze of streets and highways; airplanes drone overhead; voices are more numerous because people live closer together; television blares in every living room; and even deep in the forest we may meet a youth with a transistor radio.

Daniel Boone probably welcomed sounds. We have learned to shut them out, to ignore them, to insulate ourselves against them. Insulation is a protective device useful in its way. It is often an aid to concentration. Besides, if we were exquisitely conscious of every sound, we might, to parody Alexander Pope, die of a song in auscultative pain. But the trouble with insulation is that it shuts out both what is worthless and what is worth hearing.

In our sound-filled world we need a strainer over our ears, a strainer that will automatically exclude the sounds of no significance to us but allow the others to filter through to a responsive brain. In other words, we need to listen intelligently.

IN THE CLASSROOM

Listening Is Not Just Hearing

We listen approximately three times as much as we read, five times as much as we write, and one and one-half times as much as we speak. Yet, until fairly recently, presumably because of the mistaken belief that effective listening is an innate skill, schools paid almost no attention to this important member of the communications family. In the 1950's, though, about 100 master's and doctor's theses were devoted to the nature of listening or to techniques for teaching it, and more and more elementary and secondary schools planned units in which instruction in listening was included. Scholarly interest seems to have diminished since then, but teachers are still aware of the importance of teaching good listening habits.

Hearing and listening, we are increasingly aware, are not identical. Listening requires conscious effort, and it results in some kind of activity. One *hears* the sound of passing cars, and it leaves no impression; but one *listens* to find the source of a squeak in one's own car, and then one tries to do something about it. A fond mother *hears* the babble of children's voices, but she *listens* to her own child's voice and reacts appropriately.

Listening Creatively

It is this "appropriate reaction" that makes listening creative. In effect, we make a new decision each time we listen. We listen to a commercial for Breathless mouthwash and decide to buy or not to buy it. We listen to an appeal to vote for Joe rather than for Moe, and we perhaps find reinforced our decision to cast a ballot for Moe.

What we listen to we must evaluate and use. From those who address us we may learn how to look at the world about us, learn the unchanging verities, formulate a philosophy, and discover how to accomplish things, and why and when.

If for no other reason, creative listening is important in a democracy because it can help us to think straight about the issues that a democratic nation continuously faces. Essential to democracy is intelligent choice. There is no royal road to utopia—there may be no utopia—but we have to weigh the merits of each trail through the swamps and choose the least undesirable one. We have to distinguish between the weighed words of the scientific pleader and the weighted words of the spellbinder. Constantly we are faced with the necessity of evaluating and choosing—between two or more candidates, isms, methods, or proposed solutions.

The Objective of Classroom Listening

School is both a part of life and a preparation for later life. Since this is true, each classroom activity should have meaning and value for both the present and the future. Creative listening meets this demand, since for the student it does at least the following things. It:

1. Adds information
2. Increases interests
3. Creates wholesome attitudes
4. Improves skills and techniques
5. Improves social behavior
6. Aids appreciation
7. Aids creative expression
8. Improves discrimination and critical thinking

The objective of classroom listening, then, is to build listening ability and habits to a point where maximum progress toward each of these outcomes may be made.

Techniques for Improving Listening

So much for theory. Now for some practical suggestions concerning ways in which students may be made into creative listeners. As Lawrence Brewster said,[1] good listening habits cannot be developed in a short series of exercises. Instead, there must be many opportunities for practice, extending over a long period of time.

The Teacher as Model. John Sweet writes of one teacher, "Basic to his skill is the fact that he is first and foremost a listener. He is a whole course in how to listen. Magically, he mixes relaxation with intensity. Formal and yet warm, he respects his students as persons. The attention of the class is focused on their truths, not his own." [2]

Discussion of Listening. Students are usually amenable to reason, especially when they supply the reason. Therefore a class discussion on the why and how of listening may be valuable. It is

[1] *Speech Teacher,* Jan., 1966.
[2] "Profile of an English Teacher," *English Journal,* LVII (March, 1968), 420.

hoped that the class will stress courtesy ("listen unto others as you would have them listen unto you"), purposefulness, accuracy, and responsiveness. Young classes may need to talk about physical requirements for listening, such as having desks clear, showing interest by posture and facial expression, and being patient when a speaker has difficulty. Discussions may be followed by having a volunteer committee construct a poster naming and illustrating the qualities of a good listener; this poster may be left for some time in a conspicuous spot as a reminder. If a student is adept at cartoons or caricatures, he may use his ability in order to laugh out of existence some of the faulty listening habits.

Suggestions on What to Listen for. Before playing a record in a music-appreciation course, the teacher generally suggests that the students listen for something in particular—the function of a certain instrument, the repetition of a theme, etc. This technique may be borrowed by the English teacher when he knows fairly well what to expect in an oral presentation. Once, for instance, when several freshmen were explaining how to make things, the teacher simply asked the class members to try to follow each explanation and be ready to ask questions if there was something they did not understand. When a junior was talking about the life of Walt Whitman, the teacher asked the class to listen for what they thought was the most interesting episode in the poet's life. It is surprising how much a very little guidance will increase the intensity of listening; surprisingly also, the understanding of the entire presentation seems to be increased when the students are supposedly concentrating on one item.

A variation of the plan, with the advantage of teaching the students some of the fundamentals of note taking, is for the teacher to read something interesting related to the material being studied. The students are asked to take notes on certain points mentioned in advance by the teacher.

Still another variation, suggested in the NCTE *The English Language Arts in the Secondary School,* is to divide the class into groups, each listening for a different point:

Group 1 may be asked to listen for new ideas; Group 2, for familiar ideas aptly expressed; Group 3, for the speaker's plan of organization; Group 4 for effective ways used by the speaker to hold or to reclaim attention; Group 5, for quotable phrases or sentences; Group 6, for unsupported generalizations; Group 7, for clues to questions to be raised in the discussion period.

After the talk, each listening group is allowed five minutes to share within the group whatever was heard. One member is chosen by the five as their spokesman in the general discussion. What each representative brings out will help the entire class to see what can be done in purposeful listening. Discussion under the guidance of the teacher will also reveal how listeners can focus their attention and how they can school themselves to remember what they decide they want to recall.[3]

Note Taking. Although taking notes may be useful for all students, those who are planning to go to college will find it especially so, because they will almost certainly be subjected to lectures in college.

The teacher may help here by suggesting that the class try to write down not everything that is said but only the most important points, together with a pertinent example or illustration here and there. One teacher demonstrated the process by taking notes on an assembly address while her students made their own notes. She mimeographed hers, and the students compared what they and she had written down.

Quizzes. It is certainly a mistake to allow students to assume that they will be held responsible only for the material in the textbook. If class periods have any value, much of what is said in class is worth remembering. Examinations, therefore, may cover content presented in class in addition to that in the textbook.

Following Instructions. Any teacher can cite instances of students' failure to follow oral instructions. Probably any foreman could supply more illustrations. The school provides a worthwhile service if it offers much practice in following instructions.

Most such practice will come automatically from school activities. One teacher, though, dismayed by the fact that his students habitually did things the wrong way, held a discussion on the importance of following instructions. Then he gave oral instructions on a number of useful topics—how to open a new book, how to check a book out of the library, how to take notes on a 3 x 5-inch card, etc. He encouraged creative listening by having his students try to answer the question "Why?" after each step; for example, "Why is the page number of the reference included in the notes?" After completing each set of instructions, he had the students do what he had just explained. At a later class meeting he had each student give instructions for accomplishing some task that could be done quickly in the classroom, and other students carried out the instructions.

[3] P. 262.

484   THE TEACHING OF HIGH SCHOOL ENGLISH

Understanding Organization.   Let us assume that you have been unable to attend a lecture and that you want to find out what the speaker had to say. If you ask an acquaintance to tell you about it, the chances are perhaps even that he will say "It was good," "It was dull," "He speaks well," or "He talked about ————," but will be unable to summarize the lecture for you. Why? Because listeners are often unaware of the organization of a talk, and, having no mental outline to follow, they are unable to reconstruct it. They may have listened to every word, but if they have not understood the organization they will be able only to generalize or to refer to a point here and there.

Of double value to your students is listening to a speech or report in an attempt to understand its organization. The first value is that they can learn to give intelligent summaries of what they hear; the second, that they become increasingly conscious of the need for organization in order to assure clarity in their own speaking and writing. A procedure that may be employed is to review the possible methods of organization and to discuss ways of identifying the chief supporting points. A few comments on the use of transitions are apropos here. Then the students listen to the next assembly speaker, or to presentations by their classmates, and make analyses. Students who have been taught to listen for the organization of a talk tend to comprehend it rather well; they also tend to be highly critical of any rambling discourse.

Listening for Details and for Language Signals.   In *Using Mass Media in Teaching English* (Albany, 1960) the New York State Bureau of Secondary Curriculum Development suggests using newspaper stories for two purposes. The first is to help students listen for details. A newspaper story, perhaps about a ball game or some other topic of great current interest, is read to the class. Specific questions, prepared either by the teacher or by the students, are then to be answered; for example, "How many spectators were in the stadium?" The second purpose is to make students more aware of transitions, or language signals. After a discussion of such signals, the teacher reads from a newspaper the text of part of a speech. The class is responsible for noting such signals as those that anticipate new points (*next, then, finally, another,* etc.) and those that show other relationships (*however, for this reason,* etc.). Radio and television programs may sometimes be used for the same purposes.

Selecting Main Ideas.   A natural outgrowth, indeed a part of the study of organization, is the selection of main ideas. One procedure is to have students write papers of 150 to 200 words on such a topic as "What Our School Needs Most" or "If I Were a Czar of Television." After each paper is read, the members of the class try to reduce the main idea to one terse sentence. If the writer has not been clear, the listeners will not hesitate to tell him so.

A follow-up can be the reading of carefully selected passages from a current magazine, a newspaper editorial, or the work of a major nonfiction writer. Once more the students try to reduce the material to a single sentence.

A college teacher presented well-organized lectures to his freshmen and asked them to find the main point of each. Before instruction in listening, only 27 per cent could select main ideas. After instruction, 50 per cent of the poor listeners showed significant improvement.[4] Boys, interestingly enough, seemed to be slightly better listeners than girls.

A prepared debate between two student teams affords a different kind of summarizing activity. Here the purpose is to list the arguments on both sides.

David Levinson suggests that students may profit from reporting on speeches in the way that a journalist would.[5] He points out that here a summary is not desirable; instead, students seize upon what appears most newsworthy.

A measurement of a speaker's ability to convey his main ideas is W. H. Ewing's speaking-listening index.[6] Ewing would employ the index as a measure of a speaker's success in conveying his thoughts to his audience, but it would seem to have value as a measure of listening ability as well. While one student speaks, the others write down what they believe is the theme of his speech and each of the chief supporting ideas. What they write is then compared with the speaker's own written statements of theme and supporting ideas. The formula for measuring the success of the speaker is this:

$$I = \frac{P + 2C}{.02N_1N_e}$$

I = index. P = number of partially correct statements by all members of the class. C = number of correct statements by all members

---

[4] Charles E. Irvin, "Evaluating a Training Program in Listening for College Freshmen," *School Review*, LXI (1953), 25.

[5] "Reporting Speeches: A Writing Unit." *English Journal*, XLIX (Oct., 1960), 477.

[6] W. H. Ewing, "Finding a Speaking-listening Index," *Quarterly Journal of Speech*, XXXI (Oct., 1945), 368.

of the class. N_1 = number of speaker's items. N_e = number of listeners. For example, a class of 30 has 64 partially correct statements and 58 correct ones; the speaker had 5 items.

$$\text{Index} = \frac{64 + (2 \times 58)}{.02 \times 5 \times 30} = \frac{180}{3} = 60$$

The speaker's index would be 60 (a fairly high figure).

But each listener could measure his listening ability by simplifying the formula to

$$\frac{P + 2C}{.02N_1}$$

Thus, if a student had two partially correct statements and one correct out of a possible five, his index would be

$$\frac{2 + (2 \times 1)}{.02 \times 5} = \frac{4}{.10} = 40$$

Consistent attainment of a listening index of 60 or above should be the goal.

Listening for Contradictions and Faulty Reasoning. In a discussion or an argumentative presentation, a speaker will sometimes contradict himself, although the contradiction may be well hidden. The classic example is that of the politician who comes out in favor of lower prices, higher wages, and larger profits.

Even more common than contradictions are flaws in reasoning, and the use of propaganda tricks. Advanced high school students may be taught to identify fallacies and tricks like these:

1. Begging and ignoring the question: talking about a related subject instead of the point at issue; talking about a person's strong or weak points instead of the facts or ideas actually involved; arguing in a circle (e.g., "The Koran is the word of God. We know that, because it says so, and the word of God cannot lie."); appealing to the emotions instead of to reason; stating as a fact something that remains to be proved
2. False analogy: inadequate resemblance between the two things being compared
3. Hasty generalization: drawing a conclusion from too few examples
4. Faulty dilemma: submitting only two choices when more actually exist
5. *Post hoc, ergo propter hoc:* (after this, therefore because of this) assuming that, because one thing follows another in time, the later is based on the earlier (e.g., since the French Revolution was later

than the one in America, the French people were necessarily inspired by the Americans)

6. Hidden major premise: failure to state the generalization upon which a conclusion is based (e.g., "Giuseppe sings well because he is an Italian" has the hidden premise that all Italians sing well)

7. Incompetent authority: using the opinion of someone who is not an expert in the field being discussed (e.g., "_____ _____ the movie star believes that we should declare war at once")

The purpose of keeping students alert for flaws in reasoning is not, of course, to make them hypercritical of one another. Rather, it is to help them as speakers to reason logically, and as listeners to be aware of the types of faulty reasoning against which they should be on guard.

Bringing in One's Own Knowledge. To listen creatively, one must relate what one hears to what one already knows. That means that one should classify it, compare it with related information or ideas, reject it if it seems worthless or false, and keep it if it appears valuable and true. The person with a well-ordered mind apparently files away his information so that whatever he wants can be quickly found. If, for instance, he learns that Venezuela produces much petroleum, he tucks that fact away snugly with what he already knows about Venezuela and about petroleum production. Sometime he will receive a stimulus that will call for this particular bit of information; he will then open the mental file, and there it will be. From another part of the file he may draw another fact; he will put the two together in the form that we call a thought—actually a creative response. In contrast with this possessor of a well-regulated mind is the person with a haphazard mind. He does not regularly relate newly acquired bits of information to anything else; as a result, they drop quickly from memory or else become so badly scattered that they cannot readily be recalled. This person also has a mental filing system, but he files nearly everything under the heading "Miscellaneous."

Teaching students to relate what they learn to what they already know is one of the biggest jobs in education. In a sense it is the topic of most of this book and of hundreds of other educational writings. Here are a few suggestions concerning ways of helping students to mesh the gears between their ears and their brains:

The "post-mortem" is probably the most useful device. A challenging assembly speaker should not be ignored in the English class that follows his appearance. Talk about what he said; question his statements of opinion and possibly his facts; let the class amplify some of his remarks, and seek parallel incidents from life or literature. When a student has made an oral presentation, the same procedure may be followed. The oral work will probably improve when the class knows that more comes from its efforts than a mark in a gradebook; student attention will be heightened; and the processes of thinking will be accelerated.

The search for parallels is particularly stimulating. Suppose that a class has heard a report on James Russell Lowell in which the emphasis was upon his versatility—poet, critic, humorist, essayist, editor, professor, speaker, and international diplomat. Questions like these should be raised: "What other poet was also a humorist?" "An essayist?" "A professor?" "What other writers have held high government positions?" "Who is the most versatile person you have ever heard of?" "What versatile people do you know?" Parallels to almost anything are endless—history does repeat itself infinitely—and recognizing parallels seems to help in the improvement of mental filing systems.

Similar to searching for parallels is supplying examples. The following illustration refers to a printed selection, but the same technique may be used after a talk. Van Loon, in his *Geography*, refers to prehistoric animals that "went about their daily affairs clad in the armor of a medieval knight." What were some of these animals? Other creatures, he says, have gone "into domestic service." For example? Man, van Loon goes on, has taken possession of the earth "by right of his superior brain and by the strength of his foresight and his shot-guns." What has man conquered by his brain? By foresight? By shot-guns? This searching for examples helps students to listen more attentively, to straighten up their mental files, and possibly to include more examples in their own writing.

Three more devices may be mentioned briefly. (1) Supplying contrasts is desirable. Suppose, for instance, that a student has been explaining to a senior class how plays were staged in ancient Greece. Pointing out the contrasts between Greek and modern, or between Greek and Elizabethan, staging will be valuable. (2) Sometimes a statement by a speaker will recall a proverb or a famous quotation. Let the students think of it. (3) When a talk has been about a person—fictional or otherwise—a clever teacher may construct certain hypothetical situations and ask what that person would do in each situation. As illustrations: "What would Hamlet do if an enemy army invaded Denmark?" "What would Wordsworth do if he were living today and were told that he had to spend the rest of his life in New York City?" Questions like these lead students to bring together what they have heard about a person and what they already know about life.

Of all the aspects of creative listening, this relating of the known to the previously unknown is most important. It leads to minds that are awake, to critical response, and to retention of what has been heard.

Evaluation. If a debate like that suggested on page 485 is held, or if political candidates representing diverse points of view may be heard on radio or television, it is useful to have students evaluate the opposing arguments. After listing contrasting arguments in parallel columns, they may see which opinions have been refuted in whole or in part and may then compare the merits of the remaining opinions or arguments. Some students may tend only to count the points on each side, but they can soon be shown that one strong, unanswerable argument may be worth a half-dozen trivial bits of reasoning or evidence.

Often a class will conclude that neither side is right or wrong, but that some compromise is desirable. When the students reach that stage, they have advanced far toward an understanding of one of the principles upon which democracy is based—the principle that alternative or compromise solutions are often the only practicable ones.

"The important part of the listening and reading process is not the tape-recorder type of reception," says Sam Duker, of Brooklyn College. "The real emphasis should be on evaluative and critical listening and reading." [7] Dr. Duker points out that the poor listener is swayed unduly by a speaker's appearance and eloquence. "A person with a pleasing, dynamic, and outgoing personality may not have anything worthwhile to say, while another, who has a jarring personality, which makes it impossible for you to feel any sort of rapport with him, may have a real message for you."

Additional Devices. Guy Wagner [8] lists fourteen suggestions for building good listening habits. Among them: (1) Use the last five minutes of the class hour to review highlights. (2) Give some tests

[7] "Basics in Critical Listening," *English Journal*, LI (Nov., 1962), 565.
[8] *Education*, Nov.–Dec., 1967.

orally. (3) Have students summarize, for students who were absent, what was done in class. (4) Have some writing done from dictation. (5) During a class hour, ask for occasional oral summaries. (6) Use sociodrama to dramatize good and poor listening.

IN FRONT OF THE RADIO OR THE TELEVISION

Educational Programs

Since the early days of radio, many schools have made extensive use of broadcasts. As early as 1923, Haaren High School, in New York, broadcast accountancy lessons; the WLS (Chicago) Little Red Schoolhouse program, which originated in 1924, in a short time had an audience of 27,000 schoolroom users. Through the intervening years many classes have tuned in on radio broadcasts intended specifically for classroom audiences. Educational television stations in many cities now transmit programs, many of them superbly planned and executed, watched by thousands of students and large numbers of interested adults. An airplane once circled over Indiana, beaming television programs into the classrooms of five states. Kinescopes of hundreds of programs are available and can be used as motion pictures would be.

Some educators once worried about the possible spread and influence of educational television, fearing a monolithic educational system in which, for example, every ninth grade English class in the nation would tune in on the same lesson: "A million students on one end of a coaxial cable and Mark Hopkins on the other." Not only would such a system fail to provide for individual differences, but it could also tend toward indoctrination and thought control out of harmony with American ideals of democracy. The role of the teacher would be reduced to policing, supervising written work and physical activities, and giving grades. Fortunately, the likelihood that education will become so monolithic appears slight, but the danger does exist: Arguments on the grounds of economy and effectiveness will perhaps be heard increasingly.

Commercial television is also being used for educational purposes, though few programs suited to those purposes are available during school hours. As for the assignment of evening viewing, a Newtonville, Massachusetts, teacher once summarized the difficulties:

. . . the enrichment provided by television was only sporadic; for adapting night telecasts to the day's recitation presents problems of preparation, content, and scheduling. Because I cannot preview, I am totally dependent on the study guides occasionally provided by a producer or a sponsor. Usually I must devote hours *after* the night telecast to planning classroom follow-up. Nor can I expect from the entertainment provided by commercial television the continuity, repetition, and progression that insure learning. . . . Even the opportunity to extend the viewing experience through reading the play is rare, for textbooks cannot be obtained on short notice. The demands made on our school library are heartening but symptomatic of interests generated and opportunities lost.[9]

As we shall see, commercial television may have its classroom uses, but they are more likely to be incidental than direct.

Teaching Discrimination

Comparatively few teachers ever bothered to teach discrimination in radio listening. If they had, perhaps the public would have clamored enough to effect some improvements. Now comparatively few teachers help students to be discriminating television viewers and writers of convincing letters to sponsors, advertising agencies, and networks. As a result, much of television is still a "wasteland."

Hearing no roaring demands for quality, TV sponsors and producers (with praiseworthy exceptions) have filled the channels with visual adaptations of the same kind of stuff that was accepted on radio, and have added new varieties on the same level of immaturity. Hence the endless retellings of the same tale in the pseudowesterns, the sagas of suds, the annually changing fads for programs about detectives or lawyers or doctors or hillbillies, the often ridiculous audience-participation and quiz shows; hence the depictions of life as it never was nor can be; hence, perhaps worst of all, the shallow stereotypes of characterization.

Teachers are usually inept reformers. They can effect no sudden improvements in TV fare. But, if they can teach what quality is, teach distrust of the tawdry and respect and liking for the meritorious, their students, becoming adults, may join in cries for more significant programs.

Here, sketched very briefly, are a number of devices for helping students toward higher standards for their listening and viewing. Some of these ideas may be combined in an "On the Air" unit, or

[9] Miriam Goldstein, "Humanities Through Television," *English Journal,* XLIX (April, 1960), 250.

some may be used as a change-of-pace activity between units. Probably each school system should agree to pay some systematic attention to TV and radio once in grades seven, eight, or nine, and once again in grades ten, eleven, or twelve, with emphases differing according to the ages of the children.

Analyzing Amount of Time Spent. To help both teacher and class discover how large a share of a 168-hour week is devoted to broadcasts, students and teacher may prepare a simple questionnaire on listening and viewing habits. The number of hours spent each week on different kinds of programs should be included. Students are often impressed when they realize that as much as a seventh or a sixth of the 168 hours may be devoted to broadcasts, as much as a fourth of their waking hours. The questionnaire may be supplemented by another, on the listening time of other members of the family or other adults.

Discussing "Getting Your Time's Worth." A logical follow-up of the questionnaire is a discussion of how large a role broadcasts *should* have in one's life. What does one sacrifice by staying glued to a set? What other activities are worthwhile? Why is time often called man's most priceless possession? What would be a sensible amount of time per week for broadcasts? We often hear about getting our money's worth. How can we decide whether we are getting our time's worth?

Preparing a Class List. Students may be asked to keep up to date a section of the bulletin board called "Worthwhile Programs." The personnel of the responsible committee should change frequently. Students may obtain information about future programs by writing to the networks.

Letter Writing. Individuals and classes may be encouraged to write thoughtful letters to both sponsors and networks. Some of these letters may be critical of programs that seem too shallow, too improbable, too stereotyped. Perhaps more should be letters of reasoned praise for good programs. Dozens of such programs have been taken off the air because the audience response was disappointingly small.

Discussing Changing Tastes. "When I was a child, I spake as a child, I understood as a child, I thought as a child; but when I became a man, I put away childish things." (I Cor. 13:11.) Children are constantly struggling to elude childhood; they look longingly toward adulthood. Discussion of programs they have outgrown may lead toward a desire for still more mature programs.

Reading and Writing Reviews. Some of the best newspapers have excellent review columns (which should be sharply distinguished from mere uncritical puffs.) Weekly news magazines and some other magazines, especially *Saturday Review*, contain columns of penetrating analysis. Some of these reviews will appeal only to your brighter or more mature students, but other students will often enjoy reading someone else's reactions to programs with which they are familiar. A natural sequel to the reading of reviews is the writing of them.

Summarizing Plots. A good exercise in writing and in criticism is to have students summarize, in the fewest words possible, radio or TV dramas. A frequent summary may be: "Good guys beat bad guys." A virtue of this device is that it shows up the monotony of plot of many programs, especially those in a series; "Teen-ager gets into trouble and out," for example, is the plot of an amazingly large number of plays about young people. In contrast, although plots of good plays may be similarly capsuled, these summaries less often are repetitive.

Estimating Probability and Truth to Life. With a little training, students in both junior and senior high school can learn to pick out at least the glaring improbabilities in dramatic broadcasts. For instance, they can realize how unlikely it is that one man can be shot at week after week, year after year, and never suffer more than a flesh wound, or they can decide that sudden and complete reformations are questionable. Conversely, they can learn to recognize and praise those dramas in which the events might actually happen and in which people act like people. Although in their study of literature they need to learn about "the willing suspension of disbelief," and although they need to appreciate fantasy for fantasy's sake, they should come to condemn, more or less vigorously, artistically unwarranted distortions of human portraits and the laws of chance.

Applying Literary Tests. In their study of literature, students acquire at least partial answers to such questions as these: "What are the characteristics of a good story?" "Of a good play?" It is not unfair to apply the same or similar criteria to dramatic broadcasts, even though television drama is showing evidence of becoming a unique genre. A comparison of the techniques used by TV writers

and writers of printed stories or stage plays, with particular attention to the demands made by limitations of time, space, or dramatic
conventions, is useful. In addition, classes may discuss nonliterary
characteristics peculiar to the medium, such as plausibility of the
acting, excellence of the photography, or quality of the direction.

Reading Books on Which Broadcasts Are Based. A comparison
of the book and its dramatization may be fruitful. Lively and informative discussions may result from such questions as these:
"What important episodes or characters were left out?" "Why?"
"What differences in characterization did you notice?" "Why were
these changes probably made?" "What alterations were made in
the arrangement of events?" "Why?" "What depth of meaning did
you observe in the original but not in the dramatization, or vice
versa?" "What other differences did you see?" "Was the ending
the same in both versions?" Sarah Roody has pointed out that some
movie and radio versions of *Pygmalion* end with Eliza Doolittle's
marriage to Henry Higgins, although "Shaw considered that outcome most unlikely and wrote an epilogue for the express purpose
of telling why such a marriage would have failed to attract Eliza
in the first place or to satisfy her in the long run." "Which version,
Shaw's or a later one, is preferable?" "Why?" "How does *My Fair
Lady* (based on *Pygmalion*) end?" "Is this ending satisfactory?"

Showing Kinescope or Film Versions of Good Programs. More
and more good kinescopes and film versions are becoming available
for use in classrooms. Showing these, and discussing what makes
them better than average, is worthwhile.

Writing Radio and Television Plays. Not only does this activity
provide well-motivated writing experience, but also it sharpens critical acumen. As the students try to avoid the weaknesses to which
they have learned to object, they become even more aware of those
weaknesses. And, as they attempt to bring into their plays what
they have learned to approve, they develop a keener appreciation
of the professionals who succeed. Some of their efforts may be to
create original dramas; others may involve the rewriting in play
form of short stories studied in class. Both individual and group
creations are possible. Some of the best work may be presented in
assembly programs or in other classrooms.

Teaching the Power and the Responsibilities of the Mass Media.
When twenty million or more persons watch the same program, the
television writer and producer and sponsor may exert a strong in-

fluence on twenty million minds. The influence may be good or bad. In the control of the unscrupulous, television can contribute toward mental and moral bankruptcy, but fortunately the potential for good is no less. A nation addicted to the mass media must learn to question ceaselessly the integrity of the purveyors. Students in the senior high school can understand and should discuss the implications of the immense power the mass media have placed in the hands of a few hundred or a few thousand people.

Analyzing Speeches. The English Language Arts in the Secondary School says that, in listening to speeches intended to influence thought or to inform,

"Who is speaking?" students learn to ask. "Why? Under what sponsorship?" and "On what authority?" Ability to detect bias in point of view, unsubstantiated generalizations, or inferences inadequately drawn is particularly important in a land where freedom of speech gives equal rights to the informed and to the uninformed, to the straight and to the crooked thinker, to the sincere and to the insincere. Critical examination of what is heard is vital in today's world.[10]

Reporting Events. Students may profitably write or present orally, as if they were newscasters, descriptions of events that they have witnessed in person or on TV. This activity will give a better understanding of the problems real newscasters face.

Discussing Subjects Not Treated or Seldom Treated. Mature classes may find profitable discussion of the fact that the large network shows infrequently treat realistically such topics as race relations, unfair or unethical practices of employers, abuses by labor of its privileges, the fact that the white race is numerically a minority, and the like. "What are the reasons for such omissions?" "Are the omissions defensible?"

Encouraging Variety. Just as some students read only the sports page or the comic page in the daily newspaper, so some stick to the same monotonous radio and TV fare. Encourage them to shop around, to develop varied tastes. To choose the good, they must know both bad and good.

Developing a Class List of Standards. An important goal in any series of activities dealing with the mass media—in fact, *the* goal— is the creation of a set of standards that will guide students in the future. These standards cannot be teacher-prepared or teacher-imposed. They must come from the observations and the discus-

[10] P. 229.

sions of the students themselves. It is good to draw up a list of the major kinds of programs—drama, comedy, speeches, quiz shows, music, and so on—and have the class decide the characteristics of the programs to which they could conscientiously attach the label "Good."

Planning Units. In 1961 the NCTE published *Television and the Teaching of English.* This paperbound book devotes about seventy pages to "The Educational Significance of Television" and about fifty-five pages to "The Classroom Study of Television." Although the examples inevitably became dated very quickly, the basic information and suggestions remain valid. Among the recommendations are some on brief units isolated from the regular curriculum, brief units within the regular curriculum, and an extensive unit. The first kind of unit would make possible a planned discussion of important drama on television, such as a play by Ibsen. Before the production the class discusses topics related to the theme of the play; during the telecast they listen for answers to specific questions; and after the telecast they discuss these questions and others. In a brief unit within the curriculum, the teacher has the class read a play or story to be televised; the students then compare the printed and the televised version. A possibility for an extensive unit is summarized in this way: "An ambitious project for a class would involve the study of television programs as an expression of American life, a study that would extract from television plays, comedies, musicals, and commercials the values that television seems to find inherent in American life."

THE IDEA BOX

How Much Ear-Exercise Do Students Get?

Stanford E. Taylor, in *Listening* (NEA Dept. of Classroom Teachers), says that high school and college students spend nine of each ten class hours in listening, mostly to their teachers. Is the proportion too high?

Techniques That Brought Results

Nettie B. Lewis, in Oklahoma City, brought her class from a listening test percentile rank of 35 in October to 57 in May. She used records, tape recordings, directions to be followed, and sometimes tricky exercises such as "If New York is west of San Francisco, write the word

Chicago on the first line of your paper." "Listen, Please," *Clearing House*, XXX (May, 1956), 535.

A Student Panel

Some teachers use panels in which students discuss the characteristics of good listeners.

Continuing a Story

One student starts an original story and designates a second person to continue the telling. He designates a third, etc. No one may bring in anything that is incompatible with previous statements.

Tuning Out Distraction

A good listener tunes out distractions. You might try playing a rock and roll record while students are asked to listen to a serious presentation.

Recordings

A library of carefully chosen recordings may add to the enjoyment of literature as well as sharpen listening skills. Many excellent recordings are available at reduced prices to members of the NCTE. Numerous commercial companies also sell recordings.

A Plan for Teaching Auding

Don Brown, of Redwood City, California, who prefers the term "auding" to "listening," advocates "speaking and writing assignments based upon auding experiences." For this discussion of the importance and the techniques of teaching auding, see his "Concepts and Practices in Teaching Aural English," *English Journal*, XLV (Dec., 1956), 540. Different plans are described in detail by Gertrude Elliff in "A Direct Approach to the Study of Listening," *English Journal*, XLVI (Jan., 1957), 20; and by Alexander Frazier in "Making the Most of Speaking and Listening Experiences," *English Journal*, (Sept., 1957), 330.

Listening Tests

The Brown-Carlsen *Listening Comprehension Test* (New York: Harcourt Brace Jovanovich, 1953), measures immediate recall, following of directions, recognition of transitions, recognition of word meanings, and lecture comprehension. Educational Testing Service (Princeton,

N.J.) has a newer (1957) listening test measuring plain-sense comprehension, interpretation, and evaluation and application.

A Listening Guide

Joseph Mersand (Bulletin of the NASSP, May 1958) uses prepared guide sheets with a recording of Poe's "Cask of Amontillado." Students answer questions about the time of year, the name of the narrator, the kind of background music, etc.; they also summarize the story in 100 words or write a 50-word opinion.

Educational TV Programs for Your School

Many 16-mm educational TV programs, both films and kinescopes, on literary and other subjects, may be rented at modest rates from various university AV centers.

Pros and Cons of Educational TV

The two strongest arguments in favor of educational TV are that it affords opportunity to expose students to an exceptionally able teacher who has ample time to prepare and that this teacher may employ expensive or difficult-to-obtain teaching aids and materials not available in most classrooms.

Students in Danville, Illinois, High School, however, after a semester of viewing air-borne television, objected on these grounds: can't take notes fast enough; can't ask questions; too easy to daydream; "If your attention wanders a second, you're lost"; no helpful discussion; too much outside reading; vocabulary too large; boring.

Teachers objected on these grounds: format too confining and inflexible; arbitrary time allotment; teacher a mere monitor, relegated to "warming up a TV dinner"; too much emphasis on lecturing, listening, note taking; inadequate provision for individual differences; curriculum, in effect, organized by "outsiders."

Literature Via TV

Bob Donaldson criticizes television teaching of literature on these counts: (1) teaching should involve more than telling; (2) TV does not provide for individual differences; (3) discussion and language practice are not provided by TV; (4) in large TV classes, too little written work can be required; (5) the TV teacher cannot be argued with; (6) TV tends to avoid the controversial; (7) students need to give, not just receive. *Newsletter* (Michigan Council of Teachers of English, April, 1959).

Television Drama

Television plays may provide a wedge for literary study, William R. Martin argues ("Television Drama in the Junior High School," *Speech Teacher*, X [Sept., 1961], 225). Building upon the students' interest in "How does it end?" Mr. Martin would move to discussion of various components of a story and the way they lead to a resolution of the conflict. The discussion may turn to dialog, characterization, and "stage effects," all of which, except possibly the last, are pertinent in consideration of fiction and drama.

TV: A Rung On a Ladder

Build on students' interest in TV plays by taking them a few more steps up the literary ladder, Patrick and Mary Hazard urge ("What's TV Doing to English?" *English Journal*, XLVIII [Oct., 1959], 414). "If TV goes half-cocked on westerns, push Walter Van Tilburg Clark, A. B. Guthrie, and Francis Parkman for all they're worth. Use the unmotivated violence of mysteries and police films to explain the artistic integration of violence in the Greek tragedies, Elizabethans like Shakespeare, and moderns like Tennessee Williams."

How Much Time for TV?

The average American high school senior has watched TV for 15,000 hours and has been in school 10,800 hours, says John M. Culkin, S.J., *Saturday Review* (July 16, 1966). What are the implications for English teachers and for the students' futures? Students with low verbal ability, however, watch much less TV than do the verbally proficient, according to Eugene Best, *New Jersey Education Association Review* (May, 1967). What implications are here?

Does TV Affect Grades?

In Ontario, California, 2,428 seventh and eighth graders' TV-watching habits were studied. Joyce Marion reported in *Journal of Educational Research* (Dec., 1963) that no significant relation exists between amount of time spent watching TV and English grades. Two-fifths of the students said that they did homework while watching TV.

Duologues

We have too many "duologues" in schools, churches, cocktail parties, and the Congress, says philosopher Abraham Kaplan. Duologues are structural exercises in non-listening. "You have to give the other his turn, and you give signals during his turn, like saying 'uh, huh' or laughing at what he says, to show that he is having his turn. You must also refrain from saying anything that really matters to you as a human being, as it would be regarded as an embarrassing intimacy." (Reported in *Time*, Jan., 24, 1969.)

Bridges to Literature Through Listening

In introducing students to "Richard Cory" (a lonely man) Edmund J. Farrell opened with a discussion of loneliness. As a bridge to "To an Athlete Dying Young," he ascertained that his class couldn't recall four All-Americans from four years back. And before going into "The Lottery," he told his students that though all had done well on their last tests, he would let them draw names to see which three students should be given failing grades. ("All hell broke loose.") Many other suggestions on both listening and literature are in "Listen, My Children and You Shall Read," *English Journal*, LV (Jan., 1966)) 39.

Listening and Reading

According to research reports by Sam Duker and by Thomas Devine, there is a high correlation between listening ability and reading ability. Perhaps this implies that improvement in one of these areas may lead to improvement in the other. *Language Arts and Fine Arts, Review of Educational Research* (April, 1964, and April, 1967).

14

Speech in the English Classroom

SPEECH ACTIVITIES FOR THE ENTIRE CLASS

Increased Emphasis on Oral English

The late 1960's and early 1970's saw a new emphasis on oral English in the classrooms. In part this may have been a delayed response to structural grammarians' insistence that spoken language is *the* language, while written language is a derivative from spoken. In part it may have been a result of teachers' and students' frequent dissatisfaction with some of the content and methods in conventional English classes, and consequent search for something new or at least different. The popularity of Marshall McLuhan, who downplayed the importance of the written or printed word, may have been a smaller contributing factor. Probably much more important was the influence of British experimental schools, in which improvisation and dramatization occupied a central role. Thousands of English teachers learned about these schools through reports and demonstrations at conventions and through reading books like John Dixon's *Growth Through English* and other outgrowths of the Dartmouth Conference of 1967. Students in many methods courses learned about the British procedures and carried them into the schools where they obtained their first jobs.

In earlier chapters of this book, particularly those dealing with the teaching of literature and the teaching of composition, we have seen various ways in which oral work may affect the conventional concerns of the English classroom. In this chapter we shall be dealing more with activities of the sort more traditionally labeled "Speech." In schools where all students take Speech courses, not everything described in this chapter need be offered in English courses. But since many schools have no required work at all in Speech, the English Department must take up the slack and incorporate in its program many of the activities described below.

In this section we shall look at activities suited for an entire class. In the second section our concern will be with effecting improvements in the speech of individuals. Nothing will be said about the correction of serious speech defects such as stuttering, because that is in the province of specially trained personnel.

Objectives

The intention in oral English is not to make platform speakers but to develop citizens who can participate satisfactorily in the everyday situations that demand spoken English. These situations may be grouped roughly according to their frequency in adult life, as follows:

Group I, often needed. Conversation, telephoning, making introductions, giving directions, telling stories, reading aloud, informal discussions.

Group II, important but less frequently needed. Interviewing or being interviewed, making announcements, introducing a speaker, giving reports, following parliamentary procedure, defining, taking part in panel discussions.

Group III, possibly important for superior students. Giving book reviews, dramatizing, debating, platform speaking, after-dinner speaking, choral reading, reciting of memorized passages, participation in radio or television programs.

Group IV, needed for professional work. Techniques of salesmanship may serve here as a single example.

All students should be given enough practice to become reasonably proficient in the situations named in Groups I and II. Less emphasis need be placed on Group III, and none at all on Group IV, except when a particular student wants assistance.

Organizing Oral Work

A typical but probably mistaken procedure is to devote each Friday to oral work—talks of various kinds, panel discussions, dramatizations, and the like. The weaknesses of this procedure are that it interrupts whatever the class is doing and that it seems to point to a nonexistent dichotomy between English and oral English. It seems better to allow most oral work to grow naturally out of other class activities and to prepare short concentrated units for those phases that have no particular relationship to the other activities.

From the study of literature and composition arise many opportunities for oral work. Oral reading, class and panel discussions, reports, definitions, giving directions, dramatizations, telling of stories, choral reading, and recitation are natural outgrowths of the "regular" study. A good class discussion is actually a conversation, but diffident students may be given more chance to converse if the class is occasionally divided into small groups, each of which is to talk about one aspect of the work. Telephoning, making introductions, and conversation may well be combined as part of a courtesy unit. Other short units may be devoted to the interview, parliamentary procedure, and additional speech activities that do not grow readily out of the work in literature and written composition.

The Role of the Teacher

To develop students who can speak well, the teacher himself must be a reasonably competent speaker. That does not mean that he should be an orator or a lecturer—few teachers could make a living on the lecture platform—but he should have a satisfactory voice and the ability to express his thoughts clearly and pleasingly. He should occasionally hear recordings of his speech and try to correct whatever deficiencies he discovers.

An occupational hazard of teaching is that it tends to create objectionable speech habits. Three of these are common enough to merit consideration: unnaturally precise enunciation, rising inflection, and a "know-it-all" tone. In the effort to serve as a model and to wean students away from sloppy enunciation, "Cher turn tspell, 'enry," teachers tend to pronounce each syllable with unnecessary distinctness: "It is your turn to spell, Henry." The happy medium is that of a capable radio or TV announcer, who would say something like this: "It's your turn tuh spell, Henry." The excessively correct enunciator tries to give each word its dictionary pronunciation regardless of context; however, in such a sentence as "He said that that was a mistake," the two *that's* should not really be pronounced in the same way. The second fault, that of ending a sentence with a rising inflection, is probably attributable to the fact that teachers ask so many questions that the rising inflection becomes habitual; then, even when they are making a statement, they make it sound interrogative. The third fault, the particularly obnoxious "know-it-all" tone, sometimes develops in the teachers who have taught the same thing in the same way for a half-dozen years; the tone leaves the impression, "I am Sir Oracle; when I ope my lips, let no dog bark." When this tone is used, students are likely to speak with hesitation.

Sir Oracle is unlikely to be a successful teacher, because he unintentionally discourages class participation. It should be the teacher's role to help each student make his best contribution to the class. That means that the teacher must be a leader and a guide, but not a dictator. It means that the class atmosphere must be such that each student knows that what he has to offer will be welcome, that he has a share in making the class a success. A class is like an automobile: The teacher provides both lubrication to reduce friction and water for cooling, but the students supply much of the fuel that results in forward movement.

Some Teaching Techniques

Some techniques that have been employed successfully in teaching each of the oral activities listed on page 502 are the following:

Group I

Conversation. The small-group technique lends itself most readily to conversation, but one warning is in order: Each group should have a fairly definite subject to discuss. Before the first such conversation, there might well be a class discussion of the characteristics of good conversation: alertness of each speaker and listener, tactfulness, courtesy, attempting to make real contributions, avoidance of showing off or talking too much, avoidance of interrupting, the asking of leading questions, and so on.

To illustrate how conversation via the small-group method may grow out of literature, let us assume that a freshman class has read the first twelve chapters of *Treasure Island*. The students may be divided into five or six groups; one group may talk about which character is the most fascinating; another, what it has learned about eighteenth-century customs; another, what sea terms it has added to its vocabularies; another, what its members would have done if they had been in Jim's place in the apple barrel; another, what kinds of treasure hunting are carried on today; and another, the life and customs of buccaneers. The teacher may move from group to group, putting in a word here and there. If teacher and class wish, the results of each conversation may be summarized for the rest of the class by a member of each group.

Some classes may profit from role-playing conversations. A boy, for instance, wants to go to a summer camp, but his parents have some practical objections. Students act out the conversation. A tape recorder plays it back, being stopped at any points where something should be discussed, such as what should have been left unsaid or what added arguments could have been offered or how a statement could have been made more tactfully.

Telephoning. A junior high school class may spend a profitable hour in discussing telephone ethics and courtesy, telephone pests, and the qualities of a pleasing voice, as well as in dramatizing certain familiar instances when the telephone may cause friction within the family. Dramatization of good and bad telephone habits is also helpful.

Making Introductions. Unless he has observed the right people very carefully, the student is likely to have difficulty in introducing one person to another. Class discussion should cover the topics of when introductions are in order, who should be presented to whom, what the acceptable phrases are, what should be included besides the exchange of names, and how introductions should be acknowledged. The discussion should be followed with demonstrations and practice. Groups of three students may work together effectively, taking turns in acting as various imaginary persons both old and young.

Giving Directions. Almost any student can relate instances in which he was given unclear directions concerning the location of the post office or some other place he wanted to find. The reason for the lack of clarity may have been the director's ignorance, inability to visualize, or poor speech habits. Junior high school students, working in small groups, may take turns being complete strangers in town and asking for assistance. Those giving the directions must remember that the "strangers" do not know any of the landmarks and may not even know the points of the compass. Giving directions in a rural area—for instance, how to find a spring or a certain tree—may pose a still more difficult problem.

Telling Stories. Since nearly everyone enjoys stories, it is unfortunate that most persons do not tell them well. There is a tendency to bring in irrelevant statements, add unnecessary *see's* and *you know's*, relate events in illogical order, laugh before the hearers know what is funny, leave out important details, and spoil the climax. The best cure is discussion of the characteristics of effective storytelling, plus plenty of opportunity to practice. A teacher should encourage students to include pointed anecdotes in their reports on authors, to relate to the class stories or parts of stories that they have found interesting, and to bring into class discussion pertinent illustrative stories, funny or otherwise. For years a storytelling unit has been included in many English classes of Pontiac, Michigan, on the ground that the ability to tell stories well is useful in camp life, church schools, law, acting, broadcasting, medicine, teaching, ministry, clerking, and parenthood.

Reading Aloud. In the past few decades many elementary schools have stressed silent reading to the near exclusion of reading aloud, although good modern programs have corrected that tendency. If the secondary schools likewise ignore oral reading, students will receive no assistance in mastering an activity that has at least the following values: meeting the adult needs for reading newspaper items, announcements, letters, reports, and prepared papers; reading to children or others for pleasure; reading in order to increase enjoyment of literature; providing incidental help on speech; and giving opportunity, through reading announcements and the like, to make students feel that they "count."

Often the understanding and appreciation of literature may be improved by oral reading. The teacher will need to help the students improve their phrasing, their emphasis, and their tempo. Some students will need assistance in modulating their voices or adjusting their pauses to reveal the emphasis suggested by the punctuation: the change of pitch for a question, the change of stress for an exclamation, the difference in length of pause for a comma and a period.

The importance of emphasis may be shown by having members of the class pronounce a monosyllable like "Oh," "Yes," or "No," or a sentence like "John didn't say that" to indicate different meanings. By changing the place of emphasis in "John didn't say that," the speaker may indicate (1) that someone else said it, (2) that the speaker is denying that John said it or is astonished that he did, (3) that John implied it even though he didn't say it, or (4) that John said something else. In connection with literature, classes may often discuss how a given speech should be interpreted. Perhaps the most famous example is Lady Macbeth's "We fail" (Act I, scene vii). Does Lady Macbeth say matter-of-factly, "We fail," or does she pause after "We" and say, "fail" in a tone of disbelief, as if failure is impossible?

Tempo likewise should be appropriate. Teacher and class ought to see, for instance, that the movement in humorous selections should be brisk and sometimes even breathless, that the reading of "How They Brought the Good News from Ghent to Aix" or "The Ballad of East and West" should suggest the rapid hoofbeats of the horses, that "Thanatopsis" demands a slow, thoughtful reading.

Oral reading, then, provides much opportunity for developing flexibility—a flexibility that may be carried over into other speech activities. It permits also a study of meaning, and the clarification of meaning through effective use of the voice.

In recent years the use of Readers' Theater (also called Interpreters' Theater or Theater of the Mind) has become increasingly popular, first because it is fun and secondly because it may contribute substantially to improved oral reading. Readers' Theater is a blend of acting, public speaking, critical reaction, and sympathetic sharing. It differs from a play in that the performers do not ordinarily memorize their parts (though they should if possible practice before a performance); it differs also in that the audience through its imagination must furnish the scenery, action, costumes, make-up, and the physical appearance of the characters. Readers' Theater centers attention upon the author's text, which is brought to life by two or more performers who are usually seated behind lecterns (music racks are good), and each of whom may read two or more roles, one of which may be that of narrator. The action happens in the minds of the audience (hence the alternative name Theater of the Mind), although the readers are not necessarily completely invisible and may sometimes move away from their lecterns.

An Illinois teacher, Mrs. Regina Foehr, has described how moving an effective Readers' Theater performance may be. One of the student readers was describing a hole in the back of a cave: "His description and expression were so vivid that members of the class turned around to look toward the back of the room where his eyes were focused. The literature had come alive. Their 'mental image' had made them forget that they were in a classroom and not in a cave at all."

Student-written plays and stories can sometimes be adopted by students for Readers' Theater production in the classroom. Some of the best of these may find wider audiences in other classrooms, at PTA meetings, or in student assemblies.

Choral reading (already discussed in Chapter 7) is often enjoyable. William H. Cullen recommends starting with unsophisticated material like rhythmic folksongs, moving then to poems like Sandburg's "Fog," "Chicago," and "Jazz Fantasia," and on to longer poems like James Weldon Johnson's "God's Trombones." The teacher–director, Cullen stresses, must be uninhibited and must stress student initiative.[1]

Informal Discussions. In school, students need to participate in numerous class discussions; in later life, most of them will take part in business conferences, club and political meetings, and family discussions. The principles underlying good conversation are also basic to these discussions involving larger groups.

A satisfactory discussion requires progress toward a recognized goal and involves contributions of all, or nearly all, the members of of the group. As aimless discussion is of little value, a topic of discussion should usually be phrased as a problem to be solved. Perhaps no unquestionable solution exists, but at least tentative conclusions may often be drawn.

Getting all students to take part is sometimes a problem. However, if the teacher remembers the particular strong points of each student, he may occasionally supply a lead or a question that will bring in some of the silent ones. The attitude that each person has something worthwhile to offer usually brings results, and a few words of praise sometimes can transform a shrinking violet into a rose, or at least into a carnation. Some teachers like to have a discussion topic determined in advance, with each student responsible for preparing and being ready to present three reasons for believing as he does.

---

[1] "The First Thirty Minutes in Choral Reading," *English Journal,* LVII (March, 1968), 395.

Group II

The Interview.   Although most students will take part in only a few interviews during their lifetimes, those few may be of major importance. Their chances of employment in their chosen work will sometimes depend upon the success of one interview. Some colleges also require interviews with their prospective students. Yet many employers and college interviewers complain that young people are often careless in appearance and manners, that they slouch and sprawl, that their answers to questions are delivered in a slovenly fashion, and that they have nothing positive to contribute. These complaints suggest that a valuable project for the junior or senior year is a short study of techniques of the interview, and dramatizations of good and bad techniques. Then the small-group plan can be employed to allow each student practice in interviewing and being interviewed for mythical positions. Students who have had such training, artificial though the situation is, are often loud in its praise.[2]

Making Announcements.   The good announcement is not unlike the lead of a news story, in that it usually answers the questions who, what, where, and when, and sometimes why and how. In school many announcements must be made, and conscientious teachers see to it that each student occasionally has such responsibility. It is desirable to have committees in charge of bulletin boards, the classroom library, special occasions, and the like; with such committees, the need for announcements often appears. Homerooms and assembly programs also frequently necessitate announcements. Since in adult life almost everyone is occasionally expected to announce something to a group, practice in giving announcements based on the "five W's" is desirable.

Introducing a Speaker.   Although opportunities for introducing outside speakers are rather rare, one student may sometimes present another to a school group. The chairman of a discussion panel, for instance, may remind his classmates of some pertinent qualification of the next speaker. Or, in those schools where students sometimes appear before other classes to talk about their specialties, someone, preferably a student, must introduce them.

---

[2] The technique of a quite different kind of interview, that of a speaker or other personage who visits the school, may well be left for the journalism class, since it has value for comparatively few students.

Giving Reports.   Reports in English and other classes are frequent and may be valuable.   Too often, though, a report is dull and
almost worthless because the student chooses too big a subject (e.g.,
The Publishing Business), fails to narrow it, takes notes on only an
encyclopedia article, and for his report simply summarizes what the
encyclopedia says.   Guided, the same student will cut the subject
down to workable size, consult more than one source, and employ
his own plan of organization for the material.

The report subjects should grow from the classwork and not be
chosen merely for the sake of having reports.   Second, students
should usually be given some degree of freedom in choosing the
subjects of their reports, because they are more likely to make interesting whatever they themselves find interesting.   Third, ordinarily
not many reports should be given on the same day.

As an illustration, suppose that a senior class is studying eighteenth-century English literature.   The teacher suggests that certain
reports will enlighten and enliven much of the study.   He invites
the students to be on the alert for subjects that they would like to
investigate, and in addition he lists a rather large number of topics
including such subjects as Whigs vs. Tories, eighteenth-century etiquette or dress or amusements, Fielding's *Tom Jones,* the story of
Johnson's dictionary, etc.   Each student should choose the topic
that interests him most and should talk with the teacher concerning
sources of information and the most appropriate time for his report.
The subject of etiquette should probably be discussed when the
class is reading Addison and Steele, Johnson's dictionary when the
class is reading from the *Rambler* essays, and so on.   In other words,
the reports are interspersed within the rest of the work, and each
student makes his contribution when it is most meaningful.

The principles of organization—chronological, inductive, etc.—
are as important in oral as in written English.   Time should be taken
occasionally to refresh students' memories concerning the possible
types of organization and how to employ them.   The usefulness of
outlines—at least topic outlines—can be more easily demonstrated
for oral work than for written compositions.

Some shy students are extremely hesitant about giving reports;
the thought of standing before the class terrifies them so much that
they will even feign illness to escape.   Sympathy for these students
is better than scorn.   Also, a gradual building up to reports is better

than a sudden assignment. If a teacher is aware that some students are excessively shy, he may first encourage participation while the students are seated, later have them place written work on the board and explain it, and then allow them to use notes freely in their reports. A friendly, cooperative atmosphere within the classroom is desirable and may be encouraged by the teacher's frequent praise of the student audience.

One teacher anticipates the most common troubles in oral reports by dramatizing the types of difficulties. She herself, before students have given any reports, presents a little talk as it would be given by a "mouse," a bashful boy, Miss And-uh, Mr. Bored Sophisticate, Mr. Unprepared, Miss Phonograph, and finally, Mr. Average Student, whose tone is pleasant and enthusiastic.

Sometimes the teacher may remark that he himself has had to overcome stage fright, and may refer to famous stage actors and actresses who feel frightened or even nauseated before each performance (including the great Ethel Barrymore).

In evaluating reports, as John B. Newman advises,[3] teachers should not overemphasize mechanics of delivery. Newman says that content, semantics, and general effectiveness are all more important than mechanics.

Following Parliamentary Procedure. Since parliamentary procedure is of marked importance in our life (business, church, and club meetings, as well as local, state, and federal government), students should become familiar with the order of business and should be able to trace a motion, with amendments, from origin to disposal. In addition, they should know such technicalities as the procedure in electing officers, the method of addressing the chair, and the order of precedence of motions.

Class following of parliamentary procedure, however, need not be mere routine. In some classes, discussion of controversial issues is a more or less regular practice. A chairman and a secretary are elected, the topic is explained and then discussed, and the opposing points of view are summarized at the end of the hour. Students must be recognized by the chair before speaking. Discussion must be kept free of personalities. Courtesy should be the rule, with frequent use of such remarks as "Mr. Chairman, I believe that Jim

[3] *Speech Teacher,* March, 1967.

is partly right, but I should like to disagree with one statement." Opinion should be supported by as much factual evidence as is available.

A value inherent in such a plan of discussion is that it helps students to think about issues of importance to them. It is important for all students to develop the ability:

1. To employ a reflective and analytical technique rather than the argumentative technique in approach to controversial problems.
2. To display competence in, and inclination toward, defining key words and phrases used in discussion.
3. To display competence in reinforcing general or abstract concepts with appropriate concrete details.
4. To master and to apply the principle that the truth of a solution depends upon the degree to which it corresponds with the basic assumptions.

The types of subjects that may be considered in parliamentary discussions vary widely. Some teachers prefer national and international issues. Others advocate consideration of problems nearer the students: home difficulties, cheating, athletics, courtesy, movies, etc. Community issues (generally non-political ones) may be discussed; class consideration of such an issue as school-district reorganization has even been known to affect a community's decision on an important problem. It would seem advisable to begin with subjects in which students have an immediate personal interest and gradually to branch out into topics with wider implications.

Defining. Perhaps defining should not be listed as a special speech activity, since it is needed frequently in reports and discussions, but it provides enough pitfalls to seem to require separate treatment. Much disagreement or confusion may be avoided if terms are carefully defined. Therefore, when Ray is talking about a "good football team," he should be expected to define "good"; when Katherine is talking about the education of Indians, both "education" and "Indians" need definition; when any student uses a technical term that may be unfamiliar to the class, he should pause to explain it.

Every good definition, students should learn, does two things: it places the thing being defined in a general category and then distinguishes that thing from others in the same category. For instance, if one is defining *psychiatry*, he says first that it is a science (the general category); then he distinguishes it from other sciences by saying that it involves the treatment of mental diseases.

Panel Discussions. In many ways the panel discussion is preferable to debate. It is less formal and more natural; it permits audience participation; and, as has often been said, unlike debate it searches for truth rather than victory.

Careful preparation is essential to success in panel discussion. Students must be familiarized with the usual pattern: opening remarks by the chairman; introduction of speakers; rather formal presentation of differing points of view by members of the panel; informal exchange of comments, additions, and rebuttals; and audience participation. (There are, of course, many possible variations of this pattern; in a less formal panel, there may be no set order for the speakers.) If the topic is a controversial one, care must be taken to have approximately an equal number of speakers for each side. The members of the panel must know exactly what issue or issues are involved, and who is to present which points of view. Material must be sought and organized as carefully as it would be for a debate.

Loren Reid suggests an ingenious method of appraising individuals' contributions to discussions of almost any type. He suggests that the teacher mark a tally each time a student speaks, even only a sentence or two. A *plus* indicates a helpful contribution, a *zero* a neutral one, and a *minus* a contribution that is "digressing, sidetracking, blocking or overly-aggressive." Thus, some students may be marked like this:

Crews 0++0000000000
Goold ++++
Mutti 00-0-00-0-0
Page 0000+0 [4]

It should be useful, too, for students to employ this device occasionally in evaluating their classmates' contributions: It should lead to good listening and to critical thinking.

Group III

The types of speaking listed under Group III—book reviews, dramatizing, debating, platform speaking, after-dinner speaking,

[4] *Teaching Speech* (Columbia, Mo.: Artcraft Press, 1960), p. 188.

choral reading, reciting of memorized passages, and participation in radio programs—are of varying value as class activities. Dramatization and choral reading have considerable worth in aiding literary appreciation and, therefore, deserve class time; book reviewing (which is not necessarily the same as book reporting) may likewise possess merit for some students. It is doubtful, though, that class hours, limited as they are, should be spent on debating, after-dinner speaking, and principles of microphone technique.[5] The old practice of reciting long memorized passages—to which the rest of the class paid scant attention—was wasteful of time.

In general, the activities in Group III demand little class attention, except where dramatizing and choral reading seem advisable.

Group IV

Teaching the types of speaking needed for professional work is primarily the responsibility of the college, not of the high school. The foundations for a salesman's speaking habits, a minister's speaking habits, and so on, are laid in the elementary and secondary schools, but detailed work is possible only on a more specialized level.

THE IMPROVEMENT OF THE INDIVIDUAL'S SPEECH

The class activities that have been described should lead to improvement of speech habits by giving class members practice in numerous situations requiring speech. But there is still something more that the teacher can do to help individuals better their oral English. This is remedial and developmental work aimed at reduction or elimination of faults in speech.

It must be stressed that the teacher who is not a trained speech correctionist should never try to remedy faults that may be organic. Some persons have serious nervous maladjustments or malformed speech organs; for anyone but a specialist to attempt to apply treatment for these persons may be dangerous.

The majority of students, however, have speech defects that can be corrected by the non-specialist. Some of these flaws appear in what is said; others, in how it is said.

[5] Radio or TV work, of course, does have value if a class is fortunate enough to be granted air time occasionally. Also, a class may sometimes happily prepare a radio script and present it over a public-address system or closed-circuit TV—or even with just a dummy microphone.

Improving Content and Organization

In most speech activities, class and teacher should focus attention upon what is said. The delivery is, after all, only the vehicle for conveying thought; the thought itself is the important thing.

In class discussions the teacher may do much to encourage attention to facts. When George glibly condemns Congress as incompetent, he should be pinned down to specific accusations and asked for definite evidence to prove his statements. When Margaret says, "All French people are frivolous. I knew a French girl and she . . . ," there is the opportunity to demonstrate that an assuredly valid conclusion cannot be drawn from only one or two instances. When Clarence, whose family has voted Republican for seventy-five years, remarks bitterly that wars usually start during Democratic administrations, he not only is revealing personal prejudice but also is guilty of *post hoc, ergo propter hoc.* Whenever a student shifts from issues to personalities (a favorite trick of politicians), he is ignoring the question. Louise's remark, "Everybody's wearing whozits now, so we ought to get some," has the hidden premise that we should do what "everybody" is doing. Examples could be multiplied, but the point is simply that the teacher should be constantly alert for weaknesses in reasoning and lack of evidence; he should encourage the class to challenge demonstrable fallacies. The intent is not to make a class argumentative but, rather, to make it a mentally awake one that thinks about what it hears.

The teacher should also remove some of the snags of content and organization before the students come to them. Unaided, most students will find little material for reports and discussions, and will not organize what they do find. With the teacher's help, however, they will uncover information in addition to that offered by the old stand-by, the encyclopedia. They will see how examples add to the interest and clarity. The teacher also is responsible for showing the students how they can apply to their more formal talks the principles of organization they use in written composition. For a report, they learn, a good plan is to have an interest-rousing opening, a body with not more than four well-illustrated main points (the most important usually last), and an ending that summarizes or restates in memorable fashion what has previously been said.

On the matter of permitting notes for rather long presentations, opinions differ. Students seem usually to do their best work if they are allowed to have notes on small cards—notes that will remind them of the steps in their talks. These notes should consist only of words or phrases, not complete sentences, because students tend merely to read anything written in sentence form. The little cards provide comfort, if nothing else; the students know that they cannot become completely lost when they have a few scribblings to which they may refer. There is nothing disgraceful about consulting notes; college professors who have given the same lecture a dozen or more times make extensive use of them. And one cannot help wondering how a teacher can conscientiously forbid his students to use any notes when he himself refers frequently to a bundle of cards as he addresses the PTA.

In the follow-up after rather formal work in oral English, most of the remarks should concern the content and organization. Although the class must be kept constantly aware of the importance of good enunciation, accepted pronunciation, and so on, the comments should be more meaningful man "He said 'and uh'" or "He mispronounced 'Italian.'" Judicious praise of what was said is superior to random criticism of the method of saying it. Additions to the content are in order, as are questions addressed to the speaker to elicit further information. Sometimes the teacher may speak favorably of the careful way in which Sally or Pete organized a presentation, or may pause to comment approvingly on an especially happy illustration. Adverse criticisms should, as a rule, be given following a number of presentations, and ought to refer to weaknesses observed in several of the talks. If one of the speakers has a unique fault in content or organization, it may be mentioned to him in privacy, unless some of the questions and comments bring it out incidentally.

Improving Vocal Quality

Almost certainly among your students there will be a fairly large number whose vocal quality is poor. The three defects you will find are throatiness, thinness, and either nasality of denasality.

The throaty voice is unpleasantly deep and husky; the sound seems lost in the throat or even in the chest. The prevalence of throatiness, which results in making words hard to understand, accounts in large part for the fact that "Whadja say?" is the sentence most frequently spoken in the United States.[6]

Exercises in throat relaxation and in clear articulation may be recommended to throaty-voiced students. If several in one class have the same handicap, they may perform some of the exercises as a group, while other groups are working on faulty pronunciation or on overcoming other defects. A good exercise for throat relaxation is to sit upright, drop the head forward until the chin touches the chest, turn the head slowly to the right until the chin touches the right shoulder, then turn to the left, and repeat several times. Another is to take an imaginary drink of water and say "Oh" as the throat is open, a second drink and "Ah," and other imaginary drinks for the other vowel sounds. Still another exercise is to open the jaws wide and say the vowel sounds, to be followed later by words in which each vowel sound appears.

In all such exercises, it is perhaps needless to say, no individual should be made to feel ashamed or self-conscious. A teacher sometimes has an entire class perform certain exercises when he knows that only two or three students need them. The small-group plan, though, with each group working on something that it needs, is less wasteful of time.

The thin voice lacks resonance, is usually high in pitch, and sometimes degenerates into an unpleasant whine. Humming is often mentioned to students as a means of increasing resonance. Long practice in sustaining the *m*, *n*, and *ng* sounds is also beneficial; these sounds may later be combined with vowels, as *am*, *em*, etc., and, still later, sentences with many *m's*, *n's* and *ng's* may be used.

Only the sounds of *m*, *n*, and *ng* should be allowed to pass through the nose. If any others do so, speech is described as nasal. The reverse of nasality, called denasality, occurs when the sounds of *m*, *n*, and *ng* do not pass through the nose. A speaker then sounds as if he has a cold; he says "ted tidy Idiads" instead of "ten tiny Indians."

A student may test his nasality by placing his finger beside his nose as, with his mouth open, he prolongs the sounds of *m*, *n*, and *ng*, and then of other consonants and the vowels. If he can feel

[6] Some years ago researchers for Funk and Wagnalls made this interesting but disconcerting discovery.

distinct vibration for the *m, n,* and *ng* sounds, and not for the others, his nasal resonance is normal. If, however, he feels much vibration when he pronounces vowels, he should practice making the sound issue from his mouth instead of his nose; unless there is something organically wrong, he should be able to overcome his difficulty. Denasality, though, is often due to stoppages and perhaps can be corrected only by a speech pathologist.

Improving Pitch

Most persons are unaware of their own vocal shortcomings, because they have never actually heard themselves speak. If your school has a tape recorder, let each of your students hear himself. More than likely he will say, or at least think, "Do I really sound that bad?"

One of the causes of "sounding that bad" is defective pitch. Very high-pitched voices are offensive, and very low-pitched ones are often monotonous. Frequently the only step needed for a cure is a conscious attempt to vary the pitch—for the low-pitched near-monotone to reach toward higher levels and for the person with high pitch to try to bring the voice down. The vocal apparatus in most persons can be used flexibly if it is given a chance, but nearly everyone tends to use it in the easiest way, regardless of whether that way is pleasant to his hearers. Throat-relaxation exercises, like those described on page 517, are helpful, but primarily the treatment for most students is simply to make them aware of the deficiency and to suggest reasons for doing something about it.

Improving Enunciation

Americans are breath-lazy, throat-lazy, jaw-lazy, tongue-lazy, and lip-lazy. As George Arliss declared, the chief defect of British speech is snippiness, and the chief defect of American speech is sloppiness. As a result of our lazy habits, we say "Uh dunno," "Whurya gawn?" "Whuh timezut?" etc. Although overprecise articulation seems affected, there is a happy medium in enunciation as in all things else.

Unless there is something wrong physiologically, anyone can improve his enunciation if he wishes. That fact implies that the teacher, or someone else, must supply motivation if enunciation is to be improved. One clever but possibly not very humane teacher told her class that she was going to read to them the questions that would be asked on the examination the next day, but that she would read as she had heard some of them talk. She proceeded to mumble through the questions so that only a word here and there was distinct. Most of the students understood what she was trying to do! Other teachers have had their students note the enunciation of favorite TV stars and movie actors, and a few have skillfully led students to a realization that recognized leaders in almost all spheres of activity enunciate clearly. Still other teachers have used friendly ridicule—not of individual students but of people who habitually sound as if their mouths are filled with mush.

Poor enunciators tend to mumble, to insert extra syllables into words, or to omit syllables. The mumblers habitually speak indistinctly. Mouthers say, "abaout" for "about," "baud" for "bad." The omitters tend to ignore middle syllables: "telscope" for "telescope," "connent" for "continent." All three defects, unless they are cured early, seem to increase with age. So, if you can motivate your students to struggle effectually against them, you can save many people hundreds of hours of unpleasant listening.

Improving Pronunciation

It is not a criminal offense to mispronounce a word; in fact, if one could go back far enough into the past, one might find a time with the mispronunciation regarded as correct. Pronunciations do change; Alexander Pope and his contemporaries, for instance, said "tay" for "tea" and "jine" for "join."

Right there is your entering wedge for correcting errors in pronunciation. Your students are modern—aggressively so. They want to do almost everything the way it is done today—none of this old-fashioned stuff for them. Encourage them to be as modern in their pronunciations as they are in their clothes or their music. Certainly, Grandpa said "crick," but we say "creek" today; Mark Twain's friends said, "genuwine," but we don't.

Let them know, too, how dictionary makers determine what is correct pronunciation. The diacritical marks do not reflect someone's opinion; rather, they are determined by a careful study of how each word is pronounced by the majority of the educated people who use it. When one keeps up with the dictionary, one is keeping up with the Joneses—as well as with the Smiths and the Smythes.

If you use pronunciation drills, be sure to concentrate on words that you have heard your students mispronounce. Such drills are usually better than stopping each student whenever he mispronounces a word; you should make a mental note of his error and include the word later in a list. Thus, you will save yourself the fate of the wife who always corrected her husband's mistakes:

> I whammed her on the cerebellum
> Her beating brain to overwhelm;
> I hung her body on an elm—
> And as she died, she whispered, "Elm." [7]

You will also save your students from embarrassment and dislike of speaking. Your list will probably consist mostly of common words: *asked, column, February, government, get, idea, just, library,* and so on.

Some teachers devote two or three minutes per class hour on pronunciation demons. For instance, the class each day for a week may pronounce the same five or ten words, printed on large cards. New cards are introduced the following week, with some of the older ones brought back for review.

A less time-devouring method is to have daily class drills on 10 words, changed each day for 20 days, with occasional reviews. Then comes a test in which each student is given, entirely at random, 10 of the 200 words. He gets 100 per cent if he pronounces all 10 correctly, barely passing if he misses 1, and zero if he misses 2 or more. The weakness of this plan is its excessive emphasis on grades.

One caution: Be sure that the pronunciations you attack are actually unaccepted. Some teachers have been surprised to learn that their favorite pronunciations of such words as *bouquet, gratis, isolated, menu,* and *panorama* are not the only ones listed in reputable dictionaries. Some dictionaries list Feb-yoo-ary, li-ber-y, and guver-ment as accepted alternatives.

Improving Body Control

Bernard shuffles up to the front of the class, glances in final desperation at the teacher, sways a little, puts both feet close together and sways some more, fidgets with his hands, and focuses

---

[7] By Morris Bishop, quoted in *Word Study,* April, 1943.

his gaze on his toes as he begins to mumble at the floor. Bernard, with numerous variations, is in almost all classes. What can be done for him and his sister?

The importance of having a friendly class atmosphere has already been emphasized. That in itself will help Bernard and Bernardine, will give them confidence that their efforts will be received cordially, will contribute to the knowledge that they are before the class because they have something to offer and not because teacher wants to criticize them. But there is something more that the teacher can do, something too rarely done in English classes. The teacher can give all the students practice in walking, in pantomiming, and in using the hands.

Here is how one teacher accomplishes this. In connection with vocabulary work, she and the class list as many synonyms as possible for *say* and *walk*. The ostensible purpose is to add words like *orate* and *saunter* to students' vocabularies. Then she asks for volunteers to act out some of the words in front of the class: Doris shouts, Jimmy strolls, and so forth. When the volunteers have performed, words are still left; the teacher asks the non-volunteers, in pairs, to act out some of the words in order to demonstrate the contrast: Bernard skips while Roy totters. Having the shy ones work in pairs makes each less self-conscious.

Then, when all the words have been pantomimed, the teacher temporarily abandons vocabulary work and casually inquires what are the characteristics of an attractive style of walking. "How do movie stars usually walk?" Gradually she elicits the information that graceful walkers carry the weight on the balls of the feet, keep the abdomen flat, have the shoulders relaxed, and lead with the chest. She emphasizes leading with the chest, because that is perhaps the most important essential. "Let's try it," she says to the class. "We'll have a little parade around the room, with everybody walking the way we have described. Bernard, you lead, and we'll all fall in behind you." Later, she frequently reminds the class of the principles of graceful walking, asks for more illustrations, and tactfully suggests that it is worth their while to walk well, in class and out.

She makes more use of pantomime on other occasions. (The British often do so, frequently having groups pantomime simple everyday acts such as brushing the teeth, applying make-up, or making tea. They sometimes also incorporate dance routines into classwork, on the theory that dance is itself a form of expression and that anything that helps to liberate the body can aid in communication.) She also has her students make many explanations at the blackboard and give a chalk talk now and then. In the students' minds, the purpose is only to explain something to the class, but the teacher knows that, when people use their hands in public, they think less about them.

This teacher says little about gestures, because she believes that no gesture is worthwhile unless it is a natural accompaniment of the thought; the patterned arm-waving of the elocutionists she deplores. She says more about looking at the audience, and herself puts on a little act in which she alternately addresses the floor, the ceiling, the window, the door, and the portrait of Longfellow.

Perhaps the methods of this teacher seem too unorthodox to you. However, they do get results—her students appear more happy and cooperative and less self-conscious than those of dozens of other teachers.

"Trippingly on the Tongue"

You recall Hamlet's famous advice:

Speak the speech, I pray you, as I pronounced it to you, trippingly on the tongue; but if you mouth it, as many of your players do, I had as lief the town-crier spoke my lines.

We teachers may not succeed in getting all our students to speak as well as Hamlet advised, but we should, in the years that we teach them, be able to help them to find something worth saying, plan how to say it, and say it reasonably well.

Speech is but the incorporation of thought.—JOSEPH JOUBERT

Let him be sure to leave other men their turn to speak.—FRANCIS BACON

As a vessel is known by the sound, whether it be cracked or not, so men are proved, by their speeches, whether they be wise or foolish.— DEMOSTHENES

The voice is a human sound which nothing inanimate can perfectly imitate. It has an authority and an insinuating property which writing lacks. It is not merely so much air, but air modulated and impregnated with life—JOSEPH JOUBERT

THE IDEA BOX

Guiding Class Discussions

Examples of remarks that can improve discussions:

1. "What evidence is there for this belief?"
2. "This digression has been interesting, but let's get back on the subject."
3. "Should we bring out the facts before we attempt a solution?"
4. "Is it true that so far we have agreed on these points . . . ?"
5. "Let's hear now from those who haven't said anything."
6. "Could it be that we are letting personal prejudices sway us too much?"
7. "I don't understand. Can you think of an example?"
8. "Is a middle-of-the-road position more sensible than either extreme?"
9. "Can anyone think of circumstances in which this suggestion would not work?"

A Tip to a Discussion Leader

A simple but effective opening for a youthful discussion leader is to ask, "Do all of you agree with George (or Lucille)?"

Woodrow Wilson on Eloquence

"Eloquence lies in the mind, not in the throat."

"Effective Speaking in the Classroom"

John J. Chalmers, a Canadian, uses an "Oral Report Score Sheet," with point allocations for Voice, Physical, Organization, Language, Manner, Speech value, and Effectiveness. The scale for each part is 15, 12, 9, 6, or 3, except for Physical, where it is 10, 8, 6, 4, or 2. *English Journal*, LVI (Dec., 1967).

"Small-Group Training and the English Classroom"

For an introduction to group dynamics (it's "back again") and specific suggestions for small-group responsibilities and tactics, see David M. Litsey's article, *English Journal*, LVIII (Sept., 1969), 920.

"Dramatic Improvisation: Path to Discovery"

Today, spurred by British schools, many American teachers are experimenting with improvised classroom drama. Marianne P. Simon and

Sidney B. Simon offer specific suggestions. *English Journal*, LIV (April, 1965), 323.

"Creative Dramatics and the Slow Learner"

George E. Keyes tells how his very slow students profited first from simple pantomimes and then by creating their own dramatic version of "The Pied Piper." *English Journal*, LIV (Feb., 1965), 81.

Videotaped Speeches

Students' prepared speeches may be videotaped. Each student then watches himself on the screen and determines ways in which he would like to improve.

"A Proposal for Improving Class Discussions"

Joseph P. Fotos has a student keep a daily chart showing the number of times each student contributes to discussion; he emphasizes strongly the importance of such contributions, stressing quantity more than rightness or wrongness. *English Journal*, LVII (Oct., 1968), 1036.

More Imaginative Choral Reading

At Macalester College, Mary Gwen Owens' students serve as directors of choral reading. The groups make their own selections and arrangements, and sometimes use music or props for special effects—even doing some square dancing at times. Marilyn E. Stassen, "Choral Reading and the English Teacher," *English Journal*, LVIII (March, 1969), 436.

Overcoming Speech Fright

A survey reported by Charles Gruner in *Speech Teacher* (Sept., 1964) shows that 101 of 121 students said that practice is the best way to overcome speech fright; 75 said that increased understanding of speech techniques helps; and 62 said that attitudes of the teacher and classmates are determining factors; better understanding of self was named by 53, and understanding the nature and cause of speech fright was cited by 52.

Impromptu Speeches

Students (slow junior high) draw a topic from a box, take a minute or two to think, and then talk briefly on it. Representative topics: "Nothing turns me on like . . . ," "It burns me up when . . . ," "How to lose friends . . . ," "The part of the dress code that I most dislike is. . . ."

Speech As Preparation for Writing

Elkhart, Ind., students who took a speech and literature course did as well or better in a later writing course in comparison with students who took a conventional course in composition, grammar, and literature. So G. L. Wenger and A. L. Schilling report in *The Speech Teacher* (March, 1965).

"A Speaking Approach to Composition"

A student gives the teacher a written thesis sentence for his talk. When he finishes, each classmate writes what he thinks this sentence is—or should be. Discussion follows. Good practice in listening, and useful for providing focus in written composition, too says R. W. Higbee, *English Journal*, LIII (Jan., 1964), 50.

Correlating Speech and Literature

Before studying short stories, students may relate anecdotes and expand upon them; later, stories may be read interpretively. Before studying essays, students may give informal talks on essay-like topics. Before studying lyric poetry, they may discuss and illustrate an emotion that poets often treat, such as feelings about death; later, they may interpret. And drama, of course, should be performed. These are among the suggestions by William J. Reynolds, "Let's Talk Speech," *English Journal*, LVII (Jan., 1968), 105.

Combating Stage Fright: More Suggestions

1. Advise fearful students to start a talk with something funny. Doing so may relax them and the audience too.

2. Help students select topics that they are genuinely interested in, even concerned about. Thinking about the subject will leave less time to think about the self.

3. Advise rehearsing the talk but not memorizing it. Fear of forgetting contributes to fright.

Overcoming Shyness

1. "A good device for overcoming initial reticence is to introduce a subject which contains much controversial matter. As soon as the teacher sees that the subject matter has caught the fancy of the class,

he allows students to select a chairman and plan their own talks." (Arigo La Tanzi, Braintree, Mass.)

2. Another teacher begins by having students make an announcement of a real or imaginary event, including time, place, purpose, cost, and any other needed information. Generally, the more imaginary the event, the livelier the announcement. Second step: a prepared (but not memorized) three-minute oral reading of anything the student likes.

3. A useful device for overcoming shyness and teaching thinking on one's feet is a modification of the old *commedia dell'arte*. The teacher or a student briefly summarizes a simple story with few characters. Students then act it out, improvising the dialog. Once the students have become accustomed to making it up as they go along, they may be given a story with the ending omitted; the actors must then work out a reasonable solution by themselves *while* they are acting.

Getting Them All to Talk

Donald W. Hensel, Boulder, Colorado, pits class against class in a "discussion race." He has a student note the percentage who contribute to class discussion and announces it to the next class, who try to exceed it. Students urge their fellows to "Say *something*." The shy gradually become less shy, and slowly the quality of discussion also improves because of the general participation. (Probably not a useful device for more than a few weeks.)

The Speech Consultant

West Canada Valley High School, Middleville, N.Y., employs for eighty half-days a year a speech consultant from a nearby college. He has worked out a specific schedule of speech teaching and gives instruction beyond the scope of most English teachers. For details, see "The Speech Consultant Teaches Speech in the English Classroom," *English Record*, XIII, No. 2 (1962), 30.

A Simple Speech Plan

In an extraordinarily compact but specific article, "Let Any Student Speak" (*Illinois English Bulletin*, Feb., 1961), Wilmer Lamar describes a highly successful program for teaching speech in the English classroom. One of the many techniques suggested is the following of a simple outline, especially useful for inexperienced teachers. The five divisions of a speech are (1) awakener (question, striking statement, narration, arousing of suspense, quotation, personal incident), (2) point (statement of what the speaker is driving at), (3) reason (why the point is important), (4) examples (the body of the talk), (5) conclusion (restatement, quotation, relevant question, or call to action).

Measuring Change of Opinion

Before an argumentative or persuasive presentation or discussion, ask class members to indicate on slips of paper whether they favor or oppose the proposition or are undecided. After the presentation, have them indicate "more strongly favor," "favor to about same degree," "more strongly oppose," "oppose to about same degree," "still undecided," "shifted from favor to undecided," "shifted from oppose to undecided," etc. Have a pair of students tally the number and direction of opinion shifts.

Audio-Visual Aids and Demonstrations

Encourage use of maps, charts, pictures, diagrams, and the like in talks and reports. These may be especially useful in how-it-works or how-to-do-it explanations.

Demonstrations, with actual objects, may help shy students forget themselves. For example, a basic dance step, artificial respiration, tuning a musical instrument.

Brainstorming

As a problem-solving technique (to be used only in the face of a *genuine* problem) try a brief brainstorming session. The rules: (1) Allow no adverse criticism, even if a suggestion seems utterly ridiculous. (2) Welcome imaginative ideas. (3) Try for many and diverse ideas. (4) Combine and improve ideas (called "hitchhiking").

A recorder notes all suggestions. A day later, the group appraises the ideas to see whether any of them or any combination of them may afford a solution.

Student Responsibility

Let students conduct bees, vocabulary tests, and dictations, and carry messages, make announcements, etc. Put poor speakers in the back of the room so that they have to speak distinctly to be heard.

Planning To Do Things

In a class that really does things—dramatizes, takes field trips, interviews, etc.—discussions involving the planning for these things are usually lively.

Improving Reports

A West Virginia ninth grade class taught by Anna Brochick made these decisions about ways to improve its reports: (1) Every oral report must show that the reporter "went out of his way" to make it good. (2) The beginning and ending should show some originality. (3) The reporter must try to use acceptable speech. (4) Material should be well organized. (5) The reporter should try to make himself easily heard. (6) Each report should be subject to group evaluation and to evaluation by the reporter.

Oral English in Community Affairs

The Speech Department of Reno, Nevada, recommends: "The speech program can help to promote community affairs such as Red Cross and Community Chest campaigns. Student participants become more civic conscious. Presenting such programs before adults makes for excellent public relations because the citizens of the community have an opportunity to see one thing that the schools are doing." This department also recommends inviting guests to class periods when there are special oral presentations.

Speaker's Bureau

In Roosevelt High School, Chicago, a "Speaker's Bureau," with a faculty sponsor, is in charge of publicizing school activities. Members make announcements in homerooms, etc., and sometimes are sent to speak before civic organizations such as Kiwanis, Union League Club, etc. (Lynne Harford)

Oral English in Vocational Guidance

Students may write to trade schools or colleges in which they are interested. Then, in class, they present prepared talks on entrance requirements, courses and training offered, social life, and rating.

Breathing

"To obtain clear, distinct speech, the most valuable technique is the regular practice of diaphragmatic breathing and vowel sounding in class, in chorus. This need only be done enough to educate pupils to the idea that speech is always more clear and forceful when supported by well-controlled breath." (John Ferrett, Braintree, Mass.)

Tongue Twisters with a Purpose

Many students who are slovenly in enunciation do not distinguish clearly between the voiceless and voiced consonants: *f* and *v, t* and *d, p* and *b, k* and *g, s* and *z, ch* and *j, sh* and *zh, th* as in *thin* and *th* as in *this*. Tongue twisters, written by teacher or students, will help. Examples from *Better English* (published by Ginn & Co., Boston, 1959):

Face the fancy vase and find the fine vine, Vinnie.
Mat's satin hat had saddened Dad, hadn't it?
Proud papa babbled, played, bubbled, clapped, and boasted.
Come goat, come goat, come goat, come goat, come goat!
Chug-chug-jug-jug-chug-jug-chuck-chuck-junk-chuck-junk-junk-chunk-chuck.
Big black pigs bickered blatantly by papa's big pig pen, Ben.

Using "Weeks"

"Book Week," "Good Manners Week," etc., often supply excellent motivation for oral activities.

Standards for Oral Reading

Positive Qualities
1. Correct pronunciation of every word
2. Distinctness and open tones
3. Suitable speed
4. Correct phrasing
5. Observance of punctuation marks
6. Variety of tone
7. Smoothness
8. Showing the reader's interest
9. Ability to glance away from the book for brief glances at the audience
10. Comfort while reading
11. Good habits of speech
12. Correct emphasis on words
13. Ability to read as if telling something
14. Vitality in reading

Negative Qualities
1. Carelessness
2. Tight jaw, closed mouth, lazy lips
3. Too slow, too fast, jerky
4. Wrong pauses
5. Not understanding the meaning
6. Monotone
7. Repetition of syllables or words
8. Lack of preparation
9. Indifference to audience, hanging head, wrong position of book
10. Breathlessness
11. Adding syllables not in print (such as *uh, an*)
12. Extra stress given to wrong syllables or words
13. Singsong
14. Lack of vigor

From *Minimum Essentials in the Mechanics of English Composition*, prepared for use in Albuquerque, N.M., schools.

To Eliminate Singsong Reading

"Copying poetry in prose paragraphs is a valuable help in destroying the singsong so common with beginning readers of poetry." (Frances Albright, Portales, N.M.).

Puzzles

An excellent way to make students aware of the need for clear presentation is to have them explain the solutions of certain puzzles. For example, two trains, each 1,000 long, meet. The only sidetrack is 500 feet long. How can they get past each other?

Tall Stories

To make students forget themselves in their subjects, try a tall-story contest.

Acting Companies

In Princeton, N.J., two hundred students in three "companies" (ninth grade, tenth, and eleventh and twelfth) get instruction in dramatization, and perform plays for junior high schools and other area schools. Don Evans, "Educational Theater in the High School," *English Journal,* LVII (March, 1968), 587.

Dramatized Research Papers

In Red Bank, N.J., "Our research paper is submitted in the form of a ten-minute radio program. . . . Students choose their topic, do their research, write their script, rehearse their performance, tape the script at home or during a class period, play the tape, preside over a question period . . . and then assume a receptive attitude for evaluation by their peers. The peers will be marked for their listening arts." Marie E. O'Connor, "The Research Paper and the Tape Recorder," *English Journal,* LVII (May, 1968), 652.

"Directing Your First Play"

Useful suggestions from John Sweet for the neophyte. *English Journal,* LIV (Dec., 1965), 806.

15

Teaching Film

WHY STUDY FILM?

Our students live increasingly exposed to the visual media of our image-saturated culture. They have grown up on visual stimulation. Say what you will about the quality of the stimulation, it is a dominant visual factor in their lives. Teaching a child to discriminate between high and low quality should be a primary objective of the schools—in every classroom, in many school experiences.

"The fact that film is both an art and a mass medium places it in a unique context and explains some of the ambiguous reactions to it within our culture."[1] This ambiguity actually should be fruitful because it provides the opportunity to deal with a mass communicator that is not only a factor in our students' lives, but is also capable of being great art. The film and many of its conventions are quite familiar to our students. It is desirable to amplify and sharpen this acquaintance with films to deepen artistic experience.

The purpose of teaching film is to introduce students to the language of film, to its aesthetics, to its cultural dimensions, and to its techniques and history, and to enhance the understanding of specific films as a means of cultivating an ability to order and judge the millions of visual images the students deal with. The more information and experience, direct and vicarious, a student can

[1] John Culkin, *Film Study in the High School* (New York: Fordham Film Study Center, Fordham University, 1965), p. 3.

bring to a situation, whether it concerns love or art or life, the more intelligent his judgment and expectations will be.

English classes have proved natural for film study. The reason is that film study very closely parallels literature study, because films, like novels and poems, are naturally discussable along the same lines, as they both involve attention to form, symbols, levels of meaning, criticism, and historical development. However, film and literature are entirely different art forms, and films are not necessarily less demanding. It is a common thought that anyone can watch a movie—it is true that anyone who is not physically blind *can* watch a movie—but very few people actually *see* a film; most people are visually illiterate. The English teacher is in a unique position because he has a natural structure in his own class to work on visual literacy as well as reading literacy.

A book called *The Motion Picture and the Teaching of English*, prepared under a grant to the NCTE, listed in 1965 the following reasons "to consider the role of the moving picture in the teaching of English . . . : First, the film has an unparalleled power to transmit information and inferences. Second, it may illuminate and augment the study of literature. Third, it has form, structure, theme, irony, metaphor, and symbol—aspects of any work of art, hence subject to examination and isolation. And finally it is concerned with ethics, values, and truth—which may be embodied or distorted in films as in any other medium." [2]

The kind of film study advocated in this chapter is based on the screening, discussion, and analysis which involves the "exchange of ideas in an honest and personal way." [3] This chapter, in Culkin's words, advocates "a total human approach which will harmonize aesthetic, moral, technical, social and economic judgments. [Perhaps] all of these goals will eventually be part of the school program at all levels of education." [4]

If this kind of teaching is to make any impact, it must directly relate to the young people's experiences and selves. If films are studied in terms of techniques, how films are made and how they have developed, at the expense of each individual's reaction and emotional response to the meanings in a film, film study will not differ greatly from often hated school work. But, if discussion leads

[2] Marion Sheridan, *et al.*, *The Motion Picture and the Teaching of English*, p. viii.
[3] Culkin, p. 20.
[4] Culkin, p. 4.

to "an exploration of the structure of the film, its levels of meaning, its symbolism, its non-verbal clues, its recurring themes," [5] the classroom should open many understandings about art and people and the students themselves. The communal experience of seeing and discussing films "equips the student and the teacher with a backlog of shared experiences which can be used to facilitate inter-personal communication and to establish relationships with situations in literature or social studies." [6]

In the last ten years film study has grown tremendously so that now it is not uncommon to find high school students offered the choice of one approach or another to film study before they graduate. Generally, film study has been approached along these lines:

HISTORICAL—the origin and development of motion pictures
AESTHETIC—film as art; relationships within the form
THEMATIC—study of films under themes, e.g., war
SOCIOLOGICAL—film and its impact on society, e.g., propaganda
CREATIVE—film making
COMPARATIVE—how a film is related to other arts, e.g., literature, photography

Film has been used in English classes for decades for instructional purposes; excerpts from novels have been used in English classes to "enhance literature." But now, as English teachers, we have come to the place and time that film must be considered on its own—as an art in itself that can be dealt with successfully in the English classroom. We have in the past built our classes around works of art and we welcome yet another art form: one that is not embedded with constrictions and restrictions, expectations and traditions of literature that inhibit free teaching and open responses. Film can integrate several areas that we consider English: thinking, creating, expressing, and relating. And that is what this chapter is about: how film as an art form relates to and can become part of the English experience.

A word or two of warning and advice. Teaching film is not easy—it requires an accumulation of many intelligent perceptions and abilities. The production of long-awaited curriculum aims for teaching film has begun, and these guides can help fill in many gaps, but nothing will replace alive awareness of the environment. Showing films can be personal, and each classroom experience with film

[5] Culkin, p. 9.
[6] Culkin, p. 13.

must in the end be uniquely that of the individual class. Use films that you like—just as you should use books that you like—it makes the experience a pleasant and stimulating one to share.

THINGS TO KNOW ABOUT FILM BEFORE YOU START

Nothing can replace the knowledge and undying love of film that the generation of people have whose eyes light up at the mention of Sidney Greenstreet, or "Play it again, Sam," or "There is a new sucker born every minute," or Monica Vitti, or *Breathless*, or *The Bicycle Thief*, or Kurosawa, or Dalton Trumbo, or—on and on. In other words, as in all teaching, nothing is as good as a thorough knowledge of the subject. However, all English teachers are familiar with many elements of film through their acquaintance with literature, most English teachers have seen a large number of films, and more and more help is coming along as increasing numbers of teachers experiment with films in class.

In preparation for any kind of film study, the teacher probably should acquaint his students with the general technical terms used in film production, often called "the language on film," and a brief summary of how a film is made. Such technical matters, though, should not be a major concern. However, if the teacher provides a minimal background, the student will better understand and appreciate the film as a separate art form.

The 'Grammar' of Film

The grammar of film relates to the piece of celluloid that runs before the projector at the speed of twenty-five frames (individual pictures) per second. The moving image is created by the fact that the eye retains an image approximately one tenth of a second longer than the image is actually present. So, the individual pictures, or frames, appear to be connected, as our brains are fooled into seeing a "moving" picture. The standard width of that piece of celluloid, or film, is thirty-five mm for feature films, sixteen mm for most film used in schools, and eight mm for most home uses of film.

Film has its own syntax or grammatical structure. The basic unit, comparable to words in a sentence, is called a *shot*. A shot is best defined as that which takes place in front of the camera from the time the camera starts until it stops. For example, if you are shooting a girl walking across a field, and turn the camera on as she begins to move and stop the camera as she gets across the field —that is a shot.

The next term is *scene*. A scene, like a sentence, is a series of connected shots, just as a sentence is a series of connected words. For example, in the situation above, suppose the next shot is of the girl meeting her boyfriend at the edge of the field; these two shots become a scene.

The "paragraph" of film is called a *sequence*. A sequence is a group of related scenes that develop part of a story in a given time and location. If the boy and girl begin to argue and the scene eventually builds up to the girl running away in tears, then switches to the girl crying at home—the time the action is centered in the field is called a sequence.

The next techniques to discuss are the "switches" or *transitions*. The most common is the *cut*. A cut is a straight switch from one shot to another. For example, during the argument between the boy and the girl, the film may have switched from the boy's face to the girl's without the camera seeming to move. This is called a cut (the script might order, "Cut to the boy's face"). A cut is done in one of two ways: 1) the camera is turned off, moved, and turned on again, or 2) the film is spliced to make it appear that the camera moved. Cuts usually occur between shots.

Between scenes or sequences the transitions can become more complicated. The film may *fade* into the next scene, which means that the screen darkens to blackness and gradually lights up to a new scene. Or it may *dissolve:* the last scene of one sequence melts into the first scene of another. It could be said that cuts are the equivalent of punctuation, while fades and dissolves are paragraph or chapter transitions. Film makers use variations of these transitions, plus other, more complicated ones, for various purposes.

Point of View: The Camera and Editing

Everything in a film is controlled by the camera and by editing. Although we can see no more than the camera shows us, the camera is a very facile instrument with many shot variations. The most common shots are the *long shot*, the *medium shot,* and the *close-up.* The long shot is a shot of an entire scene from about 50 yards to 20 feet away, the medium shot focuses on one or two people and includes background, and the close-up is of one person's face. The camera can *angle* in from any direction, and it can *pan* (sweep across a scene) and *tilt* (move up and down). A camera can move in to a close-up, for example, with a *zoom* shot (a lens adjustment that produces a rapid close-up), or *dolly* shot (actually moving the camera in). When the camera is transported for such uses as following the getaway car, the shots are called *traveling* or *trucking* shots.

An awareness of shot composition is also important. Students should be aware that a whole film is a continuous visual composition of images that are fused together to create a complete work. The quality of the whole depends on the compositional excellence of each individual scene.

The last fundamental to be considered is the editing process. Briefly, editing consists of *splicing*, or putting together pieces of film, in a coherent and ordered sequence. Since films are not shot in sequence (it's more economical in terms of time and money to shoot at one time all the scenes of a film that occur at a given place), it is the editor's job to put it all together to create a unified work. The film editor's work, usually done with the director present, is analogous to an author's final editing and rewriting.

Many people contribute to making any given film: far more than for a play or certainly for a novel. Unmentioned above are the cameramen, script-writers, actors, costume designers, make-up people, sound men and on and on. Making a film is a shared experience. So can studying a film be.

THE FILM IN THE ENGLISH PROGRAM

The English classroom is a good place to study film because film as an art is better dealt with in relation to other art forms—not necessarily to support other art forms, but in comparison with them. It is unfortunate that many English teachers have subordinated film to purely instructional function or to "enhance" literature by showing as a film of a play or novel studied and never treating it by itself as a cinematic product. This makes film serve as a supplement to literature, and fails to educate the students about film.

Film does fit into the English class on its own merit, whether for thematic study, or for an analysis of one or two long films, or for documentary study—or as a means of personal expression. "The study of film when integrated with the study of literature allows students to see how each medium works and to explore the similarities and the differences between the two media. When students study film and literature together, they are able to understand not only the meaning or message of a particular work of art, but also what each medium is forced to do, what it is able to do most successfully, and what it seems unable to do." [7]

The remainder of this chapter will relate film to what already exists in the English program: fiction, drama, and forms of personal expression such as writing and poetry.

Most film study is based on viewing films, discussing them, and then producing a response—either writing of some kind or a visual product, such as a student film. There have been literally hundreds of guides to specific films written to assist the teacher; the bibliography and Idea Box suggestions at the end of the chapter offer some advice and suggestions about where to begin looking for specific film guides. For a general discussion, the following comment is useful:

How do you teach film? You don't. You sit in the back of the darkened room and watch. . . . After sharing a film, you talk with the kids, but more important, you listen to them. Listen to them discuss their feelings, their thoughts, themselves. Don't worry about your questions. Listen for theirs. Lead them back to the film when they get too far astray: move them, without pushing, toward making connections, toward seeing relationships; but don't belabor the old kinds of relationships: setting to theme, mood to plot, character to language. Explore relationships that are relevant to kids, to their own lives. Let them free-wheel with their imaginations. How very little attention we've paid to the inward eye, the vision, the "stuff that dreams are made on." Encourage discussion which is honest and free. Above all, don't force them to see the film your way. Don't, in your infinite wisdom, tell them how and what it means. Don't intellectualize it to death. [8]

This method makes the discussion almost more important than the film itself. David Sohn, in his National Film Study pamphlet, *Film Study and the English Teacher*, has listed the following guidelines for film teaching that have proved effective:

1. Do not lecture before showing the film. Do not tell the students what to look for!
2. Show the film under the best possible conditions for viewing and hearing. Darken the room and put the speaker in front of the audience.

[7] Katz, John Stuart, "An Integrated Approach to the Teaching of Film and Literature," *The English Quarterly*, 2:1 (Jan. 1969), p. 27.

[8] Grenier, Charles F., "Film Study Hang-Ups," *Media and Methods*, 5:5 (January, 1969), p. 33.

3. Have a short break after showing the film, if possible. [A long break is sometimes preferable.]
4. Discuss the picture—not ideas in general.
5. Give specific examples when you discuss.
6. As a moderator, be brief, Do not let a few students dominate the discussion.
7. Try to relate each remark to the remark of the previous speaker.
8. Indicate the way in which the camera conveys ideas.
9. The success of a discussion does not depend on whether students agree with the moderator or not.
10. After the class has seen several films together, the moderator should expect or suggest cross-references and comparisons among films.
11. After the discussion, comment on the way the discussion progressed, without giving answers to the film or the discussion. The ideas are important, not the number of "right answers." [9]

Father John Culkin also recommends that the students feel that "this is not 'school.' No exams. No failures. No teachers."

The Relation of the Novel and Short Story to Film

That films and novels are closely related is proved by the fact that many films are taken from or adapted from novels. It is sad, but too often we hear people comment after seeing a feature film, "Oh, that was just like the book!" or "They changed the ending!" or "My favorite scene was left out!" These comments reveal (1) that people feel the print medium is superior to film and, because print is superior, the film must remain "true" to the book or the film has somehow cheated; and (2) that people do not understand that print and film are different media with different restrictions and advantages. Looking at the restrictions and advantages has proved rewarding to both novel study and film study.

Let us begin with the points of similarity. Both novels and films use the imagination to recreate life in a meaningful way; both use narrative to reveal what a person feels; both concentrate on the individual and his relation to his environment; both attempt to order experience; both try to make the audience feel a situation; and both use symbols and emphasize character, setting, and theme. The core of the novel and the film are almost identical.

But each also has unique qualities. The major difference lies in the fact that film better depicts action and relies on visual images,

[9] David A. Sohn, *Film Study and The English Teacher* (New York: Fordham Film Study Center, Fordham University, 1968), p. 8. (Sohn borrowed some of these from Father Culkin.)

and the novel better depicts abstractions and inner thoughts and relies on mental images. Because film is largely limited to action, the characters cannot often relate their feelings as they do in a long Shakespearean soliloquy without hurting the film. It is the film's burden to *show* the audience its meaning, not tell it. Consequently, much more attention is paid to visual components, such as movement from one place to another, flashbacks, etc. A person with a sense of film, one who knows how to see a film as he knows how to read a novel, can see connections and relationships in the setting and characterization and mood, and can see symbols throughout; in other words, such a person can discuss a film using the same tools he uses to approach a novel, but constantly realizing that the application of the tools varies with the medium. This is the approach to concentrate on in English class. This does not mean a casual viewing of the film after the class has studied the book; it means approaching the film as an art form in its own right.

A General Guide to a Novel-Film Discussion or Comparison

The following questions may be useful as a guide for a comparative discussion of a film and a novel:

What symbols occur and recur throughout? Are they the same in both media?

What is the theme or themes? What scenes directly relate to the theme? To the plot? What is the difference between these scenes in the novel and in the film? What can you conclude about the difference between plot and theme, as they are developed in each form?

Are there many subplots in the film? (Here is frequently a difference between film and fiction: film cannot pursue many details effectively, and hence subplots are fewer in films.)

Does the story end the same way? What scenes are different in the novel and the film? How does this affect the film?

What characters are strongly developed in each? How is this development accomplished? Which characters do you like? Why? Can you separate the actor from the character he is portraying? Compare the ways character is developed in a novel and a film.

Setting is much easier to establish in a film than in a novel. Why? What methods are used in both?

Is mood also easier to establish in a film? What are some ways mood is established in a novel and in a film?

Compare the sense and development of space and time in both forms.

How do you separate or deal with the camera eye and point of view in a film? How is point of view established in a film? Or is the point of view always impersonal, i.e. do we see things objectively? Do we get the point of view from a character as we often do in a novel? Study the author's voice in a novel and compare it to the director's. Where does the screen-writer fit in?

Editing can be compared with rewriting. How has the film been edited? Do you notice the cuts, where they occur and why? Could you change the film by re-editing it? Could you add a scene? Remove one? How does this craft compare to the novelist's?

The Film and Drama

In a theater, everyone knows and accepts the fact that nothing is real, but in film the environment can be more realistic. A film is hurt by elements that are not authentic. Imitation of film weakens the theater just as films made to be like plays are inevitably weak.

Why? Because drama is a form that relies on verbal communication almost entirely—in a way that even a novel does not. In fact, the novel is closer to the film because it, in a sense, can *show* things (real places, close-ups that show people's feelings, what is happening at any moment somewhere, etc.) as film does. Drama, however, is much more stationary than either the novel or the film and must *tell* everything that cannot be staged. Because of this, theater can explore relationships and psychological inner problems and complexities through its dialogue better than its partners, novels and films.

Plays and films can be dealt with in class to the benefit of both. Scripts of many screenplays are available in paperback. They are usually illustrated with still photographs from the films and are interesting and quite acceptable for classroom use. It is rewarding to find a copy of a screen play that was taken from a stage play and to compare dramatic techniques with cinematic techniques.

The Feature Film: Rewards and Difficulties

Feature films are difficult to obtain and difficult to show within the confines of a school day broken up into fifty-minute segments. The rewards are the opportunity to explore a complex piece of cinematographic art in satisfactory detail. The optimum conditions for showing a film are a two or three hour block of time, an undisturbed, uncrowded, darkened room, and a good film. The showing can be after school if necessary. Also, some film teachers have obtained the last hour in the day for film class; then if a film runs over, perhaps the students can stay. There are many teachers who claim that breaking a film up into a three-day viewing doesn't hurt at all; in fact, some say the break enhances the film because it gives time for contemplation that is impossible in a continuous showing.

Film as Expression, or as Rhetoric, or as Personal Experience

Because they are short and fit into school schedules, and can be obtained more easily than feature films, the experiential-experimental short films are generally best to use in the schools. Short films cover a wide variety of themes and subjects and are made to create an experience for the viewer; hence they are named "experiential." The magazine *Media and Methods* offers frequent bibliographies and reviews of these films.

Such films are the most adaptable and are exceptionally rewarding because: (1) they are usually shorter than thirty minutes; (2) they are timely—they concern immediate problems; (3) they are the most avant-garde—that is, they utilize the most current techniques and often invent new ones; (4) they encapsulate all the characteristics of feature film and literature; (5) they are easily obtainable and are widely distributed, they are much lower in cost than feature films; and (6) there is an incredible amount of excellent and exciting film offered in this category.

The short film is probably best taught in thematic units, since study of themes facilitates comparisons. Topics for such units might be alienation, the individual and society, violence, love, satire, comedy, the western, fantasy and reality, and responsibility.

These films must be screened before they can be included in the curriculum. Even though guides are published on most of the good short films, the teacher cannot adequately prepare without advance screenings.

The "Film as Rhetoric" staff at the University of Illinois has suggested the following general questions for studying the experiential film:

1. What is the film maker trying to *say?* Is there a message to his work?
2. Is the title of the film an arbitrary label, or does it give some structure or meaning to the work?
3. Is the film *effective?* (i.e., does it persuade you or convince you of the validity of its point?) Why does it work?
4. What *cinematic* techniques does the film maker use and why? (e.g., Why color rather than black and white, or vice versa; why

one kind of background music rather than another; why one photographic style rather than a different one?)

5. What general *rhetorical* techniques does the film maker use and why? (e.g., irony, juxtaposition, repetition, etc.)
6. What structure is evident in the film? (e.g., linear or cyclical, general to particular, static or progressive, etc.)
7. *Tone:* how does the film maker treat his audience?
   Mood: how does the film maker treat his subject?
8. Emphasis: what object or objects does the camera choose to focus upon? To a certain extent, a film is just as important for what it excludes as for what it includes. What are the film maker's criteria for his selection of details?
9. What assumptions about the sympathies and viewpoints of his audience does the film maker make? What kind of audience is the film geared to?
10. What are the predominant visual images of the film? Which ones do you remember and why? What visual qualities of the film most appealed to you?

An effective film, like an effective essay, story, or poem, consists of a variety of elements all working together to achieve a unified effect. The ability to analyze a piece of writing and the ability to analyze a short film are analogous talents. And although works of cinematic rhetoric and those of written rhetoric lie basically in two different spheres, the student who can perceive the workings of a film can, to his betterment, transfer these perceptions to his own reading and writing.

All forms of expression are easily integrated under this kind of study. Novels, plays, essays, poetry, newspaper articles, experimental and experiential films, documentaries, TV, comics—almost any media in the student's environment could easily fit into this kind of thematic study. This approach to the English class provides the student with the opportunity to respond to and with the forms that best suit him. If this kind of study is attempted through sharing responses and materials by everyone in the class, the classroom can truly become a live community where learning and thinking flourish.

THE IDEA BOX

Nothing Really Moves

Some fast-working artistic students can make a series of very simple drawings (e.g., a man mounting a horse). They arrange these at the edges of pages. When the pages of this flip chart are flipped, action appears to be taking place. It is upon such an illusion that all movies, animated drawings, etc., are based.

Using the Comics

William Kuhns and Robert Stanley suggest study of comics to observe such things as switching from one scene to another. "Reading" the pictures without the words (and vice versa) is also useful. Students can learn much, too, from writing their own comics. *Teaching Program: Exploring the Film* (1968), 27–33.

Play Into Film

Another suggestion from Kuhns and Stanley: take a familiar play (or part of it). Discuss how it would have to be changed to make it a film, how words could be changed to images. If possible, attempt the filming.

Documentary vs. Fiction

Given a theme or a situation, e.g., a harbor threatened by pollution. Describe the documentary film you might make. Describe a fictional film on the same situation.

Avant Garde

Film makers keep experimenting with techniques and ideas. In 1969, said Stan Van Der Beck (*Screen Experience,* 18–19), they found these very interesting: simultaneous images and compression, abstractions, superimpositions, discontinuous information, social surrealism, and episodic structure.

"An Integrated Approach to the Teaching of Film and Literature"

John S. Katz describes a composite approach like this: "We approach the theme of man's relationship to machines in three ways. First, we consider works of literature and film which depict man in the absence of, or unaffected by machines, including some Utopian and pastoral works. Secondly, we consider those works in which the machine is praised or even apotheosized for the role it plays in man's existence. And finally, there are those works in which the machine is shown as the physical or spiritual destroyer of mankind.

"The students are involved in three activities related to this thematic approach. They see films, discuss them and write about them; they read books in an individualized reading program, discuss them and write about them; and they make movies and discuss them. . . . The students write on the theme as well as on the ways in which film and literature deal with the theme. . . . As a corollary to the writing, they are given 8-mm cameras. . . . As a final project, students are given the opportunity to work in a group on the production of their own 16-mm film, including the script writing, acting, directing, shooting and editing." *English Quarterly*, 2:1 (Jan., 1969), 25.

Film Society

If there is no film program in your school, start a film society that meets after school, and look carefully through the catalog of your school's film source to pick the films that sound the best—or that you've heard of—and show them to the film lovers after school. Or, have a film festival in your class—you might find yourself in the middle of the best discussion all year.

Perhaps the function of the film festival could be to screen films, with class members to choose films to show. The class members could lead the subsequent discussions.

"Using Films in Teaching English Composition"

Adele H. Stern of Montclair, N.J., offers a list of about twenty available films for class sharing, and describes their use as stimuli. *English Journal*, LVII (May, 1968), 646.

In the Magazine

The class or school library magazine may have a film section. Acclaimed films may find a place in next year's program.

Use of Montages

Preparation of montages on a theme can help show students the relationships between ideas. Look also at montages put together as film; e.g., Norman Braverman's *American Time Capsule* and *The Sixties*. See David Sohn's *Film: The Creative Eye* (1970) for more ideas.

Films Without Sound

Occasionally play a film with the sound track off. Analyze what sound contributes, and where it may distort or sway.

Mixed Media

Say something in various media about the same problem or theme: film, filmstrip, filmscript, play, poem, dance, etc. Compare the results.

On Commercial Movies

1. Help students to set up criteria for judging movies. Authenticity, quality of acting, moral tone, propaganda values, informational values, plot, theme, setting, and characterization are among the points that might be included. (Lois Roquemore, Las Vegas, N.M.)

2. The teacher should help students to recognize movie stereotypes, propaganda, glittering generalities, and misrepresentation of social facts; for example, suggestions that winning the girl means lasting happiness or that the good life is the acquisitive life or that catching the criminal solves the crime problem.

3. The students establish standards for judging movies. Then, after having seen particular films, they indicate their quality by a traffic light display: red if the movie is poor, yellow if mediocre, and green if good.

4. Try to preview each commercial film shown in class. Also, do a little preteaching to point out certain things for which to look. A long movie may be presented in instalments. After showing, discuss such. points as casting, acting, directing, theme, plot, significance, dialog, balance, music.

Previews by Students

Students may sometimes preview short films and prepare descriptions for the information of the class.

"Occurrence at Owl Creek Bridge"

"Occurrence at Owl Creek Bridge," a fine story by Ambrose Bierce, has been made into an equally excellent film by Robert Enrico. There have been several studies written to help the teacher use this film and short story: The Geo. A. Pflaum Publishing Company has put out a booklet that compares the two versions very closely; The *Willowbrook Cinema Study Project* (in bibliography) includes a unit on the subject; and William Kwapy in *Screen Experience: an Approach to Film* asks some good questions.

Multimedia Unit on Satire

Satire allows flexibility of choice in the selection of material. A unit could include books and films such as *Gulliver's Travels, Catch 22,*

Dr. Strangelove, and *Zabriskie Point;* songs such as the Beatles' "Maxwell's Silver Hammer" and "Taxman" and Simon and Garfunkel's "Bright Green Pleasure Machine"; *Mad* magazine; Art Buchwald's columns; and short films such as *Automania 2000* and *Pow Wow.* Visual irony, students find, operates on basically the same principles as verbal irony but is sometimes more immediately apparent.

Useful Works for the Teacher of Film

Amelio, Ralph J. *Willowbrook Cinema Study Project.* Dayton: Geo. A. Pflaum, 1969. (Guide.)

Bluestone, George. *Novels into Film.* Berkeley: University of California Press, 1961. (General.)

Culkin, John. *Film Study in the High School.* Fordham Film Study Center, Fordham University, Bronx, N.Y., 1965.

Feyen, Sharon, ed. *Screen Experience: An Approach to Film.* Dayton: Geo. A. Pflaum, 1969. (General, film guide.)

Fulton, A. R. *Motion Pictures: The Development of an Art from Silent Films to the Age of Television.* Norman: University of Oklahoma Press, 1960. (General; good section on literature and film.)

Hall, Stuart, and Paddy Whannel. *The Popular Arts.* Boston: Beacon Press, 1964. (General.)

Knight, Arthur. *The Liveliest Art,* New York: New American Library, 1957.

Kuhns, William, and Robert Stanley, *Exploring the Film* and *Teaching Program: Exploring the Film.* Dayton: Geo. A. Pflaum, 1968. (Guide.)

Kuhns, William. *Themes: Short Films for Discussion.* Dayton: Geo. A. Pflaum, 1969. (Guide.)

MacCann, Richard Dyer, ed. *Film: A Montage of Theories.* New York: E. P. Dutton & Co., Inc., 1966. (Anthology of articles on film.)

Mallery, David. *The School and the Art of Motion Pictures.* Boston: National Association of Independent Schools, 1966. (General.)

Media and Methods. Philadelphia, Pennsylvania. (An outstanding magazine for teaching film and other media.)

Sheridan, Marion, Harold H. Owen, Jr., Ken Macrorie, and Fred Marcus. *The Motion Picture and the Teaching of English.* New York: Appleton-Century-Crofts (available through the National Council of Teachers of English), 1965. (General and guide.)

Sohn, David A. *Film: The Creative Eye.* Dayton: Geo. A. Pflaum, 1970. (Guide to short film.)

Sohn, David A. *Film Study and the English Teacher.* Bloomington, Ind.: Field Services, Indiana University Audio Visual Center (available through NCTE), 1968. (General.)

Stewart, David C. *Film Study in Higher Education.* Washington, D.C.: American Council On Education (available through NCTE), 1966.

Sullivan, Sister Bede, O.S.B. *Movies: Universal Language; Film Study in High School.* Notre Dame, Ind.: Fides Publishers, Inc., 1967.

Talbot, Daniel, ed. *Film: An Anthology.* Berkeley: University of California Press, 1966. (Anthology of articles on film.)

Young Filmmakers

This book by Rodger Larson and Ellen Meade (published by E. P. Dutton, 1969) offers useful and generally concrete suggestions for students who want to make a movie. Among the items covered are photography, visual language, planning a movie, shooting the picture, and relationships among director, cameraman, and actors.

16

The Teacher Who Grows

THE PALACE OF ART

The teacher of English is not a creature apart. Despite what he knows that the majority in the community do not know, despite his travels in the realms of gold, he is still a human being, with human strength, human weakness, human need.

You remember Tennyson's "The Palace of Art." The poet says that his soul built a magnificent palace, "full of great rooms and small," splendidly decorated with tapestries depicting landscapes and myths, and adorned with portraits of Milton, Shakespeare, Dante, Homer, and others. There dwelt the poet's soul,

> Communing with herself: "All these are mine,
> And let the world have peace or wars,
> 'Tis one to me.
>
> "I take possession of men's minds and deeds,
> I live in all things great and small,
> I sit apart holding no forms or creeds,
> But contemplating all."

"Three years she throve, but on the fourth she fell," because in her lovely palace were excessive solitude, "uncertain shapes," and "dull stagnation." The air needed changing. Tapestries portraying homes and rivers and wood nymphs were inadequate substitutes for real homes, real rivers, real people; the tapestries would become more meaningful if they were not separated completely from actuality; Milton and his "L'Allegro" would mean most to one who knew firsthand of upland hamlets and shepherds who tell stories "under the hawthorn in the dale." So, Tennyson says, his soul "threw her royal robes away."

> "Make me a cottage in the vale," she said . . .
> "Yet pull not down my palace towers, that are
> So lightly, beautifully built:
> Perchance I may return with others there."

Regardless of how much the teacher loves literature—and he must love it—he cannot afford to immerse himself in it and ignore reality. Literature is a reflection and interpretation of life, but it is not life itself. The teacher, like the poet, must not lose contact with life, must not climb into the tower of a Palace of Art. His students are alive; the people in the community are alive. The teacher of English is a living link between the life about him and the life depicted in literature, just as the teacher of music is a link between "rock" and Beethoven. To his students the English teacher brings something fine—an enrichment of knowledge concerning themselves and their heritage. If he is to succeed in effecting this enrichment, though, he must know people as they are, as they breathe, work, play, sweat, eat, drink, love, talk, and dream. A teacher who knew only literature would be like a physician who knew only medicine and was ignorant of the bodies he was to strengthen.

THE TREADMILL

So the successful teacher cannot isolate himself in the Palace of Art. No more, however, can he place himself on a treadmill. You have perhaps seen pictures of a treadmill: One or more persons move a large cylinder by climbing steps mounted upon it; as their weight pushes one step down, another takes its place. Over and over they repeat the process, hour after hour and day after day, climbing the same steps, looking always at the same monotonous fixtures, reaching no higher point, while the massive cylinder slowly turns. Those long on the treadmill lose their human qualities and become automatons or less—mere physical forces, part of a mechanical assemblage of weights and counterweights.

Almost any kind of work can become a treadmill. Teaching can, very readily, but it need not. The danger lies in the ease with which the teacher, after a few years, may fall into a routine.

> Today I teach as I taught before;
> Tomorrow I work as I wrought before;
> Friday I cry as I cried before;
> Monday I die as I died before.

> Bowed by the weight of tediousness he stands
> Behind his desk and glowers at the class,
> The emptiness of ennui in his face,
> And in his eyes dull hate of all he sees.

How can a teacher avoid the treadmill? Perhaps a minister gave the clue. For more than fifty years he had followed the routine of his calling: a sermon every Sunday, prayer meeting every Wednesday, christenings, weddings, funerals—each week much like 3,000 others. His hair had become white, his face was wrinkled, but his eyes were still vivacious as he rose to speak at the banquet on the occasion of his retirement. "I have been excited for fifty-five years," he began. "People excite me. They interest me. During my fifty-five years in the ministry I have learned much about people. I know how they blunder, how they err, how they stumble and often fall. I know how they need leadership both human and divine. But I am perpetually excited by the sparks I find in them—sparks of goodness and kindness and self-sacrifice, sparks of promise for the future. In my small way I have spent my life fanning sparks."

He concluded with quotations from Kahlil Gibran and Elizabeth Barrett Browning:

You have been told also that life is darkness, and in your weariness you echo
　　what was said by the weary.
And I say that life is indeed darkness save when there is urge,
And all urge is blind save when there is knowledge,
And all knowledge is vain save when there is work,
And all work is empty save when there is love,
And when you work with love you bind yourself to yourself, and to one another,
　　and to God.[1]

> The world waits
> For help. Beloved, let us love so well,
> Our work shall still be better for our love,
> And still our love be sweeter for our work.[2]

Need more be said about how to avoid the treadmill?

---

[1] Kahlil Gibran, *The Prophet* (New York: Alfred Knopf, Inc., 1923).
[2] E. B. Browning, "Aurora Leigh."

THE TEACHER AND THE STUDENT

"Should we try to be pals to our students?" an earnest young prospective teacher once asked the author of this book.

"Heavens, no!" was the reply. "You people are already old men and old women in the eyes of most high school students, and every year you'll become more ancient. You can hope to become an older friend; maybe, if you're so inclined and really prepared for the job, a respected counselor. But a pal—never. Pals have to have much in common including similarity in age. Thirty-two and twenty-two may be pals, but not twenty-two and fifteen.

"Despite what I've said about your antiquity, though, some of you are young and attractive enough that one or more of your students will dream of you in a quite unorthodox teacher-student relationship. In other words, some of them may get what used to be called a 'crush on you.' When you suspect it, ignore it if you can. Pretend that it doesn't exist. It will probably go away. If pretense becomes impossible, if there is an open avowal, be gentle. Say how flattered you are, but how impossible the situation is. Make the break gentle, but clean and complete. Leave no room for hope. The student's pain and bitterness will last no more than a week or so—about the time it lasts when a going-steady pair breaks up.

"While we're on the general subject of relationships with students, let me urge you to continue learning about young people. You'll never know enough. Take a graduate course in adolescent psychology. A bit of sociology and anthropology may answer a question or two. Some fiction for teen-agers is realistic and filled with insights. You'll learn most, of course, about young people from your own students, from their writing, from their class responses, from their participation and behavior in cocurricular activities. Try to meet them socially on some occasions. Dinner at a student's home can be both revealing and pleasant.

"All this is relevant to the original question about 'palship.' Give them your best efforts. You are a teacher. You can be a teacher—friend. That's the end of the line. Next year you're teacher—friend to another generation."

THE ENGLISH TEACHER AND HIS COLLEAGUES

The English teacher has an especially strong motive for cooperating with his fellows. Since English overlaps all other fields to some extent, working with other teachers will pay large dividends to any English instructor. As has been said earlier, the English teacher hopes that all teachers in the school will constantly illustrate the attitude that good English is important. Happy relationships with members of other departments may help to translate that hope to reality.

In meetings of his own department, the young teacher may best be rather quiet in his first year or so. Maybe, fresh from his exhilarating college experience, he sees ways in which the department should be reformed. Let him postpone the reform for a little while. Let him try in his own classes as much as possible of the reformed program, but let him prove *himself* as a teacher before he reforms others (who have presumably already proved themselves). If his teaching is outstandingly successful, if some of his new methods and materials work miracles, the other members will be more receptive when, dry behind the ears, he speaks up in meetings.

A small but important matter: A teacher should find out about channels of communication in his school. If, for example, supplies are needed or a recommendation of some kind is to be made, should the information be channeled through a course chairman, the department head, the business office, the assistant principal, or someone else? Sad to say, some teachers and administrators resent being bypassed; sometimes bypassing will, indeed, result in confusion. Following channels, then, is the most sensible procedure. Only if a clearly unnecessary block develops is another procedure justified.

THE ENGLISH TEACHER AND THE COMMUNITY

Although in most communities a teacher is not now required to be so straitlaced as formerly, he is (quite rightly) looked upon as a leader and to some extent a model for youth. In the not-so-old days teachers sometimes had to sign contracts containing some rather absurd provisions: that they would not leave town on more than four week ends during the school year, that they would teach a Sunday-school class, that they would not use makeup, that they would not dye their hair, and even—in at least one community—that they would not fall in love! Today such stipulations are rarely found, because teachers are becoming increasingly regarded as responsible adult citizens who are entitled to lead lives of their own.

Nevertheless, just as a doctor or a minister assumes certain professional obligations when he voluntarily chooses his profession, so does the teacher. The obligations are a part of the profession. The bricklayer may carouse nights and week ends and still do what he is paid for—lay so many bricks a day. The milliner's assistant may be guilty of some variety or varieties of turpitude without impairing her trimming of hats. But the teacher, as a leader of youth, cannot conscientiously set an example that he would not want young people to follow.

This does not mean that the teacher should be a prude—far from it. The teacher of English should be one of the most broad-minded persons in the community, because he knows the mainsprings of human action, and because he knows the weaknesses as well as the strengths of people. So he is not a prude, but he does try to live in such a way that young people would not find him an unwholesome example.

He chooses clothes that are reasonably conservative without being dull or hopelessly outmoded. Unless he receives advice to the contrary (this seldom happens today), he smokes if he wishes at times when he is not on duty. In most communities he will not be criticized if he drinks a cocktail in his own or someone else's home, though he should not be a habitue of the neighborhood tavern. He dances and plays cards and goes bowling if he likes and, in general, leads a normal social life.

It is encouraging to note the increasing amount of political freedom being given to teachers. Whereas in former years a teacher might lose his position if he went to a Republican rally in a Democratic town (or vice versa), today a teacher is expected to maintain as active an interest in politics—even local politics—as anyone else. That is, in this area also, he is being regarded more and more as a responsible adult citizen of a democracy. It is his duty, as a well-informed member of the community, to express himself on matters of political importance. This does not mean that he electioneers in his classroom, but it does mean that in public meetings he does not hesitate to speak his mind.

Another question that merits consideration is this: What does the community, especially the small one, expect of the English teacher as his special contribution to the life of the community?

The English teacher is usually thought of as a person who can speak and write reasonably well and who knows much about literature. If he can act or if he has musical ability or other talents, the small community will consider him an especially welcome addition and perhaps will overburden him with requests, some of which he may have to refuse. Even though he has no special talents, he will occasionally be asked to review a current book or play, give a talk at a meeting of the PTA, write a feature or a review for the local newspaper, or possibly give a talk over the air. Oral readings from literature, if well selected and well delivered, afford excellent entertainment and may win friends for himself and his school. If the teacher has a good subject and enough time, he may occasionally speak before men's luncheon clubs or women's gatherings.

Words are the English teacher's chief stock in trade, and his chief value to the community outside of school hours lies in what he does with words. He should not consider himself a missionary bringing sweetness and light to the uncultured heathen, but he may bring wholesome entertainment and worthwhile information to his community through what he writes and says. Although the welfare of students is his first responsibility, he may, if he has time and energy remaining, enjoy himself and give pleasure to others by using his skill with words.

THE ENGLISH TEACHER AND HIS BOOKS

The English teacher should be the most omnivorous reader among the faculty. Books are his specialty, and all learning is his province. Never, of course, can he catch up on his reading. The presses clatter and rumble ceaselessly.

Inevitably, much of his reading will be in Western classics that he has missed or largely forgotten: Homer, Aeschylus, Aristotle, Vergil, Ovid, Dante, Racine, and many more. Some reading is necessary to refresh his memory of the giants of English and American literature. He is aware of vast gaps, too: The literature of the Orient, of Australia, of Latin America may be almost unknown to him. Literature by black Americans, shamefully ignored for many years, has now become part of the curriculum. The emerging literature now being written in English in several African nations contains rich surprises in style and content. Books for adolescents the teacher should at least skim. Philosophy, sociology, the fine arts, science for laymen, good current magazines—the list goes on and on.

Then there is professional reading. The *English Journal* tops the list, but he has found that *College English, College Composition and Communication,* and even *Elementary English* have many relevant articles. *Abstracts of English Studies* gives him a glimpse of what is happening in literary scholarship, and *Research in the Teaching of English* keeps him up to date in that field. *The Journal of Reading* and *Educational Leadership*, the NEA *Journal, Media and Methods*—he expands the list to suit his special interests. Important new books on teaching and on literary and linguistic scholarship appear every year.

A hopeless task? Yes, in a way, for the days and the nights and the summer are never long enough. Yet, in another way, it isn't hopeless and it isn't a task. There is always a book to look forward to, a magazine crying to be read, the pleasure of new knowledge to be savored. How can any English teacher's life be dull?

THE ENGLISH TEACHER AS EXPERIMENTER

There is an easy way to teach English in the second year and forever after. That way is simply to repeat whatever was done in the first year, to follow exactly the same outlines, the same lesson plans. So easy! But so deadening to teacher and students alike! So futile—for whose first year of teaching (or thirtieth) has ever been so nearly perfect as to deserve endless repetition?

The lively, exciting classroom is the one where something new is always being tried—new books, other new materials, new procedures. It is the classroom where the teacher isn't always sure how something will turn out, because part of what he is doing he has never done before. At least once a week, maybe even once a day, he conducts a little experiment. Some of the experiments fail; some succeed; but they all help to keep him alert.

No big experiments are needed—just a substitution of this poem for that; just a little more room for student initiative this hour, an unusual kind of test tomorrow, a filmstrip, a tryout of a programed textbook. Sometime, perhaps, there *will* be a big experiment—*Research* maybe—with all the trimmings of control groups and coefficients of correlation and a picture in the paper. But that isn't necessary. Lots of little experiments are enough to keep sap flowing.

THE ENGLISH TEACHER AS JOINER

In some schools it is made clear that every teacher is "expected" to join the National Educational Association (NEA) and the state association. Such associations have helped greatly in the fight to increase teachers' salaries and pensions; they have made some contributions to educational research; and occasionally an article useful to a classroom teacher appears in their publications. For these reasons, joining should be voluntary, before anybody needs to say "It's expected" or "We're always a hundred per cent."

The organization that addresses itself exclusively to English teachers is the National Council of Teachers of English. In addition to publishing half a dozen important magazines, the NCTE has sixty or so committees working on problems of the profession, publishes pamphlets and a few books on curricular and other matters, sponsors literary tours abroad, manages a talented-student competition that has helped many young people obtain college scholarships, works toward a reasonable teacher load, and makes available to its members, at reduced cost, large numbers of recordings, filmstrips, literary maps, and other teaching aids. Its conventions, held annually at Thanksgiving time, move to a different city each year in accordance with a set geographical pattern; the leaders of the profession are often at the speakers' tables there, but competent young persons—tomorrow's leaders—are constantly being sought. The NCTE is the one organization that an English teacher cannot afford not to join.

Most states and some communities or other areas within a state have English-teacher organizations, of which most are affiliated with the NCTE. Because these organizations concern themselves with state or area problems in English teaching, they are worth support. Some of them publish excellent small magazines or newsletters, and most of them hold one or more professional meetings each year.

For those especially interested in reading, the International Reading Association has a strong program and a good magazine. The Association for Supervision and Curriculum Development appeals to those who do the things suggested by its title; it, too, has a good magazine, of which perhaps a fourth is pertinent to English teaching. Other special-interest associations exist and may appeal to individual teachers.

"Should I join a teachers' union?" The answer to that may best be left to your conscience. Unions have effected considerable improvements in salaries and working conditions in a number of places. But, since strikes are a union's chief weapon, a basic question is whether it is ethical for members of any profession to strike. This question has arisen in the medical profession in countries that have government control over compensation for doctors, and has been a focus of discussion in teachers' strikes in the United States. It is not a question that permits an easy answer.

ADVANCEMENT IN THE PROFESSION

In several ways a devoted and hardworking teacher of English can advance professionally. Some school systems require earning additional college credits, educational travel, in-service study, or contributions to curriculum development as a prerequisite to certain upgradings in salary. But aside from these rather obvious means, in what ways may a teacher move upward?

There is, of course, a chance to move to a "better" school. "Better" should not, however, be confused with "bigger." Some relatively small schools have English departments, English programs, and salary schedules superior to those of many larger schools.

Some English teachers become interested in part- or full-time work in guidance and counseling. A graduate degree in this field may be required. The penalty involved is likely to be abandonment of the classroom in favor of individual work with students and perhaps the conduct of a testing program.

Administration beckons some English teachers. This is most likely to take the form of a department headship, which in large schools generally involves an increase in salary and a reduction of teaching responsibilities. Administration may also mean a principalship or even a superintendency. For either of these posts, special graduate work is almost essential. Although the loss of able classroom teachers to administrative posts is in a way lamentable, it is good for a school to have administrators with strong academic interests and preparation.

College teaching offers another attraction. However, unless the teacher is willing to expend the time and effort to earn a Ph.D., he will almost inevitably never rise above the lower echelons in college teaching.

Some universities have developed doctoral programs in the teaching of English. These degrees, which often require a major in English and a minor in education, and which have high school teaching as a prerequisite, prepare teachers to take over college methods courses and to counsel prospective teachers; they also prepare the candidates for headships in large high school English departments and for supervisory positions in city or county school systems, or in state departments of education.

Committee work and writing for local, state, and national organizations of teachers offer a different road for advancement and do not take the teacher from his classroom. Able people are always needed to help with research in these organizations, and their editors are always looking for excellent manuscripts. No money, as a rule, is paid for such work or such articles, but professional prestige and personal satisfaction may be sufficient remuneration. Some school districts recognize professional contributions in their salary schedules.

Individual research is a special means of advancement, open to a few persons who are patient and thorough. Such research may be in conjunction with work toward an advanced degree, but it need not be. Occasionally the U.S. Office of Education offers financial support for needed research studies.

Writing is attractive to some English teachers. Good textbooks, which are usually developed cooperatively by teachers and by representatives of a publishing firm, are always needed. Writing for children or adolescents also appeals to some teachers. So do other kinds of writing: A fairly large number of today's novelists, poets, and writers of non-fiction were or are teachers of English.

Unfortunately, several of the roads to advancement tend to take the teacher partly or entirely out of the classroom. For most teachers the best route may be the one that keeps them in the classroom doing the job each day as well as they are able, experimenting on a small scale, working with children, spending most of a lifetime in the same community, growing old and honored in Littleville or in Bigg High. Perhaps no other road leads to greater satisfaction.

THE IDEA BOX

Who Is the Good Teacher?

"The difference between a good and a mediocre teacher lies mainly in the emphasis the former puts on the exploring part of the mind, the aspects of learning that reveal meanings and lead to further understanding. . . . Mediocre teachers . . . stress memory at the expense of intelligence." Northrop Frye, *Design for Learning*, 12–13.

Talking Too Much: An Occupational Disease

"Of the talking that goes on in schools, 70 per cent is teacher talk. That leaves, barring child differences, approximately one per cent for each child," says John M. Kean, *Educational Leadership* (April, 1967). Is one per cent enough? Are teachers' words seventy times as important? Could we settle for fifty? forty? thirty?

The Widening Circle

Can you use this in what must be your constant struggle, the fight against provincialism?

Each of us lives inside a small circle, the circumference of which is our own experience. Timidity or complacence restricts many of us to a never expanding circle; we live our one life and die in its narrow confines. Others of us are battering constantly against the rim, seeking new knowledge and new experiences, reaching out geographically, hunting for what those younger and those older know that we do not, searching backward through time; we bulge the circle here and there, and gradually it becomes a larger circle. The seekers, the bulgers, live a richer, more exciting life than do the provincials—maybe not a happier life but a more rewarding one. The provincials are vegetables; the seekers are Daniel Boones.

Worth Thinking About

1. Maybe we English teachers try to do too many things. Maybe it is better to do a few well than to do many poorly. Maybe it is better to hit a clean single than to strike out trying for a home run.

2. Everybody has to have certain skills to make a living; besides, he has to know how to live with his fellow men. English contributes richly to the fulfilment of both needs.

Growing Downward and Upward

It is possible to grow downward and upward at the same time? Beginning teachers may find that they can grow upward in their appreciation of literature by looking at it through the unspoiled eyes of high school students instead of the horn-rimmed, possibly pedantic eyes of their college professors. For an illustration of this enigmatic statement, read "Literature and the Beginning Teacher," by Georgia Christopher, *English Journal*, XLVIII (Sept., 1959), 321.

I've Been Reading . . .

A few social evenings each year may provide both pleasure and profitable interchange, especially if elementary, junior high, senior high, and possibly college teachers participate. After dinner, instead of having a formal program, each person present may talk informally for no more than five minutes on "I've been reading. . . ." Literature, professional books and articles, even popular magazine articles may be included.

"Does English Have a Chance?"

William H. Evans discusses three kinds of "barriers to the improvement of English instruction": community-made barriers, administration-made barriers, teacher-made barriers. In the last category he includes unnecessary repetition, reluctance to experiment, fostering ridiculous traditions, and too little participation in professional organizations. *English Journal,* LII (Jan., 1963), 22.

If Conferences Are Coming

1. Little has been written about techniques of the conference with a student. Edgar Logan, of Detroit, makes these suggestions: (1) Make definite appointments. (2) Use no sarcasm. (3) Don't pry into the student's personal life. (4) Stick to the subject, for example, the compositions that the student has written recently. (5) Stress the things *this* student needs as an individual, not something the whole class will soon be taught. Mr. Logan comments that sometimes it is good to talk over a student's paper that the teacher has not yet graded or even read. "Composition Conference," *Clearing House,* XXXV (May, 1961), 524.

2. A detailed discussion of values and techniques of teacher–student conferences is in "We Are Trying Conferences," by Janet Emig, *English Journal,* XLIX (April, 1960), 223. Praise and individualized suggestions for improvement are the chief goals of each biweekly conference.

Enlisting Student Aid

1. Often ask classes for ideas about procedure or content; doing so will increase their interest.

2. Assign routine tasks to students. The experience will be good for them, and the aid will be helpful to you.

Making the Classroom Attractive

1. Ideally, each English teacher should have a classroom of his own.
2. Enlist student aid in improving the appearance of your classroom. Students' interest will carry over into their classwork.

To Encourage Students

On the bulletin board each week, list the authors and titles of the best pieces of student writing prepared during the preceding week. Given similar recognition for other "bests." Irving C. Poley recommends checking the class roll weekly to see that each member has had the opportunity to "distinguish" himself in some way.

Thoughts on Discipline

1. If the teacher knows his subject and is truly courteous (not merely polite), troubles with discipline seldom arise.
2. Troublemakers are often students who have too little to do or who cannot do what has been assigned. The cures should be obvious.
3. The potential "bad boys" may be given special positions with high-sounding titles: Chairman of the Classroom Library Committee, etc. They may also be won over by having them do special favors for the teacher (not vice versa).
4. Probably a student should never be scolded before the class. A friendly private conference, with an attempt to get at the cause of the difficulty, brings much better results.

To Keep Things in Order

1. Have a file for pictures, maps, notes, and other supplementary aids.
2. Keep an assignment book.
3. Keep your grade book up to date.
4. Return papers promptly.
5. Use the NCTE Cumulative Reading Record for book reports.
6. Follow a set procedure in recording absences.

Free and Inexpensive Materials

In each September issue of the *English Journal* for a number of years, John Searles has listed useful free and inexpensive materials newly developed for secondary English

Keeping the Public Informed

An NCTE pamphlet, "Informing the Public about the English Language Arts," has been prepared particularly for teachers of English in the elementary and secondary school to help them inform the public about the teaching of English.

Good-By Quill Pen

Dr. Joseph Mersand, a past president of the NCTE, asserts, "We shall have to become acquainted with many new materials of instruction, with newer methods of utilizing them, with better ways to understand our students, and devices for evaluating our instruction. The English teacher, armed with a grammar, a literature anthology, and a piece of chalk, may have been acceptable in my high school days, though he was rarely popular; but in the demanding days ahead, he will be as out of date as the quill pen." SRA *Insight* (Winter, 1963), 6.

On Freedom

" 'They'—the public, the administrators, the critics—have no right to take freedom from us, the teachers; but freedom is not something one wins and then possesses; freedom is something we rewin every day, as much a quality of ourselves as it is a concession from others. Speaking and writing and exploring the books of the world are prime fields of freedom." When you need inspiration, look up Lou La Brant's "The Rights and the Responsibilities of the Teacher of English," *English Journal*, L (Sept., 1961), 379.

A Teacher's Happiness

Happiness, according to Lin Yutang, consists of moments. A teacher cannot expect an endless series of joy-filled hours, success after success. A reasonable goal may be one or two moments a day—on the average. They will make an impressive array by retirement age.

Humanities Week

Brea-Olinda Union H.S., California, has tried a Humanities Week, with concerts, debates, art exhibits, lectures on music appreciation, interpretive dance, poetry readings, etc.

"Humanities Abroad"

A wave of the future? Hazel R. Anderson and Paul E. Healy escorted a number of their students on a 4,300-mile, 30-day trip through Europe.

In preparation they read about what they expected to see, as well as literature appropriate to the places. Each evening on the trip they discussed the day's events and prepared for the next. No disciplinary problems arose. *English Journal,* LV (May, 1966), 585.

"An Alternative to the Traditional Grading System"

For her bottom classes, Marla Sparks of Ohio got permission to substitute written comments (largely positive) for report card grades. Students read more, wrote more, and discussed more freely; only four of eighty-five did not receive credit for the course. The wave of the future? *English Journal,* LVI (Oct., 1967), 1032.

Professional Meetings

Professional conferences are valuable for exchange of points of view, getting new ideas, and examining new textbooks and other materials. Yet William A. Jenkins, past-president of NCTE, said in a speech that over four-fifths of English teachers have never attended a national meeting, about half never a state meeting, and about a quarter not even a local meeting.

Advice From a "Teacher of the Year"

Illinois English teacher Alice Grant, "teacher of the year" in 1964, has this advice for other teachers:

Think like a man.
Look like a girl.
Act like a lady.
And work like a dog.

Keeping Up with Research Findings

It is very difficult for a busy teacher to keep *au courant* with recent research. The *English Journal* and ERIC publications will help. (ERIC is an acronym for Educational Research Information Center.) About once a year the *English Journal* briefly summarizes "Investigations Relating to the English Language Arts," and English ERIC prepares numerous up-to-date "state of the art" papers on specific topics.

For Comfort on Your Blue Days

In a comic strip, Priscilla's Pop laments that all of Priscilla's classmates can tell a hyphen from a comma. Priscilla comforts herself, "But can they tell a pinto from a palomino?" (Philosophical question: What knowledge is of most worth?)

"I Have a Dream"

"I have a dream . . . that someday all English teachers will spend a minimum of one day each week keeping in touch with reality—that someday all English teachers in all of our schools will sit down together for at least a half day each week to determine how to make their subject relevant to their students in today's world . . . and that these same teachers will work in solitude during another half day each week, working up practical applications of the creative ideas stimulated during the interaction sessions—for their own students in their own classes!

"I have a dream—of a day when English teachers will help their students inquire into the use and misuse of language in human affairs . . . of a day when English teachers will use literature to help each student inquire into the problems that concern him . . . of a day when all teachers will have their students use writing every day to develop their learning and thinking process, instead of writing boring compositions for bored English teachers to correct and return." Gerald Kincaid, *Minnesota English Journal* (Fall, 1968).

Name Index

Subject Index